LGBTQ Politics

A Critical Reader

Edited by
Marla Brettschneider
Susan Burgess
Christine Keating

NEW YORK UNIVERSITY PRESS
New York

NEW YORK UNIVERSITY PRESS
New York
www.nyupress.org

References to Internet websites (URLs) were accurate at the time of writing. Neither the author nor New York University Press is responsible for URLs that may have expired or changed since the manuscript was prepared.

Library of Congress Cataloging-in-Publication Data
Names: Brettschneider, Marla, editor. | Burgess, Susan, 1961- editor. | Keating, Christine, editor.
Title: LGBTQ politics : a critical reader / edited by Marla Brettschneider, Susan Burgess, and Christine Keating.
Other titles: Lesbian, gay, bisexual, transgender, queer politics
Description: New York : New York University Press, 2017. | Includes bibliographical references and index.
Identifiers: LCCN 2017003765 | ISBN 9781479893874 (cl : alk. paper) | ISBN 9781479834099 (pb : alk. paper)
Subjects: LCSH: Sexual minorities—Political activity. | Sexual minorities—Civil rights. | Sexual minorities—Political activity—United States. | Sexual minorities—Civil rights—United States.
Classification: LCC HQ76.5 .L49 2017 | DDC 306.76—dc23
LC record available at https://lccn.loc.gov/2017003765

New York University Press books are printed on acid-free paper, and their binding materials are chosen for strength and durability. We strive to use environmentally responsible suppliers and materials to the greatest extent possible in publishing our books.

Manufactured in the United States of America

10 9 8 7 6 5 4 3 2 1

Also available as an ebook

LGBTQ POLITICS

To Shane Phelan, with deepest gratitude for your work and friendship

CONTENTS

ACKNOWLEDGMENTS

We are enormously grateful to the many activists and political scientists whose work has forwarded the LGBTQ movement over the years. Since they are too numerous to mention by name, we sincerely hope it suffices to say that truly, this volume would have been impossible without their devotion and generosity to the cause. Extra special thanks to Shane Phelan, to whom this volume is dedicated. Shane's visionary thinking made it possible for lesbians to become more visible in political science, no small feat, creating a regular meeting place for us, and other disciplinary outcasts, in our intellectual home away from home: the Western Political Science Association's Feminist Theory Pre-Conference.

Editing this collection was a labor, but it was a real labor of love. It deepened our appreciation of each other's talents and strengthened the bonds of friendship between us. While we were working on this volume, each of us faced difficult challenges, including the deaths and serious illnesses of family members and friends, and we were buoyed by each others' support and intellectual companionship. The wisdom, energy, and goodwill of those who contributed essays to this volume were phenomenal. Some have said that editing a collection such as this is like herding cats. To that we say: we love cats! Ilene Kalish and Caelyn Cobb at NYU Press are exceptional editors whose expertise and support made it possible for us to see the work through from start to finish. If fortune smiles on us, we'll all be working together again on a second edition before too long.

Marla offers many thanks to the University of New Hampshire Women's Studies Program and the Department of Political Science, and to Felicia Nadel, Emerson Doiron, and especially Elisabeth Lohmueller for crucial assistance during summer 2016. Working with Susan and Cricket has been a real gift—they are amazing to work with and have taught me so much. Thanks to Toni and to Paris for sharing their mom and to my sisters Beth and Nina for their support.

Susan is grateful to work in Ohio University's Department of Political Science, where research and teaching in the area of LGBTQ politics is not just tolerated but valued. It was a real treat to work on this project with Marla and Cricket—I learned so much from both of them, but equally importantly, I laughed a lot with them both too. Thanks beyond words to Kate Leeman, who understands as always, and to my dear aunt, Cassie Tiogoly, who always did.

Cricket thanks Marla and Susan for the wonderful experience of putting this volume together. She also thanks the colleagues, students, and staff at the gender, women's, and sexuality studies departments at the Ohio State University and the University of Washington for making these schools such fabulous places to grow as a scholar, an activist, and a teacher. Thanks as well to past and present members of la Escuela Popular Norteña for profoundly and radically shaping my understanding of politics, coalition, and resistance. As always, I'm deeply grateful to my friends and family for their love, wisdom, laughter, and support.

Thank you to our indexers: Nina Judith Katz and Leonid S. Blickstein.

1

Introduction

MARLA BRETTSCHNEIDER, SUSAN BURGESS, AND
CHRISTINE KEATING

Lesbian, gay, bisexual, transgender, and queer (LGBTQ) activism has gained a good deal of visibility in recent years and has had some significant successes.[1] Worldwide, the number of countries in which same-sex acts are illegal is decreasing. An increasing number prohibit employment discrimination, punish hate crimes, and recognize same-sex marriage and adoption. LGBTQ activism has also led to path-breaking scientific discoveries of life-saving treatments for people with AIDS. In the United States, hate crimes against LGBTQ people may be prosecuted under federal law, and LGBTQ people may serve openly in the military. Barriers to LGBTQ families adopting and fostering children have been lifted in many states. Many states and localities have added sexuality to antidiscrimination laws that protect basic civil rights such as equal housing, public accommodation, and employment. Indeed, this book was conceived as the United States Supreme Court recognized the right of same-sex couples to marry in *Obergefell v. Hodges* in June 2015. Readers will note the presence of that dramatic political turn of events in many chapters in this volume.

However, this history has been neither linear nor necessarily progressive, including in recent years. The killing of forty-nine people in a gay nightclub in Orlando, Florida in June 2016 dramatically demonstrated that violence against LGBTQ populations persists despite legal and political gains. Also, as this book was about to go to press, Donald J. Trump was elected the forty-fifth president of the United States in 2017. While specific policy development remains open, it is clear that anti-LGBTQ elements worldwide have experienced a tremendous political boost from his election. The struggle for sexual and gender diversity and justice is far from over.

At the same time that the LGBTQ movement has gained greater visibility in local, national, and international politics, the study of LGBTQ politics has gained traction in the discipline of political science in the United States. This is distinctly different from the situation just twenty years ago, when research on LGBTQ political issues was scant and formal recognition of LGBTQ professional interests was virtually nonexistent. Today, in contrast, the American Political Science Association includes a committee that studies the status of LGBT people in the profession as well as a caucus that provides a place for LGBT scholars to organize their interests. Further, an organized section on sexuality and politics promotes scholarly research on a variety of topics. This critical reader gathers together contemporary essays in political science that address LGBTQ politics in the context of a variety of issues, including activism, law, coalition building, community, education, erotics, technology, marriage and families, globalism, intersections with other progressive movements, the politics of political science professional associations, teaching issues, public opinion, organizational strategies, right-wing resistance, and visions for the future. These themes are approached from a variety of subfields in political science as it is studied in the United States, including comparative politics, political theory, American politics, public law, and international relations. Taken together, these essays provide a snapshot of the contemporary study of LGBTQ politics in the discipline of political science in the United States.

This volume analyzes both the successes and obstacles involved in building the LGBTQ movement over the past twenty years, and offers analyses that point to potential directions that the movement might take in the future. Rather than aiming for a seamless narrative, the volume presents a wide range of methodological, ideological, and substantive approaches to LGBTQ politics that exist in political science. Essays that focus on more mainstream institutional and elite politics appear alongside contributions grounded in grassroots movements and critical theory. While some essays are celebratory of the movement's successes and prospects, others express concerns that the democratic basis of the movement has become undermined by a focus on funding power over people power and on legal and state-centered rights over community solidarities. Some contributors suggest that mainstream successes have diminished the transformative potential of the LGBTQ movement and corroded its linkages to overlapping and allied progressive movements.

In preparation for this volume, we organized several roundtables at political science conferences such as the American Political Science Association, the Western Political Science Association, and the Midwest Political Science Association meetings. These roundtables brought together scholars working on LGBTQ politics across various subfields of the discipline in order to deepen our collective understanding of the LGBTQ movement and research on it over the past twenty years or so. During the panels we asked scholars to consider the history of the study of LGBTQ politics, where it is now, and where it might be headed in the future. One theme that emerged in the panels was the pressure that scholars often felt to deradicalize or "tone down" their work in the discipline of political science, a pressure that interestingly parallels the way in which LGBTQ activists often feel compelled to work within the politics of respectability. We encouraged authors to consider moving against that pressure in their contributions to the volume.

One common theme that emerges across many of the essays is that a focus on LGBTQ politics can help us to understand the complexities of politics more generally. For example, the rapid acceptance of marriage equality in the United States in recent years suggests that we need to rethink mainstream public opinion frameworks and models that do not account for the possibility of such a swift change. To be sure, even the study of mainstream LGBTQ political issues with the traditional tools of political science has challenged longstanding assumptions, allowing us to see the limitations of U.S. politics and political science more clearly, and providing a basis from which to anticipate new forms of politics and imagine new ways to study them. In addition, this volume includes several chapters that directly challenge the way politics has been defined and studied from within the mainstream, using analytic tools drawn from critical frameworks such as queer theory, feminist theory, critical race theory, and global justice theory to destabilize and reimagine the boundaries of politics and political science.

Another central argument that runs through the essays in the volume is that a political science approach can usefully inform LGBTQ politics. To take the development of public support for marriage equality in the United States as an example again, the use of survey research allows us to chart its surprisingly quick rise and to pay attention to its complexity vis-à-vis other social movements. Further, a political science approach also helps us to think about the broader political contexts, motivations, and consequences of what often might seem to be individual preferences or attitude. For example, in LGBTQ political movements, anti-LGBTQ sentiment, sometimes referred to as "homophobia," is often taken as a personal belief or attitude. Given its focus on political agendas, institutions, and structures, a political science approach can highlight the ways in which homophobia is mobilized politically, for particular political interests, even if the central political issue being addressed does not directly implicate LGBTQ people or concerns. Such sentiment can be mobilized within various modes of power in different historical and cultural contexts.

A third theme that echoes across the chapters is that the study of LGBTQ politics is best situated within an intersectional framework that takes up oppressions and identities as mutually constitutive, or co-created. This framework, developed over the past two decades primarily by feminists of color, underscores the analytic importance of looking at the ways in which systems of power such as race, gender, sexuality, class, and others work in conjunction with each other and the political importance of building movements that address such interconnections. Indeed, in addition to being at a crossroads for the LGBTQ movement, we are also at a critical juncture in progressive political activism more generally. Social media has enlivened movements for social change, with some lauding the ways digital technologies have widened conversations, facilitated organizing, and enabled people to share information across time and place, while others have warned that social media activism runs the risk of becoming a form of armchair politics. Environmental crisis and climate change have led activists to organize at the grass roots and press for change through more institutional channels around the globe. Further, building upon the antiglobalization protests in relation to the 1999 World Trade Organization meeting in Seattle, and gaining momentum through the 2000s, the Occupy movement has prompted a rethinking of questions of economic justice in terms of the 1 percent over and against the rest of us. In the United States, a vibrant #BlackLivesMatter network has drawn international attention for its sustained and vital work against police brutality and other forms of persistent racial inequality. In this time of intense social contestation, several of the contributors to the volume argue that intersectional approaches to the study of politics are vital in order to analyze and understand why progressive movements emerge and how they can be sustained.

This reader offers six main sections containing essays focused on the following themes: the politics of social movements and interest groups; LGBTQ politics within the discipline of political science in the United States; U.S. public opinion and politics; marriage equality politics; global politics; and visions for the future. Each section includes a short introduction that highlights key issues and questions raised by the essays offered therein. Each essay offers an in-depth analysis of an issue important to the LGBTQ movement, while self-consciously overlapping with other essays in the volume, to encourage connections across central analytic and conceptual categories that serve to structure (and often limit) the discipline of political science. The specifics of each of the six sections of the book are described below.

Part I: Building LGBTQ Movements

The Chicago Society for Human Rights (1924) is credited as the first main homosexual rights organization in the United States, followed by the Daughters of Bilitis (1955) and the Mattachine Society (1950). Historians and other scholars often date the explosion of a widespread popular LGBTQ movement to the acts of resistance at the Stonewall Inn in New York's Greenwich Village in 1969. That series of rebellions was multiracial, and participants emerged from a variety of diverse LGBTQ positionalities.

The contributions to this section update the exploration of movements and groups to more recent years with an interesting array of focal points for analysis and on-the-ground social justice work. Zein Murib examines social movements and interest-group advocacy related to LGBTQ people during the period 1968–2003. Looking at disputes regarding political objectives and coalition building, Murib demonstrates important divisions among organizations based on race, class, and gender. Using a critical discourse analysis, Murib articulates how movements for LGBTQ marriage and military issues came to obscure other significant agenda items in LGBTQ political movements. B Lee Aultman and Paisley Currah develop the concept of epistemic justice to critique the erasure of lives and experiences of trans politics, which remains largely illegible in more mainstream political science scholarship on LGBTQ equality movements. Providing an overview of trans political movements in the United States, the authors present a comprehensive history in the field as well as a cogent argument on the needs of trans politics today.

J. Ricky Price examines the links among race, gender, and sexuality within contemporary HIV activism and prevention efforts, exploring these issues from a feminist-science and criminal-justice standpoint. Kimala Price offers her expertise on queer reproductive-justice politics by women-of-color activists beginning in the 1990s, exploring the direction of coalitions and agenda setting between LGBTQ and reproductive-justice movements when many LGBTQ activists were claiming that reproductive issues were not pertinent to their movement. Moving through the divides, Price offers a rich analysis of difficulties and possibilities associated with such coalitions for activists and theorists.

Charles Anthony Smith, Shawn Schulenberg, and Eric A. Baldwin discuss critically how political science often overlooks the bisexual members of the LGBTQ community. Countering a common presumption in political studies of bi-, multi-, and pansexuals, the authors demonstrate that the community is significantly politically engaged.

While much scholarship identifies and relies on binary understandings of sexuality, Joseph Nicholas DeFilippis and Ben Anderson-Nathe complicate this typology, analyzing models of redistributive agendas of class-based LGBTQ movements and recognition-based frameworks of organizations led by queer people of color. We see in these contributions the crucial roles movement and activist politics play in interacting with action in more formal and legal arenas on LGBTQ political issues. Sean Cahill works with LGBTQ and questioning incarcerated adults and with youth examining issues that emerge from the frame of LGBTQ experience in the criminal justice system.

Part II: LGBTQ Politics in the Discipline of Political Science

The essays in this section focus on LGBTQ politics and movement issues in professional political science associations and academic institutions. Here we ground the examination of the role of LGBTQ politics in the discipline of political science, focusing on the American Political Science Association, the central professional organization for the study of politics in the United States. Angelia R. Wilson and Martha Ackelsberg critically survey the development of the Sexuality and Politics Section and the LGBT Caucus in the American Political Science Association, integrating interviews from key participants who have led the development of this field over the last twenty-five years. Susan Burgess and Anna Sampaio offer an intersectional reflection on the controversy over whether to hold the 2012 APSA meeting in Louisiana, which presented a variety of conflicting interests that threatened to undermine fragile alliances among groups representing LGBTQ, racial, gender, and class interests, in part due to persistent attachments to single-issue politics.

Barry L. Tadlock and Jami K. Taylor survey trends in publishing articles on LGBTQ topics in the top fifty journals in political science and the top twenty journals in public administration and international relations, as well as books published by the top ten university presses in political science. Jyl Josephson and Thaís Marques then examine the relationship between LGBTQ politics and its study in political science and the development of the field of feminist political theory, arguing that mainstream LGBTQ politics and political science have shaped feminist political theory more significantly than did queer theory. In this section, readers will note familiar themes in LGBTQ studies and see how knowledge production in the academy forms and contributes to the contours of political activism and examination in the broader civic and governmental arenas. From here we can critically take up the most active area of LGBTQ research in the discipline of political science, which includes public opinion research, given that subfield's centrality to the discipline.

Part III: LGBTQ Politics and Public Opinion in the United States

This section contains essays that explore public opinion regarding LGBTQ politics and its relation to mainstream politics in the United States. It is now legal for gays and lesbians to marry, serve in the military, and express their sexuality privately without fear of criminal prosecution, leading some activists and scholars to suggest that the LGBTQ movement has reached a victorious conclusion, an end to marginalization. Yet, as many critical scholars have noted, LGBTQ people who do not or will not conform to mainstream sex, gender, race, and class norms continue to be politically marginalized. The chapters in this section use the tools of mainstream political science to assess recent developments in LGBTQ politics, providing evidence that sometimes supports and at other times challenges the discipline's understanding of American politics. Taken together, these essays suggest that integrating the study of LGBTQ politics into the standard subfields of political science (such as public opinion, public policy, the presidency, campaigns and elections, and Congress) can both confirm and disrupt what the discipline thinks it knows about how politics works in the United States.

Jeremiah J. Garretson begins by offering a critical analysis of various explanations that political science has offered to explain growing support for LGBTQ rights in the United States, focusing on unexplained variance among subgroups such as African Americans and conservatives. Donald P. Haider-Markel and Patrick R. Miller suggest that survey data reveals a longstanding division between individual policy preferences for marriage equality and broader movement priorities. They argue that such divisions undermine mobilization towards more transformative political goals, such as alternative gender and family structures, calling for a broader approach to public opinion. Through interviews, a discussion of Victory Fund support, and an analysis of various campaign materials, Ravi K. Perry and X. Loudon Manley argue that President Obama's decision to support marriage equality in 2012 was a crucial factor not only in changing Black public opinion on marriage equality but also in promoting a number of electoral victories for LGBT African American candidates from 2012 to 2014. Paul Snell explores the establishment of the LGBT Equality Caucus as a means of addressing the underrepresentation of such interests in Congress. He suggests that the institutionalization of the caucus contributes to a transformation of LGBTQ politics from morality to interest-group politics. In the final chapter of the section, Mandi Bates Bailey and Steven P. Nawara offer a survey-based experiment that suggests that gay and lesbian candidates, particularly lesbians, are disadvantaged by campaign advertising that activates gender and sexuality stereotypes.

Part IV: Marriage Equality Politics

This section addresses the thorny issue of marriage equality, easily the most visible issue in LGBTQ politics in the United States in the last several years. While marriage has long been a contentious issue among LGBTQ people, opposition to it has diminished (but not disappeared) within the movement in recent years, paralleling its greater acceptance within mainstream politics in the United States. Mainstream support culminated in the 2015 case of *Obergefell v. Hodges*, arguably the single most important case to address LGBTQ rights issued by the U.S. Supreme Court. The chapters in this section critically assess the cases prior to *Obergefell* and their import in shaping the gay and lesbian community, the meaning of *Obergefell* itself, and the effect that marriage equality may have in defining the parameters of the LGBTQ movement going forward.

Noting tensions between what are often referred to in the political science literature as liberal LGBT and radical queer activists, Courtenay W. Daum assesses the viability of their sometimes competing policy goals and their import for the future development of LGBTQ politics in the United States. She argues that the *Obergefell* ruling protects those in the LGBTQ community who are more socioeconomically privileged, concluding that this may well subvert the ability of the LGBTQ movement to radically challenge, disrupt, and transform traditional institutions and identities, as well as the mainstream sex and gender norms upon which they are built. Ellen Ann Andersen explores various sociolegal factors that led couples to choose to become married in state and local venues offering same-sex marriage before the *Obergefell* ruling, noting the central role that political and legal contexts played in shaping more personal influences.

Addressing LGBTQ liberty and equality through a queer theoretical lens, Jerry D. Thomas argues that same-sex marriage privileges heteronormativity at the expense of queer sensibilities. His essay performs an enraged and profane "fagchild" identity that centralizes the concerns of the "here and now" queer citizen, who both challenges and yet remains subject to mainstream norms. Connecting the same-sex marriage debates with a different area of grassroots LGBTQ politics, Jason Stodolka offers a case study of LGBTQ homeless youth activism in Chicago. Stodolka argues that this at-risk population has been able to utilize mainstream LGBTQ marriage-rights advocacy to increase recognition of its own grassroots concerns. Nonetheless, he also finds evidence that suggests that normative debates about same-sex marriage have tended to reify local political structures that perpetuate the very conditions of LGBTQ youth homelessness.

Part V: LGBTQ Politics in Global Context

The essays in this section focus on LGBTQ politics in the Global South as well as on transnational LGBTQ politics. Julie Moreau provides an overview and a critical analysis of central trends in the study of LGBTQ movements in the Global South. Miriam Smith explores competing approaches to the comparative study of LGBTQ politics. The first approach foregrounds the advances and setbacks to the legal and political incorporation of LGBTQ issues in different national contexts, while the second approach focuses on homonationalism, that is, the way in which states seek to create a more positive image of their government by promoting LGBT rights; Smith argues that each approach could benefit from incorporating insights from the other. Cynthia Burack provides an overview of U.S.-government-funded international LGBTQ human rights programming and analyzes the relationship between the U.S. government and local LGBTQ groups. Burack argues that despite a conception that the U.S. government imposes a particular agenda upon these groups, the programs themselves are actually developed through close negotiation with local groups. Finally, Christina Kiel and Megan E. Osterbur look at transnational advocacy networks (TANs) in relationship to LGBTQ politics and use hyperlink data to generate a map of global LGBTQ networks. They argue that while much research seeks to understand the role of TANs in issue framing in different national contexts, it is also important to understand the networks themselves, paying particular attention to connections across regions and levels of development.

Part VI: Queer Futures

The essays in this section present, envision, and analyze different possible futures for LGBTQ politics. What do political scientists think about the future of LGBTQ activism based on the last twenty years of LGBTQ scholarship and politics? Gary Mucciaroni's essay analyzes and assesses alternative futures for the LGBTQ movement, looking at the possibilities of building a movement that aims for broad-based social transformation. Judy Rohrer's essay explores the import of contemporary controversies about sexuality and gender identity in the Boy Scouts and Girl Scouts and what they reveal about generational anxieties regarding the future in the United States. Drawing on the emphasis on fun in scouting practice and philosophy, she argues for an approach to gay futurity that goes beyond inclusion. Melissa Meade and Rye Young consider what it means to invest in feminist and queer futures and argue for the development of alternative models of philanthropy and funding. Finally, Heath Fogg Davis critically analyzes the benefits and limitations of women's colleges and the single-sex college admissions policies based on race-sex identity.

This volume does not aim to be exhaustive. Rather, it includes creative, cutting-edge essays from scholars reflecting on the development of the field, writing about contemporary LGBTQ issues in political and historical context. Our intention has been to bring together the best contemporary work on LGBTQ politics from a range of emerging and established scholars in mainstream and critical political science. We hope that the essays in this volume taken together will further the long trajectory of creative and transformative work being done in the field of LGBTQ politics, provoking continued critical discussion of the parameters of LGBTQ politics and the import of its study for the discipline of political science as a whole.

NOTE

1 In this volume, we use the term "LGBTQ politics" ("LGBTQ" standing for "lesbian, gay, bisexual, transgender, and queer") to refer to struggles to end discrimination, persecution, and marginalization based on sexual orientation and gender identity. The question of naming is a hotly debated political question. In general, there has been a trend towards inclusivity in nomenclature, with the acronym expanding to incorporate minority sexual and gender identities as they gain political traction as well as more open-ended identities such as "queer" or "questioning." One important critique of the acronym itself is that it is based on English-language terms for minority sexual and gender identity and thus serves to erase cultural and linguistic variation of both identity and practice as well as reinforce Western cultural and linguistic dominance. In order to avoid this problem, the human rights community in particular has turned to the acronym "SOGI" (standing for "sexual orientation and gender identity") instead of "LGBTQ" in order to focus attention on sexual and gender diversity in general. At the time of the writing of this book, however, this naming practice has not become widespread. Because the question of naming is an important and ongoing political question, we do not impose conformity of nomenclature in this volume and leave the choice of how to refer to the movement up to each contributor.

PART I

Building LGBTQ Movements

MARLA BRETTSCHNEIDER

Looking at what Dean Spade has called "impossible people," these chapters explore a range of movement organizations, strategies, and theoretical orientations. In keeping with the theme of the whole volume, we find many scholars interested in differences between, and tensions among, specific groups and basic premises that span a reformist and more radical range for LGBTQ activists and issues. We begin this section with a look at how GLBT emerged as a coalitional identity that over time narrowed its agenda. From there chapters explore a range of "trickle-up social justice" perspectives, including those of race, class, gender, sexuality, citizenship and national affiliation, culture, and religion as these play out in various cross-cutting arenas such as immigration, economic and labor policy, youth, homelessness, reproductive justice, carceral studies, and the terrorism industry.

Zein Murib examines how gay, lesbian, bisexual, and transgender identities became joined by movement leaders in the United States during the late 1990s and early 2000s to produce a new coalition and overall category: GLBT. In "Rethinking GLBT as a Political Category in U.S. Politics," Murib reviews National Policy Roundtable archived meeting transcripts to explore the political processes that shaped the newly created "GLBT" coalition and identity category. In this chapter, the author demonstrates that the activist and academic grouping of these communities "limits questions to addressing dynamics between groups," such as GLBT and straight. Whereas relatively little scholarly attention has been paid to examining politics within a GLBT umbrella, Murib shows that "interest group coalitions are shaped by political circumstance, influence the boundaries of political identities for members, and reproduce inequalities."

Developments for trans rights in accepted formal arenas of politics (such as the courts, executive arenas, and law) have been relatively fast-paced in the past fifteen years. However, if one looks beyond these formal spheres, the picture is quite different. In "Politics outside the Law: Transgender Lives and the Challenge of Legibility," B Lee Aultman and Paisley Currah articulate the limitations of conceiving of the political in these structured formal arenas. They identify the ways in which such imagination of the political co-creates a "transnormative" categorization that seeks inclusion into existing political structures instead of transformation of them and continues to marginalize those facing multiple axes of oppression such as race and class. The authors perform an "examination of an expansive notion of the 'transgender political,' one that brings normative questions of justice to bear on empirical examinations of lives as their *being* and politics as its *being enacted in the quotidian*."

J. Ricky Price, in examining the links among race, gender, and sexuality within contemporary HIV activism and prevention efforts, calls for a look back at activist principles from the early days of the AIDS epidemic to help us move forward. Price explores how preventive treatment campaigns for HIV overlook intersectionality, particularly the ways in which race, class, and sexuality often intersect in ways that can lead to criminalization of marginalized people with HIV. In the beginning of AIDS activism, these issues were more readily at the fore, and Price argues that unless we look at these sorts of community-based strategies, the biological and social problem that is HIV cannot be tackled in the present day.

Kimala Price argues against a common view that reproductive justice issues are not queer issues in "Queering Reproductive Justice: Toward a Theory and Praxis for Building Intersectional Political Alliances." This approach is problematically limited by an unconsciously raced, classed, gendered, sexed, and cultured view of what constitutes LGBTQ issues. Price lays out what it can mean to "queer" reproductive justice in an intersectionality framework looking at cross-movement alliances and coalitions from LGBTQ and reproductive justice organizations. The author explores the potential for transformation as well as LGBTQ resistance to the project of queering reproductive justice.

In "The 'B' Isn't Silent: Bisexual Communities and Political Activism," Charles Anthony Smith, Shawn Schulenberg, and Eric Baldwin discuss critically how political science often overlooks the bisexual members of the LGBTQ community. Situated in a binomial distribution of sexuality—straight or not—research tends to lump bisexuals in a general "not straight" category. While contestations over rights priorities and strategies among gay men, lesbians, trans persons, and the broadly defined queer persons are more well known and often studied, the "B" is often treated in the literature as if it is silent. Politically, some assume that bisexuals are not politically active as they are seen as situated between straight rights bearers and social change demands from the "gay" world. In this chapter, the authors present evidence of a politically active and politically astute bisexual community nested not in the traditionally defined LGBTQ groups but in the polyamory and BDSM communities. Using survey data and in-depth open-ended questions, they find that self-described bisexuals comprise up to one-half of the polyamory community and nearly two-thirds of the BDSM community. These communities are politically aware and politically active.

In "Embodying Margin to Center: Intersectional Activism among Queer Liberation Organizations," Joseph Nicholas DeFilippis and Ben Anderson-Nathe argue that we can see clear trajectories within a mainstream gay rights movement that the authors state has pursued a limited political agenda focused on equality for people identifying as LGBTQ. Partly what makes this movement "mainstream" is not only the focus on equity within a given existing system, the policy arenas targeted, and the methods utilized but also that this movement has attended mainly to the interests of the most privileged members of the various LGBTQ communities: upper-middle-class, gender-conforming, white gay and lesbian citizens. The authors juxtapose this movement with what they term "queer liberation organizations," run by and aimed at concerns of the most marginal members of the LGBTQ mixed communities. The authors evaluate organizations such as Affinity Community Services, allgo, the Audre Lorde Project, National Queer Asian Pacific Islander Alliance, Queers for Economic Justice, Southerners on New Ground, and the Sylvia Rivera Law Project and demonstrate that they constitute a distinct movement grounded in "different political and theoretical foundations centering intersectional perspectives, multi-issue organizing, and working from margin to center."

We close this section with "From 'Don't Drop the Soap' to PREA Standards: Reducing Sexual Victimization of LGBT People in the Juvenile and Criminal Justice Systems," in which Sean Cahill describes his work with LGBTQ and questioning incarcerated adults and with youth who often first interact with the criminal justice system due to survival crimes such as shoplifting and sex work, or because they fight back when they are bullied or are unsafe at school. Bureau of Justice Statistics data indicate that nonheterosexual youth and LGBT adults are much more likely to experience sexual victimization in custody, mostly at the hands of other incarcerated youth or adult inmates. This chapter reviews issues faced by GLBTQ adults and youth and policies emerging to address these concerns. Here Cahill articulates an agenda for policy change to reduce victimization of LGBTQ people in corrections.

2

Rethinking GLBT as a Political Category in U.S. Politics

ZEIN MURIB

The way gay, lesbian, bisexual, and transgender identities were linked together by political actors in the United States during the late 1990s and early 2000s produced a new political coalition and umbrella identity category, "GLBT."[1] Politically, the introduction of "GLBT" as a unified political identity category with an associated agenda of political interests has been used to pose gay, lesbian, bisexual, and transgender people as a coherent and large minority group that merits rights and recognition under the law. Symbolic importance has also been attached to "GLBT," with the grouping of these identity categories hailed by many as demonstrating the high priority placed on diversity. Reflecting the growing visibility of these political objectives and the groups that these goals aim to serve, the "GLBT" initialism has quickly evolved into the most common way in which activists, community members, journalists, and politicians refer to sexuality and gender identity.

"GLBT" and its variants have also been adopted in academic discourse, and are currently the predominant ways in which political scientists index research questions pertaining to sexuality and gender identity. While this growing attention is a necessary and welcome development in political science, contributing to enhanced understandings of the way political outcomes and public opinion shape and are shaped by the regulation and stigmatization of sex, gender identity, and sexuality, the reliance on "GLBT" as an analytic and descriptive category in political science limits questions to addressing dynamics *between* groups—straight and GLBT—with relatively little scholarly attention devoted to understanding the politics that occur *within* GLBT. Consequently, political scientists do not interrogate dynamics of privilege and marginalization across the many disparate groups that constitute GLBT.

Building on these observations, this chapter asks how, why, and to what effect political actors joined these disparate identity categories into a new political coalition and identity category. Relying primarily on the archived transcripts of a series of meetings held between 1997 and 2001, where leaders of various gay, lesbian, bisexual, and transgender interest groups convened to discuss developing a national strategy, this chapter explores the political processes that shaped the new "GLBT" coalition and identity category. The analysis of these transcripts reveals evidence of a critical juncture at which political actors brokered a coalition to unite gay, lesbian, bisexual, and transgender people and disseminated "GLBT" as the preferred way to refer to sexuality and gender identity in social and political discourse. These transcripts consequently offer insight into the factors that influence the creation of a new coalition and identity category. I begin below by introducing the meetings, known as the National Policy Roundtables, as a case for exploring the processes of constructing a new identity category and interest group coalition.

The National Policy Roundtables

In March 1998, the NGLTF (National Gay and Lesbian Task Force) issued a press release detailing the third meeting of the National Policy Roundtable: "a semi-annual meeting of executive directors and leaders of national GLBT groups sponsored by the Policy Institute, a think tank inside NGLTF dedicated to research, policy analysis, and strategy development."[2] Bringing together over twenty executive directors to represent their respective interest groups and organizations at each meeting, the National Policy Roundtable was described by Urvashi Vaid—the director the Policy Institute and the founder of the National Policy Roundtable—as "a forum for the creative and strategic thinking which is the basis of united action." Reflecting these goals, the press release detailed the agenda taken up at the March 1998 meeting. The items on the agenda included the impending midterm elections, debates over the origins of sexual orientation, race and leadership in national GLBT movement organizations, and how to respond to an "increasingly shrill and hostile right."

These four agenda items provide a general overview of the goals prioritized by the leaders of national gay, lesbian, bisexual, and transgender interest groups during this time period. Specifically, questions about how to create a more diverse and representative movement, how to frame the origin of lesbian and gay identities, and how to respond to the growing aggression of the Conservative Right are significant because they indicate the importance that members of the National Policy Roundtable placed on generating a common frame, brokering a functional coalition, and developing a shared understanding of sexuality and gender identities. Taken together, these agenda items highlight the broader purpose of the National Policy Roundtable: to join gay, lesbian, bisexual, and transgender organizations into a cohesive front united by a shared agenda. In other words, they self-consciously pursued the formation of an enduring coalition and unified identity category to most effectively represent the political interests pertaining to sexual orientation and gender identity in U.S. politics.

Through the exploration of the archived meeting minutes from the National Policy Roundtables that took place during this period, I make three arguments about this new coalition and associated identity category. First, enduring interest group coalitions are strongly influenced by the political contexts in which the organizations do their work. Second, interest group coalitions—specifically those that endure over long periods of time—should be examined for the ways in which they contribute to the ongoing constructions of political identities and interests for members. This relationship among coalitions, identities, and agendas of interests is particularly important to examine because an agenda of shared interests does not emerge *sui generis* according to the particular characteristics of an interest group's membership, but is instead constructed by political actors who frame issues, identities, and interests in particular ways (Strolovitch 2007). Third, and perhaps most importantly, I argue in this chapter that internal marginalization and exclusions that are evidenced in individual organizations are often reproduced when groups come together in coalition.

I advance these arguments—that interest group coalitions are shaped by political circumstances, influence the boundaries of political identities for members, and reproduce inequalities—in four sections. In the first section, I outline a theoretical framework that connects coalition formation to shifting political contexts. After advancing some expectations for conditions in which enduring interest group coalitions emerge, I draw on the concept of frame transformation from sociology to develop an understanding of how interest group coalitions are sites that political actors can use to influence meanings associated with the identity groups that comprise a coalition.

I use this framework in the second section to examine the NPR meetings held between 1997 and 1998. I show how the political actors taking part in these meetings initially resisted uniting gay, lesbian, bisexual, and transgender identities into a coalition and associated identity category due to concerns over becoming a single-issue movement that would necessarily require a narrow agenda. In light of these worries, the eventual consensus among leaders at these meetings was that the various groups should work in loosely defined coalitions with each other to advance a range of goals, which would allow gay, lesbian, bisexual, and transgender interest groups to maintain a broad and multifaceted agenda of interests that addressed issues of race, class, and gender in conjunction with sexuality and gender identity.

The third section illustrates how the leaders negotiated this broad agenda and the need to respond to attacks from opponents that sought to challenge the very existence of gay, lesbian, bisexual, and transgender as legitimate identities. I show that although leaders disagreed about how to frame the origins of these identities, they did agree to assert the political orientation of these groups. It was during this moment that political actors introduced "GLBT" as an identity category to unite these groups in political action.

The fourth section, which centers on the meetings held between 1999 and 2001, shows how the changing political context—specifically the 2000 presidential election and the subsequent partisan shifts in Congress and the White House—encouraged some leaders to reconsider the strategy of several small coalitions. It was under these circumstances of diminishing political opportunities in the early 2000s that some interest group leaders at the NPR began to advocate uniting these disparate identity categories and organizations into a political coalition in order to pool resources, enhance political efficacy, and project an image of critical mass in politics. As I show in this section, brokering the coalition with these goals in mind resulted in the absorption of difference under the signifier of "GLBT," rather than the institutional maintenance of inclusion and a broad agenda previously favored by these leaders. I underscore this dynamic in this section by examining the ways in which leaders of gay, lesbian, bisexual, and transgender organizations worked to address the lack of racial diversity among their organizations and within the evolving GLBT coalition.

Examining these meetings together reveals the trade-offs that occur in the processes of brokering unified coalitions to merge various groups. Whereas NPR participants during the earlier meetings advocated for issue agendas that would advance goals pertaining to each of the constitutive GLBT identity categories, as well as race, gender identity, and class, the participants at the NPRs that took place after the 2000 elections made a strong case for forming a large, unified coalition to advocate for a narrow agenda of issues under the heading of "GLBT." The shift towards "GLBT" helped political actors to project critical mass behind the interests they advocated. This revised agenda after the 2000 elections, however, privileged interests benefiting a specific swath of gay men and lesbians by foregrounding issues like same-sex marriage and full inclusion for gay men and lesbians in the military to the exclusion of issues such as improving access to administrative processes for transgender-identified people seeking to change their documented sex or a transgender-inclusive Employment Non-Discrimination Act.

The next section outlines the theoretical framework that I use for understanding how it is that some agenda items, and not others, came to stand in for a unified group under the heading of "GLBT."

Combating Backlash: Interest Group Coalitions, Stigma Transformation, and Identities

It is already well established in the scholarship on American interest groups that interest group coalitions have become more common in contemporary politics, with the research indicting two main culprits for this increase. First, the number of advocacy organizations in U.S. politics has surged dramatically in the past fifty years, increasing the number of interest groups that share agendas and would thus benefit from a united approach (Berry 1977; Strolovitch 2007; Holyoke 2009). Coalitions, in other words, have become a way that interest groups avoid conflicts with each other and mitigate competition. Second, this research shows that interest group coalitions are becoming more common as policy-making processes are growing increasingly decentralized. This requires interest groups, particularly those with limited resources, to coordinate efforts when competing for the time and attention of policymakers dispersed across various institutions and agencies (Hula 1999; Loomis 1986), and Strolovitch (2007) shows that this is increasingly true for organizations that advocate on behalf of marginalized groups.

Scholars of interest groups have also examined more diffuse influences on coalition formation. These include competition from other interest groups with similar agendas and conditions of adversity, or threat, that advance opposing agendas. Holyoke's 2009 study of interest group coalition lobbying, for example, shows that growing competitive pressures provide the incentives for interest groups with ideologically similar agendas to form coalitions. These coalitions are used to mitigate challenges among groups that share political objectives and would be better served by pooling resources. Threats from opponents have also been shown to increase the likelihood of interest group coalitions forming to share resources and craft a unified agenda to mount a successful defense against opponents (McCammon and Campbell 2002; Staggenborg 1986; Meyer and Staggenborg 1996). McCammon and Campbell's 2002 study of the unlikely coalition forged by women's suffrage groups and the Women's Christian Temperance Movement succinctly captures the dynamics of threat and interest group coalition formation, explaining that "[w]hen movement goals are blocked, we find that movement organizations will attempt to seek out new advantages for the group. Forming a coalition with another organization can be just this kind of advantageous tactic" (245).

Drawing on the scholarship on threats and coalition formation, I theorize that conditions of backlash, which I define as resistance and opposition that is mobilized in response to increased visibility for minority groups, motivates the formation of interest group coalitions. Political scientists have explored this particular understanding of backlash at length. This research shows the ways in which the dynamics of backlash shape the experiences of racial minorities in electoral politics (Giles and Hertz 1994; Tolbert and Hero 1996, 2001; Tolbert and Grummel 2003), women in legislatures (Kanthak and Krause 2012), and gay, lesbian, bisexual, and transgender people (Ayoub 2014; Haider-Markel, Querze, and Lindaman 2007; Fetner 2008). While recent scholarship has indicated that backlash, as it is defined here, seldom has an enduring influence on public opinion in the United States (Bishin et al. 2015; Flores and Barclay 2014), other scholarship shows that backlash—particularly as it has been directed to gay, lesbian, bisexual, and transgender people—helps to enhance issue salience and inject dialogues about sexuality in the polity (Ayoub 2014; Fetner 2008). In other words, groups representing gay-, lesbian-, bisexual-, and transgender-identified people have been notably successful at harnessing the energy and public debates generated by opposing forces to forge a strong united front, generate effective shared agendas, and claim standing in politics.

I build on this scholarship to contend that backlash prompted the formation of a coalition comprised of gay, lesbian, bisexual, and transgender interest groups to pool resources, develop a shared agenda, and present a strong, united front to defend against opponents. Specific threats during this period were mobilized by groups that comprised the Conservative Right—epitomized by the Family Research Counsel, Focus on the Family, and the Christian Coalition—which waged increasingly visible attacks on what they considered a "radical gay agenda" (Stein 2012). These assaults from the Conservative Right compelled leaders of various gay, lesbian, bisexual, and transgender interest groups and organizations to establish a working coalition to engage in political actions like lobbying and conduct events like parades to bring people together to present a united front and project critical mass (Stryker 2008; Stein 2012; Ghaziani 2008).

An influential aspect of the unified mobilization against backlash by the new coalition of gay, lesbian, bisexual, and transgender interest groups was a concerted effort to achieve what sociologists refer to as frame transformation, specifically stigma transformation (Benford and Snow 2000; Snow et al. 1986; Berbrier 2002). Frame transformation describes a process through which political actors modify existing framings of group identity and associated political interests to generate new understandings of the group that will attract more participants and garner broad support. These frame transformations are especially pressing tasks for negatively stereotyped groups, a process Berbrier labels "stigma transformation," which uses the introduction of new frames to produce positive shifts in group perception (Berbrier 2002). To confront the opposition, the coalition of gay, lesbian, bisexual, and transgender interest groups that emerged from the National Policy Roundtable explored different ways to frame sexuality and gender identity to assert the legitimacy and political standing of the associated identity groups. Internally, this entailed debates over how to most effectively frame the origins of sexual orientation and gender identity, as well as prolonged discussions about race in the movement, both of which were significant influences on meanings associated with gay, lesbian, bisexual, and transgender identities.

Over time, the efforts at stigma transformation in response to backlash compelled political actors in gay, lesbian, bisexual, and transgender interest groups to assert the interconnected nature of these identities, with challenges to gender and sexual normativity as the perceived bond uniting them (Seidman 2001; Warner 1993). Whereas coordinated political action across gay, lesbian, bisexual, and transgender interest groups had been advanced through separate organizations that frequently sought coalitions with other marginalized groups in the early 1970s through the 1980s (Kissack 1995), in the late 1990s and early 2000s, political actors began to project sexuality as the link that bound these groups together, to the exclusion of other racial, class, or gender identifications. Previously discrete identity categories of gay, lesbian, bisexual, and transgender identities, in other words, come to be understood as linked together in coalition with each other as a new identity category: "GLBT."

Viewing the introduction of "GLBT" as an available identity category, particularly as it emerged out of a coalition of interest groups, illustrates legal scholar Kimberlé Crenshaw's provocation to consider identities as "in fact coalitions" in a rather explicit and blunt way (Crenshaw 1991, 1299). Put differently, with the introduction of this new "GLBT" identity category, the members of these interest groups were encouraged to see their agendas and identities as closely linked and, to some extent, imbricated at the most basic and essential level. While this new identity-based coalition allowed them to enhance their political power and project the image of unity that is necessary in contemporary interest group politics, this chapter shows that this unity was achieved through the exclusion of various racial groups as well as those who did not conform to perceived gender norms. Anna Carastathis (2013) directs scholars to examine identities as coalitions with exclusions and differences such as these in mind, explaining that "identities are also potential coalitions, in the sense that when viewed intersectionally they illuminate interconnections and interrelations, as well as grounds for solidarity, that reach across and reveal differences within categories of identity" (946). Strolovitch makes a related point about advocacy groups themselves, writing that an intersectional approach reveals that they "do not represent unitary constituencies with clearly defined and bounded interests." Instead, they are "coalitions of intersecting and overlapping groups that are organized around one particular axis that is *constructed* or *framed* as what they have in common" (Strolovitch 2007, 26). Drawing on these arguments, this chapter suggests that the similarities asserted in the brokering of the coalition to unify gay-, lesbian-, bisexual-, and transgender-identified people should also be read for the ways in which they indicate the differences and consequent exclusions and within-group marginalization that give identity categories meaning, particularly as these meanings are mediated by interest groups.

I thus approach this study of the gay, lesbian, bisexual, and transgender interest group coalition and the GLBT identity category through the lens of identity as coalition. This directs my attention to questions not only of how and why the coalition across these diverse groups was formed at the National Policy Roundtable but also of what effect they produced with regard to specific understandings of related identifications. Throughout this analysis, I focus on the ways in which the projection of unity and similarities across the new coalition and identity category also entailed the concomitant designation of differences that lent the evolving identity category meaning (Brubaker 2006; Connolly 2002; Hall 2000; Norton 2004). In many cases, the privileging of sexual orientation—i.e., lesbian and gay political identities and political interests—entailed silencing the political agendas for transgender and bisexual-identified people, as well as butches, fairies, cross-dressers, queer people of color, and intersex-identified people, who also comprised the margins of the new "GLBT" identity group and coalition. These silences helped to construct the emerging GLBT coalition as one concerned specifically with issues pertaining to the interests of white, middle-class lesbian- and gay-identified people, with all other identifications posed as deviant or other (Stryker 2008; Valentine 2007).

Thus, although interest group coalitions that unite a broad diversity of interests and identities are sometimes viewed in idealized or utopian terms, this chapter shows some of the costs of enduring interest group coalitions on the representation of marginalized groups—GLBT in this chapter—that have already been established by important scholarship in the field of interest group politics (Beltrán 2010; Cohen 1999; Strolovitch 2007). This research shows that since interest group coalitions cannot possibly prioritize the interests of all members, they must make choices about which issues to mobilize around and which issues will be used to project a cohesive agenda. These negotiations over priorities often result in the reproduction of marginalization *within* these coalitions, as leaders elevate the concerns of more advantaged subgroups over those members with less power and influence (Strolovitch 2007, 191).[3]

The next section explores the NPR meetings between 1997 and 1999, with particular attention to the discussions about coalitions and issue agendas to be advocated by the gay, lesbian, bisexual, and transgender interest groups in attendance.

Making Coalitions: 1997–1999

The first National Policy Roundtable was convened in Washington, DC, over two days in September of 1997.[4] Facilitating the meeting of forty executive directors who represented organizations such as the Human Rights Campaign (HRC), the Intersex Society of North America, and BiNet USA, Urvashi Vaid opened by elaborating the vision that motivated the National Policy Roundtable:

> It is my hope that ideas and collaboration will emerge from this roundtable. The first goal is to create a space, to meet, share information that can continue in an on-going manner. . . . The second goal is building trust among our organizations and us as leaders. The final goal is to establish a mechanism for the national leaders to think strategically and creatively.[5]

Conspicuously absent from Vaid's introduction was an explicit mention of forming a coalition across the organizations in attendance. However, the interest in uniting in political action was articulated by several participants from the outset. These advocates cited the perceived unity of evangelical Christians, who had only recently entered secular politics, as a model for their own coalition (Burack 2014; Fetner 2008). In 1977, for example, Anita Bryant launched her Save the Children campaign, which successfully mobilized evangelical Christians in efforts to challenge political gains made by gays and lesbians in south Florida. By the 1980s, evangelical Christians used their broad network to influence the election of Ronald Reagan and successfully mobilize the efforts to criminal-ize commercial sex in cities, and by the 1990s, evangelical Christians had led a fierce and victorious attack against the National Endowment for the Arts (NEA) to force the defunding of what evangelical Christians perceived to be sexually explicit art, typified in the photography of Robert Mapplethorpe.[6]

It was against this backdrop of unified and increasing opposition from the Christian Right in the 1990s that the National Policy Roundtables were con-vened. The perceived unity of evangelical Christians—particularly in their efforts to stigmatize homosexuality and wage attacks against the various groups participating in the Roundtable—figured prominently in the motivation to form a coalition that was articulated by some participants. As the following reading shows, the proposals for a new coalition channeled efforts into challenging the stigmas of gay, lesbian, bisexual, and transgender identities advanced by evan-gelical Christians.

Kate Kendell, the executive director of the National Center for Lesbian Rights (NCLR), illustrates the influence of threat from the Right in her articulation of the ways she saw her organization fitting into the meetings and her hopes for what the Roundtable would accomplish. Kendell characterized the NCLR as

> [m]ostly reactive as legal organization, responding to legal problems within legal structure . . . Radical Right is organized; speak with one voice on queer issues. Our community is not adequately poised to respond. Gay agenda is not capable of definition. Lack of coalescence—issues defined for us. How can we speak with one voice while honoring our differences? Would like to have an agenda for the community.[7]

Kendall identifies some of the shared concerns mobilizing gay, lesbian, bisexual, and transgender political action in the mid-1990s. Most notable is the assertion that the "gay agenda" lacked clear associations with established meanings and, by association, a defined set of political interests. For Kendall, this is due in large part to the perpetual need to respond to attacks from the Right, which effectively dictates the issues prioritized for her organization and others at the table. By posing the need to unify as "the community," alongside her assertion that the Right is organized and speaks with one voice, Kendall's comments introduced a coalition to unify the groups as a possible desirable goal. Leaders agreed to take up the question of forming a coalition at the next Roundtable meeting.

The agenda for the next meeting of the Roundtable, which was convened in March 1998, focused on educating participants about strategies to target federal agencies with the most impact and, by association, on how to effectively use coalitions—with emphasis on the plural—to effect change in politics. To educate participants on strategies, the facilitators called on a panel of experts, many of whom had been active in the struggles to urge federal action on AIDS in the face of the apathetic Reagan administration. These panelists emphasized the potential power of utilizing several coalitions to target the many large agencies that comprise the federal bureaucracy. One panelist, identified only as Marj from the Lesbian Health Advocacy Network, instructed participants to

> pick an agency to lead in an area and make a coalition and go for it. . . . I encourage the national groups to say they will do coalition building and take a lead around a department, but don't assume the department belongs to you. . . . I really fervently believe that our agenda can only be implemented if national organizations pick a department to run a coalition around.[8]

Whereas the previous meeting had focused primarily on articulating the lack of cooperation across groups and taking up the question of whether or not the groups present should unite in coalition with each other, Marj's advice here and the minutes from the March 1998 Roundtable show that by the time of the second meeting, many of the participants embraced using coalitions to advance political agendas shared by groups with similar objectives. Significantly, the coalitions imagined by participants at this meeting were seen as a way to represent a diverse agenda of interests, rather than to throw the full force of the unified organizations behind a single issue.

The newfound commitment to organizing in many loosely defined coalitions and representing a broad range of issues was demonstrated in subsequent discussions about the agendas to be pursued. For instance, in addition to committing to coalitions across different groups participating in the Roundtable, participants also explored the possibility of forming coalitions with other interest groups perceived to be unaffiliated with lesbian, gay, bisexual, or transgender interests. A participant identified as Tim encouraged others to think of political agendas in relation to coalitions with outside groups:

> Deb mentioned working with unions. People are talking about non-gender identified coalitions (e.g., GLBT elderly poor people). You can go to organizations like the AARP and ask to be included in their work. Same thing with Families, USA. I believe that many GLBT people end up in poverty. We don't need to reinvent the processes; sometimes, coalitions already exist.[9]

Another participant, who was identified as an employee at a federal agency, immediately followed Tim's comment with a plea for participants to use him and other federal employees as a coalition to advance their political interests.[10] These two alternative uses of "coalition"—this first used to propose branching out beyond gay, lesbian, bisexual, and transgender groups and the other used to describe a potential coalition across political actors and bureaucrats—effectively decentered a formal coalition of interest groups and organizations. In other words, during these early meetings of the Roundtable, participants considered but ultimately rejected establishing a single gay, lesbian, bisexual, and transgender coalition comprised of the interest groups present at the Roundtable. The participants at the March 1998 meeting instead fostered a network of several small coalitions, such as the International Conference of Transgender Law and Employment and BiNet USA joining forces to single out the Department of Labor regarding nondiscrimination in employment. By prioritizing the formation of several small coalitions during the period between 1997 and 1998, the political actors participating in these Roundtables worked hard to avoid falling into the trap of single-issue politics that preoccupied the participants of the earlier Roundtables. Having established this strategy, the leaders turned their attention to how to respond to specific threats. The next section explores how Roundtable participants engaged in debates over how to frame the content and boundaries of gay, lesbian, bisexual, and transgender identities in politics, specifically in response to opposition from those who claimed that these identities were not legitimate bases for political action.

Engaging in Conflicts over the Meanings of Sexual Orientation

The main issue taken up at the September 1998 National Policy Roundtable was how to respond to the recent surge of "gay conversion therapies" and the promulgation of conversion narratives by self-identified "ex-gays" in the media, which many Roundtable participants perceived as calling into question the very existence of gay, lesbian, bisexual, and transgender identification. Common across the therapies was the emphasis on facilitating an "ex-gay's" proper gender role—i.e., husband or wife, son or daughter—and, by association, membership in his or her family, which was considered the central unit for the dissemination of values espoused by evangelical Christians (Burack 2014).[11]

Below, I examine how the September 1998 Roundtable agenda channeled the attention of participants to the most strategic way to frame gay, lesbian, bisexual, and transgender identities in response to the stigmatizing rhetoric—i.e., backlash—advanced by evangelical Christians and the new campaign to go public on "gay conversion therapies." I show how many of the conflicts over how to frame identities in response to this backlash from evangelical Christians occurred in conjunction with questions about whether and how to develop a shared and cohesive agenda of interests to unite these groups in political action.

One strategy introduced at the Roundtable prioritized responding to these attacks by shifting the discourse on the origins of sexual orientation and gender identity. Advocates for this strategy speculated that moving the discussion away from essential characteristics—the scientific origins that evangelical Christians cited as the reason for claiming that gay, lesbian, bisexual, and transgender identities do not actually exist—and in the direction of how gay-, lesbian-, bisexual-, and transgender-identified people are model citizens. Dixon Osborn, from the Service Members Legal Defense Network, summarized the debate over the origins of sexuality and gender identity as he and other participants saw it:

> Often posed question to the community is, is this biology or choice. Seems to me to be separate sets of questions that pose false either-ors. . . . Opponents suggest that identity of self is a matter of choice or if we act on it then it's a choice. Discussion we should have is one about morality, that it's morally good to be who we are.[12]

Here, Osborn proposes reframing the relevant identifications as acts of morality, or personal authenticity, that only stand to benefit society. Proponents of the morality framing extended their arguments to the necessity of personal authenticity for the maintenance of healthy families in which each person is valued for his or her uniqueness, with one participant explaining that they "have to make the argument that we are redefining the family, but not tearing down the family, talking about families coming in different shapes."[13] In other words, gay-, lesbian-, bisexual-, and transgender-identified people and their families are valuable members of a heterogeneous and multicultural democratic society who deserve consideration under the law. This framing of sexual orientation and gender identity as manifestations of good morality and model citizenship effectively side-stepped the question of gay, lesbian, bisexual, and transgender identifications as mutable or essential, and sought to change the conversation initiated by proponents of "ex-gay therapies."

Many Roundtable participants embraced the morality and respectability framing advanced by Dixon and expressed an interest in adopting it as a strategy. Others, however, worried that the emphasis on morality and good citizenship would erode the urgency of their political demands, particularly for the most vulnerable members of their organizations. Chief among these concerns was the ways in which elevating gay, lesbian, bisexual, and transgender people as model members of society would negate the need for antidiscrimination protections and legislation to document and punish hate crimes, all of which tended to disproportionately affect people of color, the poor, and non-gender-normative gay, lesbian, bisexual, and transgender people. Historian and cultural theorist Lisa Duggan (2003) terms the efforts to align gay, lesbian, bisexual, and transgender identities with good morals, model citizenship, and paradigmatic American families the "new homonormativity," which advances

> a politics that does not contest dominant heteronormative assumptions and institutions, but upholds and sustains them, while promising the possibility of

a demobilized gay constituency and a privatized and depoliticized gay culture anchored in domesticity and consumption. (50)

When viewed through the lens of Duggan's new homonormativity, the articulation of lesbian- and gay-headed families as necessary and complementary additions to the American social landscape by Dixon and other participants effectively removes gay-, lesbian-, bisexual-, and transgender-identified people from politics by situating them squarely within the private domestic sphere. From this location, and presumably with the benefit of relatively strong consumer power, lesbian- and gay-headed families are able to assert their belonging in the polity on the basis of the necessary similarity to heterosexual families: they vote, have children, go to work, and own cars and homes, just like straight people do, and do not advocate for revolution, as their Gay Liberation counterparts did.

The discourse of homonormativity was cast as an alternative to framing gay and lesbian identities as immutable. There were, however, some participants who urged the Roundtable to see the political and legal expediency of posing sexuality and gender identity as in fact essential and a core aspect of identity. Chai Feldblum, the director of the Georgetown University Law Center, pressed participants to see the legal and political reasons for posing identity as immutable: "I would say yes there's something called orientation and defines a set of people, very hard to change or impossible to change, and it's central to the person's identity. All those things are essential for constitutional and political activity."[14] Here, Feldblum alludes to the need to pose discrete identities as fundamentally impossible to alter and consequently linked to a history of discrimination in order to merit consideration under strict scrutiny by the courts. While this position captured the support of some of the participants—particularly in the wake of the 1986 *Bowers v. Hardwick* Supreme Court decision that denied constitutional protection for gay men based on what the Court's majority represented as scientific, historical, and moral reasons—there were many participants who expressed reservations about the turn to immutability for many of the same reasons that some protested the morality framing.

Representatives from various bisexual- and transgender-oriented groups, for instance, voiced strong objections to framing sexuality and gender identity as a product of biological determinants. One unidentified participant explained that "[i]f you're really going to actually support bi and trans have to drop the immutability thing. . . . So much about being intersex or transgender it's not just a matter of feeling like I'm both with it, some of it's trying things out."[15] Comments such as these were echoed by other participants, who argued that all the members of the Roundtable would be well served to remember that, as one participant put it, "heterosexism is the common oppressor."[16] Similarly to the transgender-identified activists, who urged lesbian and gay political actors during this same time period to see gender normativity as the common oppressor that should unite transgender, lesbian, and gay activists (Murib 2015), these participants urged others at the Roundtable to keep in mind that questions of the origins of sexual orientation and gender identity were irrelevant in the face of socially constructed categories that are used to maintain the dominance of straight-identified people over all other possible relationship configurations.

The systems that structured and maintained this domination, specifically at the site of the federal government, thus informed the concluding comments of this Roundtable. One participant explained the resistance to defining the origins of gay, lesbian, bisexual, and transgender identity this way: "The Constitution doesn't differentiate between GLBT and non-GLBT. We need to call religious folks when they are trying to influence the government—the constitution does talk about that and religious right is trying to annex the Constitution."[17] Once again, the backlash in the form of stigmatization is cited as a reason for unified political mobilization. In this iteration, the speaker encourages the Roundtable members to take an explicitly political position. By agreeing to situate the political claims of gay, lesbian, bisexual, and transgender-identified people in relation to the Constitution, in opposition to heterosexual domination and with immediate concern for how marginalized groups ought to be treated under the law, the participants at the September 1998 Roundtable reasserted the political standing of these groups, as a group: GLBT. Participants at this meeting of the Roundtable introduced GLBT as a marginalized group that would make claims on political rights. The question of the origins of gay, lesbian, bisexual, and transgender identities was left unsettled, and the need to continue a strong and unified political mobilization remained a priority.

The next section explores the agenda of political interests generated by the leaders taking part in the National Policy Roundtable between 1999 and 2001. During this time period, the question of how to craft an inclusive movement—particularly with respect to race—occupied the agendas of the Roundtable.

Inclusion across GLBT

Over time, the NPR evolved into the site where executive directors discussed ways to make the movement more efficient by developing shared agendas and delegating tasks, such as lobbying and public outreach. Increasingly, these activities were conducted under the aegis of "GLBT politics." That is, rather than representing many different agendas through loosely structured coalitions around specific issues, as they had done in the past, the organizations taking part in the NPR came to be seen as representative of a new identity category that was emerging in the late 1990s: GLBT (Valentine 2007). As the coalitional work across various groups became more institutionalized in conjunction with this new identity category, part of the function for the NPR was hosting meetings to address the extent to which diverse interests and segments of the gay, lesbian, bisexual, and transgender community were represented. In what follows, I examine the minutes from meetings held between 1999 and 2001 to show how participants of the Roundtable attended to questions of inclusion in the new coalition, particularly with respect to race.

Between 1999 and 2001, several meetings of the Roundtable were convened to address the structural and attitudinal aspects of the different organizations that resulted in their predominantly white leaderships. These meetings invited leaders from interest groups representing people of color, particularly representatives from Black and Latino gay, lesbian, bisexual, and transgender interest groups, to a discussion on race with the intention of shaping the movement from within. Phil Wilson, the executive director of the AIDS Social Policy Archive and founder of the National Black Gay and Lesbian Leadership Forum, chaired one such panel. His opening for the meeting succinctly introduced the issues characterizing the questions of inclusion across the coalition and in the GLBT movement:

> What is our message? The core of the message is that "We are just like you." Well, if you can imagine this statement being said in the current Congress—with its old white men. What does it mean to be just like them? These are old racists. What does it mean to be just like them? The goal is not to make me equal by diminishing my blackness, to be just like them. That is not the goal. I once said about the definition of gay rights: "gay rights are the rights of white GLBT people to oppress the rest of us like straight people."[18]

Wilson's comments are implicitly directed to the assimilationist strategies advanced by some of the Roundtable's national interest groups, which tended to assert the political and social standing of lesbian and gay people on the basis of their fundamental similarity to their straight analogues (D'Emilio 1983). Here, Wilson illustrates how these assimilationist political strategies necessarily resulted in the exclusion of Black and Latino lesbian women and gay men whose claims to the same status as heterosexuals were inflected by race, and thus precluded the possibility of asserting that "we are just like you" because of markedly different racial and ethnic histories.

It is telling that many participants also considered intervening in the assimilationist agenda promulgated by many of the national groups as the wrong goal to advance from within the coalition active at the Roundtable. Vaid even went so far as to speculate about the possibility of forming an entirely separate movement and group of organizations dedicated to race and class:

> What we can then do is to create a progressive wing of the GLBT movement and resign ourselves to work with THE movement on the "sexual orientation" issue in COALITION and that there will be other ways in which THE movement cannot

be together. And we can work with other groups on the race and economic justice issues.[19]

Whereas the earlier Roundtables were devoted to forming many coalitions across the disparate groups representing gay, lesbian, bisexual, and transgender memberships and advancing several different but coordinated agendas, here Vaid suggests that there is, in fact, a unified GLBT coalition that has taken shape, and that the best way to address issues of marginalization within that coalition would be to form two independent wings of that coalition. The new progressive wing would join in coalition with "THE" movement—comprised of organizations presumably preoccupied only with sexual orientation—to draw attention to issues of economic and racial marginalization. While some participants supported introducing a progressive flank to the increasingly mainstream GLBT movement, others resisted this strategy on the grounds that it would serve to further naturalize the associations of "GLBT" with sexuality and whiteness. For these participants, what was needed was the reorientation of the newly unified "GLBT" agenda to prioritize issues like the Employment Non-Discrimination Act (ENDA), which would ideally help to protect Black and Latino gay-, lesbian-, bisexual-, and transgender-identified people by ensuring access to employment.

Taking Wilson's and Vaid's comments about race and class together illustrates two important features of the GLBT coalition that had taken shape at the National Policy Roundtables since its inception in 1997. First, as the transcripts from these later meetings shows, by the late 1990s the groups participating in the Roundtable had steadily evolved into a united front to address issues of sexuality in politics. The second feature to note is that this new, unified GLBT movement tended to marginalize issues at the intersection of race and sexuality, as well as political agendas pertaining to bisexuals and transgender-identified people. The paradox of the new coalition and identity category developed at the Roundtables thus emerges. While the participants at the National Policy Roundtables were seemingly successful at introducing the linked and overlapping nature of gay, lesbian, bisexual, and transgender identity categories, these links were made by naturalizing sexuality as the similarity that bound these groups together. This privileging of sexuality—understood exclusively in opposition to the categories of straight or heterosexual—effectively closed off coalitions with other political groups and completely silenced consideration for internal marginalization and exclusions produced within the GLBT category.

Conclusions

Approaching the new identity category of "GLBT" as a coalition in itself furnishes insight into the ways in which select similarities are used to project specific meanings with an identity category while also pointing to the differences through which these definitions operate. As this chapter attempts to show, the construction of this new category naturalized sexual orientation as the unifying characteristic across these various group, and effectively silenced concerns pertaining not only to race and class but also gender identification. The reliance upon "GLBT" to convey certain gender identities and sexualities in the U.S. context, in other words, comes at the cost of acknowledging the particular experiences of marginalization and exclusion experienced by bisexual men and women, those who are queer and transgender-identified, gay-, lesbian-, bisexual-, and transgender-identified people of color, and intersex individuals—among many other examples—in contemporary political agendas and representations advanced under the aegis of "GLBT politics."

Building on these observations, I want to conclude this chapter by suggesting that researchers should rethink the use of "GLBT" as an analytic and descriptive category in political science. Broadly, this assertion stems from the ways "GLBT" naturalizes unity across gay, lesbian, bisexual, and transgender identity categories, treating their coherence as a pre-political fact rooted in biological similarities as opposed to a political coalition designed to mobilize around the implementation of laws and policies, or an identity category produced and given meaning through politics. The tendency to collapse gay, lesbian, bisexual, and transgender identities into a single descriptive category, "GLBT," thus assumes a false dichotomy, wherein differences and exclusions are understood as functioning only between groups—heterosexual and GLBT. Under this paradigm of a single and unified category, hierarchies of membership consequently flourish, with certain members of the "GLBT" category, namely, those who are white, cisgender gay men and lesbians, representing the group to the simultaneous exclusion of the many others who do not match these dominant characteristics but also identify as lesbian, gay, bisexual, and/or transgender. Disaggregating "GLBT" into its constitutive subcategories for the purposes of crafting research questions will ultimately direct research towards developing better understanding of inequalities produced *within* groups as well as *between* them.

NOTES

1 There are many different orderings of this initialism. These include "LGBT," which seems to enjoy more current popularity. Others include still more groups, such as "queer," "intersex," and "allies." I use "GLBT" for this chapter because it is what many of the political actors cited used. For a concise overview of the alternate orderings of these identities, see Zein Murib, "LGBT," *Transgender Studies Quarterly* 1, nos. 1–2 (2014): 118–20.

2 "NGLTF Convenes Third National Policy Roundtable." *Oasis Magazine*, 1998. Accessed using the Internet Archive: www.waybackmachine.org.

3 See Strolovitch 2007, ch. 6, for a more comprehensive overview of findings regarding interest group coalitions and the representation of interests offered by them.

4 In 1988, a similar set of meetings was convened to gather leaders to capitalize on the momentum of the 1987 National March on Washington for Lesbian and Gay Rights. Referred

to as "The War Conference," these meetings established the intention for coordinated political action; however, they drew critiques for not being diverse and inclusive. See Darrell Yates Rist, "AIDS as Apocalypse: The Deadly Costs of an Obsession." *Nation*, Feb. 1989.

5 "National Policy Roundtable," Human Sexuality Collection 7301, Box 299, Folder 12, 1 (hereafter, "HSC"), Cornell University, Ithaca, NY.

6 For more on Mapplethorpe's photography and the significance of his eventual defunding by the NEA, see: Kobena Mercer, "Looking for Trouble." *Transition* no. 5 (1991): 184–97.

7 "National Policy Roundtable," HSC 7301, Box 299, Folder 12, 8.

8 "National Policy Roundtable: Selected Minutes on Federal Agencies and Outcome of the 2000 Election." HSC 7301, Box 299, Folder 17, n.p.

9 Ibid.

10 Ibid.

11 Cynthia Burack's 2014 study of the Christian Right shows how the 1973 declassification of homosexuality as a mental illness by the American Psychiatric Association (APA) provoked the formation of a new professional organization called the National Association for Research and Therapy of Homosexuality (NARTH) to serve as a centralized resource for conversion therapists (Burack 2014; see also Fetner 2008).

12 "National Policy Roundtable Minutes: September 17th and 18th, 1998." HSC 7301, Box 299, Folder 13, 26.

13 Ibid., 24.

14 Ibid., 21.

15 Ibid.

16 Ibid., 22.

17 Ibid., 26.

18 Ibid., n.p.

19 Ibid., n.p. Emphasis in original.

REFERENCES

Ayoub, Phillip M. 2014. "With Arms Wide Shut: Threat Perception, Norm Reception, and Mobilized Resistance to LGBT Rights." *Journal of Human Rights* 13: 337–62.

Beltrán, Cristina. 2010. *The Trouble with Unity: Latino Politics and the Creation of Identity*. New York: Oxford University Press.

Benford, Robert D., and David A. Snow. 2000. "Framing Processes and Social Movements: An Overview and Assessment." *Annual Review of Sociology* 26: 611–39.

Berbrier, Mitch. 2002. "Making Minorities: Cultural Space, Stigma Transformation Frames, and the Categorical Status Claims of Deaf, Gay, and White Supremacist Activists in Late-Twentieth-Century America." *Sociological Forum* 17, no. 4: 553–91.

Berry, Jeffrey M. 1977. *Lobbying for the People: The Political Behavior of Public Interest Groups*. Princeton, NJ: Princeton University Press.

Bishin, Benjamin G., Thomas J. Hayes, Matthew B. Incantalupo, and Charles Anthony Smith. 2015. "Opinion Backlash and Public Attitudes: Are Political Advances in Gay Rights Counterproductive?" *American Journal of Political Science* 60, no. 3: 625–48. doi:10.1111/ajps.12181.

Brubaker, Rogers. 2006. *Ethnicity without Groups*. New ed. Cambridge, MA: Harvard University Press.

Burack, Cynthia. 2014. *Tough Love: Sexuality, Compassion, and the Christian Right*. Albany: State University of New York Press.

Carastathis, Anna. 2013. "Identity Categories as Potential Coalitions." *Signs* 38, no. 4 (June 2013): 941–65. doi:10.1086/669573.

Cohen, Cathy J. 1997. "Punks, Bulldaggers, and Welfare Queens: The Radical Potential of Queer Politics?" *GLQ: A Journal of Lesbian and Gay Studies* 3, no. 4: 437–65.
doi:10.1215/10642684-3-4-437.

Cohen, Cathy. 1999. *The Boundaries of Blackness: AIDS and the Breakdown of Black Politics*. 1st
ed. Chicago: University of Chicago Press.

Connolly, William E. 2002. *Identity\Difference: Democratic Negotiations of Political Paradox*.
Revised, expanded ed. Minneapolis: University of Minnesota Press.

Crenshaw, Kimberlé. 1991. "Mapping the Margins: Intersectionality, Identity Politics, and
Violence against Women of Color." *Stanford Law Review* 43, no. 6: 1241–99.

D'Emilio, John. 1983. *Sexual Politics, Sexual Communities: The Making of a Homosexual Minority
in the United States, 1940–1970*. Chicago: University of Chicago Press.

Duggan, Lisa. 2003. *The Twilight of Equality? Neoliberalism, Cultural Politics, and the Attack on
Democracy*. Boston: Beacon.

Fetner, Tina. 2008. *How the Religious Right Shaped Lesbian and Gay Activism*. Minneapolis:
University of Minnesota Press.

Flores, Andrew R., and Scott Barclay. 2014. "Backlash, Consensus, or Neutralization? Decompos-
ing the Effect of Same-Sex Marriage Policy on Mass Attitudes." Manuscript prepared for the
2014 American Political Science Association Meeting, Washington, DC.

Ghaziani, Amin. 2008. *The Dividends of Dissent: How Conflict and Culture Work in Lesbian and
Gay Marches on Washington*. Chicago: University of Chicago Press.

Giles, Micheal W., and Kaenan Hertz. 1994. "Racial Threat and Partisan Identification." *American
Political Science Review* 88, no. 2: 317–26. doi:10.2307/2944706.

Haider-Markel, Donald P., Alana Querze, and Kara Lindaman. 2007. "Lose, Win, or Draw?
A Reexamination of Direct Democracy and Minority Rights." *Political Research Quarterly* 60,
no. 2: 304–14.

Hall, Stuart. 2000. "Who Needs 'Identity'?" In *Identity: A Reader*, edited by Paul Du Gay, Jessica
Evans, and Peter Redman, 15–30. London: Sage.

Holyoke, Thomas T. 2009. "Interest Group Competition and Coalition Formation." *American
Journal of Political Science* 53, no. 2: 360–75.

Hula, Kevin W. 1999. *Lobbying Together: Interest Group Coalitions in Legislative Politics*. American Governance and Public Policy Series. Washington, DC: Georgetown University Press.

Kanthak, Kristin, and George A. Krause. 2012. *The Diversity Paradox: Political Parties, Legislatures, and the Organizational Foundations of Representation in America*. New York: Oxford
University Press.

Kissack, Terrance. 1995. "Freaking Fag Revolutionaries: New York's Gay Liberation Front,
1969–1971." *Radical History Review* 62: 104–34.

Loomis, Burdett A. 1986. "Coalitions of Interests: Building Bridges in the Balkanized State." *Interest Group Politics* 2: 258–74.

McCammon, Holly, and Karen Campbell. 2002. "Allies on the Road to Victory: Coalition Formation between the Suffragists and the Woman's Christian Temperance Union." *Mobilization: An
International Quarterly* 7, no. 3: 231–51.

Meyer, David S., and Suzanne Staggenborg. 1996. "Movements, Countermovements, and the
Structure of Political Opportunity." *American Journal of Sociology* 101, no. 6: 1628–60.

Murib, Zein. 2015. "Transgender: Examining a New Political Identity Category Using Three
Political Processes." *Politics, Groups, and Identities* 3, no. 3. doi:10.1080/21565503.2015.1048257.

Norton, Anne. 2004. *95 Theses on Politics, Culture, and Method*. New Haven, CT: Yale University
Press.

Seidman, Steven. 2001. "From Identity to Queer Politics: Shifts in Normative Heterosexuality and
the Meaning of Citizenship." *Citizenship Studies* 5, no. 3: 321–28.

Snow, David A., E. Burke Rochford Jr., Steven K. Worden, and Robert D. Benford. 1986. "Frame Alignment Processes, Micromobilizations, and Movement Participation." *American Sociological Review* 51, no. 4: 464–81.

Staggenborg, Suzanne. 1986. "Coalition Work in the Pro-Choice Movement: Organizational and Environmental Opportunities and Obstacles." *Social Problems* 33, no. 5: 374–90.

Stein, Marc. 2012. *Rethinking the Gay and Lesbian Movement*. 1st ed. New York: Routledge.

Strolovitch, Dara Z. 2007. *Affirmative Advocacy: Race, Class, and Gender in Interest Group Politics*. Chicago: University of Chicago Press.

Stryker, Susan. 2008. *Transgender History*. Berkeley, CA: Seal Press.

Tolbert, Caroline J., and John A. Grummel. 2003. "Revisiting the Racial Threat Hypothesis: White Voter Support for California's Proposition 209." *State Politics & Policy Quarterly* 3, no. 2 (2003): 183–202.

Tolbert, Caroline J., and Rodney E. Hero. 1996. "Race/Ethnicity and Direct Democracy: An Analysis of California's Illegal Immigration Initiative." *Journal of Politics* 58, no. 3 (August 1996): 806–18. doi:10.2307/2960447.

Tolbert, Caroline J., and Rodney E. Hero. 2001. "Dealing with Diversity: Racial/Ethnic Context and Social Policy Change." *Political Research Quarterly* 54, no. 3: 571–604.

Valentine, David. 2007. *Imagining Transgender: An Ethnography of a Category*. Durham, NC: Duke University Press Books.

Warner, Michael. 1993. *Fear of a Queer Planet: Queer Politics and Social Theory*. Minneapolis: University of Minnesota Press.

3

Politics outside the Law

Transgender Lives and the Challenge of Legibility

B LEE AULTMAN AND PAISLEY CURRAH

In the United States, movements for transgender equality appear to have advanced with astonishing speed in the new millennium. From policy reforms to public opinion trends, transgender people seem to be well on their way to full inclusion in the American polity. Trans rights are fast catching up with successes of the gay, lesbian, and bisexual rights movement. Of the twenty-one states that ban discrimination based on sexual orientation, only three now exclude gender identity from that ban (American Civil Liberties Union 2015). After decades of resistance, in the last fifteen years impact litigation on behalf of transgender clients has resulted in some tremendous successes. Even in the absence of a federal nondiscrimination bill that includes gender identity, discrimination against transgender people is increasingly seen as a violation of Title VII's prohibition against sex discrimination (*Glenn v. Brumby* 2011). Many state laws now protect students from discrimination and harassment based on their gender identity or expression, and the Department of Justice views discrimination against trans students and gender-nonconforming students as a violation of Title IX's ban on sex discrimination in education (*G. G. v. Gloucester County School Board* 2015). More and more agencies, from the State Department to many state divisions of motor vehicles, now allow individuals to change the sex assignment on their identity documents without requiring proof of body modifications such as genital surgery (Eilperin 2015). A 2015 poll found that 72 percent of the millennial generation in the United States favor laws banning discrimination against transgender people—a proportion very close to the 73 percent who support protections for gay and lesbian people (Jones and Cox 2015, 42). Certainly, there have been some setbacks, such as the failure of Houston's Equal Rights Ordinance in 2015. Opponents of that legislation campaigned with the "No Men in Women's Bathrooms" slogan and defeated the ordinance by an overwhelming margin of 61 percent to 39 percent (Fernandez and Smith 2015). And there is still no federal nondiscrimination law that would ban discrimination based on sexual orientation *and* gender identity. However, that failure is not a result of lack of support but of specific institutional barriers (Smith 2008).

In general, however, the clear trajectory appears to be toward increasing transgender inclusion in the institutions that comprise American citizenship.

This was made possible, in part, because gay rights organizations, after decades of not being predisposed to seeing trans people as among their constituents, had begun to add "T" to the "GLB" umbrella (Minter 2006). It was also a result of advocacy by an initially small but determined number of transgender "pariahs" who faced not just resistance but ridicule when they first enunciated arguments for transgender rights in the last decades of the twentieth century (Sontag 2015). In the last fifteen years, then, transgender rights have entered the mainstream. When Joe Biden, a vice president in a poll-driven administration, proclaims that "[t]ransgender rights are the civil rights issue of our time" (quoted in Puar 2015, 45), it is very clear that this relatively new identity politics movement is on the cusp of respectability, of achieving the formal recognition that inclusion in normative citizenship brings. These successes have been refracted to great effect through the media, which amplifies the impression that transgender people— while still facing legal barriers to full inclusion—are just steps away from equality. In a three-month period ending July 31, 2015, the *New York Times* editorial board came out in support of transgender issues seven times—and that number does not include the several almost universally positive op-ed contributions published during the same period. The lead-off editorial in this series, on "transgender Americans," promised "heartening stories" of acceptance as well as the policy challenges still facing this newest "civil rights movement" (New York Times Editorial Board 2015).

The recognized achievements of the transgender rights movement in the United States have taken place in the institutions where politics is imagined to take place—courts, legislatures, administrative venues, and the highly resourced organizations that purportedly represent transgender people. But limiting the analysis of trans politics to a "political" field defined by formal institutions will narrow one's findings. As one commentator puts it, "the world you make inside your head, that's the one you see around you" (Jones 1989). In this chapter, we argue that if one looks elsewhere, one sees other forms of trans politics. And studying that political activity produces a very different account of the lives of transgender and gender-nonconforming people than is depicted when one looks at courts and legislatures, voters and polls. However, struggles outside these venues are much less legible to scholars of American politics. That illegibility is a product of two occlusions. First, in political science, these institutions are often constructed as the horizon and limit of legitimate politics. Indeed, over the twentieth century, an expansive notion of "the political" has shrunk radically. It is now limited to the corporate bodies of interest groups, political parties, and the various branches of state and federal government. Sheldon S. Wolin suggests that the death of the political has been brought about, ironically, by the creation of more formal mechanisms (constitutions, periodic elections, governance by experts) designed to protect the political process. As a political actor, the individual citizen has now been reduced to a mere actor within a constraining web of economic activity. "The citizen," he argues, "is shrunk to the voter: periodi-cally courted, warned, and confused but otherwise kept at a distance from actual decision-making and allowed to emerge only ephemerally in a cameo appear-ance according to a script composed by opinion takers/makers" (2004, 565). Others, such as Wendy Brown, draw on Foucault's work on neoliberalism to point to "the growth of capitalism and its overtaking of public life" to account for an increasingly circumscribed political imaginary. "*Homo oeconomicus*," Brown writes, "has displaced *homo politicus*" (2015, 92).

Second, in order to be legible as subject-citizens (from this point forward, "subject") making demands within U.S. legal architecture, or as exemplars of a cognizable social movement, subjects have generally enunciated claims for equality as a "but for" arithmetic: but for characteristic X, one would have been treated equally. This logic reduces the legal subject to a singular characteris-tic, one that defines the parameters of the group. While the boundary may be relatively porous or relatively impenetrable, rights discourse demands a sin-gular "us." For the category transgender, the defining characteristic is broadly conceived: Susan Stryker designates it as a "movement away from an initially assigned gender position," one that could be embodied by "any and all kinds of variation from gender norms and expectations" (2008, 19). Even with such an analytically broad definition, trans people, whose vulnerability and precar-ity result from imbricated structures of racism, class, (dis)ability, gender, and nonhegemonic forms of embodiment of many kinds, are much less legible to political scientists, to mainstream LGBT equality movements, and to state actors. Ironically, the inadmissibility of everything except the "but for" characteristic taken to define trans people increases the *invisibility* of the vulnerable and the *visibility* of normative trans people, thus creating "transnormative" subjects. Of course, no one is "just" transgender—one's race, ethnicity, and class, to name a few intersectional positions, also produce privilege and vulnerability. Writing in the 1980s about employment discrimination claims brought by black women, Kimberlé Crenshaw explains the effects of this "but for" single-issue framework: "sex and race discrimination have come to be defined in terms of the experiences of those who are privileged *but for* their racial or sexual characteristics" (1989, 144). Crenshaw draws a compelling analogy to show how the consideration of more than one hierarchy of social difference at a time becomes impossible in the legal imaginary:

> Imagine a basement which contains all people who are disadvantaged on the basis of race, sex, class, sexual preference, age and/or physical ability. These people are stacked—feet standing on shoulders—with those on the bottom being disadvan-taged by the full array of factors, up to the very top, where the heads of all those disadvantaged by a singular factor brush up against the ceiling. Their ceiling is actu-ally the floor above which only those who are *not* disadvantaged in any way reside.

In efforts to correct some aspects of domination, those above the ceiling admit from the basement only those who can say that "but for" the ceiling, they too would be in the upper room. A hatch is developed through which those placed immediately below can crawl. Yet this hatch is generally available only to those who—due to the singularity of their burden and their otherwise privileged position relative to those below—are in the position to crawl through. Those who are multiply-burdened are generally left below unless they can somehow pull themselves into the groups that are permitted to squeeze through the hatch. (1989, 151–52)

In this metaphor, transnormative subjects "before the law" are likely to be those in the "but for" group, closest to the floor above.[1]

A transnormative approach seeks inclusion in existing political and social arrangements, and, like its cognate, "homonormative," describes a politics in which " 'equality' becomes narrow, formal access to a few conservatizing institutions" (Duggan 2003, 65). Aren Z. Aizura describes "transnormative" as an imperative to fade "into the population . . . to be 'proper' in the eyes of the state: to reproduce, to find proper employment; to reorient one's 'different' body into the flow of the nationalized aspiration for possessions, property, [and] wealth" (2006, 295). The vulnerabilities that structure many trans people's lives will not be ameliorated when some trans people are allowed entrée into current political arrangements and rights. Nor will these vulnerabilities disappear by developing a more robust intersectional strategy that remains focused on the overdetermined term "recognition." In fact, a strategy geared toward achieving formal political emancipation/equality can actually have negative effects on the material lives of those encumbered by more than one form of social disadvantage, especially including poverty, or, in the current argot, precarity. Beyond not serving the multiply marginalized, the movement to achieve formal political equality might intensify the substantive inequality concealed by a political culture focused on liberal democratic institutions. As Judith Butler reminds us, "Paradoxically, as certain forms of recognition are extended, the region of the unrecognizable is preserved and expanded accordingly" (2015, 7). Additionally, a focus on assimilation obscures the constitutive relation between the transgender "have" and "have nots." As a result, C. Riley Snorton and Jin Haritaworn argue, "the universal trajectory of [the transnormative subject's] coming out/transition, visibility, recognition, protection, and self-actualization largely remains uninterrogated in its complicities and convergences with biomedical, neoliberal, racist, and imperialist projects" (2013, 67; see also Gossett 2013, 588). Not only does the liberal presumption that all subjects are equally legible not hold, but, Butler points out, "embodying the norm or norms by which one gains recognizable status is a way of ratifying and reproducing certain norms of recognition over others, and so constraining the field of the recognizable" (Butler 2015, 35). In sum, there is not, then, one "transgender" politics, but a plural array of political activity: one is the story of increasing political equality and recognition; the others range from daily acts of embodied resistance to more intransigent vulnerabilities that remain illegible to readers of the *New York Times*, those emerging transnormative subjects and their cisgender allies who may care but still cannot think in intersectional terms, and political scientists who are often preoccupied with polling and institutional behavior.[2]

Because most scholarship in political science has tended to equate political legibility with what occurs in courts, legislatures, executive agencies, the mainstream media, and recognized spaces of protest, it is no wonder that an expansive vision of transgender politics has generally remained out of the political scientist's view. With this chapter, we hope to redirect attention away from the institutional domain toward the less recognizably political spaces and times of provisional events, virtual networks of resistance, "subaltern counterpublics" (Fraser 1990, 67), moments of "fugitive democracy" (Wolin 1994), "micropolitical enactments" (Frank 2010), antihierarchical *horizontalidad* (Sitrin 2012), archives of violence (Gossett 2013), and "embodied and plural performative" forms (Butler 2015, 8) that comprise transgender politics outside the law.[3] Certainly, work in other disciplines, such as sociology and anthropology, has chronicled dispossessed trans communities (e.g., Valentine 2007). And many theorists of democratic politics, from Hannah Arendt to Sheldon Wolin, have extolled a conception of "the political" that comes into being outside the permanent apparatuses of governance designed to channel the chaos wrought by aleatory events and potentially revolutionary irruptions into more predictable—and thus less political—institutional spaces (Foucault 2007, 46). What's lacking, however, is an examination of an expansive notion of the "transgender political," one that brings normative questions of justice to bear on empirical examinations of lives in their *being* and politics as its *being enacted in the quotidian*.[4] Rather than limit the study of transgender politics to the large-scale arena of "the state," then, we center localized, embodied action that can "generate and continuously renew direct political experience" (Wolin 2004, 604). By foregrounding the localism of transgender bodies in revolt, of situated contests and nonconforming gender enactments, we identify a political constituted by the interaction of discourse—or collected bodies of knowledge about reality and constellations of facts—and activity.

The theoretical framework here draws on work that centers the body as a locus of particular political and discursive investments. While Foucault saw sexuality "as an especially dense transfer point for relations of power" (Foucault 1990, 103), we see the sex/gendered body as another such point. For Foucault, the power of discourse lies in its ability to discipline and normalize certain behaviors, barring others as deviant and creating a space of illegibility (1979). This space of illegibility, however, requires our attention, for it is also the place where human actors also find their agency, or will, through their imbrication within and against these very systems of power. Butler suggests,

> Although gender cannot function as the paradigm for all forms of existence that struggle against the normative construction of the human, it can offer us a point of departure for thinking about power, agency, and resistance. If we accept that there are sexual and gender norms that condition who will be recognizable and "legible" and who will not, we can begin to see how the "illegible" may form as a group, developing forms of becoming legible to one another, how they are exposed to different forms of living gender violence, and how this common exposure can become the basis for resistance. (2015, 38)

In political science, the identities of women and gay, lesbian, and bisexual people, whether cis or trans, are often construed as pre-political, as already fully formed when appearing in the domain of politics—just like those of their universal counterparts: straight, cisgender men. The processes by which these identities come into being have largely been ignored by political scientists—or at least not treated as a political phenomenon. Behind the abstract accounts of liberal LGBT strategies for rights and equality emerge trans communities defined by and subjected to a mode of being called "gender." As Claudia Hilb suggests, the "political" is any irruption at the scene of the individual within h/er social relations (1994, 109). These irruptions are multiple and unexpected.

There is no common story of transgender dispossession, embodiments of gender/sex, or the local and provisional collective actions that come into being. All seek to survive, and some seek to subvert, reformulate, or otherwise undo the discursive chains that make them illegible, and these actions are inherently political. The epistemological dimension of this work focuses on how the local knowledges of the body are themselves imbued with political meaning. These activities must all be treated as political, built within the irruptions of the everyday. But all these political efforts demand rethinking as productive of particularized and local political knowledge. That is the first step toward what we will be identifying as epistemic justice—bringing the plurality of transgender politics into the narrative of political action in the United States. The following section illustrates transgender being as it has been articulated in archived materials from the University of Victoria's Transgender Archives. In examining the varied ways transgender has been shaped by transgender people for themselves, we develop an account of political subjectivity that is in excess of the recognizably political channels and medical narratives that have defined transgender identities, actions, and daily life.

On Crossing the "Genderal" Boundary: Embodying the Political

We do not advance a "tragic trans narrative." Asserting that all trans people suffer, at the hands of either social actors or an already pathologized identity, risks appropriating the narrative power of the trans person themself. However, as much as joy and sense of community have animated transgender political action, isolation and social rejection remain salient. For example, in an undated poem from an unknown author, the speaker writes, "Is there anyone willing to give / Hope to me so I can live / I search for help, someone that's kind / But sympathy I never find." This poem, "The Agony of the Transsexual," captures the invisible life of nonnormative embodiment. It announces an outpouring for a new political regime of recognition.[5] Indeed, the narratives of early trans folx share a private, mostly secretive set of boundaries in which their identities were forged. At this point in time, transgender/transsexual being had not yet been represented in any socially supportive way (Meyerowtiz 2002). Virginia Prince, an early pioneer of the "transgenderist movement," had already illustrated this privation in her book *The Transvestite and His Wife* (Prince 1967). As Butler points out, "Not everyone can appear in a bodily form, and many of those who cannot appear, who are constrained from appearing or who operate through virtual or digital networks, are also . . . constrained from making a specific body appearance in public space" (2015, 8). For Butler, and for us, modes of presentation are partially constituted within a grid of intelligibility, norms that prefigure certain social appearances. Gender/sex is one node on this grid. Trans identifications and embodiments were often constructed within the spaces of subaltern communities, hidden away from the public sphere. In such a way, we investigate the extent to which these subaltern "gender transgressors" created distinctive grammars through which trans people could "speak," or in the very least be disclosed, to public political life (Spivak 1988).

Outside medical and legal discourses and forums, transgender "social transitions" take on multiple contexts with interconnected depths, from pronoun choices to name selections, physical appearances, the physical manifestation of "voice," clothing, hair, makeup, nonmedical body modification such as breast binding, "standing-to-pee" devices, penis-tucking, and hair removal (Reynolds and Goldstein 2014, 124–36). "Being read correctly" or "going stealth" become personal acts of survival—and in this sense political acts against social policing. Given this (nonexhaustive) range of activities, a single narrative, an unfortunate linguistic slip that describes the "transgender experience" in the singular or a "trans-ness" as essence, commits an epistemic wrong, an injustice, to the representative voice of these political communities (Fricker 2007). More to the point, "Mainstream cultural beliefs about 'transness' are so far off the mark that some of us want to be out and visible everywhere we go, to put a face on what 'trans does and does not mean'" (Reynolds and Goldstein 2014, 144). Each person defines identities and self-creates, carves out selves in private and public places, in different ways.

> The decision to live privately as a trans person is different for each of us. For most of us, every use of the right pronoun and name is an affirmation of our identity. If we choose not to tell people how we got there, that does not necessarily mean we

are ashamed of being trans. . . . For some of us, living stealth may be motivated by the desire for privacy, job or family security, or physical safety. (Reynolds and Goldstein 2014, 144)

When "[Helen] ran up against all the medical, social, and legal problems of actually becoming Helen, [she] didn't know where to turn" (Dumanoski 1975, 17). Helen turned to social networks at her disposal. Organizations like Fantasia Fair, Gender Identity Service, the Outreach Initiative, and others erected a small but supportive edifice for social connectivity.

In constructing the self, transgender men and women engage in the revelatory practice of embodied change that is marked by the "language and cultural forms at hand" (Meyerowitz 2002). Sexual characteristics, gender expression(s), the conflation of gender(s) altogether become the critical responses to a (cis) gendered system that accords individuals a this-or-that gendered legibility, and the private/public norms it prescribes. This individual legibility marks the realm of the personal. But the political is and always has been more than the personal. It exceeds the conceptual confines of such a closed sphere. As Farmer remarked, "The process of throwing off the shackles of masculinity to become a woman, I call 'Transition.' 'Transformation' has been a revolution in my awareness of myself and of my life, well beyond the matter of gender" (1993, v). Farmer revels in the emancipatory and self-creative acts that transformed her in spite of an otherwise cisnormative view that obviated her body's legibility—her very source of social recognition. In a letter addressed to "Dear," the author, Nancy, writes,

At age 46 (an unlikely age to re-start!) I am embarking on an entirely new lifestyle and, in fact, life. Each of you is unaware of a massive burden I have been carrying for most of my known life. I have, alternatively, over the years, capped, repressed, depressed, and what-ever other word is available in our language to convey the idea of pushing down a gnawing and persistent theme. . . . Briefly, Bill Griglak is Nancy Ledins—the name I have chosen to be known by in this preoperative stage and, within due time, postoperatively. (Ledins c. 1960, 1–2)

Nancy, like many transgender people (she identifies as transsexual) declares that "[s]urgery is not the final answer—not the end-all—not the magical answer" (ibid., 3). Transgender people undergoing surgeries have exclaimed, "I feel like I have been let out of a prison" (Drake 1974, 56). Another proclaimed that, following surgery, "It's like being given a second chance at life" (ibid.). The rest is recognition. "What of the future?" she asks. "I am now in the pre-operative stage—basically it means a period of living full-time in the female role, trying to bring together sexual and gender issues into an integrated life" (ibid., 4). Nancy exclaims, through all this process, which is, in one sense, out of her own hands, "I am me—and I am becoming" (Ledins c. 1960, 4).

The "prison" and "second chance" narratives indicate the presence of despair and discrimination built into some early transgender experiences. It announces a historical narrative that situates transgender people within a constraining cultural framework to be resisted. Ariadne Kane—founder of the Fantasia Fair and other social networks formed in the 1970s and '80s for the purposes of bringing what Kane and others first called "transgenderists" together—often fought against the prevailing norms that situated men as male and women as female (see figure 3.1). Dressing in an attire that is socially constrained for a particular sex was often perceived as a "disguise," as committing fraud. Further, Kane found that major magazines that were engaged in "[the] casual use of such terms as 'transvestite, transsexual, maleness and femaleness, drag queen, etc.,' coupled with clichés about the attitude and events of the [transvestite] world, serve only to confound . . . fundamental issues concerning sex and gender roles" (Kane 1974).

These misconceptions, "casual" misuses of terms, and general ignorance about the "para-culture" of transgenderists no doubt contribute to an ongoing anxiety within the community. In "The Agony of the Transsexual," the author writes,

> If I told the world my one desire
> Their laughter could not quench the fire
> that burns this man's soul, torn apart
> for in it beats a woman's heart.

Discrimination is historically commonplace. In an interview, Jan Morris, a transgender woman, explains her encounters with social prejudice as "inescapable" ([In Her Own Words] c. 1970, 26). B. Fortune's words, written in 1985, provide an exemplary expression of this dual life: "Though I still live a lie, I have a wife, who knows, a daughter and family who don't know at this point. Why upset those about you unnecessarily? Life is a compromise and I have managed to find a compromised middle ground where I can be who I am and still give those about me the person they need and want" (8–9).

These texts indicate how the truth of transgender selfhood is distorted by the social norms that makes a personally lived truth unrepresentable. One must live a life for survival. The "lie" interiorizes as self-condemnation, anxiety, and the overwhelming feeling of isolation. Overcoming this seemingly insurmountable obstacle toward self-completion, many found, and still find, solace in service-oriented organizations. Helen, for example, felt "alienated from the transvestite group in which [she'd] been so actively involved. [She] felt different from the others and slowly struggled to the realization that [she] was, in fact, a transsexual" (Dumanoski 1975, 16). Her turning to the Gender Identity Services created a safe space for her identity to come into clearer view. The epistemic error would be to embed a nonagent in the narrative of the oppressed transgender

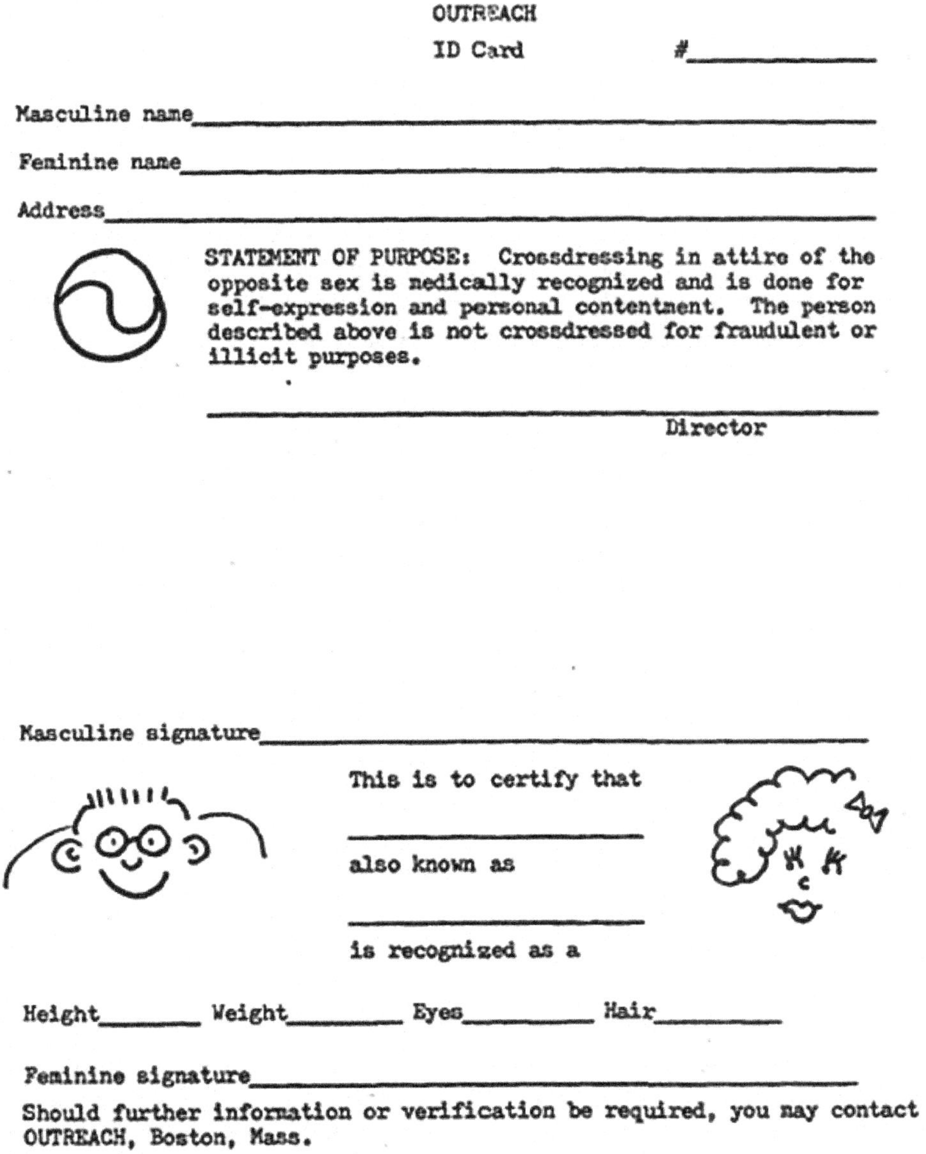

OUTREACH

ID Card # _____

Masculine name _____

Feminine name _____

Address _____

STATEMENT OF PURPOSE: Crossdressing in attire of the opposite sex is medically recognized and is done for self-expression and personal contentment. The person described above is not crossdressed for fraudulent or illicit purposes.

_____
Director

Masculine signature _____

This is to certify that

_____

also known as

_____

is recognized as a

Height _____ Weight _____ Eyes _____ Hair _____

Feminine signature _____

Should further information or verification be required, you may contact OUTREACH, Boston, Mass.

Figure 3.1. Outreach ID Card. Note the differences of gendered names and how the actual activity of signatures was also decidedly "gendered." University of Victoria, Transgender Archives, Rikki Swin Collection, Box 4.

person—a subject of both gendered and sexed terror. Each found ways to rebel and create the self that worked best for them in an inimical cultural apparatus.

The problem, so it would seem, is social and cultural. "Many trans folks experience serious mental health issues and have histories of trauma *due to transphobia*" (Sarkisova 2014, 292; emphasis ours). Thus the consequences of transphobic discourses for embodiment are many and varied. An anonymous survey of transgender youth taken in 2001 asked respondents to describe their most difficult moments in school, growing up, and coming to terms with identifying as transgender. Adjusting to a new gendered mode of existence is part of identity construction, often at odds with internalized normative genders. One youth in the same survey responds that their "physicality" was the issue. "Having to wear all this makeup just to hide the burning stinging redness from the obsessive shaving on my face. Also the fact that I do not have 'normal' sized breasts. The other body hair that I have to shave irks me to no end. The worst thing is the hair" (ibid., 15–16). Another respondent claimed that "passing most people look at me and see a dyke" (ibid.). The question of the ability to access transition-related services repeats itself. "I find it very difficult to find resources and someone to confide in because I know most people can't wrap their heads around the whole gender-bending thing" (ibid.). Even a (proper) name becomes a political preoccupation. "About a couple of weeks ago I started thinking about changing my name and pronouns. I went through my baby name books and talked to some friends. . . . Along with all that comes an extreme frustration with language. Theres [sic] only so many words to use for pronouns and genders and sometimes I feel like none of them fit me" (ibid., 17–18). Another found "finding others like myself (from baby TGs to 30 years of age), and finding our admirers"—that is, social connectivity—to be most challenging (ibid., 18).

Where these social contexts exist, they give transgender youth "peer networks where our gender identity and expression are not considered a distraction or concerning, thus enabling us to have more typical adolescent connections" (Keo-Meier and Hicks 2015, 460). These youth centers can be geographically dispersed. Many programs can be started in public schools, particularly in high school, such as Gay-Straight Alliances. These organizations are often student driven, and as a result encourage those already marginalized and bullied to come forward. "Many trans youth feel astounding pressure to prove we can fit into preexisting gender categories in our society and to prove we can live up to the standard of a 'real' man or woman" (ibid., 456). The imperative to be gender compliant and to "pass" puts particularly difficult demands on transgender youth in gender-segregated spaces such as locker rooms, sports teams, and bathrooms.

Fear and disgust (at myself). I know perfectly well that the majority of people out there at best view me with something in between revulsion and fascination. Like a circus freak on display. I'm terrified of most of the world. I feel alone and helpless and paranoid. At times it gets to the point where I can barely function. Then I become disgusted with myself: I have it so fucking GOOD! I eat well, I have a good house, my parents may be ashamed to be seen with me in public but at least they're still willing to send me to college. I'm not starving or working 18 hour days in a sweatshop or prostituting myself because I was thrown out of the house at 13.

I have no goddamn right to be so afraid. And I'm disgusted at myself for being a transsexual. (Transgender Youth Survey, 2001, 15)

The prevalence of cultural norms prescribing "passable" gender conformity brings about an internalized fear when that conformity isn't possible. The need for passability creates very real conditions for physical threats to a nonnormative body seen as trespassing on an already gender-coded social space. To overcome these anxieties and respond to the need to build communities in the face of hostile publics, many have turned to online networks (such as Facebook, YouTube, and other social media) to bridge geography and localized contexts. "I have a vlog where I talk about gender, and I'm subscribed to by a ton of transguys and their partners. It is a nice community, very supportive" (ibid., 457).

These narratives—personal experiences as described in surveys, autobiographical fragments, and poetry—highlight the challenges of legibility outside of normalizing accounts. To be transgender is to confound hegemonic external cultural expectations that the sex one is assigned at birth dictates one's gender for life. Living an authentic life under one's own authorization, without fear of the violence that misrecognition often entails, lies at the crux of these interwoven narratives. It is a politics of visibility that is deeply tied to a politics of survival. The political, as these narratives have illustrated, is grounded in the body, the everyday, and the oftentimes missed struggle of self-creative action.

In the second decade of the twenty-first century, we find that many trans people are much less likely to rely on coded language, hidden networks, and conferences whose topic is illegible to the mainstream. Indeed, given the widespread acceptance by the public of transgender people, institutions hidden from view, such as Fantasia Fair, are no longer necessary for transgender people to find support and acceptance, and to engage in embodied politics. That work has been delegated to national and regional transgender rights organizations that do engage in traditional forms of politics, focusing on impact litigation, policy work with executives, and legislation advancement. As we noted in the introduction, the trend in the United States is toward increasing equality and recognition. But these successes disproportionally benefit the "but for" element of the transgender community—those who occupy privileged positions vis-à-vis everything but their gender identity or expression (i.e., race privilege and [dis]ability). At this moment in time, then, there is an array of distinctive transgender politics: those focusing on formal equality and those lived by people whose vulnerability to private and state violence, economic dispossession, and gross health disparity cannot be resolved by a politics of (equal) recognition. These politics are so distinct that Paisley Currah goes so far as to suggest that

the transgender-cisgender binary, the grid of intelligibility that dominates so much trans studies and advocacy, possibly obscures more than it reveals. Indeed, though transgender is a category of increasing cultural currency in the language of diversity, it stitches together people whose only commonality is that their gender didn't turn out as expected, given the sex they were assigned at birth. That "transgender" purports to describe people who are so very differently situated in relation to their vulnerability to violence, to incarceration, to illness, to homelessness, and to slow death seems like one of the more miraculous feats of identity politics. (forthcoming)

In contrast to an increasingly mainstream transgender politics that increasingly meshes with neoliberal diversity discourse even as it leaves intact the structures that produce inequality, an embodied transgender politics focuses on everyday sites of creation and resistance. In challenging the mainstream trans rights discourse's erasure of vulnerabilities based on race and class, this new politics centers epistemic justice.

Epistemic Injustice and Practice: Embodied Politics of Transgender Rights

There is an inherent epistemological dimension to politics. How does one know of, let alone participate in the creation of, these "irruptions" that constitute politics? How does one make sense of difference and situate one's knowledge in some common "we"? Feminist epistemologies have included a provisional view toward the contentiousness of the epistemic domain of politics. Alcoff and Potter suggest that "feminist epistemologies must be tested by their effects on the practical political struggles occurring in a wider frame of reference than the academy" (1993, 14). As Kathryn Addelson notes, "The social worlds relevant to public problems consist of group knower/doers whose collective action involves creating and struggling over public problems" (1993, 281). They consist of the active knower/doer, of a situated set of knowledges that delink, or uncouple, what is discursively "known" to be true from a so-called reality. Collective political engagement is thus subject to an epistemology of resistance—the generation of new knowledges that create new cleavages within the world as we know it and create new ways of being and new modes of presentation.

Anticipating Miranda Fricker's claims that justice and politics converge on embodied knowledge and practice, Saidiya Hartman writes, "If through performance the enslaved 'asserted their humanity,' it is no less true that performance articulated their troubled relation to the category 'human'" (Hartman 1997, 78). This political resistance amounted to a "politics without a proper locus" whereby subjects engaged in practices that were "fragmentary" and "transient," usually not sustained attacks on the institution of domination but nevertheless assertions of their sensible, human selves (ibid., 51). For both scholars, knowing and doing are creative, productive, and inherently political acts. Miranda Fricker has, in this vein, explored the ethics of knowing through her treatise on "epistemic injustice." That knowers are denied credibility, or prevented from accessing the common pool of knowledge in order to make sense of their own experiences, constitutes unjust practice. "Eradicating these injustices would ultimately take not just more virtuous hearers, but collective social political change—in matters of epistemic injustice, the ethical is political . . . the political depends upon the ethical" (Fricker, 2007, 8). Giving revolutionary ground to Fricker's epistemological abstractions, Hartman argues that embodiment produces knowledge about the self in ways that are both emancipatory and unsettling to dominant structures. "Redressing the pained body encompasses operating in and against the demands of the system, negotiating the disciplinary harnessing of the body, and counterinvesting in the body as a site of possibility" (ibid.). Rejecting the notions that oppressive systems merely instantiate a repressed sense of self without recourse to notions of agency, Hartman argues that former theories of power do not really take difference into account. Politics and the political consist of irruption, of the generation of new conceptions of being through new grammars built on sustained community knowledge.

Finding epistemic common ground among transgender communities, given the vastness of experiences and the localized knowledges these experiences reflect, is not a self-defeating effort. Nancy Cole, commenting on her travels across the United States to various national, regional, and local support groups for transgenderists, finds the conditions for divisions (c. 1993, 1). She defines these divisions as "maladies," many of which stem from institutional organizations that compete for that one spot as advocacy. But given the internal racial, sexed, and gendered pluralisms, that competition does little to bridge differences. Personalities, too, of "leaders" and "pioneers" who speak on behalf of communities contribute to a set of problems (consider Virginia Prince, who was one of the first to define key terms, or Ari Kane, who established Fantasia Fair). Language itself is problematic, as communities use the subcultural scripts to define themselves—scripts often borrowed from dominant discourses on gender and sex (we have documented resistances to these scripts). What words *do* and *who* has access in the construction of these words in the process of identification have political consequences (cf. Fricker 2007). Further, communities are fragmented within themselves and are created by local contexts and histories. As a gesture toward overcoming these "maladies," Cole hearkens back to the discourses of the early U.S. colonies, which focused on overcoming internal differences for the sake of a common call for independence from an otherwise overarching oppression, asking leaders across organizations to transcend their internal drives to be the universal representative of the transgender community.

Others see these internal divisions as symptomatic of a larger, ideological problem. In developing resistance and "counteractions" outside of the discriminatory nature of "official" channels of politics, radical transgender activists such as Dean Spade gesture toward "[b]uilding alternatives . . . to using the police or prison system to address harm and violence. Calling the cops or going to court often escalates or multiplies violence for people and communities that are targeted for criminalization, but we need ways of dealing with harm that happens" (Spade 2015, 188). He asserts that "we should prioritize the experiences of people facing the worst manifestation of transphobia rather than being tempted to try to solve problems for those who are least vulnerable. Social justice does not trickle down" (Spade 2015, 188). The law's epistemological underpinnings often privilege cisgender conceptions of transgender experiences, undermining their epistemic capacities (Aultman 2016). In his well-known critiques of the limits of law for transgender populations, Spade insists that case law protecting the nondiscrimination rights of professional, mostly white, and middle-class transgender people does not give the pressing attention needed to these subaltern transgender groups. "When people try to make change through the law, they often end up focusing on those from the group who are most likeable . . . who fit normative standards" (Spade 2015, 188).

Conclusion

Our epistemological claim is not confined to the abstract, but rather extends to the real, lived moments for transgender people. Following José Medina, we argue that epistemology needs to "include not only (or primarily) the justification of knowledge claims, but also and more fundamentally the very production of knowledge and ignorance and the formation of cognitive and affective capacities that make knowledge possible" (2013, 53). For us, these cognitive and affective capacities are directly rooted in the body, sets of practices that we have labeled both epistemic and political. It was the intent of this chapter to capture moments, whether in Fantasia Fair or a fragment of a poem or within the activism of the Christopher Street Pier kids, the embodied practices that make up new ways of understanding the self and the body as sites of democratic projects, and as a source of pluralism. By this we have meant that either democratic projects that end in a termination of a council's curfew (Pier kids) or those that teach trans people what being trans is (Fantasia Fair) are born of a kind of "constitutive ambiguity," opening a space in which to restage our shared conception of the political (Connolly 1995, 101). For that reason, we wanted to shift our attention away from the traditional sites of politics, namely, away from institutions.

Instead, our view turned towards different forms of sociality. This led B to the Transgender Archives at the University of Victoria, archival work from which this chapter draws much of its substance. The collection of work at the archives (as yet just cracked open) demonstrates that trans identities are often left well outside the institutional field of recognition. For theorist William Connolly, democratic citizenship creates a productive tension between "the citizen as participant in representational politics of the state and as activist in social movements that interrogate previous patterns of settlement in the state and other social institutions" (Connolly 1995, 101). The "productive tension" between these two characteristics of citizens is precisely the site of subaltern sociality and micro-networks from which new patterns of self-making and political action emerge.

If either a person's knowledge can be discounted or an entire subgroup of people can disappear from political narratives, what are we missing from our common resource pool as active democratic citizens? And more, there is something materially problematic if a person who lives at the margins of society's normative grid cannot even access those networks in which experiences become legible and meaningful. Thus injustice is no longer a question of juridically defined rights and wrongs. Rather, we find an array of problems that relate to how gender-nonnormative people conceive of themselves outright. As a remedy, we pondered, if "the imagination is an exercise in perspective-taking, a way of inhabiting spaces and relating to others that connects up with our actual world" (Medina 2013, 255), then our political imaginary ought to shift as well. It ought to take from as many sites and fields of social interaction as possible, and assemble them within our continued efforts toward democratic life and social, as well as epistemic, justice.

NOTES

1 One can certainly see this "but for" tendency made literal by the race and class of many of the plaintiffs chosen by national nonprofits in their impact litigation for transgender rights.

2 Of course, violence against the most vulnerable trans people, such as assault and murder of trans women, is visible to the mainstream. But, as C. Riley Snorton and Jin Haritaworn point out, "trans women of color act as resources . . . for the articulation and visibility of a more privileged transgender subject." Initiatives such as the annual Transgender Day of Remembrance extract "value from trans of color lives" and transfer it to the transgender rights movement (2013, 70–71).

3 Fraser describes subaltern counterpublics as "parallel discursive arenas where members of subordinated social groups invent and circulate counterdiscourses, which in turn permit them to formulate oppositional interpretations of their identities, interests, and needs" (Fraser 1990, 67).

4 This is not to suggest that examining how the formal political institutions of the state distribute inequality through the law is not also of vital importance (see, e.g., Currah 2003; Currah 2013; Davis 2014; Taylor and Haider-Markel 2014; West 2014).

5 Much of the following work is taken from the Transgender Archives at the University of Victoria, the largest transgender archive in the world.

REFERENCES

Addelson, Kathryn Pyne. 1993. "Knower/Doers and Their Moral Problems." In Linda Alcoff and Elizabeth Porter, eds., *Feminist Epistemologies*, 265–94. New York: Routledge.

[Agony of the Transsexual]. Transgender Archives, University of Victoria, BC, Canada. Rikki Swin Collection, Box 3.

Aizura, Aren Z. 2006. "Of Borders and Homes: The Imaginary Community of (Trans)sexual Citizenship." *Inter-Asia Culture Studies* 7 (2): 289–309. doi:10.1080/14649370600673953.

Alcoff, Linda, and Elizabeth Potter. 1993. "Introduction: When Feminisms Intersect Epistemology." In Linda Alcoff and Elizabeth Porter, eds., *Feminist Epistemologies*. New York: Routledge.

American Civil Liberties Union. 2015. "Non-Discrimination Laws: State by State Information." American Civil Liberties Union. Accessed November 27, https://www.aclu.org.

Aultman, B. 2014. "Cisgender." *TSQ: Transgender Studies Quarterly* 1(1–2): 61–62.

Aultman, B. 2016. "Epistemic Injustice and the Making of Transgender Legal Subjects." *Wagadu: A Journal of Transnational Women's and Gender Studies* 15.

Bailey, M. M. 2013. "Performance as Intravention: Ballroom Culture and the Politics of HIV/AIDS in Detroit." In S. Stryker and A. Aizura, eds., *The Transgender Studies Reader*, vol. 2, 630–43. New York: Routledge.

Bassichis, M., L. Alexander, and D. Spade. 2013. "Building an Abolitionst Trans and Queer Movement with Everything We've Got." In S. Stryker and A. Aizura, eds., *The Transgender Studies Reader*, vol. 2, 653–67. New York: Routledge.

Beemyn, G. 2015. "U.S. History." In L. Erickson-Schroth, ed., *Trans Bodies, Trans Selves: A Resource for the Transgender Community*, 501–36. New York: Oxford University Press.

Brown, Wendy. 2015. *Undoing the Demos: Neoliberalism's Stealth Revolution*. Brooklyn, NY: Zone Books.

Butler, Judith. 2015. *Notes toward a Performative Theory of Assembly*. Cambridge, MA: Harvard University Press.

Cole, Nancy. Ca. 1993. [In Search of a Community]. Transgender Archives, University of Victoria, BC, Canada, Rikki Swin Collection, Box 16.

Connolly, William. 1995. *The Ethos of Pluralization*. Minneapolis: Minnesota University Press.

Crenshaw, Kimberlé. 1989. "Demarginalizing the Intersection of Race and Sex: A Black Feminist Critique of Antidiscrimination Doctrine, Feminist Theory, and Antiracist Politics." *University of Chicago Legal Forum*, no. 140: 139–67.

Currah, Paisley. 2003. "The Transgender Rights Imaginary." *Georgetown Journal of Gender and the Law* 4: 705.

Currah, Paisley. Forthcoming. *Not the United States of Sex: Regulating Transgender Identity*. New York: NYU Press.

Davis, Heath Fogg. 2014. "Sex-Classification Policies as Transgender Discrimination: An Intersectional Critique." *Perspectives on Politics* 12: 45–60.

Drake, D. 1974. [Crossing the Sex Barrier]. Transgender Archives, University of Victoria, BC, Canada. Rikki Swin Collection, Box 3.

Duggan, Lisa. 2003. *The Twilight of Equality: Neoliberalism, Cultural Politics, and the Attack on Democracy*. Boston: Beacon.

Dumanoski, D. 1975. "Gender Identity Serves the Transsexual," *Boston Phoenix*. Transgender Archives, University of Victoria, BC, Canada. Rikki Swin Collection, Box 3.

Eilperin, Juliet. 2015. "Obama's Quiet Transgender Revolution." *Washington Post*, December 1. https://www.washingtonpost.com.

Farmer, R. 1993. [A Great Hope: A Transsexual Rebirth]. Transgender Archives, University of Victoria, BC, Canada. Rikki Swin Collection, Box 4.

Fernandez, Manny, and Mitch Smith. 2015. "Houston Voters Reject Broad Anti-Discrimination Ordinance." *New York Times*, November 3. http://www.nytimes.com.

Fogg Davis, Heath. 2014. "Sex-Classification Policies as Transgender Discrimination: An Intersectional Critique." *Perspectives on Politics* 12: 45–60.

Fortune, B. 1985. [Letter]. Transgender Archives, University of Victoria, BC, Canada. Rikki Swin Collection, Box 4.

Foucault, Michel. 1979. *Discipline and Punish: The Birth of the Prison*. Translated by Alan Sheridan. New York: Vintage.

Foucault, Michel. 1990. *The History of Sexuality: Volume I.* Translated by Robert Hurley. New York: Vintage.

Foucault, Michel. 2007. *Security, Territory, Population: Lectures at the Collège de France, 1977–78.* Translated by Graham Burchell. New York: Palgrave MacMillan.

Frank, Jason. 2010. *Constituent Moments: Enacting the People in Postrevolutionary America.* Durham, NC: Duke University Press.

Fraser, Nancy. 1990. "Rethinking the Public Sphere: A Contribution to the Critique of Actually Existing Democracy." *Social Text*, no. 25/26: 56–80.

Fricker, Miranda. 2007. *Epistemic Injustice: Power and the Ethics of Knowing.* New York: Oxford University Press.

G. G. v. Gloucester County School Board, cv00054, E.D. Va., 2015.

Glenn v. Brumby, 663 F.3d 1312, 2011.

Gossett, Che. 2013. "Silhouettes of Defiance: Memorializing Historical Sites of Queer and Transgender Resistance in an Age of Neoliberal Inclusivity." In Susan Stryker and Aren Z. Aizura, eds., *The Transgender Studies Reader*, vol. 2, 580–90. New York: Routledge.

Hanhardt, Christina B. 2013. *Safe Space: Gay Neighborhood History and the Politics of Violence.* Durham, NC: Duke University Press.

Hartman, Saidiya. 1997. *Scenes of Subjection: Terror, Slavery, and Self-Making in Nineteenth-Century America.* New York: Oxford University Press.

Hilb, Claudia. 1994. "Equality at the Limit of Liberty." In Ernesto Laclau, ed., *The Making of Political Identities.* New York: Verso.

Hill, Robert. 2013. "Before Transgender: Transvestia's Spectrum of Gender Variance, 1960-1980." In S. Stryker and A. Aizura, eds., *The Transgender Studies Reader*, vol. 2, 364–79. New York: Routledge.

Holland, D. 1976. [The Politics of Dress. Gay Community News]. Transgender Archives, University of Victoria, BC, Canada. Rikki Swin Collection, Box 3.

[In Her Own Words: A Distinguished Man Becomes a Woman]. Ca. 1970. [Interview Fragment]. Transgender Archives, University of Victoria, BC, Canada. Rikki Swin Collection, Box 3.

Jones, Rickie Lee. 1989. "Ghetto of My Mind." In *Flying Cowboys.* Geffen Records.

Jones, Robert P., and Daniel Cox. 2015. "How Race and Religion Shape Millennial Attitudes on Sexuality and Reproductive Health." Public Religion Research Institute. publicreligion.org.

Kane, Ariadne. 1974. [Letter to the Editor: Penthouse Forum]. Transgender Archives, University of Victoria, BC, Canada. Rikki Swin Collection, Box 3.

Kane, Ariadne. N.d. "Notes on Gender Cuing." Transgender Archives, University of Victoria, BC, Canada. Rikki Swin Collection, Box 3.

Keo-Meier, Colt, and Lance Hicks. 2015. "Youth." In Laura Erickson-Schroth, ed., *Trans Bodies, Trans Selves: A Resource Guide for the Transgender Community*, 446–75. New York: Oxford University Press.

Ledins, N. Ca. 1960. [Letter]. Transgender Archives, University of Victoria, BC, Canada. Rikki Swin Collection, Box 3.

Lois. N.d. "Letter to Virginia Prince." Transgender Archives, University of Victoria, BC, Canada. Rikki Swin Collection, Box 3.

Medina, José. 2013. *The Epistemology of Resistance: Gender and Racial Oppression, Epistemic Injustice, and Resistant Imaginations.* New York: Oxford University Press.

Meyerowtiz, Joanne. 2002. *How Sex Changed: A History of Transsexuaity in the United States.* Cambridge, MA: Harvard University Press.

Minter, Shannon Price. 2006. "Do Transsexuals Dream of Gay Rights? Getting Real about Transgender Inclusion." In Paisley Currah, Richard M. Juang, and Shannon Price Minter, eds., *Transgender Rights*, 141–70. Minneapolis: Minnesota University Press.

Nelson, Lynn Hankinson. 1994. "Epistemological Communities." In Linda Alcoff and Elizabeth Potter, eds., *Feminist Epistemologies*, 121–60. New York: Routledge.

New York Times Editorial Board. 2015. "Transgender Today." *New York Times*, May 4.

Owen, N., and R. Garfield. 1984. [Fantasia Fair Legal Seminar Notes]. The Transgender Archives, University of Victoria, BC, Canada. Rikki Swin Collection, Box 3.

Pierce, Wendi. N.d. "Who Speaks for the Transsexual?" Transgender Archives, University of Victoria, BC, Canada. Rikki Swin Collection, Box 3.

Prince, Virginia. 1967. *The Transsexual and His Wife*. Los Angeles: Argyle Books.

Prince, Virginia. 1969. [Article: Men Who Choose to Be Women]. Transgender Archives, University of Victoria, BC, Canada. Rikki Swin Collection, Box 21.

Puar, Jasbir K. 2015. "Bodies with New Organs Becoming Trans, Becoming Disabled." *Social Text* 33 (3): 45–73. doi:10.1215/01642472-3125698.

Rancier, Jacques. 1999. *Dis-agreement and Philosophy*. Translated by J. Rose. Minneapolis: University of Minnesota Press.

Ranciere, Jacques. 2015. *Dissensus: On Politics and Aesthetics*. New York: Bloomsbury.

Reynolds, Heath Mackenzie, and Zil Garner Goldstein. 2015. "Social Transition." In Laura Erickson-Schroth, ed., *Trans Bodies, Trans Selves: A Resource Guide for the Transgender Community*, 124–54. New York: Oxford University Press.

Sarkisova, X. 2014. "(Beyond) Suffering as a Measuring Tool." In L. Erickson-Schroth, ed., *Trans Bodies, Trans Selves: A Resource for the Transgender Community*, 292. New York: Oxford University Press.

Simmons, Holiday, and Freshi White. 2014. "Our Many Selves." In Laura Erikson-Schroth, ed., *Trans Bodies, Trans Selves: A Resource for the Transgender Community*, 3–23. New York: Oxford University Press.

Sitrin, Marina. 2012. "Horizontalism and Territory." Possible Futures. Social Science Research Council. http://www.possible-futures.org.

Smith, Miriam. 2008. *Political Institutions and Lesbian and Gay Rights in the United States and Canada*. New York: Routledge.

Snorton, C. Riley, and Jin Haritaworn. 2013. "Trans Necropolitics: A Transnational Reflection on Violence, Death, and the Trans of Color Afterlife." In Susan Stryker and Aren Z. Aizura, eds., *Transgender Studies Reader*, vol. 2, 66–76. New York: Routledge.

Sontag, Deborah. 2015. "Once a Pariah, Now a Judge: The Early Transgender Journey of Phyllis Frye." *New York Times*, August 29. http://www.nytimes.com.

Spade, Dean. 2015. "Trans Survival and the Limits of Law Reform." In L. Erickson-Schroth, ed., *Trans Bodies, Trans Selves: A Resource for the Transgender Community*, 187–88. New York: Oxford University Press.

Spivak, Gayatri. 1988. "Can the Subaltern Speak?" In Cary Nelson and Larence Grossberg, eds., *Marxism and the Interpretation of Culture*, 271–315. Champaign: University of Illinois Press.

Stryker, Susan. 2008. *Transgender History*. Berkeley, CA: Seal Press.

Taylor, Jami K., and Donald P. Haider-Markel, eds. 2014. *Transgender Rights and Politics*. Ann Arbor: University of Michigan Press.

Transgender Youth Survey. 2001. [Maine Gender Resource and Support Service]. Transgender Archives, University of Victoria, BC, Canada. Rikki Swin Collection, Box 16.

Valentine, David. 2007. *Imagining Transgender: An Ethnography of a Category*. Durham, NC: Duke University Press.

Walker, Rachel Loewen. 2011. "Toward a FIERCE! Nomadology: Contesting Queer Geographies on the Christopher Street Pier." *PhaenEx* 6 (1): 90–120.

West, Isaac. 2014. *Transforming Citizenships: Transgender Articulations of the Law*. New York: NYU Press.

Wolin, Sheldon S. 1994. "'Fugitive Democracy.'" *Constellations* 1 (1): 11–25. doi: 10.1111/j.1467-8675.

Wolin, Sheldon S. 2004. *Politics and Vision: Continuity and Innovation in Western Political Thought*. Expanded edition. Princeton, NJ: Princeton University Press.

Wolin, S. 2006. *Politics and Vision*. Princeton, NJ: Princeton University Press.

Ziegler, Kortney Ryan, and Naim Rasul. 2014. "Race, Ethnicity, and Culture." In Laura Erikson-Schroth, ed., *Trans Bodies, Trans Selves: A Resource for the Transgender Community*, 24–39. New York: Oxford University Press.

4

The Treatment and Prevention of HIV Bodies

The Contemporary Politics and Science of a Thirty-Year-Old Epidemic

J. RICKY PRICE

Thirty-five years into the struggle against HIV/AIDS, we are still being outwitted. The rapid mutation and replication of the complex human immunodeficiency virus outpaces our bodies' immune response despite medical intervention (we have yet to find a cure or a vaccine); treatment and prevention strategies are often thwarted by systemic racism, misogyny, and homo- and transphobias; poverty and the criminalization of people with HIV further stigmatize the epidemic; and our failure to remember the lessons of the virus's three-and-a-half-decades history, all taken together, have allowed HIV to thrive. This essay critically explores our contemporary strategies to combat the virus.

Traditionally, there have been two different but connected efforts to stamp out the epidemic: treatment of people living with HIV, and prevention of "at-risk" populations from contracting the virus. Recent research has combined these efforts. The Centers for Disease Control (CDC) currently recommend a strategy of "Treatment *as* Prevention" in the effort to achieve the goal of an "AIDS-free generation." This strategy relies on two prongs: (1) that anyone exposed to HIV should be immediately put on antiretroviral therapy, which has been shown to suppress the viral load in individuals to "undetectable" levels, making it much less likely that a carrier will transmit the disease;[1] and (2) that "at-risk" populations, namely, gay and bisexual men, intravenous drug users, and heterosexual men and women who "are at substantial risk for HIV infection" should take Pre-Exposure Prophylaxis (PrEP), a once-a-day pill that drastically reduces the chances of HIV infection.[2] Treatment as Prevention, then, is a strategy of *preemption*, of intervening on "at-risk" populations before they are infected and prescribing antiretroviral therapy immediately to prevent the virus from being able to replicate itself and spread throughout the body.

In what follows, I explore the different ways in which bodies are understood in relationship to HIV. I begin with a discussion of immunology and the new ways HIV has allowed us to understand the immune system. From there I examine the research that led to the preemptive strategy of Treatment as Prevention alongside the rise of legislation aimed at criminalizing people living with HIV. Finally, I look back at the Denver Principles, one of the first activist statements from people living with HIV. Looking back at these principles reminds us of the political strategies and tactics developed in the fight against HIV, offering insight into ways forward. What emerges from this study is the portrait of a social, political, and biological problem that, to be eradicated, must be combated not merely through medical intervention but through a combined effort centering on the struggles of the affected communities, antiracist and feminist science practices, and the decriminalization of people living with HIV.

Your Body Is a Doughnut

Immunologists often employ the metaphor of a doughnut to differentiate between the inside and the outside of our bodies: "Just as the hole passes through the donut, the gastrointestinal tract passes through the body" (Weeks and Alcamo 2010, 69). This means that much of what we think of as "inside of our body," our stomach, for example, is technically outside of our physical body. Biology understands the body as a "closed container," implying that "if a microorganism is to invade the body tissues, it must pass the cellular barrier separating the interior of the body from the exterior" (Weeks and Alcamo 2010, 69). If we understand our bodies to be like doughnuts, then our immune "defenses" begin on the surface of this doughnut, namely, with our skin. It is here that our first line of "defense" against "foreign invaders" occurs. But our bodies, unlike doughnuts, have porous regions between our internal structure and the outside world: our mucosal membranes, the sticky parts of our body—the eyelids, mouth, lungs, anus, vagina, and penis—work to prevent pathogens from entering our body and also help lubricate our bodies for activities central to growth and reproduction, like eating and sex. Taken together, our tears, saliva, vaginal and penile secretions, stomach acid, and the sticky mucous in our lungs represent a significant portion of our body's nonspecific response to pathogens. These nonspecific responses work in conjunction with our white blood cells, often referred to as "microscopic foot soldiers," who constantly survey our body for pathogens and develop specific responses to particular pathogens (Weeks and Alcamo 2010, 70; Sessions and Loftus 2001, 358–63).

As A. Daniel Napier notes in his book *The Age of Immunology*, military metaphors have a long history in the study of the immune system, but these metaphors are best understood as "a microscopic parable to reconfirm our cultural predilections regarding just what it is that makes a person" (2003, 42). In Donna Haraway's 1991 book *Simians, Cyborgs, and Women*, she speaks of the illusiveness of the immune system, saying that it is "everywhere and nowhere. Its specificities are indefinite, and they arise randomly; yet these extraordinary variations are the critical means of maintaining individual bodily coherence" (Haraway 1991, 218). The immune system guards the health and longevity of the self, the body, the individual. When the immune system is threatened, the self is threatened. The immune system is tasked with bounding the self and with detecting external threats by identifying what is *nonself*. Our bodies may be doughnuts, but they also serve as host to numerous sets of bacteria, funguses, and viruses. The immune system decides what to attack and dispose of through a complicated communication system involving an array of microscopic actors. Their ability to recognize threats and purge them from the body is crucial to the maintenance of the self. "Disease is a subspecies of information malfunction or communications pathology; disease is a process of misrecognition or transgression of the boundaries of a strategic assemblage called self" (Haraway 1991, 212). To understand how HIV transgresses the boundaries of the "strategic assemblage called self," we must understand the players who orchestrate the second line of immune defense, but to do so we must enter either a world of medical jargon or a world of oversimplified metaphors.

The second line of "defense," the specific response, happens behind the scenes and starts with our white blood cells. White blood cells come in two distinct types: phagocytes and lymphocytes. Phagocytes are considered part of the nonspecific response and are tasked with seeking out foreign microorganisms and destroying them; lymphocytes make up the majority of our specific immune response and refer to T-cells, B-cells, and natural killer cells (Sessions and Loftus 2001, 359).[3] The names "T-cells," "B-cells," "macrophages," and "phagocytes" do not refer simply to a type of cell but also to the *behavior* of a cell. Memory cells do not actually remember; rather, they exchange proteins. In some ways, this jargon, these complicated descriptions, all become metaphorical at a certain point. Does a killer T-cell commit first- or second-degree murder? The way we talk about the immune system happens in two central ways: (1) use of jargon to convey complexity and specificity or (2) use of flawed metaphors unjustly creating unequal relationships between the microscopic world and our own lived experience. It seems that when we speak of the microscopic, all we have are metaphors; and they are not enough.

In her 1992 essay "The End of the Body," medical anthropologist Emily Martin showed that the manner in which scientists convey the intricacies of the immune system are laced with gendered and racialized readings of the hierarchy of action in the immune system:

> So we have T cells, masculine and high-ranking; B cells, feminine and high-ranking; and macrophages, feminine, perhaps racially marked, and low-ranking on all counts. What is missing? Low-ranking males, revealing by their invisibility in this system (even as they seem to be "invisible" in the U.S. social structure) how salient a system of race and class is to the understanding of relationships among these cells. In this system, gendered distinctions are not limited to male and female, they also encompass the distinction heterosexual and homosexual. T cells convey aspects of male potency, cast as heterosexual potency. There is evidence that T cells are for many researchers the virile heroes of the immune system, highly

trained commandos who have been selected for and then educated in the technical college of the thymus gland. . . . Some T cells, killer cells, are masculine in the
old-fashioned mold of a brawny, brutal he-man. . . . Other T cells, T 4 cells, have a
different kind of masculinity, one focused on abilities required in the contemporary world of global corporations, especially strategic planning and corporate team
participation. The T 4 cell is often called the quarterback of the immune system,
because he orchestrates everything else and because he is the brains and memory
of the team. (Martin 1992, 130)

Martin notes that the rise of immunology in the 1960s and 1970s coincided with
changes in global capitalism and argues that the way we conceive of, and consequently care for, our bodies was inflected with these broader changes. She
argues that we experienced "a transformation in embodiment, from Fordist bodies held by disciplined order in time and space and organized for efficient mass
production, to late capitalist bodies learning flexible response in rapidly collaps-
ing time and space" (Martin 1992, 134). For Martin, the image of HIV attacking
the quarterback of immune cells, resulting in the death of homosexuals, could
not be understood outside the broader contexts and neoliberal changes taking
place—from the "weakening of the liberal state" to the "withdrawal of government support from social services," making "the nuclear family seem to be the
only sources of . . . glues to the social fabric." In this way, she implies that something "subtle, invisible, and therefore insidious" is going on in the description of
bodily cells this way (Martin 1992, 132).[4] For Martin and Haraway, the words that
convey microscopic worlds structure how we understand them and mirror our
own built environments.

What then can we make of the way we understand the immune system today?
Are we in a similar moment, like the one Martin describes above, "a transformation of embodiment"? Does the biomedical knowledge we have gained change
the way we conceive of our bodies, from a conception of Fordist discipline to
the Great Recession's austerity? Should we understand PrEP in relationship to the
Global War on Terror, akin to drone warfare? Does taking PrEp follow a similar
logic to carrying a handgun at all times: for self-protection? Rather than intimat-
ing a "transformation of embodiment," the language of PrEP and of Treatment
as Prevention evokes a neurotic surveillance state: an ability to survey the body,
in flux, live, as it transforms. We are no longer simply HIV positive or negative but instead we are either seroconverted with an undetectable viral load (we
humans can detect that the body is not likely to transmit the virus, if that body
has taken its regular dose of antiretrovirals) or elite controllers (those whose
bodies can "maintain" and "manage" the virus at undetectable levels without the
help of antiretrovirals), both of which require "responsible" and "self-disciplined"
patients who regularly report to their doctor. HIV is currently understood as a
"manageable" terminal illness *if you have regular access to affordable healthcare.*

To manage is not the same as to fight. Management comes after the war. Management is the ability to cut one's losses and soldier on. Management presumes there will be something to manage tomorrow.

Scientists speak in metaphors to describe the inner workings of our bodies. Social scientists talk about what these metaphors mean. Science, for Haraway, operates as a sort of "genre of Western exploration and travel literature" (Haraway 1991, 205). To travel inwards, to the microscopic world of T-cells, B-cells, macrophages, and HIV, evokes images of "heroic quest[s]" filled with "themes of nuclear exterminism, space adventure, extra-terrestrial, exotic invaders, and military high-technology" (Haraway 1991, 205). The actors of the immune system stand in for heroes in the defense of the body, heroes we liken to soldiers, athletes, and business executives protecting the boundaries of the self. Haraway connects the invasion of the body by pathogens to Western practices of colonization:

> Expansionist Western medical discourse in colonizing contexts has been obsessed with the notion of contagion and hostile penetration of the healthy body, as well as of stunning reversal: the colonized was perceived as the invader. In the face of the disease genocides accompanying European "penetration" of the globe, the "coloured" body of the colonized was constructed as the dark source of infection, pollution, disorder, and so on, that threatened to overwhelm white manhood (cities, civilization, the family, the white personal body) with its decadent emanations. (Haraway 1991, 223)

The tools, languages, and practices we have developed to understand the body creates "a portrait of the body as a nation-state, organized around a hidden discourse of gender, race, and class. . . . In this picture, which is taught in biology classes and conveyed in the popular media, the boundary between the body ('self') and the external world ('nonself') is rigid and absolute" (Martin 1992, 126). Napier argues that we should move away from understanding our immune systems as operating on a logic of self/nonself, to help usher in new ways of thinking about our bodies in the world (2003).

How might we think of disease as a belonging rather than a cleavage? The political and medical histories of HIV are full of the creation of new institutional and activist communities, new connections, and new paths for research and funding. How might we organize our research priorities if we understood HIV as a part of ourselves, rather than as our enemy?

Haraway reminds us that the evolution of the individual, the self, was a contingent biological event, what she calls "a constrained accident, not the highest fruit of earth history's labours" (Haraway 1991, 220). And for Martin, the complex specificity of the immune system forces us to question our agency over our own body: "The 'I' who used to wear the body like a closely fitting set of clothes is now miniaturized, and is dwarfed by its body. The 'I' is made a passive and powerless witness to the doings of the components of the body. Somewhere in the system lies agency; the 'I' can only watch" (Martin 1992, 125). The flexible boundaries of our bodies and the limits to our agency over that body call into question ideologies that evangelize individuality, individual responsibility, and self-care. Thus, the response to the logic of neoliberal individuality should be towards strengthening and building community, fostering empowerment, and understanding disease as communal, not individual.

Science discourses on the immune system paint a world where white blood cells operate an intricate filing system while running an expansive army of foot soldiers, spies, and intelligence officers who report back the identifying markers of any foreign enemy, marking them for destruction; a bureaucratic military force within our bodies fighting alien invaders while coordinating for future transgressions. Despite Susan Sontag's plea to give these war metaphors "back to the war-makers," it seems as though we lack the ability to understand how our bodies work without them (Sontag 1990, 183). We lack metaphors describing a grand collective project that is not an exploration, an expansion, an occupation, a war, or a fried dough pastry.

The immune system, the protector of the doughnut, tells us as much about the organization of our world as it does the organization of the microscopic. Is it enough, though, to follow Napier and Martin's lead, and use the metaphors as sites of contestation, as places to "battle" for meaning, as a way to reconfigure the world? The complexity of the systems that maintain our body, and our inability to control them fully through medical interventions, is one of the central ways in which HIV still outwits us. Despite everything we have learned about our immune systems in the last thirty years, in no small part due to HIV research, we are still humbled by the complexity of the microscopic.

The Medical HIV Body: The Mississippi Baby

In 2012, "the Mississippi Baby," an infant born to a mother with HIV, was put on an aggressive dose of antiretroviral therapy at thirty hours old. The baby was then put on a regular regimen of antiretroviral drugs; however, after months of treatment, the mother "failed" to bring the baby to a follow-up. After a five-month absence, the mother returned her baby to the hospital and the scientists expected to see a reemergence of the virus. They were shocked, however, to find no trace of HIV. The doctors decided not to continue the antiretroviral therapy. The baby became an anonymous celebrity throughout the world, known only as the "Mississippi Baby," and was hailed as the first person to be "cured" of HIV through antiretroviral therapy (Hayden 2013; Persaud et al. 2013; National Institute of Health 2013).

After twenty-seven months of the baby testing free of HIV, the virus inexplicably returned to the "Mississippi Baby" in July of 2014: "[T]esting from a routine examination revealed that the child's viral load had spiked and that her levels of CD4+ T cells, markers of a normal immune system, had dropped" (Maron 2014). The NIH went forward with an ambitious proof-of-concept clinical study involving 472 babies in Argentina, Brazil, Haiti, Malawi, South Africa, Uganda, the United States, Zambia, and Zimbabwe (National Institute of Health 2014). The goal, however, was less hopeful; instead of finding a cure for infants born to HIV-infected mothers, the study is looking for how this treatment might lead to a "remission" of HIV. The language of remission is crucial here, because the mystery that the "Mississippi Baby" represents is not "How did we bump into a potential cure?" but rather, "How were we unable to detect the virus for twenty-seven months?"

Dr. Anthony Fauci, the head of the National Institute of Allergy and Infectious Diseases since 1984, responded to the news in an interview on the federal government's website devoted to AIDS, saying, "I certainly don't think this is a step forward but it is not a step backward. . . . [T]he real critical question is what was it that was keeping that virus from rebounding if there wasn't a detectable immune response?" (Fauci 2014). The latent reservoir is a "stealth" supply of HIV that "hangs around" on memory B-cells. It represents a final hurdle in the discovery of an HIV cure and vaccination. Consequently, this means that the short-term strategies for managing the epidemic will remain focused on biomedical solutions, pharmaceutical ethics, and self-discipline, exhibited either by the wearing of condoms or the regularly taking of pills.

Fauci is a leading proponent of Treatment as Prevention as the best possible way to create an "AIDS-free generation." He has played an outsized role in the federal government's response to HIV/AIDS. Appointed in 1984, he has advised every president since Reagan on the epidemic. He was the target of ACT-UP's "Storm the NIH" action in 1990, and one of the few officials in any administration of that era who listened to activists and people living with HIV. He was instrumental in the institutionalization of a portion of ACT-UP through the Treatment Action Group (TAG), and claims a close friendship with activists such as Larry Kramer as well as former President Ronald Reagan (Fauci 2011). He explains that throughout the history of the epidemic, research funds have been split between prevention and treatment, two similar but distinctly different goals. He believes the best possible way to turn the tide and create an "AIDS-free generation" is to treat the newly infected as quickly as possible and to promote PrEP, Pre-Exposure Prophylaxis, to at-risk populations.

> Prevention has been extraordinary. We realized early on that prevention is not uni-dimensional but requires a combination of modalities. The low tech ones . . . testing, counseling, condoms, harm reduction. The biologically based ones . . . prevention of mother to child transmission, male circumcision, microbicides, treating STDs. . . . As it turns out a landmark study has proven that treatment is actually part of prevention. (Fauci 2013)

He cites a 2011 study published in the *New England Journal of Medicine* that tested early antiretroviral treatments in over seventeen hundred serodiscordant couples (one person in the couple is living with HIV and the other is not). The results demonstrated only a 5 percent infection rate for the noninfected partner. However, the best results occurred when the partner with HIV's antiretroviral therapy brought his or her viral load down to undetectable levels (Cohen et al. 2011). This means that seroconverted individuals, if they have access to drugs and maintain an aggressive antiretroviral therapy, present a very low risk of transmission to other partners.

During this period the NIH was also conducting four clinical trials on the viability of PrEP as a prevention tool. The four trials included gay and bisexual men, heterosexual men and women in serodiscordant couples, intravenous drug users, and sexually active heterosexual men and women. The results showed that participants were between 44 and 75 percent less likely to be infected with HIV (Centers for Disease Control 2015b). On May 14, 2014, the CDC recommended that PrEP be used in at-risk populations as "a way for people who do not have HIV but who are at substantial risk of getting it to prevent HIV infection by taking a pill every day" (Centers for Disease Control 2015a). Fauci is implying not that we end our "low tech" and "biologically based" efforts like condoms, education, and microbicides but that to turn the corner on the epidemic—in the absence of a vaccine—we must also place people on antiretroviral drugs as early as possible and place at-risk populations on PrEP. Yet, when we look at the cases of the "Mississippi Baby" and the development of PrEP, questions immediately arise concerning poverty, access, and cost.

The way Fauci describes the mother of the "Mississippi Baby" is particularly telling: "a child that was born of a mother that was HIV infected but who unfortunately had no prenatal care and wasn't receiving antiretroviral care . . . and then [the baby] was unfortunately . . . lost to follow up" (Fauci 2014). The "Mississippi Baby" acts as synecdoche for the last twenty years of AIDS in America; HIV has migrated south, its mutations have taken up host bodies in rural enclaves, and while HIV still infects a disproportionate number of gay and bisexual men, particularly men of color, heterosexual black and brown women from the rural South have replaced urban gay men as the center of the epidemic. Black women make up roughly 13 percent of the overall female population in the United States, and account for 65 percent of new AIDS diagnoses among women; Hispanic women make up 17 percent of new AIDS diagnoses (Stine 2012, 334). "In the United States, ending 2012, about three-quarters of the estimated 421,000 women living with HIV and AIDS will be black or Hispanic" (Stine 2012, 334).

Gilead, the pharmaceutical company that produces PrEP, further demonstrates the growing complexity of describing who exactly is "at risk" for HIV in 2015 in America. The pharmaceutical company uses the CDC's definitions for people "at-risk" for HIV in their prescription guidelines for the pill, stating that a person at high risk for HIV either has a partner who is already infected or "[e]ngages in sexual activity within a high prevalence area or social network and one or more of the following: inconsistent or no condom use, diagnosis of sexually transmitted infections, exchanges sex for commodities (such as money, shelter, food, or drugs), use of illicit drugs, alcohol dependence, incarceration" (Gilead 2014). The body, then, is "at risk" if one has the misfortune to live in an area with a high prevalence of one or more of the following: people having sex without condoms, people using drugs, people engaging in sex work, people drinking excessively, and people who are imprisoned. These behaviors are not particular to any community exclusively, but we know that not every community is "at risk" for HIV in the same way.

The Medical HIV-body is outlined by omissions, erasures, and a false objectivity. As Cathy Cohen notes,

> If we do not address the growing discrepancy between sexual storytelling and true sexual life, we will only exacerbate the negative consequences that result from such silences, including ineffective policies to support the families who actually populate black communities and inappropriate messaging in the fight against HIV/AIDS, all of which threaten the very survival of young black people. (Cohen 2010, 54)

The inability to speak truthfully and simply at scientific, policy, and community levels about who is at risk and who is not at risk—to honestly distinguish sexual reality from "sexual storytelling"—contributes, in no small way, to the persistence of new infections in communities of color.

In the past twenty years, medical treatments have advanced, gay rights have advanced, but racial and economic inequality have advanced as well. While the identity of the "Mississippi Baby" and her mother have rightly remained unknown, we can assume, with a good deal of probability, that a mother living in Mississippi who lacks the "fortune" of prenatal antiretroviral treatment most likely also lacked access to that care, was unaware of her status, or was aware and couldn't afford the therapies. Dr. Fauci, and the medical and research establishment, rarely address systemic structural issues of poverty, racism, misogyny, and transphobia as concurrent problems in the fight against AIDS. Nor do they mention the predominant strategy that the U.S. legislative and judicial branches have used for prevention: criminalization.

The Juridical HIV-Body: Criminalization and Stigma

In 1987, Senator Jesse Helms proposed mandatory testing for the general population and the creation of quarantines for those infected. He stated at the time that his goal was "to protect the people who are innocent" (qtd. in New York Times 1987). Fortunately, Helms's attempt at prevention through prejudice never came to fruition. Despite many important legal victories for people living with HIV in the late 1980s and 1990s, such as the inclusion of HIV in the Americans with Disabilities Act and the Ryan White CARE Act, the legislative and judicial branches have primarily used punitive measures as a central strategy in preventing HIV.

Our ability to manage the disease medically has not led to full reduction in the stigma surrounding the epidemic. Disclosure of a person's HIV status is not simply a matter of "positive" and "negative." As the studies reviewed above show, if antiretroviral drugs are taken early during the onset of an infection, a person's viral load can drop to "undetectable" levels, making transmission between partners much less likely. State and local laws, though, remain deeply stigmatized, and as the Center for HIV Law and Policy notes, from 2008 to 2013, there were over two hundred prosecutions of people living with HIV for actions that are not linked scientifically with transmission of the virus. These prosecutions include a thirty-five-year sentence for a seroconverted man in Texas who spat on a police officer (HIV is not transmittable through saliva). To another extreme, a man in Iowa was sentenced to twenty-five years for not disclosing his status to a sexual partner, though he had an undetectable viral load and used a condom during intercourse (Center for HIV Law and Policy 2013). These "crimes" are often prosecuted under the various charges of "assault with a deadly weapon" and "attempted murder," and in a case in Michigan, a man was charged with "possession of a biological weapon" under an antiterrorism law. Furthermore, in ten states, "punishment includes sex-offender registration" (Center for HIV Law and Policy 2013).

The work of the Center for HIV Law and Policy, the HIV Is Not a Crime Conferences, and grassroots activism from groups such a Queerocracy, Break-Out, Streetwise and Safe, and the Sero-Project have raised the profile of this issue. Yet, according to President Obama's 2010 National HIV/AIDS Strategy for the United States, these laws remain the rule rather than the exception:

> At least 32 states have HIV-specific laws that criminalize behavior by people living with HIV. Some criminalize behavior like spitting and biting by people with HIV, and were initially enacted at a time when there was less knowledge about HIV's transmissibility. Since it is now clear that spitting and biting do not pose significant risks for HIV transmission, many believe that it is unfair to single out people with HIV for engaging in these behaviors and should be dealt with in a consistent manner without consideration of HIV status. (White House Office of National AIDS Policy 2010)

These outdated, unscientific, and discriminatory laws not only punish individuals for a communicable disease but also further stigmatize people living with HIV. At the same time that the NIH and CDC are proposing that the most at-risk should be put on regimens of PrEP, and that early detection and treatment are crucial to ending the AIDS crisis, the stigma of AIDS prevents patients from seeking treatment and doctors from recommending therapies. This is a critical flaw in the Treatment as Prevention strategy; it assumes not only that people have access to healthcare facilities but also that they feel free to talk to their doctor about an issue that could lead to stigmatization if not criminalization.

We should understand these trends as a continuation of the push in the 1980s and 1990s towards "individual responsibility" in one's healthcare "choices." The ideas that Jesse Helms held in 1987—that there were "innocent victims" of the AIDS epidemic and those who "deserved" the punishment of a life with HIV— are embedded within these HIV criminalization laws. HIV is a *transmissible* disease; you cannot get it alone. It requires the interaction of people together. AIDS is *communal*. No individual strategy will effectively eradicate this virus. Both our medical interventions of once-a-day preventative pills and lifelong regimens of antiretroviral drugs assume that the majority of the responsibility for the prevention of the disease lies with the individual. In this scenario, a person must be "fortunate" enough to live far from risk, afford HIV drugs, and have the discipline to keep up an every-day pill schedule.

The Juridical HIV-body, then, is bounded by shame, stigma, and criminalization. Minimally, seroconverting puts one in a tenuous relationship with legal and medical authorities, and maximally, one's status can send one to prison for years. While the LGBTQ community has made tremendous gains within political and cultural spheres over the past thirty years by arguing that sexuality is not a "choice," we remain stuck in a society where the diagnosis of a communicable disease continues to be seen as a "choice," or as a behavior appropriate for criminal punishment. This too is a fundamental aspect of the Juridical HIV-body: thirty-plus years since the onset of the epidemic, people with HIV are still seen as responsible for their fortunes. Health is seen as a question of guilt and innocence. The inconsistencies between the Medical-HIV body and the Juridical HIV-body force us to question why HIV is criminalized where other STIs are not. Shouldn't men carrying the human papillomavirus (HPV) be held to the same criminal scrutiny if one of their sexual partners develops cancer? Wouldn't you like to sue the person who gave you the flu? If you are living with a terminal illness, or a life-long medical condition, where do you begin and where does the disease end? How much of your biology are you responsible for? Here again, we are outwitted. By punishing all people with HIV out of fear, rather than addressing the fundamental healthcare needs of people at risk for and living with the virus, we allow the epidemic to continue.

The Activist HIV-Body: The Denver Principles

HIV/AIDS is an epidemic of acronyms. There are the medical (HIV, AIDS, ARC, ART, PrEP, PeP, TAP),[5] the institutional (CDC, NIH, NIAID, UNAIDS),[6] and the activist (GMHC, STAR, ACT-UP, WHAM, TAG, TAC, POSITIVE),[7] to name but a few. In 1983, a group that would later become known as the National Association for People with AIDS (NAPWA) released the Denver Principles, a manifesto for patients' rights at the closing of the Second National AIDS Forum (Callen and Turner 1988).

Written by activists from San Francisco and New York, and delivered in Denver, Colorado, the statement called for a patient-centered approach to dealing with the epidemic and presented a blueprint for the grassroots, direct-action, patient-oriented activism and research that would define much of HIV/AIDS protests in the 1980s and 1990s. Political scientist Michael Bosia notes how "[f]acing death, activists disrupted normal social life, forcing the disease onto the public stage and demanding accountability. In sharp contrast to the silences around the disease, activists positioned themselves and their bodies as a very physical manifestation of the growing epidemic" (Bosia 2009, 76). The document not only led to the creation of NAPWA but influenced the creation of PWA-led organizations across the United States and around the globe (Wright 2013, 1795–96; Piot 2015, 50–51). Its significance, both as a historical *and* as an ethical document, helps to outline the work of activists who inspired mobilizations that changed the way the CDC, NIH, and NIAID conducted clinical trials and tested, approved, and recommended medical treatments—but beyond that, the Denver Principles sowed the seeds for changing what it meant to be a person living with HIV. They began a movement for self-empowerment, inspired and influenced by the Women's Health movement of the 1960s–1970s, and the statement begins by stating, "We condemn attempts to label us as 'victims,' a term which implies defeat, and we are only occasionally 'patients,' a term which implies passivity, helplessness, and dependence upon the care of others. We are 'People with AIDS'" (Denver Principles 1983). The Denver Principles go further, not only reclaiming the agency of people with AIDS but also outlining recommendations for allies (supporting people with AIDS and not scapegoating them) as well as recommendations for people with AIDS (organizing strategies, demanding participation in AIDS forums, practicing safer sex, etc.), and it concludes with a declaration of the rights of people with AIDS

1) [t]o as full and satisfying sexual and emotional lives as anyone else.
2) [t]o quality medical treatment and quality social service provision without discrimination of any form including sexual orientation, gender, diagnosis, economic status or race.
3) [t]o full explanations of all medical procedures and risks, to choose or refuse their treatment modalities, to refuse to participate in research without jeopardizing their treatment and to make informed decisions about their lives.

4) [t]o privacy, to confidentiality of medical records, human respect and to choose who their significant others are.

5) [t]o die—and to LIVE—in dignity. (Denver Principles 1983)

Only a year into the epidemic, activists were trying to "flip the script," trying to change the way in which the medical establishment, the public, and they, people with AIDS, would form a response. The political savvy demonstrated by identifying particular audiences and offering open-ended yet achievable goals, while at the same time articulating the rights of people fighting a deeply stigmatized disease would not have been possible without the establishment of LGBTQ associations, organizations, and institutions. The Denver Principles were delivered at the Second National AIDS Forum, presented by the National Lesbian and Gay Health Association, founded in 1977, four years before the first cases of HIV/AIDS became public. Gay communities built health associations, political groups, and gay newspapers like the *New York Native*, the *Washington Blade*, and the *Bay Area Reporter*. Gay male histories of protest intertwined with the lesbian rights movement, the women's movement, and the Black Power movements of previous decades. These are some of the tools and networks that allowed early AIDS activists to be so successful, despite being "at risk."

In what would become known as the PWA Self-Empowerment movement, people living with the disease helped redefine what it meant to be an AIDS patient. Instead of being passive victims of a disease,

> They [the authors of the Denver Principles] argued that their experiences, and so their participation, was vital to understanding the progress of the disease as well as the benefits and costs, in human terms, of any treatment modality. And they had no faith that pharmaceutical companies and the researchers linked to those companies would provide treatments for HIV and AIDS related illnesses that were affordable and accessible. (Bosia 2009, 77)

From this document we can begin to outline what the Activist HIV-body means. The Activist HIV-body understands itself as vital, dignified, knowledgeable, and powerful. This understanding comes in direct conflict with the Medical and Juridical HIV-bodies, and understanding how these very different HIV-bodies align, overlap, and completely contradict each other demonstrates the tensions between the real live actors in research labs, in courtrooms, in bedrooms, and on the street. The medical body is at war with itself while the criminal body is guilty of the infection; all the while the body that hosts the virus reaches outwards towards a broader community, towards dignity, respect, resources, and recognition. This impasse manifests not simply in the way we talk about the epidemic but also in the way resources are allocated for HIV research, in the way people are denied housing, in the way people are treated in doctors' offices, in prison cells, and in classrooms across the country. We need these visions of a body living with HIV to align with each other in order to end the epidemic.

Wading Back into the Water

In January of 1983 the Gay Men's Health Crisis (GMHC) released its second newsletter about the epidemic. Dr. Lawrence Mass, one of the group's cofounders, authored a section of the newsletter entitled "Basic Questions and Answers about AIDS." The GMHC newsletter was one of the first and most effective means of communicating details of the burgeoning crisis to the LGBTQ community. In response to a question about how one should deal with feelings of "guilt" and "sin" in relation to the epidemic, Mass turns to metaphor, comparing gay sex to taking a swim in the ocean: "There is nothing 'immoral' or 'sinful' about celebrating your enjoyment of swimming in the ocean. If, however, your favorite beaches have posted Undertow or Oilspill warnings, it is prudent to avoid swimming in those areas as long as the signs are up" (Mass 1983, 18). The signs on the beaches have been up for over thirty years. As new generations grow up in a world of manageable HIV, they may wonder, "What is there to be afraid of? The water seems fine."

The generational debates in the gay community about the dangers of PrEP versus the potential sexual liberation these drugs might offer hint at some of the ways in which the HIV epidemic and LGBTQ politics have changed over the past thirty years. While PrEP offers a return to a beach of sexual freedom, it comes with a hefty price tag (literally and metaphorically) and requires constant vigilance. We do not know what taking this pill as prevention, every day, will mean over the course of the next thirty years, for our communities and for our bodies.

In a 1985 pamphlet published by the GMHC called *Medical Answers about AIDS*, Mass writes,

HISTORICALLY, HOMOSEXUALS HAVE BEEN STEROTYPED AS INCAPABLE OF ESTABLISHING ENDURING MONOGAMOUS RELATIONSHIPS. ILLOGICALLY, THIS PREJUDICE HAS BEEN USED AS A JUSTIFICATION FOR DENYING HOMOSEXUALS THE THEOLOGICAL, SOCIAL, AND LEGAL OPPORTUNITIES TO ESTABLISH SUCH RELATIONSHIPS. LOGICALLY, A NUMBER OF LEADING MEDICAL AND SCIENTIFIC AUTHORITIES HAVE EXPRESSED THEIR BELIEF THAT THE CULTURAL SANCTIONING OF SAME-SEX RELATIONSHIPS WOULD HELP TO ENCOURAGE THE ESTABLISHMENT OF MORE STABLE MONOGAMOUS RELATIONSHIPS AMONG GAY MEN. . . . THE PROTECTION OF THE BASIC CIVIL LIBERTIES OF ALL LESBIAN AND GAY PERSONS, WHICH WOULD INCLUDE THE RECOGNITION OF SAME-SEX RELATIONSHIPS, SHOULD THUS BE AN ESSENTIAL CONSIDERATION IN THE LONG-RANGE PREVENTATIVE MEDICINE OF AIDS AND OTHER SEXUALLY TRANSMITTED DISEASES. (Mass 1985, 38; emphasis in original)

Mass seems to have predicted, or aspired for, the Supreme Court's June 2015 ruling in *Obergefell v. Hodges*, legalizing same-sex marriage across the country. Now that LGBTQ people have a modicum of civil rights in the United States, where does that leave the LGBTQ community in relationship to the fight against HIV/ AIDS?

Rather than developing new and better metaphors to describe the AIDS crisis, we should take our lead from the virus itself. At this moment, after the sweeping and rapid victory of same-sex marriage, we need to mutate our politics and create the conditions to inspire new metaphors. Certainly we should continue to push for further education, access, and reduction of costs of antiretroviral drugs, but we should also foster more curiosity and skepticism about scientific practices, policies, and procedures. LGBTQ groups should continue to fight for anti-discrimination laws in housing and the workplace. But we must move towards fighting poverty, ending stigma, and repeating HIV criminalization laws as well. Mainstream LGBTQ groups, who have fought for marriage, should look to grassroots groups that focus on ending poverty, discrimination, and inequity. They should join in movements fighting criminalization and poverty more broadly by aligning with racial and economic justice groups already at work in the South. They should ally with groups fighting for reproductive justice, and work towards making PrEP cheaper and easier to access for rural women of color.

LGBTQ people exist, in variegated forms, within every community, making the issues of economic, racial, and gender justice central to any movement for LGBTQ rights, since economic, racial, and gender injustice often affect LGBTQ people disproportionately in comparison to their straight counterparts. We need to educate lawmakers, police departments, and our communities about the facts of modern HIV science. If we want to tear down the signs on the beach, LGBTQ groups must continue to fight against the stigma of this communicable disease. Now that we know what we know, after thirty years of science, activism, and the deaths of over twenty-eight million people, how will communities affected by HIV return to the beach?

NOTES

1 See: CDC 2015b.

2 In May of 2014, the Centers for Disease Control and the National Institutes of Health released findings from four clinical trials recommending that people "at risk" for HIV begin Pre-Exposure Prophylaxis (PrEP). This preventive therapy relies on the pharmaceutical drug Truvada (tenofovir disoproxil/emtricitabine), which, taken once a day, dramatically reduces the chances of becoming infected with HIV. The CDC defines those at "substantial risk for HIV" as heterosexual men and women who have a seroconverted partner, have a high number of sex partners, have acted as sex workers, have a history of no condom use, or are member of a "high [HIV] prevalence area or network." See: United States. Department of Health and Human Services. Centers for Disease Control and Prevention 2014.

3 The "specific" immune response to a pathogen comes in two forms: a cell-mediated response, for a pathogen in your cells (cancer, bacteria); and a humeral response, for an

infection in your blood stream. T-cells are used for cell-mediated responses; B-cells are used for the humeral response. For both a cell-mediated and a humeral response, a helper T-cell is alerted by a macrophage (a type of phagocyte) displaying an antigen protein. It then binds to the macrophage and, in a cell-mediated response, the helper T-cell directs a specific T-cell to search out and destroy cells displaying that particular antigen. After this process, some of these T-cells die, but some, called memory T-cells, stay alive much longer and are able to mount a more efficient response to a pathogen if it reenters the body, often providing you with a lifelong immunity to that particular threat.

4 I follow Cathy Cohen's definition:

By "neoliberalism" I mean . . . a governing agenda that includes the increased privatization of government programs and institutions like public schools or even prisons; the scaling back and in some cases elimination of the welfare state, that is, government assistance to the poor, low-income, and elderly; a move toward fewer economic regulations and more trade that is free of constraints that would protect jobs, the environment, and entities such as unions, in order to produce greater profits for companies that, some would argue, will lead to more jobs. Neoliberalism also involves an intensifying rhetoric that is grounded in the belief that markets, in and of themselves, are better able than governments to produce, in particular, economic outcomes that are fair, sensible, and good for all. This rhetoric is bolstered by a discourse that is more familiar to the larger public, one that emphasizes personal responsibility and the role of individual agency or choice in determining one's success. (Cohen 2010, 11)

5 Human Immunodeficiency Virus, Acquired Immune Deficiency Syndrome, AIDS-Related Complex (archaic term), Antiretroviral Therapy, Pre-Exposure Prophylaxis, Pre-Exposure Prophylaxis, Treatment as Prevention.

6 Centers for Disease Control, National Institute of Health, National Institute of Allergy and Infectious Diseases, United Nations Acquired Immune Deficiency Syndrome.

7 Gay Men's Health Crisis, Street Transvestite Action Revolutionaries, AIDS Coalition to Unleash Power, Women's Health Action Mobilization, Treatment Action Group, Treatment Action Campaign, Proactive Optimistic Sisters in Touch, Involved, Validated and Empowered.

REFERENCES

Addison, Brian. 2014. "Larry Kramer, Truvada Whores, and the Angry Divide between Two Generations: HIV Equal." HIV Equal, 6 June. www.hivequal.org.

Altman, Dennis. 1988. "Legitimation through Disaster: AIDS and the Gay Movement." *AIDS: The Burdens of History*. Ed. Elizabeth Fee and Daniel M. Fox. Berkeley: U of California P. 301–15.

Bersani, Leo. 2010. *"Is the Rectum a Grave?" and Other Essays*. Chicago: U of Chicago P.

Bosia, Michael J. 2009. "AIDS and Postcolonial Politics: Acting Up on Science and Immigration in France." *French Politics, Culture & Society* 27.1: 69–90.

Burress, Jim. 2014. "'Truvada Whore' Stigma Endures among Doctors and LGBTs." *Advocate*, 11 Aug. www.advocate.com.

Callen, Michael, and Dan Turner. 1988. "A History of the PWA Self-Empowerment Movement." The Posthumous Home Page of Michael Callen, www.michaelcallen.com. Article original originally published in 1988 Lesbian & Gay Health Education Foundation Program Booklet. Published on coauthor M. Callen's website, posthumously.

CDC. 2015a. "Pre-Exposure Prophylaxis." Centers for Disease Control and Prevention, June 25. www.cdc.gov.

CDC. 2015b. "PrEP Clinical Trials." Centers for Disease Control and Prevention, Oct. 28. www.cdc.gov.

Center for HIV Law and Policy. 2013. *When Sex Is a Crime and Spit Is a Dangerous Weapon: A Snapshot of HIV Criminalization in the United States*. Issue brief, April. www.hivlawandpolicy. org.

Cohen, Cathy J. 1999. *The Boundaries of Blackness: AIDS and the Breakdown of Black Politics*. Chicago: U of Chicago P.

Cohen, Cathy J. 2010. *Democracy Remixed*. Oxford: Oxford UP.

Cohen, Myron S., et al. 2011. "Prevention of HIV-1 Infection with Early Antiretroviral Therapy." *New England Journal of Medicine* 365.6: 493–505.

Delany, Samuel R. 1999. *Times Square Red, Times Square Blue*. New York: NYU P.

"The Denver Principles." 1983. *ACT-UP NY Documents*. ACT-UP NY, www.actupny.org.

Fauci, Anthony. 2011. "Thirty Years of HIV/AIDS: A Personal Journey." Columbia University Global Strategy Seminar, Aug. 10. Columbia University, New York City. www.youtube.com.

Fauci, Anthony. 2013. "Three Decades of HIV/AIDS Science and Policy." Annual Meeting of the American Association of Immunologists, May 28. Honolulu, HI.

Fauci, Anthony. 2014. "Interview with Dr. Anthony Fauci on 'Mississippi Baby.'" Interview by AIDS.gov, July 14. www.youtube.com.

Fox, Daniel M. 1988. "AIDS and the American Health Polity." *AIDS: The Burdens of History*. Ed. Elizabeth Fee and Daniel M. Fox. Berkeley: U of California P. 316–43.

Gilead. 2014. "About TRUVADA for a PrEP Indication." *Pre-exposur e Prophylaxis*. Gilead, June. www.truvadapreprems.com.

Glazek, Christopher. 2014. "Why I Am a Truvada Whore." *Out Magazine*, May 20. www.out.com.

Halper-Stomberg, Ari. 2015. Interview with Ari Halper-Halper Stromberg, Nussenzweig Laboratory of Molecular Microbiology, at Rockefeller University, Feb. 18.. Interview by J. Ricky Price.

Halper-Stromberg, Ariel, et al. 2014. "Broadly Neutralizing Antibodies and Viral Inducers Decrease Rebound from HIV-1 Latent Reservoirs in Humanized Mice." *Cell* 158.5: 989–99.

Haraway, Donna Jeanne. 1991. *Simians, Cyborgs, and Women: The Reinvention of Nature*. New York: Routledge.

Hayden, Erika Check. 2013. "Infant's Vanquished HIV Leaves Doctors Puzzled." *Nature*, March 5.

Hoffman, Michelle. 1996. "AIDS: A Howdunit Story." *American Scientist* 84.1: 26–27.

Malbec, M., et al. 2013. "Broadly Neutralizing Antibodies That Inhibit HIV-1 Cell to Cell Transmission." *Journal of Experimental Medicine* 210.13: 2813–21.

Maron, Dina Fine. 2014. "HIV Detected in 'Cured' Mississippi Baby, Creating Huge AIDS Therapy Setback." *Scientific American*, July 10.

Martin, Emily. 1992. "The End of the Body?" *American Ethnologist* 19.1: 121–40.

Mass, Lawrence. 1983. *Basic Questions and Answers about AIDS*. New York: Gay Men's Health Crisis Newsletter.

Mass, Lawrence. 1985. *Medical Answers about AIDS*. New York: Gay Men's Health Crisis Newsletter.

Napier, A. David. 2003. *The Age of Immunology: Conceiving a Future in an Alienating World*. Chicago: U of Chicago P.

National Institute of Health. 2013. "Toddler 'Functionally Cured' of HIV Infection, NIH-Supported Investigators Report." *NIH News*, March 3. www.niaid.nih.gov.

National Institute of Health. National Institute of Allergy and Infectious Diseases. 2014. "NIH Trial Tests Very Early Anti-HIV Therapy in HIV-Infected Newborns." *NIH News*, Nov. 3. www.niaid.nih.gov.

New York Times Editorial Board. 1987. "Senator Helms and the Guilty Victims." *New York Times*, June 17.

Persaud, Deborah, et al. 2013. "Absence of Detectable HIV-1 Viremia after Treatment Cessation in an Infant." *New England Journal of Medicine* 369.19: 1828–35.

Piot, Peter. 2015. *AIDS: Between Science and Politics*. Trans. Laurence Garey. New York: Columbia UP.

Pross, Addy. 2012. *What Is Life? How Chemistry Becomes Biology*. Oxford: Oxford UP.

Sessions, Kimberly B., and Richard Loftus. 2001. "Immune System." *The Encyclopedia of AIDS*. Ed. Raymond A. Smith. Revised ed. New York: Penguin.

Somerville, Siobhan B. 2000. *Queering the Color Line: Race and the Invention of Homosexuality in American Culture*. Durham, NC: Duke UP.

Sontag, Susan. 1990. *Illness as Metaphor and AIDS and Its Metaphors*. New York: Picador.

Stine, Gerald James. 2012. *AIDS Update 2012: An Annual Overview of Acquired Immune Deficiency Syndrome*. New York: McGraw-Hill.

Treichler, Paula A. 1999. *How to Have Theory in an Epidemic: Cultural Chronicles of AIDS*. Durham, NC: Duke UP.

United States. Department of Health and Human Services. Centers for Disease Control and Prevention. 2014. *Preexposure Prophylaxis for the Prevention of HIV Infection in the United States—2014*. By U.S. Public Health Service. N.p.: Department of Health and Human Services.

Weeks, Benjamin S., and I. Edward Alcamo. 2010. *AIDS: The Biological Basis*. Sudbury, MA: Jones and Bartlett.

Wei, Xiping, et al. 2003. "Antibody Neutralization and Escape by HIV-1." *Nature* 422.6929: 307–12.

White House Office of National AIDS Policy. 2010. *National HIV/AIDS Strategy for the United States*.

Wright, Joe. 2013. "Only Your Calamity: The Beginnings of Activism by and for People with AIDS." *American Journal of Public Health* 103.10: 1788–98.

5

Queering Reproductive Justice

Toward a Theory and Praxis for Building Intersectional Political Alliances

KIMALA PRICE

In 2007, the United States Supreme Court upheld the Partial-Birth Abortion Ban 2003, which was signed into law by President George W. Bush, in the two consolidated cases of *Gonzales v. Planned Parenthood* and *Gonzales v. Carhart*. The Court stated that the federal ban was constitutionally sound and did not impose an undue burden on the right to an abortion. The decision caused an immediate outcry from medical practitioners, feminist organizations, and other socially progressive groups, including the National Gay & Lesbian Task Force (NGLTF). In response to the NGLTF's press release decrying the decisions, James Kirchick, the assistant to the editor-in-chief of the *New Republic* at the time, published an opinion article in the *Washington Blade* in which he argued,

> I believe abortion should be, as President Clinton said, "safe, legal and rare." But just because one supports the right of women to have the control over their bodies that abortion laws seek to protect does not mean that gay people, ipso facto, believe that the gay rights movement—which has plenty of significant legal battles of its own to win—ought to take a position on abortion. . . . And as if it merited mentioning: abortion is biologically a heterosexual issue. Noting this fact does not make gays who oppose abortion selfish, it merely emphasizes further that abortion is, in its essence, something with which heterosexual women and their partners struggle. The only way in which abortion could ever be tied to gay political concerns is in the rare case when a surrogate or lesbian mother decides, for whatever reason, to abort the fetus that she agreed to carry prior to insemination. (2007, 24)

Struck by the shortsightedness of Kirchick's remarks and his privileging of gay male experience over that of others, many within the LGBTQ community took issue with his limited approach to LGBTQ politics. His remarks, however, did raise several issues: How do we determine what is a "gay rights" issue? Which issues should be prioritized by the LGBTQ movement? Who gets to decide these matters?

In response, Miriam Pérez, a Latina, LGBTQ, feminist activist, argued that reproductive justice and queer politics are intimately connected in more ways than Kirchick can ever imagine (Pérez 2007). For instance, rape and sexual assault, which can result in unintended pregnancy, are very real concerns for both hetero-sexual and queer women, and unintended pregnancy through consensual sexual activity is a very real possibility for bisexual women and transgender people. All of these potential situations make access to abortion services a genuine concern for many within the LGBTQ movement. However, Pérez argues that there is even more at stake; there are more issues beyond abortion that connect LGBTQ issues and reproductive justice. She asserts that "reproductive justice is not just about one's ability to reproduce. It's about autonomy, its [sic] about respect, its [sic] about shared principles based in the human right to health and a desire for real social change" (Pérez 2007). Her essay was ultimately a call to "queer" reproduc-tive justice. What exactly does it mean to "queer" reproductive justice, though?

There have been LGBTQ advocacy organizations, such as the National Cen-ter for Lesbian Rights (NCLR) and the National Gay and Lesbian Task Force (NGLTF), that have embraced reproductive justice as a part of their political agendas, as well as reproductive justice organizations, such as the National Latina Institute for Reproductive Health (NLIRH) and Forward Together (for-merly known as Asian Communities for Reproductive Justice), that have incor-porated LGBTQ issues into their grassroots organizing. Moreover, the Lesbian, Gay, Bisexual & Transgender Community Center (the Center) in New York has created the "Causes in Common" project, which "brings together activists rep-resenting the LGBT Liberation and Reproductive Rights and Justice Movements to work toward a shared vision of reproductive freedom, sexual liberation and social justice" (LGBT Center 2015).

This essay explores the ways in which activists have attempted to build coali-tions and develop a shared agenda between the LGBTQ and reproductive justice movements, despite protestations from some that abortion and reproductive health in general are not LGBTQ issues. Drawing from the experiences of sev-eral reproductive justice and LGBTQ advocacy groups and informed by queer and feminist theory and the scholarly literature on reproductive justice, queer politics, and social movements, this essay is part political history of the organiz-ing efforts of these groups and part narrative analysis of the discourse that has emerged from this work. Storytelling is the most typical form of communication that we use in our daily social interactions. It is the way we make sense of our experiences and construct identities—our own and others'—make sense of indi-viduals and groups, and make claims about the world and the nature of reality (Bruner 2003; Price 2010; Stone 1989). Storytelling is used by social movements to frame issues, construct a collective identity, and recruit and mobilize new members (Polletta 1998a, 1998b; Price 2010). Last, storytelling is a performance. We are not just reporting what we see and experience; we actually are "doing things with words" (Langellier and Peterson 2004). In other words, activists *are* building coalitions and solidarity just by merely sharing stories about their commonalities.

Finding the Intersection: Reproductive Justice and LGBT/Queer Politics

Coined in 1994 by a group of women of color activists at a reproductive rights conference in Chicago (Loretta Ross quoted in Avery 2005), "reproductive justice" is not synonymous with "reproductive rights" or "pro-choice" (Price 2010; Silliman et al. 2004). It is a distinctive conceptual and political organizing framework that is rooted in human rights and social justice principles, and it questions the concepts of choice and the right to privacy that are at the center of mainstream reproductive rights politics (Luna 2009; Mason 2013; Smith 2005). Feminist legal scholar Dorothy Roberts (1997) argues that the concept of privacy—which is predicated on a negative view of liberty (i.e., freedom from governmental intervention)—ignores the many obstacles to reproductive decision making, such as social prejudices, economic inequality and injustice, and the instances of state intervention in the lives of poor people, particularly through social welfare programs. Moreover, the concept of privacy ignores the social hierarchies that actually play a part in limiting the number of options that an individual may or may not have. In other words, how can we talk about access to abortion, when, historically, there have been women who have not had adequate access to healthcare in general?

The reproductive justice framework also critiques the centrality of abortion within the mainstream reproductive rights movement; the pro-choice framework narrowly focuses the debate on abortion, which has been to the detriment of other important reproductive and sexual health issues. This framework strives to move the discussion on reproductive freedom beyond the right to obtain an abortion (that is, the right *not* to have children) to include the right to *have* children and the right to raise the children that one has in a safe and healthy environment (Price 2010; Silliman et al. 2004; SisterSong 2015). This initial definition of reproductive justice has been expanded to include the right to give birth in dignity and to determine the conditions of one's birthing process, the right to adult consensual sexuality and sexual pleasure, the right to gender expression, and the right to access medically accurate, nonjudgmental, comprehensive sex and sexuality education (SisterSong 2015; Black Women Birthing Justice 2015; LGBT Center 2003).

In order for women and girls to achieve reproductive freedom, activists must address and dismantle reproductive oppression, which is defined as

> [t]he control and exploitation of women and girls through our bodies, sexuality, and reproduction[, which] is a strategic pathway to regulating entire populations that is implemented by families, communities, institutions, and society . . . [T]he regulation of reproduction and exploitation of women's bodies and labor is both a tool and a result of systems of oppression based on race, class, gender, sexuality, ability, age, and immigration status. (Asian Communities for Reproductive Justice 2005, 1)

As the last sentence of this definition indicates, intersectionality is also a central principle of the reproductive justice framework. Gender is not the only source of reproductive exploitation and oppression. In order to truly understand reproductive oppression, we must understand how all of these aspects of identity, oppression, and privilege interact with one another to produce the conditions through which we experience reproduction and sexuality. Moreover, an intersectional analysis of reproduction and sexuality goes beyond our individual experiences. It is about understanding the collective history of reproductive oppression of communities, not just about preserving individual autonomy. After all, some communities, such as communities of color and low-income communities, have historically been the targets of coercive sterilization campaigns sanctioned by the federal and several state governments (Gutiérrez 1999; Nelson 2015; Roberts 1997; Silliman et al. 2004).

With the reproductive justice framework, reproduction does not happen in a vacuum; it is connected to other social justice issues. It is impossible to truly achieve reproductive freedom if one, for instance, does not have adequate housing for one's family, lacks reliable transportation in order to make health appointments, or lives in a community that is located near a waste site or chemical plant that releases toxins in the air, soil, and local water supply that can cause major health problems. Other issues that may constrain one's options include the reduction of welfare benefits for women with children, the prohibition of the use of federal Medicaid funds to pay for abortions for poor women, and the ban on immigrants receiving governmental benefits. Accordingly, over the last decade, there has been a steady increase in scholarship and activism that explore the connections between reproductive justice and other social justice issues, such as environmental justice, immigration, disability rights, fat studies, and LGBTQ liberation (Gaard 2010; Generations Ahead 2009; LGBT Center 2003; NAPAWF 2007; Piepmeier 2013; Richardson 2006; Roberts and Jesudason 2013). While many self-identified reproductive justice organizations have addressed multiple social justice issues, no one organization or movement can possibly address *all* of these issues effectively. This means that an intersectional approach to reproductive politics relies on the formation of alliances within the movement and with other social justice movements.

There have been calls from various LGBTQ activists and scholars to the mainstream LGBTQ movement, which includes groups such as the Human Rights Campaign and GLAAD, to broaden its agenda and scope. The movement must be more representative of the diversity of the LGBTQ community, and has a responsibility to address the broader social justice issues that affect their lives (Cohen 1997; PPFA 2005; Vaid 2012). The focus on marriage equality and military service is too narrow, and in the long run only benefits those who are already privileged in other aspects, such as race, ethnicity, socioeconomic class, gender identity, and citizenship status. It is an agenda that reflects a "white, middle-class conception of the 'status queer'" (Vaid 2012, 39). This parallels the discussions in which women of color, queer women, low-income women, and other groups have expressed feeling marginalized by the political agenda of the mainstream reproductive rights movement, which has largely ignored the effects of racism, homophobia, economic injustice, and other social injustices on reproduction. That is, the norm of the "universal woman" in reproductive politics has been largely based on the experiences of white, middle-class, heterosexual women. Taking a cue from the reproductive justice movement, the LGBTQ movement could benefit from an intersectional approach to its political work.

With reproductive justice organizations looking to building cross-movement alliances and the calls to broaden the LGBTQ political agenda, the time seems ripe for coalition building between the reproductive justice and the LGBTQ movements. Even though the histories of these respective movements are inter-twined, there generally has been little organizational collaboration between the LGBTQ and reproductive rights and justice movements, but this seems to be slowly changing (Generations Ahead 2009; Nixon 2013). The rest of this essay examines how these LGBTQ and reproductive justice organizations have attempted to build alliances with each other by addressing the following questions: How and in what spaces is this organizing happening? What is the potential for social and political transformation from such coalition work? How have activists addressed resistance to the project of queering reproductive justice?

Methodology

I collected narrative data from documents from fourteen LGBTQ and reproductive justice advocacy organizations as well as multi-issue feminist organizations that incorporate reproductive justice issues in their organizing work. I deliberately chose groups that explicitly work on LGBTQ and reproductive justice issues. The initial group of organizations included in the sample were the National Center for Lesbian Rights, the National Gay and Lesbian Task Force, the National Latina Institute for Reproductive Health, Forward Together (formerly known as Asian Communities for Reproductive Justice), the Lesbian, Gay, Bisexual & Transgender Community Center in New York (the "Causes in Common" project), and the National Center for Transgender Equality (NCTE).

Founded in 1973 and 1977, respectively, the National Gay and Lesbian Task Force and the National Center for Lesbian Rights are among the oldest of national LGBT advocacy organization; while the Task Force is primarily a grassroots organization, NCLR is a public interest law firm that litigates precedent-setting cases and provides free legal assistance to LGBT individuals and their families, as well as advocates for public policies and conducts community education campaigns (NCLR 2015; NGLTF 2015). National Latina Institute for Reproductive Health (NLIRH) and Forward Together are reproductive justice organizations that incorporate LGBTQ issues into their respective missions. Founded in 1994 and located in New York City, NLIRH is a national reproductive justice organization that focuses on Latinas; its main issues include abortion, reproductive and sexual health equity, and immigrant women's health and rights. Founded in 1989 as Asians and Pacific Islanders for Reproductive Health (APIRH), Forward Together (which was most recently formally known as Asian Communities for Reproductive Justice) is an Oakland, California–based multiracial organization that works with community leaders and organizations to transform culture and public policy in order to facilitate social change (Forward Together 2015a, 2015b). The LGBT Community Center (the Center) has been a home and resource hub for the LGBT community in New York City since its founding in 1983 (2015). Based in Washington, DC, the National Center for Transgender Equality was founded in 2003 by transgender activists, and has quickly become the nation's leading social justice advocacy organization for transgender people (NCTE 2015).

After the initial search for and analysis of documents produced by the above-mentioned groups, it became clear that I needed to expand the list of organizations; there were other groups that were involved in this cross-movement alliance building. The groups that were added to the sample are Law Students for Reproductive Justice, Pro-Choice Public Education Project (PEP), Funders for Lesbian and Gay Issues, National Women's Law Center, Center for Women's Policy Studies, Woodhull Sexual Freedom Alliance, Lambda Legal, and the Zuna Institute.

The sample includes forty-six documents, including reports, fact sheets, blog entries, issue briefs, and op-ed articles. These documents were published between 2003 and 2014, with the majority of the documents dated between 2010 and 2014. Some of these documents include articles from the LGBTQ press, such as the *Washington Blade* and the *Advocate.com*, and articles from the feminist press, such as RH Reality Check (blog) and *On the Issues* magazine. These documents were found through Google keyword searches of websites. I used various combinations of the following terms: "reproductive justice," "reproductive rights," "abortion," "LGBT," "LGBTQ," "queer," and "politics." (This strategy presupposed a connection among these terms.)

This essay also draws from an oral history interview of Carmen Vázquez, a prominent feminist and LGBTQ activist, who is a cofounder of Women's Building in San Francisco and Somos Hermanas, a Central American women's solidarity network. Her interview is from the Voices of Feminism Oral History Project housed at Sophia Smith Collection at Smith College (Vázquez 2005). This essay draws from her experience as the director of public policy for the LGBT Community Center in New York City (from 1994 to ca. 2005), which created the Causes in Common project. Last, this essay draws from Reproductive Justice for All: A U.S. Policy Conference, which was held at Smith College in Northampton, Massachusetts, in November 2005. Sponsored by the Smith College Women Studies Program and Planned Parenthood Federation of America, the conference was a gathering of academics, activists, and policy wonks to discuss and propose a policy agenda for reproductive justice (PPFA 2005). It included sessions that focused on sexuality and LGBTQ issues and included participation from the National Center for Lesbian Rights and prominent scholars who specialize in LGBTQ topics, such as political scientists Cathy Cohen and Anna Marie Smith, and historian Nancy Ordover.

With the aid of Atlas.ti qualitative data analysis software, I coded the documents for narrative themes. I coded for specific social and political issues such as abortion, marriage equality, parenting, HIV/AIDS, violence, and economic justice, as well as for abstract concepts such as privacy, choice, liberty, and sexual freedom. Second, I coded for activism and social justice–oriented themes such as coalition building, intersectionality, racism, sexism, homophobia, and transphobia. Last, I coded for specific historical and contemporary events (e.g., U.S. Supreme Court decisions), organizations, and political slogans. I used a reiterative process for the coding strategy. I started with a list of themes that I cultivated from an initial reading of the documents. The list was refined after each round of coding. Once the coding was in place, the analysis entailed noting the frequency with which these themes occurred, examining the context in which they are discussed, and determining the relationships among them.

The Search for Common Ground

The search for common ground between these two social movements has taken place in many places over the years (particularly since the early 2000s). As we shall see, this work has mainly occurred in the programming and political and policy activities of individual advocacy organizations, through opinion articles published in print and online media, and through meetings and conferences created specifically to discuss the potential for coalition building between these two movements.

The Oakland-based reproductive justice group Forward Together has incorporated LGTBQ issues in its programming. For instance, its youth organizing program was created specifically to "create a safe space for Asian youth of all genders and sexualities," and its "Let's Get It On" campaign advocates for public schools to provide comprehensive sexuality education that offers medically accurate and culturally sensitive information about sex, the body, and healthy relationships, which includes covering gender and LGBTQ identity. Its "Strong Families" campaign includes support for marriage equality in addition to the advocacy for equitable and fair immigration policy, affordable childcare, and after-school programs. Moreover, LGBTQ liberation is one of the advocacy issues for the National Latina Institute for Reproductive Health (NLIRH). Two notable fact sheets by NLIRH include "Queer Immigrants and Affordable Health Care" (ca. 2014) and "At the Margins of Care: The Need for Inclusive Health Care for Transgender and Gender-Nonconforming Latin@s" (2013). It is important to note that the former publication was also sponsored by the National Asian Pacific American Women's Forum and the National Gay and Lesbian Task Force Action Fund. It is also important to note that NLIRH uses the "@" sign in its publications to "represent the diversity of [its] community and to include persons who do not conform to traditional gender identities" (NLIRH 2013).

Likewise, the National Gay and Lesbian Task Force has publicly supported abortion and reproductive rights. For instance, in 2014 NGLTF weighed in on the Hobby Lobby court case, in which the U.S. Supreme Court ruled that closely held corporations (such as the plaintiff, a chain of crafts stores) have the right to refuse to cover contraceptive prescriptions, as mandated by the Affordable Care Act, if their owners' personally held religious beliefs dictate that certain contraceptives are abortifacients. Forcing such corporations to participate in the no-cost contraceptive program violates the Religious Freedom Restoration Act of 1993. In an opinion piece entitled "Birth Control Is Not My Boss's Business," Arlie Schwartz connects the denial of birth control coverage to LGBTQ liberation by arguing that

> [c]orporations must not be allowed to deny birth control coverage to their employees based on their own personally held religious beliefs. . . . This is your paycheck and your healthcare, and private corporations have no business telling you otherwise. We at The Task Force recognize the intersectionality between the reproductive justice movement and the LGBT community—our bodies are not a battle ground for the world to vote on and we cannot allow people (or corporations) to decide how we live our lives. (Schwartz 2014)

While the previously mentioned groups have incorporated either reproductive justice or LGBTQ issues into their work, it can be argued that the National Center for Lesbian Rights has always employed a reproductive justice framework, even though its founding predates the term. It was originally founded to protect lesbians' right to parent their children. As NCLR's policy director Shannon Minter explains,

> NCLR was started back in 1977 precisely in order to deal with issues around parenting and reproduction and, in particular, to represent mothers who were coming out as lesbians, leaving heterosexual marriages or relationships, and were very often losing their children in custody battles because their lesbianism was seen as, per se, evidence that they were unfit to be parents. . . . [I]t was thought necessary to start a whole new legal organization . . . because the existing gay rights organizations at the time were run almost exclusively by men [who] didn't see that as a civil rights issue. They saw it as a personal problem that some women were having. . . . [I]ssues relating to parenting and family continue to be our core program areas at

NCLR, only now we've expanded that framework to include trying to create legal protections for same sex couples and their children, for couples that are creating intentional families. So that includes relationship protections like working for the right to marry . . . fighting for lesbians to have access to alternative insemination, [and fighting] for gay men to have access to adoption and, in some cases, surrogacy, which raises a very complex set of issues. (PPFA 2005, 64)

As this narrative reveals, NCLR's original mission (i.e., legally representing lesbian mothers) reflects two of the tenets of the reproductive justice framework: the right to have children and the right to parent children in a safe and healthy environment. With its now-revised mission, it is continuing to expand the boundaries of reproductive justice to include the protection of intentionally created families, and it has collaborated with and supported reproductive justice organizations such as Forward Together, National Latina Institute for Reproductive Health, and the DC Abortion Fund (Nixon 2013). Moreover, this narrative mirrors the example at the beginning of this essay; it is an earlier manifestation of the struggle to define what constitutes a "gay rights" issue. Although NCLR now legally represents all types of same-sex/queer couples and families, it was founded specially to represent lesbians, as child custody cases were not considered a "gay rights issue" by many gay male activists at the time.

The first effort to explicitly bring these two movements together is the Causes in Common program of the LGBTQ Community Center of New York City. According to founding program director Carmen Vázquez (2005),

[W]e did some workshops, Terry [Boggis] and I did. We wrote some things and finally got funding from the Ford Foundation to actually develop a project [Causes in Common]. [T]he project involved inviting reproductive rights leaders and LGBT leaders together to come and have a conversation about what we understood to be the political and policy links between the two movements and what sort of common ground could we agree on as places where we could support each other's work and really understand that reproductive rights are intimate, I mean, deeply, profoundly about sexual and gender rights and, therefore, about LGBT liberation. (12)

Although these workshops fostered fruitful dialogue among activists from these respective movements, Vázquez believed that the group needed to produce a compelling, visionary statement that outlined the group's goals and principles. However, she insisted that the statement be a philosophical treatise that was rooted in the legal history of the right to privacy rather than merely an impassioned rhetorical argument (Vázquez 2005). After two years of extensive legal and historical research, on May 16, 2003, the program convened a roundtable of twenty-five activists to develop a statement of principles and recommendations for action. Additionally, this roundtable created the Causes in Common Pledge of Commitment, which has been signed by seventy-five groups, including many regional affiliates of the Planned Parenthood Federation of America (LGBT Center 2003).

Undoubtedly, the Causes in Common statement and the pledge were instrumental in broadening the definition of reproductive justice to encompass sexual justice, which includes, but is not limited to, the right to adult consensual sexuality with whomever one chooses, the right to sexual pleasure free from moral judgment and shaming, the right to gender expression, and the right to form the relationships and families of one's choosing—and to have those relationships legally recognized and supported. Furthermore, the statement was among the first to explicitly discuss the legal connection between the two movements, specifically between abortion and antisodomy laws. It acknowledged that earlier U.S. Supreme Court cases regarding reproductive rights, such as *Roe v. Wade* (1973), which legalized abortion in the United States, paved the way for the *Lawrence v. Texas* (2003) decision, which deemed antisodomy laws unconstitutional. *Roe v. Wade*—along with the *Griswold v. Connecticut* (1965) and *Eisenstadt v. Baird* (1972) decisions that allowed the right to use contraception—established the right to privacy for the most personal, intimate matters. *Roe v. Wade* was cited as precedent in the *Lawrence* decision (LGBT Center 2003).

A little over a decade later, in 2014, two nonprofit organizations, Funders for LGBTQ Issues and the Funders Network on Population, Reproductive Health and Rights, continued the conversation started by Causes in Common by convening a day-long meeting of funders and activists in New York City. Sponsored by the Arcus Foundation, the Ford Foundation, and the Moriah Fund, the meeting was convened to discuss the intersections between the reproductive justice and LGBTQ movements, which had "work[ed] principally on separate tracks, while sharing core values and common adversaries" (Funders for LGBTQ Issues 2015). Although it included the participation of representatives from the National Gay and Lesbian Task Force, the LGBTQ Community Center of New York City, the Transgender Law Center, Spark, Forward Together, and Choice USA, this meeting differed from the Causes in Common project in that funders were front and center. One of the meeting's main objectives was figuring out the role of funders in providing the institutional and financial support that can foster more collaborative work among these organizations, which can be difficult considering that funders face institutional constraints that make it more difficult to fund intersectional alliances than to fund single-issue advocacy groups (Funders for LGBTQ Issues 2015).

Building Solidarity Rhetorically

While there has been some cross-issue and coalitional work between these two movements, most of this work has been discursive in nature. For instance, we have seen how Causes in Common has explicitly made the connection between abortion regulation and sodomy laws, showing how these issues are tied by the legal principle of the right to privacy. Many activists represented in this sample have told multiple stories about the need for the legal recognition of relationships and families. These and many other stories are told by activists to foster solidarity—a sense of unity and mutual respect—between these two movements. By focusing on shared principles, common goals and interests, mutual enemies, and similar histories of oppression, activists have attempted to find common ground rhetorically. There are certainly similarities in the social and political histories of these movements.

Members of both movements have been vilified via moralist judgments and pronouncements by religious conservatives, especially right-wing Republicans (Pizer 2014; Wellek and Yeung 2015; Yeung 2011/2012). Women who use contraceptives, have sex outside of marriage, have unintended pregnancies, and seek abortions are constructed as being promiscuous, irresponsible, and selfish, while homosexuality (queerness) is considered a crime against nature and God's will (Shorto 2006). Accordingly, members of both communities are viewed as immoral, wrong, and harmful to society because of their nonconformity to traditional gender and sexual norms. Feminists and the LGBTQ community are often blamed for the breakdown of the traditional nuclear family by conservative pundits; this condemnation, in turn, justifies any proposed laws and policies that politically, socially, and financially disenfranchise these communities (LGBT Center 2003). Sharing a common opponent can quickly create a sense of unity among different communities.

These two movements also have similar histories of oppression. Members of both movements have been the targets of eugenic policies in which some social groups (i.e., white/middle-class/able-bodied/native-born) are considered "fit" to reproduce, while other groups (i.e., people of color/poor/disabled/criminal/ immigrant) are deemed to be unfit to bear and raise children (Ordover 2003). Entire communities have historically been socially controlled through their bodies through the creation and implementation of coercive laws, public policies, and medical practices. In 1907, for instance, several states began passing laws that mandated the sterilization of people deemed unfit to reproduce. For several decades afterward until the early 1980s, large segments of communities of color—particularly African American women in the South, Puerto Rican women, women of Mexican origin in the Southwest, and Native American women through Indian Health Services—were sterilized, often without their full knowledge or consent (Gutiérrez 1999; Roberts 1997; Silliman et al. 2004). On the other hand, white women have historically been strongly encouraged to have children, and policies were put in place to make it difficult for them to obtain sterilizations or other contraceptive methods. Until 1973, homosexuality was considered a mental disorder by the American Psychiatric Association

(Ordover 2003). There has been "a long history of diagnosis and treatment of LGBTQ people [in the U.S.]. . . . include[ing] electric shock treatments, lobotomies, hysterectomies, clitoridectomies, vasectomies, all performed on queers in this country," with "gay conversion therapy" being the most recent incarnation of this history (Nancy Ordover quoted in PPFA 2005, 95).

In addition to telling stories about the historical connections between the movements, activists tell stories that make contemporary connections; this is often done through the telling of personal stories and stories that use hypothetical situations to humanize the issue. In a blog posting for LGBT HealthLink, Megan Lee (2011) argues,

> If a transman needs a pap smear, what does he do? Will his insurance cover this preventative care (an effective means of preventing cervical cancer) if he is listed as "male" on his insurance? And if he is diagnosed with cervical cancer and needs to receive care, will his provider be able to adequately serve him? Will he even be able to find a provider that's willing to talk to him?

This exemplar jibes with the assertion by many activists that reproductive healthcare is gendered and that many medical providers are not prepared to treat transgendered patients (Law Students for Reproductive Justice 2014). Many medical providers are not equipped to deal with health issues that may arise from sex-reassignment/gender-confirming surgery, nor are they likely to be aware that they should conduct pap smears and deal with pregnancies for an array of transpeople, not just those who are female-identified. Moreover, transpeople are more likely to be refused care by health providers because of their gender identity or expression, and they are more likely to postpone healthcare because of anticipated disrespect or discrimination by healthcare providers (NLIRH 2011, 2013).

Many of the documentary sources in the sample addressed transgender issues, with many of the stories focusing on healthcare, HIV/AIDS, violence, and economic justice. Many activists purposefully include transpeople in this discourse because of their marginalized status in both movements and their greater vulnerability in society at large. Indeed, transwomen of color are the most likely to be the targets of violence among those in the LGBTQ community, and transgender immigrant detainees experience sexual assault at the hands of detention officers, are often denied healthcare (including hormone treatment), and even risk death in many situations (NCLR 2015; NLIRH 2011, 2013). According to the National Latina Institute for Reproductive Health, 28 percent of Latin@ transpeople live in poverty (NLIRH 2011, 2013).

In a guest blog entry for URGE (United for Reproductive and Gender Equity, formerly known as Choice USA), Tanisha Humphrey (2013) of the Gay & Lesbian Victory Institute asserts that reproductive justice is a queer rights issue. She contends that reproductive justice is relevant for

[t]he 19 year old gay man who was kicked out of his house for coming out, moved to a big city for the first time in his life, and is just trying to figure out what his identity means. The married lesbians who are thinking about having a baby. The teenage couple facing an unintended pregnancy. All are searching for that necessary freedom. We want to share our families and therefore our lives without the cultural or political pressure invading our decisions. We want to get married, to have a baby, to not have a baby, to have sex, to not have sex. We can and should be working together to guarantee this for each of [sic] interlocking and intersecting communities.

By rhetorically joining these hypothetical scenarios (which are essentially condensed stories) together in this one narrative, Humphrey forces the audience to consider how these seemingly disparate social issues are in fact interrelated. Humphrey's framing of these scenarios as examples of the freedom to make personal decisions allows the audience to see how sexual identity development, family formation (presumably via marriage recognition, adoption, and/or donor insemination), safe shelter, pregnancy, contraception, abortion, and sex for pleasure all fall within the confines of reproductive justice, and her framing reminds us of the diversity of experiences within both movements.

Toward a Theory and Praxis of Intersectional Coalition Building

In this essay, I have shown how some reproductive justice and LGBTQ advocacy groups have attempted to form alliances through discourse and political collaboration. Their solidarity-building strategies have included identifying mutual foes, comparing historical connections, and recognizing shared values. Another important strategy has been the attempt to develop a shared vision, or a common goal. Given the many references to freedom, autonomy, liberty, and privacy, and declarations that "our bodies are not a battleground for the world" (Schwartz 2014) that run throughout this discourse, the right to bodily integrity emerges as the top contender for that shared vision. An intersectional approach to coalitional politics allows us to see how bodily integrity and autonomy unite these two movements.

As feminist scholars Sônia Correa and Rosalind Petchetsky (1994/2013) explain, bodily integrity is one of the four ethical principles of reproductive and sexual rights (as developed through United Nations human rights doctrine), along with personhood, equality, and diversity (i.e., the respect for differences). Defined as the personal autonomy and self-determination of human beings over their own bodies, bodily integrity is an individual and social right that encompasses the right to security in and control over one's body, the right to safety of one's physical person, the right to health, well-being, procreation, and sexual expression, and the right to not be alienated from one's sexual and reproductive capacity (Correa and Petchetsky 1994/2013). These different components of bodily integrity are reflected in many of the narratives in this discourse.

Reflecting back to Miriam Pérez's observations at the beginning of this essay: What, then, does it mean to "queer" reproductive justice? Eschewing identity politics, "queerness" suggests that identity—sexual and all other forms—is irreducible, malleable, and unstable, and it emphasizes affinity and solidarity over identity (Marcus 2005; Walters 1996). Some would argue that intersectionality and queerness are incompatible frameworks, for they claim that intersectionality by definition emphasizes identity. However, that is not necessarily the case. Intersectionality is not just about intersecting *identities*; it is also about the intersecting nature of *oppression* (e.g., racism, sexism, classism, and heterosexism/homophobia) and *privilege*. Political intersectionality is not an identity-based politics; it is a coalitional politics that seeks to eradicate institutionalized oppression and inequality. A critical approach to political intersectionality moves us from individual subjectivity to political collectivity. Duong (2012) contends that it moves us from "I am" (which is identity based) to "I want this for us" (which fosters a sense of affinity and solidarity). Individuals and groups do not have to personally identify with each other in order to work together. It is the common goal that unites them.

In order for intersectional coalition building to work, we must go beyond traditional notions of (single) identity politics—the notion that people form social and political alliances solely on the basis of a shared, single identity, whether it is race, ethnicity, gender, sexual orientation, nationality, or some other social or cultural marker. The reality is that we all belong to multiple social groups, and most people within the reproductive justice and LGBTQ movements experience multiple forms of oppressions (that may be tempered by some privileges). This means that many of us are situated between two or more movements and are often forced to prioritize one over the other(s) (Carastathis 2013; Cohen 1997). This compartmentalizing of political loyalties does not help the project for social, political, and economic transformation and justice in the long run. Taking a cue from the reproductive justice movement, which envisions itself as a coalition of smaller social groups, such as African American women, Latinas, Arab American/Middle Eastern women, and lesbian/bi/queer women, the LGBTQ movement should cease identifying itself as a single-identity movement and instead think of itself as a coalitional movement. It must also critique, challenge, and detach the implicit association of LGBT rights and "queerness" with the white, gay male subjectivity, embrace the full diversity (i.e., race, socioeconomic status, etc.) of its community, and tend to the most vulnerable within its ranks if it truly wants to be liberatory. Acknowledging the coalitional nature of its own movement may make it easier for the LGBTQ movement to form cross-movement alliances.

Intersectional, coalitional politics is not easy; it requires compassion, mutual respect, trust, and patience. Carastathis stresses, "Coalitions are usually contrasted with identity-based groups in the following way: identity-based groups are spaces of similarity, seclusion, and safety, whereas coalitions are spaces of difference, confrontation, and risk. Coalitions are born of necessity, not in order to fulfill needs of recognition, belonging, solidarity, or inclusion" (Carastathis 2013, 944). Acknowledging differences does not necessarily mean divisiveness, but it does require us to move out of our comfort zones in order to understand the perspectives of others who may have had different experiences. Meaningful social transformation cannot be possible without the contribution of these different perspectives.

REFERENCES

Asian Communities for Reproductive Justice (ACRJ). 2005. "A New Vision for Advancing Our Movement for Reproductive Health, Reproductive Rights and Reproductive Justice." http://forwardtogether.org/resources.

Avery, Byllye. 2005. Interview by Loretta Ross. Transcript of video recording, July 21 and 22. Voices of Feminism Oral History Project, Sophia Smith Collection, Smith College, Northampton, MA.

Black Women Birthing Justice. 2015. "What Is Birth Justice?" Accessed on May 26, 2015, at www.blackwomenbirthingjustice.org.

Bruner, Jerome. 2003. *Making Stories: Law, Literature, Life*. Cambridge, MA: Harvard University Press.

Carastathis, Anna. 2013. "Identity Categories as Potential Coalitions." *Signs* 38(4): 941–65.

Cohen, Cathy J. 1997. "Punks, Bulldaggers, and Welfare Queens: The Radical Potential of Queer Politics?" *GLQ: A Journal of Lesbian & Gay Studies* 3: 437–65.

Correa, Sônia, and Rosalind Petchetsky. 1994/2013. "Reproductive and Sexual Rights: A Feminist Perspective." In *Feminist Theory Reader: Local and Global Perspectives*, 3rd ed. Edited by Carole R. McCann and Seung-kyung Kim, pp. 134–47. New York: Routledge.

Duong, Kevin. 2012. "What Does Queer Theory Teach Us about Intersectionality?" *Politics & Gender* 8(3): 370–86.

Forward Together. 2015a. "Name Change FAQ." Accessed on June 9, 2015, at www.forwardtogether.org.

Forward Together. 2015b. "Our Mission." Accessed on June 9, 2015, at www.forwardtogether.org.

Funders for LGBTQ Issues. 2015. "The Power of Two: Funding at the Nexus of LGBT Rights and Repro Rights/Repro Justice, June 25, 2014." Accessed on March 22, 2015, at www.lgbtfunders.org.

Gaard, Greta. 2010. "Reproductive Technology, or Reproductive Justice? An Ecofeminist, Environmental Justice Perspective on the Rhetoric of Choice." *Ethics & the Environment* 2(2): 103–29.

Generations Ahead. 2009. *Bridging the Divide: Disability Rights and Reproductive Rights and Justice Advocates Discussing Genetic Technologies*. http://www.generations-ahead.org.

Gutiérrez, Elena R. 1999. *The Racial Politics of Reproduction: The Social Construction of Mexican-Origin Women's Fertility*. Minneapolis: University of Michigan Press.

Humphrey, Tanisha. 2013. "Queer Rights Are Reproductive Rights because Queer Folks Have Reproductive Systems." Urge, June 14. Accessed on March 22, 2015, at www.urge.org.

Kirchick, James. 2007. "It's Not a Gay Issue." *Washington Blade*, May 24, p. 24.

Langellier, Kristin M., and Eric E. Peterson. 2004. *Storytelling in Daily Life: Performing Narrative*. Philadelphia: Temple University Press.

Law Students for Reproductive Justice (LSRJ). 2014. "Reproductive Justice in the Transgender Community." Fact Sheet. http://www.ifwhenhow.org.

Lee, Megan. 2011. "Queering Reproductive Justice: The Intersection of Reproductive Health and LGBTQ Liberation." LGBT HealthLink blog, Feb. 5. Accessed on March 22, 2015 at blog.lgbthealthlink.org.

Lesbian, Gay, Bisexual, and Transgender Community Center (LGBT Center). 2003. *Causes in Common: Reproductive Justice & LGBT Liberation*. New York: LGBT Community Center.

Lesbian, Gay, Bisexual, and Transgender Community Center (LGBT Center). 2015. "About the Center." Accessed on June 9, 2015, at www.gaycenter.org.

Luna, Zakiya T. 2009. "From Rights to Justice: Women of Color Changing the Face of US Reproductive Rights Organizing." *Societies without Borders: Human Rights and the Social Sciences* 4: 343–65.

Luna, Zakiya T. 2010. "Marching toward Reproductive Justice: Coalitional (Re) Framing of the March for Women's Lives." *Sociological Inquiry* 80(4): 554–78.

Marcus, Sharon. 2005. "Queer Theory for Everyone: A Review Essay." *Signs: Journal of Women in Culture and Society* 31, no. 1: 191–218.

Mason, Carol. 2013. "How Not to Pimp Out Reproductive Justice: Adventures in Education, Activism, and Accountability." *Frontiers: A Journal of Women's Studies* 34(3): 226–41.

National Asian Pacific American Women's Forum. 2007. "Immigration Reform and the Impact on Pregnant and Birthing Asian and Pacific Islander Immigrant Women." Issue Brief, Feb. https://napawf.org.

National Center for Lesbian Rights (NCLR). 2015. "About Us." Accessed on June 9, 2015, at www.nclrights.org.

National Center for Transgender Equality (NCTE). 2015. "About Us." Accessed on June 9, 2015, at www.transequality.org.

National Gay and Lesbian Task Force (NGLTF). 2015. "About." Accessed on June 9, 2015, at www.thetaskforce.org.

National Latina Institute for Reproductive Health (NLIRH). 2011. "LGBTQ Latin@s and Reproductive Justice." Issue Brief, June. http://www.latinainstitute.org.

National Latina Institute for Reproductive Health (NLIRH). 2013. "At the Margins of Care: The Need for Inclusive Health Care for Transgender and Gender-Nonconforming Latin@s." Fact Sheet, Jan. http://www.latinainstitute.org.

National Latina Institute for Reproductive Health (NLIRH). 2015. "Who We Are." Accessed on June 9, 2015, at www.latinainstitute.org.

National Latina Institute for Reproductive Health (NLIRH), National Asian Pacific American Women's Forum and the National Gay and Lesbian Taskforce. 2014. "Queer Immigrants and Affordable Health Care." http://www.latinainstitute.org.

Nelson, Jennifer. 2015. *More Than Medicine: A History of the Feminist Women's Health Movement*. New York: NYU Press.

Nixon, Laura. 2013. "Celebrating *Roe v. Wade* and Keeping Its Promise." National Center for Lesbian Rights website, March 22. Accessed on March 22, 2015, at www.nclrights.org.

Ordover, Nancy. 2003. *American Eugenics: Race, Queer Anatomy, and the Science of Nationalism*. Minneapolis: University of Minnesota Press.

Parker, George. 2014. "Mothers at Large: Responsibilizing the Pregnant Self for the 'Obesity Epidemic.'" *Fat Studies* 3(2): 101–18.

Pérez, Miriam. 2007. "Queering Reproductive Justice." *RH Reality Check* (blog), May 31. Accessed on March 22, 2015, at www.rhrealitycheck.org.

Piepmeier, Alison. 2013. "The Inadequacy of 'Choice': Disability and What's Wrong with Feminist Framings of Reproduction." *Feminist Studies* 39(1): 159–86.

Pizer, Jennifer C. 2014. "What the Supreme Court's Hobby Lobby Decision Means for LGBT People." Lambda Legal website. Accessed on March 22, 2015, at www.lambdalegal.org.

Planned Parenthood Federation of American (PPFA). 2005. "Reproductive Justice for All: A U.S. Policy Conference" (summary report). Reproductive Justice for All Conference Records, Sophia Smith Collection, Smith College, Northampton, MA.

Polletta, Francesca. 1998a. "Contending Stories: Narrative in Social Movements." *Qualitative Sociology* 21(4): 419–46.

Polletta, Francesca. 1998b. " 'It Was Like a Fever . . .': Narrative and Identity in Social Protest." *Social Problems* 45(2): 137–59.

Price, Kimala. 2010. "What Is Reproductive Justice? How Women of Color Activists Are Redefining the Pro-Choice Paradigm." *Meridians: feminism, race, transnationalism* 10(2): 42–65.

Richardson, Chinué Turner. 2006. "Environmental Justice Campaigns Provide Fertile Ground for Joint Efforts with Reproductive Rights Advocates." *Guttmacher Policy Review* 9(1): 14–17.

Roberts, Dorothy. 1997. *Killing the Black Body*. New York: Pantheon.

Roberts, Dorothy, and Sujatha Jesudason. 2013. "Movement Intersectionality: The Case of Race, Gender, Disability, and Genetic Technologies." *Du Bois Review* 10: 313–28.

Schwartz, Arielle P. 2014. "Birth Control Is Not My Boss's Business." National Gay and Lesbian Task Force blog. Accessed on March 22, 2015, at www.thetaskforce.org.

Shorto, Russell. 2006. "Contra-Contraception." *New York Times Magazine*, May 7, pp. 48–55.

Silliman, Jael, Marlene G. Fried, Loretta Ross, and Elena Gutierrez. 2004. *Undivided Rights: Women of Color Organizing for Reproductive Justice*. Boston: South End Press.

SisterSong. 2015. "What Is RJ?" Accessed on May 26, 2015, at www.sistersong.net.

Smith, Andrea. 2005. "Beyond Pro-Choice versus Pro-Life: Women of Color and Reproductive Justice." *NWSA Journal* 17(1): 119–40.

Stone, Deborah A. 1989. "Causal Stories and the Formation of Policy Agendas." *Political Science Quarterly* 104(2): 281–300.

Vaid, Urvashi. 2012. "Still Ain't Satisfied: The Limits of Equality." *American Prospect*, May, pp. 38–42.

Vázquez, Carmen. 2005. Interview by Kelly Anderson. Transcript of video recording, May 12 and 13 & Aug. 25. Voices of Feminism Oral History Project, Sophia Smith Collection, Smith College, Northampton, MA.

Voices of Feminism Oral History Project, Sophia Smith Collection, Smith College, Northampton, MA. Webpage. Accessed on May 25, 2015, at www.smith.edu.

Walters, Susan Danuta. 1996. "From Here to Queer: Radical Feminism, Postmodernism, and the Lesbian Menace (or, Why Can't a Woman Be More like a Fag?)" *Signs* 21(4): 830–59.

Wellek, Alisa, and Miriam Yeung. 2015. "Reproductive Justice and Lesbian, Gay, Bisexual & Transgender Liberation." Accessed on March 22, 2015, at www.protectchoice.org.

Yeung, Miriam W. 2011/2012. "Reproductive and Genetic Justice." *Scholar & Feminist Online* 10(1/2). Accessed on March 22, 2015, at www.sfonline.barnard.edu.

6

The "B" Isn't Silent

Bisexual Communities and Political Activism

CHARLES ANTHONY SMITH, SHAWN SCHULENBERG, AND
ERIC A. BALDWIN

In 2015, President Barack Obama became the first president to mention bisexuals in his state of the union speech. While President Bill Clinton mentioned "gays" in his 2000 speech, no president had ever before acknowledged the existence of bisexuals, lesbians,[1] or transgender people in this important forum. Just like presidents, political scientists have largely ignored the "B" in LGBT. We make an initial foray towards extending the literature in this area.

The "B" in LGBT is frequently neglected in the investigation of sexual minorities in American political processes (Smith 2011). In the bimodal model of sexuality assumed by much of the political science literature, bisexuals are categorized and incorporated within the larger LGBT community simply as "not straight." The goals, challenges, and rights claims of the bisexual community are assumed to be identical to, and therefore subsumed within, the same struggles shared by all sexual minorities.

The literature reflects the reality of political discourse for bisexuals in the United States. They are mostly invisible within both LGBT communities and our larger political system as a whole—a notable exception being the recent national attention given to openly bisexual Oregon governor Kate Brown. Lesbians and gay men have historically served as the primary faces of the LGBT movement, although lately many transgender activists have also emerged as recognizable figures with their own policy priorities, including fighting transphobia within LGBT communities. Bisexual "issues," while overlapping in some areas with those of other sexual minorities, are distinct as bisexuals face unique forms of discrimination (biphobia and monosexism to name two, for example) from both LGTs and heterosexuals. In the end, the agendas of the major national LGBT activist groups have mostly not incorporated the independent claims of the bisexual community. Moreover, the broader public does not distinguish bisexuals as a marginalized group with specific concerns. Given this lack of visibility and power within the LGBT community and more generally in the public at large, some bisexuals have instead found themselves better incorporated into other sexual minority communities. Here we discuss bisexuals in the polyamory and BDSM political communities, which provide them with a venue for political action and interaction as well as a simpatico community in which to locate.

We proceed as follows. First, we review the relevant literature and discuss the political activism of sexual minorities in the United States. From there, we provide background about the BDSM and polyamory communities. We follow with a description of the research methodology and the empirical findings. We finish with a synthesis of our findings, our explanation of the prevalence of bisexuals in these communities, our postulations based on the evidence, and several points for further inquiry.

Extant Literature

How and where bisexuals engage in politics are important questions to consider in order to understand their political attitudes and political behaviors. Political scientists have long established group identification in American politics as a source of unified civic engagement and sociopolitical participation (Barreto and Pedraza 2009; Uslaner and Brown 2005; Bobo and Gilliam 1990; Sanchez 2006). There is substantial research in the canon of political and social inquiry that explains how group identification is relevant in the formation of political values and the degree of collective influence on political systems and public opinion (Bishin et al. 2015; Bishin and Smith 2013; Smith 2007). Much of the existing literature on group identification addresses ethnicity and social identities, finding that individuals usually derive their concept of self from their sense of belonging within social groups. Membership in a group carries emotional significance and causes attitudinal and perceptual values (Greene 1999, 393). The group and its collective values and biases become affective attachments and individual members are likely to behave in ways consistent with their group identification.

Humans construct dichotomous oppositional binaries that posit "us" against "them," a tendency that frequently plays out in partisan American politics. Preference for one platform often pairs with negative attitudes towards the opposition (Greene 1999, 394–95). An individual's social identity is intrinsically linked to his or her behavioral patterns, and for political scientists this proves to be a largely accurate way to predict voting patterns, political activism, and political affiliations.

An understanding of how group membership influences individual preferences and biases can also lay the foundation for an explanation of how and why certain groups advance particular agendas. Regardless of the degree of assimilation, the political behavior of ethnic groups tends to fall uniformly along group lines (Parenti 1967, 717; Dahl 1961, 59; Wolflinger 1965). Michael Parenti suggests that the political system—which includes party, precinct, candidates, elections, and so forth—continues to rely on group strategies that reinforce ethnic, religious, and social group differences (Parenti 1967, 717). Both Parenti (1967) and

Raymond Wolflinger (1965) establish that political affiliation is strongly related to an ethnic, religious, or social group's long-term historical values, short-term residual political loyalties, and an individual's psychological attachment to a group. The psychological attachment—what we might think of as the developed feeling of belonging or "groupness"—is a critical link between the group identity and the individual identity.

Contemporary research demonstrates that the arguments of Parenti and Wolflinger remain both accurate and relevant. Matt Barreto and Francisco Pedraza (2009) revisit Wolflinger's claims through the lens of Latino group identification. Second- and third-generation Latinos in the United States have assimilated in the techno-legal domain but have held onto ethnic ties and a strong sense of in-group solidarity (Barreto and Pedraza 2009). Previous research, including perhaps most notably the American National Election Survey (ANES), have underestimated the degree of group identification and overestimated the impact of different individual life conditions on voting behavior (Barreto and Pedraza 2009). Contrary to intuitive hunches and some existing research, Barreto and Pedraza show that ethnic identity has grown stronger (not weaker) as Latinos move away from an "immigrant" identity, and they have become more distinctly partisan, supporting the Democratic Party (Barreto and Pedraza 2009, 604). Gabriel Sanchez (2006) examines how demographic reality translates into political influence. While he agrees that Latinos are not as politically influential across all issue areas as their numbers might suggest, they are very cohesive in their political attitudes and behavior when they perceive that a policy is motivated by discrimination. Questions about minority group representation are at the core of democracy, where majority rule can come into conflict with other values like liberty and equality. Sometimes elected representatives support minority rights over the majority preference (Bishin and Smith 2013), and sometimes the public supports minority rights despite the preferences of elected officials (Bishin et al. 2015). We situate this work at the confluence of general identity politics and the more specific work on LGBT politics. Understanding the political attitudes and behavior of the bisexual community depends upon properly situating that community in this context.

George W. Bush's reelection to a second term in the White House is for many the most defining event of the 2004 general election in the United States, but this election carries a different significance to those concerned about the LGBT community or rights contestation generally (Smith 2007). On that same day in 2004, eleven states approved state constitutional amendments explicitly banning same-sex marriage, all by ample margins indicating widespread resistance to same-sex families (Smith 2007). Charles Smith demonstrates widespread homophobia, which results in the "electoral capture" of gay and lesbian Americans (Smith 2007). Electoral capture may happen in a two-party system when a specific demographic group very closely aligns with one political party but not the other (Smith 2007; Frymer 1999). In essence, one party has no interest in gaining votes from the demographic groups captured by the other, so the party that has captured the group does not have to expend political capital to deliver policy because the group will never vote for the party that ignores or attacks the group. Recent events, led by the Supreme Court, have brought the Democratic Party and the public in general to a very gay-friendly position (Bishin et al. 2015). Issues of concern to the trans community have come to the forefront thanks to celebrities such as Caitlyn Jenner and Laverne Cox and academic efforts such as the new political science journal *TSQ: Transgender Studies Quarterly.* Still, bisexuals have been largely left out of the public discourse.

LGBT Americans, and especially bisexual Americans, represent a distinct type of group because their members come from every category of demographic, including, age, income, religiosity, gender, ethnicity, socioeconomic status, and so on. The only universally shared trait or experience is the animus from some sectors of society and a lesser roster of rights than those enjoyed by heterosexuals. One significant difference for bisexual Americans is that at some points they may appear to many as indistinguishable from heterosexual Americans because they may form durable, even legally recognized, sexual relationships with members of the opposite sex. It is this ability to glide from the targeted group or lesser rights group, LGBT, to the dominant and full rights group, heterosexual, that perhaps accounts for the invisibility of the "B" in LGBT political science.

Cases: Bisexuality in BDSM and Polyamory Communities

While conducting research on a separate and larger project about the political attitudes and political activities of nontraditional sexual minorities, which include the BDSM and polyamory communities, we discovered that substantial numbers of our subjects identified as bisexual. Before we discuss our findings, we explain our definitional parameters of these two communities.

Like the LGBT community, the BDSM community is comprised of people of all sexual and gender identities from all demographic categories, including but not limited to age, race, sex, religiosity, income, education, and region. BDSM is an acronym for Bondage and Discipline, Dominance and Submission, and Sadism and Masochism. The experience and engagement of people who identify as part of the BDSM community vary. Some may engage in mundane casual experimentation like light spanking, role playing, or mild bondage like blindfolding or tying one partner to the bedposts. Others are engaged in more hardcore BDSM play, and their activities might be shocking to those more who are, in the parlance, "vanilla" (or engage in routine or nonexotic sexual activities). These activities might include extreme role-playing scenarios, intense bondage, scarification, and a host of activities only bounded by the imagination and the dictates of safety and consent. Many engaged in the BDSM life attend professional, organized BDSM conventions and have local communities that host activities that include learning about and engaging in many types of BDSM play. BDSM involves various subgroups of sexual activity that frequently overlap and sometimes are practiced together. Bondage and Discipline refer to the desire to bind, restrict, or control others or to be bound, restricted, or controlled by one's sexual partner(s). Dominance and Submission refer to role play where the submissive partner gives all (play) power to the other dominant player. Sadism and Masochism refer to the desire to inflict or receive pain from a sexual partner. These activities are not mutually exclusive but rather represent a range of activities that might, indeed often do, overlap.

Under the umbrella of BDSM we include two other closely related, often overlapping subsets of identities of sexual practice: the "leather" and "puppy play" communities. These communities utilize the foundational premise of BDSM but carry out specific types of scenarios and manifest BDSM in particularized fashion fetishes. "Leather" constitutes the use of leather clothing and the fetishization of leather equipment used during dominant and submissive sexual role playing. The use of black leather carries connotations of masculinity and sexual power differentials, and may impose a degree of discomfort—caused by the tightly bound leather clothing/accessories—that invokes themes of sadism and masochism. The leather fetish community as currently constructed originated in the United States out of the post–World War II military culture of the mid-twentieth century.

A second group that we include in our BDSM analysis is "puppy play." Puppy play is the execution of submissive and dominant sexual role playing specifically through the roles of puppy (submissive) and handler (dominant). Puppy play often includes the use of leather clothing and plastic props, including masks and anal plugs that resemble tails, to make the participants more closely present themselves as canines. They engage in dog/human and dog/dog interaction scenarios using the mannerisms and behaviors typically seen between humans and dogs and among dogs. Handlers are not always involved: sometimes puppy play involves just the puppies playing with one another, meanwhile establishing dominant/submissive relationships among the pack. For our purposes, we have collapsed these two subgroups into the larger BDSM category. We use the acronym "BDSM" to refer to the traditional bondage-discipline-dominance-submission-sadism-masochism community in addition to the leather and puppy play community. We feel confident with this choice because the latter two subgroups are simply distinct subcultures within BDSM.

Polyamory is the practice of engaging in intimate and sexual relationships with multiple partners. In other words, polyamory is any form of consensual nonmonogamy. These relationships may take a multitude of forms and involve a variety of numbers of adults. They vary in degree of commitment and range of nonmonogamy, with some being long-term, committed relationships and others being occasional nonmonogamous sexual partnerships. Like bisexuals, these sexual identity groups are largely absent from political science scholarship as well as the consideration of the rest of society. These are invisible communities for most people and certainly most politicians other than those who are members of the communities. They are frequently marginalized, and when they are not invisible they are labeled as sexual deviants by policymakers and the public at large. Despite the lack of attention given to these groups, our other research shows that the polyamory and BDSM communities are both larger and more politically engaged than previously assumed. Their members represent a diverse and sizable group with clear political attitudes and a more active political life than the general public. This research also revealed that the identity of bisexuality intersects with these two subsets—polyamory and BDSM—in a significant way. For our purposes here, we focus specifically on the bisexuals in these communities. We find they represent a significant portion of these politically engaged and active communities. Note that in our analysis of those who identify as bisexual and as members of either the BDSM or polyamory communities, we collapse all of the terms that are surrogates at some level for "bisexual" that were used by our subjects to self-identify. These terms include include "bisexual," "pansexual," "switch," "bicurious," and "heteroflexible."

Methods

We used a mixed-methods approach to examine the political attitudes and political activity of the polyamory and BDSM communities. Recall that we discovered the prevalence of bisexuals in these communities as we gathered our data. Our work here includes surveys, interviews, participant observation, and modified ethnographic studies. To measure the political attitudes and activities of our subjects, members of the polyamory and the BDSM communities, we administered two sets of surveys. The first set consisted of twenty-nine multiple-choice questions asking about our respondents' demographic characteristics and political attitudes/behaviors, mostly drawn from the Pew Research Center for the People and the Press (various years) (see Appendix A). Because the Pew multiple-choice questions may constrain answer options and do not allow for elaboration, we also asked a second set of eleven open-ended questions (see Appendix B). The open-ended questions allowed for as expansive a response as the subject desired. Some gave brief answers of perhaps a few sentences; others gave much longer responses encompassing several paragraphs. We took the responses to both the surveys and the questionnaires anonymously.

We obtained our first round of data through a convenience sample that we then leveraged through a virtual-snowball technique. We began by contacting elites and group organizers representing each of our communities to see if we could attend their events to promote our survey and talk with attendees. We began polyamory data collection through a large polyamory support group in Albuquerque, New

Mexico. We began BDSM data collection (including leather and puppy play) at the "Beyond Vanilla" annual BDSM convention in Dallas. Our first forty-eight responses for polyamory and our first seventy-five responses for BDSM were obtained in person. We then utilized a virtual-snowball technique to continue data collection. By "virtual-snowball technique," a term we have coined, we mean that we asked our subjects to share the survey and questionnaire with others in their communities via Facebook, social networking, blogs, and email. That is, we asked those who participated in person to share the links to the questionnaires with anyone else they knew who identified as a member of the polyamory or BDSM community, respectively. Ultimately, we were led to several closed Facebook groups for polyamory and BDSM communities, where our surveys were shared. In each case, we asked the group administrators for permission to post our survey in their group before we moved forward. Within three weeks for the polyamory community, we obtained 527 respondents for the multiple-choice survey and 178 respondents for the open-ended questionnaires. For the BDSM groups we obtained 162 respondents for the multiple-choice survey and 68 respondents for the open-ended questions. We anticipate that since we are using a novel, virtual-snowball sampling strategy, our sample may be younger, perhaps more educated, and certainly more technologically sophisticated than the population as a whole.[2] Moreover, because we were able to reach some otherwise very difficult-to-study sectors of the polyamory and BDSM communities this way, some sectors of those groups may be represented more than others. Most importantly for our purposes here, we discovered that in our samples, a substantial portion of these communities identifies as bisexual. We do not assert that all bisexuals fall into these communities; indeed, we do not make any claims that these bisexuals are representative of all bisexuals. Rather, we are making the claim that a meaningful proportion of the polyamory and BDSM communities also identify as bisexual.

Findings

For a number of the demographic characteristics, our sample is not representative of the U.S. population. However, given that polyamory and BDSM are understudied communities, we have no way of unambiguously identifying what the distribution of polyamorists or BDSM adherents is among the U.S. population generally. We might expect the polyamory community to be younger than the population as a whole because evolving social norms are less inhibitory than in the past. We might also expect these sexual communities to be younger than the population as a whole because of the role of social media in organizing the community. What this unfortunately means is that we have no way of knowing how closely our sample aligns with the actual demographics of the entire polyamorous-identified and BDSM-identified population in the United States. Without further data allowing us to weight our results on the basis of population demographics, we will make the uneasy assumption that our data are essentially representative of those most active in polyamory and BDSM circles. Given all of this, we can say a few things about each sample.

For polyamory:

1. *Sex.* More of our respondents identified as women than the general U.S. population: 60 percent are women, 34 percent identify as men, and 6 percent identify as other. (figure 6.1)

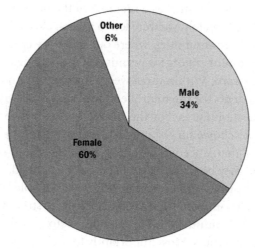

Figure 6.1. Polyamory, sex.

2. *Age.* Our sample skews young, with 46 percent between the ages of eighteen and twenty-nine. (figure 6.2)

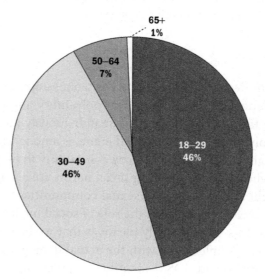

Figure 6.2. Polyamory, age.

3. *Race.* Whites make up 83 percent of our sample—much larger than the U.S. population generally—perhaps indicating that polyamory is more of a white identity. (figure 6.3)

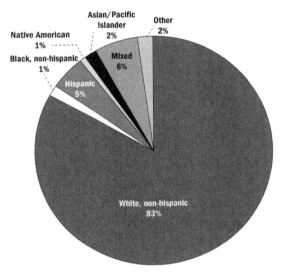

Figure 6.3. Polyamory, race.

4. *Education.* Our sample is very educated, with 58 percent of our respondents saying that they have a college and/or postgraduate degree. (figure 6.4)

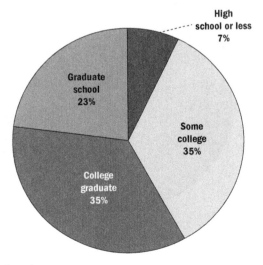

Figure 6.4 Polaymory, education.

For BDSM:

1. *Sex.* There are more men involved in BDSM compared to polyamory: 63 percent are men while 37 percent identify as women. (figure 6.5)

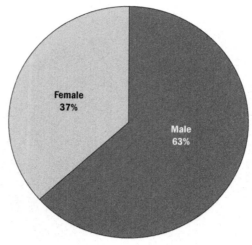

FIGURE 6.5. BDSM, SEX.

2. *Age.* Our sample skews towards the middle-aged demographic, with 49.4 percent between the ages of thirty and forty-nine. (figure 6.6)

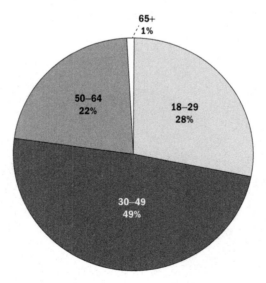

Figure 6.6. BDSM, age.

3. *Race.* Whites make up 82 percent of our sample and represent the vast majority of BDSM participants. (figure 6.7)

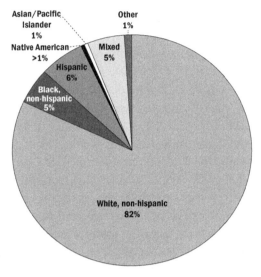

Figure 6.7. BDSM, race.

4. *Education.* Our BDSM sample is very educated, with 44 percent of our respondents saying that they have a college and/or postgraduate degree. (figure 6.8)

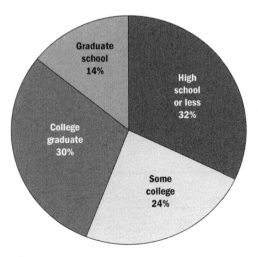

Figure 6.8. BDSM, education.

In addition to this demographic data, we also asked our respondents to list their other sexual identities (beyond polyamory/BDSM) in question one of the open-ended survey. We ask, "Do you identify as part of the polyamory (or BDSM, leather, puppy play) community? How do you identify sexually? Do you carry one identity or multiple? If you carry multiple, are some more dominant than others?" Interestingly, the number of people who identify as bisexual in one form or another was much larger than we expected (see table 6.1). Remember, as stated earlier, we include a handful of identity labels here to demarcate bisexuality: "bisexual," "bicurious," "heteroflexible," and those who "switch" between preferences. While each of these labels is not identical and may vary in nuance of identity, they all signal resistance to the idea that one must choose a singular sex of preference.

Moreover, we also see that the polyamory and BDSM communities have distinct political views and political affiliations apart from the general population. These views are easily imputable to the bisexuals in the sample. In other words, given the prevalence of bisexuals in these two communities—well over half in each—we can draw conclusions from the entire sample without too much concern that the bisexuals within these groups are radically different than the group as aggregated. Here we see the aggregate response percentages for a series of questions that indicate their political tendencies and activities. Although we cannot be sure that our sample is representative of the entire polyamorous or BDSM communities, or generalizable to all bisexuals who are members of these communities, our data still reveal several generalizable points of interest.

First, the BDSM community closely mirrors the U.S. population in terms of party identification while those in the polyamory community are far more likely to identify as a Democrat or Independent than the typical voter (see table 6.2).

TABLE 6.1. Aggregate Bisexual Identification

Polyamory	53% (98 out of 184)
BDSM	62% (100 out of 161)
Aggregate Bisexuals	57.4% Total sample: 198 bisexuals out of 345

TABLE 6.2. [Question #12]
PARTY ID: In politics today, do you consider yourself:

	Polyamory	BDSM	U.S. Population*
Republican	4%	24%	24%
Independent	48%	35%	37%
Democrat	38%	30%	31%
No Answer	11%	11%	9%

*Source: Pew Research Center for the People & the Press Poll, August 2014.

A remarkably small percentage of our polyamory respondents—just 4 percent—identify as Republican compared to both 24 percent of the BDSM community and the general population—a 20 percent gap.

However, when we look at ideology instead of party identification, only 1 percent of our polyamory respondents identified as "Very Conservative" compared to 6 percent of the general U.S. population; moreover, 38 percent identify as "Very Liberal" compared to 6 percent of the general population (see table 6.3). This seems to indicate that although many in the polyamorous community prefer to identify as politically Independent (instead of as Democrat), they consider their political philosophy to be very liberal and consistently hold policy positions very far to the left. The BDSM community appears more liberal when we ask about ideology instead of party identification: only 15 percent of respondents have conservative tendencies ("Conservative" or "Very Conservative") compared to 32 percent in the general U.S. population. We see that this ideology holds consistent when asking about the Supreme Court in both groups: both polyamory and BDSM respondents generally agree that the Supreme Court is too conservative across the board (see table 6.4). This may mean that the Democratic Party might be able to pick up more support, money, and votes from both the BDSM

TABLE 6.3. [Question #14]
IDEOLOGY: In general, would you describe your political views as:

	Polyamory	BDSM	U.S. Population*
Very Conservative	1%	2%	6%
Conservative	2%	13%	26%
Moderate	11%	24%	35%
Liberal	20%	19%	16%
Very Liberal	38%	8%	6%
No Answer	29%	33%	11%

*Source: Pew Research Center for the People & the Press Poll, July 2014.

TABLE 6.4. [Question #16]
SCOTUS: Thinking about the Supreme Court . . . in your view, do you think the current Supreme Court is:

	Polyamory	BDSM	U.S. Population*
Conservative	47%	29%	27%
Middle of the Road	20%	27%	38%
Liberal	3%	12%	26%
No Answer	30%	33%	8%

*Source: Pew Research Center for the People & the Press Poll, August 2014.

and polyamory communities if they were to (1) speak more directly to political issues that affect these people and (2) move further to the left on a range of social policy positions.

This may mean that many in the polyamorous community choose to consider themselves as politically Independent, but not politically moderate, mainly because they fall to the left of the Democratic Party. We can see this clearly from one of our questions. When we asked Democrats and Democratic-leaning respondents in the polyamory community which direction they would like Democratic leaders in Washington to move, 63 percent responded "more liberal direction" compared to 37 percent in the general population. Conversely, 26 percent of our polyamorous sample answered "more moderate direction" compared to 53 percent of all of the U.S. population.

While the data show that both groups are left leaning, our findings indicates a crucial distinction between the two groups; polyamory is left leaning, but its members are more evasive of specific party classification while avoiding specific party affiliation. BDSM participants are less likely to identify ambiguously as "Independent" and instead choose a specific party affiliation. This reveals a broader motif of these sexual communities: just as polyamorous individuals are evasive of classificatory systems in their gender, sexual identity, and sexual practices, they are equally as eager to avoid specific classifications in the political realm; on the other hand, BDSM (including leather and puppy play) participants are more apt to identify both with fixed social roles within their sexual and organizational hierarchies and with fixed political identities

Our evidence also indicates that individuals in the polyamory and BDSM communities closely follow politics, they discuss political issues frequently, and they want the polyamory community to become more politically active. Of our polyamorous respondents, 70 percent indicate that they frequently (daily or weekly) discuss political issues with others in the community. As a follow-up, many said that they feel comfortable discussing politics because they (correctly) identify that others in the community share their values. Moreover, they tend to vote as frequently in primary elections as the general U.S. population, as shown in table 6.5. Finally, nearly 57 percent of our respondents believe that the polyamorous community should become more politically active in the future.

When asked about their sexual identity, the largest contingency within polyamory are bisexuals, representing 53 percent of all identifications (see table 6.1). This is the single largest sexual identity (bisexual/bicurious/heteroflexible/switch) within the group other than the overarching identification of "polyamorous." Following bisexual, 26 percent of the sample identified as straight/heterosexual, 11 percent identified as queer, and a sprinkle of the respondents carried other identities such as asexual (2 percent). Bisexuality in the BDSM community

TABLE 6.5. [Question #11]
PRIMARY VOTING: How often would you say you vote in primary elections—that is, the elections in which a party selects its nominee to run in a general election. Would you say you vote in primary elections:

	Polyamory	BDSM	U.S. Population*
Always	25%	37%	35%
Nearly Always	24%	17%	22%
Part of the Time	16%	11%	17%
Seldom	26%	25%	24%
No Answer	8%	10%	2%

*Source: Pew Research Center for the People & the Press Poll, August 2014.

is even more prevalent: 62 percent of the BDSM respondents identify as bisexual. Although some respondents have rigid sexual identities, our data show that sexuality in these communities is much more fluid than the traditional labels of gay vs. straight. For comparison, the Williams Institute reports that only 1.8 percent of adults who identify as LGB (3.8 percent of the population) identify as bisexual (Gates 2011).

This preliminary glance at the data suggests that affiliation with the polyamory community or the BDSM community acts as a primary identity for many of the members, and many of those members also identify as bisexual. One of the more interesting aspects of the data is that the "B" in LGBT research may no longer be silent. We have revealed two communities that rely heavily on self-identified bisexuals for membership.

Implications

With these general findings established, our data points to an important discovery: many bisexuals, who may have had their collective voice omitted from the choir of rights demands in gay and lesbian political movements, have found themselves politically nested in polyamory and BDSM communities. They are politically aware, they participate, and they have clear ideas about what direction the political system should take. As the largest single bloc within these communities, they represent a potential but as yet unrealized influence on the political system. Although minority groups are often faced with an inability to easily affect policy (Smith 2007), on occasion politicians will defy their constituents to expand rights for minorities (Bishin and Smith 2013). Moreover, once sexual minorities obtain rights, whether through litigation, legislation, or executive action, the public will embrace that progress (Bishin et al. 2015). Of course, upon reflection, it should perhaps come as no surprise that bisexuals find themselves welcome in these particular communities. With both polyamory and BDSM, making a choice of sexual partner on the basis of gender alone is not required, and variations on hetero-normative or homo-normative expectations are not shamed or shunned by these communities.

Practically, why are the B's invisible in electoral politics? Why don't candidates and campaigns attempt to garner votes and curry favor with sexual minorities, especially bisexuals? One possible explanation recalls Smith's argument (2007) of electoral capture of gay and lesbian Americans by the Democratic Party. Democrats did not, until very recently, feel compelled to deliver policy for members of the LGBT community because the Republican Party, both historically and currently, aggressively demonizes members of the LGBT community. Until very recently, Democrats could simply deliver cheap talk and secure over 85 percent of the LGBT vote. That is, Democrats did not have to deliver for the gay and lesbian community because the alternative party subjected them to constant derision and denigration. A similar concept might be applicable here: given the sensitive nature of politics surrounding sexual minorities and sexual practices in this country, politicians may be hesitant to court bisexual voters— assuming the political class is even aware that bisexual voters exist—in order to avoid alienating long-established and prominent voting blocs. Moreover, as long as no party competition exists for the bisexual bloc, then at best what the community can hope for is cheap talk short of actual enlightenment similar to the recent Democratic push for marriage equality. Unless and until there is some party competition for the votes of bisexuals, there may be no effort to engage them. However, this premise assumes the passivity and lack of coherent political organizing of bisexual communities. Perhaps contemporary politics, including for instance the fallout associated with Indiana's recent controversial Religious Freedom Restoration Act and President Obama's statements at the 2015 State of the Union address, indicates a move from passive electoral capture to a more open acknowledgment and pursuit of the voting blocs represented by sexual minorities.

A shift towards active and aggressive political organizing could demonstrate to the American binary political system that these communities, regardless of what the parties choose to campaign on or whom they choose to court, can influence elections in meaningful ways. Mobilization of the bisexual communities embedded in other sexual minority communities might lead the major political parties to reconceptualize their platforms and address the concerns of the more diverse set of sexual minorities beyond lesbian and gay. The political binary need not be trapped in the artificial sexual binary. Just because we are limited to Democrats and Republicans, we need not be limited to gay and straight.

In the case of bisexuals, their current approach lacks real political influence because while many collectively identify in the polyamory and BDSM community, they lack formal organizational structure and they lack a broader participation in an interest group sector. To acquire access to a broader interest group sector, they first need to engage the political system and make their existence known through the BDSM and polyamory communities or any other sexual minority community in which they are nested. If a cohesive and formalized organizational structure, a grand sexual minority coalition perhaps, is constructed, bisexuals could influence discourse about policy, create a specific rights roster, and attract media and public attention. This might lead to changes in the political reality in favor of sexual minorities and specifically in favor of bisexuals. In areas such as family law, employment nondiscrimination, and healthcare policy, there certainly could be bisexual-specific policies that might not be implemented through advocacy oversight or low salience among the activist groups that align the boundaries of debate.

Our research suggests several avenues of additional inquiry. We have established that communities of sexual minorities exist that include very large numbers of bisexuals. These bisexual communities act as cohesive and politically astute political groups, albeit nested within the other sexual minority groups of BDSM and polyamory. Further research should assess the viability of expanded political activity by bisexuals identified as an insular sexual minority and the potential such an increase in activity might hold for an impact on the political system. Additional research should be conducted to determine what tactics these groups might use in order to achieve movement goals and a prioritization of the policy preferences.

Bisexuals have been overlooked in the primary venues of the LGBT movement and have successfully found a home at least in the BDSM and polyamory communities. Additional research should also be conducted to determine whether there are additional sexual minority communities that house large numbers of bisexuals. Nested within these communities, bisexuals may represent a potential force equal to or greater than the gay and lesbian movement.

Appendix A: Survey Questions

Demographic Questions
1. Sex: Male, Female, Other
2. Age: 18–29; 30–49; 50–64; 65+
3. Race: White, Non-Hispanic; Black, Non-Hispanic; Hispanic; Native American; Asian/Pacific Islander, Mixed, Other
4. Education: High School or Less, Some College, College Graduate, Graduate School
5. Income: More Than $75,000, $30,000—$74,900, $20,000—$29,000, Less Than $20,000, Prefer Not to Answer
6. Religion: Evangelical Christian, Protestant, Catholic, Islamic, Jewish, Other, None
7. Attendance of Religious Services: Weekly or More, Monthly, Yearly, Seldom or Never

8. Marital Status: Single, Never Married; Single, Divorced or Widowed; Married; Married More Than One Time

9. Employment Status: Employed Full-Time, Employed Part-Time, Not Employed, Not Employed But Searching For Work

Political Attitudes and Participation

1. Which of these statements best describes you? Are you absolutely certain that you are registered to vote at your current address; are you probably registered, but there is a chance your registration has lapsed; or are you not registered to vote at your current address?

2. And how often would you say you vote in primary elections—that is, the elections in which a party selects its nominee to run in a general election. Would you say you vote in primary elections always, nearly always, part of the time, or seldom?

3. In politics today, do you consider yourself a Republican, Democrat, or Independent?

4. (In politics today, do you consider yourself a Republican, Democrat, or Independent?) (If Independent/No preference/Other party/Don't know/Refused, ask:) As of today do you lean more to the Republican Party or more to the Democratic Party?

5. In general, would you describe your political views as very conservative, conservative, moderate, liberal, or very liberal?

6. Would you say news organizations . . . are liberal, or conservative?

7. Thinking about the Supreme Court . . . In your view, do you think the current Supreme Court is conservative, middle of the road, or liberal?

8. Would you like to see Republican leaders in Washington move in a more conservative direction or a more moderate direction?

9. Would you like to see Democratic leaders in Washington move in a more liberal direction or a more moderate direction?

10. Thinking about the Republican Party's position on some issues, do you think the Republican Party is too conservative, not conservative enough, or about right when it comes to . . . government spending?

11. Thinking about the Republican Party's position on some issues, do you think the Republican Party is too conservative, not conservative enough, or about right when it comes to . . . abortion?

12. Thinking about the Republican Party's position on some issues, do you think the Republican Party is too conservative, not conservative enough, or about right when it comes to . . . gay marriage?

13. Thinking about the Republican Party's position on some issues, do you think the Republican Party is too conservative, not conservative enough, or about right when it comes to . . . immigration?

14. Thinking about the Democratic Party's position on some issues, do you think the Democratic Party is too liberal, not liberal enough, or about right when it comes to . . . government spending?

15. Thinking about the Democratic Party's position on some issues, do you think the Democratic Party is too liberal, not liberal enough, or about right when it comes to . . . abortion?

16. Thinking about the Democratic Party's position on some issues, do you think the Democratic Party is too liberal, not liberal enough, or about right when it comes to . . . gay marriage?

17. Thinking about the Democratic Party's position on some issues, do you think the Democratic Party is too liberal, not liberal enough, or about right when it comes to . . . immigration?

18. How often do you discuss political issues with your friends and family? Daily, weekly, seldom, hardly ever?

19. Have you contributed more than $25 to a political campaign or cause in the last two years?

20. What state do you live in? (Open Response)

Appendix B: Interview Questions

Open-Ended Questions

1. Do you identify as part of the [insert community here]? How do you identify sexually? Do you carry one identity or multiple? If you carry multiple, are some more dominant than others?

2. How did you learn about and become involved in [insert community here]? Friends? Online?

3. Do you feel a sense of community with others involved in [insert community here]? If so, how important is the "community" aspect of [insert community here] to you?

4. Does being a member of the [insert community here] have any impact on your attitudes about politics or political issues? Do you see any connecting underlying themes among the following issues: government spending, abortion, gay marriage, immigration? If so, how? If yes, what are they?

5. Do you discuss political issues with people in [insert community here]? If yes, is it because you believe they share the same values? If no, are you afraid it will cause conflict? If sometimes, are you selective? What type of information do you share and with whom? How often do you discuss political issues with the other people in [insert community here]?

6. Are there any political issues that unite the [insert community here]? If so, what are they?

7. As a follow-up, in what forms of political activism (petitions, lobbying, fundraising) does the [insert community here] engage?

8. Do you think the [insert community here] should be more politically active, less active, or is it just right?

9. Do you think people who are not part of the [insert community here] know about or understand the [insert community here]?

10. What, if anything, do you think politicians think about the [insert community here]?

11. Is there anything else you think we should know or you would like to share?

NOTES

1 Although some argue that Clinton's 2000 speech implicitly included lesbians with his use of the word "gays," the inclusion was not explicit.

2 As a caveat, we do not assert that this is a representative sample of all members of the respective communities.

REFERENCES

Barreto, Matt A., and Francisco I. Pedraza. 2009. "The Renewal and Persistence of Group Identification in American Politics." *Electoral Studies* 28(4): 595–605.

Bishin, Benjamin G., Thomas J. Hayes, Matthew B. Incantalupo, and Charles A. Smith. 2015. "Opinion Backlash and Public Attitudes: Are Political Advances in Gay Rights Counterproductive?" *American Journal of Political Science* 60(3): 625–48. Doi:10.1111/ajps.12181.

Bishin, Benjamin G., and Charles A. Smith. 2013. "When Do Legislators Defy Popular Sovereignty? Testing Theories of Minority Representation Using DOMA." *Political Research Quarterly* 66(4): 794–803.

Bobo, Lawrence, and Franklin D. Gilliam. 1990. "Race, Sociopolitical Participation, and Black Empowerment." *American Political Science Review* 84(2): 377–93.

Conover, Pamela Johnston. 1984. "The Influence of Group Identifications on Political Perception and Evaluation." *Journal of Politics* 46(3): 760–85.

Dahl, Robert A. 1961. *Who Governs? Democracy and Power in an American City.* New Haven, CT: Yale University Press.

Frymer, Paul. 1999. *Uneasy Alliances: Race and Party Competition in America.* Princeton, NJ: Princeton University Press.

Gamson, William A., and David S. Meyer. 1996. "Framing Political Opportunity." In *Comparative Perspectives on Social Movements: Political Opportunities, Mobilizing Structures, and Cultural Framings*, eds. Doug McAdam, John D. McCarthy, and Mayer N. Zald. New York: Cambridge University Press, pp. 275–90.

Gates, Gary J. 2011. "How Many People Are Lesbian, Gay, Bisexual, and Transgender?" Williams Institute, University of California, Los Angeles.

Greene, Steven. 1999. "Understanding Party Identification: A Social Identity Approach." *Political Psychology* 20(2): 393–403.

Greene, Steven. 2004. "Social Identity Theory and Party Identification." *Social Science Quarterly* 85(1): 136–53.

Herek, Gregory. 2004. "Beyond 'Homophobia': Thinking about Sexual Prejudice and Stigma in the Twenty-first Century." *Sexuality Research & Social Policy* 1(2): 6–24.

Jeffreys, Sheila. 1999. "Bisexual Politics: A Superior Form of Feminism?" *Women's Studies International Forum* 22(3): 273–85.

Koch, Jeffrey W. 1994. "Group Identification in Political Context." *Political Psychology* 15(4): 687–98.

Leighley, Jan E., and Arnold Vedlitz. 1999. "Race, Ethnicity, and Political Participation: Competing Models and Contrasting Explanations." *Journal of Politics* 61(4): 1092–114.

Miller, Arthur H., Patricia Gurin, Gerald Gurin, and Oksana Malanchuk. 1981. "Group Consciousness and Political Participation." *American Journal of Political Science* 25(3): 494–511.

Parenti, Michael. 1967. "Ethnic Politics and the Persistence of Ethnic Identification." *American Political Science Review* 61(3): 717–26.

Rambukkana, Nathan Patrick. 2004. "Uncomfortable Bridges." *Journal of Bisexuality* 4(3–4): 141–54.

Sanchez, Gabriel R. 2006. "The Role of Group Consciousness in Latino Public Opinion." *Political Research Quarterly* 59(3): 435–46.

Smith, Charles A. 2007. "The Electoral Capture of Gay and Lesbian Americans: Evidence and Implications from the 2004 Election." *Studies in Law, Politics, and Society* 40(1): 103–21.

Smith, Charles A. 2011. "Gay, Straight, or Questioning? Sexuality and Political Science." *PS: Political Science* 33(1): 35–38.

Uslaner, Eric M., and Mitchell Brown. 2005. "Inequality, Trust, and Civic Engagement." *American Politics Research* 33(6): 868–94.

Wolfinger, Raymond E. 1965. "The Development and Persistence of Ethnic Voting." *American Political Science Review* 59(4): 896–908.

7

Embodying Margin to Center

Intersectional Activism among Queer Liberation Organizations

JOSEPH NICHOLAS DEFILIPPIS AND BEN ANDERSON-NATHE

Over the past several decades, the mainstream gay rights movement (GRM) has achieved stunning success in its pursuit of a limited political agenda oriented toward achieving "equality" for LGBT people. Securing policy wins in terms of LGBT people's access to the military, passage of hate crime legislation, and, most recently, the 2015 *Obergefell v. Hodges* Supreme Court decision legalizing same-sex marriage, this movement has advanced a narrow agenda under the guise of representing the interests of LGBT communities across the country. In galvanizing public support around this limited agenda, national gay rights organizations, including but not limited to the Human Rights Campaign (HRC), the National LGBTQ Task Force, Lambda Legal, and GLAAD, as well as the statewide equality groups, have positioned themselves as de facto representatives of LGBT people across the United States, and their victories are framed as victories for all these communities. However, a strong countercurrent in LGBT activism and organizing has existed alongside the dominant movement, challenging the GRM's claim to represent LGBT interests and arguing instead that the movement's agenda has privileged the interests of White, middle-class, and wealthy gays and lesbians to the exclusion of more marginalized LGBT people. Activist organizations in this countercurrent, here called "queer liberation organizations," present a nuanced, complex, and radical vision of organizing that attends directly to the interests of the most marginal among queer communities.

This chapter grows out of a study examining the relationships between and strategies used by several of these queer liberation organizations. We begin with an overview of the tensions between the GRM, in its position of dominance relative to public perception of LGBT interests, and the interests and goals of these queer liberation organizations. We present how these organizations build on the political and philosophical roots of Black feminism to prioritize the interests of the most marginal among queer people, enact a drastically different form of LGBT organizing, and resonate with an emerging form of intersectional radical politics. And finally, we suggest that these organizations may signify the emergence of a new queer social movement that is markedly different from its mainstream gay rights counterpart.

Tensions with the GRM

LGBT communities face many life-and-death issues more pressing to them than the GRM's political agenda and often related to systems of marginalization and oppression beyond simply homophobia. Nevertheless, tens of millions of dollars have been poured into the GRM's agenda, and economic and racial justice are still not generally considered "gay issues" by LGBT national organizations, elected officials, funders, statewide organizations, or media: "Today's mainstream LGBT movement is strangely silent on the broader social-justice challenges facing the world, oddly complacent in its acceptance of racial, gender, and economic inequalities, and vocal only in its challenge to the conditions facing a white, middle-class conception of the 'status queer'" (Vaid, 2012b, para 9).

Numerous activists have claimed that these issues are ignored because the leadership of the GRM does not reflect the diversity of the communities they claim to represent (Carter 1999; Cohen 1999; D'Emilio 2012; Vaid 2012a). With few exceptions, directors of the national LGBT organizations have been White and middle-class, as has the majority of the movement's constituent and donor base. Consequently, "gay issues" have for the most part been determined on the basis of a perceived unifying experience of homophobia but with little or no lived experience of other axes of oppression. Critics have claimed that, for many GRM leaders, what constitutes a "gay issue" is limited by and to the concerns of White, gender-conforming, financially secure American citizens like themselves. Consequently, in the last twenty years, activists of color have increased their demands for an intersectional analysis and multi-issue organizing that incorporate issues of race, class, economics, gender, nationality, and sexual orientation (Applied Research Center 2012; Cohen 1999; D'Emilio 2012; Duggan 2003; Gore, Jones, and Kang 2001; Hutchinson 1999; McMichael and Wallace 1999; Richardson 1999; Vaid 2012a).

In the context of these divides between the GRM movement and more marginal LGBT communities (people of color, poor LGBT people, transgender people, queer immigrants, and others), dozens of queer organizations across the country are involved in multi-issue intersectional activism. While their individual work is significant, collectively they present a countercurrent to the dominance of the GRM and its limited policy and activism agenda. Seven such multi-issue organizations (Affinity Community Services, allgo, the Audre Lorde Project, National Queer Asian Pacific Islander Alliance, Queers for Economic Justice—which closed in 2014—Southerners on New Ground, and the Sylvia Rivera Law Project) received Movement Building grants from the Astraea Lesbian Foundation for Justice in 2006–2010 and were included in the 2014–2015 study from which this chapter draws. That study found that these groups present a rich and transformative model of organizing and intersectional activism and suggested that dozens of other organizations across the country might also be counted in their number. Together, they may constitute a distinct social movement, separate from the GRM and rooted in substantively different political and theoretical foundations, which center intersectional perspectives, multi-issue organizing, and efforts to work from margin to center (hooks 2000) to privilege the voices and experiences of the most marginal among queer communities.

Conceptual Foundations of Intersectional Organizing

These queer liberation organizations orient themselves around a set of shared principles, most significantly related to intersectional analysis and critical attention to centering the needs and interests of the most marginal, shifting the focus of analysis from those assumed to be in a movement's center (the most advantaged and normative) to those on the margins, who are often pushed out or ignored, even in movements that purport to include them. Originally published in 1984, bell hooks's *Feminist Theory: From Margin to Center* (2000) is a highly influential work of Black feminism and grounds this shift in perspective.

One of hooks's central themes was her claim that feminism should not merely seek equality between sexes but should work to end the "ideology of domination" that undergirds sexist oppression. She contended that feminism has the potential to challenge not only patriarchy but also racism, capitalism, and other oppressive systems. Consequently, she was, like many feminists of color, frustrated with second wave feminism's limited agenda, claiming that "feminism has so far been a bourgeois ideology" focused on "liberal individualism" (9). She critiqued second wave feminism for accepting small victories benefiting primarily White women rather than fighting for broader social change. She maintained that "society is more responsive to those 'feminist' demands that are not threatening, that may even help maintain the status quo" and insisted that feminist reforms often reinforce "capitalist, materialist values (illustrating the flexibility of capitalism) without truly liberating women economically" (23). These critiques of second wave feminism informed contemporary liberal feminism and are almost identical to these queer liberation organizations' critiques of the GRM.

In addition, hooks (2000) claimed that White women and Black men can be both the exploited and the exploiter, by virtue of simultaneously experiencing privilege and oppression based upon race and gender. hooks argued that both groups have sought equality with White men, promoting their own interests in ways that perpetuate the exploitation and oppression of others. Black women, on the other hand, have the lowest social status (experiencing both racism and sexism) and work in the lowest-paying jobs, thus preventing them, as a group, from functioning as "exploiter/oppressor," because there is no one lower than they to exploit. Consequently, Black women's experience inherently challenges racism, sexism, and classism. From their position on the margins, Black women possess a unique perspective that allows them to develop both individual and organized strategies of resistance, and to understand and critique hegemonic structures and ideas, creating a counterhegemony.

The queer liberation organizations approach their work from this starting point, understanding that privileging the dominant within a marginal group (in hooks's case, White women within the broader category "woman") does further violence to those on the margin and ultimately replicates the power imbalances the movement may originally have sought to resolve. In contrast, by centering the interests and needs of poor queers, queer people of color, queer immigrants, and others who live on the margins of dominant conceptions of the LGBT community, these organizations call attention to the power dynamic that marks White, middle-class gays and lesbians and their interests as normative. This not only leads to a focus on the interests of the most marginal queer people but also drives these organizations to intersectional and multi-issue organizing; when the needs of poor queers are centered, for instance, organizing around gay rights but not poverty is insufficient.

Impossible People

In some ways building from hooks's notion of moving from the margin to the center, Dean Spade (Barnard Center for Research on Women 2009) has discussed the concept of "impossible people" to describe people whose very existence contradicts dominant social expectations. Put differently, when White, affluent gays and lesbians are centered and treated as representatives of all LGBT people, those queer people on the margins are rendered impossible; no recognized social narrative exists to acknowledge them. Their exclusion from the agenda of the dominant, then, goes unquestioned. The queer liberation organizations draw on this notion of impossible personhood to illustrate hooks's call for movement from the margin to the center, naming the majority of their constituencies as impossible people.

Spade specifically describes transgender people as impossible people; the gender binary is so prevalent throughout society that countless systems exclude or reject the very existence of transgender identity. He quotes fellow transgender scholar Paisley Currah: "When trans people walk up to an institution, it's like the computers break down and the walls fall down, it's like they can't understand us, they are just like 'you can't exist!'" This quotation illustrates how social structures and policies indicate that trans people cannot or should not be possible. "We are being told that we are impossible people, we are told that constantly by every single person that can talk" (Barnard Center for Research on Women 2009). Precisely because society ignores or rejects them, these impossible people are a central focus of the work of the queer liberation organizations. Homeless gay White men, or incarcerated Black lesbians, or undocumented Latino queers are similarly centralized by the queer liberation groups. Their statuses, as people without homes, full civil rights, or legal identities, make them similarly impossible people. The choice to centralize these types of impossible people reflects what Spade would later refer to as a commitment to "trickle-up social justice."

Trickle-Up Social Justice

These conceptual foundations—margin to center (hooks 2000), impossible people, and their associated intersectional and multi-issue perspectives—come together for the queer liberation organizations in a commitment to equity and activism unlike that of other single-issue identity movements (including but not limited to the GRM). These organizations are committed to the belief that the interests of people who experience the greatest oppressions must be prioritized over those of the most privileged. In doing so, people with more privileges will also benefit from work that benefits those who are less privileged:

> Social justice doesn't trickle down . . . so we should center the experiences of the most vulnerable first. That's how we should determine our agenda. So . . . if we address the problem that White gay people who want to marry immigrants have, you won't necessarily have addressed the problems of two undocumented queer people who aren't partnered with a citizen. Although if you address the problems of undocumented queer people, you will address the problems of somebody who wants to marry an immigrant. And if you address the issues of professional White lesbians and their parental rights, you won't solve the problem of low-income mothers of color or imprisoned mothers who the child welfare system targets for separation from their families. But if you do the reverse, if we really upended the child welfare system, and made it about reunification of families and communities, then inevitably, that would have beneficial effects on rich, White gay people who want to make sure that they have parental rights. So it does trickle up, but it doesn't trickle down. (Barnard Center for Research on Women 2013)

Sylvia Rivera Law Project's (SRLP) mission statement illustrates the queer liberation organizations' commitment to this principle: "We believe that justice does not trickle down, and that those who face the most severe consequences of violence and discrimination should be the priority of movements against discrimination."

The queer liberation organizations that were studied provided numerous examples of how they deliberately employed this "trickle-up social justice" framework, whether or not they used that phrase. These groups clearly prioritized the needs of the most marginalized queer people over their more privileged peers. Some stated this philosophy outright, such as Audre Lorde Project's (ALP) Cara Page: "We are creating a liberation movement that is centering people of color and trans and queer leadership . . . taking the most marginalized and centering our relationship to systems of state that are controlling our bodies and lives." Others conveyed the same values in sarcastic quips, such as Paulina Helm-Hernandez from Southerners on New Ground (SONG): "I have not heard a particularly transformative idea of how if we win same sex marriage, the most vulnerable people in our community will be lifted up as well." This chapter explores how this commitment to intersectional work and trickle-up social justice shapes the work of these queer liberation organizations.

Employing the Trickle-Up Framework

Whom They Organize

Because of this commitment to trickle-up social justice, these organizations focus their community organizing efforts on mobilizing a very different set of people than those of the mainstream gay rights movement. Rather than targeting White, middle-class gays and lesbians, these groups mobilize the most marginalized queer people. They focus on organizing those at the bottom. The groups in this study have membership and leadership that reflect this commitment. They are comprised of queer people of color, low-income queers, LGBT immigrants, and/or transgender people. Several (Affinity, allgo, ALP, and National Queer Asian Pacific Islander Alliance are specifically organizations for people of color, while others (Queers for Economic Justice, SONG, and SRLP) are multiracial and multiclassed. Both independently and in their collective work, these organizations have prioritized communities that are often ignored by the GRM. They have chosen to focus on the needs of communities who are part of multiple marginalized identity categories.

This concept requires some clarification. With such a broad focus, how do these groups decide who is the most marginalized? Spade specifically references the identities of high-priority communities: low-income people, undocumented queers, people of color, and imprisoned people. In so doing, Spade (and SRLP, by extension) prioritizes a number of groups rather than just one identity category deemed the most oppressed. These groups are defined merely in opposition to those with greater privilege, not by any specific single identity category of their own. This approach of trickle-up social justice is thus flexible enough to accommodate a variety of different identity categories while consistently pulling the margin in toward the center of the organizations' efforts.

Other queer liberation organizations share similarly fluid definitions of the most marginalized people. Sometimes, as is the case with SONG, those identities are deliberately broad and encompassing of many different identity categories:

> There are more and more people we know that are relying on the collective safety
> net of our communities, that are relying more and more on street economies, that

are relying more and more on underground economies, both as undocumented people, but also as gender nonconforming people who don't have identification that matches their gender identity. (Paulina Helm-Hernandez, SONG).

At other times, however, specific identity categories are prioritized as the most oppressed in particular contexts. For instance, describing a controversy in immigration activism, NQAPIA's Ben de Guzman stated clearly who experienced the most oppression: "The binational couples' provision, while important, should not be articulated as one gay journalist put it, 'Oh, the immigrants threw us under the bus.' You know, when, in fact, undocumented immigrants can't even drive a fucking bus." Here, de Guzman contends that undocumented straight immigrants were more vulnerable than gay U.S. citizens. Later, however, he suggested that transgender immigrants have even greater needs than gay immigrants, illustrating how these groups fluidly use the trickle-up social justice approach to prioritize a range of identity categories.

What They Organize About

A trickle-up social justice framework informs not merely *who* these groups mobilize but also *what* they mobilize around. Importantly, while the groups are explicitly queer liberation organizations, their activism targets are intersectional, not strictly (or even principally) limited to sexual orientation. To varying degrees, both individually and collectively, they have prioritized issues that impact people from multiple subordinated identity groups, including social services and public assistance, criminal justice, and immigration.

SOCIAL SERVICES AND PUBLIC ASSISTANCE

Given that their intersectional analysis recognizes that LGBT people are not all affluent White people who can afford to privatize their own health, these organizations work on issues including poverty, TANF, homelessness, Medicaid, and HIV, and have devoted substantial resources towards influencing public benefits and healthcare systems. In fact, government programs that provide public benefits and health services are a major focus for the queer liberation groups, both individually and in their collaborative and collective work.

> We're impacted by all the intersections of our identities and how those then are reflected in what our choices are. . . . If you're poor, if you're transgender, if you're a person of color, if you're HIV positive, and you're homeless, the ability to be safely somewhere . . . is unlikely. And QEJ works in a lot of places like shelter systems, when in a traditional LGBT analysis, you would never know that there are queer people that are homeless. You would never know that there are low-income people

who are LGBTQ and that we're actually the majority of who shares that identity, not a minority. (Amber Hollibaugh, QEJ)

QEJ targeted the policies and practices of New York City's Department of Homeless Services and coordinated with other organizations, including ALP and SRLP, to successfully change policies in the shelter system that impacted LGBT people. One victory allowed transgender people to self-determine whether they wanted to reside in male or female shelters, while another allowed domestic partners to access family shelters and expanded the definition of domestic partnership beyond merely romantic couples. Similarly, ALP, QEJ, and SRLP jointly targeted the NYC welfare system, Human Resource Administration, and Medicaid, striving to eliminate the transgender discrimination in access to TANF and in healthcare:

> For example, the mayor has the power to change NYC's birth certificate policy. Currently, the birth certificate policy requires trans and nonconforming people to have a certain kind of surgery that they may or may not want and most often cannot afford. So that's another policy that we work on. (Reina Gossett, SRLP)

Queer liberation groups' work on healthcare extends beyond New York and is more expansive than solely transgender healthcare. For instance, health systems have always been among allgo's targets of influence. Initially, this meant targeting the Department of Health with work on HIV/AIDS and sexual freedom. allgo was the first openly gay and lesbian organization that got funding from the Texas Department of Health and during the AIDS crisis was threatened with defunding by that department due to Texas law criminalizing gay and lesbian sexual activity. allgo's work has since expanded to include other sexual health issues, including reproductive justice. By making the connections between HIV rates among communities of color and queer people (and also recognizing that these are not mutually exclusive categories), and by making connections among healthcare, HIV, and reproductive justice, allgo demonstrates another example of work grounded in an intersectional analysis that prioritizes those queer people who are most marginalized.

CRIMINAL JUSTICE

The criminal justice system is a major target of influence among the organizations in this study, but they have a different focus from that of the GRM. While the GRM focuses on obtaining access to the protection of a criminal system and focuses its work almost entirely on legislation to enhance criminal penalties for hate crimes (Kohn 2001; Mogul, Ritchie, and Whitlock 2011; Whitlock and Kamel 2001), queer liberation organizations seek to reform the entire criminal justice system. Much of this work responds to the surveillance and harassment of low-income neighborhoods and communities of color by police.

They argue that poor people are subject to multiple forms of criminalization. SRLP staff contends that criminalization is highly ritualized and gendered in terms of who gets monitored and then arrested. ALP participates in a coalition organizing for police reform, specifically resisting police targeting of low-income communities and advocating for increased police accountability. Explaining that this work is "about moving against a right-wing agenda that further marginalized our communities and policed our bodies . . . [and] struggling with city government on how the increase of policing is connected to the racial and economic injustices of our communities," ALP's Cara Page demonstrates an intersectional understanding of queer people's lives that prioritizes those with multiple subordinated identities (sexual orientation and gender identity are inseparable from race and class).

Beyond policing, however, these groups take on the criminal justice system altogether, organizing for complete overhaul of a system they view as harmful to their multiple communities. Their work is different from the GRM's criminal justice agenda; in fact, most of these organizations stand in direct opposition to the GRM with regard to hate crime legislation. While they recognize that hate crimes against LGBT people are a huge problem, these activists argue that hate crime laws do not prevent antigay or antitrans violence or murders. Rather, they share the opinion of QEJ's Kenyon Farrow: "decreasing homophobia or homophobic violence requires shifting the culture and the dynamics of violence in the country," not criminalization.

Further, these organizations oppose hate crime legislation because of how they prioritize those at the bottom; they see the criminal justice system as fundamentally racist and classist. White middle-class gays and lesbians may feel comfortable calling the police for help, but queer people of color and transgender people have no reason to trust law enforcement. Given that prison populations disproportionately consist of people of color and poor people in prison for crimes related to poverty, these groups are deeply critical of enhanced criminal penalties for hate crimes. In 2009, three organizations (ALP, QEJ, and SRLP) took a public stand against the addition of hate crimes legislation to New York's Gender Employment Non-Discrimination Act (GENDA). GENDA would have added transgender people to the classes of people covered by hate crime laws, and it was supported by many GRM organizations. Yet queer liberation groups opposed it because they resisted further empowering the criminal justice system. These activists believe that their communities experience more violence at the hands of the carceral state than they do from homophobic strangers on the street. Consequently, they argue that hate crime legislation helps to strengthen a system that should instead be disempowered, if not completely abolished. Rather than embracing the GRM's push for hate crime legislation, most of these organizations openly oppose these efforts and seek significantly different solutions. According to QEJ's Kenyon Farrow, these organizations "are moving to stop prisons or policing strategies."

Some of the groups have found ways to create safety in their communities that do not rely upon the police or the criminal justice system. Cara Page described a project of ALP's "Safe Outside the System" Collective, which challenges hate and police violence by using community-based strategies, rather than relying on the police, in order to build safe spaces within Brooklyn. These safe spaces are public spaces that visibly identify as willing to open their doors to community members fleeing from violence, and whose staffs have been trained on homophobia, transphobia, and how to prevent violence without relying on law enforcement:

> So our strategy is about saying, yes, there are hate crimes, so what are we doing inside of our communities with allies, with families, with other queer and trans people of color? What are we identifying as strategies that define safety for us, and help us reimagine how oppression has divided us and created a narrative of hatred between us? So how are we building relationships to each other that are not defined by state but are instead defined by our livelihood, our survival, our cultural and political existence? (Cara Page, ALP)

Here, Page makes clear that in ALP's approach to criminal justice, it is trying to influence community members, rather than the state. ALP is working to transform relationships in local communities, and build safety by training neighbors to take care of each other, rather than to fear each other. Rather than empowering the state to further criminalize their communities, Page seeks to empower those communities to collaborate and support each other as allies.

> And we are really pursuing a strategy of redefining safety in central Brooklyn. And saying a space of predominantly (straight) Caribbean and African immigrant communities, and African American communities, and newer communities coming in—as people of color, where are we building safety that's not defined by police? And how are we thinking about hatred and oppression and violence around how we are going to transform that amongst ourselves? (Cara Page, ALP)

So while the GRM works to expand the criminal justice system via hate crime legislation, these queer liberation organizations target other entities as sites in which to create safety, while simultaneously targeting the criminal justice system to decrease its power. In fact, prison abolition lurks in the background of much of the queer liberation organizations' work. Although the day-to-day work of some of these organizations involves providing direct legal services for individual prisoners, class action suits, or sensitivity training for prison staff, their long-term goals appear to be creating safety outside of the criminal justice system while also pursuing prison abolition. Some of the interviewees implied this, while others stated it outright, such as SRLP's Reina Gossett: "A lot of my energy goes into a movement to abolish the prison industrial complex." These radical goals are derived from their commitment to prioritizing the needs of those on the bottom.

IMMIGRATION

Immigration policy is a major priority among these organizations, which devote substantial resources to this issue. They do so because of their commitment to trickle-up justice, which includes, in the words of SONG's Paulina Helm-Hernandez, "undocumented folks working very low-wage jobs, working in the very informal economies that have no benefits, no safety net built into them."

To influence the debates about immigration reform, these groups work inside immigrant rights coalitions, pushing them to be more inclusive of LGBT people and families. ALP, for instance, radicalizes the existing immigrant-justice movement to include concerns related to sexuality and gender, "by looking at gender violence. By looking at sexuality and politicalizing the role of what that means in terms of body, and sovereignty, and state. And taking the immigrant justice movement to another level" (Cara Page, ALP).

These organizations also work inside the LGBT movement to influence the conversation about immigration policy. They challenge the GRM's work on immigration, because they view that work as principally focused on American citizens and their right to keep their foreign-born partners in the country. For instance, NQAPIA's Ben de Guzman described how they work to explain to the LGBT movement that immigration was not just about binational couples, and that "there are all these other ways in which LGBT folks who have immigrants in their families or who are immigrants themselves are affected and have a stake." This highlights the difference between a single-issue analysis, such as the equality organizations' exclusive focus on sexual orientation (e.g., immigration policy as experienced by a White American citizen who is gay or lesbian), and the intersectional analysis offered by these queer liberation groups, which simultaneously focuses on sexual orientation, immigration status, and race (e.g., immigration policy as experienced by an LGBT immigrant of color) in their efforts to focus on the most marginalized.

By extension, these groups push a broader view of immigration, making explicit connections between immigration and other social movements including the gay rights movement as well as the struggles of Palestinians, Indigenous Americans, Black Americans, and people with disabilities:

> We see [comprehensive immigration reform] as a step in our longer goal to actually transform the idea of citizenship, to talk about indigenous sovereignty and the role of indigenous communities in defining that conversation. Of the pushing back

of the White nativist movement that assumes that only White people have claim to the U.S., only White people have claim to legitimate citizenship in this country. . . . We think our people need and have demanded citizenship as one of the main ways to also be able to honor the reality of most undocumented communities being reduced only to labor. This assumption that we're disposable, and as long as you can stand up and work and produce, then you can be here. In the shadows, but you can be here. And as long as you don't become a person with disabilities, as long as you're not queers, as long as all of these other things, because then [it's] thank you for your labor and good day. (Paulina Helm-Hernandez, SONG)

Through various means, such as organizing against guest worker programs for their exploitation of workers and undercutting of the U.S. labor market, these organizations make multi-issue interconnections and parallels explicit in their work. Their analysis explicitly draws connections between immigration policy and economic policy while implicitly situating all workers (LGBT people and heterosexual cisgendered people, citizen and noncitizen) in solidarity with each other. This argument is clearly rooted in an intersectional framework that prioritizes those from marginalized communities.

In 2007, QEJ worked for a year with organizations from across the country to identify a platform of issues impacting LGBT immigrants (DasGupta 2012), which fifty immigrant-rights and queer organizations eventually signed and used in their advocacy work (although most national LGBT organizations declined). The platform required a complicated analysis of immigration:

Part of our work has been to do political education with the LGBT community about understanding what does immigration even mean? What actually are the root causes of immigration? What are some of the most common misconceptions—not just about who comes here and [the narrative that says] "everybody wants to come to the U.S." But the fact that immigration is a global issue, that people are migrating all over the world all the time. . . . [The United States is] one of the major players of driving people out of, you know, exiling people out of their own countries by destroying their economies. . . . We are actually even interrogating this assumption that "citizen" should equal "safety." Why are we assuming that? Given what we've seen in this country about what black citizenship actually looks like . . . [we are questioning] the assumption that with this demand only for citizenship, that it's going to fix everything else. . . . And to examine how citizenship, historically, has always been used to define our proximity to privilege. And so for us it's been really important to do that level of political education with our communities. (Paulina Helm-Hernandez, SONG)

The organizations in this study take an approach to U.S. immigration policy that avoids single-issue analysis and, instead, addresses the complexities of immigration policy. They work to influence the entire immigration system and expand the current parameters of the immigration debate. ALP and the other queer liberation organizations seek to expand the national dialogue beyond merely the questions of guest workers and fences, and to put those questions in the larger context of links between immigration and capitalism:

> We must understand that the War on Terrorism is a war abroad and at home, and that when we say our people are being unfairly incarcerated for the benefit of a few, we mean an American prison population which is largely citizens of color, the detention industry, and the illegal incarceration of prisoners of war. When we talk about the War at Home we mean the militarization of the border and the use of local police officers and immigration enforcement agents. . . . We must make the connections between the detention industry and the prison industrial complex, war profiteering and disaster profiteering. (Trishala Deb, ALP)

Here Deb included the criminal justice system, ICE, and the military. Like SONG, ALP centers these analyses in its expansive treatment of and work on issues related to immigration. The analyses put forward by these groups require engaging a vastly different set of targets, from a much more intersectional perspective, than does an analysis (such as the GRM's) limited to seeking access for gay and lesbian American citizens to marry their foreign-born partners. Trickle-up justice requires overhauling the entire immigration system.

How They Do This Organizing

These queer liberation groups may well represent a new expression of organizing and social activism, different from other movements (such as the mainstream gay rights movement) not only in whom they organize but also in how they organize. Social movement scholar Chris Dixon (2014) describes twenty-first-century social movements that hold much in common with the strategies and foundational values of the queer liberation organizations. Based upon interviews with hundreds of activists in the United States and Canada working in many different social movements, Dixon (2014) argues that these organizations are building twenty-first-century social movements that differ from preceding movements. He refers to this new form of social movement as "another politics," describing a new form of activism aligned with anti-authoritarian, anticapitalist, and anti-oppression politics. He explains that the twenty-first century has seen the emergence of new models of social justice organizing that involve non-hierarchical organizing, leadership from below, and transformation of power relations. We situate the queer liberation organizations in this context, particularly in examining how they operate. The decision to focus on the needs of the most marginalized not only informs the organizations' agendas; it also impacts how they work in pursuit of those agendas.

Dixon (2014) argues that the particular form of institution being built is not as important as how the institution building is done. "The question is how self-conscious these organizations are about what they're trying to do and who they're trying to work with. What are the ways that their form helps or hinders that?" (200). The queer liberation groups are clearly self-conscious about how their form helps and hinders their work. For instance, over the years, Affinity has embraced a concept called "critical justice." Kim L. Hunt described that concept and how they use it to think about how they work within their 501(c)3 structure:

> And that's the idea of really examining how you do your work and being aware if you are guilty of creating the same hierarchies and structures that we fight against in our social justice work. So that there is a constant critical look at how we do what we do. And we don't always do that well. But we try to examine. It's really hard. Especially when you've become a part of the nonprofit industrial complex. There are just some things that come with that. We fight it at other places and then we create it in our organizations and in our work. And it's a constant battle.

Hunt clearly recognizes how Affinity sometimes fails to live up to its own values, yet the organization continues to try. Most participants expressed similar sentiments regarding the contradictions within which they operate, and Dixon (2014) contends that living with these contradictions is both inevitable and necessary: "We can't bring a new world into being as long as current systems call the shots. And yet we can't bring a new world into being unless popular movements can envision and create something new here and now" (83–84). I turn now to an exploration of the specific and concrete ways these queer liberation groups try to envision and create something new here and now.

Since these organizations center the interests of the most marginal in their communities, their work must take different forms than those common in other movements. For instance, several of the groups schedule organizing meetings at times that allow their low-income members to attend and sometimes have to provide them money to be able to attend. Some organizations do outreach at locations like homeless shelters or welfare offices, which are not usually understood to be recruitment sites for LGBT organizing. Some have provided community members with cell phones so they have technology needed to participate in community organizing campaigns or serve on the board of directors. Other groups provide childcare at their events so low-income parents can participate. Most do outreach in multiple languages. In all cases, the organizations' work with people from multiple subordinated identity categories demands multiple strategies for including them.

In addition, these organizations carefully select the campaigns they will support, because of their focus on trickle-up social justice. For example, while the groups in this study attempt to make incremental change, working on winnable battles that move forward a larger vision of liberation, they simultaneously critique the way social movements often utilize that strategy. Too often, when social movements have chosen "winnable" battles, the most vulnerable communities have been discarded, such as when New York passed a sexual orientation act that excluded transgender people. These activists argue that people with multiple subordinated identities are often deliberately omitted in order to make battles more winnable, yet those same people are usually the ones to bear the brunt of subsequent backlashes. This realization drives the queer liberation groups toward organizing strategies that not only align with the interests and needs of the most marginal but center the active involvement (from agenda development to concrete action) of those at the bottom.

ORGANIZING THAT IS GRASSROOTS AND BOTTOM-UP

Dixon (2014) identified a core principle of some twenty-first-century social movements as the prioritization of grassroots organizing, which involves developing relationships in the community that connect people to long-term struggles. This is carried out through democratic processes and collectives, where leadership is developed from below (the grassroots). Most of the groups in this study have deliberately built their organizations to elevate the leadership of community members, especially those most disempowered in general society. SRLP provides a clear example of this organizational structure; its Prison Advisory Committee (comprised of seventy incarcerated people) guides the organization's work, and a larger collective membership structure leads the organization. SRLP (2009) makes explicit their commitment to leadership from the bottom: "SRLP's commitment to maintaining a collective body that is diverse, our commitment to developing new leadership and under-heard voices in our community . . . may sometimes result in a determination that an applicant is not suitable for membership at this time." Other organizations have similar advisory structures. The queer liberation groups ground their commitment to leadership from the bottom, as expressed by ALP's Mission Statement: "Understanding that services and organizing efforts are most successful when they involve the communities served, ALP is committed to creating and supporting decision-making/organizational structures that are representative of our communities." Among some organizations, leadership from below guides their highest level of authority: the board of directors. The typical nonprofit model often involves having wealthy board members, because they are assumed to be able to help with fundraising. Many queer liberation organizations' groups differ in their commitment to having community members on their boards of directors. For instance, QEJ was committed to having a multiclassed board of directors and always had homeless shelter residents serving as members of their board.

Leadership does not only follow conventional lines of organizational hierarchy for these groups. Affinity also works to build leadership from within its constituents, on the basis of a belief that community members should lead: "Individuals don't need to really look for a leader. Everybody is capable of having a leadership role. Everybody is capable of being a change agent" (Kim L. Hunt). Affinity is intended to be an organizing space, one that functions as "a vehicle for folks to use to do that work to change the world or just build community. So that's the thing that underlies the work that we do." Hunt's quotation illustrates the commitment among these groups to building institutions to provide infrastructure for projects that are determined and led by community members. Caitlin Breedlove described how SONG, which always utilized this model, has moved even further:

> We see the usefulness of still being a nonprofit, but we are trying to shrink the non-profit while we grow the organization. And the main mechanism we use for that is membership. . . . The staff become more and more just the coordinators and the administrative side of the organization to help boost member-led work.

She went on to talk about how the typical nonprofit model limits leadership to those, like her, in paid positions. Breedlove believes that this model is antithetical to movement building.

> There's literally just too few people at work in nonprofits. And where do people enter movements now? What are the entry points? What one of five jobs in a non-profit can you work? Or you are in academia. What are the other places that people can enter? And it's not a movement if there are not opportunities for new leaders to be coming in. Building a movement is about constant leadership development.

By building leadership at the grassroots level through multiple strategies and organizational structures, these groups illustrate what Dixon (2014) called "the Ella Baker thing—the role of the leader is to make more leaders" (188). Most of the organizations engage in deliberate and comprehensive leadership development efforts, building new leaders who direct the organization in participatory modes of governance.

ORGANIZING VS. SOCIAL SERVICES OR POLICY ADVOCACY

The way these organizations structure their work—indeed, even the work itself—highlights existing and pervasive tensions in activism, organizing, and social service responses to marginalization and need. The line between social service delivery and activism is often a murky one. When mobilizing, organizers often have to choose between working towards the world they envision and responding to the pain they see in the world that exists. As these queer liberation groups engage in radical social change, they sometimes provide services. However, they prioritize mobilizing community members and building a base of activists. They recognize the importance of direct services and advocacy in the lives of individual people, but they do not think that larger change results from direct service provision, as SRLP's Reina Gossett stated directly: "We think that services and legal strategies are important and have their place but are not necessarily the central way to change structures, to change people's behaviors and their hearts and minds." Instead, they walk a sometimes tense line between social service and activism, mirroring other organizations, like the Black Panthers, which provided social services (e.g., organizing community health clinics) as a means to both care for their community and also to recruit people into their radical organizing efforts.

The queer liberation organizations also engage the tensions they see between movement building and policy advocacy. One of the ways the queer liberation groups' work differs from the equality organizations is in their focus on community organizing and movement building over advocacy or litigation. The queer liberation organizations in this study prioritize movement building but do not oppose advocacy or policy work. They engage in policy work but disagree with the mainstream movement's tactic of measuring successful social change by successfully changing laws. These organizations believe that policies and laws alone cannot achieve material change in people's lives. For example, *Roe v. Wade* remains legal, yet access to abortion services is scarce in many states. They contend that movement building is more important than policy advocacy, and that building a base creates power that can bring about both cultural and material changes.

NONHIERARCHICAL ORGANIZING

Some twenty-first-century social movements reject corporate hierarchies and have developed alternative ways to lead their organizations and movements, often called "nonhierarchical organizing," or organizing with "horizontal orientation." This orientation aspires to direct democracy, self-management, and autonomy, rather than representative democracy or the empowerment of leaders; it seeks to build collective power and create more participatory and freer spaces for all (Dixon 2014; Sitrin 2012). A central part of this practice is nonhierarchal decision making, such as collective leadership structures or consensus decision making.

Owing largely to their commitment to grassroots organizing, queer liberation organizations engage in this practice in a variety of ways, including consensus-based decision making. Sometimes this happens at the board level, sometimes at the staff level, and/or sometimes among volunteers. Several of the organizations have distinct shared leadership structures, including codirectorships and collectives. allgo and SRLP, for instance, are designed "so that each of the staff positions are all titled director. And they all work as kind of a collective, so that no single person has authority over the other ones. People just work together" (Rose Pulliam, allgo). This model illustrates the participatory leadership representative of horizontalism. Even in those queer liberation organizations with executive directors, most do not follow typical models. From explicit limits on unilateral decision making to mandatory director-level consultations with community members prior to any formal action, even these relatively conventional organizational structures share important similarities with the other groups in their practice of horizontal leadership.

TRANSFORMING POWER RELATIONS

Transforming power relations involves deliberate plans to avoid replicating the dynamics of power found in general society, where some groups hold domination over other groups. It requires intentionally building consciousness and creating organizational structures that challenge power and privilege (Dixon 2014). These organizations address this issue repeatedly in their work. It shows up overtly on their websites and in their mission statements. For instance, SRLP works "to build a non-hierarchical collective organization that internally practices what we're struggling for by developing the leadership of low-income transgender, intersex, and gender nonconforming people of color." Similarly, QEJ's Mission Statement stated that one reason it was created is that "although poor queers have always been a part of both the gay rights and economic justice movements, they have been, and continue to be, largely invisible in both movements." These organizations recognize how their constituencies have been oppressed and ignored by larger society, and their organizations operate differently.

One way these groups transform power relations is by making sure that people in subordinated positions in the outside world take leadership within the organizations. Participants talked extensively about how and why they prioritize the leadership of marginalized people:

> We believe that the people who are navigating these issues are the experts on these issues and are really powerful and capable of changing these issues. So that's who we imagine we are most accountable to. . . . Often those are the very people, whether they are incarcerated or whether they are low income—the very people who are navigating an issue are historically pushed out of social movements. So we think it's really important to not replicate that and to have people be central to the movement if it's an issue that they are facing. (Reina Gossett, SRLP)

These organizations commit themselves to transforming power dynamics evident in other movements, where certain groups are regularly pushed out. SONG and other groups, for instance, have been "working against the continued attack and undermining and pushing out of LGBT people of color leadership, particularly trans people of color leadership being pushed out of the main LGBT movement" (Paulina Helm-Hernandez). It is no surprise, then, that most leaders of queer liberation organizations are people of color, transgender, and/or low-income.

All the organizations shared a commitment to this ideal, and each group knows this to be true of the others. For instance, when SRLP's Reina Gossett talked about QEJ's closing, she said, "QEJ was not just talking about issues of poverty. It was being led by and centered people who were currently living in poverty." The shared commitment to the principle of transformed power relationships for the benefit of the most marginal unites the queer liberation organizations and is reminiscent of activism that arose from the New Left and centered people from multiple subordinated identity categories. These groups align themselves with that legacy; SRLP's Reina Gossett invoked two iconic, low-income, transgender activists of color from the 1970s in articulating how these groups set priorities: "Sylvia Rivera and Marsha P. Johnson said that the way to change homophobia and transphobia is to support the lives of people who are *most* affected by that." Others draw on the legacy of the Stonewall Riots, led by low-income trans people of color:

> One of the powerful things about legacy is that once you invoke legacy you actually have to be accountable to it. It's not good enough to name, like, Stonewall as a buzzword without actually talking about who was in the lead of that? Who was it that was actually so enraged by the condition of what's happening in our communities, and saw that there was no other option but to rebel, when a lot of people were in hiding and were completely unwilling? And so when we look at that, who has, historically, been those folks? And who are the people who have always stepped to the line and have encouraged the rest of us to step to that line as well? (Paulina Helm-Hernandez, SONG)

These groups take their lead from the most oppressed members of LGBT communities, centering the contributions and legacies of these people as an act of transforming power relations in their movement. In one final example, the Miss Major–Jay Toole Building (home of several of the organizations in this study) was named to honor two low-income, gender-nonconforming elder activists, not only because of their significant individual work but also because low-income people, gender-nonconforming people, and elders are too often ignored. Similarly, SRLP's Reina Gossett said,

> A lot of times our elders are not honored. A lot of times the people who helped create the possibilities for this work are treated as disposable. . . . So we named the building after these two people because they have an extraordinary legacy. And

also because we want to prefigure how we treat people who have done incredible work but are often not considered valuable.

hooks claimed that the strategies, critiques, and agendas created by Black women from their place on the margins must be centralized by feminism, in order to abolish all forms of domination and oppression. This principle is put into practice by the queer liberation groups when they centralize the leadership of people with multiple subordinated identities and prioritize their issues. The queer liberation organizations look to the people whose knowledge about oppressive systems came from living under those systems, and in doing so, these groups transform power relations such that the most marginal become most central. SRLP's Reina Gossett illustrates this when she discussed why a group of low-income queer people of color developed the focus and strategies of one of the antipoverty projects that she staffed: "Those are the folks who know the best, who can say these are the questions we should focus on, and these are the ones that we shouldn't."

Implications

Different from the GRM

By pursuing trickle-up social justice, these groups' priorities position them as profoundly different from the mainstream gay rights movement. The national and statewide equality groups are doing little work on racial and economic justice issues. Although several of these groups named "Issues Affecting People of Color" among their program priorities, the actual content of these efforts only involved "outreach" or diversifying the organizations' membership; they reported little substantive or programmatic work on racial or economic justice issues (MAP 2010). The mainstream groups' focus on issues of concern to White, middle-class gay and lesbian American citizens has failed because the solutions that benefit the most privileged segment of a marginalized group often end up not helping those below them. Worse, these solutions frequently stigmatize further those people on the bottom. The queer liberation groups in this study contend that the reverse strategy is needed. They believe that prioritizing the needs of those at the bottom of the economic or social ladder will result in solutions that will benefit everyone above them. This approach distinguishes them from their mainstream counterparts.

Not the Only Ones

While this chapter has focused on seven organizations, numerous others across the country share their philosophy. In particular, the organizations in this study have worked closely with other Astraea Movement-Building grantees, members of the Roots Coalition, and others actively engaged in queer organizing aligned with the principles of margin-to-center and trickle-up justice. An exhaustive list is impossible, but several of these organizations warrant explicit mention: Break-OUT! (New Orleans, Louisiana), Buried Seedz of Resistance (Denver, Colorado), the Center for Artistic Revolution (Little Rock, Arkansas), the Disability Justice Collective (national), the Esperanza Peace and Justice Center (San Antonio, Texas), Familia: Trans Queer Liberation Movement (Los Angeles, California), FIERCE (New York City), the First Nations Two Spirit Collective (national), the Freedom Center for Social Justice (Charlotte, North Carolina), GLOBE: The LGBTQ Justice Organization of Make the Road by Walking (Brooklyn, New York), the Queer Women of Color Media Arts Project (San Francisco, California), SPARK (Atlanta, Georgia), Streetwise and Safe (New York City), Trans Women of Color Collective (Washington, DC), the Transgender, Gender Variant, and Intersex Justice Project (Oakland, California), and the Transgender Law Center (San Francisco, California). In addition, dozens of queer organizations across the country, with whose work we are less familiar, are involved in multi-issue work. It is possible that some or all of them may share the characteristics described in this chapter. Collectively, these organizations represent an important shift away from the single-issue politics that have dominated the GRM and other identity-based movements for almost half a century.

New but Not Unique

Dixon (2014) is not alone in noticing recent developments in twenty-first-century social movements (Crass 2013; Farro 2014; Khatib, Killjoy, and McGuire 2012; LaMarche 2014; Lustiger-Thaler 2014; Touraine 2014). Some scholars have observed that recent years have seen many progressive organizations working outside of the "silos" that have characterized the Left of the last thirty years, and standing in solidarity with other movements (Kriegman 2006; LaMarche 2014). Activist Chris Crass (2013) also writes about contemporary social movements and shares Dixon's analysis. Both Crass and Dixon see contemporary movements for economic justice, immigrant rights, environmentalism, global justice, prison abolition, reproductive justice, and racial justice as interconnected, situated within a larger movement for collective liberation, and less siloed off from each other than the social movements of the 1980s and 1990s.

Although these authors do not focus on queer organizations, we contend that their analysis applies to the queer liberation groups. In their pursuit of trickle-up social justice, these organizations have developed agendas that transcend the limitations of the single-issue politics pursued by the GRM. They work on issues not commonly understood to be "gay issues"; this is a new form of LGBT activism. Although there is a long history of intersectional work by queer activists dating back to the New Left of the 1960s and 1970s, those groups did not build long-term institutions. The queer liberation organizations in this study are building a new kind of LGBT social movement—one with commonalities among other contemporary movements. The dynamics we see in these organizations are reflected in other (non-queer-specific) social movements emerging in the twenty-first century. The queer social movement being built by these groups, though new in LGBT activism, is not unique, and much may be gained by bolstering the connections between this emerging movement and others currently beyond the queer umbrella.

Conclusion

By focusing on organizations doing intersectional, multi-issue work that are led by people with multiple subordinated identities, this project demonstrates that LGBT lives are, in fact, much more complicated than hegemonic unidimensional notions have captured. It also provides real-world examples of how theories about intersectional identities can be put into practice, and it suggests that if LGBT lives are complicated, then so too must be the organizations queer people build for themselves. These examples hold significant value for those studying social movements, gender/queer studies, political science, or social work.

These queer liberation organizations enact Spade's trickle-up construct, informed by hooks's concept of margin to center and aligned with Dixon's "another politics." These groups signify the creation of an important social movement model because of its intersectional focus on the issues of queer people who experience multiple forms of oppression, from multiple systems. It prioritizes the issues of concern to queer people in multiple subordinated identity categories and simultaneously creates structures for those same people to lead the organizations. By putting into practice hooks's (2000) concept of margin to center, this new social movement is distinct from the mainstream gay rights movement, as well as many other identity-based movements.

REFERENCES

Applied Research Center. 2012. *Better together in action: Organizations working to integrate racial justice and LGBT issues.* Retrieved from www.arcusfoundation.org.

Barnard Center for Research on Women (producer). 2009. *Dean Spade: Impossible people.* Available from www.youtube.com.

Barnard Center for Research on Women (producer). 2013. *Dean Spade: Impossibility now.* Available from www.youtube.com.

Carter, M. 1999. The emperor's new clothes; or, How not to run a movement. In K. Kleindienst (ed.), *This Is What Lesbian Looks Like* (pp. 62–69). Ithaca, NY: Firebrand Books.

Cohen, C. 1999. What is this movement doing to my politics? *Social text, no. 61, Out front: Lesbians, gays, and the struggle for workplace rights,* 111–18.

Crass, C. 2013. *Towards collective liberation: Anti-racist organizing, feminist praxis, and movement building strategy.* Oakland, CA: Pm Press.

DasGupta, D. 2012. Queering immigration: Perspectives on cross-movement organizing. *A new queer agenda: The scholar and the feminist online* 10(1–2). Retrieved from sfonline.barnard .edu.

D'Emilio, J. 2012. Creating change. *A new queer agenda: The scholar and the feminist online* 10(1–2). Retrieved from www.sfonline.barnard.edu.

Dixon, C. 2014. *Another politics: Talking across today's transformative movements.* Oakland: University of California Press.

Duggan, L. 2003. *The twilight of equality: Neoliberalism, cultural politics, and the attack on democracy.* Boston: Beacon.

Farro, A. L. 2014. A new era for collective movements: The subjectivization of collective action. In A. L. Farro and H. Lustiger-Thaler (eds.), *Reimagining social movements: From collectives to individuals* (pp. 15–34). Burlington, VT: Ashgate.

Gore, D. F., T. Jones, and J. H. Kang. 2001. Organizing at the intersections: A roundtable discussion of police brutality through the lens of race, class, and sexual identities. In A. McArdle and T. Erzen (eds.), *Zero tolerance: Quality of life and the new police brutality in New York City* (pp. 251–69). New York: NYU Press.

hooks, b. 2000. *Feminist theory: From margin to center.* Chicago: Pluto Press.

Hutchinson, D. L. 1999. Gay rights for gay whites: Race, sexual identity, and equal protection discourse. *Cornell Law Review* 85: 1358–91.

Khatib, K., M. Killjoy, and M. McGuire (eds.). 2012. *We are many: Reflections on movement strategy from occupation to liberation.* Edinburgh: AK Press.

Kohn, S. 2001. Greasing the wheel: How the criminal justice system hurts gay, lesbian, bisexual, and transgendered people and why hate crime laws won't save them. *Review of Law & Social Change* 27: 257–80.

Kriegman, O. 2006. Dawn of the cosmopolitan: The hope of a global citizens movement. *GTI Paper Series.* Retrieved from www.greattransition.org.

LaMarche, G. 2014. How the left is revitalizing itself. *Nation*, Aug. 13. Retrieved from www. thenation.com.

Lustiger-Thaler, H. 2014. Occupying human values: Memory and the future of collective action. In A. L. Farro and H. Lustiger-Thaler (eds.), *Reimagining social movements: From collectives to individuals* (pp. 35–50). London: Ashgate.

MAP: LGBT Movement Advancement Project. 2010. *Standard annual reporting: A financial and operating overview of the leading organizations of the LGBT movement.* Retrieved from MAP website: www.lgbtmap.org.

McMichael, P., and C. Wallace. 1999. Who is the "we"? In K. Kleindienst (ed.), *This is what lesbian looks like* (pp. 152–65). Ithaca, NY: Firebrand Books.

Mogul, J. L., A. J. Ritchie, and K. Whitlock. 2011. *Queer (in)justice: The criminalization of LGBT people in the United States.* Boston: Beacon.

Richardson, M. 1999. What you see is what you get: Building a movement toward liberation in the twenty-first century. In K. Kleindienst (ed.), *This is what lesbian looks like* (pp. 210–19). Ithaca, NY: Firebrand Books.

Sitrin, M. 2012. Horizontalism and the Occupy movements. *Dissent.* Retrieved from www.dis sentmagazine.org.

Sylvia Rivera Law Project. 2009. *SRLP Collective member handbook.* Retrieved from www .srlp.org.

Touraine, A. 2014. Afterword: Globalization and the war of gods. In A. D. Farro and H. Lustiger-Thaler (eds.), *Reimagining social movements: From collectives to individuals* (pp. 273–81). London: Ashgate.

Vaid, U. 2012a. *Irresistible revolution: Confronting race, class, and the assumptions of LGBT politics.* New York: Magnus Books.

Vaid, U. 2012b. Still ain't satisfied: The limits of equality. *American Prospect.* Retrieved from www .prospect.org.

Whitlock, K., and R. Kamel. 2001. *In a time of broken bones: A call to dialogue on hate violence and the limitations of hate crimes legislation.* Philadelphia: American Friends Service Committee.

8

From "Don't Drop the Soap" to PREA Standards

Reducing Sexual Victimization of LGBT People in the Juvenile and
Criminal Justice Systems

SEAN CAHILL

Prisoners who are LGBT, or perceived to be gay or gender nonconforming, are at high risk of sexual abuse and other forms of abuse in prison.[1] Until recently, cultural homophobia prevented many prison and jail administrators from taking prison rape seriously: "Don't drop the soap!" and other jokes were often made, implying that prisoners deserved to be raped. Related to this is the belief that gay prisoners deserve or enjoy rape.

The 2003 Prison Rape Elimination Act (PREA), and its implementation standards developed under the Obama administration, have brought increased attention to sexual abuse in the corrections system, but much more needs to be done.[2] About 93 percent of inmates in U.S. prisons are men.[3] In male facilities, gay men, particularly those exhibiting stereotypically effeminate characteristics or behavior, and transgender women are extremely vulnerable to sexual abuse.[4]

In a landmark report on male prisoner rape in U.S. prisons, Human Rights Watch reported a number of characteristics that can make prisoners more likely to be raped:

> These include youth, small size, and physical weakness; being white, gay, or a first [-time] offender; possessing "feminine" characteristics such as long hair or a high voice; being unassertive, unaggressive, shy, intellectual, not street-smart, or "passive"; or having been convicted of a sexual offense against a minor. . . . [P]risoners with several overlapping characteristics are much more likely than other inmates to be targeted for abuse.[5]

Giller notes that "[r]ace and sexuality intersect at the heart of prison rape."[6]

> An anonymous ex-prisoner painfully recounted the role that race played in his sexual assault recalling, "[s]ince I'm light skinned the first dudes that raped me were blacks who thought I was white. After word got out that I was black, they left me alone but then the whites took me off. After that I was a 'black' punk and passed on to whites."[7]

The disproportionate burden of prison rape on gay and bisexual men has remained constant over the past several decades. A 1982 study found that 41 percent of gay men were sexually assaulted in prison, as opposed to 9 percent of heterosexual men.[8] A 2012 U.S. Bureau of Justice Statistics (BJS) report that surveyed former state prison inmates on sexual victimization found that gay or homosexual men were eleven times as likely as heterosexual men to report being sexually victimized by another inmate (38.6 percent versus 3.5 percent); bisexual males were ten times as likely (33.7 percent versus 3.5 percent), as in table 8.1.[9]

Many male inmates consent to sexual acts against their will to avoid violence, apparently feeling that there are no other options.[10] The *New York Times* reported in 2004 on the case of Roderick Johnson, a gay man forced into "daily sex acts" of sexual slavery in a Texas prison:

> "The Crips already had a homosexual that was with them," Mr. Johnson explained. "The Gangster Disciples, from what I understand, hadn't had a homosexual under them in a while. So that's why I was automatically, like, given to them." According to court papers and [Johnson's] own detailed account, the Gangster Disciples and then other gangs treated Mr. Johnson as a sex slave. They bought and sold him, and they rented him out. Some acts cost $5, others $10. . . . "I was forced into oral and anal sex on a daily basis. . . . Not for a month or two. For, like, 18 months."[11]

T. J. Parsell, former board chair of Stop Prisoner Rape (now Just Detention International) and author of the autobiography *Fish*, was sentenced to prison in Michigan at age seventeen for armed robbery. On his first day in jail, Parsell was drugged and gang raped. "When they were done, they flipped a coin to see which one I belonged to," Parsell said.[12]

In women's facilities, lesbians and other women who are seen as transgressing gender boundaries are often at heightened risk of sexual torture and other ill treatment. Actual or perceived sexual orientation was found to be one of four categories that make a female prisoner a more likely target for sexual abuse, as well as a target for retaliation when she reports that abuse.[13]

BJS data on lesbian and bisexual women indicate some disproportionate experience of sexual abuse when compared to heterosexual women, but the

TABLE 8.1. Sexual abuse reported by men in state prisons by sexual orientation

Group	Inmate-on-inmate sexual victimization (% reporting)	Staff sexual misconduct (% reporting)
Heterosexual men	3.5	5.2
Bisexual men	33.7	17.5
Homosexual or gay men	38.6	11.8

Source: Beck, A. J. and C. Johnson C. 2012. Sexual victimization reported by former state prisoners, 2008. U.S. Department of Justice, Office of Justice Programs, Bureau of Justice Statistics. http://www.bjs.gov.

disproportionality is not as pronounced as among men. As a group women experience inmate-on-inmate sexual victimization more than three times as often as men (13.7 percent versus 4.2 percent).[14] However, significant differences are seen by sexual orientation, as in table 8.2.

BJS pooled data from 2007 through 2012 indicate that 34.6 percent of transgender people in state and federal prisons and 34.0 percent in jails reported some kind of sexual victimization while incarcerated (see table 8.3). Some 24.1 percent of prisoners report victimization by another inmate, and 16.7 percent report staff sexual misconduct. Among those formerly held in local jails, the rates are 22.8 percent and 22.9 percent, respectively.[15]

A national survey of transgender people conducted by the National Gay and Lesbian Task Force and the National Center for Transgender Equality found high rates of sexual victimization reported by former transgender prisoners.[16] Sixteen percent of the nearly sixty-five hundred transgender people surveyed said they had spent time in a jail or prison, compared to 2.7 percent of the general public.[17]

Placing transgender women in men's prisons because they have not surgically altered their genitalia places them far too often into a "virtual torture chamber of incessant sexual humiliation."[18] The National Transgender Discrimination Survey found significant racial/ethnic and gender differences in experience among formerly incarcerated individuals:

- 32% of Black, 21% of Latino, and 13% of all transgender prisoners reported sexual assault by another prisoner;
- 9% of Black, 7% of Latino, and 6% of all transgender prisoners reported assault by a prison guard (corrections officer) or staff; and
- 17% of male-to-female transgender people reported experiencing sexual assault while in prison or jail, compared to 2% of female-to-male former prisoners.[19]

Survivors of rape in prison often leave prison in a state of "extreme psychological stress, a condition identified as rape trauma syndrome."[20] Other conditions often brought on by the experience of prison rape include low self-esteem, shame, depression, nightmares, self-hatred, suicidality, uncontrollable anger, and violence.[21] The psychological problems caused by being raped while in prison likely play a major role in ex-prisoners' frequent difficulties reintegrating into society upon release. They could be a major factor in high recidivism rates. Higher rates of HIV, other sexually transmitted infections (STIs), and Hepatitis C among prison populations also mean that prison rape can put victims at risk of these STIs.[22]

Many of those subjected to such abuse are reluctant to report their experiences, fearing retaliation by both prisoners and staff, and having justifiably little faith in receiving the appropriate relief. When instances are reported or claims filed, victims are frequently subjected to further abuse, ignored, or told that the incident was their fault or that they deserved what happened to them.

TABLE 8.2. Sexual abuse reported by women in state prisons by sexual orientation

Group	Inmate-on-inmate sexual victimization (% reporting)	Staff sexual misconduct (% reporting)
Heterosexual women	13.1	3.7
Bisexual women	18.1	7.5
Homosexual or lesbian women	12.8	8.0

Source: Beck A. J., and C. Johnson (2012, May). Sexual victimization reported by former state prisoners, 2008. U.S. Department of Justice, Office of Justice Programs, Bureau of Justice Statistics. www.bjs.gov.

TABLE 8.3. Sexual abuse reported by transgender people in prisons and jails

Facility type	Overall prevalence of sexual victimization (% reporting)	Inmate-on-inmate sexual victimization (% reporting)	Staff sexual misconduct (% reporting)
State and federal prisons	34.6	24.1	16.7
Local jails	34.0	22.8	22.9

Source: Beck, A. J., and C. Johnson. 2014. Sexual victimization in prisons and jails reported by inmates, 2011–12. Supplemental tables: Prevalence of sexual victimization among transgender adult inmates. U.S. Department of Justice, Office of Justice Programs, Bureau of Justice Statistics. http://www.bjs.gov.

Those who report rapes are often not believed or are told that they consented. They are often accused of being gay, the implication being that if they were gay, they wanted it.[23] When prisoners known to be gay or transgender report prison rape they are often told that they enjoyed the act, and that it was consensual. Others have reported that if they do not have physical evidence of an attack (e.g., wounds, scratches), their claims are not believed and are considered unsubstantiated by prison authorities. Prisoners who report rape are not protected from other inmates, who may retaliate against the prisoner for being a "snitch."[24]

This disproportionate impact of sexual abuse on LGBT prisoners is the reason why the National Gay and Lesbian Task Force, Gay Men's Health Crisis, and other LGBT groups submitted comments to the Department of Justice on how to implement the Prison Rape Elimination Act in ways that reduce risk to LGBT prisoners.

LGBT Youth in Juvenile Justice Systems

LGBT and questioning youth face unique issues in custody:

> The juvenile justice system is characterized by a profound lack of acceptance of LGBT identity, based in large part on misconceptions about sexual orientation and gender identity. These include myths that youth, by virtue of their age, cannot be LGBT or that LGBT youth simply do not exist within the juvenile justice population.[25]

This finding, in a 2009 analysis of LGBT youth in juvenile detention by three leading legal organizations, underscores the challenges facing justice-involved LGBT youth. LGBT youth are overrepresented in the justice system generally, with approximately 13 percent of youth in detention facilities across the country identifying as LGBT.[26] This compares to about 7 percent of youth on the Massachusetts Youth Risk Behavior Survey (YRBS) who identify as lesbian, gay, or bisexual.[27] Family rejection of LGBT youth, harassment in school, and "survival" crimes such as robbery or sex work make LGBT youth more likely to become involved in the juvenile justice system.[28] Massachusetts YRBS data from 2013 indicate that gay, lesbian, and bisexual youth are more than twice as likely to be gang involved as heterosexual youth.[29] LGB youth in Massachusetts are five times as likely to skip school because they feel unsafe, and experience higher rates of getting in fights at school and being attacked or threatened with a weapon at school or on the way to school.[30]

There is emerging research indicating that LGBT youth are punished more harshly than their heterosexual and nontransgender peers. A 2010 article in *Pediatrics* found that LGB youth are punished more harshly in schools and in the court system, even though they are less likely to engage in serious misdeeds—such as using a weapon, selling drugs, or burglary—than their heterosexual peers.[31] This analysis was based on a national sample of fifteen thousand middle and high school students. LGB youth also report being expelled from school at higher rates than heterosexual students, perhaps because of getting in fights resulting from bullying. This disparity in treatment by law enforcement is especially pronounced among girls. Lesbian and bisexual girls are 50 percent more likely to be stopped by police, and twice as likely to be arrested and convicted, even though they do not engage in higher levels of misconduct compared to heterosexual females.[32]

Youth workers often punish justice-involved LGBT youth or attempt to change their sexual orientation or gender identity. Gender variance is often perceived as rebellious behavior for which the youth are punished.[33]

LGBT youth are treated more harshly in sentencing than heterosexual peers. They are sometimes viewed as sexually predatory, and detained as a result. Sometimes youth flee prior placements due to anti-LGBT harassment; courts and probation officers see them as flight risks, further detaining them without providing supportive counseling to address the victimization they experience. It is common when a youth is released to his or her parents that he or she must obey "home rules" even if the parents' rules are not LGBT-affirming, putting the youth at further risk of violation and of coming back into the system. "At every stage of the process, services and placements competent to serve LGBT youth are lacking," write Majd, Marksamer, and Reyes in *Hidden Injustice: LGBT Clients in Juvenile Courts.*[34]

The disproportionate involvement of LGBT youth in juvenile justice systems is related to their disproportionate involvement in other "out-of home-youth" populations. Often youth who are justice involved are also in the foster care system, homeless, and/or receiving residential treatment for substance use and/ or mental health issues. A 2014 study of youth involved in the Los Angeles foster care system found that 19.1 percent identified as LGBT, meaning that sexual- and gender-minority youth were one and a half to two times as likely as other youth to be foster care–involved.[35] LGBT youth in foster care often encounter a hostile atmosphere that forces them to hide their identity and subjects them to abuse.[36] Sometimes this is due to a lack of institutional acknowledgment or awareness that LGBT youth are in the system. One of the problems transgender youth in foster care face is not being allowed to dress according to their gender identity. Fully 100 percent of LGBT youth surveyed in group homes run by New York City's Administration on Children's Services reported being verbally harassed, and 70 percent suffered physical abuse because of their sexual orientation.[37] As a result of cultural incompetence or experiences of discrimination or worse, many LGBT youth run away from foster care placements. Youth in foster care are more likely to encounter difficulty finding a long-term living situation and to suffer multiple interruptions in their education. This discontinuity, combined with school-based harassment, often causes LGBT youth to drop out of school.[38]

LGBT youth are overrepresented in the homeless population, especially in cities.[39] Clatts et al. estimate that up to 35 percent of homeless youth identify as gay, lesbian, or bisexual.[40] Gay and lesbian teens in Massachusetts are eight times as likely to be homeless, and bisexual teens five times as likely, compared with heterosexual peers.[41]

Youth often leave home due to an inability to get along with their parents and to domestic violence. But LGBT youth run away more frequently, and are more likely to leave home as a result of physical abuse and parental alcoholism, according to a 2002 study.[42] Left on their own to support themselves, many LGBT youth turn to "survival" crimes such as robbery or sex work. Gay male homeless youth are more likely to be sexually victimized while homeless than heterosexual males. LGBT homeless youth are more likely to abuse substances, experience higher rates of depression, have sex with more partners, and are younger when they have their first sexual experience (average age, thirteen). The majority do not use a condom during sex "most of the time."[43]

Support networks, which LGBT youth in schools may be able to access, are almost completely absent for homeless LGBT youth. Homeless shelters are segregated by sex and usually do not properly integrate transgender youth according to their gender identity.[44]

LGBT youth in detention facilities experience physical, sexual, and emotional abuse from heterosexual youth and facility staff. The U.S. Bureau of Justice

Statistics (BJS) reports that nonheterosexual youth in custody are twice as likely as heterosexual youth in custody to report sexual victimization while in detention—14.3 percent of nonheterosexual youth report any sexual victimization versus 8.9 percent of heterosexual youth.[45] Nonheterosexual youth are nearly seven times as likely as heterosexual youth to report sexual victimization by another youth (10.3 percent versus 1.5 percent); they are about as likely to report sexual victimization by facility staff (7.5 percent of nonheterosexual youth report sexual victimization by facility staff versus 7.8 percent of heterosexual youth).

There are some racial/ethnic differences in the BJS data on LGB youth in juvenile justice systems: White, non-Hispanic youth report more victimization by another youth (4.0 percent) as compared to Black youth (1.4 percent) and Latino youth (2.1 percent). Black youth report higher rates of staff sexual victimization (9.6 percent) compared to White and Latino youth (both at 6.4 percent).[46]

Youth in state-owned juvenile facilities were nearly twice as likely to report sexual victimization as those in local or privately run facilities (8.2 percent v. 4.5 percent). Youth in large facilities (twenty-six or more youth) reported two to three times the abuse that youth in smaller facilities reported. Male youth reported staff sexual misconduct at higher rates than females (8.2 percent v. 2.8 percent), while females reported forced sex with another youth more than males (5.4 percent v. 2.2 percent).[47]

Protocols designed to offer better safeguards for LGBTI youth in detention are a critical piece of efforts to effect safer and more respectful management of youth. These protocols stand to benefit all youth in custody. Heterosexual youth and nontransgender youth can be victimized by prejudice motivated by bias against homosexuality and gender nonconformity. Strict enforcement of nondiscrimination and nonharassment policies for LGBT youth can benefit other youth as well.

Important Court Precedents and the Prison Rape Elimination Act

The Eighth Amendment of the U.S. Constitution protects incarcerated individuals against cruel and unusual punishment. Inmates in prisons and jails have the right to be safe and to receive adequate medical care. Corrections officials can be liable if they do not take reasonable steps to protect inmates against physical and sexual harassment and abuse. The U.S. Supreme Court first ruled in 1976 that a correctional agency's deliberate indifference to an inmate's serious medical needs violates the Eighth Amendment.[48]

The first call for an end to prison sexual abuse on the Supreme Court came from U.S. Supreme Court Justice Blackmun in his dissent in *U.S. vs. Bailey* (1980), in which Blackmun was joined by Justice Brennan.[49] In 1994, for the first time the U.S. Supreme Court ruled that prisoners have a right to be free from sexual abuse by other inmates and staff. The case, *Farmer v. Brennan* (1994), involved a transgender woman placed in a men's prison who was raped repeatedly and physically beaten by other inmates.

In *Farmer*, the majority ruled that "[a] prison official may be held liable under the Eighth Amendment for acting with 'deliberate indifference' to inmate health or safety only if he knows that inmates face a substantial risk of serious harm and disregards that risk by failing to take reasonable measures to abate it."[50] Prison administrators are liable for abuse of prisoners when they know of and disregard "an excessive risk to inmate health or safety." An excessive risk can exist when an inmate belongs to "an identifiable group of people who are frequently singled out for violent attack by other inmates." Since *Farmer*, a number of courts have ruled that an inmate's status as gay or gender nonconforming can be sufficient reason for prison officials to be aware of this prisoner's vulnerability and take steps to protect the prisoner against abuse.[51] For example, in 2004 a federal district court held prison officials liable for the routine abuse experienced by Roderick Johnson, a gay male prisoner in Texas, who was forced to be a sex slave for other prisoners.[52] In 2015, U.S. Attorney General Eric Holder supported a transgender woman's case against the Georgia Department of Corrections, holding that the Georgia DOC's denial of hormone therapy to Ashley Diamond, who was on hormone therapy when she entered the system, was an unconstitutional violation of the Eighth Amendment.[53]

In 2003 Congress unanimously passed the Prison Rape Elimination Act (PREA).[54] PREA calls for a comprehensive study of the issue of prison rape and the issuance of national standards to end this practice. These include an annual statistical review of data on prison rape. Since 2007, BJS has collected data and looked at differences in experiences between heterosexual and nonheterosexual prisoners. Recently it has collected data on transgender prisoners.

Standards to implement PREA were adopted by DOJ in 2012.[55] During public comment on the implementation standards, a number of LGBT organizations submitted comments calling for "heightened protection for vulnerable detainees" and for homosexual and bisexual orientation, and transgender and intersex status, to be added to a list of other vulnerabilities to rape, including youth, disability, and slight build.[56] The LGBT organizations also called for accommodations to be made for LGBT and intersex prisoners in regard to placement, housing, searches, and showering facilities. The coalition also called for consensual sex in prisons not to be punished as sexual abuse.

The final PREA standards focus on inmate vulnerability. PREA Standard 115.41 calls for gathering information on "whether the inmate is or is perceived to be gay, lesbian, bisexual, transgender, intersex, or gender nonconforming."[57] The PREA standards establish clear legal obligations for correctional officials to vulnerable inmates, particularly those who identify as or are perceived to be LGBT, intersex, or gender nonconforming. The standards require that prisons and jails conduct a screening of a new inmate within seventy-two hours of his or her arrival. On intake into a juvenile detention facility or adult jail or prison, inmates who could be perceived to be LGBT or intersex or who identify as LGBT or intersex are flagged as being more vulnerable to sexual and physical abuse in that facility. Corrections staff should take steps on a regular basis to ensure that that inmate or youth is not being sexually victimized.

When investigating allegations of sexual abuse against an inmate or youth in custody, agency officials must "[c]onsider whether the incident or allegation was motivated by . . . gender identity; lesbian, gay, bisexual, transgender, or intersex identification, status, or perceived status[;] . . . or . . . other group dynamics at the facility."[58]

Other key provisions of PREA in relation to LGBT prisoners include the ending of "protective custody" for gay and transgender prisoners. Often the practice of prison administrators has been to place gay and transgender prisoners in a segregated housing unit ("the SHU") for their own safety. However, this means solitary confinement, which the Supreme Court ruled in 1978 "is a form of punishment subject to scrutiny under Eighth Amendment standards."[59]

Some big-city jails, such as Rikers Island in New York City, had a gay and transgender unit in the men's jail for decades. In 2005–2006, former transgender inmates at Rikers approached the National Gay and Lesbian Task Force Policy Institute, which I then directed, and asked for our help maintaining the separate gay and transgender unit at Rikers, which dated back to the 1960s. The former inmates said that the segregated unit helped protect them against rape. However, despite our advocacy, New York City Commissioner Martin Horn eliminated the separate unit.

Under PREA, LGBT and intersex inmates may not be placed in dedicated wings or units unless an existing consent decree or legal settlement or judgment exists with that prison or jail system.[60] PREA mandates training of corrections staff on LGBT and intersex issues.[61] Given a perception by some corrections staff that LGBT and intersex prisoners may be getting singled out for special treatment, it is preferable that LGBT content be integrated into a broader training curriculum about ensuring safety for inmates and staff. While PREA allows bans on same-sex sexual activity to remain in place (no prison or jail allows same-sex sexual behavior), the PREA standards state that same-sex activity should not be considered sexual abuse if the facility staff determine that the conduct was not coerced.[62]

Same-Sex Behavior in Prisons and Jails and Condom Use

While sexual activity between staff and inmates as well as relations between inmates is prohibited in prisons, sexual interaction does occur. Under PREA standards, sexual activity of any kind is not allowed. Prisons, jails, and juvenile facilities generally have a "zero tolerance policy" that bans any sexual activity.

However, the PREA standards state that facilities may not "deem such activity to constitute sexual abuse if it determines that the activity is not coerced."[63]

Most prison professionals and former prisoners think that consensual sex is not possible in corrections settings. Power dynamics are such that same-sex relationships between two prisoners inevitably involve some degree of coercion, and one partner in the relationship—a weaker, younger prisoner of slighter build—is usually engaging in "protective coupling" in order to obtain the protection of a stronger inmate against random sexual assault. Because of this phenomenon, prison administrators and some former prisoners are concerned that providing condoms and lubricant in prison—thereby tacitly acknowledging that same-sex activity is occurring—could send the wrong message that sexual activity is being condoned and is acceptable to prison administrators and staff.

At the same time, the high rates of HIV, STIs, and Hepatitis C among the prison population raise concerns about sexual transmission of infection and prisoners' health. The Bureau of Justice Statistics reported in 2010 that the U.S. prison population had four times the rate of HIV as the general U.S. population. [64] Chronic Hepatitis C (HCV) is a growing concern. While HCV is largely transmitted via needle sharing, recent evidence suggests that HIV-positive men who engage in unprotected anal sex with other men (MSM) are at a higher risk of contracting HCV.[65] HIV-positive MSM with a CD4 count of 500 cells/mm3 or lower were shown to be particularly vulnerable to infection.[66]

In 1992, the World Health Organization recommended that preventive measures, including safer-sex education and condoms, be made available to prisoners in order to reduce the risk of HIV/AIDS transmission during detention. Despite the fact that HIV and STIs are prevalent among U.S. inmates at four times the rate affecting the general population,[67] allowing prisoners access to condoms in the United States has remained controversial. As of 2010, only two state prisons in the United States had implemented condom provisions.[68] Major concerns exist among prison staff that condoms will be used to conceal contraband or as weapons.

Stigma surrounding homosexuality and sex between inmates also acts as a potential barrier to the success of condom-access programs. The hypermasculine, homophobic environment of men's prisons also exacerbates the issue of identifying HIV-positive prisoners. Some inmates are reluctant to be screened for HIV/AIDS for fear of judgment or harassment from other prisoners.[69]

A few prison facilities place individuals identifying as gay, bisexual, or transgender in a specific unit to prevent abuse from other prisoners or separate HIV-positive inmates from the others to control transmission. Segregation is only allowed under limited circumstances, as delineated by the Prison Rape Elimination Act (PREA). In general, only prison or jail systems under a court order can have a separate gay and transgender unit. Provision of condoms in prisons has the potential to markedly reduce instances of unprotected sex between inmates, thereby decreasing the prevalence of sexually transmissible infections such as HIV/AIDS and hepatitis in prisons.

Several pilot programs have been carried out and monitored in which condoms were made available in prisons and jails. A 2010 study examined the effect of installing a condom-dispensing machine in a San Francisco jail. From 1989 to 2010, condoms were only accessible via one-on-one counseling sessions. Sexual health education was also offered along with condoms. By the end of the study, most prisoners and staff were supportive of the provision of condoms. Data did not indicate an increase in sexual activity as a result of expanded condom access.[70]

An evaluation of a condom-access pilot program in a California state prison found that dispensers placed in more discreet areas of the facility were utilized more frequently and were less likely to be vandalized by inmates.[71] Some prison administrators have expressed concerns about condoms being used as weapons or to smuggle contraband. Whereas prior to the California pilot program, 76 percent of staff were concerned about the potential risks of prisoners misusing condoms, post-intervention only 13 percent continued to express such concerns.[72]

These findings suggest that condom dispensers could benefit gay and bisexual male and male-to-female transgender prisoners in particular. Overall, studies do not show any association between condom access and increased sexual activity. Provision of condoms and sexual education in prisons could be beneficial from a public health standpoint and poses minimal threat in terms of promoting sexual activity or increasing the rate of rape or coercive sex. Gay Men's Health Crisis and other HIV/AIDS organizations support the distribution of condoms as an effective means of preventing the transmission of HIV and other STIs among inmates.[73] Distribution of condoms should also be accompanied by an educational component, led by either health services staff or peer educators. Condom-access programs can be a cost-effective strategy for reducing the prevalence of HIV, HCV, and STIs in prisons and preventing further transmission as inmates are released from detention.

In terms of same-sex behavior among youth in juvenile detention, it is important for administrators to understand that youth are developing their identity during adolescence, and that same-sex experimentation—particularly in sex-segregated environments, which is the case for many juvenile facilities—is a normal part of human development, including for people who eventually identify as heterosexual in adulthood.[74] Also, often girls and young women in juvenile facilities hold hands and show affection that is not sexual. PREA prohibitions on sexual behavior should not be misinterpreted to ban such innocent displays of friendship. Nor should reasonable rules against adult-youth physical contact be taken to such an extreme than an adult staff person is not allowed to console a youth who has just learned of a death in the family, for example.

Other Issues Affecting LGBT and Intersex Youth and Adults in Corrections

A number of municipalities have adopted model policies for managing LGBTI adults in custody (e.g., Denver, Colorado, and Harris County, Texas) and LGBTI youth (the Commonwealth of Massachusetts Department of Youth Services). The National Institute of Corrections in the Bureau of Prisons at the U.S. Department of Justice has developed best practices for managing LGBTI populations in corrections and juvenile justice systems.[75] Among the best practices are the following.

Creating a Safe and Nondiscriminatory Environment

American society is a violent and dangerous place for LGBT people. Twenty-one percent of hate crimes reported in the United States in 2014 were motivated by anti-LGBT bias, making this kind of hate violence second only to racial hate violence in prevalence.[76] Gay men, people of color, and transgender women are disproportionately targeted.[77] Prisons, jails, and juvenile detention facilities, and especially men's prisons, can be violent places. Men's facilities are often more hypermasculine and homophobic than our society in general. It is therefore important that prison administrators set a tone that ensures safety for all prisoners, and especially gay and transgender prisoners.

The National Institute of Corrections' *Quick Guide for LGBTI Policy Development for Adult Prisons and Jails* recommends that prisons and jails start by assessing their culture, including current knowledge and attitudes of staff toward LGBTI inmates.[78] Developing policies and procedures to manage and protect LGBTI inmates is also essential. It is important that policies do not discriminate against LGBT prisoners. For example, if married heterosexual couples are allowed to hug during visitation, then a prisoner with a same-sex partner or spouse should also be allowed to hug his or her partner or spouse during visitation. Training staff to understand these policies, and liability that may ensue if LGBT inmates experience discrimination, is also essential.

Ensuring respectful communication, privacy, and safety is also important. Staff can set the tone by using preferred name and gender pronouns for transgender and gender-variant prisoners. Another option is to use gender-neutral language when addressing inmates, such as "inmate." It is also important that staff not use slur words to refer to LGBTI prisoners.

NIC also encourages prisons to educate inmates on sexual-orientation and gender-identity issues "to encourage respect between inmates and to ensure that LGBTI inmates understand their rights and the resources available to them."[79] These include the right of an inmate to report "discrimination, bullying, violence or the threat of violence."[80]

Classification, Placement, and Housing

As noted, the 2012 PREA standards require prisoners to be screened for being LGBTI or appearing to be LGBTI within seventy-two hours of entering a juvenile or adult facility.[81] Inmates have a right for this information, which can put them at risk, to be kept confidential. It should only be shared with other staff on a need-to-know basis and not shared with other inmates.[82] Placement of LGBTI inmates should prioritize the physical safety and emotional well-being of the inmate. Placement in segregated housing should only be allowed as a temporary measure (seventy-two hours maximum)[83] and as a last resort.[84] In general, transgender women should be placed in women's prisons. Transgender men should be handled on a case-by-case basis in a way that "respect[s] the gender identity of individuals to the extent possible within security guidelines." In many instances, transgender male adults are safer in women's prisons.

Searches

PREA standards prohibit cross-gender searches except in emergent situations and by medical personnel. Cross-gender pat-downs of female inmates are also prohibited. While NIC has not issued a best practice for searches of adult transgender inmates, the National Center for Transgender Equality suggests that transgender inmates be allowed to designate the gender of the corrections officer they prefer to do the search.[85] This is also the policy of the Massachusetts Department of Youth Services for both transgender and intersex youth.[86] A number of federal court rulings have ruled that voyeuristic strip searches of transgender inmates by prison staff violate the Eighth Amendment's prohibition against cruel and unusual punishment.[87]

Showering and Restrooms

PREA standards require that transgender and intersex inmates be allowed to shower separately from other inmates,[88] and that all inmates be free of being forced to expose their breasts, buttocks, or genitalia to staff of the opposite sex except in emergent situations or "when such viewing is incidental to routine cell checks."[89]

Medical Care

Health care issues affecting LGBTI people in prison include HIV/STI prevention and care, particularly for gay and bisexual men and transgender women, who represented 68 percent of new HIV infections in the United States in 2013.[90] The federal Bureau of Prisons also promotes Hepatitis C testing for persons at risk, including HIV-positive individuals and those infected with Hepatitis B, which disproportionately affects gay and bisexual men.[91] Issues affecting lesbians and bisexual women include higher rates of obesity and overweight,[92] and lower rates of cancer screenings, including mammograms[93] and Pap tests.[94] Transgender health care issues are controversial in prisons. Some courts have ruled in favor of access to hormone therapy, while other courts have ruled that transgender inmates do not have a basic right to this treatment.[95] In *Kosilek v Maloney*, the U.S. District Court for the District of Massachusetts ordered the Massachusetts Department of Corrections to cover gender-reassignment surgery for a transgender inmate.[96] However, a 2014 federal appeals court overturned this ruling, finding that Kosilek, a convicted murderer, did not have a right to state-funded gender surgery.[97]

Accommodation—Makeup, Clothing, Commissary

One final issue relates to transgender prisoners' ability to access clothing and grooming items consistent with their gender identity. While NIC has not yet issued guidance in this area, transgender advocates have encouraged prison and jail administrators to allow transgender inmates to access what nontransgender or cisgender inmates who share their gender identity are able to access. In other words, if female inmates can access lipstick, then transgender female inmates should also be able to access lipstick.[98]

Gender Nonconformity and Protective Coupling

It is important to balance respect for transgender inmates' gender identity with safety for those in protective coupling relationships. Because of homophobia, sometimes dominant prisoners in men's and women's prisons force a weaker partner to present as the opposite gender in order to make same-sex behavior more acceptable to the dominant partner. While administrators and corrections officers should refer to transgender inmates by their chosen names and pronouns, they should make sure that this is a choice and not something that is being forced on a relatively weaker inmate who is being exploited in a "protective coupling" relationship with a predatory, stronger inmate. To use opposite-gender pronouns and names in the latter instance could inadvertently send the message of condoning exploitative relationships, which prison leaders should not do.

Conclusion: The Way Forward toward Eliminating Prison Rape and Its Disproportionate Impact on LGBT Prisoners

Over the past decade the passage of PREA and the development and implementation of PREA standards have transformed the way America views prison rape for the better. They have also provided an opportunity to train administrators and staff working in juvenile justice and adult corrections on broader issues affecting LGBT people in custody. Marriage equality and emerging judicial precedent regarding sexual-orientation and gender-identity nondiscrimination will require further clarification regarding LGBT prisoners' right to medical care, especially transgender prisoners' right to care. Attorney General Holder made it clear in 2015 that the Department of Justice believes transgender prisoners have a fundamental right to hormone therapy.[99] We must improve social services for LGBT youth, promote family acceptance, and reform our juvenile justice system to reduce the disproportionate involvement of LGBT youth in the juvenile justice system. We must also continue to closely monitor the implementation of the 2012 PREA standards to ensure that sexual and other victimization of LGBT people in adult prisons and jails and juvenile systems is reduced and eliminated.

NOTES

1 Cahill, S. (2006). Prison sexual abuse and LGBT prisoners. National Gay and Lesbian Task Force Policy Institute.
2 PREA Resource Center (no date). Prison Rape Elimination Act. www.prearesourcecenter.org.
3 Federal Bureau of Prisons. (2015, June 27). Inmate gender. www.bop.gov.
4 Mariner, J. (1999). *No escape: Male rape in U.S. prisons.* New York: Human Rights Watch. P. 71. *Roderick Keith Johnson v. Gary Johnson,* 385 F.3d 503, 512 (5th Cir. 2004).
5 Mariner, J. (2001). *No escape: Male rape in U.S. prisons.* New York: Human Rights Watch. P. 5.
6 Giller, O. (2004, summer). Patriarchy on lockdown: Deliberate indifference and male prison rape. *Cardozo Women's Law Journal* 10: 659.
7 Anonymous. (2001). The story of a black punk. In D. Sabo et al. (eds.), *Prison masculinities.* Philadelphia: Temple University Press. P. 127. Cited in Giller 2004, p. 3.
8 Wooden, W., and J. Parker. (1982). *Men behind bars.* New York: Plenum Press. P. 18.
9 Beck, A. J., and C. Johnson (2012, May). Sexual victimization reported by former state prisoners, 2008. U.S. Department of Justice, Office of Justice Programs, Bureau of Justice Statistics. www.bjs.gov.
10 Man, C., and J. Cronan. (2001/2002). Forecasting sexual abuse in prisons: The prison subculture of masculinity as a backdrop for "deliberate indifference." *Journal of Criminal Law & Criminology* 92: 153.
11 Liptak, A. (2004, October 16). Ex-inmate's suit offers view into sexual slavery in prisons. *New York Times,* A1. Cited in Ries, D. (2005). Duty-to-protect claims by inmates after the Prison Rape Elimination Act. *Journal of Law & Policy* 13: 915–16.
12 Associated Press (2006, January 17). Disputed study: Prison rape, sexual assault rare. Accessed January 20, 2006, from www.msnbc.msn.com.
13 Curtin, M. (2002). Lesbian and bisexual girls in the juvenile justice system. *Child and Adolescent Social Work Journal* 19(4): 285–301.
14 Beck and Johnson 2012.
15 Beck, A. (2014). *Sexual victimization in prisons and jails reported by inmates, 2011–12. Supplemental tables: Prevalence of sexual victimization among transgender adult inmates.* Washington, DC: U.S. Department of Justice, Office of Justice Programs, Bureau of Justice Statistics. www.bjs.gov.

16 Grant, J., L. Mottet, and J. Tanis. (2011). *Injustice at every turn: A report of the National Transgender Discrimination Survey.* Washington, DC: National Center for Transgender Equality and National Gay and Lesbian Task Force.

17 Ibid.

18 Rosenblum, D. (2000). "Trapped" in Sing Sing: Transgendered prisoners caught in the gender binarism. *Michigan Journal of Gender Law* 6(499): 517.

19 Ibid.

20 Ibid., 112.

21 Ibid.

22 Flanigan, T. P., N. Zaller, L. Taylor, C. Beckwith, L. Kuester, J. Rich, and C. C. J. Carpenter. (2009). HIV and infectious disease care in jails and prisons: Breaking down the walls with the help of academic medicine. *Transactions of the American Clinical and Climatological Association* 120: 73–83.

23 Letter to Human Rights Watch from J. G., Florida, September 4, 1996. Mariner 2001.

24 Lee, A. (2003). Nowhere to go but out: The collision between transgender and gender-variant prisoners and the gender binary in America's prisons. Berkeley: Boalt Hall School of Law. P. 14. Posted on Sylvia Rivera Law Project website, accessed January 20, 2006, from www.srlp.org. *Roderick Keith Johnson v. Gary Johnson*, 385 F.3d 503, 512 (5th Cir. 2004).

25 Majd, K., J. Marksamer, and C. Reyes. (2009). *Hidden injustice: Lesbian, gay, bisexual, and transgender youth in juvenile courts.* Washington, DC: Legal Services for Children, National Juvenile Defender Center, and National Center for Lesbian Rights. www.equityproject.org. Accessed January 15, 2013.

26 Majd, Marksamer, and Reyes 2009.

27 Massachusetts Department of Elementary and Secondary Education. Massachusetts high school students and sexual orientation: Results of the 2011 youth risk behavior survey. www.mass.gov. Cited in Cahill, S., and J. Wilson. (2014, March). LGBT youth of color: Disparities and resilience. Harvard University Graduate School of Education.

28 Majd, Marksamer, and Reyes 2009.

29 Massachusetts Department of Elementary and Secondary Education. (2013). Massachusetts high school students and sexual orientation: Results of the 2013 Youth Risk Behavior Survey. Malden, Massachusetts.

30 Ibid.

31 Himmelstein, K., and H. Brickner. (2010, December). Criminal-justice and school sanctions against nonheterosexual youth: A national longitudinal study. *Pediatrics*. Published online December 6, 2010.

32 Ibid.

33 Majd, Marksamer, and Reyes 2009.

34 Ibid.

35 Wilson, B. D. M., K. Cooper, A. Kastanis, S. Nezhad. (2014, August). *Sexual and gender minority youth in Los Angeles foster care.* Los Angeles: Williams Institute, Los Angeles LGBT Center, Holarchy Consulting, Permanency Innovations Initiative. williamsinstitute.law.ucla.edu.

36 Lambda Legal Defense and Education Fund. (2001). *Youth in the margins.* New York: Lambda Legal Defense and Education Fund.

37 Feinstein, R., A. Greenblatt, L. Hass, S. Kohn, and J. Rana. (2001). *Justice for all: A report on lesbian, gay, bisexual, and transgendered youth in the New York juvenile justice system.* New York: Urban Justice Center.

38 Mallon, G. P. (1998). *We don't exactly get the welcome wagon: The experiences of gay and lesbian adolescents in child welfare system.* New York: Columbia University Press. This study

examined the experiences of fifty-four gay and lesbian youth in the New York City foster care system.

39 Dylan, N. City enters partnership to assist lesbian and gay homeless youth. (2004, March 8). *Nation's Cities Weekly*, p. 8.

40 Clatts, M., L. Goldsamt, H. Yi, M. Gwadz. (2005). Homelessness and drug abuse among young men who have sex with men in New York City: A preliminary epidemiological trajectory. *Journal of Adolescence* 28: 201–14.

41 Corliss, H., C. Goodenow, L. Nichols, B. Austin. (2001). High burden of homelessness among sexual-minority adolescents: Findings from a representative Massachusetts high school survey. *American Journal of Public Health* 101(9): 1683–89.

42 Cochran, B., A. Stewart, J. Ginzler, and A. Cauce. (2002). Challenge faced by homeless sexual minorities: Comparison of gay, lesbian, bisexual, and transgender homeless adolescents with their heterosexual counterparts. *American Journal of Public Health* 92(5): 773–76.

43 Ibid.

44 Motte, L., and J. Ohle. (2013). *Transitioning our shelters: A guide to making homeless shelters safe for transgender people.* New York: National Gay and Lesbian Task Force Policy Institute, National Coalition for the Homeless. www.thetaskforce.org. Accessed January 16, 2013.

45 Beck, A. J., D. Cantor, J. Hartge, and T. Smith. (2013). *Sexual victimization in juvenile facilities reported by youth, 2012.* Bureau of Justice Statistics. www.bjs.gov. Accessed June 26, 2014.

46 Ibid.

47 Ibid.

48 *Estelle v. Gamble*, 429 U.S. 97 (1976).

49 Stop Prisoner Rape (now known as Just Detention International). (1994, June 7). Hailing Supreme Court decision: Supreme Court hailed for "historic breakthrough" in prison rape decision. Press release about *Farmer v. Brennan*. www.justdetention.org.

50 *Farmer v. Brennan* (92–7247), 511 U.S. 825 (1994).

51 Smith, B., M. Loomis, J. Yarussi, and J. Marksamer. (2013). *Policy review and development guide: Lesbian, gay, bisexual, transgender, and intersex persons in custodial settings.* Washington, DC: U.S. Department of Justice, National Institute of Corrections. www.nicic.gov/library.

52 *Johnson v. Johnson*, 385 F.3d 503, 527 (5th Cir. 2004).

53 Apuzzo, M. (2015, April 3). Transgender inmate's hormone treatment lawsuit gets Justice Dept. backing. *New York Times*. www.nytimes.com.

54 PREA Resource Center (no date). Prison Rape Elimination Act. www.prearesourcecenter .org.

55 Marksamer, J., and H. J. Tobin (no date; 2013 or later). *Standing with LGBT prisoners: An advocate's guide to ending abuse and combating imprisonment.* Washington, DC: National Center for Transgender Equality. www.transequality.org.

56 National Center for Transgender Equality, National Center for Lesbian Rights, American Civil Liberties Union, et al. (2011, April 4). *Protecting lesbian, gay, bisexual, transgender, intersex, and gender-nonconforming people from sexual abuse and harassment in correctional settings.* Comments submitted in response to Docket No. OAG-131; AG Order No. 3244–2011. National Standards to Prevent, Detect, and Respond to Prison Rape. www.srlp.org.

57 28 C.F.R. § 115.41(c)(7) (2012). Cited in Smith, B., M. Loomis, J. Yarussi, and J. Marksamer. (2013). *Policy review and development guide: Lesbian, gay, bisexual, transgender, and intersex persons in custodial settings.* Washington, DC: National Institute of Corrections. www.nicic.gov.

58 28 C.F.R. § (115.386)(d)(2). Cited in Smith et al. 2013, 12.

59 *Hutto v. Finney*, 437 U.S. 678, 685 (1978).

60 28 C.F.R. § 115.42(g). Cited in Smith et al. 2013, 25.

61 28 C.F.R. § 115.31(a)(9). Cited in Smith et al. 2013, 25.

62 28 C.F.R. § 115.78(g). Cited in Smith et al. 2013, 12.

63 28 C.F.R. § (115.378)(g). Cited in Smith et al. 2013, 12.

64 Lovinger, E. (2012). Fenced in: HIV/AIDS in the US criminal justice system. New York: Gay Men's Health Crisis.

65 Ard, K., H. Goldhammer, and H. Makadon. (2014). Emerging clinical issue: Hepatitis C infection in HIV-infected men who have sex with men. *National LGBT Health Education Center.*

66 Ard, et al. 2014.

67 Lovinger 2012.

68 Harawa, N. T., J. Sweat, S. George, and M. Sylla. (2010). Sex and condom use in a large jail unit for men who have sex with men (MSM) and male-to-female transgenders. *Journal of Health Care for the Poor and Underserved* 21(3): 1071–87.

69 Derlega, V. J., B. A. Winstead, and J. E. Brockington. (2008). AIDS stigma among inmates and staff in a USA state prison. *International Journal of Sexually Transmitted Diseases and AIDS* 19(4): 259–63.

70 Sylla, M., N. Harawa, and O. Grinstead Reznick. (2010). The first condom machine in a US jail: The challenge of harm reduction in a law and order environment. *American Journal of Public Health* 100(6): 982.

71 Lucas, K. D., J. L. Miller, V. Eckert, R. L. Horne, et al. (2014). Risk, feasibility, and cost evaluation of a prison condom access pilot program in one California state prison. *Journal of Correctional Health Care* 20: 184.

72 Ibid.

73 Lovinger 2012.

74 Greenfield, J. (2015). Coming out: The process of forming a positive identity. In H. Makadon, K. Mayer, J. Potter, and H. Goldhammer (eds.). *Fenway guide to lesbian, gay, bisexual, and transgender health,* 2nd ed. Philadelphia: America College of Physicians, 2015. Pp. 49–77.

75 National Institute of Corrections. (2012). *A quick guide for LGBTI policy development for adult prisons and jails.* Washington, DC: U.S. Department of Justice, National Institute of Corrections. www.nicic.gov. Smith, B., M. Loomis, J. Yarussi, and J. Marksamer. (2013). *Policy review and development guide: Lesbian, gay, bisexual, transgender, and intersex persons in custodial settings.* Washington, DC: U.S. Department of Justice, National Institute of Corrections. www.nicic.gov.

76 Scaccia, A. (2015, June 29). Four LGBT issues to focus on now that we have marriage equality. *Rolling Stone.* www.rollingstone.com.

77 National Coalition of Anti-Violence Programs. *Lesbian, gay, bisexual, transgender, queer, and HIV-affected hate violence in 2014.* www.avp.org.

78 National Institute of Corrections 2012.

79 Ibid.

80 Ibid.

81 28 C.F.R. § 115.41(c)(7) (2012). Cited in Smith et al. 2013.

82 National Institute of Corrections 2012.

83 Marksamer and Tobin, no date.

84 Ibid.

85 Marksamer and Tobin, no date.

86 Massachusetts Department of Youth Services. Policy of harassment and discrimination against youth. Policy # 03.04.09. Effective date: July 1, 2014.

87 Smith et al. 2013.

88 PREA Standard § 115.41, cited in Marksamer and Tobin, no date.

89 National Institute of Corrections 2012.

90 CDC. (2015, February). *HIV surveillance report, 2013A.* Vol. 25. www.cdc.gov.

91 Federal Bureau of Prisons. (2014). Interim guidance for the management of chronic hepatitis C infection. *Clinical Practice Guidelines.*

92 Boehmer, U., D. J. Bowen, and G. R. Bauer. (2007). Overweight and obesity in sexual minority women: Evidence from population-based data. *American Journal of Public Health* 97: 1134–40. Cited in K. H. Mayer, J. B. Bradford, H. J. Makadon, R. Stall, H. Goldhammer, and S. Landers. (2008). Sexual and gender minority health: What we know and what needs to be done. *American Journal of Public Health* 98: 989–95.

93 Institute of Medicine. (2011). The health of lesbian, gay, bisexual, and transgender people: Building a foundation for better understanding. Washington, DC: National Academies Press. www.iom.edu.

94 Valanis, B. G., D. J. Bowen, T. Bassford, E. Whitlock, P. Charney, and R. A. Carter. (2000). Sexual orientation and health: Comparisons in the Women's Health Initiative Sample. *Archives of Family Medicine* 9(9): 843–53.

95 Smith et al. 2013.

96 *Kosilek v. Spencer*, 889 F. Supp. 2d 190, 2012 WL 4054248 (D. Mass. Sept. 16, 2012). Cited in Smith et al. 2013.

97 Ellement, J., and T. Andersen. (2014, December 16). Court denies inmate's sex-change surgery. *Boston Globe.* www.bostonglobe.com.

98 Marksamer and Tobin, no date.

99 Apuzzo, M. (2015, April 3). Transgender inmate's hormone treatment lawsuit gets Justice Dept. backing. *New York Times.* www.nytimes.com.

PART II

LGBTQ Politics in the Discipline of Political Science

MARLA BRETTSCHNEIDER

The American Political Science Association was founded in 1903 and is the leading professional organization for the study of politics. Given its list of lofty core objectives, which include concern about standards, the environment for those researching, teaching, and engaging in the study of politics, and the promotion of excellence, one might get the impression that the discipline of political science in the United States has achieved its goals of professionalization and rigor.

For more than thirteen thousand members in over eighty countries, the APSA largely sets the standards of legitimacy in the discipline. At the same time, we find a long-standing resistance to the objective assessment of new fields of inquiry, such as LGBTQ studies. Any new field has the potential not only to add new knowledges but also to disrupt existing paradigms taken for granted. Additionally, new subjects often require new methodologies.

The U.S. discipline of political science has developed somewhat in the face of tremendous activity in LGBTQ scholarly production in teaching, research, and service on the ground. However, despite a longer history of activism on the ground, publishing developments in the academy—for example—have largely taken place within the past fifteen years. Additionally, the closer a project has been, generally, to more recognized methods and fields already existing within the discipline, the more likely those projects are to be recognized, and published, in association outlets.

We often find that there are differentials between different types of people studying and teaching in various LGBTQ subfields. While often still facing discrimination, those who are LGBTQ themselves but do not participate in LGBTQ political science work do not necessarily have the fruits of their labors blocked in disciplinary venues because of their identities. Also, scholars and professors known not to be LGBTQ might have more leeway to work in LGBT and queer fields, including theory. Those who are known to be LGBTQ and who also work in these fields face more difficulty.

In the past thirty years there has been much activity in the U.S. discipline of political science by and on LGBTQ scholars and subjects. A great deal of work within the APSA has yielded a small amount of growth in the legitimacy and publication of LGBTQ work. The studies in this section explore this history in the APSA, which is by no means linear and complete. Additionally, in this section, chapters provide clear evidence of the distinctions between the relative success of scholarship that follows the mainline norms in the discipline, utilizing empirical methods, relying on attitudinal research, and focusing on explicit subjects in the U.S. policy arena (such as same-sex marriage), which dominates the growth areas thus far, and theoretical work, activity in comparative and international relations fields, as well as work with more complex race, class, gender, sexuality, national, religious, and cultural orientations across fields, which have not found as much acceptance in the discipline as a whole.

While one may find more work in various LGBTQ fields in the U.S. discipline of political science than in some other disciplines (perhaps classics and the hard sciences), political science also lags regarding the openness and creativity recognized in LGBTQ studies by some other U.S. academic disciplines, such as sociology and history. The chapters in this section cover a range of approaches and spheres enabling readers to make their own assessments and arguments regarding the state of LGBTQ studies in politics and to ascertain areas in need of attention. Looking at the organizational history within the APSA and publications in disciplinary journals and by presses esteemed in the discipline, the pieces here offer a clear view of where things have been and where they might go—topics that we take up again in the final section of this volume. Looking also specifically at theory and sex/gender issues in university admissions and educational policy, we get a rounded portrait of developments and remaining issues before us in the study of politics and for those engaged professionally in such study. Trans studies, race, diversity, and intersectionality more broadly lag in representation in what has emerged thus far. In keeping with a theme readers will find throughout this volume, tensions—sometimes productive and sometimes exclusionary—have long existed between slower and reformist notions and what are often categorized as more radical ones in the study of politics and in the politics of the U.S. discipline of political science.

In "Our Stories," Angelia R. Wilson takes into account the history of the APSA Sexuality and Politics Section in particular, as related to but distinct from the LGBT Status Committee and the LGBT Caucus in the association. The author relies on interviews with self-selected scholars in the APSA in conjunction with her own experience working with others to chart the course of this new section for the academic study of LGBTQ politics in the U.S. discipline of political science. Wilson notes that the APSA is a leading professional organization and "plays an important role in its ability to frame and embody good practice in nondiscrimination and wider issues of equality." We each have a responsibility to recognize the hard work of those who came before us and worked with us to make the APSA as open as it is today, as well as those still coming in new to the discipline. Connecting this analysis to the siting debate, Wilson takes stock of tensions, limits, difficulties, comradery, and developments in the APSA of import in the discipline of political science, in LGBTQ studies, and in movement politics generally.

Martha Ackelsberg's "Politics of LGBTQ Politics in APSA: A History (and Its) Lesson(s)" provides an analytic case study of institutional change and limitations in the APSA and in the discipline of political science as a whole by looking at the LGBT organizing and presence within the discipline as well as at shifts in the acceptance of the study of LGBT issues. We see a significant shift in scholars being out and in the study of LGBT topics, which coincides with the development of U.S. AIDS activism and then LGBT activism at large. With change we also see a continued discrimination against LGBT political scientists within some departments and a continued marginalization of the study of LGBT politics in the U.S. discipline.

In "Power, Politics, and Difference in the American Political Science Association: An Intersectional Analysis of the New Orleans Siting Controversy," Susan Burgess and Anna Sampaio reflect on the controversy over whether to hold the 2012 APSA meeting in Louisiana. For many APSA members, New Orleans was a compelling site for the meeting due to its location in the South, its historical significance for people of color, and perhaps most especially, its contribution to the economic rebuilding that was occurring in the wake of Hurricane Katrina. However, Louisiana also had adopted one of the most draconian anti-same-sex-marriage laws in the country, presenting the possibility of conflicting interests regarding the New Orleans siting that threatened the vitality of the newly organized Sexuality and Politics section. This essay critically analyzes the promise and problems that arose in the context of an attempt to broker an intersectional approach to the siting issue.

In "Where Has the Field Gone? An Investigation of LGBTQ Political Science Research," Barry L. Tadlock and Jami K. Taylor explore trends in LGBTQ political science research in two ways: (1) by including a content analysis of abstracts from the field's leading journals, and (2) by conducting an analysis based upon the Library of Congress's last fifteen years, when the majority of LGBTQ-focused political science research has been published. Further, same-sex marriage is a favored topic in the field and is the most common area of research. When compared to normative approaches, empirical work is more commonly published in leading political science journals. The vast majority of articles and books ignore transgender-related policy or identity, as there is also a lack of attention to intersectionality.

Arguing that queer feminist political theory has much to offer the discipline of political science as a whole, Jyl Josephson and Thaís Marques offer an interesting assessment of the relationship between queer feminist political theory and the discipline. Looking primarily at political science journals, in "Unfulfilled

Promises: How Queer Feminist Political Theory Could Transform Political Science," the authors argue that the discipline of political science generally has not yet taken in/on queer theory sufficiently. They find, however, that queer theory has significantly influenced feminist political theory so that we can note a distinct subfield of queer feminist political theory.

9

Our Stories

ANGELIA R. WILSON

In "The Will to Remember," Joan Nestle describes the motivation for establishing a Lesbian Herstory Archives thus: "We wanted our story to be told by us, shared by us, preserved by us."[1] Anyone who has had the privilege of researching at that Brooklyn-based collection knows exactly how wonderful it is to dive into that voluptuous archive and get lost for hours. The array of lives and ephemera recorded there form a vast resource from which one can choose to hear one voice or multiple narratives. The cacophony of voices housed there offers truths about the shoulders upon which we stand—their journey, and ours.

The first part of this collection, devoted to histories, gives a snapshot of the wide-ranging tales of LGBT political scientists. The authors here construct stories from organizational records, others' voices, and personal memories. While I am tasked with highlighting the emergence of the APSA Sexuality and Politics Section, my words sit alongside those provided by Martha Ackelsberg, Susan Burgess, and Marla Brettschneider. Our individual chapters collectively endeavor to provide an account of a professional past in hopes of informing, and inspiring, the future. In the telling of stories, the final chapter, the outcome, is not the aim. The aim is to share the journey. So, while I report the procedures by which the Section came to be, the significance of the emergence of the Section to the profession of political science lies in the stories that predate its birth and give caution regarding its success.

As lesbians writing in this volume, we take our cue from the herstory movement and are keen to preserve histories of LGBT activism within the profession of political science. Just as in many other academic disciplines, white heterosexual men have dominated the profession due to better access to education, financial support, gender normativity, and old-fashioned patriarchy. Some of those gay men who could "pass" and/or who had privileges of education and finances did make it into the academy and, as in many other disciplines, professional success as a political scientist came at a cost. Usually this came in the form of staying in the closet and living with relentless job insecurity. As heterosexual women in political science grew in numbers, some of those women could not entertain the need to push the boundaries further and grew suspicious of the "lesbian menace." Some lesbian political scientists stayed in the closet, some left for more welcoming disciplines, some left academic life, and some continued, either inside or outside of feminist politics movements, to be menacing. All of those stories could be written as individually sad, as organizationally damning, or as collectively echoing the push and pull of power and privilege. Here, I choose to don the rather tattered hat of modernity and tell a tale of progressive change because it is my authentic experience, and it is my continued hope for the future of the profession.

My account of the establishment of the Sexuality and Politics Section includes the details of strategy and negotiation with APSA. But it simply would not be sufficient to recount that in isolation. For example, the work of the APSA LGBT Caucus and the LGBT Status Committee paved the way for LGBT scholars to travel from the margins towards the mainstream.[2] With an awareness of the tricky nature of writing a history, I asked others for their stories. My intention was to offer a space to those who have a much longer and more varied relationship with APSA as an organization. In an attempt to balance my power to frame these stories and their own authentic experience, I have presented their words without my reinterpretation or analysis. Taking as my template open-ended questions, I invited people to participate by answering a few "starter questions" via email. Invitations were sent to the LGBT Caucus listserve and to senior individuals I knew had been involved in APSA for over twenty years. Some suggested I contact others, and there was a snowball effect, albeit a small one. In total, over a dozen people wrote back to me with their own histories and recollections of professional tectonic shifts. This is a self-selecting, not representative, group. Given the trajectory of academic history noted above, it is unsurprising that many of the voices are those of gay men. I am also keenly aware of those voices that we will never hear again: Len Hirsch, Tim Cook, Don Rosenthal, to name a few whom I personally witnessed push this discipline a little closer towards equality and justice. Despite these shortcomings, the voices here set a context for the emergence of the APSA Sexuality and Politics Section—one that evidences how hidden we were, how hard it was, and how far we have come.

Hidden

The history of LGBTs in the profession of political science begins somewhere in the 1970s and, in many ways, mirrors the history of the larger American LGBT movement. That the original sparks for change were graduate students should be inspiring for current younger scholars:

> I was a member of APSA for six or seven years before Stonewall happened. In the fall of 1972, I decided to use the methods I had learned studying the civil rights movement to study the LGBT rights movement (then the "gay rights movement") by doing a study of leaders and followers in New York's Gay Activists Alliance.[3] . . .

In the winter of 1972, Phil Ryan, a CUNY political science grad student, told me that a group of gay academics were forming an organization [which turned into the Gay Academic Union] . . . I told Phil we should form a gay caucus in APSA. I approached the APSA national office and asked for a room at the 1974 Annual Meeting to have a panel and a business meeting. To our delight, we got it with no problem. . . . Phil and I put flyers announcing these events all over the convention hotel and I think we were listed in the program. Virtually no one showed up to either the panel or the business meeting. We tried again in 1975. . . . [A]gain we put up fliers. . . . [A]gain virtually no one came to the panel or the business meeting. At that point, I decided not to keep on trying. (Ken Sherrill)

By the 1980s, others tried again:

Bob Bailey, who had been one of my graduate students, told me that Mark Blasius and a bunch of people were getting a caucus started. I think there was a small meeting at the conference hotel and then a larger gathering at Len Hirsch's home . . . I remember being surprised at how many people were there and at their range of interests. (Ken Sherrill)

The first meetings of the caucus were small and informal. There was a real camaraderie that I liked, and a willingness to work together whatever our political differences. It was, not surprisingly, male dominated, and white, though there were influential women like Shane Phelan in the early days as well. I recall no one in my early days who identified as bisexual or trans . . . Ken Sherrill had been a leader in the attempt to form a caucus in 1974, and was one of the core supporters of a more sustained push in 1984, alongside Len Hirsch, Mark Blasius, Bob Bailey. Once Len moved to Washington, DC, he hosted meetings and parties at the house that he shared with Kristian Fauchald near Dupont Circle. As Tim Cook points out in his 1999 review of empirical literature on LGB politics, there had been an informal Lesbian and Gay group formed in the 1974–76 period, but the 1984 gathering appears to have been larger and more sustaining, leading to the formal establishment of the caucus in 1989.[4] (David Rayside)

The first meeting [of the caucus] was in the mid-80s, when the conference was in DC, at Len Hirsch's apartment. At the time I was 32 and an assistant professor at Harvard. I remember someone mouthing to someone else, when I introduced myself and answered a question about where I taught, "I don't believe it!" (Harry Hirsch)

The original goals were to get to know one another, to provide a venue for presenting our work, and to start to talk about the kinds of things we might do to protect us against discrimination within the profession. . . . At first there was no questioning that our single-minded focus should be on LGBT issues—at least on LGB issues. T is relatively a newcomer [on the caucus] but now has greater attention and inclusion than before. There was a period recently when people felt that we should not be a single-interest organization and this created great tension in the caucus, including some serious personal hostility. . . . [A]fter 20 years, more of us have rank and tenure. We are now included in editorial boards, on the Council and we have been Vice-Presidents of APSA. (Ken Sherrill)

Under Ken's tutelage, I left the practice of law and matriculated as a graduate student in political science at Yale in the Fall of 1984. And that year was the first time I attended an APSA annual meeting (in Washington, DC). Indeed, the Washington conference was my first formal introduction to the discipline of political science. Ken made sure I attended the gay and lesbian caucus meeting, which was held at the home of Len Hirsch and his partner Kristian Fauchald. I don't remember the get together particularly well, except that it was in the evening, consisted mostly of men, and wasn't held in a conference hotel. (Dan Pinello)

One described that the early days of the mid-1980s were "so pre-Stonewall— organized in secret and taking place in living rooms" away from the conference. I myself was fortunate enough to attend one of these gatherings at Len's house in the early 1990s. I think Shane Phelan and I were the only two women. What I do remember clearly were the stories of being in the closet and of professional risk. For example, when attending the Caucus meetings some would take off their nametags in an attempt to stay anonymous. Others recounted how heads of departments with suspicions about the sexuality of their staff would come to look in sessions or be conveniently standing outside meeting rooms to spy. At a time of few employment-discrimination protections, this intimidating behavior would be worrying for any young scholar. I was the first graduate student representative on the Caucus executive and initially very grateful for the additional line on my rather sparse c.v. My naivety was lost when a British-born elections expert, who asked about my PhD topic, gently placed her hand on my arm, leaned toward me, and whispered, "If you want to succeed in this profession, you really need to write on something else." In many ways, she wasn't wrong. At my first Caucus meeting, as an American doing my political theory doctorate in the UK, where academic sexuality studies was welcomed in sociology only, I was just relieved to know there was some home for me and my work in political science.

I first joined APSA in 1978 when I was a graduate student, but I did not have much contact with either the Caucus or the Status Committee even after I "came-out" in all aspects of my life in the 1990s. I went to the occasional LGBT reception at the annual meeting but that was about all. (Gary Macciaroni)

My first APSA was in 1989 when I was a grad student. I was out, and even though I wasn't doing work on sexuality, I sought out panels/paper/people who were LGBT or doing work on sexuality. I didn't worry about being out or associating with known queers, possibly because at that time I didn't have much of a sense of professional identity . . . [I]t was tough to imagine being an academic so I didn't worry about the professional consequences of being openly lesbian. (Cindy Burack)

While I haven't been as active with the caucus or with APSA for a while, as someone who was in the process of coming out in the mid-1980s, it was just great to know that a caucus like this one existed in our profession, especially a very conservative profession like political science. (Craig Rimmerman)

The early caucus was both an intellectual and social community. It was a small enough group in a huge sea of political scientists that we could all meet each other. I remember a great deal of excitement whenever a bunch of queer political scientists were together for a panel—even if we were all in different subfields and did completely different kinds of research! (Cindy Burack)

Some of those who pushed the professional boundaries to make space for LGBT colleagues were unable to participate in this questionnaire or are no longer with us. Personally, I was inspired by Shane Phelan, whose voice is in a separate chapter of this collection. I found a copy of her book *Identity Politics* towards the end of my PhD and, reading the back cover, had that panic about originality we all have had: "Oh god, someone has already written it!" I wanted to meet and talk with her but in the days before email and Facebook, the geographical distance between us made a casual encounter impossible. So, while visiting my parents in the Texas Panhandle, I rang Shane and said that I would be passing through where she lived in Albuquerque on other business and that I would like to have a coffee. I now confess, that was a complete lie. When she agreed, I got in the car and drove the 470 miles one way, had coffee, and got in the car and drove back. The inspiration was worth it! The email responses I received mentioned other outstanding figures such as Gary Lehring and Greg Lewis; Steve Sanders has quietly managed the Caucus email listserv for years; Valerie Lehr, with whom I served on the Status Committee, has managed the Caucus finances diligently for as long as anyone can remember. Martha Ackelsberg, Joan Tronto, Wendy Brown, and Cathy Rudder have encouraged many of us with their research and their leadership within APSA. Before moving on to more discussion of developments within APSA, it is worth pausing to remember a few of those who inspired us:

Once I got to know Len, I recognized in him a consummate Washington insider, but also a relentless activist completely engaged in advancing LGBT rights. He organized the first meeting of the Gay, Lesbian, Bisexual, and Transgender

Employees of the U.S. government (the federal GLOBE), and never stopped working to improve the rights of sexual and other minority rights. In the endless preparation of my book *On the Fringe*, Len and Christian were my Washington hosts,
and at crucial times Len helped me secure important interviews, and bolstered my
morale when it flagged. . . . Len's "insiderist" approach to political advocacy did
not always sit well with everyone in the caucus after the formative years, but he
never flagged in his political commitments, and in his belief in scholarly engagement with change. . . . Other early figures prominent in those early years were
Ken Sherrill, Don Rosenthal, Sarah Slavin, Shane Phelan, Mark Blasius, Robert
Bailey, Tim Cook, and Harry Hirsch. Bob Bailey was one of the first to publish a
large and wide-ranging study of LGBT politics, adding activist commitment and
good humour to caucus meetings. Shane and Mark were pioneers in treating sexual diversity as a central starting point in political theory. Ken was an intellectual
leader in treating American public attitudes to sexual minorities seriously. (David
Rayside)

Bob Bailey and Tim Cook are two people that were central for a long time, both
are no longer with us. Both brought a degree of intellectual seriousness that was
quite essential. . . . David Thomas . . . and Wendy Brown were also involved early
on. (Harry Hirsch)

I was a grad student with the late Tim Cook. In addition to being one of the best
students in our cohort, Tim was also the only openly gay man in our program (and
he had a partner). I admired Tim very much for his courage and integrity, for his
ability at such a young age and in such a repressive era, to live as his true self (especially when compared to me). I told Tim about my admiration for him years after,
and he said the university was a liberal place so he felt comfortable but I know that
still took a lot of guts to do what he did. (Gary Macciaroni)

I completed my dissertation and received my PhD in 1998 . . . I secured a "movement" job in 1999 working for the NGLTF Policy Institute. I have published and
taught at several universities as an adjunct. I attended APSA every year until
2006, when my focus shifted to health policy . . . [and in the caucus] I met many
leading LGBT political scientists and social scientists, policy people . . . I established research partnerships with leaders like Bob Bailey, Alan Yang, Paisley Currah, Cathy Cohen and Ken Sherrill and expanded that network through APSA
and the caucus. . . . Bob Bailey was a visionary leader. His work analysing Voter
News Service exit poll data and gay, lesbian and bisexual voting behaviour was
instrumental in the emergence of our movement's political power in the 1990s. . . .
Another visionary was Urvashi Vaid at the National Gay and Lesbian Task Force
Policy Institute in the late 1990s—launching the Racial and Economic Justice Initiative, supporting analysis of the US Census data by Judy Bradford that showed

same-sex couples living in more than 99% of US counties, promoting transgender inclusion—did a great deal to document our existence, our community's diversity and help establish political alliances with communities of color and other progressive movements. (Sean Cahill)

One of the intellectual and professional powerhouses of the Caucus was Shane Phelan. Shane was very supportive when I was just learning to toddle as a scholar and she was kind enough to include me in her 1997 book *Playing with Fire: Queer Politics, Queer Theories*. (Cindy Burack)

I was fortunate to land a tenure track appointment at Temple University in the early 1990s. The chair of the department, Lynn Miller, was an openly gay man. He did not suspect I was gay because I had no interest in living in downtown Philadelphia where many gay men lived. I did not come out to my colleagues until after I earned tenure in 1995. While the university and department created a liberal atmosphere, I was not comfortable coming out in front of my older colleagues who were all men. (Gary Macciaroni)

Don Rosenthal and I worked on the board of Equality North Carolina together and he took an interest in my work while I was in grad school. That provided some needed encouragement at a time when I was really floundering. I will greatly miss him . . . Paisley Currah's work on trans rights was important scholarly and in creating spaces for other trans scholars. I feel indebted. . . . As one of the few trans people around, I've always felt pretty alienated from most of the caucus . . . I have never really experienced open hostility but I feel a lack of inclusion unless I force myself into a discussion, task or social gathering. What inclusion exists can sometimes feel a bit tokenish: I was introduced once to the APSA Executive Director by another caucus member as "H, a trans woman and a Republican." . . . That being said, some folks like Tony Smith, Barry Tadlock, Charles Gossett, Don Rosenthal, Angie Wilson, Greg Lewis, Ken Sherrill, Ellen Andersen, Don Haider-Markel, and Susan Burgess have always been great . . . [W]e have collaborated, [and] I have gone to [them] for career advice. (Jami Taylor)

Kenneth Sherrill is the person most responsible for my becoming a political scientist . . . Ken was an activist politician on Manhattan's Upper West Side for many years. In 1977, he was elected as a Democratic district leader (comparable to a ward captain or precinct leader) and served for two or three two-year terms. Ken was the first openly gay or lesbian person to be elected to public office in the State of New York, just as Harvey Milk became the first openly gay man elected in California in the 1977 race for San Francisco Supervisor . . . I'm convinced the single most important player in the history of the LGBT Caucus has been Ken Sherrill. My observations over three decades of his indefatigable energy and generosity of spirit in organizing the caucus, participating at meetings, and mentoring young scholars attest that Ken has been a unique guiding force for American LGBT political scientists and their research. (Dan Pinello)

Hard Times

Given the cultural and political climate of the United States, it is not surprising that claiming professional territory was contentious for LGBT political scientists. There are a thousand small battles fought by social movements; unfortunately the worst ones leave internal scars. As witnessed above, the profession had difficulties acknowledging its homophobia and respecting LGBT scholarship. I begin this section noting tensions and problems within the organization. Another chapter in this collection gives an account of the siting of the APSA Annual Conference in New Orleans in 2012. The siting of the NOLA conference was not the only challenge faced by LGBT scholars but was a defining moment—a moment when some in APSA articulated their homophobia clearly and when some challenged it vociferously. The stories below capture the experience of those LGBTs in APSA leadership at the time, and the effects of the debate on LGBT scholars.

For me, there are three points worth acknowledging. Firstly, movements for equality, including this one for professional respect of LGBT scholars, are often controversial because they touch upon issues of power—challenging the historical power of others, asserting power as an interloper, and struggling with our own internal divisions and intersections of power. Secondly, rarely do movements for change happen within a clear frame of "us" and "them" and yet neither institutions nor movements are particularly good at operationalizing intersectionality. Finally, despite the battle scars, made by foes, friends, or ourselves, the current outcome within the organization of the APSA is a structural recognition of LGBT scholars and scholarship through the LGBT Caucus, the LGBT Status Committee, and the Sexuality and Politics Section and in the increasing openness of leading APSA journals to LGBT political science. This professional recognition is worthy of celebration and of gratitude to those who fought for it over the last fifty years.

How do you challenge the profession by insisting on good practice and respect? The voices below give us a flavor of how that process was undertaken in the early days of the Caucus and then within the remit of the LGBT Status Committee:

> I was asked to join the Committee on the Status of Lesbians and Gays in the Profession in 1995, just after a survey had gone out to all association members posing a range of questions about status issues. Somehow, Martha Ackelsberg and I agreed to draft a report[5] based on those rather flawed data. . . . We worked well as a team, and produced a draft report in the spring of that year, and the full Status

Committee, with Mark Blasius as chair, then met to hammer out a final report. There were plenty of strongly held views expressed during a day-long meeting to finalize the report, though I mostly remember a cooperative feeling among members, and a relative absence of categorically different approaches to the report. . . . As chair of the committee, Mark was an advocate of taking seriously our relationship with other status committees, and in that he had pretty full support from other committee members. Martha and I also drafted a separate document with recommendations. During that time, and for the remainder of my term on the Status Committee, I recall the APSA staff being nothing but helpful, and encouraging. That was particularly true of the then executive director of the Association, Cathy Rudder. . . . The Status Committee, with the support of the caucus, was then focused on securing approval of the report's recommendations from the full APSA Council. The most difficult of those recommendations was one that essentially called for the inclusion of sexual diversity in the Association's affirmative action programing. Eventually that was approved but not without encountering stiff opposition from some Council members. (David Rayside)

One issue for the LGBT Status Committee in the mid-1990s, when I was a member, was trying to get a scholar with expertise on LGBT politics onto the editorial board of the APSR which was resistant. We went to the Council and they eventually agreed. . . . Other members of the Status Committee that worked hard on that issue were David Rayside, Cathy Cohen, Christine DiStefano. It was a lot of hard slogging. (Harry Hirsch)

Tim Cook was, I believe, the first member of the caucus or Status Committee to be chosen for the Council, a few years before that. When I served [on the Council in 1999], the push to broaden the APSR beyond its relatively narrow intellectual base was at its peak, and of course those of us in the caucus were champions of that cause. . . . Tim published his extraordinary review essay in the APSR, reflecting Tim's broad range and intellectual sharpness. It provided helpful profile to a wide variety of empirical scholarship, and to the relative silence in the broader profession. At that point, anything focused on LGBT politics was immediately categorized as marginal, and of no broad significance to our understanding of public policy, social movements, electoral politics, public opinion, and so on. In my view that is still widely the case, but then it was completely standard for even the most significant of LGBT-related scholarship to be marginal to the discipline, and for even the highest profile issues to be invisible in the textbooks on American or comparative politics. . . . During this time, I continued to find the APSA staff supportive, though I know that in a few years there were some who disagreed with that view. (David Rayside)

There was controversy, even back then [1990s], about the conference siting issue. [Caucus leaders] accepted a policy on behalf of the caucus—acknowledging the legitimacy of geographical balance, which meant [the conference taking place occasionally in] the South [with its] sodomy laws—without consulting the membership. That caused turmoil. (Harry Hirsch)

The complexity of conflict around the siting issue would continue when, in the wake of extensive DOMA and super-DOMA legislation across the South, Dan Pinello led the 2009 challenge to APSA's decision to hold its annual conference in New Orleans. While the decision to hold the conference in Louisiana was made long before Hurricane Katrina's devastation, many felt that the APSA conference could bring much-needed economic support to the city. Some framed the two concerns as opposing agendas, and difficult debates took place within the Caucus, the Status Committee, and, ultimately, in the APSA Council as to how to move forward. Dan instigated a boycott of the APSA conference in New Orleans and approximately one thousand APSA members supported it, including the LGBT Status Committee. The Status Committee also tried to work closely with the staff of APSA to minimize risk to LGBT participants attending the conference in NOLA and to plan events at the conference that would try to heal remaining animosity between members.

Cindy Burack reminds us that the relevant documents are still available online in the APSA website, including the Status Committee's Statement in Support of the Boycott of the 2012 APSA Annual Meeting in New Orleans and two related papers: Martha Ackelsberg and Mary Lyndon Shanley's "Discrimination and Inclusivity: Why APSA Should Not Meet in New Orleans" and Wendy Brown's "Why I Favour a Boycott of the 2012 New Orleans APSA Meetings and What I Object to in Post-Katrina Arguments against Such a Boycott." Given the significance of this conflict, my questionnaire did ask about it specifically, and more than one who had served in APSA leadership positions at the time emailed me directly to acknowledge their strong support of the boycott but asserted that they just didn't want to talk about it anymore. Having served on the Status Committee at the time, and witnessed some homophobia over this issue from APSA staff and fellow APSA members myself, I have some sympathy with this perspective. However, sometimes it is better to share our histories, even if they are hard to hear. Below I offer reflections from some of those serving on the Caucus, the Status Committee, and the APSA Council during that time. That is followed by reflections about the aftermath in terms of LGBT scholars' relationship to APSA, changes within APSA, and futures made possible by the conflict.

The first really serious conflict I experienced in the Caucus was over New Orleans. It was in my view an immensely complicated issue, inevitably intersecting race, but there were highly contrasting views. There were also some within the Caucus who felt that the APSA leadership was not as supportive, or even as sympathetic, as it ought to have been. Knowing the then-ED of the association, I found it hard to believe that the Association was as indifferent to concerns expressed in the Caucus as some claimed, and my later involvement as a member in the Siting Committee (designed to establish policy and practice for the future) reinforced my view. Nevertheless, I cannot deny the strong feelings on the other side, including by smart academics who I respected. (David Rayside)

In 2004, voters in 13 American states approved amendments to state constitutions prohibiting civil marriage for same-sex couples. Nine of those states (including Louisiana) adopted constitutional language that also banned every other form of governmental relationship recognition for lesbian and gay pairs, such as civil unions, domestic partnerships, or reciprocal benefits. The only thing that same-sex couples could be to one another in those jurisdictions was legal strangers. . . . I served on the APSA's LGBT Status Committee from 2004 to 2007. At our March 2005 meeting, we asked the executive director whether the Association had scheduled an annual meeting in New Orleans (because one of our members heard a rumor to that effect). He told the committee bluntly that no conference had been scheduled in Louisiana. Several years later, however, when a chronology surrounding the New Orleans controversy was posted on the APSA website, the Association acknowledged that its contracts with New Orleans hotels had indeed been signed in 2004. Thus, the March 2005 assurance to the LGBT Status Committee that no conference would be held in Louisiana was an utter lie. . . . In 2007–2008, when the APSA Council finally got around to considering the LGBT Status Committee's 2005 resolution to relocate the 2012 annual meeting away from New Orleans, members of the LGBT Caucus of political scientists met with the President to persuade her to support the resolution. Unfortunately, she mistakenly believed that federal law protected gays and lesbians from sexual-orientation discrimination, and no amount of advocacy by Caucus members would disabuse her of that erroneous belief. Thus, the APSA president whose action was the most crucial in determining the Association's conference-siting policy most relevant to LGBT political scientists refused to allow actual facts to influence her judgment. Needless to say, she opposed the Status Committee's proposal regarding the New Orleans meeting. (Dan Pinello)

I served on the Status Committee from 2007–2010. For better or worse, my tenure coincided with the introduction of, and debates over, the boycott of the 2012 annual meeting in New Orleans. While I served on the Status Com, we were operating in the wake of a wave of anti-LGBT state statutes and constitutional amendments, and I didn't find APSA leadership supportive of LGBT political scientists' concerns about discrimination. I'd describe my experience as a member of the Status Com during the debates over NOLA as profoundly disheartening but also instructive. When Dan Pinello announced that he would lead a boycott of the meeting . . . my first thought was that I probably wouldn't either sign the boycott or attend the meeting. However, being on the Status Com during the boycott debates led me to change my mind about lending support to the boycott . . . I supported it not because I thought it would or should punish New Orleans or Louisiana, but because I came to believe the leaders and members of our own professional association didn't understand or appreciate what it meant to be political scientists and, at the same time, members of a group that substantial numbers of our fellow citizens wanted to harm with discriminatory public politics. I still believe it was a debate worth having, even though many of us in the LGBT Caucus and Section disagree among ourselves. I also understand why many of my colleagues disagreed with the boycott. (Cindy Burack)

I was on APSA Council 2007–9 when the NOLA issue erupted. I don't mind saying that I felt quite beat up by that fight, both within the caucus and more generally. . . . [When] Cathy Rudder was executive director APSA was, on the whole, quite coop- erative during her tenure. There was a staff member [then] who was hostile and that caused some problems although she eventually became more open. There was another APSA staff member during the NOLA fight who was quite hostile, at least on the NOLA issue. I remember him interrupting me and shouting at me several times during the two meetings when the Council debated the NOLA siting. (Harry Hirsch)

First, most people don't really know what happened, and there were a lot of assumptions made about people in the LGBTQ community of APSA being racist, when in fact there was a great deal of homophobia, misogyny, and racism to go around. [The year before the NOLA conference, when I was Chair of the Status Com] we worked to build relations with other Status Committees, to greater and lesser success depending on the groups. We had plans for various coalitional activi- ties in 2012. But honestly, I was almost relieved that the meeting was cancelled. And I have not been back to APSA since. I will reengage sometime, but by the end of my term I was just exhausted . . . I think there are limits to what we can expect from a professional association. (Jyl Josephson)

I was well aware of the NOLA debate (how could anyone LGBT in APSA not be?). I supported the boycott and didn't register for the meetings that year. I understand the passion that many people had about the issue, but I was turned off by the way that some people argued and attacked others. (Gary Macciaroni)

The New Orleans issue was just awful for those of us who were on the market. I felt bullied by one or two senior members in the section to publicly boycott something that was against my direct career interest. It is one thing to boycott something when you are in a safe position but for those of us who were not protected, the whole thing stunk. I was in a no win situation and I ended up [avoiding] emails, agree[ing] that there was a problem but [saying] that I [could not] make a public stand . . . conveniently missing the [conference] deadline and telling the department personnel committee that I wanted to attend MPSA instead. . . . SPSA has their conference in New Orleans . . . [I]t is one of the better places in the South on LGBT issues. All of this being said, I get why people wanted to boycott. I don't do much business with the state of Ohio because of its birth certificate policies on transgender people. (Jami Taylor)

The boycott of the annual meeting in New Orleans left a bad taste in my mouth. I did not understand why many LGBTQ professionals were insisting on radical actions such as changing the meeting site altogether. On the one hand, I admired the activism. I have come to loathe political scientists who remain apolitical and loathe the discipline that rewards "objectivity" as the norm. So I was encouraged that there were LGBTQ members (Dan Pinello was a loud voice) who demanded the APSA take a stand against Lousiana's discriminatory policies. On the other hand, perhaps in my naivety, I could not understand why members were so angry towards and distrustful of the administration. Looking back, I understand that I was naïve. I have come to understand queer politics like Larry Kramer: You do not get more with honey than with vinegar. (Jerry Thomas)

How Far We Have Come

Debates from 2009 to 2010 were heated and, for a few, irreparably changed their relationship with APSA. The grievances around this conflict aside, what can be heard clearly from the forty-year history recounted here is that LGBT issues are now firmly on the APSA agenda. For example, some have argued that the siting debate prompted discussions that might have otherwise progressed more slowly:

It was a time when a lot of healing was needed and I tried to facilitate some of that although to some extent it was also not possible. I believe that those who pushed for changing the 2012 meeting, and then for the boycott, made it possible for the association to listen more to the voices of the LGBT Caucus and the LGBT Status Committee. There are always limits to what you can expect from a professional association like APSA, but there were moments of real democratic engagement on the part of the LGBT community and allies in the discipline, and I think this was very important. (Jyl Josephson)

Jyl continues by highlighting how APSA responded to concerns raised by LGBT members regarding an APSA workshop that was to run in Uganda. The country's criminalization of homosexuality undoubtedly would present a risk to participants and potentially could send a signal of endorsement of this policy to the Ugandan government. She believes that despite some opposition, APSA leaders did listen eventually and acted to avoid this risk.

I have no illusions that APSA would have even cared about Uganda's proposed legislation in 2010 had it not been for the organizing done around the New Orleans boycott. One of the first meetings that I chaired (held by conference call) was in early 2010, as APSA was trying to decide what to do about the Africa workshops, which that year were supposed to be held in Uganda, and were on gender. Ultimately APSA moved the meeting to Tanzania, and this was really an executive and Council decision, and based on legal advice, but the Status Committee was very much consulted. I think that there were those who thought the LGBT Status Committee controlled the decision, but it was APSA that made the decision to move the workshop. (Jyl Josephson)

One of the most important indications that the organization, and the discipline, has shifted over time is the formal recognition of the Sexuality and Politics Section. At various points over the years, members of the Caucus and Status Committee discussed the possibility of petitioning for a formal section. Most thought there was not enough research in this field of the discipline to gain support, but by the mid-2000s, with significant numbers of paper presentations at the APSA annual conference and other regional conferences, it began to seem just a little more possible. The importance of APSA section recognition should not be understated—it is the profession acknowledgment that sexuality research is a "substantial interest in the discipline":

> Organized sections provide an opportunity for groups of APSA members who share a common interest in a particular subfield to organize meetings and coordinate communications under Association auspices. Sections provide the membership with outlets for research and opportunities for scholarship. Sections help encourage the study of political science. They have become a vital part of the Association by sponsoring panels at the Annual Meeting, producing informative newsletters, and recognizing scholarly achievements of their members. As components of the Association, sections are accountable to its Constitution and are regulated by the Organized Section Committee. Sections also receive logistical support from the national office in collecting dues and maintaining membership lists. (APSA section regulations)[6]

The original aims as outlined in the section application are included at the end of this chapter. Susan Burgess and I drafted these and led the process of negotiating the APSA procedures towards recognition. We publicly advocated for this in our article in *PS* in 2007, "Sexuality and the Body Politic."[7] In order for the APSA to grant such status, over two hundred members must sign a petition of support and the section must maintain a membership of 250. The former was fairly easy. We first gained support of the Caucus members, and then I emailed over a hundred individuals who had either published on LGBT issues or copublished or worked closely with those who had. Everyone I contacted offered his or her support. Moreover, all included words of encouragement and were glad APSA would be recognizing LGBT research, "finally."

There were many in the Caucus, including most of those contributing to this history, who were involved in discussions about the Section. Most agreed with Susan and me that the name should be "Sexuality and Politics" rather than "LGBT Politics." Our reasons were pragmatic: we needed to garner support from not just a range of members who worked on LGBT issues but also those who worked on topics such as sex trafficking, legislation regulating pornography, family policy, etc. In addition, because many departments do not yet have nondiscrimination policies that include sexual orientation, scholars without tenure or on the job market might find it harder to find employment if they had presented work on an LGBT research panel. The reality of homophobia in the profession played a role in the name selection. For these practical reasons, the Sexuality and Politics label seemed to fit the remit. The petition was sent to the APSA in January 2007 and approved by the full council when it met in the following April. During this process, the APSA staff and council members were very supportive. I heard a few homophobic grumblings in the larger membership, but it did not seem to have an impact on the recognition of the section. Moreover, during the siting debate, the LGBT Status Committee had assurances from the APSA leadership that the APSA would take into account how that debate and incidences of homophobia might affect the long-term membership of the Section. They agreed that should membership fall below the 250 needed, the Section would be allowed to continue. This commitment was a symbol of understanding of the political and professional climate and how the APSA needed to better support LGBT research and its LGBT members. It is important that we make sure APSA maintains an institutional memory of this commitment, and Jyl Josephson and others in leadership roles since then have continued to "lobby APSA to continue to support the section":

It is very important to have a section, the Caucus, and the Status Committee—they all serve different functions. LGBT political scientists do research in many different areas and the Status Committee support all LGBT political scientists—I think having a separate research section makes this clear. It is also very important to have a place for sexuality research to be supported. (Jyl Josephson)

I was pleased to be one of the original members of the Sexuality and Politics section. Members of the LGBT Caucus had talked off and on for years about organizing a section for scholars of sexuality in political science. Even though the Section has struggled at times to meet the threshold for membership, it performs an indispensable service in validating and institutionalizing political science research and scholarship on sexuality. (Cindy Burack)

Ten years later, the Section continues and, while it struggles to maintain membership numbers, it serves the laudable purpose of offering a home to LGBT scholarship and is a symbol of professional respect for LGBT members. There are even moves afoot to launch an academic journal associated with the Section. Of course, there remains some room for improvement:

> I became active in APSA and the Caucus around the time the organization was establishing the Sexuality and Politics Section. When I joined APSA, the caucus was already established. I have never known APSA without it . . . I attended the business meeting of the newly found Section and volunteered for service. I, as well as three other graduate students, were voted onto the executive board as "members at large." . . . [T]his role was not clearly defined so I made special efforts to contact the chair and reiterate my willingness to work [but] I was never asked to do anything. Senior researchers and faculty could do a better job growing new leaders. Growing leaders is important for any organization, but it is especially important for LGBTQ groups whose younger [members] identify more . . . openly . . . as LGBTQ. . . . The [Caucus and Section] could do a better job reaching out to younger queers, capitalizing on their increased visibility and lack of assimilation as a source of strength. . . . Working with African-American groups, I have learned the importance of being able to "lift as you climb." (Jerry Thomas)

> I joined APSA and MPSA as a grad student [about 2005] . . . [Those] conferences offered more LGBT friendly research environments than did public administration. . . . I think the section can provide an important avenue for legitimizing LGBT and other sexuality related political science and public administration research. A good journal would help that. While we have made a lot of progress, the vast majority of such work is still published in a handful of journals . . . [M]any areas of sexuality (transgender, intersex, LGBT in developing regions, LGBT in IR) don't see much attention in the discipline. (Jami Taylor)

As a space to present research and gain professional respect, the Section serves the LGBT community and APSA well. In 2011, the Section launched the Cynthia Weber Best Conference Paper Award, which recognizes the best paper exploring sexuality and politics presented at the previous year's APSA annual meeting. At the same time, the Section set up the Kenneth Sherrill Best Dissertation Award, which recognizes the best dissertation on sexuality and politics completed and successfully defended in the previous two calendar years. The award is open to all scholarship that falls under the broad rubric of sexuality and politics, including studies concerning the regulation of sexuality, political responses to the regulation of sexuality, the uses of sexuality as a political construct, the intersections of sexuality with gender, race, and class, or LGBT politics and mobilizations.

As a leading professional academic organization, APSA plays an important role in its ability to frame and embody good practice in nondiscrimination and wider issues of equality. Those of us who have been around long enough to secure tenured positions and serve in APSA leadership continue to work to make sure the professional path is easier for others. The discrimination faced by scholars in the 1970s, the homophobia that crept into the siting debate, as well as the professional successes such as the establishment of the Sexuality and Politics Section, serve to remind us of the distance traveled and the distance we have yet to go.

In 2013, the U.S. Supreme Court decided two hugely important marriage-equality cases. There were amicus ("friend-of-the-court") briefs filed in those appeals by the American Anthropological Association, the American Psychological Association, the American Sociological Association, the American Studies Association, and the Organization of American Historians, as well as one by 13 political science professors. But nothing from the American Political Science Association.[8] In other words, numerous national professional organizations of academics acknowledged the value of their collective efforts before the Court. But not so for concerned political scientists, who were obliged to file a brief by themselves, without the aid of their own national association, because the APSA itself would not act. (Dan Pinello)

My identity has been a major hindrance within the profession. I "transitioned" while early in grad school. I had no safety net, no job, no money, no protections and no rights. There was some harassment, one or two threats of violence and some overt discrimination (both for staff jobs and academic positions) . . . I have been fairly lucky in getting offers and the conditions in academia are better for LGBT people. I think many scholars in our section and allies have helped to improve the academic environments at their home institutions. Our research is more accepted now. So, it is not all bad and I credit the people in the Caucus and Section for paving the way. (Jami Taylor)

Conclusion

In this piece I have attempted to give voice to those who witnessed, and many who made, LGBT history in this profession. Institutional memory is important and, as Joan Nestle wrote, "we wanted our story to be told by us." Of course it is the prerogative of the author to frame these stories, and I hope I have accomplished this with integrity. In my own experience as graduate representative and later chair of the Caucus, my service on the Status Committee at a time of turmoil, my involvement in the establishment of the Section and, later, as a member of the APSA Council, I have found that the space for LGBT scholars and scholarship within the APSA has grown more welcoming. In the past, homophobia was pervasive in the profession, much as it was in the larger American culture. LGBT political scientists faced significant challenges over the years. It reached a crescendo in the profession at the point of the siting debate, which presented an opportunity for some APSA staff and members to articulate an increasingly politically and culturally unacceptable homophobia. Unfortunately, it was also an opportunity for some to participate in "us and them" and "divide and conquer" politics, stoking what Ange-Marie Hancock labels the "Oppression Olympics"[9]—none of which was helpful for LGBT members or for the profession as a whole. The histories here attest to the complex relationship LGBT scholars have had with APSA. They testify to the importance of speaking truth to power when necessary as well as the need to recognize that relationships and views of staff and other members change over time.

Just as importantly, they speak of accomplishments: getting LGBT scholarship into the conference program, protecting LGBT academics from homophobia, helping APSA establish good-practice policies for the profession, and, more recently, gaining recognition for the Sexuality and Politics Section. The cacophony of voices here, despite collective and individual pain, tells a story of progress within the profession. Progress is often slow, and occasionally not without a fight. But it does happen. From the moment I sat on the floor at Len Hirsch's home listening to more senior scholars give witness to their journeys and as my own unfolded through the years, I have been determined professionally to assume that everyone values equality and, if not, to be comfortable demanding their respect—to meet head on the challenge of living with complexity and to entertain the possibility of change for the better. It is because we stand on the shoulders of our professional ancestors that that we can reach higher.

Appendix A

The Sexuality & Politics Formal Application to APSA

The purpose of the Section is:

- to foster the study of sexuality and politics within the discipline of political science;
- to encourage rigorous but respectful research in the area of sexuality and politics;
- to promote, where appropriate, the interests of political scientists researching sexuality and politics within a larger interdisciplinary and political community.

The objective of the Sexuality & Politics Section is to bring together those currently working in a variety of areas within political science in order to facilitate the sharing of knowledge and to increase the intellectual community and expertise within the APSA. Given the centrality of issues of sexuality to the American political agenda, we believe the APSA has a responsibility to facilitate research and expertise in this area and that the establishment of a Sexuality & Politics Section is essential to such a goal.

There is a growing body of scholarship within the discipline of political science addressing issues of sexuality within a variety of subfields including public policy; local, state and national governance; international relations, elections, public administration and political theory. Moreover, the increasing political attention given to issues of sexuality e.g. citizenship, welfare, rights, health, and construction of identities necessitates the establishment of a forum for professional discussion across the discipline of political science.

To date, this discussion has happened in an ad hoc manner within the LGBT Caucus, an APSA related group, and amongst members across a variety of APSA Sections e.g. Law and Courts; Women and Politics; Elections, Public Opinion and Voting Behaviour; and Human Rights. The research field of sexuality and politics includes a wide range of APSA scholars producing cutting edge research including but not limited to topics addressed by the LGBT Caucus, for example sex education in schools, international sex trade, HIV/Aids as well as same-sex marriage, LGBT voting patterns and citizenship. The proposed Section will bring these scholars together and provide synergy for this research across the APSA. Just as the "Women and Politics Research" Section and the Women's Caucus are distinct entities, the Sexuality & Politics Section will provide fertile ground for a wide variety of intellectual exchange, while the Caucus, as an APSA related group, will continue to address concerns of specific interest to LGBT scholars.

NOTES

1 Joan Nestle, "The Will to Remember." *Feminist Review* 34 (Spring 1990): 86–94.

2 The Committee on the Status of Lesbians, Gays, Bisexuals, and Transgenders (LGBT) in the Profession assesses the status of gay, lesbian, bisexual, and transgender scholars in the profession; advances the research on LGBT issues; develops curriculum materials; and works to ensure tolerance toward LGBT political scientists. Founded in 1987, the Lesbian, Gay, Bisexual, Transgender Caucus (LGBT Caucus) is the principal association of lesbian, bisexual, transgendered, and gay men and women within the American Political Science Association and an important arena for the presentation of research on the interaction of sexual identity, theory, and political behavior. There are currently over two hundred members of the caucus from the United States and Canada, as well as Australia and several nations of the European Union. All academically affiliated social scientists, practitioner political scientists, and graduate students interested in the goals of the caucus are welcome to join.

3 Ken Sherrill: "This resulted in my 1973 APSA paper, 'Leaders in the Gay Activist Movement: the Problem of Finding the Followers.' I would like to thank Michael Lipsky, who organized the panel, for his willingness to include a paper on a topic many would have shunned."

4 Timothy E. Cook, "The Empirical Study of Lesbian, Gay, and Bisexual Politics: Assessing the First Wave of Research." *American Political Science Review* 3 (1993): 679–92.

5 David Rayside and Martha Ackelsberg, "Report on the Status of Lesbians and Gays in the Political Science Profession: Prepared by Committee on the Status of Lesbians and Gays in the Profession of the American Political Science Association." *PS: Political Science & Politics* 28 (1995): 561–74. doi:10.1017/S104909650005798X.

6 APSA section regulations may be found at www.apsanet.org/membership.

7 Angelia R. Wilson and Susan Burgess, "Sexuality and the Body Politic: Thoughts on the Construction of an APSA Sexuality & Politics Section." *PS: Political Science & Politics* 40:2 (2007): 377–81. doi:10.1017/S1049096507070734.

8 The same phenomenon happened in 2015, when the APSA refused to sponsor amicus briefs for *Obergefell v. Hodges*.
9 Ange-Marie Hancock, "Intersectionality as a Normative and Empirical Paradigm." *Politics & Gender* 3:2 (2007): 248–54. doi:10.1017/S1743923X07000062.

REFERENCES

Stories were provided by the following via personal communication on the dates noted.
Anonymous 1, personal communication, July 17, 2015.
Anonymous 2, personal communication, July 30, 2015.
Burack, C., personal communication, July 18, 2015.
Cahill, S., personal communication, September 2015.
Hirsch, H., personal communication, July 16, 2015.
Josephson, J., personal communication, October 5, 2015.
Macciaroni, G., personal communication, July 20, 2015.
Pinello, D., personal communication, July 21, 2015.
Rayside, D., personal communication, October 5, 2015.
Rimmerman, C., personal communication, July 30, 2015.
Sherrill, K., personal communication, July 31, 2015.
Taylor, J., personal communication, July 23, 2015.
Thomas, J., personal communication, July 23, 2015.

10

The Politics of LGBTQ Politics in APSA

A History (and Its) Lesson(s)

MARTHA ACKELSBERG

In the aftermath of the Supreme Court's decision in *Obergefell v. Hodges* (June 26, 2015), it seems especially important to be aware of the complicated history of both *LGBTQ organizing and LGBTQ presence*, and also changes in the acceptance of the *study* of LGBTQ issues—not only within APSA but within the discipline as a whole. In fact, I argue here, that history provides an interesting case study in the politics of institutional change: how might we explain the relative success of a small minority in achieving some significant changes within the Association and the profession? And how might we understand the limits of what has been achieved?

As has been the case with LGBTQ awareness and struggles for rights within the United States more broadly, transformations in some arenas of the discipline have proceeded at an extraordinarily fast pace, while progress in other arenas has been much slower. Since 1987, for example, we have seen the founding and chartering of the Lesbian, Gay, Bisexual (now the Lesbian, Gay, Bisexual, Transgendered) Political Science Caucus, the establishment of a Committee on the Status of Lesbians and Gays (now including Bisexuals and Transgendered) in the Profession, the establishment of an organized section on Sexuality and Politics, and growing numbers of papers and panels on a variety of aspects of LGBTQ politics in both national and regional conference programs. Further, if we compare the results of two surveys of the status of LGBTQ folks in the profession (one undertaken by the original Status Committee in 1993, and published in 1995; and a more recent one undertaken in 2007, and published in 2010), we find considerable progress, in terms of both visibility within the profession and the acceptability of scholarship on LGBTQ issues.

Nevertheless, the picture is not entirely positive. The stories of the founding of the Caucus and of the Status Committee reflect considerable uneasiness around these issues in the profession (including among gays and lesbians), which has not necessarily totally disappeared. More significantly, although the number of "out" gays and lesbians in political science has continued to grow, there is also significant evidence both of continued discrimination against LGBT political scientists within some departments and of continued marginalization of the *study* of LGBT politics within the discipline. Thus, although much has been accomplished, much also remains to be done.

The Situation of Gays, Lesbians, Bisexuals, and the Transgendered within APSA and the Discipline of Political Science

Professor Kenneth Sherrill, the informal "dean" of LGBT studies and activism within APSA, reports that he gave his first paper on gay/lesbian issues at the APSA meetings in New Orleans in 1973, and that he tried to start a caucus in 1975, but without much success (it limped along for a few years and then died out for apparent lack of interest).[1] It's not that there were not gays and lesbians in APSA then—even gays and lesbians attending annual meetings. But, it would seem, those who were present were more than hesitant about identifying themselves, even in a "private" caucus, and apparently did not feel safe putting their names on paper as engaging in research about gay/lesbian issues.[2]

There were papers presented here and there through the late 1970s and into the 1980s, particularly on panels sponsored by the New Political Science Caucus, or by the Women's Caucus. By the mid-1980s, another effort was underway—spearheaded by Mark Blasius, Len Hirsch, Bob Bailey, and Ken Sherrill—to start a gay and lesbian caucus, and this time it "took." The Gay and Lesbian Caucus of the American Political Science Association was officially founded in 1987, and began to serve both as a support group for lesbian, gay, or bisexual political scientists within the Association and as a lobbying organization to press for greater visibility of lesbian and gay political scientists, and for the legitimacy of the study of lesbian and gay issues as "appropriate" to political science. The basic strategy for the latter was to host panels on gay/lesbian politics but also to encourage members to submit papers to other sections and to propose panel cosponsorships.

It cannot be a total coincidence that the LGB Caucus was founded during the same year as ACT-UP, the New York–based AIDS advocacy organization. Largely in response to the AIDS crisis, the late 1980s saw major increases in gay and lesbian activism and advocacy; and more and more people felt both compelled to come out and (ultimately, as a consequence) safer to do so. While it took many years for stigma and fears about the consequences of visibility to diminish—and, of course, the advocacy, itself, was spurred by the horrific toll taken by AIDS on the gay community—the sense of community and empowerment that grew out of AIDS activism was critical both to the greater visibility of gays (and lesbians) in the broader culture and to increasing acceptance. Further, the extraordinarily high mortality rates from AIDS probably generated a sense of obligation to engage; and the activism, itself, may also have contributed to the development of organizing skills in the context of a radical Left that was, otherwise, rather skeptical, if not distrusting, of structured organizing.[3] It seems clear that a similar process was unfolding, both within the profession as a whole and within APSA. More people "signed on" to the LGB Caucus, more papers were delivered at meetings, both regional and national, and courses dealing (either in whole or in part) with LGB issues in politics—particularly around the AIDS crisis—began to be offered in colleges and universities around the country.[4] While progress on getting research articles into political science journals was slower, nevertheless, attention to AIDS and the activism it engendered did begin to be reflected in published research.

But although the LGB Caucus was founded in 1987, it was not until the fall of 1991 that APSA established a Task Force on the Status of Gays and Lesbians in the Profession to "explore the question of establishing a Committee on the Status of Lesbians and Gays in the Profession and to recommend a charge for such a committee should one be established."[5] The following February (1992), the Task Force reported back to the Administrative Committee of APSA, recommending that a committee be established and offering a proposed "charge" to the committee. The Administrative Committee brought the proposal forward to the APSA Council at the Council's April meeting, at which time the Council accepted this recommendation to establish a committee. In September of 1992, *PS* announced the formation of a standing Committee on the Status of Lesbians and Gays in the Profession, which was to begin its work officially on January 1, 1993. The Task Force recommended a fairly broad set of responsibilities for the Status Committee, though its main charge was to "articulat[e] and promot[e] a policy of non-discrimination against and collegiality towards lesbians and gays in the profession of political science." The charge also listed four specific goals toward which (among others) the work of the Committee should be directed:

- Undertake an empirical study of the current status of lesbians and gays in the profession, culminating in a report to the Council and distribution to the membership;
- Explore the need for a senior political scientist with an *ex officio* status on the Committee to serve as a resource for the Committee and as advisor to individual political scientists and departments regarding issues of non-discrimination and collegiality;
- Underscore that research about lesbians and gays in politics should be judged by standards ordinarily used for evaluating scholarship in the discipline;
- Facilitate the distribution of curricular materials on lesbian and gay politics;
- Develop a working relationship with the Committee on Professional Ethics, Rights and Freedoms.[6]

The Report of the Task Force,[7] which provided additional details and a rationale for its recommendations, offers an interesting window into the perceptions of gays and lesbians at the time. For example, the report provided five paragraphs of explanation on what it means to "articulate and promote a policy of non-discrimination against, and collegiality toward, lesbians and gays." It stated that "the ultimate objective is to create an environment in which sexual orientation, expressed or perceived, is not an issue," and went on to suggest that "non-discrimination is the fundamental imperative," directing the new committee to meet with the Committee on Professional Ethics, Rights, and Freedoms to develop a nondiscrimination statement for the profession. Much of the language is somewhat cumbersome, or even defensive, for example: "The Task Force views collegiality as respect for people's reasoned choices, whether the choices are about sexual orientation or about personal and private decisions of whether to disclose one's sexual orientation."[8] There was clearly concern about people being *forced* to come out; and also an assumption that people would not want to be perceived to be gay or lesbian: "[I]t is a matter of fairness not to make presumptions about sexual identity." In fact, the Task Force seems to have suggested that it would be a good idea to have at least one person on the Committee who is "known" to be heterosexual, so as to counter the presumption that anyone who is in any way involved with LGB issues is, perforce, gay, lesbian, or bisexual. The Task Force was concerned about the marginalization of individuals within their departments on the basis of such presumptions. As its report stated, "[T]here is genuine pathos in being *in* a department but not *of* it—of being excluded from all but the strict formalities of academic life. Colleagues work to dignify each other."

The recommendation that received the briefest explanation or rationale in the report was that the Committee study the current status of lesbians and gays in the profession, and report its findings to the Council and to the Association's membership. In fact, the preparation of such a survey, its administration, and then the analysis and reporting of findings were the main business of the Committee (on which I served) during its first years. More on that below.

Extremely revealing—at least in terms of the way the situation of gay and lesbian political scientists was viewed by the Task Force—was its recommendation that the Committee "explore the need for a senior political scientist . . . to serve as a resource for the Committee and as advisor to individual political scientists and departments." This was a recommendation that had no parallel in other APSA status committees. As the Task Force report noted, "[T]he status of lesbians and gays . . . differs in one significant way from that of other groups served by Status Committees—some lesbians and gays wish not to disclose their sexual orientation, and may be reluctant to risk the loss of confidentiality by contacting a committee of five people."[9] Interestingly, the Committee itself, once it was formed,[10] did not take this recommendation very seriously. It was, at the time, composed of a number of "senior political scientists," who were well known and respected within the discipline, and with whom many individuals (at various stages of their careers) had already consulted over the years. The Committee saw no need for a special "ombudsperson" of this sort. Indeed, members felt that the call for creation of such a position reflected a lack of awareness on the part of the Task Force about how informal networks and mentoring were already functioning within the profession.

Equally significant, perhaps, was the Task Force recommendation that one important goal of the Committee was to "underscore that research about lesbians and gays . . . should be judged by standards ordinarily used for evaluating scholarship in the discipline." A number of assumptions and concerns seem to be reflected in this charge. First, the explicitly stated one, was "to dispel any presumption that all research on lesbians and gays in politics is conducted by lesbian or gay scholars, or that lesbian and gay scholars are interested only in lesbian and gay research." Such a concern is, again, related to fears about visibility, or about discrimination against those who are *perceived to be* or *believed to be* gay or lesbian. Also, however, and this assumption was not quite so explicitly stated, the charge suggests that such research was *not* always treated seriously by others in the discipline and, even more, that it was thought to be less academic/scholarly than research on more "traditional" topics. Further, it seems to be addressing a fear, at least on the part of some in the profession, that including scholarship on gay and/or lesbian politics *as* legitimate topics for research would, somehow, undermine the standards of political science. Why else emphasize that it be "judged by standards ordinarily used for evaluating scholarship"? Relatedly, the Task Force suggested that the Committee might want to "assist in recommending reviewers familiar with the field of work which journals could draw upon to review submissions dealing with lesbian and gay politics." Interestingly, when—a few years later—the Committee recommended to Council (in its report on the survey) that someone with expertise in gay and lesbian politics be appointed to the editorial board of the *American Political Science Review*, the recommendation was rejected by the Council. Among the arguments adduced in opposition was that the *Review* could not afford to have "nonworking" members on it (betraying an assumption, of course, that those who work in the field of gay and lesbian politics had no other expertise!) and, in addition, that the appointment of a scholar with expertise in gay and lesbian politics would be the beginning of a "slippery slope": if someone were added with expertise in this field, it would require adding people in any number of others![11]

Findings of the First Survey on the Status of Gays and Lesbians in Political Science

As noted above, the Committee's first major task was the creation, distribution, and analysis of a survey of the Association's members to evaluate the status of LGB members, and of scholarship on LGB issues. Accordingly, the Committee (with significant additional help from colleagues outside the Committee) developed two surveys, one for department chairs and one for members at large. The chair survey was sent out to all chairs along with the Association's annual Departmental Services survey; and the member survey was distributed at the annual meeting in September 1993, and also included in the fall mailing of *PS*. The full report was published in the September 1995 issue of *PS*.[12] I summarize its major findings here.

The report was organized around the theme of visibility/"outness" and its consequences, for a number of reasons. First, as had been noted by a variety of researchers (and activists) at the time, visibility was believed to be key to challenging the "codes of silence that prevent or slow institutional change." In 1993–94, when the report was first being drafted, coming out was on the increase, both in the society at large and within APSA, at least in terms of growth in membership in the LGB Caucus. In addition, more papers and panels on LGB issues were finding their way into the APSA program. Nevertheless, as Verta Taylor and Nicole Raeburn had noted in a report on the status of gays and lesbians in the sociology profession, coming out was still a form of "high-risk activism" that had various dangers associated with it.[13] The Committee, therefore, decided to focus on what the consequences of "coming out" had been in terms of barriers to full participation in the profession. It explored three major areas: (a) experiences or perceptions of discrimination; (b) the acceptability of research/writing on gay or lesbian themes; and (c) curricular change.

There were a number of striking findings. First, compared to the disciplines of history and sociology (according to recent reports for each of those professional associations), political science had relatively lower rates of visibility. Thus, 54 percent of LGB sociologists reported themselves as being out to their chairs (up from just 32 percent in 1982), with roughly the same percentages among historians. Among political scientists, however, only about 40 percent of LGB respondents said they were out to their chairs; and, of all of the departments for which chairs sent back information, only forty-nine of twenty-three hundred full-time faculty members (about 2 percent) were known to their chairs to be lesbian or gay.

More men were out than women (46 percent versus 32 percent), and more tenured than nontenured; but grad students and part-time faculty were out in greater percentages than either. What might have accounted for these figures? For one thing, they were obviously related to perceptions of discrimination and hostile climate—the reality of which certainly came through in the surveys. We were quite shocked by the evidence of homophobia/hostile attitudes on the part of both chairs and members-at-large, who complained about the legitimacy of the questionnaires, the importance of the issues, and the appropriateness of even asking questions about "personal practices." Further, about one-third of LGB respondents said they believed they "certainly" or "probably" had been discriminated against because of sexual orientation, and another 17 percent said they didn't know whether they had. Interestingly, there were significant differences by gender: 41 percent of men, but 26 percent of women said probably or definitely yes—percentages that were similar to those reported in surveys of historians and sociologists. One explanation: it was difficult, if not impossible, for female respondents to know whether they had experienced discrimination on the basis of sex or on the basis of sexual orientation! There were also significant differences, based on sexual orientation, in awareness of discrimination. Thus, 40 percent of LGB respondents said they had experienced or witnessed situations in which the belief that a person was LGB had prejudicially affected personnel decisions or collegial relations, whereas only 10 to 25 percent of heterosexuals responded to this effect (though, consistent with the point above, women were more likely to have perceived discrimination than were men).

There were also some interesting differences in what was considered "acceptable." Thus, both chairs and most members reported that doing research, and publishing, on LGB issues would not be problematic in their department, nor would simply being identified as LGB. However, there was a sharp drop-off in acceptability when it came to being *public* about one's sexual orientation—i.e., doing advocacy work in the community or coming out in the classroom. Not surprisingly, most LGB members reported a significant drop-off in *social inclusion* at the level of their institutions, and, for some, even at the level of their department.

Overall, as the Committee summarized its findings for the Council in April of 1996, while there had been improvements in visibility, in acceptability of research, and in some curricular integration, there was still considerable marginality:

- Reports of discrimination were higher than should be acceptable, and gays and lesbians had markedly different perceptions of its pervasiveness and impacts than did heterosexuals.
- There was still relatively little serious integration of gay/lesbian themes into the curriculum.
- There were severe visibility problems for gays and lesbians of color.

The Council accepted the Committee's report, which included recommendations that APSA promote among its members the adoption of institutional nondiscrimination policies and domestic partner benefits; that it encourage members to attend to issues of social inclusion; that training sessions for new professors include materials on discrimination of various sorts and the ways they have an impact on the classroom; that the major disciplinary journals increase the visibility and availability of people qualified to review submissions on LGB issues; and that the Council promote the Committee's upcoming "curriculum infusion project" to legitimize the study of LGB issues within the profession, and to take fuller advantage of resources that were already available.

Findings of the 2010 Survey on Lesbians, Gays, Bisexuals, and the Transgendered in Political Science

What changed in the roughly fifteen years between these two surveys? Most obviously, the terms of the discussion (and even the name of the Committee) had changed. Whereas the initial committee was titled "Committee on the Status of Lesbians and Gays in the Profession" (although the survey also incorporated some attention to bisexuality), by 2010 the committee had renamed itself the "Committee on the Status of Lesbians, Gays, Bisexuals and the Transgendered in the Profession" and the survey, as well, reflected that change.

Beyond that, the survey results[14] reflected that the growing acceptance and visibility of LGBT persons in the larger society had also had an impact on APSA. For example, over 56 percent of LGBT respondents said that they definitely or probably had *not* experienced discrimination based on their sexual orientation or gender identity (as compared with the 1993 survey, in which close to 50 percent of the respondents said that they definitely or probably *had* experienced such discrimination). Not surprisingly, the percentages of respondents who reported that they had witnessed or experienced discrimination varied with institutional location and points in the academic ladder—with higher percentages at Catholic or evangelical institutions, and somewhat higher percentages in situations of reappointment, tenure, and promotion—but overall, the perception of climate was much improved, as compared to the findings in the 1993 survey. Thus, for example, more than 60 percent of LGBT respondents reported being "out" in their professional lives, though less than a quarter were out to senior administrators. Nevertheless, there were still a number of people (8 percent of the LGBT sample) who believed that their jobs would be in danger if their supervisors or chairs knew of their LGBT status.

LGBT respondents still reported some social marginalization, though at levels considerably lower than in 1993. And the most significant issue for many had to do with the availability of domestic partner benefits. This was particularly an issue for those in states that not only disallowed gay marriage but also specifically *denied* the "incidents of marriage" to those in same-sex relationships. In the aftermath of *Obergefell*, however, at least that issue should mostly disappear.

Another major change from the earlier survey was in the arena of the acceptability of research and teaching on LGBT issues. I will explore this in greater detail below; but note, here, simply that the latter survey found that substantial numbers of political scientists (both LGBT and not) considered it "appropriate" to include materials on LGBT politics in research and teaching, and actually did so. Nevertheless, there were still reports of respondents either being actively discouraged from engaging in research on LGBT topics or choosing, themselves, to avoid them, for fear of the work's not being taken seriously as political science.

Overall, the report concluded that the picture for LGBT members of the profession was "mixed." Both research and teaching about LGBT topics had made some headway (more on this below); but "troubling questions about discrimination both against those who conduct research concerning LGBT issues and LGBT individuals themselves remain."[15] The report called for more attention to sexual orientation and gender identity in the academy in general—e.g., adding questions on orientation and identity to the National Survey of Earned Doctorates—so that patterns of discrimination could be identified and tracked. It suggested a need for further study of how LGBT individuals experience different types of institutions (e.g. conservative, or religiously based), and the impact of individual state marriage laws on benefits and status. It also called attention to the very different situations of LGBT political scientists who live and work *outside* the United States, noting that, for some, local laws normalize and, for others, they create much more complexity and even danger. Finally, it called on future committees to attend more fully to a variety of issues related to gender identity, as well as to sexual orientation.[16]

The Siting Controversy

Another major landmark in the saga of LGBT issues within APSA is the so-called Siting Controversy, which came to a head over the scheduling of the 2012 APSA convention in New Orleans, Louisiana.

In 1990, at the request of the LGBT Caucus, APSA had amended its annual meeting siting policy to include protection for the civil rights of LGBT members. Council voted that APSA should only meet "in cities where all members are welcome." The contract language agreed upon focused on the *behavior of the city*, with particular focus on discrimination in employment, housing, and access to public accommodations. That language read,

> 10.02 APSA has selected [name of city] as a site of its annual meeting in light of the city's anti-discrimination record. APSA reserves the right of termination of this agreement, without penalty or liability, if the government of the city in which the hotel is located establishes or enforces laws that, in the estimation of APSA, abridge the civil rights of any APSA member on the basis of gender, race, color, national origin, sexual orientation, marital status, physical handicap, disability, or religion.[17]

In 2004, the state of Louisiana enacted a constitutional amendment (sometimes referred to as "Super DOMA") that not only banned same-sex marriages in Louisiana but also denied recognition of same-sex marriages performed elsewhere, as well as recognition by the state or any of its entities of any "incidents of marriage" for same-sex couples. In reaction to this, in 2005, the Committee on the Status of Lesbians, Gays, Bisexuals, and the Transgendered in the APSA requested that, consistent with its stated policy, APSA change the annual meeting venue, on the grounds that the law was "denigrating to committed same-sex partners" and "could potentially put them at risk." Meanwhile, others argued that it was important to hold the meetings as scheduled in New Orleans, both to support the city after the disaster wrought by Hurricane Katrina (in 2005) and to use the meeting as an opportunity for broader communal education.

The controversy was extensive, and often extremely bitter, extending over the course of almost four years. Unfortunately, it was frequently presented/experienced as an opposition between "supporting the black community of New Orleans" and "assuring the (legal) safety of LGBT members," a no-win situation if ever there were one. Further, it had the effect of threatening to undermine coalitions and alliances (e.g., among the caucuses and status committees) that had taken years to cultivate and build. After the initial requests (in 2005 and 2007) from the Committee that APSA relocate its 2012 meeting, the APSA Council created a "siting committee" in the spring of 2008 to explore the issue. Meanwhile, some members had privately started a petition campaign, asking individuals to boycott the meetings in 2012, if they were held in New Orleans. In May 2008, on the recommendation of the siting committee to the Council, then president Dianne Pinderhughes requested feedback from the entire membership in response to two proposals on siting. In addition, organized sections and status committees were polled separately. Based on the feedback it received, the Committee submitted its final report and recommendations in June of 2008, and the Council approved a siting policy at that time.[18]

While the debates were extended and complex, I will summarize here the policy outcomes. In effect, the Siting Committee considered three options: (a) retaining the policy as it was (as stated above); (b) instituting a new policy that would ban meetings in any states with a *constitutional* ban on same-sex marriage and its "incidents"; and (c) modifying the existing policy to take account of *state* actions as well as of the efforts of the relevant *city* to create a welcoming environment. The final policy read,

> In locating its future meetings, APSA presumes that states with legal restrictions on rights afforded recognized same-sex unions and partnerships create an unwelcoming environment for our members in cities where we might meet. We would notify authorities at all levels that these conditions make it difficult for us to site our meeting in these states. APSA would closely examine practices on a case by case basis in cities within these states to assess whether demonstrated positive local practices or other Association goals warrant holding our conferences there.[19]

The Committee on the Status of LGBTs in the Profession opposed this decision, but proposed to work with the Council (and the Annual Meeting Committee) and program chairs for the meeting to develop procedures for carrying out the recommendations. Specifically, "to *engage intellectually*: The annual Meeting Program should incorporate scholarly content relevant to matters of concern, such as same-sex policies, socioeconomic inequality, poverty and other matters of consequence to the urban areas where we meet." The Committee requested that space be set aside on the program for panels specifically devoted to siting issues, that a special issue of *PS* be devoted to exploring various dimensions of the siting issue, that information be provided to members in advance of the meeting about putting in place whatever legal protections they might need, and that clear criteria be developed for making siting decisions in the future.[20]

Debates and organizing continued over the ensuing years. The Status Committee and others worked to try to affect the *content* of the meeting so that attention was directed to LGBT issues, so that local activist organizations would be engaged, and so that plenaries would focus on equity issues. Meanwhile, an independently organized effort to boycott the meetings garnered many signatures, and it was clear that attendance would be lower than usual. In the end, yet another hurricane scare precluded the meeting from happening at all.

Now, post-*Windsor* and *Obergefell*, the legal situation for LGBT participants should be less in question. Nevertheless, there will still be local differences with respect to the passage and implementation of nondiscrimination laws, which APSA policy requires be taken into account when sites for the annual meeting are chosen. What this brief history shows, however, is how complex the situation was; and, in fact, how divided the membership (both of APSA in general and of LGBT groups within it) was on how to respond to the New Orleans siting decision. Strong arguments—in favor of boycott and in favor of "constructive/critical engagement"—were made on each side; and the decisions people made did not sort themselves simply into "pro-" or "anti-" LGBT. In some respects, it became a classic example of a serious, and complicated, situation that was, for many, turned into "us" versus "them," in ways that were profoundly disturbing to the Association and to relationships of individuals and groups within it. I don't know whether the tensions have yet healed.

The Status of Research and Teaching on LGBT Topics within Political Science

Even in 1993, there was more general support for *inclusion* of LGB topics as "legitimate" subjects of research, and as appropriate for political science courses, than might have seemed to be the case, given reported levels of anti-LGB discrimination. Yet, here, too, there were significant differences between heterosexual and LGB respondents. For example, 39 percent of heterosexual versus 70 percent of LGB respondents said research on LGB topics was very appropriate for political scientists, 22 percent of LGB respondents reported having been discouraged from doing research, and 39 percent had avoided doing it, for fear of its not being taken as "serious political science" (versus only 3 percent and 5 percent, respectively, for respondents who identified as heterosexual).

Similar perceptions were reflected in a variety of open-ended comments, and in reports of hiring processes. With respect to curriculum, while there was support, in theory, for the integration of topics on LGB politics, very few departments reported courses. Only 1 percent of reporting departments said that they had a graduate-level course, and 3 percent had undergraduate courses with LGB topics as a primary theme. About 6 percent had at least one course at the graduate level with LGB topics as *a* theme within a course; and about one-third had undergraduate courses with LGB topics as *a* theme. Indeed, a variety of articles in *PS* (in 1992 and 1999) sharply criticized the lack of attention to AIDS activism, in particular, whether in the classroom or in political science journals.[21]

This situation had changed *markedly* by the time of the 2007 survey. The 2010 report on that survey indicated that more than half of those who identified as LGBT incorporated LGBT issues into their teaching at least "on occasion," and less than a quarter never did. But nearly 60 percent of heterosexually identified respondents also reported teaching LGBT issues and topics at least on occasion. Further, 72 percent of all respondents replied that it was either "appropriate" or "very appropriate" to have courses on LGBT politics at the undergraduate level; 73 percent said it was "appropriate" or "very appropriate" at the graduate level; and 79 percent said it was either appropriate or very appropriate to integrate topics on LGBT politics into undergraduate courses in general.[22] (This survey did not report data on numbers of courses actually being offered.) There were comparable changes in perceptions of the *appropriateness of research* into LGBT issues and with respect to the percentages of respondents actually *undertaking research* on LGBT-related issues. Overall, 63 percent of respondents said they did not address LGBT topics in their research, but 15 percent did so "extensively or somewhat," and another 22 percent said they did so "a little." Responses about the "appropriateness" of research on LGBT topics varied with rank (peaking at the associate professor level, with over three-quarters of respondents at that level seeing it as either "appropriate" or "very appropriate"),[23] and also by subfield, with respondents in the fields of public law, American politics, and political theory most enthusiastic about inclusion.

Nevertheless, some respondents continued to be concerned that "LGBT politics is not fully accepted as legitimate political science."[24] And data certainly bore out their concerns: a small percentage of respondents evinced clearly hostile attitudes, suggesting that research on LGBT issues by LGBT political scientists is insufficiently objective, or contributes to "voluntary marginalization." Others suggested (harking back to concerns manifest in the original Task Force report) that LGBT scholarship somehow crosses a line between "science and advocacy," one claiming that it "borders on academic fraud."[25] So, although there has clearly been progress, there is still work to be done, both in terms of full inclusion of LGBT members within the profession and in terms of recognition of the validity of scholarship on LGBT issues.

What Could LGBT Scholarship Offer to the Profession?

What might the study of LGBT politics have to offer to what has been, heretofore, a mainstream political science that is still largely heterosexual and heterosexist? What would it mean to move beyond questions of overcoming discrimination (in both attitudes and policies) toward a rethinking of the boundaries and content of political science, itself?

There are, of course, a number of different ways of thinking about what political science is, and what it would mean (on each of these views) to fully incorporate attention to LGBT politics within those frameworks.

(a) According to a behavioral/empirical approach, political science is the study of groups, movements, power, and policy. Lesbian, gay, bisexual and transgendered individuals—and groups—engage in activities designed to influence power and policy, as do the members of other interest groups. Therefore, political science ought to be studying lesbian, gay, bisexual, and transgendered groups in order to get a fuller picture of the U.S. political arena. In a sense, then, this perspective argues that LGBT politics are *just like* the politics of other interest groups; and the study of LGBT groups would, therefore, add to the overall store of data about political life.[26]

(b) A second approach might make a somewhat stronger claim: political scientists should study LGBT politics because it does *not* fit simply or neatly into empiricist/pluralist models of political life in the United States. That is to say, the exploration of LGBT politics might have something *different* to add to our understandings of the workings of politics and power in the United States. For example, one might argue that (along with feminist analyses of political life), attention to the forms, practices, and goals of LGBT politics broadens the definition of issues that are taken *as* political (e.g., questions of personal status, identity, family formation, and the like). Or, attention to the concerns and engagements of LGBT persons could push us to think about issues or policy outcomes that cannot be understood simply through interest-based analyses—for example, what it would mean to have an "identity-based," rather than an interest-based politics.[27] Ultimately, this perspective could result in a challenge to the interest-group model itself.

(c) Finally, and again in a parallel to feminist political analysis, we might argue that the study of LGBT politics is important because it throws into relief not just the limits of the empirical focus of much political science research, but, even more significantly, it points to the limits of some of political science's central categories of analysis. That is to say, the study of LGBT politics can pose explicit challenges to the dominant paradigms of political science, and do so in important ways. First, it brings sharply into view the (hetero-) sexual assumptions underlying many analytical frameworks.

Second, it challenges the distinction between so-called public (that is to say, "politically relevant") and so-called private (assumed to be politically *ir*relevant) that frames so much contemporary political thought and practice. Third, it challenges the distinction between empirical and theoretical work. And finally (and relatedly), a study of LGBT activism can provide valuable case studies to expand our understanding of the range and content of U.S. political life (for example, including movement-based as well as lobbying strategies, confrontation versus assimilation, to name just a few). It could offer some purchase on just which of the "weapons of the weak" are effective, and in what contexts. And a focus on the *social construction of identities and interests* could help us to understand what otherwise appear to be "outlying" policy outcomes.[28]

By Way of a Preliminary Conclusion

In short, as both the 1995 and the 2010 reports on the status of gays, lesbians, bisexuals, and the transgendered in the profession make clear, we have made significant progress in some areas, and somewhat less in others.

The most significant gains in the profession have been achieved—not surprisingly—in tandem with gains in the broader society: in the realms of visibility and acceptance. Much higher percentages of those who identify in "nonnormative" ways are comfortable being out now than was the case twenty years ago. While discrimination has surely not ended, the perception of the *risk or danger* that would be run by coming out (as a graduate student, or before tenure) is, in general, much lower. And reports of experiences of discrimination suggest that those perceptions are accurate: in many institutions, in multiple regions of the country, it *is* more acceptable to be out as lesbian, gay, bisexual, or even (to a lesser extent, perhaps) transgendered than it was even ten years ago. How much this can be attributed to any initiatives undertaken from *within* the profession, as opposed to the impact of broader societal changes *on* the profession is, of course, questionable. But the difference in the day-to-day quality of life for most LGBT political scientists is surely significant.

Probably not coincidentally, the growth in acceptance of LGBT *people* within the profession has run parallel with (or perhaps even been exceeded by) the burgeoning of the field of LGBT and/or queer studies. While it is certainly the case that there remain within the profession (and outside it) those who continue to view the study of LGBT activism/politics as not "real" political science, or as "mere advocacy," it is also the case that the field of queer studies (both in political science and beyond it) is large and growing. It would be difficult to imagine a serious department of political science now that does *not* offer courses that deal with LGBT politics, in whole or in part, and that does not recognize the significance of queer perspectives within, for example, the subfield of political theory. The numbers of articles and books on LGBT topics has grown dramatically; and ever higher numbers of political scientists (both LGBT and not) are including attention to the *politics* of LGBT people within the study of both U.S. and comparative politics.

Within the profession, as well, change is significant, if not always unidirectional. We have come a long way from the days when the Task Force felt it would be important to have a publicly identified *heterosexual* political scientist on the CSLGB, to "protect" vulnerable scholars from presumptions of their homosexuality. Openly LGB scholars have repeatedly been elected to the Council—including some who have been on the nominating committee slate and those whose candidacies were presented by member nominations. And LGB scholars are now commonly asked to serve on the editorial boards of many of our major journals—though the number of *research* articles on LGB topics published in many of those journals remains low.

* * *

What can we learn from this history about the *politics* of change in political science?

For one thing, political science (whether the profession or the Association) is not an island. Political scientists in the United States (where these studies have been focused) are located within academia, with its own particular culture, as well as within the U.S. political context. As social movements pushed for changes in U.S. culture and politics, those changes affected the context of both activism and possibility within APSA. In the early 1970s, even after Stonewall, few (even among self-identified LGB political scientists) took seriously the idea that the *study* of LGB persons/politics could be of particular interest or value. Relatively few were willing to take the risk of coming out, to their families, their departments, or the Association. But the civil rights, feminist, and gay liberation movements of the '60s and '70s, and the crisis of AIDS that followed, changed the landscape—both globally and locally. What had been seen as private/personal challenges took on public, *political* form: the previously subordinated, ashamed, or marginalized began to claim standing, citizenship, a place at the table.[29] The impacts of those changes could not fail to resonate within the profession of political science (despite its relative conservatism within the social sciences more generally).[30]

Second, change within the Association was, and is, cumulative. Each of the various caucuses drew and built on the experiences of those who had gone before, and their individual and collective presence and advocacy changed the Association for all: the Caucus for a New Political Science (1967), National Conference of Black Political Scientists (1969), and Women's Caucus (1969) opened possibilities and manifested modes of organizing and activism that were taken up by the LGB Caucus (1987), Latino Caucus (1998) and Asian Pacific American Caucus (2000).

Third, coalition has been critical. On multiple occasions during those years, representatives of the caucuses (sometimes including representatives from official status committees, as well) met together to propose common panels and/or programming. For the 2000 APSA meeting, for example, Cathy Cohen, program chair of the Race, Ethnicity, and Politics section, Wendy Mink, program chair of the Women and Politics section, and I (then program chair for the Women's Caucus) decided to engage in some program-related direct action to highlight intersectionality, and what the mainstream of the profession could learn from feminist, LGB, and critical race perspectives. We sent out joint calls for papers (coordinating our efforts with CNPS and LGB Caucus); put together a plenary on intersectionality; and also proposed (and had accepted) a "Hyde Park Session" around intersectionality. Around the same time, representatives of all the caucuses and status committees started coordinating efforts to influence the APSA nominating committee to increase the racial/ethnic and gender diversity of the official slate. In the years before Skype and Google Chat, we pressured APSA to host a joint meeting of the Status Committees at the annual meeting (and succeeded—this was a regular feature for a number of years); and we organized conference telephone calls to coordinate nominees from the various caucuses and committees, so that we would not be competing with one another, and our combined recommendations would carry more weight. Over time, those efforts bore fruit: a review of the slates of officers and council members presented over the past twenty years shows evidence of the impact of that organizing, though more work can always be done.[31]

Fourth, institutional change is slow and bumpy. On one hand, one could argue that, given our relatively small numbers, LGBT members of the Association have achieved astounding successes, from the rapid growth of courses on or including LGBT topics to the growing numbers of out political scientists, both in the profession and in the Association (including on its Council), to the increased acceptability of research on LGBT topics as "legitimate," if not central, to political science. As I have suggested, those "successes" have much to do with a changed political climate in the country as a whole, as well as with the effective use of pressure points and coalition building within the Association.

Yet, of course, much remains to be done. And the contours of that work are also related to the larger political climate and the state of LGBT acceptance in the broader society. As many commentators on the *Obergefell* decision argued, the case for a right to marry was won on the basis of the claim that gays and lesbians are, effectively, "just like everyone else." It was, in large part, a reflection of the myriad "coming out" stories told to families, employers, the media, and the Court, that humanized members of a formerly demonized minority. The *publicizing* of the presence of gays and lesbians during the previous thirty to forty years effectively erased much of the stigma, and opened the way toward greater acceptance. Similarly, within APSA and the profession of political science, greater numbers of gays, lesbians, and bisexuals report being out, and being less fearful of experiencing discrimination because of their sexual orientation. Nevertheless, the situation for transgendered people, and for LGBTs of color, remains more complicated—both within the profession and within the larger society. LGBT folk of color remain potential victims of what Cathy Cohen has termed "secondary marginalization," both within communities of color and within the broader society;[32] and transgendered people may well be perceived as an overt *challenge* to, rather than as desirous of assimilating into, more traditional gender roles and norms.

What is perhaps most interesting—and difficult to interpret—is the gap between the broad acknowledgment of the "appropriateness" of studying LGBT people and LGBT politics within political science *courses* and the relative dearth of research articles on LGBT politics in the major journals of the profession (which is also coupled with some continued resistance to the legitimacy of LGBT issues as a focus of political science research). One would think that, if it is acceptable to teach courses on LGBT politics, it should be acceptable, even desirable, to publish articles *on* LGBT politics that could be taught in such courses! At least *some* of this resistance may have to do with the methodological orthodoxy of major journals. To the extent that research focuses on particular patterns of LGBT activism or influence—treating the gay/lesbian/bisexual/ transgendered population as yet another "interest group"—studies of LGBT politics may become normalized, and accepted as legitimate subjects for research and publication. On the other hand, when scholars of LGBT politics *question* those methodologies and approaches (in much the same ways that feminist and critical race scholars have questioned dominant methodologies and epistemologies), they may continue to find themselves "on the outside, looking in," at least in terms of publication in mainstream journals. While we have made some progress in recent decades, the dominance of behavioralist and rational-choice approaches within the discipline can still function to marginalize other methodologies. And, to the extent that the more critical work of LGBT scholars takes dominant paradigms to task, it should not be surprising (though it remains disturbing) that such work will have a harder time finding publication venues.

Not surprisingly, then, this brief survey of the status of LGBT persons and politics within the profession suggests that, while institutional change in APSA has been uneven, the patterns we find provide important clues to larger processes of institutional/social change. The sort of inclusion that has been most successfully achieved builds on relatively traditional strategies of visibility, coalition building, and the exertion of pressure at vulnerable points; and aims to insert individuals (or research topics) into positions that are, in theory, "open to talents." It has also taken advantage of changes in the broader society that have been impelled, at least in part, by strategies of disruption and confrontation.[33] We have been less successful in achieving inclusion in those areas of the profession (and the society) where inclusion would mean a more fundamental challenge to existing structures of power and authority—whether with respect to the fully equal incorporation of transgendered people and LGBT people of color, or with respect to the full acknowledgment of the power and transformative value of LGBT scholarship. It would be nice to think that the politics of LGBTQ politics in APSA are different from those in the society at large; but the evidence of our history suggests that this may be true only to a limited extent.

NOTES

1 Email to author, June 23, 2015.

2 For comparative purposes, it should be noted that the Caucus for a New Political Science was founded in 1967; the National Conference of Black Political Scientists (an independent organization) was founded in 1969; the Women's Caucus for Political Science was founded in 1969 as an advocacy organization within APSA; the Latino Caucus was founded in 1998; and the Asian Pacific American Caucus was founded in 2000.

3 I am indebted to Kenneth Sherrill for these two points. On the complexities of structure and "structurelessness" within the women's movement at the time, see Joreen [Jo Freeman], "The Tyranny of Structurelessness." *Second Wave* 2, 1 (1972), available at struggle.ws/pdfs/tyranny.pdf, downloaded July 11, 2016.

4 Ken Sherrill points out that Steve Sanders—who was instrumental in starting the LGB Caucus at the Midwestern Political Science Association—asked Ken if "he could use my name as well [as his] because he was a grad student and I was a Full." LGB caucuses in the Western and then Southern associations eventually followed (email to author, August 4, 2014). The comment makes clear, once again, the importance not only of mentoring but of a sense of "protection" offered by tenure and status within the association.

5 From the charge to the Task Force, reported in "Association News," in *PS: Political Science and Politics* 25, 3 (Sept. 1992): 588.

6 "Council Establishes Committee on the Status of Lesbians and Gays in the Profession." *PS: Political Science and Politics* 25, 3 (Sept. 1992): 591–92.

7 "Report of the Task Force on the Status of Gays and Lesbians in the Profession." *PS: Political Science and Politics* 25, 3 (Sept. 1992): 592–93.

8 Ibid., p. 592.

9 Ibid., p. 592.

10 The original committee, which held its first meeting in December 1992, was composed of Mark Blasius (CUNY–LaGuardia), Chair; Martha Ackelsberg (Smith College); Shane Phelan (University of New Mexico); Ken Sherrill (Hunter College); and Sarah Slavin (Buffalo State College). Michael Brintnall provided important staff support for the Committee.

11 The situation did change, however, with the appointment of Lee Sigelman as editor of the *Review* (the first issue under his editorship—vol. 96, no. 1—appeared in March 2002). The editorial board he appointed contained a number of individuals who (were known to have) worked on topics related to gay/lesbian/queer politics.

12 Committee on the Status of Lesbians and Gays in the Profession of the American Political Science Association, "Report on the Status of Lesbians and Gays in the Political Science

Profession." *PS: Political Science and Politics* 28, 3 (September 1995): 561–74, downloaded from http://www.jstor.org/stable/420329, June 26, 2015.

13 See Verta Taylor and Nicole Raeburn, "Collective Identity in the Gay and Lesbian Movement: Coming Out as High-Risk Activism." Manuscript, Department of Sociology, Ohio State University, April 30, 1993, p. 3.

14 The report, "Lesbians, Gays, Bisexuals, and the Transgendered in Political Science: Report on a Discipline-Wide Survey," was authored by Julie Novkov and Scott Barclay, and published in *PS: Political Science and Politics* 43, 1 (January 2010): 95–106.

15 Ibid., p. 103.

16 A full statement of the conclusions is found in ibid., on pp. 103–4 of the Committee's report.

17 Catharine Rudder, then executive director of APSA, was very helpful in working with the Caucus and the Council on this matter.

18 APSA Council Committee on Siting, Report to the APSA Council, June 24, 2008, and APSA Policy for Siting the Annual Meeting and Other Conferences, June 26, 2008.

19 APSA Siting Policy, June 26, 2008, p. 5. The document went on to delineate the sort of "evidence" that APSA would use to make such a determination. This included whether or not the city enforces state laws in a manner that creates a clear pattern of discrimination that substantially impedes members from freely participating in the meeting. In turn, examples of evidence of positive local practice include items such as the following:
    (a) adoption of anti-discrimination legislation for its employees;
    (b) presence of equal opportunity legislation;
    (c) opinions of and invitations to APSA of local civil rights and LGBT advocacy organizations;
    (d) recognition of medical power of attorney from city and local hospitals;
    (e) experience of other associations or groups meeting in this locality; or
    (f) other evidence of the local climate in respecting same-sex relationships. (p. 6)

20 Memoranda from Donald B. Rosenthal, Chair, Committee on the Status of Lesbians, Gays, Bisexuals and the Transgendered (LGBT) in the Profession to President Peter J. Katzenstein and others, October 7, 2008, and October 8, 2008, copies in possession of the author

21 See, for example, James D. Slack, "AIDS and the Political Science Classroom." *PS: Political Science and Politics* 25, 1 (March 1992): 78–80; Kenneth S. Sherrill, Carolyn M. Somerville, and Robert W. Bailey, "What Political Science Is Missing by Not Studying AIDS." *PS: Political Science and Politics* 25, 4 (December 1992): 688–92; and Patricia Siplon, "A Brief History of the Political Science of AIDS Activism." *PS: Political Science and Politics* 32, 3 (Sept. 1999): 578–81.

22 Novkov and Barclay, "Lesbians, Gays, Bisexuals, and the Transgendered in the Profession," p. 100, table 10.11.

23 Ibid., p. 101.

24 Ibid., p. 102.

25 Ibid., p. 103.

26 See, for example, Sherrill, Somerville, and Bailey, "What Political Science Is Missing."

27 For an exploration of the differences between identity-based and interest-based politics, and their implications for political science, see Robert W. Bailey, *Gay Politics, Urban Politics: Identity and Economics in the Urban Setting* (New York: Columbia University Press, 1999).

28 A similar presentation of the possibilities and challenges offered by the study of GLBT politics may be found in the 2010 report. See especially pp. 102–3.

29 I explored issues of privacy/publicity and political activism in "Anarchism, Radical Democracy, and Protest: (How) Does Politics Matter Anymore?" Paper prepared for presentation at the 2015 Annual Meeting of the American Political Science Association, San

Francisco, CA, Sept. 4–7. See also Martha Ackelsberg and Mary Lyndon Shanley, "Privacy, Publicity, and Power: A Feminist Rethinking of the Public-Private Distinction," in *Revisioning the Political: Feminist Reconstructions of Traditional Concepts in Western Political Theory*, ed. Nancy Hirschmann and Christine DiStefano (Boulder, CO: Westview, 1996), pp. 213–33; and Carole Pateman, "Feminist Critiques of the Public/Private Dichotomy," pp. 118–40 in *The Disorder of Women* (Stanford, CA: Stanford University Press, 1989).

30 In a variety of studies, anthropology, sociology and, to an extent, history, appear on the more "progressive" end of the spectrum of the social sciences, with political science and economics on the more conservative end. See, for example, Mary Frank Fox, "Women, Science, and Academia: Graduate Education and Careers." *Gender and Society*, 15, 5 (October 2001): 654–66; J. F. Milem and H. S. Astin, "The Changing Composition of the Faculty." *Change* 25, 2 (1993): 21–27; Maresi Nerad, "The Advancement of Women PhDs in Political Science: Defining the Problem." Paper presented to NSF-APSA Workshop on Women's Advancement in Political Science (Washington, DC, March 4–5, 2004); and Taylor and Raeburn, "Collective Identity."

31 The successes of this coalition work made particularly poignant the damage done through the siting controversy. We should have been able to handle this better!

32 *The Boundaries of Blackness: AIDS and the Breakdown of Black Politics* (Chicago: University of Chicago Press, 1999).

33 On the importance/necessity of working both inside and outside institutions, see Mary Fainsod Katzenstein, *Faithful and Fearless: Moving Feminist Protest inside the Church and Military* (Princeton, NJ: Princeton University Press, 1999).

REFERENCES

Ackelsberg, Martha A. 2015. "Anarchism, Radical Democracy, and Protest: (How) Does Politics Matter Anymore?" Paper prepared for presentation at the 2015 Annual Meeting of the American Political Science Association, San Francisco, CA, Sept. 4–7.

Ackelsberg, Martha, and Mary Lyndon Shanley. 1996. "Privacy, Publicity, and Power: A Feminist Rethinking of the Public-Private Distinction." In *Revisioning the Political: Feminist Reconstructions of Traditional Concepts in Western Political Theory*, ed. Nancy Hirschmann and Christine DiStefano. Boulder, CO: Westview, 213–33.

APSA Council Committee on Siting. 2008a, June 24. "Report to the APSA Council." Available at http://www.apsanet.org.

APSA Council Committee on Siting. 2008b, June 26. "APSA Policy for Siting the Annual Meeting and Other Conferences." Available at http://www.apsanet.org.

Bailey, Robert W. 1999. *Gay Politics, Urban Politics: Identity and Economics in the Urban Setting.* New York: Columbia University Press.

Cohen, Cathy J. 1999. *The Boundaries of Blackness: AIDS and the Breakdown of Black Politics.* Chicago: University of Chicago Press.

"Committee on the Status of Lesbians and Gays in the Profession." 1992. In "Association News." *PS: Political Science and Politics* 25.3: 588.

Committee on the Status of Lesbians and Gays in the Profession of the American Political Science Association. 1995. "Report on the Status of Lesbians and Gays in the Political Science Profession." *PS: Political Science and Politics* 28.3: 561–74.

"Council Establishes Committee on the Status of Lesbians and Gays in the Profession." 1992. In "Association News." *PS: Political Science and Politics* 25.3: 591–93.

Fox, Mary Frank. 2001. "Women, Science, and Academia: Graduate Education and Careers." *Gender and Society* 15.5: 654–66.

Joreen [Jo Freeman]. 1972. "The Tyranny of Structurelessness." *Second Wave* 2.1.

Katzenstein, Mary Fainsod. 1999. *Faithful and Fearless: Moving Feminist Protest inside the Church and Military*. Princeton, NJ: Princeton University Press.

Milem, J. F., and H. S. Astin. 1993. "The Changing Composition of the Faculty." *Change* 25.2: 21–27.

Nerad, Maresi. 2004. "The Advancement of Women PhDs in Political Science: Defining the Problem." Paper presented to NSF-APSA Workshop on Women's Advancement in Political Science, Washington, DC, March 4–5.

Novkov, Julie, and Scott Barclay. 2010. "Lesbians, Gays, Bisexuals, and the Transgendered in Political Science: Report on a Discipline-Wide Survey." *PS: Political Science and Politics* 43.1: 95–106.

Pateman, Carole. 1989. "Feminist Critiques of the Public/Private Dichotomy." In *The Disorder of Women*. Stanford, CA: Stanford University Press, 118–40.

"Report of the Task Force on the Status of Gays and Lesbians in the Profession." 1992. *PS: Political Science and Politics* 25.3: 592–93.

Rosenthal, Donald B., Chair of the Committee on the Status of Lesbians, Gays, Bisexuals, and the Transgendered (LGBT) in the Profession. 2008a. Memorandum to President Peter J. Katzenstein, Executive Director Michael Brintnall, et al., "Followup to New Siting Policy I," Oct. 7. Typescript, 3 pp.

Rosenthal, Donald B., Chair of the Committee on the Status of Lesbians, Gays, Bisexuals, and the Transgendered (LGBT) in the Profession. 2008b. Memorandum to President Peter J. Katzenstein and Executive Director Michael Brintnall. "New Siting Policy II," Oct. 8. Typescript, 5 pp.

Sherrill, Kenneth. 2014. Email to author, Aug. 4.

Sherill, Kenneth. 2015. Email to author, June 23.

Sherrill, Kenneth S., Carolyn M. Somerville, and Robert W. Bailey. 1992. "What Political Science Is Missing by Not Studying AIDS." *PS: Political Science and Politics* 25.4: 688–92.

Siplon, Patricia. 1999. "A Brief History of the Political Science of AIDS Activism." *PS: Political Science and Politics* 32.3: 578–81.

Slack, James D. 1992. "AIDS and the Political Science Classroom." *PS: Political Science and Politics* 25.1: 78–80.

Taylor, Verta, and Nicole Raeburn. 1993. "Collective Identity in the Gay and Lesbian Movement: Coming Out as High-Risk Activism." Manuscript, Department of Sociology, Ohio State University, April 30.

11

Power, Politics, and Difference in the American Political Science Association

An Intersectional Analysis of the New Orleans Siting Controversy

SUSAN BURGESS AND ANNA SAMPAIO

One of the most politically complex and engaging processes within the American Political Science Association's (APSA) history focused on the siting of its conferences in cities and states that discriminate against marginalized populations across a range of issues, particularly sexuality, race, gender, and national origin. This controversy came to a head during APSA Council (governing board) meetings between 2007 and 2008 after the state of Louisiana passed a law banning same-sex marriages and any "legal incidents thereof," one of the most restrictive laws in the nation at that time, sometimes called a super-DOMA (Defense of Marriage Act). Louisiana adopted this law two years after APSA had signed a contract agreeing to hold its annual meeting in the city of New Orleans in 2012. The question of how to respond to the restrictive state laws in a manner that would balance protection against discrimination for thousands of members within the APSA policy guidelines dominated its Council debates and meetings for almost two years. In this chapter we argue that this controversy elicited unprecedented political expression and engagement, resulting in distinct political positions grounded in three major frameworks: neutrality, interest-group politics, and intersectionality.

We argue that the intersectional framework offers the best analysis of enduring modes of subordination and discrimination experienced by members from historically oppressed and marginalized groups, revealing the way that multiple hierarchies of inequality were operating in tandem to create challenges unanticipated and unaddressed by previous APSA actions that had treated these groups as discrete populations. Moving beyond neutrality and single-issue interest-group politics, an intersectional understanding of the siting controversy draws attention to intervening contexts that exacerbated long-standing forms of inequality. These included differences in state and local laws and their implementation, variations in federal support and interaction with local officials, and unique environmental effects such as the devastating hurricane that struck New Orleans in 2005, leaving long-term political and economic damage. This chapter revisits the siting controversy, offering an intersectional interpretation of its central processes and events to the end of understanding the complex politics at play in the New Orleans decision and of promoting the use of this mode of analysis going forward within the politics of the Association and in the profession at large.

Background and Context

APSA administers many programs and provides a variety of services to its members who attend the meeting, numbering over seven thousand at the time of the siting controversy. The annual meeting is its most visible event and it produces significant revenue for the Association. There are a limited number of cities in North America that have facilities large enough to accommodate the size of the membership. Sites are chosen carefully to ensure robust attendance and to reflect the various regional affiliations of APSA members. Moreover, contracts with host cities and hotels are typically signed five to seven years in advance of the conference to keep reservation costs as low as possible and to ensure availability. Thus, the stakes are high for the Association even in years without overt political contestation. Michael Brintnall, the executive director of APSA at the time of the New Orleans controversy, described it as "an especially demanding and complex consideration of policy regarding siting of its meetings with respect to state laws that restrict rights for same-sex families recognized in other states."[1]

The dialogue on siting began a new chapter in 2005 when the Status Committee on Lesbians, Gays, Bisexuals, and Transgenders formally requested that APSA not hold meetings in states that had passed constitutional bans on same-sex marriage. The issue brought together questions about the status of various members in the Association, the protections afforded marginalized members and their families, and the allocation of the considerable resources attached to APSA's annual conference. When the issue arose in the Council in 2005, it reflected a longer conversation among members of the LGBT Status Committee, and was connected to a dialogue around member status that had led to earlier policy changes in the Association in the 1980s and 1990s. In particular, the request from the LGBT Status Committee made reference to a 1990 APSA policy protecting members from discrimination in host cities and reserving the right to terminate a contract in the event that the city established or enforced laws that "abridge the civil rights of any APSA member on the basis of gender, race, color, national origin, sexual orientation, marital status, physical handicap, disability, or religion."[2] The Committee also referenced a surge of hostile and restrictive state and local laws aimed at LGBT communities and individuals that had followed the initial passage of the 1990 policy.[3]

In response to the request, the APSA Council named an Annual Meeting Review Committee in 2005, chaired by Professor Joan C. Tronto, to explore this issue, among others. The Review Committee reported to the Council in August 2007, recommending that "APSA should continue its current practice which permits us to terminate an agreement that abridges the civil rights of APSA members" based on the policies at the city, not the state, level. The recommendation simultaneously took stock of and conveyed support for the LGBT Status Committee request, urging the Council to recognize the discrimination and vulnerabilities that were at issue.

This distinction between city- and state-level forms of discrimination became increasingly important because hostile and restrictive laws aimed at LGBT people were proliferating most notably at the state level, as, for example, in the constitutional amendment adopted by Louisiana voters in 2004. In that amendment, Louisiana effectively banned both same-sex marriage and any "legal incidents thereof," creating a host of additional exclusions and burdens on LGBT members and their families who would be visiting the state to attend the annual meeting. The language of the law threatened to nullify civil unions and marriages among same-sex individuals that were authorized in other states while such couples were in Louisiana, jeopardizing medical and parental rights, thereby impeding members and their families from safely attending annual meetings in cities such as New Orleans.

APSA had signed a contract with Marriott and Sheraton Hotels to host the annual APSA meeting of approximately seven thousand members in the city of New Orleans, Louisiana, in 2003—a year before voters in the state of Louisiana adopted the restrictive constitutional amendment. Woven within this issue about siting in New Orleans were additional questions about intersectionality and marginalization. Unlike several other host cities that have hosted APSA meetings, New Orleans was a majority-minority city as well as a focal point of African American culture and politics in the United States. It had long been an important location for struggles surrounding race and ethnicity, civil rights, and especially Black political empowerment and incorporation. The demographic make-up of the city included a well-established Black population and the city was also home to large numbers of Asian American and Latinas/os, marking it as one of the truly multicultural, multi-ethnic, and multiracial cities of the United States. The extensive convention facilities available there made it one of the few cities located in the South eligible to host an event as large as the APSA annual meeting, a significant factor for members of the region who had been deterred by financial costs from traveling to host cities that tended to privilege members on the coasts, particularly Boston, Philadelphia, San Francisco, and Washington, DC.

In August 2005, New Orleans was hit by a category 3 hurricane, causing one of the most catastrophic natural and engineering disasters in U.S. history. Damage from the hurricane and subsequent flooding in the city was disproportionately borne by the city's poor and minority neighborhoods, causing significant death, displacement, health challenges, and long-term economic dislocation and political vulnerability for those residents. While the contract with New Orleans had been signed long before Hurricane Katrina touched down, some members came to see siting the meeting in New Orleans as a way for APSA to contribute to the effort to recuperate and redevelop the city by drawing tourists back, creating a base for new forms of employment.

In fall 2007, Daniel Pinello, former chair of the LGBT Status Committee, began circulating a petition calling for members to boycott APSA's 2012 annual meeting in New Orleans due to the discriminatory and restrictive language in Louisiana's 2004 constitutional amendment. Discussion of the boycott became a focal point for dialogues around intersecting modes of subordination prompted by race, sexuality, ethnicity, and class, igniting debates on the proper role of APSA and its members. The debate brought members of the Black, Latina/o, Women's, and LGBT status committees as well as affiliated groups and individuals into unprecedented and sometimes heated exchanges about status and privilege. Diane Pinderhughes, the first woman of color to serve as the president of APSA, presided over the actions of the Association in the midst of these complex manifestations of difference and intersectionality.

As the controversy over siting in New Orleans became animated by larger questions of access and protection from discrimination within the APSA meetings, President Pinderhughes convened an ad hoc Council Committee on Siting in December 2007. The committee was charged with reviewing the New Orleans siting decision and proposed boycott in light of APSA's existing policy and contracts, and was asked to consider whether APSA should revise its policy to account for proliferating forms of discrimination occurring at the state level. It was here that we entered the debate both practically and conceptually. Practically, we were both named to the ad hoc subcommittee (Anna Sampaio served as chair along with Susan Burgess, Harry Hirsch—who subsequently resigned from the Committee—and Dennis Thompson). Pinderhughes later designated Valerie Martinez-Ebers as liaison from the Administrative Committee (the APSA Council's Executive Committee, responsible for constructing Council agendas in consultation with the executive director, Michael Brintnall of APSA). We both had extensive organizing and professional work histories within Latina/o, LGBTQ, Race/Ethnicity and Politics, and Women's groups. Conceptually, the issues facing APSA were dialogues that surrounded and imbued our own research and professional lives—dialogues that challenged the framing and exclusion of marginalized peoples in politics within and beyond the Association. Our work on the committee reflected a set of shared goals and experiences that cultivated mutual trust and confidence in each other, reflecting years of prior organizing in the Association. We believe that these shared experiences served as an important basis for formulating a more complex policy that reflected our commitments to intersectional political analysis.

Three Political Frameworks

Two proposals and a default position regarding city and state siting policy emerged from extended dialogue inside and outside the committee, while the specific question of holding the meeting in New Orleans was handled separately. Proposal 1 emerged from extensive deliberations between APSA staff, members of the Council, and the ad hoc committee. It recognized the discrimination imposed by state-level restrictions on same-sex members and their families, while proposing to "closely examine practices on a case by case basis in cities within these states to assess whether demonstrated positive local practices or other Association goals warrant holding conferences there." Proposal 2, submitted by Council members Wendy Brown and Harry Hirsch (who had earlier resigned his position on the ad hoc committee), stated, "APSA will not hold conferences in any state that, by law, severely restricts the recognition of domestic relationships legally recognized in other jurisdictions." A third, default position eventually emerged through discussion that became known as the "do nothing position," as it maintained that APSA should keep its current siting policy and contracts in New Orleans rather than alter its practices and policies with respect to discrimination.

It is worth noting that the form of discussion and dialogue around the siting issue was in many respects as unique as the content and outcome. Following a regularly scheduled APSA Council meeting in April 2008, the Council took the unparalleled step of passing a resolution calling for extensive feedback and deliberation from all members of the Association and especially the APSA status committees and organized sections on the two proposals outlined above, along with supporting documentation (e.g., a report from the Committee on the Status of Blacks in the Profession presented at the April Council meeting).

APSA posted these materials on a website accessible to members through a password-protected login. Members were notified of the issue and the feedback process via broadcast email message from President Pinderhughes and were asked to log in to view the materials and submit their responses within thirty days. All responses were confidential, and even in instances where an individual (or collection of individuals) chose to self-identify, the responses were culled and identifying information was removed by APSA staff. During the same period, APSA staff and the members of the Ad Hoc Siting Committee also reached out to status committees and organized sections inviting feedback. Following protocol for committee and section reports, the feedback from the status committees and organized sections was not anonymous.

The response was overwhelming and unprecedented. In an association where complex policy issues often go unnoticed by the preponderance of members and where business meetings have at times struggled to reach quorum, the siting issue generated over 850 comments from members as well as reports from the Black,

LGBT, and Asian Pacific American status committees, the organized sections on Urban Politics; Comparative Politics; Political Science Education; Federalism and Intergovernmental Relations; Human Rights; Information Technology and Politics; Politics, Literature, and Film; Race, Ethnicity, and Politics; Science, Technology, and Environmental Politics; Women and Politics; New Political Science; Sexuality and Politics; Foreign Policy; and Foundations of Political Theory and Political Psychology. Responses were also received from fifteen past APSA presidents.

All of these responses were read, reviewed, and processed by the Ad Hoc Siting Committee, with the three most common responses outlined below as the "do nothing" responses (the most common), support for Proposal 1 or support for Proposal 2. What we have never shared publicly before now is that among those 850 responses was a glaring number of vitriolic and hateful remarks aimed at LGBT members, racial and gendered minorities, and the respective sections and committees representing these populations. While we anticipated receiving some hateful remarks, having already experienced a bit of this through informal exchanges and emails with colleagues, the volume and intensity of racism, sexism, heterosexism, homophobia, and undaunted privileged unleashed through those messages was alarming and excruciating to process. The very presence and intensity of these responses further underscored the significance of what was happening and, more importantly, pointed to the fact that there was a clear challenge produced through the debates on siting that struck at the heart of white male privilege that had long been protected by the Association.

Advocates of doing nothing held that APSA had never taken political positions on issues pertaining to siting or other administrative matters and that it should not begin to do so now. These members believed that the Association should remain neutral, above the political fray, suggesting that involvement in larger political contexts outside the Association was neither necessary nor prudent given the wide range of political views across the membership. They argued that if some members did not wish to attend the annual meeting in New Orleans, they could opt out, but that choice should be made at the personal level, without involvement from the Association. Given the looming boycott, this position threatened to significantly decrease attendance at the annual meeting, diminishing a key revenue source of the Association. In our view, its assertion of political neutrality was fundamentally flawed due to the fact that APSA regularly makes political decisions, creating a wide array of policies that necessarily advantage some groups and disadvantage others. Attempting to distance the Association from politics seemed ironic given that the Association's very reason for being is the study of politics. We feared that if neutrality were accepted, it would reinforce the political status quo, fostering a fundamentally conservative decision to continue to advantage groups that had long been dominant in the Association, which the recent call for membership feedback had revealed to be supported, at least in part, by alarmingly discriminatory and hateful beliefs.

Grounded in a single-issue interest-group model of politics, Proposal 2 challenged the idea that the Association had ever been politically neutral. Its advocates argued that APSA had moved the annual meeting out of cities to avoid discrimination in the past, citing the Association's then relatively recent decision to move its annual meeting from San Francisco to Philadelphia when labor disputes arose at the conference hotel, a decision that incurred significant costs due to broken contracts. Given this history, members adhering to this position argued that it was both fair and reasonable to expect APSA to adopt a similar stance by moving the annual meeting out of New Orleans due to Louisiana's draconian anti-same-sex-marriage constitutional amendment. Noting that the Association had already shown itself willing to take political positions and to protect targeted groups such as workers from discrimination, they argued that APSA should be willing to do so again, this time to protect LGBT members. While this view was more compelling to us than the political-neutrality approach, we nonetheless found it limited because it forwarded a single-issue interest-group model of politics that contained great potential to divide various groups who had a stake in the siting controversy, including racial and ethnic minorities who were concerned about revitalizing New Orleans after Katrina. However indirectly, the pluralist pull and tug that underlay Proposal 2 had already exacerbated profound disagreement among these groups and seemed likely to continue to do so. We feared it might allow more conservative forces in the Association to divide and conquer the already tenuous coalition of left-leaning liberals, progressives, and radicals.

Thus, although there were important differences between the two major positions, in our view both were grounded in political frameworks with serious limitations, producing great potential to leave the Association mired in status quo politics. Our proposal, referenced as Proposal 1 above, aimed to move the debate beyond both neutrality and single-issue interest-group politics, fostering a more complex, intersectional analysis that would challenge the way that political power had long been understood and distributed in the Association. We wanted to muddy the waters in a way that would produce a discussion that was mindful of the multiple manifestations of subordination and power that are embodied in groups marked by sexuality, gender, race, and class in the membership, while also attending to the effects of location and extreme weather conditions on these groups. By challenging the framing and process of the issue, we hoped that such an engagement would move the Council and the Association beyond thinking about siting as a clearly definable problem with a simple solution based in neutrality or single-issue politics, producing instead an overtly political siting policy that would address subordination and power in all its complexity. In offering an intersectional analysis of the siting controversy, we do not mean to suggest that none of the supporters of the boycott were critical scholars or that all those who opposed the boycott were. Rather, our goal is to explore how our understanding and experience with intersectional politics informed our efforts to foster a more critical politics in APSA.

Siting Politics as Intersectionality

While the intersectional dialogue engaged the Council and membership in far more complex, dynamic, and even painful conversations around race, gender, sexuality, class, and marginalization in the Association, several principles guided this dialogue. First and foremost was the acknowledgment (both explicit and implicit) that the issue of siting involved competing interests and experiences of marginalization that had value and deserved to be included in the dialogue, even if it wasn't always clear how to do that. This was in stark contrast to the zero-sum politics that often pervaded the Association or the presumption that only a small cadre of seasoned and battle-tested interest groups had legitimacy and deserved a place at the table. It also actively resisted tendencies toward a "hierarchy of injustice" that prioritized some injustices as more pressing or damaging than others while eschewing a false sense of inclusion that demanded every criticism, complaint, or experience hold equal weight. Instead, the work acknowledged that multiple forms of discrimination would be effected by whatever proposal was chosen, and rather than prioritize one interest group over another, we sought to advance a process and dialogue that allowed for multiple forms of marginalization to be attended to while also engaging local and regional differences in specific siting locations.

One example where this expansive and intersectional approach came into play was in the recognition that several state laws and amendments existed across the country creating discriminatory exclusions aimed at racial and ethnic minorities—laws that sometimes existed in conjunction with restrictive same-sex laws but in some cases did not. In particular, at the same time states such as Louisiana were engaging in campaigns to encumber and exclude LGBT populations, parallel campaigns targeted immigrants—especially undocumented immigrants and individuals or organizations that aided, transported, shielded, or supported them. The proliferation of these anti-immigrant laws and policies disproportionately jeopardized Latina/o and Asian American families where incidences of mixed status are high. Siting the conference in a city or state that provided protections to same-sex partners without also taking into account these parallel forms of exclusion and discrimination could easily result in an entirely new barrier for minorities in the membership, even as protections for same-sex partners were secured.

Underlying this commitment to intersectionality was a context of mutual trust, confidence, and solidarity that facilitated the conversation and work. To be clear, this trust was not shared across all members of the Council, but for both of us, and for a handful of additional council members and APSA staff, the experiences we shared working for years in prior collaborations advancing justice around race, ethnicity, sexuality, gender, and class within the Association enabled a common vocabulary as well as confidence in each other that enabled the group to work through even strong disagreements. This sense of trust and solidarity shared between us is uncommon in the Association. Far more common is the pervasive tendency toward competition, rivalry, suspicion, and jealousy, all of which were evident in the Council and at varying times in the debates and responses. But the ability to hold these sentiments at bay and to work in solidarity was a key quality enabling intersectional dialogue and a more nuanced conclusion.

In addition to dealing with multiple and overlapping dimensions of subordination, the intersectional dialogue at work in the siting issue also engaged multiple levels of government and political organization, as demonstrated in the debates about the proper focus of analysis (city-level ordinances versus state laws and amendments). At this level, the ad hoc siting committee was also called to balance the inequalities around siting in Louisiana with the long-standing support within the City of New Orleans for protections from discrimination, including harm aimed at LGBT people. For example, chapter 2, section 2 of the Home Rule Charter of the City of New Orleans stipulated,

> No law shall deprive any person of any rights, privilege, or immunities secured by the Constitution of the United States or the State of Louisiana, nor shall any law discriminate against any person because of race, color, religion, or national origin. No law shall arbitrarily and capriciously or unreasonably discriminate against a person because of birth, disability, age, sex, sexual orientation, culture, language, social origin or political affiliation.
>
> It shall be unlawful and prohibited discrimination under this Chapter to discriminate against any person on the basis of his or her gender identification if said discrimination would be prohibited by this chapter when and if the act or commission that constitutes the discrimination were directed at or adversely affected a person on the basis of his or her sexual orientation. All prohibitions, defenses, remedies, procedures and privileges established or recognized by this Code, and applicable to discrimination on the basis of sexual orientation shall also apply to discrimination based on gender identification.

These protections at the city level went far beyond those of most municipalities, particularly other annual meeting host cities, and were interpreted by the city and its lawyers to provide protection against even restrictive state action on visitors. Moreover, since 1997 the City of New Orleans had extended domestic-partner benefits to same-sex partners of city employees, had maintained a registry of domestic partners since 1999, and had one of the most expansive municipal agencies in charge of enforcing the city's human rights laws. In addition, nonprofit and nongovernmental agencies working within the New Orleans LGBT community as well as the annual Southern Decadence celebration had reached out to the APSA Council in the midst of the siting deliberations, asking the Association to not avoid the city and offering to find ways to work with them and other advocates to push for change.

These factors all had to be balanced within a larger policy framework that governed APSA work and especially the meetings—policies that not only impacted individual members and sections but also affected multiple partner participants, including publishers, vendors, and political science departments in the United States and abroad. Thus, changes to the specific siting policy also had to consider rotation of meeting in locations that provide regional access to members; offer urban settings with national airport access; keep costs as low as possible; preference hotels that are unionized and/or have unionized service providers; assure accessibility to facilities, including ADA compliance; and preference working with minority contractors "wherever circumstances allow." Finally, while it was never the driving factor in our dialogue, given the Council's fiduciary responsibilities for the Association, the ad hoc committee also had to consider the financial implications involved in siting that included the potential liabilities for canceling in New Orleans, the long-term effects of such a cancellation on future contracting with hotels, the potential loss of attendance and revenue if APSA remained in New Orleans during the boycott, and the risk of successfully locating an alternative site so quickly. Internal estimates suggested that canceling the meeting in NOLA would accrue more than $1,618,972 in liability costs alone, not including the potential loss of revenue from the meeting attendance itself.[4]

In this way the dialogue on intersectionality mirrored what Leslie McCall refers to as a form of "intercategorical complexity," namely, "relationships of inequality among social groups and changing configurations of inequality along multiple and conflicting dimensions."[5] In the context of the siting issue and New Orleans specifically, this intercategorical complexity reflected the engagement between individuals and organizations struggling to be heard, with the Association and multiple forms of inequality and relief emanating from competing levels of government and political organization, all colliding with the exacerbating effects of Hurricane Katrina. The resulting recommendation from the ad hoc committee attempted to keep these levels of complexity working together and attending to the differences inherent in the intersectional dialogue.

Thus, what came from the intersectional dialogue described above was a recommendation for the Council to adopt Proposal 1 as the basic policy framework for siting future conferences both within the annual APSA meetings and within the APSA Teaching and Learning Conferences. Proposal 1 stated,

> In locating its meetings, APSA would presume that states with Constitutional restrictions on rights afforded recognized same-sex unions and partnerships

may create an unwelcoming environment for our members in cities where we might meet. We would notify authorities at all levels that these conditions make it difficult for us to site our meeting in these states. APSA would closely examine practices on a case by case basis in cities within these states to assess whether demonstrated positive local practices or other Association goals warrant holding our conferences there.

Through the intersectional lens we articulated above and the central need to balance protections for multiple modes of subordination, it became apparent that the exclusive focus on city-level conditions was insufficient and that issues affecting minority groups were also ensconced in decisions made at the local, county, and state levels and any new policy needed to account for that complexity. The idea that APSA could or should stay out of this debate and maintain the "status quo" was unsupportable if the Association wanted to see itself as advancing academic freedom, ensuring the well-being of scholars, and convening open meetings accessible to all members. Even for policy to "stay the same" in protecting the civil rights of its members (as the preponderance of responses to the member survey advocated), the Association would have to broaden its lens and examine how state-level policies could shape the city's ability to guarantee the health, safety, and freedom of expression of attendees wishing to participate fully in the scholarly exchange of ideas—APSA's core mission. However, "staying the same" was never our goal. Thus, in addition to adopting a state-level analysis as reflected in Proposal 1, we advanced a policy solution that also took stock of differences at the city level that might mitigate or otherwise impact restrictive state laws. Thus the policy compelled APSA to consider whether the city in question would enforce restrictive state laws in a manner that would create a clear pattern of discrimination and substantially impede members from freely participating in its annual meeting.

More importantly, the new policy encouraged the Association and its members to engage local political issues in the siting location on a deeper level, through active dialogue with local and state officials who assert values of nondiscrimination, and to speak out as a national body on the difficulties that legal restrictions in specific locations could pose for the rights of same-sex partners and families in the Association. Such engagement would encompass dialogue with local and state actors while also promoting and disseminating scholarly resources related to inequality. In effect, this engagement would call APSA and its members to become students of the political contexts of each conference site, while also making use of the scholarly strengths within the Association to deepen and extend analyses of inequality.

Thus, the Committee recommended the adoption of Proposal 1—shifting from an exclusive focus on city-level restrictions to also scrutinizing state-level action with a particular eye to restrictions aimed at same-sex partners and unions. At the same time, the Committee recommended that the Association maintain its contract in New Orleans and host its 2012 annual meeting in the city, cognizant of its history in acting against barriers to discrimination on the basis of sexual discrimination—a history that persisted even following the passage of Louisiana's stringent anti-same-sex-marriage constitutional amendment. Moreover, we reaffirmed our commitment to support the redevelopment of New Orleans as an important site for racial empowerment, cognizant of the heavy and disproportionate impact that Katrina had had on the racial and economic minorities of the region. Finally, the committee recommended that APSA siting policy

> be further modified to call for enhanced engagement with host cities on state and local issues of importance to APSA, including restrictions on rights for same-sex unions and the economic development of meeting cities; and that APSA policy call for the Association to promote the advancement of scholarship and enhancement of intellectual engagement among members at the annual meeting on questions of inequality that may arise in relation to the siting of the annual meeting.[6]

We also recommended that in the implementation of these policy changes, APSA approach the meeting in New Orleans with sensitivity to the needs of all members and respect for those who opted not to attend for political reasons, suggesting that the Association promote enhanced intellectual engagement among APSA members and the broader community in host cities and states on questions of inequality related to siting, including but not restricted to special sessions, additional panels, and journal articles.

Conclusion

Proposal 1 was designed to foster a direct discussion of the hierarchies of difference and power within the Association, as well as the embodied difference that members bring with them to the annual meeting. In our view, the siting controversy was only one of many possible issues through which such hierarchies of difference might be both expressed and negotiated within the Association. We hoped to dislodge the well-worn discussion about whether the Association should (or should not) be political, instead intervening into the realities of that power in a complicated and productive manner grounded in an intersectional understanding and practice of politics. The issue of siting the annual meeting in New Orleans brought the politics of race, ethnicity, class, and sexuality directly to the fore of the Association, presenting an important opportunity to offer an intersectional analysis and practice that would represent the interests of these typically subordinated groups more effectively than is usually the case in APSA. Guided by intersectional assumptions and desires, Proposal 1 offered a new, more overtly political policy that would be attentive to all the interests that had long been marginalized in the Association.

Proposal 1 was approved at a special one-day meeting of the Council convened in Chicago during the summer of 2008 to address the New Orleans siting controversy, following an intersectional and intercategorical discussion that addressed a variety of different political interests and perspectives. Nonetheless, the drive to boycott the 2012 meeting in New Orleans continued, and many members planned not to attend it. In the end, Hurricane Isaac forced the Association to cancel the meeting, an unexpected conclusion to the long struggle over the siting of the meeting in New Orleans that perhaps highlighted the unpredictability associated with the entire process of reconstituting APSA's siting policy. Despite this unexpected conclusion, the years of intense political discussion and activism that preceded and followed what could be called a constitutional-level change has mattered a great deal in the Association, even though much of the possibility of the new policy has yet to be realized in full. In the years following the passage of the policy, the drive to actively engage the politics that define every meeting site has faded somewhat into the background, papered over by a return to the everyday business of the Association. However, the fact that the policy was passed means that it remains available as a reference point for members and groups who wish to continue to forward the project of centrally defining the annual APSA meeting as a place of active intersectional political engagement, rather than capitulating to passive scientific neutrality or narrowly based interest-group plurality politics. We anticipate that a new pointed political controversy will arise in the Association before too long that once again foregrounds the always present, but sometimes ignored, hierarchies of difference, inequality, and power that lie at the heart of the American Political Science Association.

NOTES

1   Michael Brintnall, "APSA's Executive Director's Report, 2008." *PS: Political Science and Politics* 41, no. 4: 933.

2   The policy is captured in the following language that APSA routinely includes in its hotel contracts:

> APSA has selected [name of city] as a site of its annual meeting in light of the city's anti-discrimination record. APSA reserves the right of termination of this agreement, without penalty or liability, if the government of the city in which the hotel is located establishes or enforces laws that, in the estimation of APSA, abridge the civil rights of any APS member on the basis of gender, race, color, national origin, sexual orientation, marital status, physical handicap, disability, or religion.

3   Article 7 Section 15 of the Louisiana State Constitution: Defense of Marriage:

> Marriage in the state of Louisiana shall consist only of the union of one man and one woman. No official or court of the state of Louisiana shall construe this constitution or any state law to require that marriage or the legal incidents thereof be conferred upon any member of a union other than the union of one

man and one woman. A legal status identical and substantially similar to that of marriage for unmarried individuals shall not be valid or recognized. No official or court of the state of Louisiana shall recognize any marriage contracted in any other jurisdiction which is not the union of one man and one woman.

This article was added by Acts 2004, No. 926, Section 1, approved September 18, 2004, effective October 19, 2004.

4 Michael Brintnall and Robert J-P. Hauck, "Memo to APSA Council, Committee on the Status of Lesbians, Gays, Bisexuals, and the Transgendered in the Profession, Annual Meeting Committee, Regarding APSA Annual Meeting Siting Costs Related to New Orleans in 2012," March 31, 2008.

5 Leslie McCall, "The Complexity of Intersectionality." *Signs: Journal of Women in Culture and Society* 30, no. 3 (2005): 1773.

6 Council Committee on Siting (Anna Sampaio, chair, Susan Burgess, Dennis Thompson), "Report to the APSA Council," June 24, 2008. http://www.apsanet.org.

REFERENCES

Brintnall, Michael. 2008. "APSA's Executive Director Report, 2008." *P.S.: Political Science and Politics* 41, no. 4: 933.

Council Committee on Siting (Anna Sampaio, chair, Susan Burgess, Dennis Thompson). 2008. *Report to the APSA Council.* Washington, DC: American Political Science Association, June 24.

Hauck, Michael Britnall, and J-P Robert. 2008. *Memo to APSA Council, Committtee on the Status of Lesbians, Gays, Bisexuals, and the Transgendered in the Profession, Annual Meeting Committtee, Regarding APSA Annual Meeting Siting Costs Related to New Orleans in 2012.* Washington, DC: American Political Science Association, March 31.

McCall, Leslie. 2005. "The Complexity of Intersectionality." *Signs: Journal of Women in Culture and Society* 30, no. 3: 1773.

12

Where Has the Field Gone?

An Investigation of LGBTQ Political Science Research

BARRY L. TADLOCK AND JAMI K. TAYLOR

The past twenty years have seen an explosion in lesbian, gay, bisexual, transgender, and queer (LGBTQ)–related political science research. The expansion of LGBTQ-focused work has encompassed a variety of topics. These include exploration of the struggle over gay rights at the local level (Button, Rienzo, and Wald 1997), public opinion on LGBT rights (Lax and Phillips 2009), religion and sexuality (Wilson 1999), same-sex marriage, civil unions, and domestic partnerships (Gerstmann 2005), sodomy laws (Richards 2009), LGBT candidates (Haider-Markel 2010), HIV/AIDS (Jennings and Andersen 1996), violence and the criminal justice system (Herek and Berrill 1992), queer and feminist studies (Blasius 2001), military service (Lehring 2003), education and bullying policy (Cianciotto and Cahill 2012), and others. What areas have been well mined? What topics need more attention? How will increasing levels of political and social equality for LGBTQ persons, and the backlash that often accompanies it, affect research on these often-marginalized communities? What impact does the variation in state and local laws have on LGBTQ individuals and families?

This chapter looks at what has been published by leading political science journals—including public administration and international relations journals—on LGBTQ-themed topics. It also looks at books that have been published by leading publishers. It is an investigative project that attempts to map what has been done so that we can identify future veins of fruitful research.

Our attempt to map political science research on LGBTQ topics is exploratory. We entered the project with no research hypotheses. However, our exploration was informed by prior LGBTQ-focused political science research (such as that cited in the introduction to this chapter) and its topical emphases since the late 1970s. We also consulted similar reviews by Smith (2011), Mucciaroni (2011), Wilson and Burgess (2007), and Cook (1999). Collectively, these reviews illustrate the impressive developments in LGBTQ research since the mid-1990s. For example, in a book review essay, Cook documented a "vibrant interdisciplinary field of inquiry" that grew out of national conferences sponsored by the Gay Academic Union in the 1970s and also from interdisciplinary conferences at various academic institutions in the late 1980s and early 1990s (1999, p. 679). Although political science was "silent" on LGBTQ issues longer than other disciplines, "in 1996, the dam broke" (1999, p. 681). As evidence, he discussed ten empirically based political science books published between 1995 and 1997, covering topics such as AIDS activism, LGBT voting patterns, and inquiry into the political meaning of a lesbian identity.

Eight years following the essay by Cook, Wilson and Burgess authored an essay arguing for the creation of an APSA organized section centered on sexuality and politics. In their essay, they drew attention to "shifts in political discourse forcing public discussion of the role of the state in regulating the sexuality of its citizens" (2007, p. 378). As a result, political scientists expanded on the topics subjected to analytical work. These included investigations into urban politics, the connection between the Republican Party and the Christian Right, and demographic trends that favored increases in support for LGBT politics.

Finally, a 2011 *PS: Political Science and Politics* symposium on the state of LGBT/sexuality studies in political science documented various developments. For example, Brettschneider asserted that "the use of queer theory also supports the critical power of political theory more generally," enabling "other critical theorists to see the enduring presumptions and biases that persist in their work and they themselves seek to undo" (2011, p. 24). Mucciaroni (2011) noted how LGBT research has contributed to other bodies of literature within the discipline, including studies of social movements, of congruence between public opinion and public policy, of framing effects, and of the relationship between science and politics. Finally, Smith brought attention to the "range of outlets" in which LGBT research is published, including "elite general topic journals" as well as "strong subfield journals" (2011, p. 36). Furthermore, he asserted that "LGBT political science is post-Perestroikan" in that "the methodological and approach-oriented cleavages that bedeviled the discipline for some time . . . have been bridged by LGBT political science" (2011, p. 37).

Methodology

Informed by our review of the literature, a topic search was performed on article abstracts in the Web of Science database. The following search terms, based on words commonly used in LGBTQ research, were used: "gay* OR lesbian* OR transgend* OR queer* OR lgb* OR glb* OR bisex* OR homophob* OR homosex* OR 'same-sex' OR transsex* OR sexual orientation."

We used wildcard characters in the query so that a variety of similar words would be captured in the search. The journals that were searched corresponded to the top 50 political science journals as identified by *Journal Citation Reports'* five-year impact factor.[1] Additionally, the top 20 journals in public administration and in international relations were included. In addition, all of the journals published by the American Political Science Association and its section journals were included (a further 19 journals).[2] Book reviews and articles not related to

LGBTQ politics or policy (such as a piece about the *Enola Gay*) were excluded from the dataset. The bibliographic data and abstracts were then downloaded to Endnote (x7.0.2) from Web of Science.[3] In all, 331 article abstracts are included in our dataset. Our article dataset contains all articles identified in these journals through December 31, 2014.

Content analysis was performed on the abstracts for each article. The dimensions assessed in our content analysis include (see the endnotes for coding) the following:

1. Scope of inclusion: Which parts of the LGBTQ community does the abstract address?[4]
2. Intersectionality: To what extent does the abstract discuss LGBTQ issues in relation to other salient identities?[5]
3. Time frame: Is the abstract cross-sectional or does it look at the phenomenon over time?[6]
4. Normative or empirical focus: What is the methodological focus identified in the abstract (e.g., quantitative, qualitative, or normative)?[7]
5. LGBTQ topic areas (primary and secondary): What LGBTQ-specific policy areas or concerns are mentioned in the abstract (e.g., same-sex marriage or antidiscrimination measures)?[8]
6. Literature (primary and secondary): According to the abstract, what body of literature within the discipline does the article contribute to and draw from?[9]

This coded data formed several categorical variables. These variables and the bibliographic information for the articles were transferred to Stata (v.11). Bibliographic data included in the analysis include year of publication (interval level), journal (categorical), times cited (interval level), and the publishing journal's five-year impact factor (interval level). Frequency analysis and cross-tabulations were used to explore the categorical data. We also used univariate statistics such as mean and median to explore year of publication and the number of times articles were cited.

Because political scientists do not solely publish in journals, we expanded our search to include books. To identify relevant books, we searched Library of Congress (LoC) holdings using the same keywords that were used in the article search. Our search was conducted using the Endnote (x7.0.2) interface with the LoC catalog.[10] We limited the books to those published by a top-20 political science press as identified by Garand and Giles (2011) and Goodson, Dillman, and Hira (1999). We used the two combined lists to mitigate changes in perceived press quality over the period of our study. Not surprisingly, there is significant overlap between the two lists (particularly among top-ranked publishing houses). The list contains traditional university as well as trade presses. Our study also stopped with the year 2014.

All relevant bibliographic records identified in Library of Congress holdings were then downloaded to Endnote (x7.0.2). Since our analysis is concerned with what political scientists have published, we eliminated from the dataset all materials where the term "fiction" was included in the LoC keywords field. We also cleaned the data by removing items that would be picked up in our keyword search but that are not related to our inquiry. One example of this was a book by Gloria Gaynor. Additionally and given the scope of our study, we eliminated those items with music, fine arts, or languages and literature call numbers (those with LoC call numbers starting with M, N, or P).[11] After data cleaning and elimination of those call numbers we were left with a book population of 723 (n = 723).

With these 723 books, we relied on the LoC classification to review and classify the information. In part, this was done because we could not follow the same procedures as was done on the articles. Most of the books in the dataset did not have abstracts to review. However, given that Library of Congress librarians catalog and classify materials by their content and descriptions (Library of Congress 2014), we believed that it was reasonable to rely on their professional judgment as to the content of the books. Therefore, the books are sorted by main LoC class (e.g., law, LoC call numbers starting with K) and a far more detailed analysis based on LoC subclass.

Article Findings

As noted in table 12.1, the earliest piece uncovered in our search of article abstracts was published in 1977. The latest articles were published in 2014. A slight majority of the articles were published after 2007. The mean number of times cited per article was 14.88 (n = 308; 23 observations had missing data). However, this was heavily influenced by a few outliers, most notably Jost, Banaji, and Nosek's (2004) paper "A Decade of System Justification Theory: Accumulated Evidence of Conscious and Unconscious Bolstering of the Status Quo" (531 cites). The median number of times cited per paper is 5.0 while the first quartile is one citation and the third quartile is 14 citations.

Table 12.2 shows that the top five journals for the publishing of LGBTQ-related research are *Social Science Quarterly* (37 articles), *PS: Political Science & Politics* (25 articles), *Public Opinion Quarterly* (21 articles), *Political Research Quarterly* (21 articles), *New Political Science* (16 articles), and *American Journal of Political Science* (13 articles). Concerning the top two journals as judged by the five-year impact factor, *International Organization* published one article, and *American Political Science Review* published five articles. Other leading journals include *Annual Review of Political Science* (one article), *International Security*

Table 12.1. Number of Journal Articles Published by Year

Year of publication	Frequency	Percent	Cumulative percent
1977	1	0.30	0.30
1978	1	0.30	0.60
1982	1	0.30	0.91
1988	1	0.30	1.21
1992	4	1.21	2.42
1993	5	1.51	3.93
1994	6	1.81	5.74
1995	4	1.21	6.95
1996	13	3.93	10.88
1997	8	2.42	13.29
1998	8	2.42	15.71
1999	15	4.53	20.24
2000	7	2.11	22.36
2001	4	1.21	23.56
2002	11	3.32	26.89
2003	11	3.32	30.21
2004	8	2.42	32.63
2005	22	6.65	39.27
2006	20	6.04	45.32
2007	13	3.93	49.24
2008	16	4.83	54.08
2009	26	7.85	61.93
2010	19	5.74	67.67
2011	28	8.46	76.13
2012	26	7.85	83.99
2013	24	7.25	91.24
2014	29	8.76	100.00
Total	331	100.00	

(six articles), *Journal of Public Administration Research and Theory* (three articles), and *Political Geography* (ten articles).

Table 12.3 examines which portions of the LGBTQ community were noted in the abstracts. The vast majority of pieces were explicitly focused on the lesbian and gay communities. LGBT inclusion was noted in 7.25% of abstracts. Transgender-specific pieces were rare, while a small number of articles expanded beyond LGBT to notations like LGBTQ. The limited number of transgender-inclusive pieces is likely affected by the relatively late inclusion of transgender to what we now call LGBTQ advocacy. There is also less public opinion data on transgender-related policy. We admittedly did not attempt to catalog any special

TABLE 12.2. Number of Abstracts by Journal and Five-Year Impact Factor

Journal	5-Year Impact Factor	Frequency
Administration & Society	1.901	3
African Affairs	1.657	2
American Journal of Political Science	3.96	13
American Political Science Review	4.516	5
American Review of Public Administration	1.257	3
Annals of the American Academy of Political and Social Science	1.44	7
Annual Review of Political Science	4.009	1
British Journal of Political Science	2.284	5
Common Market Law Review	2.074	1
Comparative Political Studies	2.46	3
Electoral Studies	1.576	1
European Journal of Political Research	1.757	1
Global Policy	1.206	1
Human Rights Quarterly	1.217	11
International Affairs	1.227	2
International Journal of Press/Politics	1.67	1
International Organization	4.643	1
International Political Sociology	1.942	1
International Security	3.359	6
International Studies Quarterly	2.142	1
JCMS–Journal of Common Market Studies	1.624	1
Journal of Democracy	1.353	2
Journal of European Public Policy	1.667	6
Journal of Policy Analysis and Management	2.281	4
Journal of Political Philosophy	1.41	1
Journal of Political Science Education	N/A	1
Journal of Politics	2.387	8
Journal of Public Administration Research and Theory	3.337	3
Journal of Social Policy	1.195	3
Legislative Studies Quarterly	1.063	1
Local Government Studies	.912	3
New Left Review	1.643	4
New Political Science	N/A	16
Policy Studies Journal	1.177	12
Political Behavior	2.124	8
Political Communication	2.33	4
Political Geography	2.85	10
Political Psychology	2.152	13

(cont.)

TABLE 12.2. (*cont.*)

Journal	5-Year Impact Factor	Frequency
Political Research Quarterly	1.281	21
Political Studies	1.558	3
Politics & Society	2.301	2
Politics and Religion	.389	8
PS: Political Science & Politics	.547	25
Public Administration	1.583	1
Public Administration Review	1.546	7
Public Choice	1.255	4
Public Opinion Quarterly	2.941	21
Publius: The Journal of Federalism	1.224	7
Representation	N/A	1
Scandinavian Political Studies	2.122	1
Social Policy & Administration	1.157	4
Social Science Quarterly	1.407	37
State Politics & Policy Quarterly	1.099	5
Studies in Comparative International Development	1.326	1
Urban Affairs Review	1.83	3
West European Politics	1.713	1
Total	1.811	331

TABLE 12.3. Scope of Community Coverage

Scope of coverage	Frequency	Percent	Cumulative percent
LG	236	71.30	71.30
Not addressed	31	9.37	80.66
LGB	29	8.76	89.43
LGBT	24	7.25	96.68
T	5	1.51	98.19
LGBT*	6	1.81	100.00
Total	331	100.00	

focus on bisexual individuals or their policy concerns. This is an oversight by us and perhaps by other political science researchers as well.

Table 12.4 provides information about the analytical approaches identified in the abstracts. A slight majority (51.36%) of the papers used quantitative approaches. This corresponds to disciplinary trends that are often discussed. Small amounts of qualitative (4.53) or mixed-method approaches (2.11%) were identified. Additionally, a significant number (16.92%) of normative pieces have been published. We were unable to discern the approach in approximately one in five abstracts (19.94%).

TABLE 12.4. Analytical Approach

Analytical approach	Frequency	Percent	Cumulative percent
Quantitative	170	51.36	51.36
Cannot discern approach	66	19.94	71.30
Normative	56	16.92	88.22
Review article	17	5.14	93.36
Qualitative	15	4.53	97.89
Mixed approach	7	2.11	100.00
Total	331	100.00	

TABLE 12.5. Degree of Intersectionality

Intersectionality	Frequency	Percent	Cumulative percent
None	266	80.36	80.36
Gender	27	8.16	88.52
Multiple	23	6.95	95.47
Race	7	2.11	97.59
Religion	6	1.81	99.40
Ethnicity	1	0.30	99.70
Class	1	0.30	100.00
Total	331	100.00	

Table 12.5 shows that calls for more attention to intersectionality have largely gone unheeded by the discipline. Slightly more than 80% of the abstracts gave no attention to this concept. However, there is evidence that a new trend is emerging. Slightly more than half of the intersectional pieces have been published since 2008. The majority of pieces (10 of 15) from queer and feminist theory have been intersectional. It is the only body of literature, containing a substantial number of abstracts, where this was the case.

Table 12.6 looks at the study of LGBTQ-specific topics over time (by half-decade, with the small number of pre-1990 abstracts removed). Not surprisingly, same-sex-marriage-related research exploded after the 2004 presidential elections. Approximately 88% of all such work occurred after 2004. HIV/AIDS-focused work has seen a sharp decline since the 1990–1994 period. Despite the LGBTQ movement's ongoing concern with laws against sodomy, especially outside the United States after *Lawrence v. Texas* (2003), there was only one abstract mentioning the topic. Public opinion research on LGBTQ rights was the most common topic (18.65% of abstracts). In the future, we expect to see a reduction in the number of pieces focused on the armed services, given the end of the

TABLE 12.6. LGBTQ Topic Area over Time

LGBTQ Topical Area (total 1990–2014)	1990–1994; 1995–1999	2000–2004; 2005–2009	2010–2014
Armed services (10)	0; 5	2; 1	2
Criminal justice (1)	0; 0	0; 0	1
Discrimination (22)	0; 5	3; 5	9
Hate crimes (1)	0; 0	1; 0	0
HIV/AIDS (16)	7; 3	1; 3	2
LGBTQ and religion (11)	1; 1	2; 3	4
LGBTQ queer/feminist studies (16)	2; 4	1; 5	4
N/A (6)	0; 1	0; 3	2
Other (22)	0; 3	4; 6	9
Policymaking (general) (23)	0; 1	3; 9	10
PS discipline and LGBTQ (24)	4; 2	0; 3	15
Public opinion on LGBTQ (61)	1; 6	13; 18	23
Rights (33)	0; 7	6; 9	11
Same-sex marriage (58)	0; 5	2; 23	28
Social movement (general) (16)	0; 5	2; 4	5
Sodomy laws (1)	0; 0	0; 1	0
Violence (6)	0; 0	1; 4	1
Total (327)	15; 48	41; 97	126

"Don't Ask Don't Tell" policy and the removal of regulations banning transgender individuals from the armed forces. Study of LGBTQ policymaking (7.03% of abstracts), LGBTQ rights in general (10.09% of abstracts), and laws against discrimination (6.72%) are other common areas of research. LGBTQ-focused political scientists also appear to do a significant amount of introspection about their place within the discipline, given that 24 articles (7.34% of abstracts) looked at this issue.

Table 12.7 provides a look at the body of literature that the reviewed abstracts appeared to contribute to or draw from.[12] As with the LGBTQ-specific topics reported on in table 12.6, public opinion (19.34% of abstracts)–related research is by far the most common area of publication. Particularly prolific authors in this area are Paul Brewer, Greg Lewis, and the duo of Jeffery Lax and Justin Phillips. Beyond opinion, LGBTQ-specific works (a general LGBTQ-rights category), policy area studies, queer/feminist theoretical pieces, and state/local government were other common areas of research. There has also been significant attention to LGBTQ rights in European-focused comparative work.

Table 12.7 also shows that two-thirds of all published political science work relates to just 13 bodies of literature. With regard to secondary areas of study (not

TABLE 12.7. Primary Theoretical Focus of LGBTQ Rights Research

Primary Body of Literature	Frequency	Percent	Cumulative percent
Public opinion	64	19.34	19.34
LGBT specific	22	6.65	25.98
Policy area studies (health, education, etc.)	20	6.04	32.02
Queer/feminist theory	17	5.14	37.16
Local government and urban affairs	17	5.14	42.30
Comparative politics: Europe	15	4.53	46.83
Political psychology	12	3.63	50.45
Social movements	10	3.02	53.47
Ballot initiatives/referendums	10	3.02	56.50
Public administration	9	2.72	59.21
Comparative politics: general	9	2.72	61.93
Interest groups	8	2.42	64.35
State legislatures	8	2.42	66.77
Morality policy—broad	8	2.42	69.18
Elections	7	2.11	71.30
Population ecology (interest groups)	7	2.11	73.41
International relations	7	2.11	75.53
Comparative politics: Africa	7	2.11	77.64
Congress	6	1.81	79.46
Federal judiciary	6	1.81	81.27
Ethics/morality	6	1.81	83.08
Executive branch	5	1.51	84.59
Comparative politics: Latin America/Caribbean	5	1.51	86.10
Political theory (general)	5	1.51	87.61
Policymaking (general)	5	1.51	89.12
Political communication	4	1.21	90.33
Methodology	4	1.21	91.54
N/A	3	0.91	92.45
State judiciary	3	0.91	93.35
Political participation	3	0.91	94.26
Candidates	3	0.91	95.17
Federalism	3	0.91	96.07
Media	3	0.91	96.98
Race/ethnicity	3	0.91	97.89
Comparative politics: Asia	2	0.60	98.49
Comparative politics: North America	2	0.60	99.09
Policy diffusion	1	0.30	99.40
Comparative politics: Oceana	1	0.30	99.70
Political culture	1	0.30	100.00
Total	331	100.00	

shown), nearly 32% of the abstracts did not have a secondary area. Public opinion was the most common secondary body of literature, with 9.37% of abstracts. General policymaking (5.14%), policy area studies (4.23%), social movements (3.93%), interest groups (3.02%), political communication (3.02%), and race/ethnicity (3.02%) round out the top seven secondary areas of study.

Because of the diversity in research topics, it was analytically useful to condense these categories into a smaller number of research areas. Accordingly, we recoded the bodies of literature into the following broad topics:[13]

1. Attitudes
2. Movement
3. Global
4. Federal institutions
5. State/Local institutions
6. Participation and communication
7. Theory
8. Policy and administration
9. Other

As with table 12.6, we condensed the number of years into half-decades, beginning in 1990 and ending in 2014. Table 12.8 provides the broad areas of research by the half-decade in which these articles were produced. As one can see, a significant percentage of research in all categories was published within the years 2010–2014 and 2005–2009. This speaks to the increasing permeability of the strongest political science journals to a variety of LGBTQ-rights-related work. Interestingly, state and local government–focused work expanded earlier than many other categories (10 of 31 articles were published between 1995 and 1999).

TABLE 12.8. Broad Areas of Focus over Time

Broad topics (total 1990–2014)	1990–1994; 1995–1999	2000–2004; 2005–2009	2010–2014
Attitudes (74)	3; 2	13; 22	34
Federal institutions (17)	0; 3	5; 5	4
Global (48)	1; 5	5; 15	22
Movement (24)	1; 3	4; 8	8
Other (32)	4; 8	1; 5	14
Participation/communication (30)	1; 6	3; 9	11
Policy and administration (43)	4; 6	3; 14	16
State/local institutions (31)	0; 10	4; 8	9
Theory (28)	1; 5	3; 11	8
Total (327)	15; 48	41; 97	126

Perhaps this is related to the number of state and local governments that adopted various statutes and ordinances banning sexual orientation–based discrimination in the 1990s. Also interesting is the relative paucity of work on LGBTQ rights at the federal level in the United States. Only 17 abstracts were identified in this area. The federal-level work was balanced among the three branches. However, we might see more work with the federal judiciary in a post–*United States v. Windsor* and post–*Obergefell v. Hodges* world. Additionally, LGBTQ-related policy changes by the Obama administration might be a fruitful avenue for exploration by scholars interested in the executive branch. With regard to comparative work, Asia has largely been ignored despite it being home to the largest percentage of the world's population. Only two of 48 global abstracts focused on Asian nations. Europe was the most common area of focus (15 studies). Latin America and Africa had five and seven studies, respectively.

Within the public opinion-related work, we delved a little further by looking at public opinion research on various policy issues over time. The majority of studies (62.5%) tracked opinion on LGBTQ rights broadly. However, the 2005–2009 period saw the development of opinion research on same-sex marriage; all of the abstracts (18) in our study were published in 2005 or later. Interestingly, opinion work on HIV/AIDS stopped in the early 1990s. No opinion studies on these topics appeared after 1990–1994. With regards to policy and administration–coded abstracts, nearly half were policy area studies (20 of 43). A slight majority (13 of 20) of those pieces were published after 2004. In terms of theory, 28 of the 327 abstracts described an article with political theory as its broad area of research.

A quick review of the most-cited articles reveals great diversity in terms of the literatures to which they contribute, as well as the methods that they utilize in their analyses. As mentioned above, the Jost, Banaji, and Nosek 2004 *Political Psychology* article was the most often cited piece in our dataset. It is a broadly ambitious work in which the authors present evidence relating to 20 hypotheses derived from system justification theory (and related to social identification and social dominance theories). In the article, they investigate the relationship between political ideology and motivations that are used to justify the existing social order. They find that "paradoxically, it is sometimes strongest among those who are most disadvantaged by the social order" (Jost et al. 2004, p. 912). In another well-cited piece, a 2002 *Public Opinion Quarterly* article by Herek, national survey data was used to examine gender gaps in heterosexuals' attitudes toward lesbians and gay men. His findings "demonstrate the importance of differentiating lesbians from gay men as attitude targets in survey research" (2002, p. 40). In a seminal 1996 *Journal of Politics* article that contributes to both the morality-policy and interest-group literatures, Haider-Markel and Meier—using both state- and county-level data—report that when gay and lesbian political issues are not politically salient, then "the pattern of politics resembles that of interest group politics," but when such issues are salient, then "the pattern of politics conforms to morality politics" (1996, p. 332). The difference in salience results from the actions of individuals who are opposed to lesbian and gay rights and their ability to expand the scope of conflict. Another oft-cited piece, the 1993 *American Journal of Political Science (AJPS)* article by Chong, uses analysis of in-depth interview data to contribute to the opinion- formation literature. Specifically, he argues that "it would seem difficult to extrapolate from surveys of opinion to how people would actually behave in real controversies" (Chong 1993, p. 898). He comes to this conclusion as a result of his critique of polling methods, arguing that "what seems to be called for in our surveys is a method of asking questions that steers respondents to canvass their thoughts on a subject before offering their opinions" (Chong 1993, p. 897). Finally, Gamble's 1997 *AJPS* article addresses both democratic theory and theories of public policy. Through an analysis of three decades of initiatives and referenda of various civil rights areas, including gay rights, she finds that "initiatives that restrict civil rights experience extraordinary electoral success," with over 75% of them being approved (Gamble 1997, p. 245).

Book Findings

As reported in table 12.9, there were 723 books released by the analyzed publishing houses on LGBTQ politics during the years 1959–2014. These 56 years

TABLE 12.9 Number of Books Published by Year

Year of publication	Frequency	Percent	Cumulative percent
1959	1	0.14	0.14
1962	1	0.14	0.28
1965	1	0.14	0.41
1968	1	0.14	0.55
1971	2	0.28	0.83
1972	2	0.28	1.11
1974	2	0.28	1.38
1975	1	0.14	1.52
1976	1	0.14	1.66
1978	2	0.28	1.94
1979	2	0.28	2.21
1980	6	0.83	3.04
1981	3	0.41	3.46
1982	4	0.55	4.01
1983	4	0.55	4.56
1984	2	0.28	4.84

(cont.)

TABLE 12.9 (*cont.*)

Year of publication	Frequency	Percent	Cumulative percent
1985	2	0.28	5.12
1986	4	0.55	5.67
1987	6	0.83	6.50
1988	7	0.97	7.47
1989	5	0.69	8.16
1990	8	1.11	9.27
1991	10	1.38	10.65
1992	11	1.52	12.17
1993	15	2.07	14.25
1994	23	3.18	17.43
1995	33	4.56	21.99
1996	36	4.98	26.97
1997	37	5.12	32.09
1998	30	4.15	36.24
1999	44	6.09	42.32
2000	30	4.15	46.47
2001	25	3.46	49.93
2002	28	3.87	53.80
2003	28	3.87	57.68
2004	28	3.87	61.55
2005	31	4.29	65.84
2006	33	4.56	70.40
2007	21	2.90	73.31
2008	29	4.01	77.32
2009	31	4.29	81.60
2010	30	4.15	85.75
2011	30	4.15	89.90
2012	33	4.56	94.47
2013	29	4.01	98.48
2014	11	1.52	100.00
Total	723	100.00	

break down into two sharply contrasting time periods. For the first 35 years, the number of books published annually increased quite slowly. The final year of the initial time period, 1993, marked the high point, with 15 books published that year. The following year launched an era of publishing productivity. In 1994 there were 23 LGBTQ-related books published. From then on, the ensuing two decades showed a consistently increasing record of publication.

TABLE 12.10. Number of Books Published by Half-Decades

5-year time span	Frequency	Percent	Cumulative percent
1955–1959	1	0.14	0.14
1960–1964	1	0.14	0.28
1965–1969	2	0.28	0.55
1970–1974	6	0.83	1.38
1975–1979	6	0.83	2.21
1980–1984	19	2.63	4.84
1985–1989	24	3.32	8.16
1990–1994	67	9.27	17.43
1995–1999	180	24.90	42.32
2000–2004	139	19.23	61.55
2005–2009	145	20.06	81.60
2010–2014	133	18.40	100.00
Total	723	100.00	

Overall, there were 106 books published during the 1959–1993 time span, for an average of 3.03 books per year. From 1994–2014, there were 620 books published, for an average of 29.52 books per year. The years 1999, 1997, and 1996 represent the three years with the most LGBTQ books published, at 44, 37, and 36 books, respectively.

Table 12.10 shows this data from a different perspective, that being five-year blocks of time. It is notable that nearly 25% of all LGBTQ books were published in the years 1995–1999. As of this writing, this represents the high point for published works on LGBTQ politics, as each of the ensuing five-year time spans did not yield the same degree of productivity.

Table 12.11 shows top publishers for works about LGBTQ political issues. The top five publishers include Routledge (201, or 27.8%), the University of Chicago Press (86, or 11.89%), St. Martin's Press (75, or 10.37%), Columbia University Press (61, or 8.44%), and Oxford University Press (60, or 8.3%). These five presses published 483 books concerning LGBTQ politics, representing 66.8% of all publications. Collectively, the remaining 19 presses accounted for 240 books (33.20%). The nine trade presses accounted for 373 of the 723 books (51.59%) while various university presses published the remainder (350).

Table 12.12 breaks down the 723 publications into categories related to the basic classes of knowledge used in the Library of Congress (LoC) classification. These are signified by the first letter in an LoC call number. These basic classes of knowledge include ones such as agriculture or technology or education. This broad classification reveals that over 68% of all LGBTQ books have been categorized as Social Sciences texts. Only 1.11% have been categorized as

TABLE 12.11. Number of Books by Publisher

Publisher	Frequency	Percent	Cumulative Percent
Basic Books	15	2.07	2.07
Blackwell Publishers	3	0.41	2.48
Cambridge University Press	36	4.98	7.46
Columbia University Press	61	8.44	15.90
Cornell University Press	7	0.97	16.87
CQ Press	2	0.28	17.15
Georgetown University Press	1	0.14	17.29
Harvard University Press	14	1.94	19.23
Johns Hopkins University Press	6	0.83	20.06
Lynne Rienner Publishers	3	0.41	20.47
MIT Press	7	0.97	21.44
Oxford University Press	60	8.30	29.74
Princeton University Press	11	1.52	31.26
Routledge	201	27.80	59.06
Rowman & Littlefield	27	3.73	62.79
Sage Publications	29	4.01	66.80
St. Martin's Press	75	10.37	77.18
Stanford University Press	6	0.83	78.01
Temple University Press	1	0.14	78.15
University of California Press	28	3.87	82.02
University of Chicago Press	86	11.89	93.91
University of Michigan Press	13	1.80	95.71
University Press of Kansas	3	0.41	96.13
W.W. Norton	18	2.49	98.62
Yale University Press	10	1.38	100.00
Total	723	100.00	

Political Science texts. Three other classifications with a substantial percentage of LGBTQ books include those concerning Medicine (5.81%), Law of the United States (5.12%), and Christianity, the Bible (3.46%).

Table 12.13 looks a bit more deeply at only four broad categories listed in table 12.12. Specifically, table 12.13 shows changes across time in terms of the publication of books within those four classifications. For example, the number of books classified as Social Science texts increases with each successive time period through 2004, at which point the number begins to decline. Also, except for 1955–1964, Social Sciences texts outnumber all other text classifications combined. Finally, the number of texts in the other classes of knowledge also increases over the time periods, but in a less dramatic fashion as compared to those classified as Social Sciences.

TABLE 12.12. Library of Congress Classification Basic Classes of Knowledge

Class of Knowledge	Frequency	Percent	Cumulative Percent
Philosophy, psychology (B, BC, BD, BF, BH, BJ)	15	2.07	2.07
Religion (General). Hinduism, Judaism, Islam, Buddhism (BL, BM, BP, BQ)	6	0.83	2.90
Christianity, Bible (BR, BS, BT, BV, BX)	25	3.46	6.36
Auxiliary Sciences of History (C)	1	0.14	6.50
History (General) and History of Europe (D, DA-DR)	6	0.83	7.33
History of Asia, Africa, Australia, New Zealand, etc. (DS, DT, DU)	6	0.83	8.16
History: America (E, F)	13	1.80	9.96
Geography. Maps. Anthropology. Recreation (G)	19	2.63	12.59
Social Sciences (H)	497	68.74	81.33
Political Science (J)	8	1.11	82.43
Law in General. Comparative and Uniform Law Jurisprudence (K)	7	0.97	83.40
Law of the United Kingdom and Ireland (KD-KDK)	9	1.24	84.65
Law of the United States (KF)	37	5.12	89.76
Law of Europe (KJ–KKZ)	2	0.28	90.04
Education (L)	18	2.49	92.53
Science (Q)	7	0.97	93.50
Medicine (R)	42	5.81	99.31
Military Science. Naval Science (U)	4	0.55	99.86
Bibliography. Library Science. Information Resources (Z)	1	0.14	100.00
Total	723	100.00	

TABLE 12.13. Four (of 19) Key Classes of Knowledge by Year

Classes of knowledge by year	1955–1964; 1965–1974	1975–1984; 1985–1994	1995–2004; 2005–2014
Social sciences	1; 8	17; 66	238; 167
Medicine	0; 0	3; 8	18; 13
Law of the United States	1; 0	0; 3	8; 25
Christianity, Bible	0; 0	0; 3	9; 13
Total	2; 8	20; 80	273; 218

Table 12.14 looks only at the 497 books classified as Social Sciences texts. This medium-grained exploration is based upon subclasses within the Library of Congress classification system (the first two letters of an LoC call number). These books are classified as ones pertaining to human sexuality (400 books, 80.48%), the family, marriage, and women (61 books, 12.27%), social pathology (18 books, 3.62%), economics history and conditions (9 books, 1.81%), sociology

TABLE 12.14. Subclasses for Texts Classified as Social Sciences

Subclass	Frequency	Percent	Cumulative percent
Human sexuality	400	80.48	80.48
Family, marriage, women	61	12.27	92.76
Social pathology	18	3.62	96.38
Economic history and conditions	9	1.81	98.19
Sociology	5	1.01	99.20
Social history, conditions, social problems	3	0.60	99.80
Communities, classes, races	1	0.20	100.00
Total	497	100.00	

TABLE 12.15. Selected Library of Congress Categories

Library of Congress Categories	Frequency
Human sexuality: Country- and/or region/time-specific	126
Gay men	72
Lesbians	50
Transgender individuals	25
Sexual behaviors and attitudes	13
Education and sociology	10
Disease and public health	10
Personality disorders	10
Bisexual individuals	8
Total	324

(5 books, 1.01%), social history and conditions (3 books, 0.60%), and communities, classes, and races (1 book, 0.20%). Interestingly, some books that are about political science topics, but use LGBTQ subjects to illustrate those topics, such as Taylor and Haider-Markel's *Transgender Rights and Politics: Groups, Issue Framing, and Policy Adoption* (call number HQ77.9 .T7173 2014), are classified under human sexuality despite their clear disciplinary focus. Apparently, library catalogers see LGBTQ as the dominant subject and often classify books by that regardless of circumstance.

Finally, table 12.15 digs deeply into the Library of Congress classification scheme. Selected categories are based upon complete Library of Congress classification numbers assigned to individual texts. There are various things to notice in this table. First, in terms of specific communities of interest: 72 books are classified as pertaining to gay men; 50 books as pertaining to lesbians; 25 books as pertaining to transgender individuals; and eight books as pertaining to bisexual people. Second, books that are country-specific and/or region-specific number 126 (some of which also are categorized as pertaining to a specific community of interest). Other categories that show particularly high numbers include 13 published books concerning sexual behaviors and attitudes, and ten published books on each of the following categories: education and sociology, disease and public health, and personality disorders.

Conclusion

This chapter cataloged LGBTQ-related political science research that has been published in the field's top journals and by leading book publishers. In terms of the journal articles, there are more articles based upon empirical research as compared to those using a normative approach. Also in terms of the journal articles, we found that political science scholars have well mined the existing public opinion data on LGBTQ rights. Similarly, there has also been a recent spotlight on same-sex marriage. While timely, the same-sex-marriage-related work will likely lose salience for many American political scientists given the ruling in *Obergefell v. Hodges*. The possibility of losing this data-rich and popular area of inquiry raises questions about the future of LGBTQ-related policy and opinion research.

The focus on same-sex marriage and opinion work more broadly is likely an artifact of publicly available data and the very limited research budgets of political scientists. The data-availability issue also likely limits the scope of community coverage for some articles. There remains a lack of opinion data on transgender rights over time, as well as a lack of data about the size of that community. For the entire discipline, these types of data issues are likely to drive many decisions about whom to include, what policies to research, and what phenomena to address. We encourage scholars to work jointly on this data problem.

It is important to highlight the work that was focused outside of the United States. Much of this addressed Europe. Yet, there seems to be a niche for more work aimed outside of Europe or the United States. One area that seems to be viable, particularly given the LGBTQ movement's longtime concern with sodomy laws, is policy work focused on various African and Middle Eastern nations. Studies that investigate the countries of the former Soviet Union might also be fruitful. Comparative work related to transgender policy also seems viable given the variety of ways that transgender persons are accommodated (or not) in some nations. Political science research related to bisexuality also appears viable given the lack of work in this area regardless of location.

We were surprised to see the relative paucity of political/queer/feminist theory treatments of LGBTQ topics in each of our datasets. Perhaps this speaks more to a disciplinary publishing bias against these approaches than to the efforts of theorists. Despite this likely bias, we are pleased to report that more of the top journals are publishing LGBTQ-related work. We encourage scholars to keep submitting their LGBTQ-focused work to the field's top journals.

Finally, this investigation of LGBTQ work published in leading journals and by top publishers should not be viewed as an attempt to describe the state of the discipline. Many readers of this chapter are most likely familiar with the APSA publications *Political Science: State of the Discipline* (1983, 1993, 2002). The most recent edition exceeded one thousand pages in length. Clearly, this brief chapter carries with it a vastly different goal than those tomes. What we have sought to do is to characterize a historical overview of our discipline's publishing record. However, this overview is not comprehensive, as not all journals and not all publishing houses are explored. In addition, there are places where the work of the discipline occurs that are not captured in an analysis such as this one. These places include roundtables and panels at professional conferences, online blogs such as the Monkey Cage, symposia sponsored by academic departments and research institutes, and various other venues. Certainly the state of the discipline consists of all these disparate components, with published articles and books being—admittedly quite important—component parts.

NOTES

1 We used the 2012 edition of *Journal Citation Reports*.

2 There is duplication across lists and with the APSA section journals. The total number of journals searched is fewer than the 109 journals generated by summing 50 (PS)+20 (PA)+20(IR)+19(APSA).

3 Journal websites were consulted for any missing data from Web of Science.

4 Codes are: 0 Not addressed, 1 LG, 2 LGB, 3 LGBT, 4 T, 5 LGBT.*

5 Codes are: 0 None, 1 Race, 2 Ethnicity, 3 Gender, 4 Class, 5 Religion, 6 Multiple.

6 Codes are: 0 NA, 1 Cross-sectional, 2 Temporal, 3 Cannot discern.

7 Codes are: 0 Review, 1 Normative, 2 Quantitative, 3 Qualitative, 4 Cannot discern, 5 Mixed.

8 Codes are: 0 NA, 1 Same-Sex Marriage, Civil Union, Domestic Partnerships, 2 Violence, 3 Discrimination, 4 Rights, 5 Hate Crimes, 6 HIV/AIDS, 7 Criminal Justice, 8 Policymaking (General), 9 Social Movement (General), 10 Sodomy Laws, 11 Armed Services, 12 Education and Bullying Policy, 13 Public Opinion on LGBT Rights, 14 PS Discipline and LGBT, 15 LGBT and Religion, 16 LGBT Queer/Feminist Studies, 17 Other.

9 Codes are: 0 NA, 1 LGBT Specific, 2 Public Opinion, 3 Interest Groups, 4 Social Movements, 5 Congress, 6 Executive Branch, 7 Judiciary Federal, 8 State Legislatures, 9 State Executive Branch, 10 State Judiciary, 11 Political Participation, 12 Candidates, 13 Elections,14 Policy Diffusion, 15 Population Ecology (Interest Groups), 16 Ethics/Morality, 17 Morality Policy–Broad, 18 Federalism, 19 Queer Theory/Feminist Theory, 20 International Relations, 21 Comparative Politics Europe, 22 Comparative Politics Latin America/Carib, 23 Comparative Politics Asia, 24 Comparative Politics North America, 25 Comparative Politics Africa, 26 Comparative Politics Oceana, 27 Political Theory–Not Queer Theory, 28 Political Economy, 29 Political Communication, 30 Ballot Initiatives/Referendums, 31 Law, 32 Political Culture, 33 Methodology, 34 Policymaking General, 35 Public Administration, 36 Political Psychology, 37 Local Government and Urban Affairs, 38 Policy Area Studies (Health, Education, Social, Criminal . . .), 39 Media, 40 Comparative-General, 41 Race/Ethnicity.

10 This keyword query used a "contains" search on the selected bibliographic field. Therefore, the keyword "gay" would pick up words like "gay," "gays," "gaylord," "gaynor," and so forth.

11 See www.loc.gov/catdir/cpso/lcco/ for a Library of Congress classification outline.

12 We also identified secondary bodies of literature in our data collection. However, these are not reported.

13 Codes are: Attitudes includes Public Opinion/Political Culture/Political Psychology; Movement includes Interest Groups/Population Ecology/Social Movements; Global includes Comparative/International Relations/All Comparative Regions; Federal Institutions includes Congress/Executive/Judiciary Federal; State/Local Institutions includes State Executive/State Legislature/State Judiciary/Local Government/Federalism; Participation and Communication includes Political Participation/Campaigns/Elections/Initiatives and Referenda/Media/Political Communication; Theory includes Queer Theory/Feminist Theory/Political Theory/Ethics and Morality; Policy and Administration includes Policy Diffusion/Policy Area Studies/Morality Policy/Policymaking General/Political Economy/Public Administration; Other includes all other literature codes.

REFERENCES

Blasius, Mark, ed. 2001. *Sexual Identities, Queer Politics*. Princeton, NJ: Princeton University Press.

Brettschneider, Marla. 2011. "Heterosexual Political Science." *PS: Political Science & Politics* 44, no. 1. doi: 10.1017/S1049096510001794.

Button, James W., Barbara A. Rienzo, and Kenneth D. Wald. 1997. *Private Lives, Public Conflicts: Battles over Gay Rights in American Communities*. Washington, DC: CQ Press.

Chong, Dennis. 1993. "How People Think, Reason, and Feel about Rights and Liberties." *American Journal of Political Science* 37(3): 867–99. doi: 10.2307/2111576.

Cianciotto, Jason, and Sean Cahill. 2012. *LGBT Youth in America's Schools*. Ann Arbor: University of Michigan Press.

Cook, Timothy E. 1999. "The Empirical Study of Lesbian, Gay, and Bisexual Politics: Assessing the First Wave of Research." *American Political Science Review* 93(3): 679–92. doi: 10.2307/2585582.

Finifter, Ada W., ed. 1983. *Political Science: The State of the Discipline*. Washington, DC: American Political Science Association.

Finifter, Ada W., ed. 1993. *Political Science: The State of the Discipline II*. Washington, DC: American Political Science Association.

Gamble, Barbara S. 1997. "Putting Civil Rights to a Popular Vote." *American Journal of Political Science* 41(1): 245–69. doi: 10.2307/2111715.

Garand, James C., and Micheal W. Giles. 2011. "Ranking Scholarly Publishers in Political Science: An Alternative Approach." *PS: Political Science & Politics* 44(2): 375–83.

Gerstmann, Evan. 2005. "Litigating Same-Sex Marriage: Might the Courts Actually Be Bastions of Rationality?" *PS: Political Science & Politics* 38(2): 217–20.

Goodson, Larry P., Bradford Dillman, and Anil Hira. 1999. "Ranking the Presses: Political Scientists' Evaluations of Publisher Quality." *PS: Political Science & Politics* 32(2): 257–62.

Haider-Markel, Donald P. 2010. *Out and Running: Gay and Lesbian Candidates, Elections, and Policy Representation*. Washington, DC: Georgetown University Press.

Haider-Markel, Donald P., and Kenneth J. Meier. 1996. "The Politics of Gay and Lesbian Rights: Expanding the Scope of the Conflict." *Journal of Politics* 58(2): 332–49. doi: 10.2307/2960229.

Herek, Gregory M. 2002. "Gender Gaps in Public Opinion about Lesbians and Gay Men." *Public Opinion Quarterly* 66(1): 40–66. doi: 10.1086/338409.

Herek, Gregory M., and Kevin T. Berrill, eds. 1992. *Hate Crimes: Confronting Violence against Lesbians and Gay Men*. Thousand Oaks, CA: Sage.

Jennings, M. Kent, and Ellen A. Andersen. 1996. "Support for Confrontational Tactics among AIDS Activists: A Study of Intra-Movement Divisions." *American Journal of Political Science* 40(2): 311–34. doi: 10.2307/2111626.

Jost, John T., Mahzarin R. Banaji, and Brian A. Nosek. 2004. "A Decade of System Justification Theory: Accumulated Evidence of Conscious and Unconscious Bolstering of the Status Quo." *Political Psychology* 25(6): 881–919. doi: 10.1111/j.1467-9221.2004.00402.x.

Katznelson, Ira, and Helen V. Milner, eds. 2002. *Political Science: State of the Discipline.* New York: Norton.

Lax, Jeffrey R., and Justin H. Phillips. 2009. "Gay Rights in the States: Public Opinion and Policy Responsiveness." *American Political Science Review* 103(3): 367–86. doi: 10.1017/s0003055409990050.

Lehring, Gary L. 2003. *Officially Gay: The Political Construction of Sexuality by the U.S. Military.* Philadelphia: Temple University Press.

Library of Congress. 2014. "Frequently Asked Questions about Cataloging." Retrieved June 10, 2015, from www.loc.gov.

Mucciaroni, Gary. 2011. "The Study of LGBT Politics and Its Contributions to Political Science." *PS: Political Science & Politics* 44(1): 17–21. doi: 10.1017/s1049096510001782.

Richards, David A. J. 2009. *The Sodomy Cases: Bowers v. Hardwick and Lawrence v. Texas.* Lawrence: University Press of Kansas.

Smith, Charles A. 2011. "Gay, Straight, or Questioning? Sexuality and Political Science." *PS: Political Science & Politics* 44(1): 35–38. doi: 10.1017/s1049096510001824.

Wilson, Angelia R. 1999. *Below the Belt: Sexuality, Religion, and the American South.* Herndon, VA: Continuum.

Wilson, Angelia R., and Susan Burgess. 2007. "Sexuality and the Body Politic: Thoughts on the Construction of an APSA Sexuality & Politics Section." *PS: Political Science & Politics* 40(2): 377–81. doi: 10.1017/s1049096507070734.

13

Unfulfilled Promises

How Queer Feminist Political Theory Could Transform Political Science

JYL JOSEPHSON AND THAÍS MARQUES

In this chapter, we join the chorus of political scientists who argue that political science as a discipline and the contribution by academics to actual knowledge of political life would be very much improved if the discipline attended more to the insights of queer, feminist, and trans political theory.[1] We begin by highlighting the voices of that chorus, who for at least three decades have called on political theory and political science to deepen its ability to analyze political life by attending to LGBTQ political activism and to the arguments of feminist, queer, and trans political theory and theorists. We then discuss the extent to which queer feminist political theory has developed as a field within the discipline of political science. We argue that there has been much significant and important work that we will call queer feminist political theory developed by political theorists associated with the discipline of political science. Among this work is an emerging field of trans feminist political theory, a promising development. We conclude the essay with some speculations as to some key ways in which queer/trans/feminist political theory might change the discipline, political theory, and the study of politics for the better.

What the Study of LGBTQ Politics and Queer Feminist Political Theory Have to Offer the Discipline

One key reason why political scientists should be interested in queer feminist political theory and in LGBTQ politics is that these fields have a great deal to contribute to the discipline as a whole. We examined the literature in both LGBTQ empirical research and in queer feminist political theory over the past two decades, and there is a persistent theme in this literature about how the discipline might learn from these fields of inquiry. From the beginning of these fields, scholars have consistently argued in disciplinary journals that questions central to the discipline of political science are central questions of these fields. Further, scholars have argued that the central questions of traditional approaches to the study of political science would be transformed, and political science scholarship thus made more accurate, relevant, interesting, and vital by taking seriously *and being changed by* the concerns of these fields.

Thus, the argument that the discipline needs to treat the questions raised by queer feminist political theory as questions fundamental to the study of politics have been present from the beginning of these fields. And they have been arguments not just about the objects of study, or the questions being asked by political theorists but also about the epistemology of the discipline of political science. Taking seriously the work of queer feminist political theorists would require a rethinking of some of the foundational assumptions of the discipline about the nature of power and the best methods for studying the operations of political, social, and cultural power, the problem of inequality in democratic political life, and the most useful questions to ask about families, intimate life, and political life. As just one example, placing lesbian families at the center of analysis fundamentally transforms traditional understandings in political theory of families and of the relationship between families and state (Brettschneider 2006; Lehr 1998; Phelan 1994). Making this analysis intersectional, attending to multiple aspects of identity such as race, religion, and culture, deepens the questions that we must ask about the role of the state in securing the well-being of families through the provision of rights and benefits, while also limiting state control over families and intimate life (Brettschneider 2016; Cohen 1997; Josephson 2016; Fogg Davis 2014; Currah 2014).

The chorus of voices that we mention above were present both in the empirical study of LGBTQ politics and in the developing field of queer feminist political theory. An early essay that made the point that the discipline was missing questions important to the study of politics by not addressing the concerns of the LGBTQ community is a piece on failure to study HIV/AIDS (Sherrill, Somerville, and Bailey 1992). The authors outline many questions that multiple subfields of political science could gain by addressing HIV/AIDS as "a focus of study" (689). They particularly note that political theory, especially feminist political theory, should have had much to say on this topic but had not done so. The authors note that Carole Pateman's then recent and very prominent book, *The Sexual Contract*, had made no mention of HIV/AIDS (Sherrill, Somerville, and Bailey 1992, 692). And they note that more generally, such "classic themes" of political theory as "entitlements, the relationship between the individual and the state, the nature of liberty, sexuality and self-actualization, the social contract, human rights, power and the central ideologies at the core of mainstream American political theory—liberalism, utilitarianism, and proceduralism" (1992, 692)—could be explored through the case of HIV/AIDS.

Fortunately, as we discuss in the next section, a body of work in political theory was already developing that addresses many of these questions, and does not simply treat LGBTQ politics as "a focus of study" but asks how centering queer feminist subjects and subjectivity transforms our understanding of the basic questions that political theory needs to ask. This is the field of work that we call queer feminist political theory, and it draws on multiple traditions from the history of political thought.

The empirical study of LGBTQ politics using traditional political science methods had a growing presence in the disciplinary journals by the 1990s (Cook 1999). Studies of the LGBTQ movement, of public policies that affect the LGBTQ community, of courts and legal decision making, and of political behavior and public opinion related to LGBTQ people and the policies for which the movement advocates have had a greater presence in the discipline than has queer feminist political theory.

Meanwhile, empirical work on same-sex marriage and LGBTQ politics developed rapidly in response to the successes of the marriage-equality movement, including in a forum on same-sex marriage in 2005, and a recent article on the causes of changed votes on same-sex marriage (Lewis 2005; Haider-Markel and Joslyn 2005; Hillygus and Shields 2005; Egan and Sherrill 2005; Gerstmann 2005; Theriault and Thomas 2014). None of the articles address or even draw upon queer feminist political theory. This illustrates the central place of empiricism and the study of political behavior in the discipline, and in our view has meant that empirical studies of LGBTQ politics have had a more prominent place in the discipline than the theoretical work that we discuss below.

Nevertheless, other scholars have continued to argue for changes in the discipline itself. Picking up on some of the themes of the Sherrill, Somerville, and Bailey article, Angelia R. Wilson and Susan Burgess urged the establishment of the Sexuality and Politics section of APSA (Wilson and Burgess 2007). The authors argue that sexuality studies is already very much a part of most subfields of the discipline, and that the establishment of a sexuality and politics section is overdue. They note the point made by multiple authors over the course of the period we have examined: sexuality is already present in the practice as well as the study of politics. Given the moral conservative agenda that seeks to repress sexuality in all facets of political life, from welfare to health to education, bringing together scholarship on sexuality and politics is crucial to the study of contemporary political life. Political science especially needs to study these matters, given that public opinion in the United States is moving towards issues of sexual equality, while, simultaneously, the moral conservative agenda is moving towards policies of discrimination (Wilson and Burgess 2007).

In 2011, PS published a forum on LGBTQ issues and political science that was put together by the LGBT Status Committee and edited by Paisley Currah. As Currah notes in the introductory essay, the idea that research that does not address LGBTQ politics is somehow politically neutral has been thoroughly discredited by a wide range of kinds of political science research. Rather, such research shows how heteronormativity has been equated with political neutrality (Currah 2011, 14). Both Brettschneider and Mucciaroni make similar points about how the study of LGBTQ politics and sexuality studies can contribute to many different subfields of political science, including "politics, power, social movements, public opinion, policymaking institutions, urban politics, and the relationship between science and public policy" (Mucciaroni 2011, 17). Thus, the theme of arguing that the discipline would benefit from integration of queer feminist political theory into the study of politics has persisted for more than two decades.

The scholars who initiated these fields of research were innovative and were taking risks by pursuing these fields of inquiry, and they also saw how the discipline could be made more relevant by attending to questions important to the movement, and argued for broader applications in the discipline. But we also believe that the empirical study of LGBTQ politics has had a more visible presence in the discipline than has queer feminist political theory. We believe this reflects the fact that it is more comfortable for the discipline of political science to take its existing methods and apply them to "new" questions than it is to reflect on and change the foundations of inquiry of the discipline. Taking seriously the work and the insights of queer feminist political theory would require deeper changes to existing methodologies. Unfortunately, contrary to the recommendations of the pioneers in the empirical study of LGBTQ politics, the discipline has not, for the most part, changed the way that it asks empirical questions as a result of the development of this field of inquiry.

This phenomenon is, we suggest, another manifestation of what Mary Hawkesworth has identified as the establishment of a "constitutive outside," where queer feminist political theory (our example) is by definition "outside" of the discipline of political science (Hawkesworth 2010). Thus, even scholars who might seem to attend to the existence of queer feminist political theory's ideas and concerns proceed to construct their arguments in ways that exclude these ideas and concerns. Hawkesworth's critique of political theory for treating critical race and feminist theory in this way is also true of the discipline as a whole in relation to critical race, feminist, trans, and queer feminist political theory. Thus, focusing on empirical research is a way to not change as a discipline, even as you are "incorporating" empirical study of LGBTQ politics, while maintaining queer, trans, and feminist political theory and the politics of sexuality as "outside" the scope of the discipline.

The Development of Queer Feminist Political Theory

How did queer feminist political theory develop as a field? As early as the 1980s we see the beginning of this literature in what are important contributions and contributors to feminist political theory (Brown 1988; Hawkesworth 1988). These authors' later essays show integration of feminist political theory with the interdisciplinary queer theory literature (Hawkesworth 2006; Brown 2002). In this section we outline the contributions of political science–based queer theory both to the discipline of political theory and political science and also to interdisciplinary queer theory.

What do we mean by queer feminist political theory? What concepts has the field contributed to political theory and to the discipline of political science? It is helpful to start with Cathy Cohen's definition: queer theory "focuses on and makes central not only the socially constructed nature of sexuality and sexual categories, but also the varying degrees and multiple sites of power distributed within all categories of sexuality, including the normative categories of hetero-sexuality" (Cohen 1997, 439). This definition helps us to think about how the discipline of political science might be informed by queer feminist political theory.[2] As queer feminist political theory has developed, the field has addressed power and inequality, including all of the arenas in which power operates. Of course, queer feminist political theory has analyzed sexuality and the politics of sexuality, including hetero- and homonormative sexuality. But a queer feminist political theory also addresses gender and gender (in)equality, and here is one place where the queer feminist political theory that has been produced by political theorists associated with the discipline of political science could significantly contribute to interdisciplinary queer theory. There are significant strands in both feminist theory and trans theory that have been critical of some strands of queer theory for developing an analysis of sexuality that is insufficiently attentive to gender (Stryker 2008; Namaste 2010). We believe that the versions of queer theory developed by political theorists and political scientists have been more successful in attending to gender and sexuality simultaneously, and we believe the emergence of trans studies in political theory provides some hopeful impetus towards a queer/trans/feminist political theory that is deeply attentive to sexuality and to gender. A queer/trans/feminist political theory could inform the study of politics in a very deep way, as we think about the categories of public and private, and the realm of state power as well as the operations of power throughout social and cultural institutions and practices.

For example, Cathy Cohen's rich empirical work on the politics of HIV/AIDS in African American communities also develops a very useful intersectional theoretical framework (Cohen 1999). In more recent work Cohen has developed her critique of Black respectability politics and highlighted the political mobilization of Black youth, showing the contradiction between promises of equality and ongoing discrimination (Cohen 2009, 2010). A number of queer feminist theorists have highlighted the promise and necessity of democratic renewal, and the extent to which the intersectional political work and mobilization of marginalized groups holds great promise for a more democratic future for American politics (Brettschneider 2006; Cruikshank 1999; Smith 2007). As Susan Burgess notes in a different context, queer theory provides a way to understand "political struggle," and in this way can contribute to political theory's understanding of democracy (2006, 401).

Burgess notes some additional potential conceptual contributions of queer theory to political science (Burgess 2006). As she notes, "sexuality is central, not marginal, to the construction of meaning and political power" and further, "identity is performative, not natural" (Burgess 2006, 401).

Burgess's first point, that sexuality is central to understanding political life and that "all citizenship is sexual citizenship" (Bell and Binnie 2000) has been central to queer, trans, and feminist political theory from the start and is a key contribution of queer feminist political theory to the study of political life. This point is made perhaps most clearly in Shane Phelan's book *Sexual Strangers*; Phelan asks, "Is the United States a heterosexual regime?" and answers in the affirmative. But this argument is made in many ways throughout the queer feminist political theory literature: sexuality is a central feature of how political regimes are organized, and understanding this is crucial to any adequate analysis of politics (Wilson and Burgess 2007; Phelan 2000; Smith 2002). A recent argument that all citizenship is sexual citizenship is Josephson's analysis of how sexual regulation operates through public policy to control and regulate many different groups in the United States (Josephson 2016).

Burgess's second point, that identity is not natural but socially constructed, is made in a range of ways throughout the queer, trans, and feminist political theory literature (Burgess 2006; Brettschneider 2011; Disch 1999; Beltrán 2004; Barvosa 2007; Carvell and Chambers 2007). Marla Brettschneider sees queer theory as challenging the idea of the "natural" (Brettchneider 2011). The concept of identity as socially constructed is central to feminist political theory and to women's, gender, and sexuality studies, and has also had an influence on policy studies (Schneider and Ingram 1993). Given how much attention the political theory canon has traditionally paid to the importance of the subject, this idea of socially constructed identity has deep implications for political thought (Dietz 2002; Hirschmann 2003). A number of queer feminist political theorists have developed ideas about the complexity of socially constructed identities. For example, in *Getting Specific*, Phelan is critiquing essentialism while also arguing for the need to continue to form alliances and coalitions; to do so she draws on Gloria Anzaldua's work and the idea of *mestiza* consciousness (Phelan 1994). Beltran argues that this is a useful intervention, though she is critical of what she sees as Anzaldua's essentialism (Beltrán 2004, 604). Beltrán (2004) and Barvosa (2008) develop this concept of hybrid or nonunitary identity, and Beltrán draws explicitly on Phelan's work. As Beltrán notes, "The hybrid subject gained prominence in the 1980s, as postmodern, feminist, and postcolonial theorists sought out alternative ways of theorizing identity and experience" (Beltrán 2004, 596). The idea of hybrid identity and of the socially constructed subject also deeply challenges many of the assumptions of traditional political theory and of empirical political science.

A related concept that is more deeply developed in the feminist literature but that queer feminist political theorists have developed is the concept of intersectionality (Brettschneider 2016; Strolovich 2008; Hancock 2011). There is a great deal of literature here but most of the literature that we are citing in this section as queer feminist political theory is intersectional in that it is attentive to more than one aspect of identity and structural inequalities, and thus draws on and develops the concept of intersectionality. This takes different forms depending upon the focus of the author. For example, Cynthia Burack has analyzed the sexuality politics of the Christian Right, in relation to the LGBTQ community and in relation to reproductive rights, thus bringing together feminism, queer as well as conservative identities, and analysis of religious beliefs and identities in her work (Burack 2008, 2014). She has also brought a critical race perspective into analysis of group identities, showing how Black feminist thought has a reparative, progressive politics at its core (Burack 2004). From a different perspective, Marla Brettschneider's body of work brings together critical race scholarship, an analysis of religious identities and cultures, queer theory, and feminist theory. Her book *The Family Flamboyant* did this work masterfully, weaving together analysis of family policies and the relationship between families and the state with analysis of the politics of identity with respect to race, class, religion, gender, and sexuality (Brettschneider 2006). She has continued this deeply intersectional analysis in her more recent work (Brettchneider 2016).

Among the other concepts that a queer feminist political theory has contributed to the discipline of political science is the concept of heteronormativity (Cohen 1997; Carvell and Chambers 2007). Heteronormativity, now a key concept in queer feminist political theory, is developed by Cohen to argue for the commonalities shared by all those with what are perceived as nonnormative sexualities, including, for example, "welfare queens," and to argue for coalition building among these groups (Cohen 1997). Carvell and Chambers develop the concept, drawing on Judith Butler's work, arguing that the critique of heteronormativity leads to "what [Gayle] Rubin named as the goal of feminism: to effect a revolution in kinship" (Carvell and Chambers 2007, 446). Given how deeply heteronormative the entire canon of political theory has been until very recently, this revolution in kinship and in the understanding of kinship would require that political theory find new grounds for most of the ways that it imagines and analyzes political life. Queer feminist political theorists have developed these concepts; the discipline has yet to adopt them in meaningful ways.

The critique of heteronormativity is thus linked to another contribution: the critique of kinship and family as commonly understood in political theory (Brettschneider 2006; Burack 2014; Carvell and Chambers 2007; Lehr 1998; Kaplan 1997; Josephson 2005, 2016; Smith 2002, 2007). This critique has taken many forms, but the key argument is that the rethinking of kinship, which is so central to political theory even when it is not much discussed explicitly, requires a deep rethinking of all of political life. One way of looking at this is to say that the traditional public sphere depends upon a private sphere in which families provide most of the unpaid caring for vulnerable family members (Lehr 1998;

Okin 1989; Pateman 1988). This creates the conditions for deeply unequal political rights for those who have duties to care for others (Tronto 2013). In turn, these inequalities are threats to democratic egalitarianism, and to the possibility for a just political order that is not based on the systematic exploitation of some groups by those with more political power. Thus, the critique of heteronormativity and its role in understandings of kinship leads directly to the question of how to form a just democratic polity.

Another concept that has been developed in different ways has to do with how political theorists might understand the creation of what might be called "queer public spheres," or what Kevin Duong has called queer "world-making" (Duong 2012, 372). One of the earliest essays developing this idea by specifically theorizing "gay and lesbian existence" was by Mark Blasius (Blasius 1992). Blasius argued for understanding gay and lesbian communities through the concept of ethos, rather than identity or the derogatory "lifestyle." He defined "ethos" as "the creation of ethical agency within and through lesbian and gay community" (Blasius 1992, 654). He was arguing in particular that the sense in which the community comes into existence and creates a public sphere is through the process of coming out: a lifelong process of creating meaning. Thus, Blasius argued that the communities created by lesbians and gay men, through geographic proximity in urban settings, the creation of community centers and publications, and other aspects of gay and lesbian urban community life, were and are deeply political, and that attending to lesbian and gay existence has deep implications for political thought and political life (Blasius 1992). This argument is also the central thesis of Blasius's books, *Gay and Lesbian Politics* and *Sexual Identities, Queer Politics* (Blasius 1994, 2001). Kevin Duong develops this through the idea of world making. For Duong, "it is the case that accounting for who we are, our queerness, is already a political claim about how the world is and how it ought to be" (Duong 2012, 382). Making collective political claims requires "an emergent normative vision of justice" and in this sense is at the center of political life (Duong 2012, 382).

Perhaps more controversially, given the fact that interdisciplinary queer theory has in general critiqued and rejected rights-based frameworks, we also see a contribution in the development of a critical political theory of sexuality that still argues for the importance of rights and rights claims, and thus for the role of the state, for political subjectivity. Paisley Currah recently made this point in relation to what he terms "fetishiz[ed]" views of the state, noting that a "generalized idea of the state . . . can obscure what is actually happening" (2014, 199). The particular point that we want to emphasize is this: he argues that fetishizing the state, and seeing it as one entity when it is actually a complex array of contradictory practices "risks substituting the conceptual for the concrete" (2014, 199). We believe that a queer feminist political theory, with its relationship to the discipline of political science, has much here to contribute to queer theory more generally. Queer feminist political theorists have grounding in a discipline that, as part of its purview, studies the state, and has at least some basic insight into the concrete workings of the complex and multifaceted set of institutions that make up "states." Queer feminist political theory thus could help inform an interdisciplinary queer theory that has a concrete analysis of the state, and a more nuanced and complex understanding of what it means to makes claims, including rights claims, before the "state."

Karen Zivi has taken up some of these questions, looking at the problem of how political theorists should think about making rights claims in the era of the deconstructed subject (Zivi 2012). Another theorist who utilizes rights-based frames in developing what we are here calling queer feminist political theory is Heath Fogg Davis (2014). Fogg Davis uses a modified liberalism to argue that most sex classifications should be eliminated, and that this would be beneficial to many people, not just people who identify as trans. This article, drawing on feminist political theory and critical race theory as well as legal theory and con-stitutional law, constitutes just the kind of broad argument in political science and theory that Shane Phelan suggested could emerge from the LGBTQ litera-ture in political theory (Phelan 2000). It certainly shows the deep contribution that scholars such as Fogg Davis have to make to the discipline and the field.

We also see Shane Phelan developing an argument in her work about the importance of rights, and of a modified liberalism. In "(Be)Coming Out: Les-bian Identity and Politics" Phelan argues for a postmodern lesbianism that rests on work by Gloria Anzaldua, Diana Fuss, Judith Butler, and Teresa de Lauretis (Phelan 2000). Phelan uses Blasius to argue against the "coming out" discourse that lesbians and gay men use, and for a shift towards the idea of "becoming" lesbian or gay. This builds the concept of subjectivity and of political subjects as socially constructed, not as fixed or unchanging. This essay lays the groundwork for understanding the central issues to a political theory that does not start from the lives of heterosexuals but rather places people who identify as LGBTQ at the center (Phelan 2000). For Phelan, it is not queer theory that can provide a foun-dation or starting point, but rather the deeply flawed but nevertheless essential political theory of modernity, liberalism. In the six very different books that she reviews, Phelan sees emerging a common theme of rights as protection, rights that are founded in a modified idea of liberalism.

This argument is made with nuance, and Phelan notes that these theorists also hold in common a critique of what she terms "orthodox liberalism" as inadequate to understanding the lives or providing for the political well-being of people who identify as LGBTQ. The self of liberal theory is not imagined as queer. But a political theory that centers LGBTQ people must see at least two things, accord-ing to Phelan: it must see selves as constructed and relational, and it must pro-vide for rights that protect those selves—however rights might be conceived. "[I]t is precisely the intense need for rights that leads minorities to continually reencounter, reformulate principles that are so obviously defective on logical, ontological, and (finally) political grounds" (Phelan 2000, 441). Phelan argues that authors as diverse as Morris Kaplan and Valerie Lehr in their views of liberalism do not reject liberalism, but rather "transpose it to a new key" (Phelan 2000, 441). And, as she argues, "Basing rights not in a sovereign self but in a constructed and vulnerable one makes all the difference" (Phelan 2000, 438).

Phelan is not laying out this ground as a fan of liberalism—she makes clear (as in the quotation above) that it is deeply flawed. But in a sense Phelan is making a pragmatist argument: she notes that in the then-current political climate, liberalism is the best hope for the defense of the rights of minority groups. And her argument also makes clear the necessity of feminism for any adequate LGBTQ political theory—she critiques authors who inadequately attend to feminist concerns and arguments, and briefly notes that queer theory as it developed in the 1990s had inadequately attended to gender.

Of course, Phelan's book *Sexual Strangers*, which develops some of these themes more extensively, was published the year after this review (Phelan 2001). The book was reviewed in *APSR* in 2002 by Anna Marie Smith—and one critique is that it fails to engage queer theory. We are reading in the margins here, but it seems possible, given Phelan's critique of the absence of feminist analysis in queer theory, that perhaps she came to the conclusion that queer theory could not provide the grounds, at least at that time, for a satisfying and useful feminist LGBTQ political theory that attended to gender as well. Phelan sees a queer liberalism—with a need for rights as a form of protection—as a thread running through the queer political theory of the 1990s, and a concern for rights that is also evident in other realms such as in critical race theory.

The state, rights, liberalism—these are traditional concepts and concerns of political theory. In the hands of queer feminist political theorists, we can see these concepts in a new light, and see the necessity of rethinking and regrounding political theory and political science differently. This is why queer feminist political theory is so crucial to any understanding of politics and political life, and why the contributions of this body of literature are so important.

We offer one final example of the kind of integrative political theory that is possible given the contributions of queer feminist political theory. Concerned not specifically with the state, or with rights per se, but with the concept of democratic justice, Joan Tronto draws on queer feminist political theory, critical race studies, disability studies, and many other fields to argue for a rethinking of democratic justice, with the United States as her most concrete case or example (Tronto 2013). The book brings together a wide range of literatures and insights to make an argument about the construction of a just democratic polity. Drawing on queer feminist political theory's insights about the multiplicity and constructed nature of the subject, Tronto argues that if we were to change our conception of the political subject to the idea of a vulnerable person, in need of care, this would help us to rethink all of our political institutions to make them more democratic and just. Traditional ideas of the political subject imagine all humans as independent, self-sufficient, male, heterosexual adults. Drawing on a broad range of scholarship, including what we have called "queer feminist political theory," Tronto's argument shows how some of the concepts discussed above might be integrated to build more just societies, and to develop a political theory that imagines all humans as deserving of care and justice (Tronto 2013).

Conclusion

Lee Sigleman noted in his overview of the first one hundred years of the *APSR* that the politics of race and of gender "were among the topics that failed to attract much attention in the *Review*"; this is also certainly true of queer feminist political theory (Sigelman 2006, 471). Indeed, as we discuss above, much of the field of queer feminist political theory has developed in deeply intersectional ways, bringing together analysis of race, class, ethnicity, gender, sex, sexuality, and gender identity in complex, interesting, and analytically useful ways. Of course, there are limits to what one can expect from the *APSR*, which sees itself and the discipline in a very particular way. *Perspectives on Politics* has a much broader view of the discipline, and as such has been much more inclusive of work on gender and sexuality, on subjects that we have identified as queer feminist political theory (Isaac 2014; and see Isaac 2015). Nevertheless, as we have seen, a rich field of queer feminist political theory has developed, some of it in political science journals, much of it elsewhere, that has much to say to political theory and the discipline of political science, and much to contribute to the analysis of politics and political life.

We noted above that Mary Hawkesworth (2010) argues that feminist political theory and critical race theory are constructed by the field of political theory as external to the discipline of political theory, as a "constitutive outside," even by political theorists such as Timothy Kaufmann-Osborne who draw on feminist political theory, and could certainly be seen by some as feminist political theorists. Further, she argues that there is a "politics of extinction" practiced by the field of political theory, claiming to be postfeminist and postracist even as it erases and ignores the work and the claims of critical race and feminist theorists. Because

> feminist theory and critical race theory expose multiple fault lines in traditional political theory, then we begin to see why caricature or dismissal and neglect are the tactics of choice for a theoretical project as incomplete as mainstream political theory. For it is far easier to misrepresent and ignore the intellectual challenges raised by feminist theory and critical race theory than to engage them on their merits. (Hawkesworth 2010, 693)

We would like to see queer feminist political theory engaged on its merits, integrated into all aspects of political theory and political science inquiry. Heteronormativity, the socially constructed nature of sexuality and of political subjects, intersectionality and the multiple aspects of identity that are relevant to all aspects of life, including political life, the concept of sexual citizenship, the socially constructed nature of kinship and families and the many political implications of this insight, the implications for democratic politics of all of these insights—taking just one of these insights seriously would reground most of political theory. The discipline of political science, taking queer feminist political theory on its merits, would need a new epistemology. We look forward to a discipline, and a political theory, that takes up this challenge.

NOTES

1   The authors gratefully acknowledge the support of the Office of the Dean, FASN, Rutgers University–Newark, for an undergraduate research fellowship that supported the work on this chapter.

2   As we reviewed the literature in political science journals, a question we faced was, How might we locate work informed by queer theory in political science journals? Searches for "queer theory" yielded limited results; searches for "feminist theory" yielded many results unrelated to our question. Our instinct to use references to and uses of Judith Butler's work proved useful. Butler, along with Michel Foucault, Eve Sedgwick, and Teresa de Lauretis, are among the most commonly cited theorists who "founded" the field of queer theory. But political scientists and theorists make very little reference to Sedgwick and de Lauretis, and Foucault's work casts the net too wide for our purposes. So we found that using references to Judith Butler's work was a useful way to identify political theorists whose work drew upon the field of queer theory.

REFERENCES

Barvosa, Edwina. 2007. *Wealth of Selves: Multiple Identities, Mestiza Consciousness, and the Subject of Politics*. College Station: Texas A&M University Press.

Bell, David, and John Binnie. 2000. *The Sexual Citizen: Queer Politics and Beyond*. New York: Polity Press.

Beltrán, Christina. 2004. "Patrolling Borders: Hybrids, Hierarchies, and the Challenge of *Mestizaje*." *Political Research Quarterly* 57 (4): 595–607.

Blasius, Mark. 1992. "An Ethos of Lesbian and Gay Existence." *Political Theory* 20 (4): 642–71.

Blasius, Mark. 1994. *Gay and Lesbian Politics: Sexuality and the Emergence of a New Ethic*. Philadelphia: Temple University Press.

Blasius, Mark, ed. 2001. *Sexual Identities, Queer Politics*. Princeton, NJ: Princeton University Press.

Brettschneider, Marla. 2002. *Democratic Theorizing from the Margins*. Philadelphia: Temple University Press.

Brettschneider, Marla. 2006. *The Family Flamboyant: Race Politics, Queer Families, Jewish Lives*. Albany: SUNY Press.

Brettschneider, Marla. 2011. "Heterosexual Political Science." *PS: Political Science & Politics* 44 (1): 23–26.

Brettschneider, Marla. 2016. *Jewish Feminism and Intersectionality*. Albany: SUNY Press.

Brown, Wendy. 1988. " 'Supposing truth were a woman . . .': Plato's Subversion of Masculine Discourse." *Political Theory* 16 (4): 594–616.

Brown, Wendy. 2002. "At the Edge." *Political Theory* 30 (4, What Is Political Theory? Special Issue: Thirtieth Anniversary): 556–76.

Burack, Cynthia. 2004. *Healing Identities*. Ithaca, NY: Cornell University Press.

Burack, Cynthia. 2008. *Sin, Sex, and Democracy: Antigay Poliitcs and the Christian Right*. Albany: SUNY Press.

Burack, Cynthia. 2014. *Tough Love: Sexuality, Compassion, and the Christian Right*. Albany: SUNY Press.

Burgess, Susan. 2006. "Queer (Theory) Eye for the Straight (Legal) Guy: *Lawrence v. Texas'* Makeover of *Bowers v. Hardwick*." *Political Research Quarterly* 59 (3): 401–14.

Carvell, Terrell, and Samuel Chambers. 2007. "Kinship Trouble: *Antigone's Claim* and the Politics of Heteronormativity." *Politics and Gender* 3 (4): 427–49.

Cohen, Cathy. 1997. "Punks, Bulldaggers, and Welfare Queens." *GLQ* 3: 437–65.

Cohen, Cathy. 1999. *The Boundaries of Blackness: AIDS and the Breakdown of Black Politics*. Chicago: University of Chicago Press.

Cohen, Cathy. 2009. "Black Sexuality, Indigenous Moral Panics, and Respectability: From Bill Cosby to the Down Low." In *Moral Panics, Sex Panics: Fear and the Fight over Sexual Rights*, ed. Gilbert Herdt. New York: NYU Press, 104–29.

Cohen, Cathy. 2010. *Democracy Remixed: Black Youth and the Future of American Democracy*. New York: Oxford University Press.

Cook, Timothy E. 1999. "The Empirical Study of Lesbian, Gay, and Bisexual Politics: Assessing the First Wave of Research." *American Political Science Review* 93 (3): 679–92.

Cruikshank, Barbara. 1999. *The Will to Empower: Democratic Citizens and Other Subjects*. Ithaca, NY: Cornell University Press.

Currah, Paisley. 2011. "The State of LGBT/Sexuality Studies in Political Science." *PS: Political Science & Politics* 44 (1): 13–16.

Currah, Paisley. 2014. "The State." *Trans Studies Quarterly* 1 (1–2): 197–200.

Dietz, Mary. 2002. *Turning Operations: Feminism, Arendt, Politics*. New York: Routledge.

Disch, Lisa. 1999. "Judith Butler and the Politics of the Performative." *Political Theory* 27 (4): 545–59.

Duong, Kevin. 2012. "What Does Queer Theory Teach Us about Intersectionality?" *Politics & Gender* 8 (3): 370–86.

Egan, Patrick J., and Kenneth Sherrill. 2005. Marriage and the Shifting Priorities of a New Generation of Lesbians and Gays." *PS: Political Science & Politics* 38 (2): 229–32.

Fogg Davis, Heath. 2014. "Sex-Classification Policies as Transgender Discrimination: An Intersectional Critique." *Perspectives on Politics* 12 (1): 45–60.

Gerstmann, Evan. 2005. "Litigating Same-Sex Marriage: Might the Courts Actually Be Bastions of Rationality?" *PS: Political Science & Politics* 38 (2): 217–20.

Haider-Markel, Donald P., and Mark R. Joslyn. 2005. "Attributions and the Regulation of Marriage: Considering the Parallels between Race and Homosexuality." *PS: Political Science & Politics* 38 (2): 233–39.

Hancock, Ange-Marie. 2011. *Solidarity Politics for Millennials: A Guide to Ending the Oppression Olympics*. New York: Palgrave MacMillan.

Hancock, Ange-Marie. 2013. "Neurobiology, Intersectionality, and Politics: Paradigm Warriors in Arms?" *Perspectives on Politics* 11 (2): 504–7.

Hawkesworth, Mary E. 1988. "Feminist Rhetoric: Discourses on the Male Monopoly of Thought." *Political Theory* 16 (3): 444–67.

Hawkesworth, Mary E. 2006. *Feminist Inquiry: From Political Conviction to Methodological Innovation*. New Brunswick, NJ: Rutgers University Press.

Hawkesworth, Mary E. 2010. "From Constitutive Outside to the Politics of Extinction: Critical Race Theory, Feminist Theory, and Political Theory." *Political Research Quarterly* 63 (3): 686–96.

Hillygus, D. Sunshine, and Todd G. Shields. 2005. "Moral Issues and Voter Decision Making in the 2004 Presidential Election." *PS: Political Science & Politics* 38 (2): 201–9.

Hirschmann, Nancy J. 2003. *The Subject of Liberty: Toward a Feminist Theory of Freedom.* Princeton. NJ: Princeton University Press.

Isaac, Jeffrey C. 2014. "Gender and Politics." *Perspectives on Politics* 12 (1): 1–6.

Isaac, Jeffrey C. 2015. "For a More Public Political Science." *Perspectives on Politics* 13(2): 269–83.

Josephson, Jyl. 2005. "Citizenship, Same-Sex Marriage, and Feminist Critiques of Marriage." *Perspectives on Politics* 3 (2): 269–84.

Josephson, Jyl. 2016. *Rethinking Sexual Citizenship.* Albany: SUNY Press.

Kaplan, Morris B. 1997. "Liberté! Egalité! Sexualité! Theorizing Lesbian and Gay Politics." *Political Theory* 25 (3): 401–33.

Lax, Jeffrey R., and Justin H. Phillips. 2009. "Gay Rights in the States: Public Opinion and Policy Responsiveness." *American Political Science Review* 103 (3): 367–86.

Lehr, Valerie. 1998. *Queer Family Values: Rethinking the Myth of the Nuclear Family.* Philadelphia: Temple University Press.

Lewis, Gregory B. 2005. "Same-Sex Marriage and the 2004 Presidential Election." *PS: Political Science & Politics* 38 (2): 195–99.

McIvor, David W. 2012. "Bringing Ourselves to Grief: Judith Butler and the Politics of Mourning." *Political Theory* 40 (4): 409–36.

Mucciaroni, Gary. 2011. "The Study of LGBT Politics and Its Contributions to Political Science." *PS: Political Science & Politics* 44 (1): 17–21.

Namaste, Vivian. 2011. *Sex Change, Social Change: Reflections on Identity, Institutions, and Imperialism,* 2nd ed. Toronto: Canadian Scholars' Press.

Okin, Susan. 1989. *Justice, Gender, and the Family.* New York: Basic Books.

Pateman, Carole. 1988. *The Sexual Contract.* Stanford, CA: Stanford University Press.

Pateman, Carole, and Nancy Hirschmann. 1992. "Controversy." *American Political Science Review* 86 (1): 177.

Phelan, Shane. 1994. *Getting Specific: Postmodern Lesbian Politics.* Minneapolis: University of Minnesota Press.

Phelan, Shane. 2000. "Queer Liberalism?" *American Political Science Review* 94 (2): 431–42.

Phelan, Shane. 2001. *Sexual Strangers: Gays, Lesbians, and Dilemmas of Citizenship.* Philadelphia: Temple University Press.

Reynolds, Andrew. 2013. "Representation and Rights: The Impact of LGBT Legislators in Comparative Perspective." *American Political Science Review* 107 (2): 259–74.

Schneider, Anne, and Helen Ingram. 1993. "Social Construction of Target Populations: Implications for Politics and Policy." *American Political Science Review* 87(2): 334.

Segura, Gary M. 2005. "A Symposium on the Politics of Same-Sex Marriage: An Introduction and Commentary." *PS: Political Science & Politics* 38 (2): 189–93.

Sherrill, Kenneth, Carolyn Somerville, and Robert W. Bailey. 1992. "What Political Science Is Missing by Not Studying AIDS." *PS: Political Science & Politics* 25 (4): 688–93.

Sigelman, Lee. 2006. "The Coevolution of American Political Science and the American Political Science Review." *American Political Science Review* 100 (4): 463–78.

Smith, Anna Marie. 2001. "The Politicization of Marriage in Contemporary American Public Policy: The Defense of Marriage Act and the Personal Responsibility Act." *Citizenship Studies* 5 (3): 303–20.

Smith, Anna Marie. 2002. "Political Theory-Sexual Identities, Queer Politics/Sexual Strangers: Gays, Lesbians, and the Dilemmas of Citizenship." *American Political Science Review* 96(1): 172–74.

Smith, Anna Marie. 2007. *Welfare Reform and Sexual Regulation*. New York: Cambridge University Press.

Strolovitch, Dara. 2007. *Affirmative Advocacy: Race, Class, and Gender in Interest Group Politics*. Chicago: University of Chicago Press.

Stryker, Susan. 2008. *Transgender History*. Berkeley, CA: Seal Press.

Theriault, Sean M., and Herschel F. Thomas. 2014. "The Diffusion of Support for Same-Sex Marriage in the U.S. Senate." *PS: Political Science & Politics* 47 (4): 824–28.

Tolleson-Rinehart, Sue. 1988. *Gender Consciousness and Politics*. New York: Routledge.

Tolleson-Rinehart, Sue, and Susan J. Carroll. 2006. "'Far from Ideal': The Gender Politics of Political Science." *American Political Science Review* 100 (4): 507–13.

Tronto, Joan. 2013. *Caring Democracy: Markets, Equality, and Justice*. New York: NYU Press.

Valelly Richard M. "LGBT Politics and American Political Development." *American Political Science Review* 15: 312–32.

Wilson, Angelia R., and Susan Burgess. 2007. "Sexuality and the Body Politic: Thoughts on the Construction of an APSA Sexuality & Politics Section." *PS: Political Science & Politics* 40 (2): 377–81.

Zivi, Karen. 2012. *Making Rights Claims: A Practice of Democratic Citizenship*. New York: Oxford University Press.

PART III

LGBTQ Politics and Public Opinion in the United States

SUSAN BURGESS

The LGBTQ movement in the United States has made several gains in political equality in recent years. Gays and lesbians are allowed to marry. LGBT people can serve openly in the military. Antisodomy laws are no longer constitutional. Some acts of violence against LGBTQ populations can now be classified as hate crimes under federal law. These advances have led some mainstream political analysts to declare victory, suggesting that a once-marginalized LGBTQ population has gained more or less full rights of citizenship and thus has largely been assimilated into mainstream politics in the United States. However, more critical scholars have challenged this conclusion, suggesting that populations that do not readily conform to mainstream sex, gender, race, and class norms continue to be politically marginalized. The chapters in this section employ various theories that have long been accepted in the study of political science, critically exploring recent developments in LGBTQ politics in the context of several subfields of mainstream American politics, including public opinion, public policy, elections and campaigns, and political institutions such as Congress and the presidency. These chapters provide evidence that sometimes supports and at other times challenges the discipline's understanding of American politics, suggesting that integrating the study of LGBTQ politics into political science can both confirm and disrupt what the discipline thinks it knows about how politics works in the United States.

For example, standard explanations of how public opinion changes over time cannot adequately account for the dramatic rise in public support for gay rights in recent years. Social scientists have suggested that factors such as shifting demographics (e.g., age), new media framings (e.g., people are born gay), or interpersonal and mediated contact (e.g., coming out) can account for change in public opinion over time. In "The How, Why, and Who of LGBTQ 'Victory,'" Jeremiah Garretson argues that these theories fail to fully explain increased support for LGBT rights, suggesting that they are a product of a longstanding assumption in mainstream political science that political elites lead public opinion and the masses follow. Abandoning this assumption, Garretson shifts attention to the political behavior of marginalized populations, such as the political radicals in ACT-UP who skillfully used the media to gain public support for their cause during the breaking years of the AIDS crisis in the late 1980s and early 1990s. In doing so, he suggests that grassroots and radical political activities are an important, but often overlooked, source of political transformation.

The recent recognition of right of gays and lesbians to marry and to serve in the military has led many political analysts to declare "victory" for the LGBTQ movement. However, Garretson cautions that increased visibility and the intergroup contact that accompanies coming out have also served to reinforce profound resistance to gay rights among ideological and religious conservatives, who have consistently blocked policy change, such as legislation that would address LGBT employment discrimination. Further, he argues that it remains unclear whether the advances that gays and lesbians have achieved will translate into greater public support of bisexual, transgender, and other queer populations who may challenge mainstream sex and gender norms more profoundly.

Picking up on this theme, Don Haider-Markel and Patrick R. Miller argue in "Equality or Transformation?" that the recent focus on marriage equality has diverted attention from more progressive, perhaps even radical, policy preferences in the LGBTQ movement that aim to transform sex and gender norms at a more systemic level. Using attitudinal data, they suggest that traditional political science approaches to public opinion and agenda formation have led scholars to overlook a diversity of political interests at the grassroots level of the LGBTQ movement. They argue that support for policies that address alternative gender identities and family structures within the movement challenge commonly held assumptions about issue cohesion. They conclude that the enormous attention given to marriage may well continue to obstruct broader political mobilization, as the LGBTQ movement reassesses its priorities and goals in the wake of the U.S. Supreme Court's recent marriage-equality ruling in *Obergefell v. Hodges*.

Political scientists and pundits have long referred to the "bully pulpit" to suggest that modern presidents are particularly well situated to influence the shape of public opinion. In "Case Studies of Black Lesbian and Gay Candidates," Ravi K. Perry and X. Loudon Manley find evidence of the bully pulpit at work, arguing that President Obama's decision to support marriage equality in 2012 not only increased Black public opinion on the issue but also fostered a number of electoral victories for LGBT people of color running for state and local offices from 2012 to 2014. Further, they suggest that the intersectional understandings fueling the victors' campaigns may well have longer-term transformational effects, promoting a more diverse pool of candidates in the future who also embrace progressive policy agendas.

In "Equality in the House," Paul Snell suggests that LGBT interests have gained better representation in Congress despite persistently low numbers of LGBT-identifying members. He argues that this is due in no small part to the establishment of the LGBT Equality Caucus in Congress in 2009, signifying that once-marginalized LGBT interests have become institutionalized in Congress. Although the caucus is led by gay and lesbian members, most of its members identify as straight. The caucus has provided important leadership on pivotal LGBT bills such as the repeal of "Don't Ask, Don't Tell." Snell suggests that the institutionalization of the caucus challenges the traditional political science characterization of LGBT politics as a form of morality politics focused on a redistribution of values, suggesting instead that it is now best understood as a form of issue-based politics motivated by electoral and partisan concerns. Caucus members are more likely to cosponsor bills consistent with LGBT interests, providing an important voice for a group that is not well represented numerically. As might be expected, larger concentrations of evangelical constituents are associated with lower levels of cosponsorship activity, leading Snell to conclude that while LGBT interests are better represented, significant barriers to gaining the rights and liberties associated with full citizenship remain.

Political scientists have long thought that voter stereotypes about candidates offered in the media can negatively affect electoral success. Some evidence suggests that deep-seated prejudicial attitudes may weaken the likelihood that greater numbers of LGBT public officials will be elected in the future. In "Gay and Lesbian Candidates, Group Stereotypes, and the News Media," Mandi Bailey and Steven Nawara present a survey-based experiment designed to activate gender and sexuality stereotypes in order to explore media influence over voter choice. While respondents are less likely to vote for both gay and lesbian candidates, they are particularly reluctant when it comes to lesbians. Indeed, greater exposure to lesbian candidates appears to activate antilesbian stereotypes, strongly affecting candidate preference.

14

The How, Why, and Who of LGBTQ "Victory"

A Critical Examination of Change in Public Attitudes Involving LGBTQ People

JEREMIAH J. GARRETSON

"Victory," "Revolution," "Winning." These are some of the words one encounters when surveying the titles of newly published accounts of recent events in LGBTQ politics (Hirshman 2012; Faderman 2015; Solomon 2015). The sense that the pendulum has swung from the dark times of the early AIDS crisis and prior is palpable. This is especially the case on college campuses. Most students have no direct memories of the "culture wars" of the 1990s and early 2000s. Events like the 1993 Don't-Ask-Don't-Tell debate, the coming out of "Ellen" in 1998, and even the 2003 *Lawrence v. Texas* Supreme Court decision occurred before young people's earliest memories. Events further back in time, even those that are relatively recent—the Reagan-Bush years and the height of ACT-UP—are as distant to younger people as the Depression or World War II. The perception of most young people is that the rights and opportunities of LGBTQ people are approaching those of heterosexuals, or that equality will be achieved shortly, within a generation.

The most profound effect of this cultural shift has been on the lives of LGBTQ youth. While I could point to changes in law or the rhetoric of political elites to demonstrate this change in climate, I find it effective to point to the results of a set of opinion polls to illustrate this sea change. Increases in mass support for laws banning discrimination on the basis of sexual orientation or growth in support for same-sex marriage, both of which are commonly studied by academics and mentioned by the press, are often used to describe this shift. However, I think the one question asked on surveys that is most reflective of the qualitative change in LGBTQ life was asked by a set of *Los Angeles Times* polls and more recently by the Pew Organization.[1] "If you had a child who told you he or she were gay or lesbian, what would your reaction be?" Respondents could choose options to express their attitudes on the *L.A. Times* version of the question, which included "very upset," "somewhat upset," "not very upset," and "not upset at all."

In 1983, fully 61% of the public said they would be "very upset": the most negative and disapproving choice that could be selected. Having been a child in the 1980s, I do not think it is unimaginable that a sizable proportion of individuals indicating this response would be likely to disown or abandon a gay or lesbian child, although this is a much more severe act than merely indicating "upset" on a survey. The percentage stating this least tolerant response actually increased to 63% in 1985.

However, by 2000, attitudes had begun to shift. The percentage saying that they would be very upset nearly halved, to 34%. In 2004, it was down to 29%. When Pew asked the question in 2013, only 19% of the public—*only one-third of the 1983 number*—said they would be very upset if their child told them they were lesbian or gay. Even more surprising, the combined percentage that said "not very upset" or "not upset at all" rose from a measly 9% among the 1983 respondents to a full majority of 55% in 2013. If a 40%+ decrease in being "very upset" at having a lesbian or gay child is not meaningful change in public opinion, I don't know what is. This shift in attitudes towards potential gay and lesbian children is larger than changes in support for same-sex marriage (Flores 2015a) and other views relating to policy attitudes discussed in politics. Considering how much more personal and emotional this question is when compared to support for abstract rights like employment protections or military service, the magnitude of this shift in only twenty years is shocking. The probability that coming out as LGBT or Q will result in a loss of employment or rejection from friends or family has dropped substantially. This has radically transformed newer generations of LGBTQ youth born after 1990.

While political scientists like to focus on change in the viewpoints of political officials and policy attitudes—like employment protections and allowing gay and trans people in the military—my own perception is that when we speak of a shifting society and growing acceptance of LGBTQ in the United States, at the most fundamental level, we are not referencing merely political changes or shifting mass support for this or that abstract right. At a gut level, it is the change that LGBTQ people now see in the way their own neighbors, friends, coworkers, and family members respond to them in their everyday lives that is the real cultural shift. Especially among younger people, there is no longer a fear that stating one's sexual orientation or talking about a romantic partner to a friend, coworker, or family member will activate some latent negative prejudice. Rejection in such a situation is no longer assumed. Even if such rejection were to result from an offhand disclosure of sexuality, many LGBT people, especially younger people, would label such a person as being unrepresentative of most other people—an anomaly in his or her intransigent prejudice—a relic of the past. The end of the assumption, conscious or subconscious, that an "average" person will react prejudicially to an LGBTQ person has resulted in a new everyday openness, seen most prominently among LGBTQ youth. I believe this is the change that characterizes the LGBTQ "revolution" more than any other shift.

At the same time as this revolution has taken place, LGBTQ legal rights have failed to advance. The social climate for many LGBTQ people has improved in such an unexpectedly quick fashion, resulting in this shared sense of "victory," that many students in successive versions of my Sexuality and Politics class have reacted with shock when they have learned that employment discrimination is still legal at a federal level (as of 2016) and that most members of Congress and state legislatures are against even the modest LGBTQ rights that are supported by super-majorities of the public. To some extent, changing views do appear to be geographically bound, advancing faster in the Northeast and West and more slowly in the South (Lax and Phillips 2009).

I believe that the changed perceptions of LGBTQ people (and especially LGBTQ youth) are a direct result of a shift in American public opinion (and more generally, the mass attitudes of the populations of other liberal countries, see Ayoub and Garretson 2016). Most surveyed attitudes on LGBTQ issues involve specific political rights of gays and lesbians. Examples include the public's support for laws allowing same-sex marriage and employment protections based on sexual orientations. Shifts in support for these policies are reflections of a more elemental, affective change experienced by LGBTQ people in their interactions with others. Although also important, other obvious markers of "victory" that have occurred since the middle of the 1990s—the election of out LGBT officials, Supreme Court victories, and endorsements of gay rights by political leaders—have all been made possible by shifts in mass opinion occurring since roughly the end of the 1980s. Examining these surveys, even with their imperfect and narrow questions, can track this shift in a more precise fashion and allow for some understanding of just why American society has changed.

It is this change in mass opinion that is the focus of this chapter. When did this occur? Why did this occur? What are the boundaries and limitations of this cultural change? In the pages that follow, I want to provide my interpretation of what the political science and social science literature has to say in terms of answering these questions and what are fruitful grounds for this literature in the future. Understanding the causes of this change is important, because few mass reductions in prejudicial attitudes towards out-groups have been observed in as much detail as the reduction in overt antigay and antilesbian attitudes.

When Did Attitudes Change? Polling Data on LGBTQ Rights

In figure 14.1, I include a number of different trends in responses to LGBT-rights issues that have been discussed in the news since the 1980s. Mass viewpoints on the legality of homosexuality, allowing gays in the military, laws banning discrimination in employment based on sexual orientation, allowing same-sex marriage, allowing adoption by same-sex couples, and the general approval of the public for same-sex relations are all depicted in figure 14.1.[2]

While each specific gay rights issue has a different level of support across time (Mucciaroni 2008), the overall trend on each issue is similar. For instance, laws

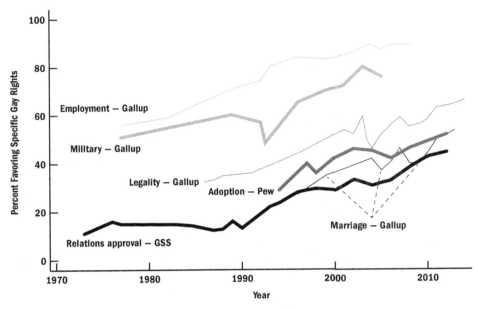

Figure 14.1. Trends in Lesbian and Gay (LG) Rights Attitudes.

banning discrimination in employment have been supported by a majority of the public since the 1970s. That majority has grown to near unanimity (as far as public surveys go) since the mid-1990s. This support has been consistently higher than support for allowing gays and lesbians to serve openly in the military (with the exception of a dip in support on that issue in 1993).

When examining questions about the public's views on whether or not homosexuality should be legal (when respondents were not first asked a question about a different gay rights issue),[3] one finds that only about 30% of the public supported the legality of homosexuality in the 1980s. This has increased to over 60% today, though the trend on legality fluctuated wildly in 2003 and 2004. This was at the same time as the *Lawrence* decision and when same-sex marriages first began to be performed in Massachusetts, Portland, and San Francisco.

Issues involving lesbian and gay families, such as gay marriage and adoption, have traditionally been less supported by the public (Mucciaroni 2008). The longest trend in opinion that exists on these issues is the General Social Survey's (GSS) trend on approval of same-sex relations by the public. Depicted in figure 14.1 is the percent of the public that states that these relationships are "not wrong at all." In the 1970s and 1980s, only between 10% and 20% of the public chose this option. By the 2010s, for the first time a plurality of the public indicated that same-sex relations were "not wrong at all." Trends in same-sex adoption from the Pew poll and same-sex marriage from Gallup are similar, although these issues only started to be polled semi-regularly in the mid-1990s. About 10% more of the public favors same-sex adoption as compared to approving of same-sex relations. Support for same-sex marriage is generally in between the levels of support for same-sex relationships and support for same-sex adoption. These relationship-based issues inched over the 50% support mark around 2012 as President Obama endorsed same-sex marriage.

Although I have described each trend individually, we shouldn't miss the forest for the trees. When we look at change in all of these issues together, it is clear that they are different manifestations of the same trend. There is little change in gay rights support across issues until at least the late 1980s or early 1990s. At that point, perhaps a little earlier on employment protections, the public starts to liberalize on all gay rights issues at once. The liberalization trend may have slowed in the early 2000s—the data are a little unclear—but even if that were the case, the liberalization trend appears to have started again around the late 2000s. There are a few anomalies. Specifically, support for gays in the military dropped in 1992 and 1993. Support for legality of homosexuality and same-sex marriage fluctuated in the mid-2000s. By and large, though, there is a clear pattern of change starting around the transition from the 1980s to the 1990s, the same time period of the height of ACT-UP and its push to get the government and national media to take the AIDS crisis and its victims seriously.

Why Did Attitudes Change? Theories from Political and Social Science

That mass attitudes on LGBT issues have shifted in a twenty-five-year period is not unique—it has happened before on race and gender roles from the 1940s to the 1980s (Page and Shapiro 1992)—but what is unique is the sheer amount of survey data collected as this change was unfolding. Outside of these examples, however, sustained and enduring shifts in mass attitudes are quite rare (Page and Shapiro 1992; Stimson 2004). For this reason, attitude change involving lesbian and gay rights does not fit neatly into the larger contours of the public opinion literature. One would think that many political scientists who purport to study public opinion and attitude change more generally would have taken the opportunity presented by this observed mass change in attitudes involving lesbians and gays to expand our basic knowledge of political change and the interrelation of mass attitudes with political actors and institutions more generally. After all, when something does not fit our current theoretical understanding of a phenomenon, like opinion instability on sexual minorities, it suggests that new understandings of public opinion at a fundamental level can result from determining exactly what has made lesbian- and gay-related attitudes exceptional on this account.

Despite the opportunity that change on LGBTQ issues has provided, few book-length studies or top journal articles about mass attitude change on LGBTQ issues have made it into print (although there are exceptions: Lax and

Phillips 2009; Bishin et al. 2015). The larger discipline of political science still appears to either ignore or marginalize LGBTQ politics research. Hopefully, the opportunities to leverage the knowledge that can be gained by exploring the unique features of the mass attitude change on LGBTQ issues will not slip away before the larger field takes notice.

A handful of scholars—some affiliated with the LGBT Caucus and/or the Sexuality and Politics section of the American Political Science Associations, some political scientists unaffiliated with these groups, and some scholars in other disciplines—have taken up the task of explaining why the American public (or liberal publics more generally) have changed. As I see it, these generally break into three sets of theories: (1) theories that implicate shifting demographics of the public (mostly from sociologists), (2) theories that implicate information coming from news media (from political science and the communications discipline), and (3) theories based on the Intergroup Contact Hypothesis (from the larger LGBTQ movement, social psychologists, and the communication discipline within academia).

The first class of theories involves the shifting demographics of the public (Loftus 2001; Treas 2002; Andersen and Fetner 2008; Baunach 2012; Olsen, Cadge, and Harrison 2006). Generally, more educated people, more secular people, and people born after 1970 have been much more supportive of gay rights. As these groups make up a larger proportion of the population over time, gay rights support has naturally increased.

However, while demographic change has appeared to contribute to more tolerant views, when put to the test, demographic change largely falls flat as a comprehensive theory of attitude change. Indeed, most studies that examine demographic change have concluded that a large proportion of attitudinal change has to be coming from elsewhere, largely because virtually every demographic group has seen increases in support for gay rights (Loftus 2001; Baunach 2012). Something else has to be at play, persuading people to support gay rights over the decades, rather than just the replacement of older, less educated, and more intolerant groups with younger, more educated, and more tolerant people. About half or more of the observed change in mass viewpoints is left unexplained by such theories (Loftus 2001).

As theories of attitude change based in shifting demographics simply cannot explain the scale of shifting attitudes, many political scientists have applied various theories from communications and social psychology in an attempt to explain the distinctiveness of change involving lesbian and gay rights. This second class of theoretical explanations stresses how changing understandings of homosexuality and gay rights have been communicated to the mass public through television news stories. All of these theories directly implicate the early 1990s as a critical transitional time period, as this is the time period in which the press started to report on several different developments relating to lesbian and gay life in the United States and elsewhere due to intense pressure from activist groups such as ACT-UP. In that sense, they are consistent with the trends described above indicating the start of large-scale change across gay right issues around 1990.

For example, building on attribution theory in social psychology, Don Haider-Markel and Mark Joslyn (2008) suggest that new beliefs that homosexuality has a biological basis—that people are perhaps "born gay"—are the key to the shift. These viewpoints began to increase dramatically in the early 1990s. Theoretically, adopting a "born gay" viewpoint may also shift individuals in favor of gay rights. News stories on genetic and physiological research on a biological basis for sexual orientation also started becoming common in the early 1990s and continued across the course of the decade. Thus the timing of articles and news stories covering this research matches up nicely with opinion shifts seen in figure 14.1.

However, there is reason to doubt the impact of attributional change for homosexuality as a major cause of the advancement of gay rights. Although changing attributions are associated with increases in support for lesbian and gay rights during this time period, attributional change was heavily concentrated among political liberals. This naturally limits its impact on mass attitude, as this group comprises only about 30% of the public or less (Garretson and Suhay 2016). Furthermore, experimental evidence (from more recent years) suggests that changing attributions do not always lead to increased support for gay rights (Suhay and Garretson 2015).

The media has an even more central role as an agent of change, according to value-framing theories of gay rights (Brewer 2003a, 2003b, 2008). According to these theories, as lesbian and gay rights began to be discussed in the news media in the early 1990s, reporters began to shift the ways in which gay rights were discussed. Specifically, news stories began to include quotations from activists or phrases in the text that mentioned lesbians and gays as seeking equality or equal rights like other minority groups (Brewer 2003b). These "egalitarian frames" brought fundamental values of equal treatment—which are held strongly by most members of the public—to the fore of people's thoughts when forming a conclusion on support or opposition to specific lesbian and gay rights (Brewer 2003a, 2003b). Since a large proportion of the public expresses support for egalitarianism (in principle), these frames led the public to use norms of egalitarianism as guides when accessing their support for specific lesbian and gay rights, thus increasing gay-rights support among the public. At the same time, alternative frames, those describing homosexuality in religious terms as "sinful" or immoral, also connected lesbian and gay rights with mass values of "moral traditionalism," resulting in decreased likelihood to support lesbian and gay rights among those who endorsed such values. This generally led to polarization on gay rights, but with gay rights support initially so low, support among egalitarians increased faster than it dropped among moral traditionalists.

An additional prominent theory of the origins of attitude change is also dependent on media coverage, although not in the way it was originally formulated: the theory of issue evolution. According to this theory, when elected officials and political elites polarize (along partisan lines) on an issue, people in the public who psychologically identify with that party (i.e., Democrats and Republicans) will slowly bring their views on that issue in line with their party's leaders. Prior issue evolutions have occurred on race and women's rights (Carmines and Stimson 1989; Wolbretch 2000). Starting in the 1970s, Democrats became increasingly in favor of lesbian and gay rights, while Republicans stayed almost universally opposed over the years. Beginning in the late 1980s, a majority of the Democratic Party in Congress became supportive of gay rights. Democrat Bill Clinton ran for president on an explicitly pro–gay rights platform in that same year.

Although media coverage is not explicitly mentioned in the theory of issue evolution, it seems that coverage of pro-gay Democrats and antigay Republicans is a necessary prerequisite to trigger attitude change among members of their parties (Lindaman and Haider-Markel 2002), something that did not happen until the 1990s. There does appear to be a small increase in polarization between Democrats and Republicans on lesbian and gay rights in 1992 and 1993, as predicted by the theory (Wilcox and Wolpert 1996; Bailey, Sigelman, and Wilcox 2003).

Lastly, many studies have confirmed that policy change on gay rights does not result in a backlash in support for gay rights among the public, as many gay activists had feared was the case in the 2000s after Massachusetts legalized same-sex marriage (Bishin et al. 2015). In fact, there is firm and persuasive evidence that legalizing same-sex marriage in localities moves public opinion on gay rights in a pro-gay direction both at the individual (Flores and Barclay 2015) and at the mass level (Flores and Barclay 2014). Although just how policy change results in attitudinal change is not always clear, the simplest causal mechanism that seems to fit involves citizens being exposed to a policy debate on same-sex marriage transmitted through news media.

These news-based theories are among the most prominent theories accounting for attitude change on lesbian and gay rights. The timing of changes on gay rights, as well as the disproportionate shift of those on the Left toward a pro-gay position, is easily explained. However, the more one thinks about the unique characteristics of attitude change on gay rights, the more one gets the feeling that the bits and pieces of these theories do not quite fit into a complete explanation.

In figure 14.2, I include counts of news stories devoted to gay rights specifically on the big three (ABC, NBC, CBS) television evening news programs.[4] The first thing one notices is that there was a moderate amount of coverage in the late 1970s, of which the assassination of Harvey Milk in 1978 was the dominant event. This coverage seems to have largely failed to result in any substantive attitude change. Furthermore, although coverage was at its most intense in 1992 and 1993 (although coverage of the AIDS crisis and gay activism were prominently covered in the TV news as early as 1990), much of the 1993 coverage involved allowing gays in the military. Recall from above that this was the one issue and year when support for gay rights *dropped* before recovering in successive years. Certainly "egalitarian frames" in this coverage were not pushing the public in a net liberal direction. The last peak in coverage in 2003 and 2004 involved mostly coverage of *Lawrence*, which involved the legality of homosexuality, as well as shock over the first same-sex marriages occurring in various localities across the country. Again, support for these issues fluctuated or flattened during this times, rather than liberalizing, which does not seem to support the thesis that news coverage is the primary cause of the upward trend in gay rights support across issues.

The reasons why these theories of news-media-transmitted mechanisms of attitudinal change do not seem to fit with the larger picture of attitude change actually run a bit deeper than just issues of timing. First, no one disputes that younger people have changed faster and more deeply in their support for gay rights since the mid-1990s than other segments of the population. At the same time, younger people have been the *least* likely demographic to consume the news. And it is not just young people who exhibit this pattern. When one looks at the increase in support for employment protection for lesbians and gays as reported by respondents of the American National Election Study from 1988 to 2008 as a function of self-reported television consumption, one finds that those who reported watching the news five days a week or more increased in strong support for such antidiscrimination laws by 21.3% over that twenty-year period. But astonishingly, those who reported watching the news an average of zero days a week saw their support increase by 30%, a full *10%* higher (Garretson 2015c). Clearly, news coverage, in and of itself, is not responsible for the bulk of attitude change if those who report avoiding the news are the most likely to change. The news may dominate the study of political communication and public opinion more generally, and framing and issue evolution may be the primary drivers of attitude change on most other issues, but they appear to be ill-fitting explanations for the distinctiveness of change on lesbian and gay rights. My own opinion is that news coverage may explain why specific gay rights issues deviate from the overall liberalizing trend since the late 1980s, but the ultimate cause for the liberalizing trend in general lies elsewhere.

The last group of theories as to the origin of mass opinion change on gay rights have their origin in social psychology, communications, and the LGBTQ movements themselves. These predicate that increases in the rates of intergroup contact between LGBTQ people and others are largely responsible for the mass public's changed viewpoints on issues of gay and lesbian rights. In essence, LGBTQ people have come out of the closet, and this is the primary driver of the public's change of heart on homosexuality. Coming out to others as LGBTQ—an act whose encouragement has been a key aspect of lesbian and gay culture since the 1970s—is predicted to result in more liberal attitudes toward LGBTQ people among individuals who meet others who are LGBTQ (Herek 2003; Lewis 2011) via the Social Contact Hypothesis of social psychologist Gordon Allport (1954). A long list of studies validates that positive interpersonal contact can effectively reduce prejudice through multiple psychological mechanisms (Hewstone and Swart 2011), especially contact where two individuals meet multiple times and share a common identity or other aspect of their lives, like a hobby or occupation (Pettigrew and Tropp 2006). Likewise, communications scholars and political scientists have shown that mediated contact with recurring fictional characters (in books, films, or television) who are members of out-groups can also result in positive change when individuals lack contact with members of these groups in their everyday lives (Riggle, Ellis, and Crawford 1996; Schiappa, Gregg, and Hewes 2006; Garretson 2015a, 2015b). That said, superficial or negative contact that reinforces stereotypes—interpersonally or mediated—can strengthen prejudicial attitudes in some situations (Hewstone and Swart 2011; Harrison and Michelson 2012).

Figure 14.2 also plots the percentage of people who report knowing lesbian or gay individuals according to the Pew poll in various years. In 1985, less that one-quarter of the public knew lesbians and gays. By the mid-1990s, this had risen to over 40% of the public and to over 50% by the late 1990s. By the late 2000s, it had approached

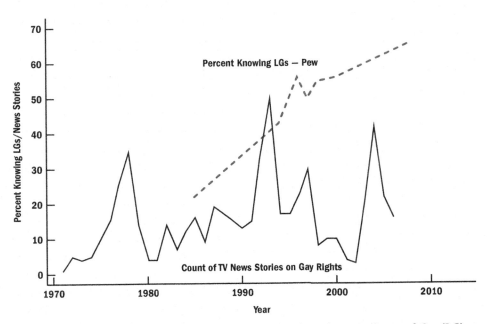

Figure 14.2. Trends in Factors Thought to Cause Change in Attitudes on Lesbian and Gay (LG) Rights.

70%. Some contemporary polls (not depicted) find the percentage closer to 80% or 90% as of 2015. Clearly, this is an important change and one that appears to directly parallel the trend lines in gay-rights public opinion. Counts of recurring LGB television characters in these years, a measure of the amount of mediated contact with LGBs, also show an almost identical trend (Garretson 2015c).

Just as with other theories of attitude change, there is a concern that increases in interpersonal and mediated contact with LGBTQ people may be a problematic explanation for attitude change. The principle critique of such theory involves *selection effects*, the notion that LGBTQ people will only come out to those already reliably pro-gay and that only people with pro-LGBTQ attitudes will watch shows with LGBTQ characters. Generally, though, evidence from recent research using experimental and quasi-experimental methods (Altemeyer 2001; Garretson 2015a), which largely control for selection effects, finds intergroup contact with lesbians and gays to be effective in reducing prejudice. Importantly, these effects of prejudice reduction are more powerful in younger people, finally explaining why younger people are generally more liberal on gay rights than older individuals and why youth liberalism on homosexuality had emerged largely in the late 1990s (Garretson 2015a, 2015c).

This leaves one lagging question involving the underlying causes of attitudinal change, though. If increases in coming out since the late 1980s are the major cause of the trends we see in figure 14.1 (along with some change due to the effects of fictional television characters that are LGB), what led individuals to suddenly start coming out at higher rates in this time period?

One solution to this problem may be to bring back the old public opinion concept of a *two-step communication flow*, but to reimagine it in a radically different fashion. Traditionally, a two-step flow of communication involves "opinion leaders" in local communities being exposed to viewpoints and information via the news. This new information affects the attitudes of these individuals: "opinion leaders" in the original formation (Lazarsfeld, Berelson, and Gaudet 1948). Others in the same immediate social environment as the opinion leaders then have interpersonal discussions with them, resulting in their attitudes also being affected by the same information in a second-hand fashion. This is important, because their attitudes are not *directly* affected by reading the newspaper or watching the TV news, but *indirectly* by encountering it from opinion leaders.

I propose that the missing piece that draws together the various trends in news coverage of lesbian and gay issues, coming out, and attitudinal change is a two-step flow of communication of a radically different sort than that originally proposed by Lazarfield and coauthors.

LGBTQ people naturally paid attention to the ongoing developments and information on lesbian and gay politics being broadcast on the national news in the early 1990s, and, later, to representations of lesbians and gays in popular culture in the mid- and late 1990s. Although public opinion had scarcely changed on gay rights by 1990, LGBTQ people responded to events covered in the news—first sympathetic coverage of ACT-UP and AIDS victims, Clinton's 1992 endorsements of gay rights, Oscar wins for *Philadelphia*, liberal Democratic support for gays in the military—and began to feel more comfortable sharing their lives with others. As they started to do so, they came out to individuals in their immediate personal lives in large enough numbers to affect national public opinion. The American public started to become less antigay, lessening the stigma among many in the population and, importantly, triggering additional waves of coming out across the course of the 1990s and after.

This also explains why pro-gay attitudes increased faster in states that legalized same-sex marriage than in states that did not (Flores and Barclay 2014). Furthermore, it would explain why the liberalizing effects of pro-gay policy seem to continue in the years after same-sex marriage became legal (Flores and Barclay 2014), rather than occurring only in the year when the policy changed. Same-sex marriage and other pro-gay policies made LGBT individuals feel more comfortable sharing their lives with others, resulting in attitudinal change. This positive climate and the coming out that it encouraged persists long after any policy debate ends.

In this way, a two-step information flow formed. But those who were the intermediaries of this flow were not "opinion leaders," the professional elite of local communities, but rather those who were marginalized—or potentially risked marginalization—because of their sexuality or gender identity. Rather than an "opinion elite," those most interested in the issue of gay rights served as the medium through which change occurred. In doing so, they triggered change across the United States and elsewhere. This is a markedly different two-step process, one not affecting opinion leaders but members of a marginalized group, and perhaps one without a known observed parallel in the social science literature.

The media climate of the early 1990s may have even created the impression of a changed society before change in the mass public actually began. Regardless of this, the perception of momentum on lesbian and gay rights probably encouraged additional coming out, ironically making the impression of a more liberal country a reality. Naturally, those who were most affected were the millennial generation, who became the first generation to then learn about lesbians and gays by meeting them in person (or by seeing them sympathetically portrayed on late-1990s television), rather than through the prism of a homophobic and heterosexist mass culture.

Who Changed (or Who Didn't)? Those Left behind by Attitudinal Change

Although most demographic groups have liberalized considerably, change has been less concentrated among political conservatives, Republicans, and those who hold identities as evangelical or born-again Christians (Baunach 2012; Burack 2008). Attitudes have generally improved among these groups, but the data suggests that intergroup contact either is less effective or, in some cases, can paradoxically result in *decreased* pro-gay attitudes among these groups (Skipworth, Garner, and Dettrey 2010; Garner 2013; Dyck and Pearson-Merkowitz 2014; Bramlett 2012). Although these groups generally report lower contact rates with LGBs in general (Lewis 2011), it is the reduced effectiveness of interpersonal contact that has resulted in lower levels of support, as reported rates of contact among conservatives have increased at the same rate as among political liberals and moderates (Garretson 2015c).

While strong prior attitudes or commitments to prejudice can close people off to attitudinal change in the social and political psychology literature (Lodge and Taber 2013), these findings generally contradict the LGBTQ movement line that coming out to others always results in positive change. Coming out may always be beneficial for the psychological health and general well-being of the person coming out, but in terms of a program of attitudinal change, those who are very ardent in support for ideological conservatism or are part of a religious tradition that endorses heterosexism are much less likely than others to see their antigay attitudes lessened when then meet LGBTQ people.

Unfortunately, this explains why super-majorities of the American public now support fundamental gay rights, but little legal change has occurred to advance gay rights. As the political parties have polarized in American politics more generally, virtually every elected Republican official has become an ardent conservative, and thus a member of one of the handful of social and political groups in which contact appears to have little to no effect. This means that in legislative arenas that are disproportionately dominated by ardent conservatives and Republicans, LGBTQ rights will not advance except under extraordinary circumstances. Thus public opinion change, as remarkable as it has been, has not translated into change in public policy. Any declaration of "victory" on LGBTQ rights is, unfortunately, incomplete. Few could have anticipated twenty years ago that a federal law banning employment discrimination on sexual orientation would be supported by 80% to 90% of the public, yet still be a nonstarter in Congress.

Future Directions for Attitudinal Research on Gendered Beliefs and LGBTQ Issues

While I believe this is a coherent explanation for the social changes we have seen in public opinion regarding lesbians and gays, there is still a massive amount that we don't know. Throughout this article, I have jumped back and forth between using "lesbian and gay," "LGB," and "LGBTQ," perhaps unfortunately giving the reader a sense of whiplash. I have done this primarily because, while it has been the entire LGBTQ movement (or movements) that has successfully effected change, the reality is that the survey data used to measure change mostly only asks about "gays" or, at most, "lesbians and gays." We simply do not know the extent to which "lesbian," "gay," "bisexual," "transgender," and "queer" are overlapping concepts in the public mind, and if changing attitudes regarding lesbians and gays have, through this conceptual overlap, resulted in more acceptance for bisexual, transgender, and queer people over the years. My own sense is that this may well be the case for a portion of the public, particularly young people.

At the same time, however, there are reasons to suspect that this might not have been the case. Early theoretical explanations of heterosexism strongly stressed its root in persistent beliefs among the public in distinctive and natural differences between men and women (Altman 1993; Wittig 1992; Butler 1990). Stated another way, for one to believe that men should only sexually desire (and be with) women, and that women should only sexually desire (and be with) men, one must first hold beliefs that men and women are separate and distinct groups of people with natural or God-given distinct roles. Without some sort of intrinsically sexist beliefs—that women and men are different and are meant for different social (and sexual) roles—heterosexism loses its logical grounding. No doubt there is a strong reason to suspect that LGBTQ rights would not have advanced without the success of the feminist movement in weakening the belief among much of the public in the naturalness of some forms of gender differences from the late 1960s onward (i.e., employment in the professions and politics).

As lesbians and gays have become perceived as a legitimate minority group in the United States and elsewhere, similar to racial and ethnic minorities, the relationship between sexist roots and heterosexist beliefs may have become weakened. The logic of intergroup contact itself is based strongly on the notion of those with static in-group (i.e., the mass public) and out-group (i.e., lesbian and gay) identities interacting. What I suspect this means is that, to the extent that lesbians and gays have become thought of as just another social group, the correlation between sexist beliefs in the public and lesbian and gay rights has diminished. If I were to guess, I would strongly suspect that negative views toward transgender, bisexual, and other queer people are still strongly rooted in notions of natural differences between men and women (as well as the belief in the binary of "men and women" itself).

Thus, if intergroup contact and its grounding in (heterosexual) in-groups and (homosexual) out-groups, has been the key reason for this "victory," does this mean that a post-identity queer liberationist politics is less likely to succeed at a mass level, versus a politics based around a shared identity like "gay" or "lesbian"? If so, that is a naturally troubling outcome for those who would support a liberationist agenda. Or, if bias and gendered beliefs are reduced through intergroup contact with out-groups, is it possible that successive exposure of the public to out-groups who are progressively more queer (i.e., feminist, then lesbian and gay, then bisexual, then transgender, then genderqueer) will eventually allow for the emergence of a post-gender, liberationist politics, one in which the distinctive social categories that brought about social change then evaporate and recede? For instance, contact with lesbians and gays may raise support for transgender rights (Flores 2015b), potentially creating a more conducive climate for transgender people to interact with others, which could in turn then lessen beliefs in the "naturalness" of gender roles and advance feminist goals. To answer these questions, we need more basic research into transgender rights, lesbian and gay rights, beliefs on the appropriateness of gender roles, contact with various sexual and gender minorities, and their interrelationship. This all suggests the need for, and the potential for, a stronger working relationship between those who research LGBTQ politics, women and politics, and other organized research sections of the APSA.

As I mentioned above, as meaningful as mass opinion change has been for the lives of lesbians and gays, it has still not translated into policy change, probably because of the ineffectiveness of contact to affect both strong conservatives and strong believers in the doctrines of anti-LGBTQ religious denominations. What is it about the beliefs of people in these groups that reduces the effectiveness of exposure to lesbians and gays? What psychological process specifically closes off the possibility of change, and can this process be disrupted? If Republican and conservative elites switch their stances on lesbian and gay rights, will their adherents finally bend, or will they merely elect more thoroughly antigay elites in the next round of party primaries? Are younger, ardent conservatives as committed to resisting lesbian and gay rights as their older brethren?

None of these questions have clear and obvious answers based on current events and the political science literature, but answering these questions—as well as understanding the interrelations among sexism, heterosexism, and intergroup contact—is crucial to both translating mass opinion change into policy change in the United States and broadening the limited "victory" that has been achieved in changing mass opinion into a real "victory" worthy of the term.

NOTES

1 George Gao, "Most Americans Now Say Learning Their Child Is Gay Wouldn't Upset Them." Pew Research Center Fact Tank, June 29, 2014. www.pewresearch.org.

2 These were gathered from the websites of the various polling firms that asked the questions. The employment-nondiscrimination, legality-of-homosexuality, same-sex-marriage, and allowing-gays-in-the-military series were all taken from the Gallup Poll, "Gay and Lesbian Rights," at www.gallup.com. The same-sex-adoption series was taken from the Pew poll (see Bowman and Foster 2008 and "Two-thirds of Democrats Now Support Gay Marriage," part 2: "Long-term Views of Homosexuality, Gay Marriage, and Adoption." Pew Research Center, July 31, 2012, www.pewforum.org. The same-sex-relations series was computed by the author from the General Social Survey dataset housed on the website http://sda .berkeley.edu. These questions are largely representative of larger trends in polling data across questions (see Bowman and Foster 2008).

3 This trend only includes questions that were not preceded by a prior question involving gay rights. Leading questions on specific gay rights appear to artificially raise support for legality due to a question order effect. See Egan, Persily, and Wallsten (2008) for more details on this specific question.

4 See Garretson (2015ab) for notes on the construction of this news series from the abstracts of the Vanderbilt Television News Archive.

REFERENCES

Allport, Gordon W. 1954. *The Nature of Prejudice*. New York: Addison-Wesley.

Altemeyer, Bob. 2001. "Changes in Attitudes toward Homosexuals." *Journal of Homosexuality* 42(2): 63–75.

Altman, Dennis. 1993. *Homosexual Oppression and Liberation*. New York: NYU Press.

Andersen, Robert, and Tina Fetner. 2008. "Cohort Differences in Tolerance of Homosexuality: Attitudinal Change in Canada and the United States, 1981–2000." *Public Opinion Quarterly* 72(2): 311–30.

Ayoub, Phil, and Jeremiah J. Garretson. 2015. "Getting the Message Out: Media Context and Global Changes in Attitudes involving Homosexuality." Working paper.

Bailey, Michael, Lee Sigelman, and Clyde Wilcox. 2003. "Presidential Persuasion on Social Issues: A Two-Way Street?" *Political Research Quarterly* 56(1): 49–58.

Baunach, Dawn Michelle. 2012. "Changing Same-Sex Marriage Attitudes in America from 1988 through 2010." *Public Opinion Quarterly* 76(2): 364–78.

Bishin, B. G., T. J. Hayes, M. B. Incantalupo, and C. A. Smith. 2015. "Opinion Backlash and Public Attitudes: Are Political Advances in Gay Rights Counterproductive?" *American Journal of Political Science*. Online First. doi: 10.1111/ajps.12181.

Bowman, Karlyn, and Adam Foster. 2008. "Attitudes about Homosexuality & Gay Marriage." American Enterprise Institute Studies in Public Opinion. https://www.aei.org.

Bramlett, Brittany M. 2012. "The Cross-Pressures of Religion and Contact with Gays and Lesbians, and Their Impact on Same-Sex Marriage Opinion." *Politics and Policy* 40(1): 13–42.

Brewer, Paul R. 2003a. "The Shifting Foundations of Public Opinion about Gay Rights." *Journal of Politics* 6: 1208–20.

Brewer, Paul R. 2003b. "Values, Political Knowledge, and Public Opinion about Gay Rights: A Framing-Based Account." *Public Opinion Quarterly* 67(2): 173–201.

Brewer, Paul R. 2008. *Value War: Public Opinion and the Politics of Gay Rights*. Lanham, MD: Rowman & Littlefield.

Burack, Cynthia. 2008. *Sin, Sex, and Democracy: Antigay Rhetoric and the Christian Right*. Albany: SUNY Press.

Butler, Judith. 1990. *Gender Trouble: Feminism and the Subversion of Identity*. New York: Routledge.

Carmines, Edward. G., and James A. Stimson. 1989. *Issue Evolution: Race and the Transformation of American Politics*. Princeton, NJ: Princeton University Press.

Dyck, Joshua J., and Shuanna Pearson-Merkowitz. 2014. "To Know You Is Not Necessarily to Love You: The Partisan Mediators of Intergroup Contact." *Political Behavior* 36(3): 553–80.

Egan, Patrick, Nathaniel Persily, and Kevin Wallsten. 2008. "Gay Rights." In *Public Opinion and Constitutional Controversy*. Nathaniel Persily, Jack Citrin, and Patrick J. Egan, eds. New York: Oxford University Press.

Faderman, Lillian. 2015. *The Gay Revolution: The Story of the Struggle*. New York: Simon & Schuster.

Flores, Andrew R. 2015a. "Attitudes toward Transgender Rights: Perceived Knowledge and Secondary Interpersonal Contact." *Politics, Groups, and Identities* 3(3): 398–416.

Flores, Andrew R. 2015b. "Examining Variation in Surveying Attitudes on Same-Sex Marriage: A Meta-Analysis." *Public Opinion Quarterly* 72(2): 580–93.

Flores, Andrew R., and Scott Barclay. 2014. "Backlash, Consensus, or Naturalization: The Impact of Policy Shift on Subsequent Public Opinion Levels." Paper presented at the 2014 meeting of the Western Political Science Association.

Flores, Andrew R., and Scott Barclay. 2015. "Backlash, Consensus, Legitimacy, or Polarization: The Effect of Same-Sex Marriage Policy on Mass Attitudes." *Political Research Quarterly* 69(1): 43–56.

Garner, Andrew. 2013. "Ambivalence, the Intergroup Contact Hypothesis, and Attitudes about Gay Rights." *Politics and Policy* 41(2): 241–66.

Garretson, Jeremiah J. 2015a. "Exposure to the Lives of Lesbians and Gays and the Origin of Young People's Greater Support for Gay Rights." *International Journal of Public Opinion Research* 27(2): 277–88.

Garretson, Jeremiah J. 2015b. *Why Tolerance Triumphed: The Origins of America's Changed Views on Lesbian and Gay Rights*. Unpublished book manuscript.

Garretson, Jeremiah J. 2015c. "Does Change in Minority and Women's Representation on Television Matter? A Thirty-Year Study of Television and Social Tolerance." *Politics, Groups, and Identities* 3(4): 615–32.

Garretson, Jeremiah J., and Elizabeth Suhay. 2016. "Scientific Communication about Biological Influences on Homosexuality and the Politics of Gay Rights." *Political Research Quarterly* 69(1): 17–29.

Haider-Markel, Donald P., and Mark R. Joslyn. 2008. "Beliefs about the Origins of Homosexuality and Support for Gay Rights: An Empirical Test of Attribution Theory." *Public Opinion Quarterly* 72(2): 291–310.

Harrison, Brian F., and Melissa R. Michelson. 2012. "Not That There's Anything Wrong with That: Messaging, Source Credibility, and Marriage Equality." *Political Behavior* 34(2): 325–44.

Herek, Gregory M. 2003. "Why Tell If You're Not Asked? Self-Disclosure, Intergroup Contact, and Heterosexuals' Attitudes toward Lesbians and Gay Men." In *Psychological Perspectives on Lesbian, Gay, and Bisexual Experiences,* 2nd edition. Linda D. Garnets and Douglas C. Kimmel, eds. New York: Columbia University Press.

Hewstone, Miles, and Hermann Swart. 2011. "Fifty-Odd Years of Intergroup Contact: From Hypothesis to Integrated Theory." *British Journal of Social Psychology* 50: 374–86.

Hirshman, Linda. 2012. *Victory: The Triumphant Gay Revolution*. New York: HarperCollins.

Lax, Jeffrey R., and Justin Phillips. 2009. "Gay Rights in the States: Public Opinion and Policy Responsiveness." *American Political Science Review* 103(3): 367–86.

Lazarsfeld, Paul F., Bernard R. Berelson, and Hazel Gaudet. 1948. *The People's Choice: How the Voter Makes Up His Mind in a Presidential Campaign*. New York: Columbia University Press.

Lewis, Gregory B. 2011. "The Friends and Family Plan: Contact with Gays and Support for Gay Rights." *Policy Studies Journal* 39(2): 217–38.

Lindaman, Kara, and Donald P. Haider-Markel. 2002. "Issue Evolution, Political Parties, and the Culture Wars." *Political Research Quarterly* 55(1): 91–110.

Lodge, Milton, and Charles S. Taber. 2013. *The Rationalizing Voter*. New York: Cambridge University Press.

Loftus, Jeni. 2001. "America's Liberalization in Attitudes toward Homosexuality, 1973 to 1998." *American Sociological Review* 66(5): 762–82.

Mucciaroni, Gary. 2008. *Same-Sex, Different Politics: Success and Failure in the Struggles over Gay Rights*. Chicago: University of Chicago Press.

Olsen, Laura R., Wendy Cadge, and James T. Harrison. 2006. "Religion and Public Opinion about Same-Sex Marriage." *Social Science Quarterly* 87(2): 340–60.

Page, Benjamin I., and Robert Y. Shapiro. 1992. *The Rational Public*. Chicago: University of Chicago Press.

Pettigrew, Thomas F., and Linda R. Tropp. 2006. "A Meta-Analytic Test of Intergroup Contact Theory." *Journal of Personality and Social Psychology* 90(5): 751–83.

Riggle, Ellen D. B., Alan L. Ellis, and Anne M. Crawford. 1996. "The Impact of 'Media Contact' on Attitudes toward Gay Men." *Journal of Homosexuality* 31(3): 55–69.

Schiappa, Edward, Peter B. Gregg, and Dean E. Hewes. 2006. "Can One TV Show Make a Difference? *Will and Grace* and the Parasocial Contact Hypothesis." *Journal of Homosexuality* 51(4): 15–37.

Skipworth, Sue Ann, Andrew Garner, and Bryan J. Dettrey. 2010. "Limitations of the Contact Hypothesis: Heterogeneity in the Contact Effect on Attitudes toward Gay Rights." *Politics and Policy* 37(1): 31–50.

Solomon, Marc. 2015. *Winning Marriage: The Inside Story of How Same-Sex Couples Took on the Politicians—and Won*. Lebanon, NH: ForeEdge.

Stimson, James. 2004. *Tides of Consent*. New York: Cambridge University Press.

Suhay, Elizabeth, and Jeremiah Garretson. 2015. "Science, Sexuality, and Civil Rights: Does Research on the Causes of Homosexuality Have a Political Impact?" Paper presented at the 2015 NYU Experimental Political Science Meeting.

Treas, Judith. 2002. "How Cohorts, Education, and Ideology Shaped a New Sexual Revolution on American Attitudes toward Nonmarital Sex, 1972–1998." *Sociological Perspectives* 45(3): 267–83.

Wilcox, Clyde, and Robin Wolpert. 1996 "President Clinton, Public Opinion, and Gays in the Military." In *Gay Rights, Military Wrongs: Political Perspectives on Lesbians and Gays in the Military*. Craig Rimmerman, ed. New York: Garland.

Wittig, Monique. 1992. *The Straight Mind and Other Essays*. Boston: Beacon.

Wolbrecht, Christina. 2000. *The Politics of Women's Rights: Parties, Positions, and Change*. Princeton, NJ: Princeton University Press.

15

Equality or Transformation?

LGBT Political Attitudes and Priorities and the Implications for the Movement

DONALD P. HAIDER-MARKEL AND PATRICK R. MILLER

Although the lesbian, gay, bisexual, and transgender (LGBT) movement is often characterized as a unified movement, it actually encompasses a fair amount of diversity in goals and priorities, historically and currently. The Supreme Court's removal of all bans on same-sex marriage in *Obergfell v. Hodges* in June 2015, one of the publicized priorities of the movement, has provided an opportunity to reexamine the political attitudes, behavior, and goals of LGBTQ Americans through the historical lenses of the assimilationist versus liberationist philosophies that were so prominent in the movement through the 1970s but seem nearly forgotten today; some elements of the liberation perspective have persisted, especially in liberal enclaves. As Jordan Stein notes of his college experience in the 1990s,

> We were not just going to hold utopian beliefs—we were going to live them. We were going to change the world. In equal measure, we wanted to fight tyranny and to celebrate beauty. . . . In all those dreams, marriage never factored. We wanted to celebrate the queer people we were and loved. But we were queer, not gay. We didn't fit into the world as we found it. We gravitated to the hope of something better. We dreamed that, come the revolution, there will be no identity. Come the revolution, there will be no marriage. Come the revolution, we will love without rules. (2015)

Stein sums up much of what was relevant in the assimilationist versus liberationist perspectives in the LGBT movement—liberationists sought to break down traditions, ideas about normality, and barriers to seeking a greater, freer perspective on being human, while assimilationists sought to integrate the LGBT community into the broader society with an implicit acceptance of many (but not all) of its norms and subsequent institutions (see Flores and Sherrill 2013; Haider-Markel 2010; Rimmerman 2007). Indeed, although assimilationists would have reveled in the Court's same-sex marriage decision, liberationists would have viewed it as cooptation and "normalization" (see Wilkinson 2015).

This chapter explores this tension in the movement by examining recent data on the attitudes of LGBT Americans to understand whether the political priorities and beliefs of LGBT adults can be described as cohesive. In this process we especially seek to understand how an individual sense of a strong LGBT identity shapes these perspectives. Although we are unable to systematically compare the attitudes of LGBT Americans to those of past decades, we are able to draw some conclusions about LGBT attitudes based on age and cohort. Our analysis suggests that while the general political orientation of the LGBT community is relatively cohesive compared to that of other groups, there are significant differences within the community on movement priorities. These cleavages result in part because of differences in ideology and income, but also social identity as LGBT and perceptions of discrimination. We conclude that the success of the marriage-equality movement might assist in increasing cohesion on movement priorities even as the victory could reduce the strength of LGBT identity.

An Overview of Political Cohesion in the LGBT Movement

It seems to be common knowledge today that the majority of adults who identify as LGBT are politically liberal and tend to vote for Democrats, but this fact tends to downplay the reality that roughly 20–25 percent of LGBT Americans identify as politically conservative and tend to vote Republican; these figures have remained fairly steady since the 1990s, with some variation between midterm and presidential election years (Bailey 1998, 2000; Cimino 2007; Egan 2012; Hertzog 1996; Newport 2014a).[1] Indeed, as Egan (2015) clearly illustrates, in the 2012 American National Election Study survey of American voters, LG voters are on average 15 percentage points more liberal on issues such as the environment, gun control, immigration, and taxes than are non-LG voters.[2] This ideological and partisan cohesion is similar to political cohesion among African Americans, Jews, and Evangelicals (Egan 2012; Olson 2010), even though African Americans can boast above 80 percent identification with the Democratic Party (Dugan 2013). Likewise, LGBT support for President Obama is almost twenty points higher than it is among non-LGBT Americans (Newport 2014a). And LGBT Americans are almost twice as likely as are heterosexuals to indicate that they have no religious identity (Newport 2014b).

The liberal and Democratic leanings of the LGBT community do indicate broad political cohesion, but belie some significant underlying divisions on issues facing the LGBT community and the LGBT movement. Below we explore differences in attitudes on a number of issues and move to a multivariate model that seeks to explain differences among individuals who identify as LGBT.

Attitudes about Problems Facing the LGBT Community and Public Policy

There is little in the way of publicly accessible survey data from representative samples of the LGBT population, but some recent data has become available from the Pew Research Center and Gallup. In addition, several studies provide some reliable sense of LGBT attitudes, even though the individual-level data from the surveys employed is not publicly available (for example, see Egan 2012; Egan, Edelman, and Sherrill 2008; Flores and Sherrill 2013; Schaffner and Senic 2006). Unfortunately, most surveys of the LGBT population do not ask many questions pertaining to a defined liberationist perspective and instead focus on social acceptance and policies that some would consider assimilationist in nature. However, some survey questions have been asked that reference an assimilation versus a liberation perspective (also see Egan, Edelman, and Sherrill 2008; Schaffner and Senic 2006).

In polling by the Pew Research Center (2013) only 19 percent of LGBT respondents indicated that there was a lot of social acceptance of LGBT people in the country today ("some" responses were 59 percent and "only a little" were 21 percent), but 92 percent indicated that society had become "a lot" (52 percent) or "a little" (40 percent) more accepting of LGBT people over the preceding ten years. Most respondents believed that LGBT societal acceptance is helped a lot by people knowing someone who is LGBT, out LGBT public figures, LGBT people raising families, and open support from public figures who are not LGBT. Meanwhile, respondents suggested the LGBT pride events and LGBT characters in TV shows and in movies help LGBT societal acceptance to a lesser degree.[3]

To assess assimilationist perspectives, we employed responses to four questions where respondents were asked to make a forced choice between options (see appendix for full questions and coding). In table 15.1 we display the percentage of respondents providing an assimilationist response to each of the questions. On two of the issues, being seen as different and prioritizing marriage equality over other issues, majorities provided assimilationist responses. But on the two questions regarding LGBT versus mainstream culture, respondents veered away from an assimilationist response, seeming to support a more liberationist perspective. Overall, gay men tended to be somewhat less assimilationist and lesbians more so.

When asked about the most important problems facing the LGBT community, 57 percent of respondents provided open-ended answers indicating social treatment, such as discrimination, and 32 percent cited legal rights or the right to marry. As often is the case in survey research, open-ended responses offer a view of a more diverse range of attitudes than forced categories. In the case of the LGBT community, the responses could not be easily classified as assimilationist or liberationist, but those responses focused on social treatment and

TABLE 15.1. Percentage of LGBT Respondents Providing an Assimilationist Response, Total and by Subgroup

Response	Total	Gay Men	Lesbians	Bisexuals
Same-sex marriage should be the top priority for LGBT people right now, even if this means some other issues do not get much attention	58%	57%	71%	58%
The best way to achieve equality is for LGBT people to be a part of mainstream culture and institutions like marriage	49%	47%	55%	49%
I don't want to be seen as different because of my (*sexual orientation*/gender identity)	74%	71%	79%	75%
(LGBT neighborhoods and gay and lesbian bars) These types of places will not be important as LGBT people are more accepted into society	41%	31%	43%	48%

Notes: Adapted from Pew Research Center (2013) survey of 1,197 LGBT adults in the United States. Each question was preceded by "Which statement comes closer to your own views—even if neither is exactly right?" Here we display the percentage of respondents indicating an assimilationist response.

discrimination rather than strict policy goals involving government might be deemed as more liberationist in orientation.

Of course in recent years the most salient issue for the LGBT movement has been same-sex marriage, an institution historically considered as the ultimate bastion of traditional moral values and gender roles and assailed by liberationists (Rimmerman 2007). But this wasn't always the case. As Flores and Sherrill (2013) demonstrate, in 2003 same-sex marriage was not a top-five priority for LGBT Democrats or Republicans, and only came in fifth among LGBT Independents.

And although the LGBT population was considerably more supportive of legal same-sex marriage than was the general public in 2013 (93 to 51 percent), support was not absolute (Pew Research Center 2013). Likewise, in a 2003 poll, LGBT Republicans, college graduates, African Americans, and older respondents were statistically less likely to support same-sex marriage than were other LGBT respondents (Flores and Sherrill 2013; see also Schaffner and Senic 2006). In addition, although 58 percent of LGBT Americans did indicate that same-sex marriage should be a top priority of the movement by 2013, 39 percent indicated that marriage has pulled too much attention away from other LGBT issues (forced choice question; Pew Research Center 2013).[4]

But when marriage is compared to other issue priorities directly, as a "top priority" equal employment rights tops the list at 57 percent, same-sex marriage is second at 53 percent, and health insurance coverage of transgender health issues comes in last, at 29 percent (see table 15.2; Pew Research Center 2013). Addressing HIV/AIDS, adoption rights, and support for LGBT youth received similar levels of prioritization, just around 45 percent. This is indeed a sharp shift from the early 2000s when workplace discrimination, hate crimes, and AIDS funding were the priorities for most LGBT adults (Flores and Sherrill 2013).

TABLE 15.2. LGBT Respondent Percent Indicating a Policy Issue Should Be a "Top Priority"

Equal employment rights for LGBT people	57%
Legally sanctioned same-sex marriages	53%
Prevention and treatment of HIV/AIDS	47%
Adoption rights for same-sex couples	45%
Support for organizations that provide services to LGBT youth	41%
Legally sanctioned civil unions or domestic partnerships for same-sex couples	39%
Coverage of transgender health issues by health insurance	29%

Notes: Adapted from Pew Research Center (2013) survey of 1,197 LGBT adults in the United States. The question asked, "Thinking about some policy issues, do you think each of the following should be a top priority, a very important but not top priority, a somewhat important priority, or not a priority at all?"

TABLE 15.3. LGBT Respondent Percent Indicating a Policy Issue Should Be a "Top Priority," by Subgroup

	Gay Men	Lesbians	Bisexuals
Equal employment rights for LGBT people	62%	69%	49%
Legally sanctioned same-sex marriages	54%	69%	50%
Prevention and treatment of HIV/AIDS	57%	45%	40%
Adoption rights for same-sex couples	45%	60%	42%
Support for organizations that provide services to LGBT youth	49%	52%	30%
Legally sanctioned civil unions or domestic partnerships for same-sex couples	41%	47%	36%
Coverage of transgender health issues by health insurance	30%	38%	23%

Notes: Adapted from Pew Research Center (2013) survey of 1,197 LGBT adults in the United States. The question asked, "Thinking about some policy issues, do you think each of the following should be a top priority, a very important but not top priority, a somewhat important priority, or not a priority at all?"

Even though employment rights and marriage receive a higher priority among LGBT adults in recent years, there are differences in the policy priorities of gay men, lesbians, and bisexuals (see table 15.3). In particular, gay men are more likely to prioritize HIV/AIDS over marriage rights, while lesbians place more emphasis on adoption rights and are more likely overall to say all of the issues should be top priorities. Bisexuals do not prioritize any of the issues as a majority and were more likely to indicate that a given issue was either less important or not a priority compared to gay men and lesbians.

Explaining Differences

Of course, individual differences among those in the LGBT community could certainly lead to divergent views about the LGBT movement and goals and priorities of the movement. For example, in a 2013 survey only 16 percent of LGBT adults reported being married and another 44 percent indicated that they would like to be married someday; in the overall population of adults, 76 percent indicate that they are or would like to be married (Pew Research Center 2013). The 40 percent of LGBT adults who have no desire to be married nearly matches the 39 percent that indicate marriage is drawing attention away from other LGBT issues.

And part of the distinction between priorities of individuals is due to gender. For example, women who identify as LGBT are just as likely as non-LGBT woman to be raising children, while men who identify as LGBT are significantly less likely to be raising children (Gates and Newport 2012). This experiential difference could certainly explain part of the divergence in attitudes about movement priorities. One can also easily imagine that other demographic differences, such as age, race, income, education level, marital status, and the like could explain attitudinal preferences, just as they do in more general attitudes about political issues (Tajfel 1981).

However, our goal is to better understand how differences in social identification as LGBT and political orientation might explain preferences in movement priorities above and beyond demographic characteristics. We focus on ideology, partisanship, and social identity. Our primary analysis employs the responses to the Pew Research Center (2013) random probability sample survey of American LGBT adults.

Measurement and Analysis

As noted, many LGBT adults identify as liberal and tend to vote Democratic. However, at least one-quarter of LGBT Americans have ideological identities that are conservative or moderate, and have partisan identities that are Independent or Republican. Given the liberal and Democratic leaning of the LGBT movement overall, we would therefore expect LGBT respondents who identify as liberal or Democrat to consider all movement goals as major priorities. However, our analysis focuses more directly on the role of assimilationist attitudes, social identity strength as LGBT, and exposure to an "LGBT culture."

Dependent Variables: We examine several different measures of attitudes related to the LGBT movement. First, we assess respondent support for "allowing gays and lesbians to marry legally" and "allowing gays and lesbians to adopt children." Responses on both items are scaled from "strongly favor" to "strongly oppose." Among Pew LGBT respondents, 94 percent support same-sex marriage and 95 percent support gay adoption to some degree. We then explore movement priorities via two questions. In the first, respondents were asked to name "the most important problems facing" LGBT people. Pew posed this as an open-ended question and content analyzed responses into twelve categories of policy and social problems. In the second, Pew named seven policy areas and asked respondents to rank how much of a priority those issues should be on a scale ranging from "a top priority" to "not a priority at all" (unless otherwise noted, see the appendix for the full questions, response category labels, and coding).

Political Orientation: We assess the impact of political ideology and partisan identification on LGBT attitudes. To measure ideology we employ responses to a question about political ideology in which respondents are asked to describe their political views on a scale ranging from "very conservative" to "very liberal," with a midpoint indicating "moderate" ideology. Among respondents, 11 percent identify as conservative, 35 percent as moderate, and the remaining 54 percent as liberal to some degree. To measure partisanship, we use a standard partisanship question; only 8 percent of LGBT respondents identify as Republicans in our sample, whereas 57 percent label themselves Democrats, and the remaining 35 percent as Independent or "other" party.

Social Identity: The Pew survey allowed for a variety of gender self-identifications and sexual-orientation identifications. Self-labeling is the most basic and necessary indicator of social identity (Tajfel 1981), but we are more concerned with an individual's strength of identity as an LGBT person. Research indicates that psychological identification with a social group is a choice and that even if a person is technically part of a group by some objective standard, she may not have accepted and internalized that identity (Flores 2014; Huddy 2004). Conover (1988) agrees and argues that social identity has two components: a self-awareness of one's membership in the group and a psychological sense of attachment to the group.

To measure social identity as an attachment to a group, we focus on several components of identity that are addressed in the literature. These include individual identity importance, linked fate to members of the group, and perceived discrimination. These elements of social identity have received little attention in political science literature on the LGBT population.[5] Identity importance refers to how central individuals feel a particular identity is to their sense of self, a concept that has been applied to the study of partisan identity (Miller and Conover 2015), among others. To measure identity importance, we employ a question asking respondents to score how important they feel being LGBT is to their "overall identity" on a scale from "not at all important" to "extremely important" (ranges 0–4; $M = 2.01$, $SD = 1.21$).

Linked fate refers to the belief that one's own condition in life and social standing is connected to the status of the broader group—in other words (Hurwitz, Peffley, and Mondak 2015), an LGBT individual believing that her personal life fortunes in part depend on the social status of LGBTs as a group. Scholars of race in political science have effectively assessed linked fate in racial subgroups, revealing important behavioral patterns (e.g., Dawson 1994; Gay 2004; Tate 2003). Pew respondents were asked to rate from "not at all" to "a lot" how much they feel that they share "common concerns and identity" with gay men, lesbians, bisexuals, and transgender people separately. These ratings are combined into an additive scale where higher values indicate that respondents have stronger senses of linked fate with other LGBT people (α = .77; ranges 0–9; M = 4.93, SD = 2.31).

Perceived discrimination against one's ingroup has also been found to be an indicator of social identity (Flores 2014; Miller et al. 1981). However, there is often a complex and disconnected relationship between how much individuals think their ingroups are discriminated against socially and how much discrimination they perceive themselves to have faced (Crosby 1984; Flores 2014; Fuegen and Biernat 2000; Oskooii 2015; Sigel 1996). As the two types of discrimination have been shown to have significant behavioral effects (Oskooii 2015), our models include measures of each from the Pew survey. Group-level discrimination is measured via one survey item asking respondents how much discrimination they believe there is against "gays and lesbians" (ranges 0–3; M = 2.45, SD = .69), whereas individual-level discrimination is an additive scale of six types of poor treatment respondents believed they have experienced because of their LGBT status.

Assimilationist Attitudes: To assess respondent dispositions toward LGBT assimilation, the four dichotomous-choice questions detailed in table 15.1 are combined into an additive scale (ranges 0–4; M=2.34, SD=1.07). Higher scores on the scale indicate that a respondent holds more assimilationist attitudes.

Control Variables: We employ standard control measures for demographic characteristics, including age, income, education, sex, and race (Flores and Sherrill 2013). Additionally, we are also concerned with the social-network connections individuals have to the LGBT community given the often powerful effects that social context has on political behavior, so our models include two contextual measures: whether the respondent reports living in a "neighborhood known for being an LGBT neighborhood" and how many of the respondents' close friends are LGBT.

Results and Discussion

Table 15.4 displays the results of our models predicting support for LGBT adoption and marriage rights. Though responses on both items lean overwhelmingly towards "strongly favor," the performance of the independent variables in the model reveals some opinion cleavages among LGBT respondents; however, given the skew of the data, in substantive terms those divides only produce differences in the predicted probabilities of "favor" and "strongly favor" responses. In short, although differences exist, the differences are not large.

Assimilationist attitudes positively predict support for adoption and marriage rights, both of which would allow LGBT individuals to form legal familial bonds that more closely mimic traditional heterosexual nuclear families. Respondents who consistently give nonassimilationist responses still overwhelmingly favor

TABLE 15.4. LGBT Support for Adoption and Marriage Rights

	Adoption	Marriage
Assimilation Scale	.211**	.519***
	(.081)	(.087)
Identity Importance	.158*	.193*
	(.078)	(.082)
Linked Fate	.227***	.269***
	(.040)	(.042)
Group Discrimination	.589***	.674***
	(.114)	(.118)
Personal Discrimination	.088+	.040
	(.049)	(.050)
LGB Friends	.231*	.382**
	(.108)	(.110)
LGB Neighborhood	−.035	−.210
	(.280)	(.279)
Ideology ^ liberal	.668***	.803***
	(.106)	(.111)
Partisanship ^ Democrat	.163*	.163*
	(.065)	(.066)
Age	−.205***	−.236***
	(.057)	(.058)
Education	.211+	.092
	(.110)	(.113)
Female	.493**	.352+
	(.178)	(.181)
Income	.084*	.120**
	(.042)	(.044)
Married	−.068	−.202
	(.213)	(.218)
White	.525**	.427*
	(.192)	(.199)
τ_1	2.532	2.959
τ_2	3.796	4.968
τ_3	6.191	7.284
LR	363.25***	457.09***
McFadden's Pseudo-R^2	.235	.292
N	1166	1172

Notes: Entries are unstandardized ordinal logistic regression coefficients; SE in parentheses; +p<.1, *p<.05, **p<.01, ***p<.001; data are from a Pew Research Center (2013) survey of 1,197 LGBT adults in the United States.

both rights, but their support is somewhat more tepid than that of the most assimilationist LGBT persons. Those scoring the minimum on the assimilation scale have a 78.18 percent predicted probability of strongly favoring adoption rights, holding all other predictors at their respective means. That increases to 89.27 percent for respondents scoring at the scale maximum value. That shift comes almost exclusively from "favor" responses, the probabilities of which decline from the scale maximum of 19.34 percent to the scale minimum of 9.65 percent. Marriage support demonstrates a similar but more pronounced pattern. The least assimilationist Pew respondents have a 67.67 percent change of giving a "strongly favor" response versus a 27.83 percent chance of answering only "favor," but those probabilities shift to 94.33 percent and 5.08 percent for the most assimilationist.

The three indicators of LGBT social identity are also statistically significant and positively predict adoption and marriage support, but again they only really differentiate between "favor" and "strongly favor" responses. For identity importance, the predicted probability of strongly favoring adoption rights increases from 80.98 percent for respondents claiming that LGBT identity is not at all important to them to 88.91 percent for those saying it is extremely important. That same change for marriage rights is 82.70 percent to 91.17 percent. Respondents demonstrating zero sense of linked fate still have a 65.66 percent chance of strongly favoring adoption rights and a 65.18 percent chance of answering the same for marriage rights, but those respect probabilities increase to 93.64 percent and 95.46 percent for respondents scoring the maximum on the linked fate scale. And for group-level discrimination, respondents perceiving no discrimination against LGBTs still have a 58.02 percent probability of strongly favoring adoption and a 57.44 percent probability of strongly favoring marriage rights, with those respective likelihoods increasing to 89.01 percent and 91.06 percent among those perceiving a lot of discrimination. Personal-level discrimination perceptions have no relationship to attitudes on either policy.

Likewise, for the remaining statistically significant predictors, LGBT respondents, even in the "least supportive" categories on each variable, still overwhelmingly favor both rights and are more likely than not to give a "strongly favor" response for both policies. Response patterns across the two models are fairly consistent. Younger, higher-income, white, more liberal, and more Democratic LGBT respondents are more likely than other respondents to provide a strongly favor response in both models, as are those who report that a higher proportion of their close friends are also LGBT. Women are more likely than men to strongly favor adoption rights, but that relationship does not reach conventional levels of statistical significance for marriage. Thus, on questions of policies that would expand LGBT rights and allow them to mimic legally more traditional family structures, LGBTs across all significant individual characteristics overwhelmingly support those policies despite differences in the strength of their support.

Table 15.5 presents models for responses on the open-ended question about the "most important problem" for LGBTs. Respondents are asked to mention up to three important problems. The first column provides the percentage of the Pew sample naming each category as an important problem regardless of whether it was the first, second, or third mention. Although 88 percent of respondents identify at least one problem (the other 12 percent providing either a "don't know" or a blank answer), the sample is substantially divided on the problems they perceive as important. The most popular response captures answers related to equality generally and discrimination, but only 32 percent of respondents provide an answer that Pew codes in that category. Generally, the three most popular answers—discrimination, rights, and marriage—are all related to legal equality for LGBT people. The fourth and fifth most frequently provided responses—ignorance and acceptance—are both related to social equality.

The next three columns in table 15.5 provide the percentage of gay male, lesbian, and bisexual respondents providing an answer in each problem category. The differences among the three subgroups are generally small. The most pronounced division emerges on the general legal rights category; 43 percent of lesbians identify this as an important problem, but only 28 percent of gay men and 21 percent of bisexuals do so. Most other subgroup differences are minor, but bisexuals seem marginally more concerned with ignorance and acceptance than other respondents, and gay men slightly more concerned with self-esteem issues.

Table 15.6 models the likelihood that respondents provide a given open-ended response for each category. We only present the models where either the assimilation scale or indicators of LGBT social identity are statistically significant predictors, and where the likelihood ratio test is statistically significant. Assimilation only differentiates responses on two items: the most assimilationist LGBTs have an 18.78 percent predicted probability of naming marriage as a problem versus

TABLE 15.5. Percent of LGBT Respondents Mentioning Each Category as Most Important Problem

Most Important Problem	Overall (N=1197)	Gay Men (N=412)	Lesbians (N=262)	Bisexuals (N=433)
Lack of general equality/discrimination/prejudice/bigotry/stigma	31.83%	34.22%	33.20%	30.95%
Legal rights (general)	27.65%	28.40%	42.75%	21.02%
Right to marry	15.62%	15.29%	17.94%	15.94%
Ignorance/misunderstanding/stupidity/fear/stereotyping	13.12%	11.65%	11.07%	16.63%
Lack of acceptance	17.96%	15.53%	18.33%	20.55%
Violence/bullying/hate crimes	7.69%	8.25%	8.40%	7.39%
Religious opposition/the religious Right	9.69%	11.16%	10.31%	9.24%
Unprotected sex/STDs/AIDS	1.09%	1.70%	.38%	1.15%
Republicans/conservatives	1.25%	2.43%	1.15%	.23%
The same issues as other people	1.25%	.97%	1.91%	1.39%
Issues specific to transgendered people	1.58%	1.46%	1.91%	1.85%
Self-esteem/self-acceptance/problems of own making	3.43%	5.83%	1.53%	2.31%

Notes: Adapted from Pew Research Center (2013) survey of 1,197 LGBT adults in the United States.

TABLE 15.6. LGBT Respondents Naming Each Category as Important Problem

	Equality	Rights	Marriage	Violence	Religion	Self
Assimilation Scale	−.036	.064	.201*	−.357**	.009	−.218
	(.062)	(.066)	(.080)	(.107)	(.096)	(.159)
Identity Importance	−.130*	.204**	.080	−.171	.015	−.403*
	(.062)	(.067)	(.080)	(.112)	(.096)	(.162)
Linked Fate	.073*	.015	.058	.058	.117*	−.043
	(.031)	(.033)	(.040)	(.056)	(.050)	(.079)
Group Discrimination	.358**	.370**	.040	.295	.356+	−.626**
	(.111)	(.123)	(.141)	(.215)	(.185)	(.221)
Personal Discrimination	.097*	.075+	−.001	.156*	.053	.063
	(.038)	(.040)	(.049)	(.066)	(.057)	(.099)
LGB Friends	−.023	.099	−.016	.199	.170	.354
	(.089)	(.095)	(.115)	(.161)	(.141)	(.226)
LGB Neighborhood	.159	−.522*	−.193	−.264	−.104	.391
	(.198)	(.225)	(.267)	(.364)	(.311)	(.449)
Ideology ^ liberal	.068	.125	.066	.264+	−.079	.211
	(.083)	(.089)	(.107)	(.152)	(.130)	(.213)
Partisanship ^ Democrat	.039	.028	.166+	.174	.073	−.023
	(.061)	(.067)	(.085)	(.137)	(.100)	(.150)
Age	−.057	−.008	−.234***	−.068	.043	.164
	(.044)	(.047)	(.058)	(.077)	(.068)	(.113)
Education	.226*	.264*	.196	.540**	−.020	.182
	(.096)	(.106)	(.124)	(.194)	(.147)	(.246)
Female	−.061	.384**	.242	.323	.125	−.625+
	(.137)	(.146)	(.177)	(.242)	(.213)	(.365)
Income	.068*	.099**	.019	−.052	.026	−.012
	(.033)	(.034)	(.042)	(.056)	(.050)	(.080)
Married	−.072	−.436*	−.540*	−.452	−.471	−.231
	(.172)	(.190)	(.241)	(.362)	(.299)	(.478)
White	.157	.323+	.415*	.005	−.471	−.361
	(.161)	(.174)	(.210)	(.274)	(.299)	(.394)
Constant	-3.175***	-5.043***	-3.913***	-6.387***	-4.822***	-2.568*
	(.479)	(.552)	(.640)	(1.030)	(.801)	(1.065)
LR	56.33***	105.05***	54.63***	57.68***	31.12**	33.42**
McFadden's Pseudo-R^2	.038	.075	.053	.092	.041	.094
N	1176	1176	1176	1176	1176	1176

Notes: Entries are unstandardized logistic regression coefficients; SE in parentheses; +p<.1, *p<.05, **p<.01, ***p<.001; data are from a Pew Research Center (2013) survey of 1,197 LGBT adults in the United States.

a 9.37 percent chance for the least assimilationist, holding all other predictors at their means. Conversely, the least assimilationist have an 11.98 percent chance of naming violence, whereas the most assimilationist have just a 3.16 percent chance. The assimilation scale has no effect on the likelihood of naming any other problem.

The social identity indicators yield more mixed results. Respondents who say that their LGBT identity is more important to them are less likely to name general equality and LGBT adults themselves as problems, but more likely to name general rights. LGBT respondents with a stronger sense of linked fate are more likely to name problems categorized as general equality and religion. And those who perceive greater discrimination against LGBTs as a group are more likely to name general equality and general rights as problems, but less likely to say that LGBTs themselves are a problem. Relatedly, respondents who claim to have experienced greater personal discrimination are more likely to name general equality and violence as problems. Interestingly, the two explicitly political variables—ideology and partisanship—fail to reach conventional significance levels across all of the models. And the two measures of social context—share of friends who are LGBT and living in an LGBT neighborhood—also fail to yield consistent effects across the models, though respondents residing in LGBT neighborhoods are less likely to name general rights as a problem.

Overall, then, the table 15.6 models fail to show a consistent pattern of division in attitudes among LGBT respondents. Certainly, differences in assimilationist attitudes are associated with some dimensions of LGBT social identity and perceptions of certain problems, but not in a systematic manner across issues, as evidenced by the fact that no one variable yields a consistent effect across the models. And indeed, as none of the predicted probabilities associated with the significant predictors in table 15.6 exceed 50 percent, even when effects do appear, those respondents who are most likely to label a certain issue as a problem have a greater likelihood of not naming that issue than they do of mentioning it.

The lack of systematic effects across models in the most important problem analysis may partly be an artifact of the open-ended nature of the question. Perhaps if respondents are given an issue and asked to assess it, more consistent patterns may emerge. Table 15.7 applies our model to the problems mentioned in table 15.3 where respondents are asked if certain issues should be a "top priority" for LGBTs.

Indeed, table 15.7 reveals a more consistent pattern of division in LGBT issue attitudes when respondents evaluate closed-ended survey questions. Assimilationist attitudes divide respondents on legal equality issues that have more prominently been part of the national LGBT-rights debate: marriage, civil unions, adoption, and approaching statistical significance on employment. For example, respondents scoring at the assimilation scale minimum value have just a 29.02 percent predicted probability of labeling marriage a "top priority," all other predictors at their means. But those scoring at the scale maximum—the most assimilationist LGBTs who, recalling the earlier analysis, are also the ones most likely to strongly favor marriage rights—have a 79.49 percent chance of calling marriage a top priority.

Among the three social identity indicators, identity strength only influences prioritization of marriage and transgender health issues. However, linked-fate

TABLE 15.7. LGBT Respondents Naming Each Category as a Priority

	Employment Rights	Marriage Rights	Adoption Rights	HIV/ AIDS	Civil Unions	LGBT Youth Support	Trans Health
Assimilation Scale	.120+ (.063)	.562*** (.063)	.143* (.056)	−.005 (.054)	.147** (.053)	.042 (.055)	.017 (.052)
Identity Importance	.100 (.061)	.175** (.060)	.040 (.056)	.007 (.055)	.038 (.052)	.070 (.055)	.176** (.052)
Linked Fate	.130*** (.031)	.140*** (.030)	.143*** (.028)	.109*** (.028)	.074** (.027)	.156*** (.028)	.202*** (.027)
Group Dis- crimination	.528*** (.097)	.614*** (.095)	.521*** (.091)	.335*** (.090)	.374*** (.086)	.537*** (.091)	.428*** (.088)
Personal Dis- crimination	.103** (.038)	.062+ (.037)	.091** (.034)	.050 (.034)	.008 (.032)	.094** (.034)	.050 (.032)
LGB Friends	.201* (.087)	.215* (.085)	.212** (.080)	.241** (.078)	.183* (.075)	.208** (.078)	−.069 (.075)
LGB Neighborhood	−.132 (.204)	.050 (.204)	−.358* (.180)	.082 (.179)	.018 (.173)	−.115 (.178)	.209 (.168)
Ideology ^ liberal	.354*** (.082)	.385*** (.080)	.433*** (.075)	.097 (.073)	−.165* (.070)	.266*** (.072)	.292*** (.070)
Partisanship ^ Democrat	.070 (.055)	.202*** (.054)	.159** (.052)	.143** (.052)	.073 (.049)	.148** (.051)	.032 (.050)
Age	.086+ (.044)	−.084* (.043)	−.088* (.040)	.087* (.039)	.080* (.037)	.092* (.039)	.092* (.037)
Education	.238** (.089)	.091 (.088)	.079 (.082)	−.186* (.083)	−.092 (.078)	.117 (.080)	.009 (.078)
Female	.160 (.138)	.299* (.134)	.510*** (.124)	−.259* (.120)	.328** (.116)	.043 (.122)	.254* (.116)
Income	−.001 (.033)	.070* (.032)	.021 (.029)	−.057* (.029)	−.008 (.027)	−.051+ (.029)	−.097*** (.028)
Married	−.135 (.166)	−.104 (.168)	−.057 (.154)	−.105 (.148)	−.365* (.142)	−.262+ (.149)	.243+ (.144)
White	.317* (.153)	.383* (.149)	.203 (.141)	−.459** (.143)	−.048 (.133)	−.059 (.139)	−.256+ (.135)
τ1	2.122	3.900	2.137	−1.783	−.534	1.340	1.202
τ2	3.455	5.290	3.746	.066	.721	3.313	2.962
τ3	5.219	6.862	5.727	1.968	2.122	5.224	4.569
LR	242.19***	410.25***	321.26***	142.54***	91.98***	273.09***	253.18***
McFadden's Pseudo-R^2	.110	.163	.120	.055	.031	.100	.082
N	1176	1176	1176	1176	1176	1176	1176

Notes: Entries are unstandardized ordinal logistic regression coefficients; SE in parentheses; +p<.1, *p<.05, **p<.01, ***p<.001; data are from a Pew Research Center (2013) survey of 1,197 LGBT adults in the United States and group-level-discrimination perceptions positively predict prioritization of every issue, indicating two consistent divides in LGBT issue opinions. On marriage, for example, LGBTs with no sense of linked fate have a 43.38 percent chance of calling it a top priority, but that increases to 72.96 percent among those scoring the maximum on the linked-fate scale. Likewise, respondents perceiving no discrimination against LGBTs only have a 25.29 percent likelihood of calling marriage a top issue, and in fact have a 13.26 percent chance of saying that it is "not a priority at all." However, LGBTs perceiving a lot of discrimination have a 68.14 percent chance of labeling marriage a top priority, and just a 2.36 percent chance of saying it is not at all a priority.

Though each issue in table 15.7 certainly has its own attitudinal idiosyncrasies, other patterns emerge across issues. In terms of social context, respondents whose friend networks are comprised of a greater share of LGBTs are more likely to say that every issue except transgender health is an important priority, though living in an LGBT neighborhood is unrelated to every issue except for placing a lower priority on adoption rights. Political orientations also matter. Ideology is a significant cleavage on every issue except HIV/AIDS; however, liberal LGBTs are less likely to prioritize civil unions than more conservative LGBTs, perhaps because they are seen as a less equal substitute for full marriage rights. More Democratic LGBTs are also more likely to prioritize several issues, but ideology yields a more consistent effect than partisanship.

Discussion

Our analysis provides evidence that the LGBT community is not as politically cohesive as many outsiders might believe. And although some divisions arise over individual characteristics, such as sex, gender identification, race, income, and education, the movement also still maintains a division over assimilationist views versus those that might be deemed more liberationist. Our analysis reveals that this divide is not simply a function of personal characteristics, and is present even when those characteristics are accounted for.

We concede that our analysis is limited in part because we do not have survey data following the effective legalization of same-sex marriage across the country and we do not have much in the way of data over time. However, our 2013 data were collected as the dominos were falling on same-sex marriage, and other studies we note do provide a sense of the assimilationist vs. liberationist views of the past.

But more importantly, our analysis and discussion do not provide a clear view of future cohesion in the LGBT movement. If we categorize those most strongly advocating prioritizing same-sex marriage as the most assimilationist (recognizing that that is not completely accurate), what does this group now prioritize since the largest battle in that struggle has been won? As same-sex-marriage advocacy groups such as the American Foundation for Equal Rights and Freedom to Marry have announced, they will be ending operations and state groups such as Equality Maryland have decided they will limit their activities (Staff Reports 2015), where will momentum move in the community? Will the community begin to lose its advocacy? Will activists go home? Or will other issues move to the forefront and find a new voice? We turn to these potential futures with our concluding thoughts.

Conclusion

Recent victories for the LGBT movement have begun to move the community towards reassessing priorities and goals. We posit that the long-term tensions between the assimilationist and liberationist portions of the movement have never gone away, even as the public face of the movement seemed largely focused on marriage equality in the past several years. With the major battle in major equality won, we explored the political cohesion of the LGBT movement using historical and recent data for analysis. Our discussion and findings allow us to draw several important conclusions and to speculate about the future of LGBT cohesion.

First, our analysis helps to demonstrate that while the push for same-sex marriage may have been top-down within the movement, by the 2010s large portions of the movement agreed with prioritizing marriage equality as the first or second movement priority. The fact that the campaign against same-sex marriage in the 1990s and again from 2003 to 2008 helped to spur this shift is not incidental and continues to indicate how the priorities and strategy of the LGBT movement can be strongly shaped by opponents as well as by LGBT leadership (see also Flores and Sherrill 2013).

Second, although our indicators of assimilationist and liberationist perspectives are imprecise, our results do indicate that these categories account for some of the division within the LGBT movement. LGBT political cohesion is fairly strong in terms of partisanship and ideology, but LGBT people who adhere to more assimilationist perspectives are somewhat more likely to prioritize issues such as marriage equality. This pattern holds even when we account for some of the demographic characteristics, such as sex, education, and income, that also influence attitudes about marriage as a priority.

Third, the data from the Pew survey we employed for our study allowed us to include measures of respondents' strength of social identity as LGBT. Here we did find that social-identity strength predicts issue prioritization for LGBT adults. In particular, a strong sense of linked fate and a higher perception of group-level discrimination were associated with prioritizing marriage equality and adoption rights. With respect to identifying problems that face the community, the social identity measures were less consistent predictors of attitudes, but strong social identity was associated with indicating that discrimination and violence are a problem.

Fourth, we included measures of a respondent's connection to LGBT culture in our analysis; we were able to account for a respondent's proportion of LGBT friends and whether the respondent lived in an LGBT neighborhood. In our analysis, living in an LGBT neighborhood is not associated with particular attitudes about problems facing the community or priorities of the movement. This may indicate that so-called gay neighborhoods are in decline, as some have suggested (Foxhall 2015; Wilkinson 2015), or may simply indicate that living in such neighborhoods does not impart distinct LGBT values, as some have assumed (Doan and Higgins 2011; Lauria and Knopp 1985). At the same time, having more LGBT friends is associated with saying that virtually all of the issues mentioned, from marriage to HIV/AIDS funding, should be prioritized. So if a decline in LGBT neighborhoods is associated with a decline in LGBT culture, it could be that LGBT friend networks might make up for that loss.

Finally, what does analysis tell us about the post-marriage era? Certainly the implementation of marriage rights will continue to be contested in a variety of venues, but the movement can also now reassess priorities. Given the high ranking of discrimination issues and workplace equality, we expect this issue will now become the top priority within the movement. However, with the adoption of marriage as an institution within the movement, perhaps a greater diversity of LGBT people will come out, including more conservative LGBT people, and this might reinforce assimilationist perspectives in the movement. Another, perhaps more troublesome aspect of the recent success could mean a decline in LGBT advocacy and LGBT organizations. Lobbying groups might see funds shrink as LGBT people perceive there is little left to fight for, and an increase in LGBT adults with an assimilationist perspective might increase this viewpoint.

Optimistically, the growing internationalization of the LGBT movement and enhanced diversity in the movement could aid in increasing activism, especially among the millennial generation, which seems to be less focused on more mundane issues. Certainly a significant portion of LGBT adults consider discrimination, adoption rights, and (long-ignored) gender-identity issues to be priorities for the movement, and this will probably continue for the near future. Researchers should continue to research the priorities of LGBT leaders and survey LGBT adults to uncover how movement priorities might shift and the extent to which activism is maintained.

Appendix: Questions and Coding from 2013 Pew Survey

Dependent Variables
Adoption Rights:

> Do you strongly favor, favor, oppose, or strongly oppose allowing gays and lesbians to adopt children?
>
> 1 = Strongly oppose
>
> 2 = Oppose

3 = Favor

4 = Strongly favor

Marriage Rights:

Do you strongly favor, favor, oppose, or strongly oppose allowing gays and lesbians to marry legally?

1 = Strongly oppose

2 = Oppose

3 = Favor

4 = Strongly favor

Most Important Problem:

What do you think are the most important problems facing lesbian, gay, bisexual, and transgender people today? [OPEN ENDED]

A. Lack of general equality/discrimination/prejudice/bigotry/stigma

B. Legal rights (general)

C. Right to marry

D. Ignorance/misunderstanding/stupidity/fear/stereotyping

E. Lack of acceptance

F. Violence/bullying/hate crimes

G. Religious opposition/the religious Right

H. Unprotected sex/STDs/AIDS

I. Republicans/conservatives

J. The same issues as other people

K. Issues specific to transgendered people

L. Self-esteem/self-acceptance/problems of own making

Top Priority:

Thinking about some policy issues, do you think each of the following should be a top priority, a very important but not top priority, a somewhat important priority, or not a priority at all?

A. Equal employment rights for LGBT people

B. Legally sanctioned marriages for same-sex couples

C. Adoption rights for same-sex couples

D. More efforts aimed at prevention and treatment of HIV and AIDS

E. Legally sanctioned civil unions or domestic partnerships for same-sex couples

F. Support for organizations that provide services to LGBT youth

G. Coverage of transgender health issues by health insurance

Response Options

0 = Not a priority at all

1 = Somewhat important priority

2 = Very important but not top priority

3 = Top priority

Assimilationist Additive Scale

(assimilationist response coded as 1; responses then summed)

Which statement comes closer to your own views—even if neither is exactly right?

0 = The push for same-sex marriage has taken too much focus away from other issues important to LGBT people

1 = Same-sex marriage should be the top priority for LGBT people right now, even if this means some other issues do not get much attention.

Which statement comes closer to your own views—even if neither is exactly right?

0 = LGBT people should be able to achieve equality while still maintaining their own distinct culture and way of life.

1 = The best way to achieve equality is for LGBT people to be a part of mainstream culture and institutions like marriage

Which statement comes closer to your own views—even if neither is exactly right?

0 = My [INSERT FOR LGB: sexual orientation, FOR T: gender identity] makes me different from other people, and I am comfortable with that

1 = I don't want to be seen as different because of my [INSERT FOR LGB: sexual orientation, FOR T: gender identity]

Which statement comes closer to your own views—even if neither is exactly right?

0 = It is important to maintain places like LGBT neighborhoods and gay and lesbian bars.

1 = These types of places will not be important as LGBT people are more accepted into society

Social Identity

Identity Importance:

How important, if at all, is being [INSERT ID] to your overall identity? Would you say it is . . .

0 = Not at all important

1 = Not too important

2 = Somewhat important

3 = Very important

4 = Extremely important

Linked Fate:

As a [INSERT ID], how much do you feel you share common concerns and identity with [lesbians/gay men/bisexuals/transgender people; all asked separately]?

0 = Not at all

1 = Only a little

2 = Some

3 = A lot

Group Discrimination:

How much discrimination is there against each of these groups in our society today? [randomize groups, including "gays and lesbians"]?

0 = None at all

1 = Only a little

2 = Some

3 = A lot

Personal Discrimination Additive Scale:

For each of the following, please indicate whether or not it has happened to you because you are, or were perceived to be, [INSERT ID]?

A. Been threatened or physically attacked

B. Been subject to slurs or jokes

C. Received poor service in restaurants, hotels or other places of business

D. Been made to feel unwelcome at a place of worship or religious organization

E. Been treated unfairly by an employer in hiring, pay, or promotion

F. Been rejected by a friend or family member

Response Options (A and B recoded as 1, C recoded as 0)

A. Yes, happened in past 12 months

B. Yes, happened, but not in past 12 months

C. Never happened

Social Context
LGBT Friends:

How many of your close friends are lesbian, gay, bisexual or transgender?

0 = None of them

1 = Only a few of them

2 = Some of them

3 = All or most of them

LGBT Neighborhood:

Would you say you live in a neighborhood known for being an LGBT neighborhood?

0 = No

1 = Yes

Political Identity
Ideology:

In general, would you describe your political views as . . .

1 = Very conservative

2 = Conservative

3 = Moderate

4 = Liberal

5 = Very liberal

Partisanship:

1 = Republican

2 = Independent-leaning Republican

3 = Independent

4 = Independent-leaning Democratic

5 = Democratic

Control Variables

Age:

1 = 18–24

2 = 25–34

3 = 35–44

4 = 45–54

5 = 55–64

6 = 65–74

7 = 75+

Education:

1 = Less than high school

2 = High school

3 = Some college

4 = Bachelor's degree or higher

Income:

Last year, that is in 2012, what was your total family income from all sources?

1 = Less than $20,000

2 = $20,000 to under $30,000

3 = $30,000 to under $40,000

4 = $40,000 to under $50,000

5 = $50,000 to under $75,000

6 = $75,000 to under $100,000

7 = $100,000 to under $150,000

8 = $150,000 or more

Marital Status:

Which best describes you . . .

0 = Not Married

1 = Married

Race:

o = Nonwhite

1 = White

Sex:

Are you . . .

o = Male

1 = Female

NOTES

1 Throughout this chapter we refer to the "LGBT" population for convenience. In fact, much of the data we employ is based on lesbian, bisexual, and gay respondents, with few or no transgender respondents in the survey samples. Currently a large-scale survey of transgender adults is being conducted by the Williams Institute at the University of California–Los Angeles to address the underrepresentation of transgender attitudes in surveys (see Lauren Jow, "Williams Institute at UCLA Launches First-of-Its-Kind Study of U.S. Transgender Population." UCLA Newsroom, March 25, 2015, newsroom.ucla.edu).

2 LGBT adults also differ in attitudes on issues such as healthcare, partly because of individual circumstance. LGBT Americans are more likely to be uninsured and to have trouble affording access to healthcare than the heterosexual population (Gates 2014a). And LGBT Americans, especially women, are more likely to indicate lower levels of health and financial well-being (Gates 2014b).

3 This is an interesting finding considering recent evidence that the increase in positively depicted LGBT characters in the 1990s had a significant positive influence on support for LGBT rights (Garretson 2015).

4 Among LGBT adults, the rationale behind why one should get married differs from that of the non-LGBT population. For example, 46 percent of LGBT adults say that gaining legal rights is a very important reason to get married, but only 23 percent of the general public provides this answer. Having children is also less likely to be seen as an important reason to get married for LGBT adults (28 percent), while 49 percent of the general population believes having children is a very important reason for getting married (Pew Research Center 2013).

5 LGBT identity strength has received some empirical attention with respect to political attitudes and behavior (Egan 2012; Egan et al. 2008; Simon et al. 1998), but the particular indicator of social identity attachment used in those studies is not measured in the Pew survey.

REFERENCES

Bailey, Robert W. 1998. *Out and Voting: The Gay, Lesbian, and Bisexual Vote in Congressional House Elections, 1990–1996.* Washington, DC: Policy Institute of the National Gay and Lesbian Task Force.

Bailey, Robert W. 1999. *Gay Politics, Urban Politics: Identity and Economics in an Urban Setting.* New York: Columbia University Press.

Bailey, Robert W. 2000. *Out and Voting II: The Gay, Lesbian, and Bisexual Vote in Congressional Elections, 1990–1998.* Washington, DC: Policy Institute of the National Gay and Lesbian Task Force.

Becker, Amy B. 2012. "What's Marriage (and Family) Got to Do with It? Support for Same-Sex Marriage, Legal Unions, and Gay and Lesbian Couples Raising Children." *Social Science Quarterly* 93(4): 1007–29.

Becker, Amy B., and D. A. Scheufele. 2011. "New Voters, New Outlook? Predispositions, Social Networks, and the Changing Politics of Gay Civil Rights." *Social Science Quarterly* 92(5): 1191–1214.

Cimino, Kenneth W. 2007. *Gay Conservatives: Group Consciousness and Assimilation*. Binghamton, NY: Harrington Park Press

Conover, Pamela Johnston. 1988. "The Role of Social Groups in Political Thinking." *British Journal of Political Science* 18(1): 51–76.

Crosby, Faye. 1984. "The Denial of Personal Discrimination." *American Behavioral Scientist* 27: 371–86.

Dawson, Michael C. 1994. *Behind the Mule: Race and Class in African-American Politics*. Princeton, NJ: Princeton University Press.

Doan, Alesha E., and Donald P. Haider-Markel. 2010. "The Role of Intersectional Stereotypes on Evaluations of Political Candidates." *Politics & Gender* 6(1): 63–91.

Doan, Petra L., and Harrison Higgins. 2011. "The Demise of Queer Space? Resurgent Gentrification and the Assimilation of LGBT Neighborhoods." *Journal of Planning Education and Research* 31(1): 6–25.

Dugan, Andrew. 2013. "Democrats Enjoy a 2–1 Advantage over GOP among Hispanics." *Gallup*, Feb. 25. www.gallup.com.

Egan, Patrick J. 2012. "Group Cohesion without Group Mobilization: The Case of Lesbians, Gays, and Bisexuals." *British Journal of Political Science* 42(3): 597–16.

Egan, Patrick J. 2015. "Will Marriage Turn Gay People into Republicans? Not Anytime Soon." *Washington Post*, June 29. www.washingtonpost.com.

Egan, Patrick J., Murray S. Edelman, and Kenneth Sherrill. 2008. "Findings from the Hunter College Poll of Lesbians, Gays, and Bisexuals: New Discoveries about Identity, Political Attitudes, and Civic Engagement." Hunter College: City University of New York.

Engel, Stephen M. 2015. "Developmental Perspectives on Lesbian and Gay Politics: Fragmented Citizenship in a Fragmented State." *Perspectives on Politics* 13(2): 287–311.

Flores, Andrew R. 2014. *Politics and Context: Public Opinion, Representation, and Group Consciousness*. PhD dissertation. University of California, Riverside.

Flores, Andrew R., and Kenneth Sherrill. 2013. "From Freedom to Equality: Marriage and the Shifted Priorities of Lesbians, Gay Men, Bisexuals, and Transgender People." Paper Presented at the InsPIRES Conference.

Foxhall, Emily. 2015. "Are 'Gayborhoods' a Victim of the Gay Rights Movement's Success?" *Los Angeles Times*, Aug. 1. www.latimes.com.

Fuegen, Kathleen, and Monica Biernat. 2000. "Defining Discrimination in the Personal/Group Discrimination Discrepancy." *Sex Roles* 43: 285–310.

Garretson, Jeremiah J. 2015. "Exposure to the Lives of Lesbians and Gays and the Origin of Young People's Greater Support for Gay Rights." *International Journal of Public Opinion Research* 27(2): 277–88.

Gates, Gary J. 2014a. "In U.S., LGBT More Likely Than Non-LGBT to Be Uninsured." *Gallup*, Aug. 26. www.gallup.com.

Gates, Gary J. 2014b. "LGBT Americans Report Lower Well-Being." *Gallup*, Aug. 5. www.gallup.com.

Gates, Gary J., and Frank Newport. 2012. "Special Report: 3.4% of U.S. Adults Identify as LGBT." *Gallup*, Oct. 18. www.gallup.com.

Gay, Claudine. 2004. "Putting Race in Context: Identifying the Environmental Determinants of Black Racial Attitudes." *American Political Science Review* 98(4): 547–62.

Haider-Markel, Donald P. 2010. *Out and Running: Gay and Lesbian Candidates, Elections, and Policy Representation*. Washington, DC: Georgetown University Press.

Henry J. Kaiser Family Foundation. 2001. *Inside Out: A Report on the Experiences of Lesbians, Gays, and Bisexuals in America and the Public's Views on Issues and Policies related to Sexual Orientation.* Washington, DC: Henry J. Kaiser Family Foundation.

Hertzog, Mark. 1996. *The Lavender Vote: Lesbians, Gay Men, and Bisexuals in American Electoral Politics.* New York: NYU Press.

Huddy, Leonie. 2004. "Contrasting Theoretical Approaches to Intergroup Relations." *Political Psychology* 25(6): 947–67.

Hurwitz, Jon, Mark Peffley, and Jeffery Mondak. 2015. "Linked Fate and Outgroup Perceptions: Blacks, Latinos, and the U.S. Criminal Justice System." *Political Research Quarterly* 68(30): 505–20.

Lauria, Mickey, and Lawrence Knopp. 1985. "Toward an Analysis of the Role of Gay Communities in the Urban Renaissance." *Urban Geography* 6(2): 152–69.

Lewis, G. B., M. A. Rogers, and K. Sherrill. 2011. "Lesbian, Gay, and Bisexual Voters in the 2000 U.S. Presidential Election." *Politics & Policy* 39: 655–77.

Miller, Arthur H., Patricia Gurin, Gerald Gurin, and Oksana Malanchuk. 1981. "Group Consciousness and Political Participation." *American Journal of Political Science* 25: 494–511.

Miller, Patrick R., and Pamela Johnston Conover. 2015. "Why Partisan Warriors Don't Listen: The Gendered Dynamics of Intergroup Anxiety and Partisan Conflict." *Politics, Groups, and Identities* 3: 21–39.

Newport, Frank. 2014a. "LGBT Americans Continue to Skew Democratic and Liberal." *Gallup,* July 30. www.gallup.com.

Newport, Frank. 2014b. "LGBT Population in U.S. Signficantly Less Religious." *Gallup,* Aug. 11. www.gallup.com.

Olson, Laura R. 2010. "Religion, Moralism, and the Culture Wars: Competing Moral Visions." In *New Directions in American Party Politics,* ed. Jeffrey M. Stonecash. New York: Routledge. Pp. 148–65.

Oskooii, Kassra AR. 2015. "How Discrimination Impacts Sociopolitical Behavior: A Multidimensional Perspective." *Political Psychology* 37(5): 613–40. doi: 10.1111/pops.12279.

Pew Research Center. 2013. *A Survey of LGBT Americans: Attitudes, Experiences, and Values in Changing Times.* Washington, DC: Pew Research Center.

Rimmerman, Craig A. 2007. *The Lesbian and Gay Movements: Assimilation or Liberation?* Boulder, CO: Westview.

Rollins, Joe, and Harry N. Hirsch. 2003. "Sexual Identities and Political Engagements: A Queer Survey." *Social Politics* 10(3): 290–313.

Schaffner, Brian, and Nenad Senic. 2006. "Rights or Benefits? Explaining the Sexual Identity Gap in American Political Behavior." *Political Research Quarterly* 59(1): 123–32.

Sherrill, Kenneth, and Alan Yang. 2000. "From Outlaws to In-Laws: Anti-Gay Attitudes Thaw." *Public Perspective* 11(1): 20–31.

Sigel, Roberta. 1996. *Ambition and Accommodation: How Women View Gender Relations.* Chicago: University of Chicago Press.

Simon, Bernd, et al. 1998. "Collective Identification and Social Movement Participation." *Journal of Personality and Social Psychology* 74: 646–58.

Smith, Raymond A., and Donald P. Haider-Markel. 2002. *Gay and Lesbian Americans and Political Participation.* Denver, CO: ABC-CLIO.

Staff Reports. 2015. "Another LGBT Rights Group to Shut Down." *Washington Blade,* Aug. 5. www.washingtonblade.com.

Stein, Jordan Alexander. 2015. "Celebrating Marriage, Mourning the Queer Revolution." *Slate,* June 26. www.slate.com.

Tajfel, Henri. 1981. *Human Groups and Social Categories.* Cambridge: Cambridge University Press.

Tate, Katherine. 2003. "Black Opinion on the Legitimacy of Racial Redistricting and Minority-Majority Districts." *American Political Science Review* 97(1): 45–56.

Vaid, Urvashi. 1995. *Virtual Equality: The Mainstreaming of Gay and Lesbian Liberation*. New York: Anchor Books.

Wilkinson, Cai. 2015. "LGBT Rights: The Perils of Becoming Mainstream." *Duck of Minerva*, July 22. www.duckofminerva.com.

16

Case Studies of Black Lesbian and Gay Candidates

Winning Identity Politics in the Obama Era

RAVI K. PERRY AND X. LOUDON MANLEY

In May 2012, President Obama came out in support of marriage equality and selected Black ABC News correspondent Robin Roberts as the interviewer. Shortly afterward, the NAACP passed a resolution supporting marriage equality. Not long after that, a group of Black pastors came out against same-gender marriage and vowed not to vote for the president in his reelection bid. Throughout the summer of 2012, many polls attempted to project the influence of President Obama's support for marriage equality on the Black community, particularly as it related to the president's chances at reelection and the Black vote. After his successful reelection, subsequent polls and research began to survey Blacks nationwide and their opinions on marriage equality, each with different outcomes. Meanwhile, an increasing number of Black openly LGBT candidates were elected to public office.

In this chapter, we argue that President Obama's support of marriage equality set into motion a series of progressive steps in the LGBT movement for African Americans, including the successful candidacies of openly LGBT Black Americans between 2012 and 2015. Through an examination of candidate personal biographies, policy proposals, and funding support, we suggest that many Black LGBT candidacies for public office were aided by President Obama's support for marriage equality and related LGBT issues.

With analysis of the Gay and Lesbian Victory Fund's support of Black LGBT candidates, we show how their candidacies differ significantly from those of White LGBT candidates for public office. Finally, we demonstrate how the broader LGBT movement throughout the twenty-first century has benefited greatly from the sociopolitical experience of Black LGBT candidates.

Methods

The data collected for this article, which aggregated a geographically homogenous group of Black LGBT candidates, focused on obtaining information from LGBT activist organizations, including the Victory Fund, the Human Rights Campaign, and others. This data set does not account for every single Black LGBT candidate who has run for elected office. It was intended to illustrate a trend in Black LGBT political mobility by focusing on candidates whose campaigns were representative of their respective peers', in terms of both campaign style and reasons for win/loss situations.

Additionally, the case studies examined in this article focus on coastal-based young, Black LGBT politicians who have run during the Obama administration's tenure in office. By looking at these individuals in particular it is possible to gain a general understanding of the social trends that have swept across the nation during the two Obama terms, leading to a more general acceptance of minority LGBT political viability.

Obama and LGBT Politics

The ascendency of the administration of Barack Obama has been a storied one, receiving heavy shares of both attention and criticism. In particular, the issue of gay rights, viewed more broadly through the spectrum of LGBT rights, casts the forty-fourth American president in a peculiar light. It is difficult to explore and properly articulate the many ways in which the tenure of the man who was dubbed the "first 'gay' president"[1] has impacted, and will impact, the LGBT community.

The president himself spearheaded a large paradigmatic shift for many Americans, appearing to favor the definition of marriage as between "one man and one woman,"[2] before switching his position to endorse same-sex marriage in 2012, soon after his reelection announcement.[3] The change in American sympathies was swift and immediate. According to poll numbers released by the Pew Research Center, the president's shift in opinion freed significant numbers of Americans to voice their own feelings with regard to same-sex marriage. Many will speculate on whether Obama's change in opinion catalyzed an intra-American social movement toward acceptance or whether, instead, he simply lent a legitimate platform to an issue that many already felt sympathetic toward. Irrespective of this apparent "chicken and egg" problem, the facts remain clear. The president's position did, in fact, move the social needle in a progressive direction. In a poll conducted in 2008, shortly before President Obama's transition to the White House, 39% of Americans favored legalizing same-sex marriage while 51% of Americans overtly opposed it.[4] Contrast that with a poll conducted in 2015, which found that 55% of Americans favored allowing same-sex marriage, while those who opposed it fell to 39%.[5]

In the context of electoral politics, the indications of these polls are significant. In a mere seven years, the percentage of Americans who actually oppose same-sex marriage, in other words, the ones who are likely to vote for an anti-LGBT platform candidate, fell by twelve points, and became the minority voice. Conversely, those who overtly support the legality of same-sex marriage found an increase of more than sixteen points and gained the majority foothold needed to secure the election of progressive candidates in the future.

While it is not possible to adequately quantify the exact impact that the president had on the passions and positions of the American electorate during this period, the election numbers don't lie. It is becoming increasingly obvious that more and more LGBT Americans felt that it was more politically viable to run for elected office during the Obama years than at any other time in American history. Yet knowing the LGBT climate in the United States is very different from understanding the impetus from which it grew. In order to more substantially explain the depth of Obama's impact, it is worth exploring not only the various ways in which he contributed to the policy aspect of LGBT acceptance but also how he used his voice and authority as a moral leader to shift Americans toward a culture of widespread social acceptance.

Post-Reelection Policy

In the years before his reelection as president, Obama's outward position on same-sex marriage wobbled back and forth quite a bit, depending upon the political viability of any one of his given stances. If we look past his surface statements to the press, Obama's actual record tells quite a solid story. In fact, he seems to be one of the most pro-LGBT presidents in American history. It is important to realize that for many non-LGBT Americans, actively addressing the topic of same-sex marriage represented a foray into previously unexplored territory. Even among outspoken LGBTQ groups, the bisexual, transgender, and queer factions of the LGBT whole had been largely marginalized, in terms of both public attention and policy change. In spite of these challenges, the LGBT community has benefited greatly from the pro-same-sex-marriage policies and rhetoric put forth by the Obama administration. In particular, the concept of same-sex unions has seemed to open the door to more open conversations about the interplay between gender identity and sexual orientation in the public sphere. Yet it seems that many of the policies enacted by the Obama administration have done a great deal to gradually adjust public opinion on the broad spectrum of LGBT issues by using the "gay marriage" issues as a jumping-off point.

One of the most important measures taken early in Obama's first term was the passage of the Matthew Shepard and James Byrd Jr. Hate Crimes Act.[6] He expanded upon the first section of the act, which classified crimes that were committed on the basis of race as "hate crimes," which thus carried more stringent punishments than their garden-variety counterparts. The Matthew Shepard Act improved upon these provisions by including sexual orientation or gender identity as bases for hate crimes, whether those categories were actual or were perceived by the perpetrator to be actual. This is monumentally important for two reasons. The first is that by openly acknowledging, with meaningful legislation, the *whole* LGBT community as a marginalized and targeted group, the president was able to lend credibility to the notion that these groups ought to be protected by the law. The second major implication was that by including the gender-identity provisions, he effectively used something that was a necessarily "gay" issue and turned it into an LGBT-universal issue. In the past and, sadly, still in the present, the aspects of an individual relating to both orientation and gender identity have received much speculative rhetoric from the conservative Right. Many of these speculations have asserted that gender identity and sexual orientation are the choice of the individual, rather than intrinsically carried from birth.[7] This has been particularly problematic, with the additional insult of con- flating trans identity and homosexuality with forms of sexual deviance such as bestiality or pedophilia.[8] By protecting sexual orientation and gender identity under federal law, the Obama administration definitively changed the narrative of and about the LGBT community to reflect a more accurate and empathetic point of view. This, in effect, legitimized the plight of the LGBT community in a way that directly defied anti-LGBT propaganda, thus opening the door for meaningful discussions of expanded legal protections.

Among other protections and rights extended to the LGBT community at large, the Obama administration led the repeal of "Don't Ask, Don't Tell,"[9] allow- ing openly homosexual individuals to serve in the military. It also directed LGBT policy reform with regard to healthcare, including LGBT families in hospital vis- itation rights, decision-making rights, family leave, spousal benefits, and retire- ment and insurance benefits for federal workers, among many more. The Obama administration also addressed public disparities between LGBT people and the rest of the population by tackling concerns with housing discrimination, public assistance, and increasing funding for AIDS research and preventative health- care, as well as focusing on LGBT-targeted bullying for school-aged children.

With these efforts, the Obama presidency not only effectively mitigated, or in some cases reversed, the decades of harmful marginalizing policies of past administrations but also encompassed the needs of several constituencies at once. As has already been stated, the LGBT community as a whole ben- efited from many of the reforms that came about to primarily address "gay" issues. Secondarily, but perhaps concurrently, the Black community and other communities of color within the LGBT sphere benefited greatly as well. Black LGBT individuals are the most likely to suffer from the exaggerated effects of dual discrimination, due to their racial and LGBT status. Preventable diseases such as HIV/AIDS, as well as disparate rates of juvenile homelessness, unem- ployment, incarceration, and drug abuse have long been known to be ailments that disproportionately affect people who are both Black and LGBT. In enact- ing policy changes and executive directives focusing on addressing the inter- sectional needs of these overlapping communities, the Obama administration was able to kill two birds with one stone. An added benefit of addressing the most universal of these issues has been providing a larger platform for Black LGBT politics.

In turn, this has given rise to an unprecedented political movement, on a national scale. What the political landscape of the United States has witnessed in the years leading up to and through the Obama presidency was a steadily increasing faction of LGBT candidates of color. This interesting trend seems to indicate two pivotal social changes within the American social climate. First, the increasing number of Black LGBT candidates, particularly candidates running for local and state-level elected office, was on an uptick throughout Obama's years in office as president. Meanwhile, since the nation evidenced its support for a Black president twice, the political viability of Black candidates in historically non-Black areas became an increasingly common reality. It would also appear as though the Obama administration's many executive actions, agency directives, and legislative pushes have had a "normalizing" effect on the nation. If only from the public opinion reflected in the Pew Research poll numbers, it is readily evident that American opinions have indeed been shifting to the tune of several million people. It appears that this shift in opinion is becoming more and more tangible to LGBT candidates, who presumably ruled out running at least partially on the basis of a supposition that many would oppose their candidacy due to their orientation. The net result of the increasing visibility of both Black and LGBT needs in the public sphere, as highlighted by the Obama administration, has meant that concepts that were previously alien to many Americans have become comfortable household topics. More impactful, perhaps, for Black LGBT candidates has been the apparent shift in Black sensibilities with regard to LGBT needs, allowing more Black LGBT candidates to run in majority-Black areas. The Black community, which has been historically perceived as *more* homophobic than other racial sects, has also seen a nullifying effect on this "antigay" doctrine since the Obama years. Prior to Obama's inauguration in 2009, only 29% of Black Americans favored the concept of "gay marriage."[10] After Obama's overt support of same-sex marriage in 2012 and the subsequent Supreme Court ruling in 2015 federally legalizing same-sex marriage, 39% of Blacks favor "gay marriage." This interesting turnaround in public opinion indicates that a larger social trend of widespread acceptance toward LGBT individuals has been engendered under the Obama White House. Indeed, even among conservatives, the numbers have risen from 20% in 2008 to 30% in 2015. It can be surmised that in many areas, homosexuality is a far cry from the political entry barrier that it once was.

Candidacy Picture Pre-Obama

Before the Obama election, the candidacy of LGBT individuals was quite limited in terms of both geographical and demographic scope. As has often been the case, the LGBT candidates represented on the mainstream circuit were typically White gay men. Historical figures such as Harvey Milk come to mind, along with recently retired Senator Barney Frank. Yet, candidates such as Jose

Sarria, the first gay person of color to run for elected office, often are swept to the side unnoticed. Because these candidates oftentimes didn't win, their campaigns have been considered a historical irregularity, perhaps warranting a mere footnote in the books. Furthermore, the most progressive areas in the nation, San Francisco, Boston, and New York, became the LGBT political strongholds for many years. Candidates were either too scarce or thought an election bid too unrealistic to mount serious campaigns in more conservative areas. Perhaps as a testament to the racial monolith of American elected officials, the faces of the LGBT political movement were more often than not White. For example, men like Frank Kameny, Harry Hay, and Allen Ginsberg are the faces and names often remembered when the days of the riots at the Stonewall Inn are recalled. Yet, other names, such as those of Marsha P. Johnson, Storme DeLarverie, and Sylvia Rivera, are oftentimes left out of the mix. Most recently, the Hollywood film *Stonewall*, which many feel inadequately depicted the riots, whitewashed much of the story, opting for a cisgendered White man as the protagonist, rather than the transgendered and lesbian women of color who are truly credited with inciting the riots.[11] It is easy to see that even in 2015, the after-effects of a racially biased media were still being felt. It is little wonder, then, that many Black LGBT would-be candidates felt that they were not politically viable in the pre-Obama years.

The candidacy numbers before the Obama election were quite dismal—in part because there was little formal structure for getting a foot in the door to the intricate world of politics. In its fledgling days during the 1980s and '90s, tthe Human Rights Campaign did not achieve the robust $38 million per year in revenue that it now commands. There were few LGBT office holders to speak of, many of whom were not in a position to risk their political credibility by either "coming out" of the closet or actively pursuing a pro-LGBT agenda. People like Rep. Barney Frank (D-MA) waited until they solidified a political foothold to announce their orientation. Frank waited a full six years after his 1981 election to the House of Representatives to come out as gay in 1987. He had been in public service for sixteen years.

To date, only twelve members of the United States Congress[12] have been openly LGBT, along with only one senator, Tammy Baldwin, who also represented Wisconsin in the House of Representatives. Unsurprisingly, of these nine, only one, Mark Takano of California, has been of color. Additionally, of the nine representatives, seven have been White men, and two were White women. The diversity problem that has long existed in electoral politics is underscored when looked at within the LGBT realm. It is obvious that, historically speaking, the White majority has enjoyed a strong foothold, even among minority groups.

Upon Obama's ascendency to the White House, however, much of that began to change. During his tenure in office, President Obama appointed more than 250 openly gay, lesbian, bisexual, and transgender people to high governmental office, more than any other president in history combined. When he entered office, he made it clear that his administration would be more than just a campaign slogan, and swore to embody the "change" that he eagerly promised Americans. His campaign promises began unfolding almost immediately, as he made huge strides toward directly addressing the LGBT diversity problem within the federal government. By appointing so many LGBT individuals, Obama has changed the landscape of American politics, by providing a strong springboard for future LGBT officials who will now have the backing of others in positions of power. Furthermore, he has created a precedent upon which future administrations can build. Knocking down the doors that were previously closed to LGBT individuals, and more specifically LGBT individuals of color, Obama positioned the Black gay community to enjoy a more robust and politically stable support system, the effects of which will outlast his tenure as president.

Candidacy Picture after Obama

The effects of the Obama administration's diversity efforts have not stopped with the president's appointees. In recent years, there has been an escalation of LGBT candidates of color who have been running and winning, in areas that were previously considered unwinnable. Ironically, it was a conservative-constitutional law case, the *Citizens United* ruling of 2010, that inadvertently paved the way for LGBT politicians to gain a stronger foothold in American politics. The Supreme Court ruling affirmed the ability of corporations and unions to give unlimited political funds to political PACs. Initially perceived as primarily benefiting the candidates in the pocket of the "old boy" network, the ruling had an unforeseen consequence, in that organizations such as Human Rights Campaign's Political Action Committee have been able to ramp up their fundraising in massive ways since the decision. According to InsideGov, in 2014, pro-LGBT-agenda PACs, Emily's List, and ActBlue raised $44 million and $280 million, respectively.[13] To put this in perspective, the National Rifle Association (NRA) PAC, which has notably supported far-right campaigns, raised only $21 million in 2014.[14]

The effects of these far-reaching and celebrity-studded left-leaning super-PACs have been swift since 2010. Many more LGBT candidates have won political office, and even greater numbers have run consistently, regardless of their election outcomes. What has been surprising, however, is the number of Black LGBT candidates who have been running in spite of interorganizational diversity issues, such as those highlighted by a scathing 2010 report of the Human Rights Campaign's inner workings. As money to these candidates has increased, in aggregate, it is reasonable to assume that more money has flowed into the elections that support White LGBT candidates, rather than their Black counterparts. Fortunately for the Black LGBT community, the lack of equal support has not translated into a candidate disparity. Conversely, Black LGBT officials and candidates seem to be on the rise in many geographically diverse areas.

Among the new class of standout candidates who have won their elections, New York City councilman Ritchie Torres and Georgia state representative Simone Bell have garnered significant media attention. Both officials represent the shifting schematic for entering viable political races for LGBT people of color.

Ritchie Torres is both Black and Hispanic, along with being openly gay, which makes him somewhat of a statistical oddity given his trajectory from the Bronx housing projects to the New York City Council, representing his home borough. Along with a slew of other fresh-faced young candidates across the nation, Torres represents a shifting dynamic in the way that Black gay politics are conducted. Rather than enter the contest closeted,[15] as many elected officials of the past have done, he and his contemporaries have been the first significant wave of elected-hopefuls who don't view their sexual orientation as a political liability. In fact, it seems almost as if acknowledging their LGBT status up front removes a major hurdle from their campaign, thus averting a media cycle and potential opposition attacks. They have also been excellent at raising money by appealing to the deep pockets of the pro-LGBT donor base. At the first campaign-finance-disclosure filing deadline for New York City elections of 2017, Torres had already significantly out-performed many of his opponents running for city council. As of January 17, 2017, he had amassed a war chest in the neighborhood of $171,894.[16] Torres has significantly out-fundraised his seventy-six peers[17] running for seats on the New York City Council, with the average fundraising total for city council candidates at $55,158.[18] Among his bigger cash donations are organizations such as the AFL-CIO, the New York School Board, the Ironworkers Union, the Hotel and Motel Trades Council, the New York State Laborers PAC, and a handful of well-to-do real estate and law firms. It seems that the narrative of the Republican Party for the "everyman" is slowly starting to dwindle as it becomes more obvious that both white-collar and blue-collar interests are being unified and universalized by a gay, Hispanic, and Black councilman from the Bronx. More importantly, the ascendancy of Torres is emblematic of a larger narrative within politics, which lends credence to the idea that Obama's "universalization" of intersectional Black and LGBT issues is manifesting itself in the real world—proving not only that these intersections are real but also that they can work together in practical ways.

Torres's speeches seem to resonate with the changing needs of younger voters as well. At only twenty-four years old, he became the youngest New York City councilman ever elected, and was heralded as a welcome change from what he described as the "business-as-usual" crowd in City Hall. On top of that, his speeches seem to center around the most unifying of issues. He sits as the head of the Public Housing Commission within the council, simultaneously serving as Deputy Majority Leader. His primary issues center around public housing reform, educational advancement, public assistance for senior citizens, and, as of 2015, securing the necessary funds for the Bronx borough to adequately recover from the devastation of 2012's Hurricane Sandy. These issues follow a similar blueprint to that of the agenda the Obama administration laid out in his early days on the campaign trail and followed through on during his presidency. Torres knows, as many others know, that Black LGBT individuals are more likely to need public housing than White LGBT individuals; they are still the victims of geographic displacement, familial instability, unemployment, underemployment, and wage disparities more than any other racial or sexual grouping across much of the United States. He also knows that LGBT and Black youth are more likely to attend public schools that are underfunded, and are victimized by bullying more frequently and more severely than their White LGBT counterparts. Among other issues, LGBT senior citizens of all races are more likely to be destitute than their straight counterparts due to lack of pension availability and Social Security access. Despite changes in federal law, many still do not have the spousal benefits they are owed due to several factors. Indeed, it is difficult to prove a long-lasting relationship that only recently became legalized. Each one of these issues is a decidedly LGBT issue, but it can just as easily be painted with a larger brush. Education, poverty assistance, and emergency funding are all able to address the most severe problems within the Black LGBT community, without taking the risk of alienating a mostly straight population. It seems that "civic universalism" has become the newest and best campaign strategy for getting meaningful things done while no one is looking.

Georgia state representative Simone Bell followed a similar trajectory as Torres, also taking a page from the Obama playbook. She was elected in 2009, shocking many in her district and becoming the first lesbian to serve in the Georgia State House. She ran again in 2010, unopposed, and won the general election. In 2010, she raised $12,000,[19] which proved adequate to secure her reelection bid for the State House. When compared with the financial statements of the New York State's council, the money Bell's campaign raised might suggest that her campaign was severely underfunded. In fact, compared to many of the other campaign finance reports for other Georgia House representatives, Bell out-fundraised the competition by a wide margin. Many other representatives raised funds south of $10,000, with some even teetering on the edge of $1,000.

What is clear with these two vastly different campaigns, in very different parts of the country, is that money makes an incredible difference in the viability of the candidacy equation. The most significant donation came from the International Brotherhood of Electrical Workers' Educational Committee—an organization that addresses the needs of its members by focusing on the broader picture, similarly to the major donors to the Torres campaign. The second-largest donations came from private citizens and professional firms. The Torres and Bell campaigns, along with many others, suggest that money flows towards the candidates who can find the most intersectionality among various, and at times conflicting, issues. Bell, like Torres, didn't shy away from the LGBT issue in the campaign; rather, she was out from the get-go. It can be speculated that the public mistrust garnered by an openly LGBT identity, at least in many parts of the country, is a thing of the past.

But, in spite of the many victories won by Black LGBT candidates, it is not the victories themselves that are most indicative of a changing American landscape. Rather, the mere act of running, the candidacies in and of themselves, constitute a very real change in the social dynamic. In order to even get a campaign off the ground, there must be significant numbers of people and organizations willing to lend their voice and dollars to supporting the candidate. Ultimately, this indicates that an increasing number of private businesses, citizens, and nonprofits are willing to align themselves not only with a candidate who carries the LGBT label but one whom they think has at least a fighting chance in an election. It is one thing to announce political candidacy. It is often only after the dollars come in, however, that a campaign becomes legitimized in the eyes of the public.

Rashad Taylor of Atlanta, Georgia, along with Marc Morgan of Washington, DC, and Lawrence Webb of Falls Church, Virginia, are among the new breed of Black LGBT candidates who, while not always successful, are nonetheless providing an important jumping-off point for their peers. Historically, cities such as Atlanta and Washington, DC, have contained large concentrations of socially conservative but politically Democratic Black constituencies. The candidacies of these three men, all of whom were openly gay at the time of their running, is symbolic of a greater shift within the Black community, where hypermasculinity and homophobia purportedly were rampant only slightly before the Obama election.

When Rashad Taylor first ran for office in 2008, he rode in on the coattails of a sweeping Democratic election year, with the first Obama presidency. He served in the Georgia State House of Representatives from 2009 through 2013, and at twenty-seven was the youngest serving member of any state legislature. He was reelected in 2010 before his defeat in 2013. Interestingly, the Taylor campaign's only significant divergence from the Torres and Bell campaigns was his status as a gay man. During both his first and second election bids, Taylor stayed closeted, and didn't make a campaign issue out of his sexuality. His primary legislative focuses were on addressing the wage gap for hourly workers and helping craft the state budget. In 2011, a factually inaccurate email chain was started, accusing Taylor of being gay and abusing his power to solicit sex. Unfortunately for Taylor, part of the rumors turned out to be true, and he came out publicly in 2011 following the short-lived scandal.[20]

It would seem that the "gay" aspect of Taylor's third candidacy was to blame for his sudden loss of office, except that others such as Simone Bell also served in the Georgia legislature at the same time. It can be speculated that rather than the Georgia voters having a problem with Taylor's sexuality, they, like many, were put off by a perceived lack of honesty on the part of their representative. The sudden ousting of Taylor must be looked at in an unconventional way, because it indeed defies the more traditional notions that openly gay candidates are less politically viable than straight ones. In the context of the new LGBT candidate wave, following the Obama presidency, the opposite seems to be true. It can be posited that it is political suicide to hide one's sexuality from the public at the risk of being exposed down the line, and thus painted as another dishonest politician mired in scandal.

Similarly, Marc Morgan, who ran for DC City Council in 2013, had issues with the cohesion of his image. Morgan entered the race against two Democrats, both of whom had strong pro-LGBT stances. Morgan, however, downplayed his sexuality and declined to take an overt stance on LGBT issues, apart from what could be inferred from his employment history. Rather, Morgan's headlines focused on the fact that he was somewhat of a political anomaly, being both Black and gay, yet running on a Republican ticket.[21] The Republican Party, which has had a history of racial discrimination, diversity problems, and an anti-LGBT agenda, seems a strange choice for Morgan. Consequently, the bulk of his media attention centered around the incongruity of his campaign, and he was ultimately defeated.

Just a few miles away from Morgan's town of Washington, DC, Lawrence Webb ran an unsuccessful campaign in 2012 to retain his seat on the city council of Falls Church, Virginia, after his initial victory in 2008. Webb then ran for the school board in 2013 and won. The candidacies of Webb and Taylor provide an interesting contrast to each other, in part because they have both won and lost elections, and have proved themselves skilled candidates, irrespective of their losses. Webb seems to prove what more and more LGBT candidates have been noticing since the Obama administration's push for diversity: that if you run often enough, you eventually win something. It is worth noting, however, that it seems Webb's 2013 campaign for council was significantly underfunded, as he raised less than $2,000 running for a position in Falls Church, where the median household income rests around $113,000 per year.

What is perhaps most revealing about the picture of Black LGBT candidates is the data collected about them in aggregate. What these numbers reveal is that for many of them, outside circumstances have a greater effect upon who is newly viable for office. First, it would appear that birth year has a great deal to do with both the electability and the political viability of the candidates. Of the sample selected for our research, all of the candidates were born around or subsequent to 1961. Perhaps not so coincidentally, this is the birth year of President Obama. If we can draw any conclusions from these cursory findings, it may be that the electorate is trending toward favoring younger candidates. This would seem to follow the trend indicated by Obama's door-opening presidency, in that both Black and relatively young candidates are considered to be politically viable.

These candidates, however, seem to be both geographically and politically limited in terms of viability. Among this same sample of Black LGBT candidates, many come from the same states, some of which are considered states that have been historically accepting toward LGBT individuals. California and Georgia, both states that function as political strongholds for Black LGBT individuals, have seen the greatest increase in candidacies over the Obama years. However, states newer to the Black LGBT landscape, such as North Carolina and the District of Columbia, are among the ranks of geographic areas that boasted multiple candidates in the elections held during the Obama presidency. Additionally, states such as Florida and Ohio, which are traditionally conservative areas, have seen an increase in Black LGBT candidates. All of this suggests that political viability is beginning to transcend geographic borders. It can also be posited that the overall trend of LGBT acceptance, as evidenced by the Pew polls, is being expressed in the most basic function of democracy, which is candidacy.

Predictably, it appears that Black LGBT candidacy is still politically confined to the Democratic Party. Of the candidates sampled, only 11.1% were affiliated with the Republican Party and ran on the Republican ticket. They were each stigmatized by their local media, and became the object of public incredulity, as the concept of a Black gay Republican still seemed to defy the political norms. In this way, it is amply evident that much work still has to be done in order to normalize the concept of minority LGBT candidates throughout both political parties. While there is still a relative monolith in political ideology, the plight of the LGBT community will remain a partisan issue, and will inevitably face an undue amount of gridlock and contention for purely political reasons. Even among Democrats, in Democratic districts, it can still prove difficult for Black LGBT candidates to win reelection. Many of them are easily edged out by straight Democratic challengers, illustrating the point that Black LGBT candidacy is still in its infancy.

In spite of the challenges still faced, what is perhaps most encouraging to the LGBT community at large, and more specifically the Black LGBT community, is that there seems to be a new way forward into the political fray for candidates who can follow the Obama blueprint. In the cases of the Black gay and lesbian candidates who went on to win elected office, very often the key to victory was adequate financial resources coupled with a universally appealing agenda, meant to address the intersectionality between mainstream and LGBT needs. Similarly, of the candidates who did not win, there was some sort of predictable failure that inevitably led to a defeat. The most important takeaway from the Obama White House is that a newly created pipeline exists that has carried LGBT activists from the grassroots stages of organizing for representation to actualizing that need into policy reform and pro-LGBT candidates. Ultimately, the path to meaningful representation is still one that has a long way to go, and the springboard provided by the Obama push for LGBT inclusion will still have to grow larger and broader in order for the needs of the LGBT community to cease being an underserved cause. While candidacy in and of itself is a good thing, the LGBT representation within communities of color is still a minority, even within the elected LGBT faction. More often than not, the needs of the Black community will be pushed aside in favor of addressing a binary agenda, one that focuses on the needs of the White LGBT elected majority, to the detriment of their minority counterparts. In order for the overlapping needs of the LGBT Black minority to be adequately provided for, there must be a consistent effort on the part of the candidates to universalize those needs that are most dire among their Black constituency. While the situation is improving, it is far from being fully addressed, and without continued, organized support from within the Black LGBT community, the racial disparity among LGBT individuals will continue to be pervasive throughout American society.[22]

NOTES

1 Dylan Byers, "*Newsweek* Cover: 'The First Gay President.'" *Politico*, May 13, 2012. www.politico.com.

2 Becky Bowers, "President Barack Obama's Shifting Stance on Gay Marriage." *PolitiFact*, May 11, 2012. www.politifact.com.

3 Ibid.

4 Pew Research Center, "Changing Attitudes on Gay Marriage." *Pew Research Center*. July 29, 2015. www.pewforum.org.

5 Ibid.

6 United States Executive Office, "Obama Administration Record for the LGBT Community." www.whitehouse.gov.

7 Eric Bradner and Alexandra Jaffe, "Ben Carson Apologizes for Comments on Gay People." *CNN*, March 5, 2015. www.cnn.com.

8 See, for example, the city of Houston's rejection of a nondiscrimination ordinance in November 2015. As a result of a heavily funded campaign that, in part, suggested men would be going into women's restrooms with a campaign slogan "No Men in Women's Bathrooms," Houston residents repealed a law previously passed by the city council with an 11–6 vote in May 2014. The result led to the development of an effort to force a repeal referendum that spanned more than one year of legal challenges. In July 2015, the Texas Supreme Court ordered the city to either repeal the law or place it on the ballot. By a 12–5 vote, city council opted for the latter. Early voting totals showed that 62.5 percent of Houston residents voted to repeal the law and 37.5 percent to sustain it. See Janell Ross, "Houston Decided It Had a Problem: Its LGBT Discrimination Law." *Washington Post*, November 4, 2015. www.washingtonpost.com.

9 United States Executive Office, "Obama Administration Record for the LGBT Community." www.whitehouse.gov.

10 Pew Research Center, "Changing Attitudes on Gay Marriage." *Pew Research Center*, July 29, 2015. www.pewforum.org.

11 Mary O'Hara, "The LGBT Community Is Not Happy about the New Whitewashed Stonewall Movie." *Daily Dot*, Aug. 5, 2015. www.dailydot.com.

12 Of these twelve openly LGBT congresspersons, only eight ran on an openly LGBT identity platform. Representatives Gerry Studds, Mark Foley, and Steve Gunderson, and Barney Frank, all came out during their congressional tenure.

13 U.S. Campaign Committees, "Key Facts." *InsideGov*, 2014. us-campaign-committees. insidegov.com.

14 Ibid.

15 As far as is known, Councilman Torres has never hidden his sexuality during his adult life.

16 New York City Campaign Finance Board, "Campaign Finance Summary 2017 Citywide Elections." http://www.nyccfb.info.

17 In determining these fundraising averages, candidates who had not reported any funds were omitted from the calculations. Only seventy-one of seventy-six registered candidates have reported raising funds for the 2017 election cycle.

18 New York City Campaign Finance Board, "Campaign Finance Summary 2017 Citywide Elections." http://www.nyccfb.info.

19 Georgia Government Transparency and Campaign Finance Commission, "Campaign Disclosure Reports for C2009000175." www.nyccfb.info.

20 Belky Perez Schwartz, "Georgia Politician Rashad Taylor Comes Out as Gay." *Examiner*, May 29, 2011. www.examiner.com.

21 Lou Chibbaro, "Gay Republican Enters Council Race." *Washington Blade*, Nov. 20, 2013. www.washingtonblade.com.

22 Another source informing this chapter but not directly cited is Perry, Ravi K., and Joseph P. McCormick II. 2015. "LGBT Politics and Rights through the Obama Era." In Donald Cunnigen and Marino Bruce, eds., Race in the Age of Obama, vol. 2. Bingley, UK: Emerald Publishing Group.

17

Equality in the House

The Congressional LGBT Equality Caucus and the Substantive
Representation of LGBTQ Interests

PAUL SNELL

On the evening of March 11, 2009, a rather normal event occurred in Washington. Two hundred lobbyists, congressional staffers, and members of Congress (MCs) met at a gala to network.[1] This is, by itself, unremarkable. The event, however, inaugurated a new era of formal advocacy for LGBTQ issues on Capitol Hill.[2] The gala celebrated the one-year anniversary of the Congressional LGBT Equality Caucus, formed the previous June by Rep. Tammy Baldwin (D-WI), Rep. Barney Frank (D-MA), and other allied members of Congress (Palmer 2009).[3] The Caucus "serves as a resource for Members of Congress, their staff, and the public on LGBTQ issues at the federal level. The Caucus works toward the extension of equal rights, the repeal of discriminatory laws, the elimination of hate-motivated violence, and the improved health and well-being for all regardless of sexual orientation or gender identity and expression" (Congressional LGBT Equality Caucus 2015). The Caucus's structure reflects its founding. The LGB members of Congress serve as chairs, while non-LGB members may serve as vice-chairs and regular members. The vast majority of the Caucus, therefore, is composed of allies. The Caucus has helped move LGBTQ issues from being marginalized to being institutionalized. This relatively new organization, therefore, provides the perfect vehicle for understanding the modern state of LGBTQ affairs in Congress.

This institutionalization raises new questions. What compels non-LGB members of Congress to join the Caucus, and what benefits does it provide to them? The central question of this chapter is whether the Caucus adheres to its creed; are members taking actions inside of Congress that aid the LGBTQ community? Does the Caucus *represent* the community that it was formed to serve? This chapter will begin its exploration of these questions by determining what predicts membership in the Caucus. It will then evaluate the question of representation more carefully by comparing Caucus members with other members of Congress in a variety of ways, including the roll-call vote to repeal the military's "Don't Ask Don't Tell" (DADT) policy, as well as their bill sponsorship and cosponsorship activity on pro-rights bills in two congresses.[4] The Equality

Caucus formed during the 111th Congress (2009–2010). This chapter, therefore, analyzes member activity in the House of Representatives during its founding session and the subsequent congress, in which Republicans gained control of the House of Representatives.[5] This will demonstrate whether advocacy varies under different partisan contexts. This chapter's analysis is the first to explore a broad range of congressional activities related to the representation of the LGBTQ community.

The preliminary findings of this chapter show that MCs join the Caucus for political reasons—to aid their reelection efforts. Caucus members, however, are the leading members of Congress acting consistently on LGBTQ Americans' behalf. While these results are hardly surprising, that is precisely the point. The behavior of Caucus members resembles "normal" politics rather than being a form of morality politics. This was the dominant congressional approach: to treat LGBTQ Americans as an issue rather than a constituency.

From an Issue to a Constituency

In the 1990s Congress typically considered fewer than ten bills per session specifically addressing gay and lesbian issues. Many members treated LGBTQ Americans as a marginalized group. Melissa Williams, in *Voice, Trust, and Memory*, defines a group as marginalized if it fits four criteria: there is a history of social and political inequality along the category of membership, the traits are seen as involuntary, the traits are seen as immutable, and society attaches negative meanings to the group's identity (Williams 2000, 16). There is a long line of scholarship that demonstrates the long history of legal discrimination and social stigma that LGBTQ individuals have experienced (D'Emilio 1983; Meyerowitz 2002). In order to combat this discrimination and stigma, they took a civil rights approach by proposing bills such as the Employment Non-Discrimination Act (ENDA) and the Gay and Lesbian Youth Suicide Prevention Act.

Yet these bills were counterbalanced by others that were often symbolic, such as one proposed by former Senator Jesse Helms (R-NC): "A bill to stop the waste of taxpayer funds on activities by Government agencies to encourage its employees or officials to accept homosexuality as a legitimate or normal lifestyle." Many of these early congressional bills were more than symbolic, however, and their message was quite clear. Most never became law, but two of them did. The first was the military's "Don't Ask Don't Tell" policy passed by the 103rd Congress (1993–1994). DADT prohibited those with "a propensity or intent to engage in homosexual acts" from military service because their "presence in the armed forces would create an unacceptable risk to the armed forces' high standards of morale, good order and discipline, and unit cohesion that are the essence of military capability" (U.S. House Committee on Armed Services 1993). This sample of the text evinces the federal government's moral conviction that homosexuality and its practitioners are condemnable (Wolinsky and Sherrill 1993). The Defense of Marriage Act (DOMA), which passed shortly after DADT, enjoyed wide bipartisan support, and is equally condemnatory. While the text of the act does not condemn homosexuality as an act, the title, by itself, has the same implication as that of DADT: marriage needs "protection" from deleterious influences, specifically from those with a proclivity to engage in homosexual acts.

Opponents of gay and lesbian rights did not accept a civil rights framework. Instead, LGBTQ Americans were a moral "issue." This created a situation that political scientists have referred to as "morality politics." This theory posits that when one side of a controversy defines an issue in moral terms, the issue transforms into a specific form of politics around the redistribution of values. Gay and lesbian issues fit this framework because one sect defined them in moral terms. Much of the early research understandably reflected this framework. Donald Haider-Markel (1999) evaluated previous congresses in addition to the 104th to ascertain what predicts MCs' support of or opposition to LGBTQ issues. Here, he concluded that partisan affiliation, ideology, religion, and constituency characteristics should predict members' support of or opposition to gay and lesbian issues.

The findings of the morality politics framework were largely validated by subsequent research that concluded that a member's religion was a unique predictor of support for DOMA (and opposition to ENDA) apart from partisanship and electoral variables (Campbell and Davidson 2000; Lewis and Edelson 2000). These results are still applicable, though later works have suggested that partisan and ideological factors have eclipsed religion in predicting members' roll-call voting behavior on LGBTQ issues (Lublin 2005). Research on state legislators suggests that their public positions on gay and lesbian issues is a composite of their personal beliefs as well as their political calculations (Herrick 2010).

The declining influence of religion on legislators' behavior may correspond with society's increased acceptance of same-sex sexuality. The public's attitude towards homosexuality, and LGBTQ persons, has been more accepting over the long term (Loftus 2001). The public's support for the legality of same-sex acts has increased from 44% in 1996 to 66% in 2014 (Gallup 2017). One reason for the growing acceptance of LGBTQ individuals is that society is more receptive to a civil rights framework. This receptivity has borne fruit in policy outcomes. President Obama's executive order prohibiting federal contractors from discriminating against individuals on the basis of sexual orientation and gender identity is a prominent and recent nonlegislative action at the federal level. At the state level, as of 2014, eighteen states had laws protecting individuals from employment discrimination on the basis of gender identity and sexual orientation. As a result of these changes, Gary Mucciaroni (2011a) has questioned the continued applicability of the morality politics framework to LGBTQ issues. These changes offer new research possibilities.[6]

Rather than being constrained by a morality politics framing of LGBTQ *issues*, it is now possible for scholars to ask more sophisticated questions about the LGBTQ community as a *constituency*. The latter framing offers rich opportunities for additional scholarship because it inevitably raises questions about whether that constituency receives *representation* in Congress—and how. The essence of representation is activity. What do representatives do, and whom do they do it for? They must actively further the interests of their constituents through the tangible acts that they take (Pitkin 1967, 114). How do members of Congress demonstrate that they *consistently prioritize* taking actions that furthers the interests of the LGBTQ community? This chapter suggests that there is at least one way to do so—maintaining membership in the Congressional LGBT Equality Caucus.

Congressional Caucuses

Congressional caucuses are ambiguous entities. On one side, research has shown that caucuses are highly active and stable organizations that are extensively involved with political actors both inside and outside Congress, positively affecting the policy agenda in line with their goals (Hammond 1998). On the other side, criticisms abound. One could persuasively argue that caucus membership is a cheap form of position taking, where members of Congress receive electoral benefits for the positions they take rather than for implementing concrete actions (Mayhew 1974). One could also persuasively argue that caucuses are ineffective in creating meaningful legislative changes. The Congressional Black Caucus (CBC) has had minimal success leveraging the organization's potential into legislative change (Singh 1998).

The Congressional LGBT Equality Caucus reflects this ambiguity. Proponents of caucuses can point to the Equality Caucus's regularly writing letters to government agencies encouraging them to modify policies to enhance or recognize LGBTQ issues or persons. On April 7, 2014, for example, members of the Caucus encouraged the Interior Department to conduct a study on the contributions of LGBTQ Americans to the history of the United States through its National Historic Landmarks program.[7] Yet the Caucus, unfortunately, reflects the charge of shallowness and ineffectiveness in many respects. Members of the Caucus routinely advertise their membership and their support of LGBTQ issues in local newspapers to appease LGBTQ—as well as highly liberal—constituents, but these commitments do not translate into bills coming to the floor. The behavior of some Caucus members in the 114th Congress (2015–2017) unfortunately also reinforces the idea that they think position taking should be cheap—literally. When the Caucus began charging membership dues of four hundred dollars beginning with the 114th Congress, it lost around half of its members. This is not an egregious amount; many caucuses charge over one thousand dollars for membership dues. The entertainment website *Buzzfeed* reported on this sharp decline, and many members of Congress rejoined the Caucus out of shame. In addition to the obviously political nature of membership, the Equality Caucus can claim few policy successes. The most prominent roll-call vote on LGBTQ issues in recent years, DADT repeal, was not solely due to the work of the Caucus. The vote occurred while Democrats had a comfortable majority in both houses of Congress, and the House was led by Speaker Pelosi, who represents the congressional district with the highest proportion of same-sex households in the country (San Francisco). The repeal also occurred during the first two years of President Obama's term—when his political capital was highest. It was also a Congress that welcomed LGBTQ issues. The Caucus has not been able to make progress on other pieces of legislation. ENDA, for example, has been introduced since the 1990s, yet it still is not law.

While the criticisms discussed above should kept in mind, it would be a mistake to conclude that caucuses do not serve a useful purpose. Members of Congress find caucuses to be a valuable means of fulfilling their objectives, especially because they overcome the limits of committees. Caucuses serve as a type of division of labor beyond committees that is voluntary and highly specific. MCs, in short, join caucuses because they allow members to specialize on issues that they care about in a way that committees do not (Stevens, Mulhollan, and Rundquist 1981; Miler 2011).

Caucuses also compensate for the limits of both intra- and interparty challenges. If committees have difficulties accommodating member interests, parties amplify this problem due to the breadth of issues that they address. Parties aggregate the preferences of their members and have difficulties accommodating the diversity of views within them. This applies both inside and outside of Congress. When parties monopolize the electoral competitiveness of a constituency, they are likely to take that group for granted (Frymer 1999; Bishin and Smith 2013). This is often referred to as electoral capture. If caucuses are helpful for overcoming intraparty difficulties, they are absolutely *necessary* for overcoming *interparty* difficulties. Parties often function like teams, and it is often in their interests to magnify oppositional behavior between themselves and the other party, even on nonideological matters (Lee 2009). The inherently polarizing nature of parties is evident on issues where the parties have taken positions. Caucuses provide a bipartisan bridge for members on certain issues that parties would ignore not only because of the aggregation problems described above but also due to competition between the parties that ensures that the minority's side will not receive consideration, especially in the majoritarian House of Representatives.

The Equality Caucus may compensate for these difficulties. First, there is the issue of committees. LGBTQ issues intersect many committees' jurisdictions, including Education and Labor, Judiciary, Armed Services, Ways and Means, and Commerce. Without the Equality Caucus the broader issues concerning each committee would be likely to obscure issues of specific concern to the LGBTQ community. This specific concern illustrates the importance of caucuses as places where members with specific policy interests can develop ideas with supportive colleagues that one can rely on for future efforts in that policy area.

The Caucus compensates for the problems that parties raise, too. It is overwhelmingly composed of Democrats, yet the party leadership has not aggressively pursued LGBTQ issues due to the breadth of concerns and constituencies that they must accommodate. Another difficulty for the representation of LGBTQ interests within the Democratic Party is the likelihood of electoral capture. LGBTQ voters' allegiance to the Democratic Party means that Democrats may ignore their interests without electoral retribution. In this situation, the need for a specific platform to advocate on behalf of the LGBTQ community is critical to effective representation. The electoral capture of LGBTQ voters also reinforces interparty difficulties. Democrats in Congress have supported LGBTQ rights while the Republicans in Congress have not (Karol 2012). As descriptive analyses will demonstrate, Republicans are almost completely unified in their opposition to anything remotely LGBT, yet the Caucus had three Republican members during the 112th Congress, when the Republicans retook control of the House. The Caucus is a bridge that would not exist otherwise.

There are other benefits that caucuses provide beyond overcoming the limitations of committees and parties. Some caucuses provide normative benefits as well. The Congressional Hispanic Caucus, the Congressional Black Caucus, and the Congressional Caucus for Women's Issues claim to speak on behalf of Hispanics, blacks, and women, respectively, as their surrogate representatives (Dodson 2006; Hero 1992; Gertzog 2004). They provide an institutionalized voice for groups that lose in their own district, or whose numbers are too small and diffuse to ever constitute a majority (Mansbridge 2003). These representatives, as a result, counteract the majoritarian biases inherent in geographically based congressional elections (Guinier 1994). Caucuses can provide a venue for furthering the interests of groups that may not receive representation otherwise. While some caucuses may have difficulty with consistent long-term policy success, they may still provide representation of the marginalized in other ways. Although previous research (specifically Singh 1998) has found that the CBC has had difficulty in securing policy success for black Americans, other research has found the CBC to be an effective force in the House by shaping legislation and getting black MCs appointed to influential committees and party positions (Canon 1995).

The LGBTQ community needs surrogate representatives due to their small numbers in each congressional district. LGBT individuals are, on average, 0.5% of a congressional district, and, at best, 2.9%. These numbers are too low to exert significant electoral pressure through geographic forms of representation alone.

The small number of LGB MCs also inhibits expansive representation of LGBTQ individuals by LGBTQ representatives. Recent estimates of the gay, lesbian, and bisexual population in the United States is 3.5%, and 0.3% for individuals who identify as transgender (Gates 2011). If the number of LGBTQ representatives in the House ever reaches the proportion of LGBTQ individuals in the population, then there will still only be fifteen LGB and only one transgender representative, which is too low a number to exert significant congressional influence. The Equality Caucus is inclusive of non-LGBT MCs out of principle (anyone who wants to aid the LGBTQ community is free to join), but probably also out of necessity. Yet it is not clear why MCs join the Caucus.

Membership in the LGBT Equality Caucus

Table 17.1 shows the results of a binary logistic regression model to estimate the factors that should compel MCs to join the Caucus in both congresses. These factors include MCs' party identification, religious affiliation, interest-group influence, and district characteristics (the proportion of LGBT and Evangelical residents, how liberal the district is, and whether the district is electorally competitive).[8] Given the partisan breakdown of the Caucus, one should expect Democrats to be predisposed to join the Caucus. Cursory analysis confirms this result. There were ninety Democrats in the Congressional LGBT Equality Caucus in the 111th Congress, and only one Republican: Rep. Ileana Ros-Lehtinen. She has a distinguished history of supporting LGBTQ rights. She has a child who is a transgender LGBT rights advocate, and she represents a district with a large gay and lesbian population (South Miami). Her presence in the Caucus is emblematic of the most substantively significant factor, above party, that drives MC membership in the LGBT Equality Caucus—representing a district with a large LGBTQ population.[9]

After the 2000 Census, each MC represented an average of 646,952 citizens. The district with the highest percentage of unmarried same-sex households is Rep. Nancy Pelosi's district (CA-8) with 2.9%, which is around 18,800 people.[10] The mean same-sex household percentage is 0.5%, which translates to around 3,200 individuals. Even a district that has 0.8% unmarried same-sex households (one standard deviation above the mean) still only translates to around 5,300 citizens. The results are impressive given the small proportion of unmarried same-sex households per congressional district. The higher the percentage of LGBTQ constituents, the more probable it is that MCs will join the Equality Caucus. This suggests that members join the Caucus to demonstrate their commitment to issues important to constituents with whom they share a direct electoral connection. This generalizes beyond LGBTQ constituents. Members from more liberal districts have a higher probability of joining the Caucus, too. These results are consistent with prior research (Miler 2011). The results also suggest that distinct

TABLE 17.1. Logistic Regression of Membership in the LGBT Caucus

	111th	112th
Democrat	3.027**	1.895*
	(1.116)	(0.741)
LGBTQ	3.160***	2.888***
	(0.823)	(0.839)
Evangelical	−0.0552***	−0.0306+
	(0.0165)	(0.0166)
Obama	0.0497*	0.106***
	(0.0212)	(0.0270)
HRC	0.0000896	0.000232**
	(0.0000594)	(0.0000839)
Competitive Seat	−1.263*	0.483
	(0.591)	(0.477)
Evangelical Christian	−1.122	−0.890
	(1.172)	(0.951)
White Catholic	0.298	−0.0328
	(0.465)	(0.503)
Latino Catholic	0.646	0.0849
	(0.666)	(0.701)
Jewish	0.700	1.574*
	(0.565)	(0.719)
Black Protestant	−1.084	−2.403**
	(0.792)	(0.786)
Conservative Christian	0.605	0.605
	(1.488)	(1.601)
Other	−1.041	0.158
	(0.729)	(0.779)
Constant	−7.487***	−10.31***
	(1.704)	(1.898)
N	441	439
pseudo R^2	0.480	0.554
AIC	261.5	241.3
BIC	318.8	298.5
Ll	−116.8	−106.7
chi2	215.5	265.0

Notes: Standard errors in parentheses. +p<0.10, *p<0.05, **p<.01, ***p<.001.

subsets of the population have distinct effects on the propensity of MCs to join. LGBTQ constituents increase the probability of membership in the Caucus more than the percent of evangelicals in the district depresses it, suggesting that the benefits of representing the LGBTQ community via Caucus membership outweighs possible retribution from a wider, but possibly less interested, attentive public, namely, evangelical voters. There is one district-level result specific to the 111th Congress that is particularly troubling. Members representing competitive districts (winning with less than a 10% margin) were less likely to join the Caucus. This is consistent with the theory of electoral capture, as the Democratic leadership can presume that LGBTQ voters would prefer a Democratic congress to a Republican one, and members may safely ignore joining the Caucus without electoral consequence.

Member demographics made a difference, but the results were idiosyncratic to each congress. In the 112th Congress, Jewish members were more likely to join the Caucus, while Black Protestant members were less likely to join the Caucus relative to Mainline Protestant MCs. These results are likely to be highly sensitive to specific members joining the 112th Congress; hence I would urge caution in interpreting the results.

DADT Repeal

The most crucial actions of a member of Congress are her votes on pieces of legislation. Yet there remains very little scholarship on this as it applies to LGBTQ Americans—and very little of it is contemporary.[11] Beyond DOMA, the repeal of the military's DADT policy is the most significant action on LGBTQ issues Congress has taken in over a decade. The House voted to repeal DADT on December 15, 2010. The vote passed with 57.6% (250/434) in favor. Consistent with most legislation in the modern House, the vote was almost strictly along party lines. Democrats overwhelmingly supported repeal, while Republicans overwhelmingly opposed repeal. An equal number of Democrats and Republicans voted counter to expectations: fifteen each—and most of them were moderates. Eleven of the fifteen Republicans were more liberal than the average Republican in the 111th Congress, while all of the Democrats who voted no or abstained were more conservative than the average Democrat.[12] Other subgroups voted overwhelmingly for repeal: every Black MC (save Rep. Davis [D-AL]), 84% of Latino MCs, and every Jewish MC (except Eric Cantor [R-VA]) voted for repeal. Given that these members are also Democrats, it is likely that partisanship explains these results as well. The statistical analysis confirms that partisanship is the most substantively significant predictor of voting for repeal.

Every Caucus member voted for repeal (one member abstained). This suggests that Caucus members, as expected, supported the most important piece of pro-rights legislation to reach the floor in recent congresses. Yet, they are statistically indistinguishable from other MCs in this roll-call episode.

Several electoral variables achieved statistical significance as seen in table 17.2. District liberalism, contributions from the Human Rights Campaign, and a higher percentage of LGBTQ voters in the district increased the probability of a member voting for repeal. Once again, LGBTQ voters are one of the most substantively significant predictors (second only to party in this model). This reflects the position-taking value of roll-call votes for MCs, as members' voting records

TABLE 17.2. Logistic Regression of DADT Repeal Vote

Caucus Membership	−0.769
	(0.958)
Democrat	4.496***
	(0.578)
LGBTQ	2.993*
	(1.457)
Evangelical	−0.0319
	(0.0203)
Obama	0.0814**
	(0.0315)
HRC	0.000267+
	(0.000145)
Competitive Seat	0.543
	(0.488)
Evangelical Christian	−0.212
	(0.648)
White Catholic	−0.0313
	(0.543)
Latino Catholic	0.726
	(1.200)
Jewish	1.548
	(2.020)
Black Protestants	Omitted
	Omitted
Conservative Christian	1.439
	(0.925)
Other	1.266
	(1.300)
Constant	−7.154***
	(2.023)
N	404
pseudo R^2	0.710
AIC	189.3
BIC	245.3
Ll	−80.63
chi2	395.6

Notes: Standard errors in parentheses. +p<0.10, *p<0.05, **p<.01, ***p<.001

are essential to their reelection efforts. Despite the overwhelming importance of electoral concerns, unlike in the membership model, having a higher proportion of Evangelical voters in members' districts does not decrease their support of voting for DADT repeal, as this variable does not achieve statistical significance. This validates the declining significance of religion in explaining roll-call votes on LGBTQ issues (consistent with Lublin [2005]), and this is apparently true both for a member's personal religion (none of the MC personal-religion variables were statistically distinguishable from Mainline Protestants') and for the religious affiliation of a member's constituents.

Substantive Representation beyond Roll-Call Votes I: Sponsorship

While roll-call vote analyses are an indispensable part of the study of congressional behavior and substantive representation, they conceal as much as they reveal. They may reveal preferences—but they do not reveal priorities, or what members of Congress care about, because MCs do not choose what they will vote on—their leaders do (Swers 2002, 155). A related difficulty with solely evaluating roll-call votes is the abysmally low number of LGBTQ bills that reach the floor of the House for a vote, as evidenced by this chapter's ability to examine only one roll-call vote: DADT repeal. In order for the nascent literature on the substantive representation of the LGBTQ community in Congress to continue to develop, scholars must complement the study of roll-call votes with the study of other legislative behavior reflecting members' priorities that is not constrained by leadership priorities and that is more consistent than sporadic votes.

One option is bill sponsorship. Previous scholarship on the CBC has ascertained that its members provide substantive representation through bill sponsorship (Whitby 2002). Many scholars deride bill sponsorship as another cheap legislative activity because it is does not take much effort to introduce a bill relative to other efforts (Sulkin 2005; Hall 1996). Sponsorship, too, does not account for whether a bill actually passed. Yet, in spite of these limits, we can learn much about legislators' priorities by looking at sponsorship. Sponsorship can tell us *who* has an interest in a specific policy area, it can bring attention to an issue, and it can be a signal to certain interest groups that they have an ally (Swers 2002, 33). Bills sponsored indicate what issues a legislator wants to be associated with, and the reputation that he wants to build (Schiller 1995). Therefore, it would be productive to analyze pro-rights bill sponsorship and whether Caucus members provide leadership on LGBTQ issues.

Bill sponsorship will also highlight the link between descriptive and substantive representation. This asks whether a legislator's ascriptive traits translate into legislative activity on behalf of the community with which she shares those ascriptive traits. Previous work confirms that the presence of LGBT individuals in a legislative context often furthers the LGBTQ community's interests (Haider-Markel 2007). The three lesbian and gay members of the 111th Congress (Jared Polis, Tammy Baldwin, and Barney Frank) were chairs of the Caucus, and were active sponsors of LGBTQ legislation. Table 17.4 lists the sponsors of the pro-LBGTQ bills in both congresses. Rep. Polis sponsored a student-nondiscrimination bill, Rep. Baldwin sponsored a domestic-partners-benefits bill as well as a health-data-collection bill, while Rep. Frank sponsored two versions of ENDA. They were also active leaders when the Republicans took control of the House.

The three LG sponsors were not the leading sponsors in both congresses. This distinction belongs to Caucus member Rep. Jerrold Nadler (D-NY), who sponsored four bills and two pro-rights bills in the 111th and 112th congresses, respectively. The most prominent bill was a proposal to repeal DOMA, which was controversial at the time among House Democratic leaders, including Speaker Pelosi. Rep. Frank opposed the bill for practical reasons. He thought that other items on the congressional agenda—DADT repeal, ENDA, and domestic-partner benefits for federal employees—would dominate the congressional agenda on LGBTQ issues and that it was impossible to achieve these items and DOMA repeal ("Frank" 2009). Nadler's support, therefore, is principled, but also has electoral roots. Nadler's district contains a high concentration of LGBTQ voters—as well as the Stonewall Inn. He has also faced a primary challenge from a gay man in the past ("Two Like-Minded Liberals" 1994).

Democrats sponsored twenty-eight and fifteen pro-rights bills in the 111th and 112th congresses, respectively. Republicans sponsored zero pro-rights bills in both congresses. Equality Caucus members sponsored 82% of the pro-rights bills introduced in the 111th Congress. Sponsorship of pro-LGBT bills decreased in the 112th Congress overall, coinciding with the House Republicans gaining a majority. Sponsorship trends were similar to those of the previous congress. The majority of the bills introduced were repeats, such as the Tyler Clementi bill, the Every Child Deserves a Family Act, FMLA benefits for domestic partners, and ENDA. Yet, Caucus members sponsored 86% of the pro-rights bills introduced in this Congress. This confirms that they provided consistent leadership that did not waver even when the chamber switched into Republican hands.

Substantive Representation beyond Roll-Call Votes II: Cosponsorship

MCs want not only to be reelected but also to implement good public policy (Fenno 1973). What a member believes makes good public policy, therefore, matters. Beyond sponsorship, an intuitive progression in the research would be to move from studying voting (roll-call votes) to studying "loud voting," wherein members can choose to be involved through bill cosponsorship (Swers 2002, 57). Cosponsorship is relevant in the legislative process for three reasons: sponsors commit a substantial amount of effort recruiting their colleagues to join their bills, members cite the number and diversity of members in floor speeches, and members' activity level (neither rare nor common) reflects the usefulness of cosponsorship as a tool (Campbell 1982). Previous literature suggests that roll-call votes and cosponsorship are forms of position taking, yet the latter is a way of demonstrating focused attention in a policy area, like sponsorship (Koger 2003; Rocca and Gordon 2010).

While cosponsorship may be easy to accomplish, it is still a form not just of revealed preferences but also of revealed *intensities* (Hall 1996). Prior research on the CBC demonstrates that its members form a cohesive cosponsorship network on issues relevant to the black community (Pinney and Serra 2002). In this context it is crucial to determine which members consider legislation that furthers the interest of the LGBTQ community to be good public policy and whether cosponsorship is one of the ways that they do so. The test of commitment to the LGBTQ community is not *whether* Caucus members cosponsor bills but how *frequently* they do so. Frequency of cosponsorship can be an expression of depth or intensity of activity like that of committee activity, mark-ups, and speeches, thereby making it an insightful congressional act.

In order to ascertain *depth* of substantive representation, a natural question to ask is whether Caucus members cosponsor LGBTQ bills more often relative to their non-Caucus colleagues. To address it, I used negative binomial regression (due to the fact that most MCs do not cosponsor LGBT bills) to determine the factors that predict the cosponsoring of many pro-rights bills. I examined all pro-LGBT rights bills in the 111th and 112th congresses. The statistical analysis in table 17.3 reveals, once again, the overriding dominance of partisanship, as it was the most substantively significant predictor. There were twenty-five Republican cosponsors of pro-rights bills in the 111th Congress, and nine in the 112th. The statistical analysis in table 17.3 reveals, once again, the overriding dominance of partisanship, as it was the most substantively significant predictor. There were twenty-five Republican cosponsors of pro-rights bills in the 111th Congress, and nine in the 112th. Republicans, as a whole, cosponsored one-third of one bill on average, effectively zero. Rep. Ros-Lehtinen cosponsored nine bills in the 111th and six bills in the 112th congresses, making her the leading pro-LGBTQ Republican in the House. Democrats cosponsored an average of six bills when they held the majority, and seven bills under minority control. This suggests that Democrats' advocacy under minority control was more concentrated and consistent, but Caucus members were the leading members once again.

The lesbian and gay representatives were leading cosponsors in the 111th Congress (fourteen [Polis], fifteen [Baldwin], and eleven [Frank]), but they, once again, were not the leading cosponsors of pro-rights legislation. That distinction belongs to Raúl Grijalva (D-AZ) and Earl Blumenauer (D-OR). Both Grijalva and Blumenauer are members of the Equality Caucus. Other members showed their leadership through cosponsorship, although the effect was more modest than in the sponsorship analysis. The model predicts that in both congresses Caucus members are likely to cosponsor an additional 1.3–1.4 bills than non-Caucus members, controlling for other factors, including the number of bills that a member cosponsors overall. The statistical results must be complemented with closer analysis of the data. The top 4% of pro-rights-bill cosponsors in the 111th Congress (those who cosponsored at least fourteen bills) were all members of the Caucus. The results are more compelling during the 112th Congress, where the top 10% of pro-rights-bill cosponsors (those who cosponsored at least twelve bills) were

TABLE 17.3. Negative Binomial Regression of the Predicted Number of
LGBTQ Bills Cosponsored

	111th	112th
Caucus	0.336***	0.420***
	(0.0834)	(0.0790)
Democrat	1.874***	3.338***
	(0.162)	(0.243)
LGBTQ	0.0914	0.169
	(0.138)	(0.118)
Evangelical	−0.0210***	−0.0174***
	(0.00331)	(0.00315)
Obama	0.0304***	0.0211***
	(0.00453)	(0.00471)
HRC	0.0000486***	0.0000535***
	(0.0000128)	(0.0000158)
Competitive Seat	0.0514	−0.0983
	(0.112)	(0.0989)
Evangelical Christian	−0.239	−0.260
	(0.184)	(0.201)
White Catholic	−0.176+	−0.0108
	(0.0994)	(0.100)
Latino Catholic	−0.0680	−0.0985
	(0.144)	(0.136)
Jewish	0.0749	0.0988
	(0.117)	(0.111)
Black Protestant	−0.184	−0.227+
	(0.151)	(0.137)
Conservative Christian	−0.620+	0.0445
	(0.375)	(0.343)
Other	−0.0831	0.0766
	(0.144)	(0.137)
Number of bills cosponsored	0.610***	0.233***
	(0.0926)	(0.0601)
Constant	−5.332***	−4.056***
	(0.580)	(0.475)
lnalpha		
Constant	−2.107***	−2.775***
	(0.271)	(0.456)
N	441	439
pseudo R^2	0.292	0.362
AIC	1498.3	1180.1
BIC	1567.8	1249.6
Ll	−732.2	−573.1
chi2	603.8	649.6

Notes: Standard errors in parentheses. +p<0.10, *p<0.05, **p<.01, ***p<.001.

members of the Caucus. These members are demonstrating their commitment to LGBTQ equality through their repeated bill cosponsorship activity.

Electoral factors, such as district liberalism and HRC contributions, are associated with higher levels of cosponsorship activity.[13] The more illuminating electoral variables are the effect of LGBTQ and Evangelical constituents on cosponsorship activity. Unlike the membership and roll-call models, the percent-LGBTQ variable is not statistically significant. MCs representing more LGBTQ districts, in other words, are *not* more likely to cosponsor more bills, and this is true of both congresses. While the LGBTQ community does not increase the number of bills that members cosponsor, a higher proportion of evangelical voters decreases the number of pro-rights bills that members in both congresses cosponsor, as figure 17.1 illustrates. The model predicts that members representing districts with a high level of evangelical voters (60%) in the 111th Congress, for example, are likely to only cosponsor two pro-rights bills rather than four bills (the average per member). This result is particularly puzzling given that the percent Evangelical is not statistically significant for roll-call voting, which is a more obvious statement of a member's position than the number of bills a member cosponsored, as the public probably knows little about a member's cosponsorship intensity.

These results validate the need to evaluate substantive representation of the LGBTQ community from multiple perspectives. These results are, by far, the most normatively troubling of this chapter—the inconsistent effect of LGBT voters on the behavior of MCs. The results seem to imply that while LGBTQ voters have political clout, they still face substantial barriers to their full inclusion in the polity

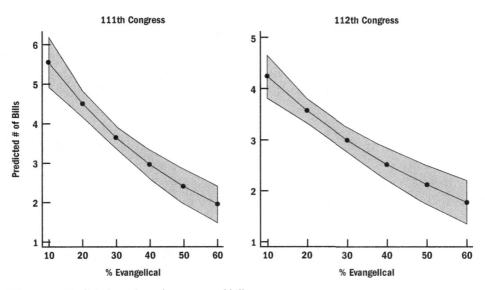

Figure 17.1. Predicted number of cosponsored bills.
Note: The shaded region depicts the 95% confidence interval.

(Sherrill 1996). LGBTQ constituents only receive the most obvious forms of representation, as the percent-same-sex variable is a statistically significant factor for Caucus membership and the vote for DADT repeal, but not for the number of bills cosponsored. They seem to drive preferences—but not priorities, or if they do so, the effect is indirect. Members' personal commitment matters. It is clear that LGBTQ representation relies heavily on Caucus members due to the ineffectiveness of LGBTQ constituents in driving the frequency of MCs' cosponsorship.

The member religion variables have inconsistent results, and only three variables achieve statistical significance, but these levels are higher than most conventional cutoffs, hence caution is warranted in interpreting these results. In the 111th Congress only, White Catholic and Conservative Christian MCs were less likely to cosponsor as many pro-rights bills as Mainline Protestant MCs. Black Protestant MCs were less likely to cosponsor pro-rights legislation during the 112th Congress (Republican control).[14]

The Representation Frontier

Although the Equality Caucus may be young by caucus standards, as the 2009 gala demonstrates, it has quickly established itself as a key force in congressional politics. The results demonstrate that Caucus members provide LGBTQ Americans the essence of representation—activity inside of Congress. Caucus members provide votes on pivotal LGBTQ bills, and are the dominant force for ensuring that issues relevant to the LGBTQ community receive congressional—and national—attention through their consistent (co)sponsorship activity independent of which party controls the chamber. This consistency bolsters the generalizability of the findings beyond these two congresses. While electoral and partisan factors affect members' decision to join the Caucus, once they join, they provide an institutionalized voice for the LGBTQ citizens who live in their districts, and as surrogate representatives to those who do not.

This chapter's analysis is the first to explore a broad range of congressional activities related to the representation of the LGBTQ community. But it also highlights additional necessary areas of research. Future work would need to extend its scope beyond two congresses and one roll-call vote episode, of course. It would need to evaluate the proto-history of the Caucus (what preconditions led to its emergence) and a wider array of congressional and executive activities such as meetings with the leadership, whip operations, congressional testimony, report writing, as well as a broader understanding of the Caucus's external efforts. The data are there. The Caucus has a partnership with the Gay and Lesbian Victory Institute, wherein LGBTQ college students may participate in a semester-long internship with a member of the Caucus, or an LGBT-friendly member of Congress, to learn about the legislative process. This is one example of an additional way in which the Caucus contributes to the national agenda on

LGBTQ issues beyond Congress. The most important outstanding question that this chapter does not address is how influential the Caucus is in tangibly furthering the interests of LGBTQ Americans. Is it an effective legislative tool that secures the passage of legislation, or is this, at root, a position-taking exercise for MCs that is incapable of overcoming the institutional powers of parties and committees to achieve its policy objectives?

There are several frontiers of LGBTQ representation research that remain unexplored, and I would like to conclude this chapter by highlighting several fruitful areas of inquiry that future scholars could pursue. In spite of calls for political scientists to make issues related to sexuality more prominent on their research agendas (Mucciaroni 2011b), there is a paucity of research on LGBTQ politics. The literature on LGBTQ issues in Congress is especially sparse (the literature on congressional caucuses is equally limited). This chapter attempts to contribute to a scholarly conversation with a small, yet passionate group of participants, but it is also an invitation for others to expand and enrich the scholarship surrounding LGBT representation in a congressional context in order to render Mucciaroni's charge moot.

There certainly needs to be more research on descriptive representation—whether the composition of a legislature mirrors the composition of society. Most defenders of descriptive representation will argue that it requires more than the mere physical presence of appropriate proportions of relevant constituencies and numerical correspondence, as normal modes of electoral accountability can ensure the representation of diverse interests. Descriptive representation has a deliberative component: do representatives who share an ascriptive trait with a group contribute a unique perspective that only they can offer to deliberative processes? In the case of black MCs, do they, for example, contribute a distinct perspective to Congress that a white member could not due to the latter's position in society and background (Mansbridge 1999)? I am certain that the lesbian, gay, and bisexual members of Congress have contributed to their colleagues' understanding of issues relevant to the LGBTQ community—but this remains an unanswered empirical question.

Scholars could also analyze the link between descriptive representation and substantive representation more comprehensively than I have done here. This is a common approach in the women and politics literature (Swers 1998; Dodson 2006; Reingold 2008; Pearson and Dancey 2011), as well as in the literature on race (Bratton and Haynie 1999; Whitby and Krause 2001; Rocca and Sanchez 2008). No one has yet comprehensively assessed the link between LGB descriptive representation and substantive representation in Congress, although other work has evaluated this link in state legislatures (Haider-Markel 2010) and across national legislatures (Reynolds 2013). This chapter has shown that Reps. Frank, Baldwin, and Polis are leading sponsors of LGBTQ legislation, and their efforts are why the Caucus formed, but they have surely provided other tangible acts of leadership beyond what this chapter has demonstrated.

Another line of research could evaluate the *substance* of substantive representation of LGBTQ interests in a more critical fashion than I have done here. Our understanding of sexuality—and the way that the government responds to it—is constantly adapting. The "first wave" of LGBTQ politics seems to be at a zenith as this chapter's opening vignette about the gala demonstrates. A question that remains for future scholars of LGBT politics in a congressional setting is what the content of substantive representation will be in the future if the politics of sexuality transitions into a "second wave." The current state of LGBTQ politics, but not necessarily the scholarship about it, is heavily centered on lesbian and gay equality, while bisexual, transgender, and queer claims often lose out, as do the intersectionally disadvantaged, such as LGBTQ people of color (Cohen 1997; Strolovitch 2012). While equal rights and protections from discrimination are important advances against marginalization—and worthy political goals—they dominate the public discourse and the congressional agenda. It remains to be seen whether the substantive representation of the LGBTQ community will include the concerns of less visible slivers of the community. Will the push for equality at a national level always be synonymous with lesbian and gay civil rights? Only time—and further research—will tell.

TABLE 17.4. LGBTQ Bills in Both Congresses

111th Congress

Bill Number	Title	Sponsor	Number of Cosponsors
*HR 1024	Uniting American Families Act of 2009	Jerrold Nadler	135
HR 1283	Military Readiness Enhancement Act of 2009	Ellen Tauscher	192
HR 1589	Bullying and Gang Reduction for Improved Education Act	Linda Sánchez	40
*HR 1616	Early Treatment for HIV Act of 2009	Eliot Engel	187
*HR 1913	Local Law Enforcement Hate Crimes Prevention Act of 2009	John Conyers	120
HR 2132	Family and Medical Leave Inclusion Act	Carolyn Maloney	32
HR 2515	Domestic Violence Leave Act	Lynn Woolsey	11
HR 2517	Domestic Partnership Benefits and Obligations Act of 2009	Tammy Baldwin	140
*HR 2625	Tax Equity for Health Plan Beneficiaries Act of 2009	Jim McDermott	133
HR 2744	Equal Rights for Health Care Act Title 42	Laura Richardson	13
*HR 2965	Don't Ask, Don't Tell Repeal Act of 2010	Jason Altmire	9
HR 2981	Employment Non-Discrimination Act of 2009	Barney Frank	12
HR 3001	Ending LGBT Health Disparities Act	Tammy Baldwin	24

(Cont.)

TABLE 17.4. LGBTQ Bills in Both Congresses

111th Congress

Bill Number	Title	Sponsor	Number of Cosponsors
*HR 3017	Employment Non-Discrimination Act of 2009	Barney Frank	203
HR 3090	Health Equity and Accountability Act of 2009	Donna Christensen	58
*HR 3567	Respect for Marriage Act of 2009	Jerrold Nadler	120
HR 3827	Every Child Deserves a Family Act	Pete Stark	14
HR 4180	Honest and Open Testimony Act	Alcee Hastings	34
HR 4376	Freedom from Discrimination in Credit Act of 2009	Steve Israel	77
HR 4530	Student Nondiscrimination Act of 2010	Jared Polis	126
HR 4806	Every Child Deserves a Family Act	Pete Stark	40
HR 4820	Fair and Inclusive Housing Rights Act of 2010	Jarred Nadler	3
HR 4828	Housing Nondiscrimination Act of 2010	EdolphusTowns	0
HR 4988	Housing Nondiscrimination Act of 2010	Joe Sestak	0
HR 6109	Health Data Collection Improvement Act of 2010	Tammy Baldwin	3
HR 6425	Tyler Clementi Higher Education Anti-Harassment Act of 2010	Rush Holt	6
HR 6500	Housing Opportunities Made Equal (HOME) Act	Jerrold Nadler	6
HR 6520	Don't Ask, Don't Tell Repeal Act of 2010	Patrick Joseph Murphy	78

112th Congress

Bill Number	Title	Sponsor	Number of Cosponsors
HR 998	Student Non-Discrimination Act of 2011	Jared Polis	171
HR 1028	Equal Access to COBRA Act of 2011	Anthony Weiner	51
HR 1048	Tyler Clementi Higher Education Anti-Harassment Act of 2011	Rush Holt	42
*HR 1116	Respect for Marriage Act	Jerrold Nadler	160
*HR 1397	Employment Non-Discrimination Act	Barney Frank	171
HR 1488	Freedom from Discrimination in Credit Act of 2011	Steve Israel	73
*HR 1537	Uniting American Families Act of 2011	Jerrold Nadler	144
HR 1681	Every Child Deserves a Family Act	Pete Stark	114
HR 1796	Reuniting Families Act	Mike Honda	78
*HR 2088	Tax Parity for Health Plan Beneficiaries Act of 2011	Jim McDermott	141
HR 2310	Equal Access to COBRA Act of 2011	Jackie Speier	69
HR 2364	Family and Medical Leave Inclusion Act	Carolyn Maloney	53
*HR 3485	Domestic Partnership Benefits and Obligations Act of 2011	Tammy Baldwin	140
HR 4609	Social Security Equality Act of 2012	Linda Sánchez	100
HR 5848	Juror Non-Discrimination Act of 2012	Steve Rothman	6

*These are bills that the HRC asked members to cosponsor as per their Congressional Scorecard.

Appendix A: Variables

Variable	Coding	Source
Caucus Membership	Scored "1" if an MC is a member of the Congressional LGBT Equality Caucus. Scored "0" otherwise.	111th Congress-Staff member of the Equality Caucus 112th Congress-Archived website of the Caucus
DADT Repeal Vote (HR 2965) Roll Call 638	Scored "1" if an MC voted for repeal, "0" otherwise.	Thomas.gov
Bill Cosponsorship	Count of number of pro-rights bills cosponsored. Also the HRC Congressional Scorecard.	Thomas.gov HRC Congressional Scorecard-111th and 112th Congresses
Democrat	Scored "1" if an MC is a Democrat, "0" for Republican.	Thomas.gov
LGBTQ	The percentage of unmarried same-sex households per congressional district.	The 2006–2010 American Community Survey 5-Year Estimates
Evangelical	The percent Evangelical (born again) per congressional district.	The Cooperative Congressional Election Study (CCES)
Obama (District Liberalism)	2008 vote percentage for Obama in each member's district for both congresses.	(insert state name). Governor and statistics. 2009. In C. McCutcheon and C. L. Lyons (eds.), *CQ's Politics in America 2010 (the 111th Congress)*. Washington, DC: Congressional Quarterly. Retrieved from http://library.cqpress.com.
Competitive Seat (CS)	The difference between the MC and her challenger. If the difference is less than or equal to 10%, the MC is scored "1," "0" otherwise.	www.fec.gov for both 2008 and 2010.
HRC	The campaign contributions given to each candidate from the Human Rights Campaign (HRC) directly.	http://www.opensecrets.org
MC Religion	Member is coded "1" if she fits one of the following categories, "0" otherwise: Evangelical Mainline Protestant White Catholic Jewish Black Protestant Latino Catholic Conservative Christian Other The baseline category is Mainline Protestant	The Pew Research Center: http://www.pewresearch.org. See Green, Guth, Smidt, and Kellstedt 1996, 188–89, for specific details as to which subdenominations the authors determine fit each category.
Count of the number of bills cosponsored (lnjoin)	I take the natural log of the number of bills each MC cosponsored per congress.	Thomas.gov

NOTES

1 I would, first, like to thank Kathryn Pearson. She has seen this chapter through almost every iteration and has contributed substantial feedback at every stage. This chapter would not be possible without her assistance. I would like also to thank Paul Goren and Timothy R. Johnson for reviewing earlier drafts and for their thoughtful feedback. Charles Anthony Smith, Benjamin Bishin, and Gregory B. Lewis provided excellent feedback on a draft of this paper presented at the Annual Meeting of the Midwest Political Science Association. Several participants of the University of Minnesota American Politics Pro-seminar also deserve special mention: Emily Baer-Bositis, Amanda Bryan, Phillip Chen, Ashley English, and Aaron Rosenthal. I would also like to thank the editors and the anonymous reviewers of this piece.

2 Throughout the chapter I will use the term "LGBTQ" (lesbian, gay, bisexual, transgender, and queer) to refer to the broad category of persons who identify as nonheterosexual or as noncisgender. While this is a simplification, it obscures the ways in which this phrase has often simply meant "gay and lesbian." Throughout this chapter, therefore, while I will refer to "LGBTQ," I will also make reference to "lesbian and gay" or "lesbian, gay, and bisexual (LGB)" when the matter is solely related to sexuality, and not inclusive of gender-identity and -expression issues.

3 This chapter will use the terms "the Caucus," the "Equality Caucus," the "LGBT Equality Caucus," and "the LGBT Caucus" interchangeably to prevent redundancy, but these all refer to the same entity: the Congressional LGBT Equality Caucus.

4 I define a pro-rights bill as one in which the primary purpose of the bill is to enhance the rights of, or prevent discrimination against, citizens on the basis of sexual orientation, gender identity, or domestic partnership status. I determined this by looking at the summary of each bill. Each bill had to be explicitly tailored to those issues. I excluded bills that covered a range of topics with only minor provisions relating to LGBTQ individuals because sexual orientation or gender identity were not the substantive focuses of the legislation. As a check on external validity of this measure, I checked my list against bills that the Human Rights Campaign's Congressional Scorecard asked MCs to cosponsor. My measure was more inclusive than theirs. Table 17.3 lists these bills.

5 The Equality Caucus is a House-based caucus. No senators are members of the caucus.

6 The results of this chapter do not refute a morality politics framework directly, as it is beyond the scope of the chapter's focus to do so, and future work would need to definitively demonstrate the declining significance of a moral issue frame over time, as well as the ascendancy of a civil rights framework. Work that predates the caucus could evaluate the expansion of the LGBTQ agenda in Congress, especially as a result of the changing fortunes of LGBTQ individuals in society.

7 See "Department of the Interior Letter," Congressional LGBT Equality Caucus, April 7, 2014, lgbt-polis.house.gov.

8 See appendix A for specification of the variables.

9 My estimate of the percent of the LGBTQ population per congressional district is the U.S. Census's estimate of the percent of unmarried same-sex households. Prior research has used this as a proxy measure of the percentage of the LGBTQ population in spite of the obvious imprecision of the measure (Haider-Markel 2010, 1997; Wald, Burton, and Reinzo 1996). I will, therefore, use LGBTQ population and percent of unmarried same-sex households interchangeably.

10 I exclude Reps. Nancy Pelosi and John Boehner from Caucus and cosponsorship models for both congresses because they do not participate in many other congressional activities due to their positions as party leaders.

11　Bishin and Smith (2013) is one of the more recent roll-call vote analyses, but it was of DOMA, passed in 1996.

12　This is according to 1st Dimension DW-nominate scores.

13　It is well established in the literature that interest groups will concentrate their efforts on allies who are already supportive of their agenda (Hall and Wayman 1990; Hojnacki and Kimball 1998). Given the limits of these data, I cannot assert that the HRC causes higher levels of activity, or whether they are rewarding supportive allies for doing what they would have done already.

14　There is prior research that predicts lower levels of black and Latino MC cosponsorship during Republican congresses due to a perceived need to preserve limited media attention for issues seen as central to those communities (Rocca and Sanchez 2008). Black Democrats, as a whole, were consistent cosponsors of LGBTQ bills, however, and I would qualify these results due to the presence of the percent Obama vote (district liberalism) in the model. Given that black districts, which black members tend to represent, voted for Obama in such overwhelming rates, the model overpredicts the number of bills that black MCs should support because these black districts appear to be the most liberal in the country.

REFERENCES

Bishin, Benjamin G., and Charles A. Smith. 2013. "When Do Legislators Defy Popular Sovereignty? Testing Theories of Minority Representation Using DOMA." *Political Research Quarterly* 66 (4): 794–803.

Bratton, Kathleen A., and Kerry L. Haynie. 1999. "Agenda Setting and Legislative Success in State Legislatures: The Effects of Gender and Race." *Journal of Politics* 61 (3): 658–79.

Campbell, Colton C., and Roger Davidson. 2000. "Gay and Lesbian Issues in the Congressional Arena." In *The Politics of Gay Rights*, ed. Craig A. Rimmerman, Kenneth D. Wald, and Clyde Wilcox. Chicago: University of Chicago Press. 347–76.

Campbell, James E. 1982. "Cosponsoring Legislation in the U.S. Congress." *Legislative Studies Quarterly* 7 (3): 415–22.

Canon, David T. 1995. "Redistricting and the Congressional Black Caucus." *American Politics Quarterly* 23 (2): 159–89.

Cohen, Cathy. 1997. "Punks, Bulldaggers, and Welfare Queens: The Radical Potential of Queer Politics?" *Gay and Lesbian Quarterly* 3 (4): 437–65.

Congressional LGBT Equality Caucus. U.S. Congress, House of Representatives. 2015. "Mission." https://lgbt-polis.house.gov/mission. Accessed October 20, 2015.

D'Emilio, John. 1983. *Sexual Politics, Sexual Communities: The Making of a Homosexual Minority in the United States, 1940–1970.* Chicago: University of Chicago Press.

Dodson, Debra L. 2006. *The Impact of Women in Congress.* New York: Oxford University Press.

Fenno, Richard F. 1973. *Congressmen in Committees.* Boston: Little, Brown.

"Frank Won't Back Marriage Act Repeal." 2009. *Politico*, Sept. 13. www.politico.com (accessed December 20, 2014).

Frymer, Paul. 1999. *Uneasy Alliances: Race and Party Competition in America.* Princeton, NJ: Princeton University Press.

Gallup. 2017. "Gay and Lesbian Rights." *Gallup Historical Trends.* http://www.gallup.com. Accessed March 26, 2015.

Gates, Gary J. 2011. "How Many People Are Lesbian, Gay, Bisexual, and Transgender?" Williams Institute, williamsinstitute.law.ucla.edu (accessed December 20, 2014).

Gertzog, Irwin N. 2004. *Women and Power on Capitol Hill: Reconstructing the Congressional Women's Caucus.* Boulder, CO: Reinner.

Green, J. C., James L. Guth, Corwin E. Smidt, and Lyman A. Kellstedt. 1996. *Religion and the Culture Wars: Dispatches from the Front*. Lanham, MD: Rowman & Littlefield.

Guinier, Lani. 1994. *The Tyranny of the Majority: Fundamental Fairness in Representative Democracy*. New York: Free Press.

Haider-Markel, Donald P. 1997. "Interest Group Survival: Shared Interests versus Competition for Resources." *Journal of Politics* 59: 903–12.

Haider-Markel, Donald P. 1999. "Morality Policy and Individual-Level Political Behavior: The Case of Legislative Voting on Lesbian and Gay Issues." *Policy Studies Journal* 27 (4): 735–49.

Haider-Markel, Donald P. 2007. "Representation and Backlash: The Positive and Negative Influence of Descriptive Representation." *Legislative Studies Quarterly* 32 (1): 107–33.

Haider-Markel, Donald P. 2010. *Out and Running: Gay and Lesbian Candidates, Elections, and Policy Representation*. Washington, DC: Georgetown University Press.

Hall, Richard L. 1996. *Participation in Congress*. New Haven, CT: Yale University Press.

Hall, Richard L., and Frank W. Wayman. 1990. "Buying Time: Moneyed Interests and the Mobilization of Bias in Congressional Committees." *American Political Science Review* 84 (3): 797–820.

Hammond, Susan W. 1998. *Congressional Caucuses in National Policymaking*. Baltimore, MD: Johns Hopkins University Press.

Hero, Rodney E. 1992. *Latinos and the U.S. Political System*. Philadelphia: Temple University Press.

Herrick, Rebekah. 2010. "Legislators' Positions on Gay and Lesbian Rights: The Personal and Political." *Journal of Homosexuality* 57 (7): 928–43.

Hojnacki, Marie, and David C. Kimball. 1998. "Organized Interests and the Decision of Whom to Lobby in Congress." *American Political Science Review* 92 (4): 775–90.

Karol, David. 2012. "How Does Party Position Change Happen? The Case of Gay Rights in the US Congress." Paper presented at the Annual Meeting of the Southern Political Science Association, New Orleans, Louisiana

Koger, Gregory. 2003. "Position Taking and Cosponsorship in the U.S. House." *Legislative Studies Quarterly* 28 (2): 225–46.

Lee, Frances E. 2009. *Beyond Ideology: Politics, Principles, and Partisanship in the U.S. Senate*. Chicago: University of Chicago Press.

Lewis, Gregory B. 2011. "The Friends and Family Plan: Contact with Gays and Support for Gay Rights." *Policy Studies Journal* 39 (2): 217–38.

Lewis, Gregory B., and Jonathan L. Edelson. 2000. "DOMA and ENDA: Congress Votes on Gay Rights." In *The Politics of Gay Rights*, ed. Craig A. Rimmerman, Kenneth D. Wald, and Clyde Wilcox. Chicago: University of Chicago Press.

Lewis, Gregory B., and Seong Soo Oh. 2008. "Public Opinion and State Action on Same-Sex Marriage." *State & Local Government Review* 40 (1): 42–53.

Loftus, Jeni. 2001. "America's Liberalization in Attitudes toward Homosexuality, 1973 to 1998." *American Sociological Review* 66 (5): 762–82.

Lublin, David. 2005. "The Strengthening of Party and Decline of Religion in Explaining Congressional Voting Behavior on Gay and Lesbian Issues." *PS: Political Science and Politics* 38 (2): 241–45.

Mansbridge, Jane. 1999. "Should Blacks Represent Blacks and Women Represent Women? A Contingent 'Yes.'" *Journal of Politics* 61 (3): 628–57.

Mansbridge, Jane. 2003. "Rethinking Representation." *American Political Science Review* 97 (4): 515–28.

Mayhew, David R. 1974. *Congress: The Electoral Connection*. New Haven, CT: Yale University Press.

Meyerowitz, Joanne J. 2002. *How Sex Changed: A History of Transsexuality in the United States*. Cambridge, MA: Harvard University Press.

Miler, Kristina C. 2011. "The Constituency Motivations of Caucus Membership." *American Politics Research* 39 (5): 885–920.

"Mission." 2015. Congressional LGBT Equality Caucus, lgbt-polis.house.gov (accessed October 20, 2015).

Mucciaroni, Gary. 2011a. "Are Debates about 'Morality Policy' Really about Morality? Framing Opposition to Gay and Lesbian Rights." *Policy Studies Journal* 39 (2): 187–216.

Mucciaroni, Gary. 2011b. "The Study of LGBT Politics and Its Contributions to Political Science." *PS: Political Science and Politics* 44 (1): 17.

Palmer, Anna. 2009. "Q Street on K Street; New Group Lobbies for LGBT Interests." *Politico*, 11 March. Accessed October 20, 2015 via LexisNexis Academic.

Pearson, Kathryn, and Logan Dancey. 2011. "Elevating Women's Voices in Congress: Speech Participation in the House of Representatives." *Political Research Quarterly* 64 (4): 910–23.

Pinney, Neil, and George Serra. 2002. "A Voice for Black Interests: Congressional Black Caucus Cohesion and Bill Cosponsorship." *Congress and the Presidency* 29 (1): 69–86.

Pitkin, Hannah Fenichel. 1967. *The Concept of Representation*. Berkeley: University of California Press.

"Q Street on K Street: New Group Lobbies for LGBT Interests." 2009. *Roll Call*, March 11. www.rollcall.com (accessed October 20, 2015).

Reingold, Beth. 2008. "Women as Officeholders: Linking Descriptive and Substantive Representation." In *Political Women and American Democracy*, ed. Christina Wolbrecht, Karen Beckwith, and Lisa Baldez. Cambridge: Cambridge University Press, 128–47.

Reynolds, Andrew. 2013. "Representation and Rights: The Impact of LGBT Legislators in Comparative Perspective." *American Political Science Review* 107 (2): 259–74.

Rocca, Michael S., and Stacy B. Gordon. 2010. "The Position-Taking Value of Bill Sponsorship in Congress." *Political Research Quarterly* 63 (2): 387–97.

Rocca, Michael S., and Gabriel R. Sanchez. 2008. "The Effect of Race and Ethnicity on Bill Sponsorship and Cosponsorship in Congress." *American Politics Research* 36 (1): 130–52.

Schiller, Wendy J. 1995. "Senators as Political Entrepreneurs: Using Bill Sponsorship to Shape Legislative Agendas." *American Journal of Political Science* 39 (1): 186–203.

Sherrill, Kenneth. 1996. "The Political Power of Lesbians, Gays, and Bisexuals." *PS: Political Science & Politics* 29 (3): 469–73.

Singh, Robert. 1998. *The Congressional Black Caucus: Racial Politics in the U.S. Congress*. Thousand Oaks, CA: Sage.

Stevens, Arthur G., Daniel P. Mulhollan, and Paul S. Rundquist. 1981. "U.S. Congressional Structure and Representation: The Role of Informal Groups." *Legislative Studies Quarterly* 6 (3): 415–37.

Strolovitch, Dara Z. 2012. "Intersectionality in Time: Sexuality and the Shifting Boundaries of Intersectional Marginalization." *Politics & Gender* 8 (3): 386–96.

Sulkin, Tracy. 2005. *Issue Politics in Congress*. Cambridge: Cambridge University Press.

Swers, Michele L. 1998. "Are Women More Likely to Vote for Women's Issue Bills Than Their Male Colleagues?" *Legislative Studies Quarterly* 23 (3): 435–48.

Swers, Michele L. 2002. *The Difference Women Make*. Chicago: University of Chicago Press.

Swers, Michele L. 2005. "Connecting Descriptive and Substantive Representation: An Analysis of Sex Differences in Cosponsorship Activity." *Legislative Studies Quarterly* 30 (3): 407–33.

"Two Like-Minded Liberals, One Job: Who'll Win?" 1994. *New York Times*, Sept. 8. www.nytimes.com (accessed October 30, 2015).

U.S. House Committee on Armed Services. U.S. Congress, House of Representatives. 1993. *National Defense Authorization Act for Fiscal Year 1994.* 103rd cong., 1st sess., Jan. 5. U.S. Government Printing Office. https://www.congress.gov. Accessed January 20th, 2017.

Wald, Kenneth, James W. Burton, and Barbara A. Rienzo. 1996. "The Politics of Gay Rights in American Communities: Explaining Antidiscrimination Ordinances and Policies." *American Journal of Political Science* 40 (4): 1152–78.

Warshaw, Jonathan, and Christopher Rodden. 2012. "How Should We Measure District-Level Public Opinion on Individual Issues?" *Journal of Politics* 74 (1): 203–19.

Whitby, Kenny J. 2002. "Bill Sponsorship and Intraracial Voting among African American Representatives." *American Politics Research* 30 (1): 93–109.

Whitby, Kenny J., and George A. Krause. 2001. "Race, Issue Heterogeneity, and Public Policy: The Republican Revolution in the 104th U.S. Congress and the Representation of African American Policy Interests." *British Journal of Political Science* 31 (3): 555–72.

Williams, Melissa. 2000. *Voice, Memory, and Trust.* Princeton, NJ: Princeton University Press.

Wolinsky, Marc, and Kenneth Sherrill, eds. 1993. *Gays and the Military: Joseph Steffan versus the United States.* Princeton, NJ: Princeton University Press.

18

Gay and Lesbian Candidates, Group Stereotypes, and the News Media

An Experimental Design

MANDI BATES BAILEY AND STEVEN P. NAWARA

Although Americans are becoming more accepting of the LGBT community and increasingly more supportive of policies impacting gay rights (see Brewer 2003), Americans' willingness to elect gays and lesbians to political office is debatable.[1] In 1987, Massachusetts representative Barney Frank's advisors were concerned about the result of his "coming out" and conducted a poll to measure the subsequent political impact. While 44% of respondents surveyed felt that Frank's disclosure would be politically damaging, when asked if they would be less likely to vote for him knowing that he was gay, only 22% of respondents agreed (Frank 2002). The concern about the impact of a candidate openly disclosing his or her sexual orientation is warranted as homophobic rhetoric has been used in American elections to lower support for opposing candidates. For example, Jesse Helms attacked Harvey Gantt for accepting money from gay interest groups in the 1990 United States Senate race in North Carolina; Linda Chavez made sexuality an issue in 1986 by implying that Barbara Mikulski was a lesbian in the U.S. Senate race in Maryland; and when Ed Koch and Mario Cuomo campaigned to become mayor of New York City in 1977, Cuomo's supporters made sexuality an issue by utilizing the slogan, "Vote for Cuomo, not the homo." Neither Gantt, Koch, nor Mikulski were "out of the closet" during these campaigns, and several vocally denied the rumors. In fact, Gantt's heterosexuality was never questioned, Koch professed his heterosexuality, and Mikulski simply did not address the issue. Regardless of the accuracy of the claims used in these examples, given that research suggests voters are less likely to vote for gay and lesbian candidates (see Herrick and Thomas 1999), such campaign tactics may be logical. But, why are gay and lesbian candidate less appealing? Does a candidate's sexual orientation override other political characteristics, such as partisanship, that could potentially impact his or her electability?

In order to understand why Americans may be less likely to vote for gay candidates and the extent to which other factors influence that decision, we must consider related stereotypes. This study proposes that stereotypes of gays and lesbians can be activated by the news media, which in turn impact voters' decisions.

We, therefore, utilize a survey-based media experiment that varies the sexual orientation, partisan affiliation, and gender of a fictional congressional candidate to find that stereotypes of gays and lesbians do in fact impact vote choice.

Stereotypes of Gays and Lesbians

Gays and lesbians may very well be evaluated in terms of relevant group stereotypes that are often negative (Golebiowska 2001; Golebiowska and Thomsen 1999). These negative stereotypes persist even though Americans are becoming more supportive of gay rights policies (as noted above). In turn, while Americans are becoming more accepting of issues such as gay marriage and civil unions, gay adoption, and gays in the workplace (Bowman 2006) and dramatically fewer Americans characterize homosexuality as "always wrong" (Brewer 2003; Wilcox and Norrander 2002; Wilcox and Wolpert 2000), research suggests that negative stereotypes of gays and lesbians may still impact Americans' perceptions of gay and lesbian political candidates. Specifically, gay political candidates are better served by waiting to disclose their sexuality when voters have information unrelated to sexuality on which to evaluate them (Golebiowska 2003). This finding corresponds to stereotyping literature that suggests that individuals rely on stereotypes in the absence of individuating information (see for example, Fiske and Neuberg 1990; Fiske and Pavelchak 1986). Thus, when evaluating gay and lesbian candidates, voters will be less reliant on the potentially negative stereotypes of gays and lesbians and may place greater emphasis on other candidate characteristics such as issue positions and experience when that information is available.

Clearly, there has been an increase in tolerance, but Golebiowska's (2003) research suggests that we should not be too quick to dismiss the potential impact of the negative stereotypes on the evaluation of gay and lesbian candidates. Further, a willingness to support policies seen as benefiting gay and lesbian Americans does not necessarily translate to a willingness to vote for a gay or lesbian candidate. This study examines the willingness of voters to rely on antigay stereotypes when expressing their willingness to vote for candidates in differing contexts.

Public Opinion Regarding Openly Gay Elected Officials

According to the Gay and Lesbian Victory Fund, in May 2014 there were four hundred openly gay, lesbian, bisexual, and transgendered individuals elected to serve at the local, state, and federal levels of government in the United States. A little over three-quarters of these elected officials served at the local level, and eighty-four openly gay elected officials served at the state level. However, only seven openly gay elected officials served in Congress. While gay and lesbian Americans are obviously underrepresented (at least descriptively) in American national politics, it is noteworthy that Americans have become increasingly willing to vote for gay and lesbian candidates, particularly at lower levels of government.

Research conducted in the last decade points to the extent to which a gay/lesbian politician's sexual orientation may impact candidate evaluations. For example, the Gay and Lesbian Victory Fund commissioned a poll to conduct in-depth interviews of residents in Kentucky and Alabama in 2005 in order to better understand individuals' attitudes toward gay public officials; they found that honesty, integrity, and job performance matter more to these southern voters than sexuality (Lake Research Partners 2006). While the Victory Fund makes no attempt to imply that this research can be generalized to the national population, the results are convincing given the socially conservative leanings of the region. Moreover, even though the individuals in this sample disagreed with the morality of homosexuality, they generally did not want to judge others, including elected officials. There was concern regarding the motives of politicians who wish to come out, however (Lake Research Partners 2005). Elected to represent a district in one of the states involved in the Victory Fund's study, Ernesto Scorsone "came out of the closet" while serving in the Kentucky state legislature. When asked if he felt that his sexual orientation would impact his reelection bid, Scorsone's response echoed the sentiment of participants in the Victory Fund study: "I feel confident that my constituents will vote on my performance as their representative, not on my sexual orientation. As long as they do that, I will be serving another term" (2006). Indeed, Scorsone was subsequently reelected.

In terms of presidential politics, according to a 2007 Gallup survey, 56% of Americans would vote for a well-qualified gay or lesbian presidential candidate. This number increased from 26% in 1978 (Bowman 2008). However, a 2006 Gallup survey indicated that 91% of respondents felt that the country was not ready for a gay or lesbian president. This percentage of respondents is greater than the percentage of respondents in the same survey who viewed Americans as not ready to accept members of other politically underrepresented groups, such as women, African Americans, Jews, Hispanics, Asians, Mormons, and atheists, as president (Jones 2006).

Media Effects

There is a great deal of evidence that media impact political attitudes and that media are capable of activating stereotypes that may bias political evaluations (see Fridkin et al. 2009; Murphy 1998; Peffley and Hurwitz 2002; Valentino 1999). Further, media prime character-related considerations during evaluations of political candidates (Mendelsohn 1996). Character evaluations are particularly relevant to this study as stereotypes of gays and lesbians (as with many other politically underrepresented groups) are typically negative, focusing on loose morals and/or ascribing masculine traits to lesbians and feminine traits to gay men.

When negative stereotypes of gay and lesbian candidates are activated, it is reasonable to assume that they would result in a more negative evaluation of those gay and/or lesbian candidates. However, the effects of the negative stereotypes may be undercut when gay and lesbian candidates fail to conform to the relevant stereotypes (Golebiowska 2000, 2001). More specifically, scholarly evidence suggests that when targets are inconsistent with their group stereotypes, the impact of those stereotypes on the evaluations of the targets is diminished (Fein and Hilton 1992; Fiske and Neuberg 1990; Peffley et al. 1997). In other words, if specific gay and lesbian candidates do not conform to commonly held negative stereotypes, individuals will be less likely to rely on those stereotypes when evaluating the stereotype-disconfirming candidates.

While there are general stereotypes impacting gays and lesbians, there are also specific stereotypes that relate to gay and lesbian politicians. For instance, gay and lesbian politicians are often seen to be primarily concerned with issues affecting the LGBT community (Herrick and Thomas 1999). Issues such as gays and lesbians serving in the military and gay marriage are linked to gay candidates, and often to the Democratic Party. As a result, many more gays and lesbians identify with the Democratic Party than the Republican Party; national exit polls for the 2012 election estimated that 76% of gays and lesbians voted for Barack Obama over John McCain (CNN 2012). Therefore, gay and lesbian candidates are stereotype confirming if they are Democrats but stereotype disconfirming if they are Republicans.

Hypotheses

We can make four summary assessments of the literature relating to the media's ability to impact evaluations of gay and lesbian political candidates. First, the media have the potential to activate stereotypes of politically underrepresented groups. Second, gay and lesbian candidates who are inconsistent with stereotypes may be evaluated more positively than those who are stereotype confirming. Third, the stereotypes activated by the media tend to be negative and can bias evaluations of gay and lesbian candidates. And fourth, individuals are more likely to rely on their personally held negative stereotypes when evaluating stereotype-consistent gays and lesbians, rather than those who are stereotype disconfirming. We, therefore, reach the following hypotheses:

H1: Individuals exposed to a gay/lesbian candidate will be less likely to indicate that they would vote for that candidate than individuals exposed to a heterosexual candidate.

H2: Individuals will be less likely to vote for a stereotype-confirming gay/lesbian candidate than a stereotype-disconfirming gay/lesbian candidate.

H3: Individuals exposed to gay and lesbian candidates are more likely to have negative stereotypes activated than are individuals exposed to heterosexual candidates.

H4: Individuals exposed to a stereotype-confirming gay/lesbian candidate are more likely to have negative stereotypes activated than are individuals exposed to a stereotype-disconfirming gay/lesbian candidate.

Methods

To test the above hypotheses, a survey-based experiment was administered to students at a midsized regional university in the Southeast in October 2010. The sample, experimental manipulation, measures utilized, and model specification are detailed below.

Sample

The analyses use a convenience sample of 268 students enrolled in an introductory course that is required of all university students regardless of major. Approximately 60% of students in this sample are women and slightly greater than 56% of the sample are white. Greater than 36% of respondents are African American, which is equivalent to the university's relatively large African American population.

While data reflecting respondents' sexual orientation and whether respondents are from the South were collected, they are not used in this analysis. Only two respondents identified as being gay or lesbian, and only fifteen respondents reported being from nonsouthern states. Similarly, we do not control for age in the models below, as there is insufficient variation.

Using a nonrandom undergraduate sample might be considered problematic and is certainly less than ideal. However, it is important to recognize that this study is more concerned with measuring an experimental effect than with generalizing cross-section survey results to a larger population. Subjects were randomly assigned to experimental conditions, and there is no reason to believe that the effects of antigay and lesbian stereotypes would be more significant among predominantly young college students than among the general population. If anything, our sample presents a more stringent test to find a significant result because public opinion surveys consistently find younger people to be the most accepting of the LGBT community, and they are therefore less likely to hold antigay and lesbian stereotypes.

Experimental Manipulation

The experimental manipulation was embedded into the survey instrument following a series of semantic differentials designed to assess respondents' feelings toward a variety of groups, including gay men and lesbians. The manipulation is presented in the form of a newspaper article introducing readers to a candidate in a fictional out-of-state (Wyoming) congressional race (no students in the sample identified as being from the state in which the race is depicted as occurring).

The candidate's gender, sexual orientation, and partisan identification are manipulated in the article while all other information remains constant. Thus, the study involves eight candidate types: (1) Democratic heterosexual male, (2) Republican heterosexual male, (3) Democratic heterosexual female, (4) Republican heterosexual female, (5) Democratic gay male, (6) Republican gay male, (7) Democratic lesbian, and (8) Republican lesbian. A photograph of the candidate with his/her spouse/partner accompanies the article. In order to eliminate as many extraneous variables as possible, the targets in the photos were selected to appear to be approximately the same age and the same relative level of attractiveness and were both presented on neutral backgrounds. Sexual orientation is addressed only in a caption below the picture (identifying the candidate and his/her partner/spouse) and in the final two sentences of the article, which read, "[Candidate's name] and his/her wife/husband/partner of 15 years, [partner's name], a Cheyenne real estate developer, live in Laramie. [Candidate's name] hopes to become Wyoming's first openly gay Congressman." No policy-specific information is contained in the article.

Model Specification

The dependent variable utilized in the analyses is the likelihood of voting for the candidate, measured by asking respondents, "If you had the opportunity to vote for the candidate in the article, how likely would you be to vote for him/her?" Responses to both of these questions were assessed on a seven-point ordinal scale ranging from "very unlikely" (1) to "very likely" (7).

The extent to which respondents hold anti–gay and lesbian stereotypes are key variables of interest in this study. We derive the stereotype variables from the semantic differential scales assessed prior to the news article manipulation in the survey instrument. These measures address respondents' previously held attitudes toward gay men and lesbians and include attitudes regarding the perceived morality, religiosity, and honesty of gays and lesbians, measured on a seven-point ordinal scale, coded so that the resulting stereotype measures reflect antigay and/or antilesbian affect. Given that gay men tend to be negatively perceived as feminine and lesbians as masculine, a measure of the perceived strength and weakness of gays and lesbians is also included. While "strong" would be considered a positive evaluation of gay men, it would be considered a negative evaluation of lesbians, however. The resulting stereotype measures can be summarized as follows:

Antigay/Antilesbian Stereotype: Evaluation of Morality + Evaluation of Religiosity + Evaluation of Honesty + Evaluation of Strength.

The antigay-stereotype variable is included in considerations of all models featuring a male candidate, and the antilesbian stereotype variable is included in all models featuring a female candidate. The models that assess both male and female candidates simultaneously utilize an antihomosexual stereotype measure that combines the antigay and antilesbian stereotypes (Antihomosexual Stereotype = Antigay Stereotype + Antilesbian Stereotype).

We employ two variables that address religiosity. The first, referred to as Protestant in tables 18.1–18.3, is a dummy variable where Protestant Christian = 1. The second, referred to as Biblical Literalism in tables 18.1–18.3, captures respondents'

TABLE 18.1. Willingness to Vote for Candidates

	All Candidates	Male Candidates	Female Candidates	All Candidates
Gay or Lesbian Candidate	−0.57** (0.22)	−0.31 (0.33)	−0.77** (0.30)	−0.44 (0.30)
Antihomosexual Stereotype	−0.05*** (0.01)			−0.05*** (0.01)
Antigay Stereotype		−0.12*** (0.03)		
Antilesbian Stereotype			−0.09** (0.04)	
Democratic Candidate	0.04 (0.22)	0.66* (0.32)	−0.60* (0.28)	0.17 (0.29)
Democratic Cand.* Gay Cand.				−0.28 (0.43)
Female Candidate	0.14 (0.21)			0.14 (0.21)
Protestant Christian	0.66* (0.26)	0.71† (0.37)	0.63 (0.39)	0.65* (0.29)
Biblical Literalism	−0.46* (0.20)	−0.65* (0.27)	−0.21 (0.27)	0.44* (0.21)
Knows a Gay or Lesbian	0.49† (0.27)	0.68 (0.42)	0.43 (0.33)	0.47† (0.27)
Ideology	−0.13 (0.09)	−0.11 (0.12)	−0.20 (0.13)	−0.14 (0.09)
Caucasian	0.11 (0.23)	−0.18 (0.32)	0.46 (0.32)	0.11 (0.23)
Male	−0.67** (0.23)	−0.85** (0.33)	−0.49 (0.32)	−0.67** (0.22)
Constant	6.13*** (0.80)	5.72*** (0.99)	6.67*** (1.05)	6.09*** (0.71)
R^2	0.22	0.32	0.22	0.23
n	258	126	132	258

Notes: OLS regression with robust standard errors in parentheses. DV= Likelihood of voting for candidate on a seven-point scale. ***p<0.001, **p<0.01, *p<0.05, †p<0.1.

attitudes toward the Bible on an ordinal scale from viewing the Bible as the "word of God," which should be taken literally (0), to the Bible as a "book of fables" recorded by men (2).

Race, respondent gender, and whether the respondent has a gay/lesbian family member, friend, or acquaintance are all dummies used as control variables (1 = White, 1 = Male, and 1 = Knows Someone Gay/Lesbian). Ideology is used rather than partisanship because many respondents in the sample of college students failed to indicate their party identification, resulting in insufficient variation within some of the experimental conditions. Ideology is measured on a seven-point ordinal scale ranging from very liberal to very conservative.

Results

Approximately 25% of respondents receiving manipulations featuring gay and lesbian candidates indicated they would be unlikely to vote for those candidates if given the opportunity, compared to 19% of respondents receiving manipulations with heterosexual candidates. Prima facie, this descriptive information would suggest that survey respondents are not very likely to view gay and lesbian candidates substantially less favorably than heterosexual candidates with the same experience. However, further examination of the data suggests varying levels of electoral support for gay and lesbian candidates. Furthermore, the activation of anti–gay and lesbian stereotypes when making the vote decision appears to vary according to candidate traits.

Table 18.1 provides a direct test of the first hypothesis. As the first column shows, people are indeed less likely to vote for a gay and lesbian candidate than a heterosexual one, as evidenced by the negative coefficient for the variable indicating that the respondent received a gay candidate ($p < 0.01$).[2] Incidentally, this relationship is present even after controlling for individuals' antihomosexual stereotypes, which also shows a statistically significant negative relationship. The antihomosexual stereotype scale ranged from eight to fifty-six in the sample, with a median of thirty-two. A voter being in the tenth percentile, indicating someone who does not subscribe to many antihomosexual stereotypes, is predicted to lower his or her willingness to vote for a gay candidate by 1.11 points on the seven-point scale, while someone being in the ninetieth percentile (who holds a great deal of antihomosexual stereotypes) is predicted to lower his or her willingness to vote by 2.33 points. This relationship is not uniform for male and female candidates, however. Somewhat unexpectedly, after the experimental conditions are split up by candidate sex, the dummy variable indicating a gay and lesbian candidate is negative but insignificant in column 2's model for male candidates (p=0.32), suggesting that this relationship is driven by an unwillingness to vote for lesbian candidates. Indeed, the coefficient indicating a lesbian candidate is quite large in column 3's model with only female candidates ($p < 0.01$).

That voters are less willing to vote for equally qualified lesbian candidates, but not gay male candidates, is an important finding and may be a sign of the increased acceptance of gays being unequally applied to gay males but not lesbians. Lesbians simultaneously belong to two marginalized groups, women and the LGBT community; like others who belong to multiple stigmatized groups, such an identity can shape the way in which others perceive members (Doan and Haider-Markel 2010; Fiske and Neuberg 1990; Jones and Shorter-Gooden 2003). To illustrate, heterosexuals have been shown to harbor more negative stereotypes about lesbians than about gay men (LaMar and Kite 1998). To some degree, an unwillingness to vote for lesbians is evidenced in real life; just 36% of all "out" elected office holders in the United States are female (Victory Fund 2014). This unequal reluctance to vote for gay and lesbian candidates according to sex may have large electoral implications and may factor into the decisions of candidates to disclose their sexuality.

The second hypothesis posits that individuals will be less willing to vote for a stereotype-confirming gay or lesbian candidate than a candidate who disconfirms stereotypes. The specific stereotype our candidates could confirm or disconfirm was their party affiliation. Hence, gay or lesbian Democratic candidates are considered stereotype confirming while gay or lesbian Republican candidates are considered stereotype disconfirming. The final column of table 18.1 tests this hypothesis by interacting the party identification of the candidate with the candidate's sexuality. The marginal effect of candidate sexuality is statistically significant in predicting the willingness to vote for Democratic candidates ($p < 0.03$) but not Republican candidates ($p < 0.16$), even though the change in the marginal effect of candidate sexuality on vote preference is small, decreasing from -0.43 for stereotype-disconfirming Republican candidates to -0.71 for stereotype-confirming Democratic candidates (Boehmke 2008; Brambor, Clark, and Golder 2006). Thus, individuals are significantly less willing to vote for gay Democratic candidates but not gay Republican candidates. This finding confirms Hypothesis 2 and the literature that suggested this relationship (Golebiowska 2000, 2001).

The third hypothesis argued that individuals will be more likely to have negative stereotypes activated when they are exposed to gay or lesbian candidates than when they are exposed to heterosexual candidates. Table 18.2 tests this hypothesis among all respondents in column 1 by using an interaction between respondents' stereotyping and whether that respondent was presented with a gay or lesbian candidate. Theory suggests that people will be less likely to vote for a gay candidate as their level of stereotyping increases. As the interaction coefficient in the first column shows, this is not the case. While it is true that the impact of stereotypes on vote choice is slightly larger when the respondent receives a gay candidate than a lesbian, the stereotype's importance to the vote is not significantly different than with heterosexual candidates. Instead, the

TABLE 18.2. Importance of Stereotypes When Voting for Gay and Lesbian Candidates

	All Candidates	Male Candidates	Female Candidates
Antihomosexual Stereotype	−0.04*		
	(0.02)		
Antigay Stereotype		−0.09*	
		(0.04)	
Antilesbian Stereotype			−0.06
			(0.06)
Gay Candidate	0.23	0.55	0.41
	(0.91)	(1.05)	(1.36)
Stereotype * Gay Candidate	−0.02	−0.05	−0.07
	(0.03)	(0.06)	(0.08)
Democratic Candidate	0.05	0.65*	−0.58*
	(0.22)	(0.33)	(0.28)
Female Candidate	0.16		
	(0.21)		
Protestant Christian	0.69**	0.70†	0.75†
	(0.27)	(0.37)	(0.41)
Biblical Literalism	−0.47*	−0.65*	−0.24
	(0.20)	(0.27)	(0.27)
Knows a Gay or Lesbian Person	0.46†	0.63	0.40
	(0.27)	(0.42)	(0.33)
Ideology	−0.15	−0.13	−0.21†
	(0.09)	(0.12)	(0.13)
Caucasian	0.14	−0.18	0.52†
	(0.22)	(0.32)	(0.31)
Male	−0.66**	−0.84**	−0.47
	(0.23)	(0.32)	(0.32)
Constant	5.79***	5.43***	6.10***
	(0.89)	(1.02)	(1.26)
R^2	0.23	0.32	0.22
n	258	126	132

Notes: OLS regression with robust standard errors in parentheses. DV= Likelihood of voting for candidate on a seven-point scale. ***p<0.001, **p<0.01, *p<0.05, †p<0.1.

marginal effect of stereotypes is significantly negative for both heterosexual and gay and lesbian candidates at $p < 0.05$ (Boehmke 2008; Brambor et al. 2006); those who hold antihomosexual stereotypes are less likely to express a willingness to vote for *all* candidates, regardless of their sexuality.

The second and third columns split the sample by candidate sex and analyze the impact of antigay and antilesbian stereotypes independently. Among male candidates, the marginal effect of antigay stereotypes is a significant negative predictor of the vote, whether the candidate is a gay or straight man, which is not

344 | MANDI BATES BAILEY AND STEVEN P. NAWARA

expected by the hypothesis and is consistent with the results in the first column of the table.

The model for female candidates (column 3) does provide some support for the third hypothesis, however. The "Stereotype* Gay Candidate" coefficient is not statistically significant because there is not a statistically significant difference in the marginal effect of an individual's level of antilesbian stereotype across gay/ straight candidates. When the respondent receives a heterosexual female candidate, the marginal effect of antilesbian stereotypes on vote preference is -0.06 and is not significantly different from zero. However, the marginal effect increases in magnitude to -0.134 when the respondent receives a lesbian candidate; this is statistically significant from zero ($p < 0.05$). This provides some, albeit quite limited, support for the third hypothesis, at least among female candidates. The substantive effect is strong as well; respondents in the tenth percentile of holding antilesbian stereotypes are expected to lower their vote preference by 0.9 points on the seven-point scale when provided with a lesbian candidate, while those in the ninetieth percentile are expected to lower their vote preference by 2.7 points.

The fourth hypothesis is that individuals exposed to a stereotype-confirming gay/lesbian candidate are more likely to have negative stereotypes activated than individuals exposed to a stereotype-disconfirming gay/lesbian candidate. The first column of table 18.3 examines this hypothesis among those respondents who received a gay or lesbian candidate using an interaction between the candidates' party affiliation and the respondents' adherence to antihomosexual stereotypes. A negative sign on the interaction is expected because negative stereotypes are expected to be a stronger predictor of vote preference when the candidate is a Democrat.

The first column shows that this is not the case; the interaction's coefficient is positive, suggesting that a respondent's negative stereotyping is a stronger predictor of the vote when the gay or lesbian candidate is a Republican as opposed to a Democrat. Indeed, the marginal effect of the stereotypes is -0.07 for a Republican candidate and statistically significant from zero at $p < 0.05$. For a Democratic candidate, the marginal effect of the stereotypes is -0.03 and is not statistically significant from zero.

Breaking up the experimental conditions by gay and lesbian candidates does not provide much insight into this confounding result. Among gay candidates in column 2's model, the marginal effect of antigay stereotypes is negative and significantly different from zero for Republican candidates ($p < 0.05$) but is statistically insignificant for Democratic candidates. The model for lesbian candidates in column 3 shows an almost identical relationship. Furthermore, this seemingly strange relationship also exists when respondents' perceptions of candidate qualifications are used as the dependent variable instead of vote likelihood.

There is precedent for this type of relationship; however, it exists in evaluations of the impact of racial stereotypes rather than of stereotypes of gays and

TABLE 18.3. Stereotype Confirmation's Importance in Vote Preference among Gay and Lesbian Candidates

	All Gay and Lesbian Candidates	Gay Candidates Only	Lesbian Candidates Only
Antihomosexual Stereotype	−0.07** (0.02)		
Antigay Stereotype		−0.16** (0.06)	
Antilesbian Stereotype			−0.09 (0.07)
Democratic Candidate	−1.10 (1.22)	−0.61 (1.24)	−0.78 (1.87)
Stereotype * Democratic Candidate	0.03 (0.04)	0.05 (0.08)	0.03 (0.11)
Female Candidate	0.00 (0.32)		
Protestant Christian	0.33 (0.40)	0.20 (0.45)	0.52 (0.73)
Biblical Literalism	−0.87** (0.33)	−0.87* (0.41)	−0.68 (0.50)
Knows a Gay or Lesbian Person	0.97* (0.47)	1.05 (0.68)	1.00 (0.66)
Ideology	−0.24 (0.15)	−0.13 (0.21)	−0.49* (0.24)
Caucasian	0.02 (0.36)	−0.15 (0.51)	0.32 (0.54)
Male	−0.57 (0.37)	−0.47 (0.45)	−0.57 (0.56)
Constant	6.16*** (1.30)	6.10** (1.98)	6.47*** (1.84)
R^2	0.32	0.37	0.35
n	120	60	60

Notes: OLS regression with robust standard errors in parentheses. DV= Likelihood of voting for candidate on a seven-point scale. ***p<0.001, **p<0.01, *p<0.05, †p<0.1.

lesbians. Specifically, Peffley et al. (1997) find that black targets that were strongly inconsistent with traditional negative racial stereotypes prompted whites to "bend over backwards" in their evaluations. While we are not concerned with racial stereotypes in this study, the extent to which targets conform to stereotypes is integral here. In turn, if this logic is applied to the impact of gay and lesbian stereotypes, we would expect respondents to be more positive in their evaluations of gay Republicans because this presentation is strongly inconsistent with expectations.

Conclusion

In spite of the evidence that Americans are becoming more accepting of gays and lesbians and policies impacting the LGBT community, the results reported in this study still point to negative attitudes toward gays and lesbians serving as predictors of willingness to vote for them. The evidence suggests that lesbian candidates bear the brunt of this negativity, however. Though people indicate less willingness to vote for both gays and lesbians, being a gay or lesbian candidate was only a significantly negative predictor of vote choice for female candidates after the experimental conditions were split by the sex of the candidate.

This experiment also sheds light on the role of stereotypes in determining how people make vote decisions. The degree to which a person held negative stereotypes of gays and lesbians was expected to negatively influence the likelihood of supporting gay and lesbian candidates but not heterosexual ones. However, this relationship was only observed among female candidates. When subjects were provided with male candidates, the belief in antigay stereotypes had a negative relationship with vote preference for all candidates, gay or straight. There are a few potential explanations for this finding, though our current data lacks the ability to settle the matter conclusively. One explanation might be that those who adhere to antigay stereotypes may have high levels of homophobia towards males, which cause them to evaluate all male candidates negatively, but not female ones. Another possible causal mechanism is that those holding these negative stereotypes may generally tend to be negative individuals, which would cause their evaluations of both gay and straight candidates to suffer. Determining the actual reason for this result, including dismissing the possibility of a Type II error, could be an interesting avenue for further experimental research on this topic.

Finally, whether a candidate conforms to existing gay and lesbian stereotypes can have electoral effects. By using the stereotype that gays and lesbians are Democrats rather than Republicans, we confirm that stereotype-confirming candidates are evaluated worse than stereotype-disconfirming candidates; our respondents were significantly less willing to vote for gay Democrats than gay Republicans. Interestingly, however, we did not find evidence that exposure to stereotypical candidates activated antigay and lesbian stereotypes. In fact, adherence to stereotypes turned out to be a slightly *weaker* predictor of the vote when respondents were exposed to stereotypical gay or lesbian candidates rather than nonstereotypical candidates. We believe that existing literature on racial stereotypes provides some explanation, however, since white respondents often "bend over backwards" to make positive evaluations of black targets that are strongly inconsistent with racial stereotypes (Peffley et al. 1997). Thus, straight voters might "bend over backwards" to provide positive assessments of gay or lesbian Republican candidates. Further research could help assess whether this speculative answer is correct. Alternatively, it could also be the case that perhaps a different stereotype other than party could produce results more in line with hypothesized expectations. Finally, we must also be open to the possibility that the unexpected finding is simply the result of sample-specific or experiment-specific anomalies and would not be replicated in further studies.

The results provided in this analysis should be interpreted cautiously for a number of reasons. First, we would expect younger Americans to evaluate gay and lesbian candidates more positively than older Americans. Given the narrow age range of respondents in the sample used in this study, we are unable to address generational effects. Likewise, we are unable to control for respondent sexuality. It is reasonable to assume that gay and lesbian respondents would evaluate gay and lesbian candidates more positively. Yet with only two self-identified homosexual respondents in the sample, we are unable to address the impact of respondent sexual orientation. Finally, given that eight manipulations are used in this study, the sample size within individual manipulations is relatively small, and a larger sample could provide more statistical power in the future.

Nevertheless, this study provides valuable insight into the media's ability to activate negative stereotypes of gay and lesbian political candidates specifically and candidates belonging to politically underrepresented groups more generally. Additionally, it suggests that the impact of ideology may be strongly undercut or erased when negative attitudes toward gays and lesbians are activated. Finally, this study provides further support for Golebiowska's (2003) conclusion that gay and lesbian political candidates may be benefited by revealing their sexuality after voters have information about those candidates unrelated to their sexuality on which to base their evaluations. As the importance of issues relating to LGBT rights continues to increase in the national consciousness and as the ranks of out-of-the-closet politicians grow, social scientists, journalists, and candidates will need a better understanding of the ways in which candidate sexuality can impact voters' evaluations. We consider our study a preliminary step in gaining such an understanding of these complex and socially evolving attitudes.

NOTES

1 The authors thank Don Haider-Markel for his helpful comments and suggestions.

2 We use OLS regression models because of their straightforward interpretation. However, since the dependent variables' seven-point scales can also be treated as ordinal, we replicated the following analyses using ordered logistic regression and found identical results in terms of the direction and significance of the important independent variables.

REFERENCES

Boehmke, Frederick J. 2008. "GRINTER: A Stata Utility to Graph Interaction Effects after Regression Models." Version 1.5.

Bowman, Karlyn. 2008. "Attitudes about Homosexuality and Gay Marriage." *American Enterprise Institute's Short Publications*. Available online at www.aei.org.

Brambor, Thomas, William Roberts Clark, and Matt Golder. 2006. "Understanding Interaction Models: Improving Empirical Analyses." *Political Analysis* 14: 63–82.

Brewer, Paul R. 2003. "The Shifting Foundations of Public Opinion about Gay Rights." *Journal of Politics* 65:1208–20.

CNN. 2012. "Election Center 2012: Exit Polls." CNN.com, http://www.cnn.com (accessed 25 January, 2013).

Doan, Alesha E., and Donald P. Haider-Markel. 2010. "The Role of Intersectional Stereotypes on Evaluations of Gay and Lesbian Political Candidates." *Politics & Gender* 6(1): 63–91.

Fein, Steven, and James L. Hilton. 1992. "Attitudes toward Groups and Behavior Intentions toward Individual Group Members: The Impact of Nondiagnostic Information." *Journal of Experimental Social Psychology* 28: 101–24.

Fiske, Susan T., and S. L. Neuberg. 1990. "A Continuum of Impression Formation, from Category-Based to Individuating Processes: Influences of Information and Motivation on Attention and Interpretation." In M. P. Zanna (ed.), *Advances in Experimental Social Psychology*, vol. 23. New York: Academic Press.

Fiske, Susan T., and Mark A. Pavelchak. 1986. "Category-Based versus Piecemeal-Based Affect Responses: Developments in Schema-Triggered Affect." In R. M. Sorenti and E. T. Higgins (eds.), *The Handbook of Motivation and Cognition: Foundations of Social Behavior*. New York: Guilford.

Frank, Barney. 2002. "Barney Frank May 1987: U.S. Representative Barney Frank Remembers when he Became the First Congressman to Come Out on His Own; Rebels & Pioneers." *Advocate*, Nov. 12.

Fridkin, Kim L., Patrick J. Kenney, and Gina Seringnese Woodall. 2009. "Bad for Men, Better for Women: the Impact of Stereotypes during Negative Campaigns." *Political Behavior* 31: 53–77.

Golebiowska, Ewa A. 2000. "The Etiology of Individual-Targeted Intolerance: Group Stereotypes and Judgments of Individual Group Members." *Political Psychology* 21: 443–64.

Golebiowska, Ewa A. 2001. "Group Stereotypes in Political Evaluation." *American Politics Research* 29: 535–65.

Golebiowska, Ewa A. 2003. "When to Tell? Disclosure of Concealable Group Membership, Stereotypes, and Political Evaluation." *Political Behavior* 25: 313–37.

Golebiowska, Ewa A., and Cynthia J. Thomsen. 1999. "Dynamics of Attitudes towards Openly Gay and Lesbian Political Candidates." In Ellen D. B. Riggle and Barry L. Tadlock (eds.), *Gays and Lesbians in the Democratic Process*. New York: Columbia University Press.

Herek, Gregory M. 1991. "Stigma, Prejudice, and Violence against Lesbians and Gay Men." In John C. Gonsiorekand and James D. Reinrich (eds.), *Homosexuality: Research Implications for Public Policy*. Newbury Park, CA: Sage.

Herrick, Rebekha, and Sue Thomas. 1999. "The Effects of Sexual Orientation on Citizen Perceptions of Candidate Viability." In Ellen D. B. Riggle and Barry L. Tadlock (eds.), *Gays and Lesbians in the Democratic Process*. New York: Columbia University Press.

Jones, Charisse, and Kumea Shorter-Gooden. 2003. *Shifting: The Double Lives of Black Women in America*. New York: HarperCollins.

Jones, Jeffrey M. 2006. "Six in 10 Americans Think U.S. Ready for a Female President." Gallup News, Oct. 3. www.gallup.com.

Kite, Mary E. 1984. "Sex Differences in Attitudes toward Homosexuals: A Meta-Analytic Review." *Journal of Homosexuality* 10: 69–81.

Lake Research Partners. 2005. "Insights into Voters' Feelings toward Gay and Lesbian Elected Officials: Informing the Victory Fund's Guide to Coming Out in Politics." Research conducted for the Victory Fund, Dec.

Lake Research Partners. 2006. "Insights into Voters' Feelings toward Gay and Lesbian Elected Officials Coming Out of the Closet." Research conducted for the Victory Fund, April.

LaMar, Lisa, and Mary Kite. 1998. "Sex Differences in Attitudes toward Gay Men and Lesbians: A Multidimensional Perspective." *Journal of Sex Research* 35(2): 189–96.

Madon, Stephanie. 1997. "What Do People Believe about Gay Males? A Study of Stereotype Content and Strength." *Sex Roles* 37: 663–85.

Mendelsohn, Matthew. 1996. "The Media and Interpersonal Communications: The Priming of Issues, Leaders, and Party Identification." *Journal of Politics* 58: 112–25.

Murphy, Shelia T. 1998. "The Impact of Factional versus Fictional Media Portrayals on Cultural Stereotypes." *Annals of the American Academy of Political and Social Science* 560: 165–78.

Peffley, Mark, and Jon Hurwitz. 2002. "The Racial Components of 'Race-Neutral' Crime Policy Attitudes." *Political Psychology* 23: 59–75.

Peffley, Mark A., Jon Hurwitz, and Paul M. Sniderman. 1997. "Racial Stereotypes and Whites' Political Views of Blacks in the Context of Welfare and Crime." *American Journal of Political Science* 41: 30–60.

Scorsone, Ernesto. 2006. Personal interview with Mandy R. Craigh, Oct. 9.

Valentino, Nicholas A. 1999. "Crime News and the Priming of Racial Attitudes during Evaluations of the President." *Public Opinion Quarterly* 63: 293–320.

The Victory Fund: Gay and Lesbian Leadership Institute. 2014. "Openly LGBT Appointed & Elected Officials." Available online at www.victoryinstitute.org.

Wilcox, Clyde, and Barbara Norrander. 2002. "Of Moods and Morals: the Dynamics of Opinion on Abortion and Gay Rights." In Barbara Norrander and Clyde Wilcox (eds.), *Understanding Public Opinion*, 2nd ed. Washington, DC: Congressional Quarterly.

Wilcox, Clyde, and Robin Wolpert. 2000. "Gay Rights in the Public Sphere: Public Opinion on Gay and Lesbian Equality." In Craig A. Rimmerman, Kenneth Wald, and Cylde Wilcox (eds.), *The Politics of Gay Rights*. Washington, DC: Congressional Quarterly.

PART IV

Marriage Equality Politics

SUSAN BURGESS

Marriage equality has been the most visible issue in LGBTQ politics in the United States for some time now, culminating in the 2015 case of *Obergfell v. Hodges* in which the Supreme Court recognized that gays and lesbians have a fundamental constitutional right to marry. The chapters in this section critically assess the cases prior to *Obergefell* and their import in shaping the gay and lesbian community, the meaning of *Obergefell* itself, and the effect that marriage equality may have in setting the parameters of the LGBTQ movement going forward. In doing so, they contribute to a longstanding discussion about whether marriage equality will lead to full rights of citizenship for all in the LGBTQ community, or whether it will marginalize those in the community who cannot or will not conform to sex, gender, race, and class norms that define the mainstream family.

In "Marriage Equality," Courtenay Daum provides an overview of the history of the struggle for marriage equality, a detailed explanation of the U.S. Supreme Court's pivotal ruling in *Obergefell v. Hodges*, and an analysis of its import for the LGBTQ movement's agenda going forward. Acknowledging that *Obergefell* is a major legal victory for gays and lesbians, Daum argues that the ruling offers legal protection to couples who are willing and able to adopt a more traditional family structure, marginalizing queer relationships and identities that more profoundly challenge patriarchal and cis-heteronormative values, differentially affecting racial minorities, the poor, and transgender and pansexual people. She concludes that the ruling offers additional protection to the more socioeconomically privileged sector of the gay and lesbian community, undermining the ability of the LGBTQ movement to radically challenge, disrupt, and transform traditional institutions and identities and the mainstream sex and gender norms upon which they are built.

In "The State of Marriage?" Ellen Ann Andersen focuses on the waves of same-sex weddings that took place before the U.S. Supreme Court's ruling in *Obergefell*. She explores various factors that led couples to choose to become married in Massachusetts following a state supreme court ruling legalizing same-sex marriage in 2003; in San Francisco and Multnomah County (Portland, Oregon) when local officials defied state prohibitions and began to offer marriage licenses to same-sex couples in 2004; and in Utah from 2013 to 2014 following the U.S. Supreme Court's ruling in *Windsor v. U.S.* On the basis of extensive mail surveying, she finds that motivations such as love, dignity, and political equality and legal benefits were all important factors that varied depending on the socio-legal context in which the weddings were taking place. For example, couples in Portland and Utah were much more likely to wed for legal benefits than those in San Francisco, because California already offered a form of legal recognition to same-sex couples in the form of domestic partnerships, whereas Oregon and Utah did not. As a consequence, same-sex marriages in San Francisco were much more likely to be motivated by political reasons. Couples across all socio-legal contexts were overwhelmingly white, highly educated, and affluent, perhaps lending credence to Daum's concerns regarding the normalizing effects of same-sex marriage.

Jerry Thomas picks up these themes in "Queer Sensibilities and Other Fagchild Tools," arguing that same-sex marriage privileges heteronormativity at the expense of queer sensibilities. Challenging what has been called "reproductive futurism," or the heteronormative idea that society should be organized around family and children yet to be born, Thomas performs the identity of the "fagchild" who centralizes the priorities of the "here and now" queer citizen, while at the same time confessing his continuing attachment to mainstream institutions such as marriage and the benefits it offers. Thomas's angry and profane fagchild provides a provocative critique of same-sex marriage, creatively presenting the harm that assimilation to the mainstream inflicts upon gays and lesbians, through a queer performance that seeks to resist the dictates of mainstream social institutions, while at the same time acknowledging that he remains at least somewhat subject to them.

Jason Stodolka's "You Don't Belong Here, Either" explores the import of the focus on marriage equality for activism on behalf of homeless LGBTQ youth. Exploring the relationship between social movement agenda definition and identity formation, Stodolka investigates whether the queer identities that inform a more radical liberationist agenda, including advocacy for homeless teens, is damaged by gay identities that ground a more assimilationist agenda, including marriage-equality activism. He offers two in-depth case studies focused on LGBTQ homeless youth activism in Lakeview, a gentrified Chicago neighborhood heavily populated by affluent gay men as well as homeless young LGBTQ sex workers. Although gay youth have often literally been left out in the cold by the city, wealthy Lakeview property owners, and the LGBTQ movement, Stodolka nonetheless finds that advocates for queer youth have been able to increase recognition of their issue due to the successes of the struggle for marriage equality. Stodolka's interviews suggest that rather than seeing advocacy issues as either/or, many LGBTQ youth advocates view marriage equality as a gateway issue that brought them into the movement, adding that success in marriage will eventually foster improvements for the homeless teens they serve. Stodolka concludes that identities and agendas of movement participants are defined by on-the-ground struggles that emerge in specific political and historical contexts, which in turn affect the shape of the movement as it develops.

19

Marriage Equality

Assimilationist Victory or Pluralist Defeat?

COURTENAY W. DAUM

Throughout the history of LGBTQ social movements in the United States, there have been disagreements about policy goals as well as the means for advancing them. One of the most contentious debates within the LGBTQ movement involves identity politics and questions about the heterogeneity of the LGBTQ community. Another debate concerns the benefits and drawbacks of pushing for equal rights and assimilating into existing legal and sociocultural institutions. Liberal activists argue that as a minority community with shared goals, LGBTQ groups should fight for equal rights and access to existing legal and sociocultural institutions, similarly to successful prior civil rights movements, whereas queer activists favor challenging the status quo and institutions such as marriage and the nuclear family structure that maintain heteronormative privileges in order to force society to adapt to the diversity of perspectives and identities (fluid and fixed) within the LGBTQ community. These disagreements informed the legal push for marriage equality, which culminated in the U.S. Supreme Court's decision in *Obergefell v. Hodges.*

In *Obergefell v. Hodges*, the Supreme Court ruled that state prohibitions on same-sex marriage are unconstitutional because they violate the Fourteenth Amendment's liberty guarantees by depriving gays and lesbians of their fundamental right to marry, effectively legalizing same-sex marriage in the United States. While this decision is rightly understood as a significant victory for lesbian and gay civil rights, the liberal arguments for marriage equality were integral to the U.S. Supreme Court's majority opinion preferencing the marriage equality movement's assimilationist strategy over the radical policy priorities of queer LGBT activists. As demonstrated throughout this chapter, the U.S. Supreme Court's legal recognition of marriage equality has significant ramifications for the queer movement and members of the LGBTQ community. Specifically, *Obergefell* privileges the institution of marriage over alternative familial and personal relationships and forecloses opportunities for a radical reconstruction of the legal institution of marriage, thereby undermining one of the strategic goals of queer activists. Second, it negatively affects those LGBTQ individuals who reject homonormativity and assimilation. By securing legal protections for gays and lesbians who are able to and/or aspire to enter into marriages, those members of the LGBTQ community who are unable to assimilate or uninterested in assimilating into systems and institutions dominated by patriarchal cis-heteronormative values may find that they are more, rather than less, marginalized post-*Obergefell*.

This chapter begins with a very brief review of the effect that the U.S. Supreme Court's prior gay rights cases had on liberal activists' strategies in the pursuit of marriage equality and proceeds to a review of the liberal arguments in favor of marriage equality. Then, Justice Kennedy's majority opinion in *Obergefell v. Hodges* will be subject to a queer critique, with attention focused on the Court's incorporation and validation of the liberal arguments in favor of marriage equality and the subsequent ramifications for the radical queer agenda and the LGBTQ community. While the U.S. Supreme Court's landmark decision constitutes a victory for the liberal gay civil rights strategy of fighting for an equal right to marry via the courts, this chapter highlights how this recognition simultaneously undermines the validity of alternative personal and familial choices and arrangements, and burdens those members of the LGBTQ community, including the intersectionally subjected, the poor, and transgender and pansexual individuals, who are not easily assimilated into cis-heteronormative patriarchal institutions. Queer theorists have long criticized liberal activists for failing to acknowledge the implicit and explicit elitism and privileges inherent in the fight for marriage equality, and post-*Obergefell* the consequences of this strategic calculation may be more evident.

A Brief Look at How Early U.S. Supreme Court Decisions Informed the Liberal Marriage Equality Movement

During the 1970s, individual gays and lesbians began to push for marriage equality by requesting marriage licenses in different jurisdictions across the United States. Those who wanted their relationships sanctioned by government for purposes of public recognition and/or legal and government benefits and their activist allies found that their goals often were at odds with those who called for the abolition of marriage and the nuclear family, identifying these institutions as oppressive heterosexist institutions (Cain 2000, 158–59). The latter group believed that the focus of the LGBTQ civil rights movement should be sexual liberation and freedom from restrictive gender roles and dichotomies.

Regardless of disagreements within the LGBTQ community about the desirability of marriage, the early push for marriage equality was not legally viable, as demonstrated by the U.S. Supreme Court's decision in *Baker v. Nelson*. In *Baker*, the justices dismissed an appeal of a Minnesota State Supreme Court decision that upheld Minnesota's prohibition on same-sex marriage because it did not violate the First, Eighth, Ninth, or Fourteenth Amendments of the United States Constitution. The Supreme Court of Minnesota explained, "The institution of marriage as a union of man and woman, uniquely involving the procreation and rearing of children within a family, is as old as the book of Genesis" (1971, 312). On appeal, the U.S. Supreme Court easily dismissed the case "for want of substantial federal question." While the *Baker v. Nelson* decision was a significant legal defeat for the proponents of marriage equality, the Supreme Court of Minnesota's emphasis on marriage as the institutional foundation for families and childrearing probably influenced the liberal movement's legal strategies moving forward.

During the early 1980s, disagreements about same-sex marriages were temporarily suspended as disparate groups and individuals within the LGBTQ movement united in opposition to restrictive sodomy statutes. Throughout the LGBTQ community, the criminalization of same-sex sexual conduct was understood as a barrier to LGBTQ liberation. As Cain explains,

> The state power to define good and bad sex was a barrier for gay and lesbian individuals who sought to redefine themselves publicly as good, moral and noncriminal. And it was a legitimate target for the more radical segments of the grassroots movement, who may not have cared about dominant definitions of morality, but certainly cared about individual freedom to transgress. (Cain 2000, 171)

In 1986, the Supreme Court's decision in *Bowers v. Hardwick* upheld state sodomy statutes on the grounds that prohibitions on same-sex sodomy did not violate the right to privacy or the fundamental liberty guarantees embodied in the Fourteenth Amendment. This case was a significant defeat for the LGBTQ community, and in its aftermath many organizations identified marriage equality as an important legal and political goal moving forward in order to extend legal protections to gay and lesbian couples and confer public recognition on these relationships (Cain 2000, 257).

At the 1987 March on Washington for Lesbian and Gay Rights, a mock wedding ceremony was held to draw attention to the need for legal protections for same-sex couples (Bernstein and Taylor 2013, 3). The AIDS crisis exacerbated the need for legal recognition of same-sex relationships as many individuals were legally barred from accessing their ill and dying partners and making medical and end-of-life decisions for their intimates. In a now-infamous exchange in *OUT/LOOK*, Thomas Stoddard—then executive director of the Lambda Legal Defense and Education Fund—and Paula Ettelbrick—then legal director at Lambda—debated the pros and cons of prioritizing and pushing for marriage equality (Ettelbrick 1992; Stoddard 1992). This public disagreement among two movement leaders demonstrated the growing saliency of marriage as a civil rights issue while simultaneously capturing the divisions within the LGBTQ community about its desirability.

At the same time that increased attention was being focused on marriage equality, the majority opinion in *Bowers v. Hardwick* made clear that legal cases predicated on privacy rights and liberty guarantees were unlikely to be viable for lesbian and gay plaintiffs, subsequently raising the saliency of equal protection claims. The nature of equal protection jurisprudence lends itself to arguments that members of one group—in this instance gays and lesbians—should be treated the same as members of another group—heterosexuals—under the law in areas such as employment, family law, and military service. Much as with the Black civil rights and women's rights movements, the most successful gay rights legal strategy sought to be predicated on equal protection arguments that emphasized similarities between gays and lesbians and heterosexuals. Accordingly, mobilization around same-sex marriage became a push for marriage equality: gays and lesbians should be granted access to the legal institution of marriage and receive the associated benefits and privileges because their relationships should be treated the same as heterosexual relationships under the law. This strategic calculation, however, prioritized assimilationist arguments and strategies over alternative pluralist paradigms and perspectives. Early court decisions such as *Baehr v. Lewin* and *Baker v. Vermont* validated that the push for same-sex marriage might be most successful as a push for marriage equality.

The U.S. Supreme Court's decision in *Lawrence and Garner v. Texas*, overturning *Bowers v. Hardwick* on the grounds that same-sex couples are entitled to the same liberty guarantees as heterosexuals, opened up opportunities to push for a fundamental right to marry but also validated legal arguments predicated on equal rights by concluding that same-sex sexual conduct should be treated the same as opposite-sex sexual conduct protected by the U.S. Constitution. In addition, the *Lawrence and Garner v. Texas* decision ended the legal debate about sodomy prohibitions, thereby enabling lesbian and gay civil rights groups to focus their attention and resources on marriage equality. For example, Freedom to Marry—a leader in the marriage equality movement—was founded in January 2003. The decision, however, to prioritize marriage equality over other issues of relevance to the LGBTQ community reflects the priorities of liberal activists and movement leaders, and their focus on the courts as a mechanism for achieving change.

In 2013, liberal activists secured an important victory in the push for marriage equality when the Supreme Court decided *United States v. Windsor*. In this case, the justices declared that the national Defense of Marriage Act could not deny federal marriage benefits to those same-sex marriages legally entered into in the states. This holding became the impetus for numerous federal court decisions negating state-level prohibitions on same-sex marriage. Then, in November 2014, the Sixth Circuit Court of Appeals ruled in six consolidated cases that Kentucky, Michigan, Ohio, and Tennessee could legally ban same-sex marriages based on the precedent of *Baker v. Nelson,* setting the stage for the U.S Supreme Court to resolve the disagreement among the circuit courts in *DeBoer v. Snyder*.

On June 26, 2015, the U.S. Supreme Court decided *Obergefell v. Hodges* and declared state prohibitions on same-sex marriage unconstitutional on the grounds that they violate the due process liberty guarantees of the Fourteenth

Amendment (*Obergefell v. Hodges*, Slip opinion, 22–23). Writing for the majority, Justice Kennedy stated that inherent in the Constitution's liberty guarantees are intimate and personal choices related to individual autonomy and dignity, including the decision to marry another individual (*Obergefell v. Hodges*, Slip opinion, 12). Citing *Loving v. Virginia* (1967, 12), *Zablocki v. Redhail* (1978, 374, 384), and *Turner v. Safley* (1987, 95), the majority stated that the fundamental right to marry is an established precedent under the Due Process Clause that should be extended to same-sex couples (*Obergefell v. Hodges*, Slip opinion, 11).

The majority also referenced the Fourteenth Amendment's Equal Protection Clause and concluded that same-sex couples' right to marry is "derived" from this constitutional guarantee (*Obergefell v. Hodges*, Slip opinion, 19). Essentially, Kennedy et al. determined that denying same-sex couples access to a fundamental liberty available to opposite-sex couples is inequitable. Yet, the justices did not engage in an equal protection analysis and identify and apply the appropriate standard of review typical in equal protection jurisprudence. Instead, the Court utilized "precepts of equality" to make the case for why it is problematic to deny gays and lesbians access to a fundamental liberty such as marriage (*Obergefell v. Hodges*, Slip opinion, 19).

The Liberal Case for Marriage Equality

By the time *Obergefell v. Hodges* was appealed to the U.S. Supreme Court, the liberal case for marriage equality had come to dominate the popular and legal narratives. While the push for marriage equality has implicated numerous legal, political, cultural, and familial considerations, in the aforementioned 1989 *OUT/LOOK* debate between Lambda Legal Defense and Education Fund leaders Stoddard and Ettelbrick, the former argued that the gay rights movement should identify marriage equality as a primary goal and take urgent action because achieving marriage equality is an essential tool for ending discrimination against gays and lesbians throughout society (Stoddard 1992, 16–18). Stoddard called this the political explanation for marriage equality, but he also offered a practical explanation—myriad economic and material benefits accrue to those who are married and the easiest way for gay and lesbian couples to get these benefits is to marry (Stoddard 1992, 14–16)—and a philosophical explanation—there is power in gaining access to the right to marry as opposed to arguing that marriage in and of itself is a desirable or ideal institution (Stoddard 1992, 18–19).

It is the political explanation that has been a foundation of the liberal movement for marriage equality. It is often operationalized as the argument that gay and lesbian relationships are the same as heterosexual relationships and worthy of equal protection and recognition under the law (Family Equality Council 2014; Freedom to Marry 2015, 19; Stoddard 1992, 16–18). Similarly, proponents of marriage equality argue that denying gays and lesbians access to legally sanctioned marriages stigmatizes them and acts as a form of discrimination against members of this community (Freedom to Marry 2015, 18–19). As articulated in the petition for a writ of certiorari in *Obergefell v. Hodges* appealing the Sixth Circuit Court of Appeals' decision that Ohio may legally prohibit same-sex marriages and deny recognition to those marriages entered into in other states, "By disrespecting their marriages, Ohio has done more than deny Petitioners basic legal rights to which they are entitled. It has treated Petitioners as second-class citizens whose most intimate relationships have been denied the dignity and respect they deserve" (Gerhardstein et al. 2014, 5). As long as discrimination against gays and lesbians is legally sanctioned in this way, it is argued that it will be difficult for these individuals to achieve equal protection and combat discrimination in other venues. In addition, for gay and lesbian couples with children, the denial of marriage equality may work to stigmatize and legally ostracize their children as well (Family Equality Council 2014).

An integral part of equal protection rhetoric is the argument that the individuals being discriminated against deserve to be treated equivalently to the dominant groups within society. Liberal proponents of using this approach in the legal battle for marriage equality believe that a key facet of ending discrimination on the basis of sexual orientation is to demonstrate to the state and society that "[g]ay people share the same mix of reasons for wanting and needing the freedom to marry and respect for their lawful marriages as non-gay people" (Freedom to Marry 2015, 19). This equality-based rhetoric, however, presupposes that assimilation is an important and desirable end goal of the LGBTQ movement. In an amicus brief submitted to the U.S. Supreme Court in *Obergefell v. Hodges*, the Family Equality Council emphasized a common theme in making the case for marriage equality, which is that "lesbian, gay, and bisexual parents do just as well as heterosexual parents at raising happy, healthy, and well-adjusted children," and subsequently they desire the same legal and social recognitions (2014, 15). Testimony from a number of children raised by gay and lesbian parents included a young woman explaining that "her mothers were 'no different from any other couple or parenting team'" (Family Equality Council 2014, 12), a young man "describing the ways in which his family 'really isn't so different from any other Iowa family'" (2014, 16), and a young woman arguing that "the similarities between her family and those of her friends with straight parents far outweighed the differences" (2014, 11).

A prominent argument in favor of marriage equality involves the positive benefits associated with conferring legal marriage recognition on same-sex parents and the protections that this provides for the long-term welfare of their children (Family Equality Council 2014; Freedom to Marry 2015, 25–26). In particular, the ability to identify both parents by name on a child's birth certificate is understood to be of the utmost importance. When states refuse to allow for or recognize same-sex marriages, this leaves children with same-sex parents unable to obtain even a birth certificate that accurately describes their families, much less have the security of a government-recognized parent-child relationship. Birth certificates are the basic currency allowing parents to fulfill their constitutionally-protected right to care for their children, providing prime evidence of parentage and allowing adults to make critical health care decisions for their children, enroll their children in school, insure their children, and freely travel with their children. (Gerhardstein et al. 2014, 20)

Similarly, for those couples thinking about starting a family and parenting together, access to marriage may sanction these decisions and provide both emotional and legal support for the nascent family unit.

Another equality-based argument utilized by liberal proponents of marriage equality is that marriage conveys important benefits and lesbian and gay couples are legally entitled to the same benefits as heterosexual married couples (Stoddard 1992, 14–16; Wolfson 2001). For example, marriage enables couples to access each other's social welfare benefits, such as health insurance and retirement funds, as well as to provide for inheritance benefits. Furthermore, same-sex marriages should be legalized so that gay and lesbian relationships are recognized in immigration proceedings, medical care and end-of-life decision making, criminal proceedings, and so on. This legal recognition and the associated economic and legal benefits are understood to be an important justification for prioritizing marriage equality over other LGBTQ civil rights issues.

In addition to the economic and legal benefits, liberal proponents of marriage equality point out that social benefits accrue to married couples as well (Wolfson 2001). Entering into marriage may validate the relationship for the couple as well as for others. For individuals interested in marrying, the ability to publicly proclaim that love and have it validated by society and the state may be emotionally, not merely materially, significant. The legal bonds that accompany marriage may bring the relationship to a new level of commitment and partnership. Similarly, entering into a marriage may encourage friends and family to be more accepting and/or supportive of the relationship as the legal contract validates its significance in the eyes of others. In interviews with thirty individuals in legal same-sex marriages in Ontario, Canada, Green found that getting married often changes familial dynamics beyond the couple; he quotes Larry, a forty-eight-year-old male, discussing how his marriage changed his family and friends:

They started recognizing, wow, this isn't just a gay relationship—this is a relationship. . . . We would have had a strong relationship regardless of being married or not, but what we've learned from the process of being in marriage to each other and how it has affected the people around us, is that the support group has become magnified in terms of their acceptance of us. (Green 2013, 384)

Similarly, married couples express that their employers and coworkers identify their relationships as more valid after marriage (Green 2013, 384–85).

In the petition for a writ of certiorari submitted in *Obergefell v. Hodges*, the benefits of marriage equality are summarized as follows:

> Petitioners seek the full panoply of protections for their families that come with recognition of a couple's marriage, ranging from acknowledgment of parental rights arising under the marital presumption; to tax, inheritance, and a range of other financial rights; to health care decision-making and visitation rights; to federal rights dependent on the state's recognition of their marital status. Petitioners also seek the dignity that comes from legal respect for their marriage and commitment to one another and to their children. (Gerhardstein et al. 2014, 8)

This statement effectively summarizes the liberal position that gays and lesbians want access to marriage because they want the same political, practical, and philosophical recognitions, rights, and benefits as those that accrue to heterosexual married couples.

Yet, this statement on behalf of a select group of petitioners is often accepted as the lesbian and gay community's universal stance on marriage equality. In reality, however, many gays and lesbians do not want access to marriages predicated on heteronormative values or monogamous legally sanctioned relationships of any kind. Despite diversity within the movement, proponents of marriage equality

> believe the right to marry will benefit all members of the LGBT community, regardless of race or class, and will advance the cause of social justice, which they interpret as the expansion of rights and recognition for underrepresented groups in American society. Since marriage is a primary means of distributing symbolic and economic capital, those who are denied the right to marry are therefore excluded from the promise of respectability, belonging, and material benefits accrued through marriage. (Stein 2013, 40)

In contrast, many queer activists have argued that fighting for and gaining marriage equality is detrimental to the interests of the LGBTQ community and undermines the movement's radical transformative potential. As a result, the Supreme Court's decision in *Obergefell v. Hodges* validating and privileging assimilation poses challenges to both queer activists' strategic goals and those members of the LGBTQ community who fail to conform to assimilationist expectations. The following section will examine what the *Obergefell* decision means for queer activists and includes an analysis of its effects on the LGBTQ community. A queer critique makes it clear that while much is gained from the *Obergefell* decision, there also are negative consequences and implications that derive from this legal victory.

The Queer Critique of Marriage Equality and *Obergefell v. Hodges*

While marriage equality increasingly occupied the time and resources of numerous liberal civil rights organizations throughout the early twenty-first century, these efforts were not universally accepted by the LGBTQ movement and communities. Organizations such as BeyondMarriage.org argue that marriage should be one viable option among many for organizing and validating relationships, whereas Gay Shame opposes marriage in its entirety (Bernstein and Taylor 2013, 13). For these organizations, fighting for access to heteronormative institutions such as marriage is counterproductive and threatens to undermine the radical transformative potential of the LGBTQ rights movement (e.g., Ettelbrick 1992; Polikoff 2008; Warner 1999). As Carl Wittman explained in *The Gay Manifesto*,

> Traditional marriage is a rotten, oppressive institution. . . . We have to define for ourselves a new pluralistic, role free social structure for ourselves. It must contain both the freedom and physical space for people to live alone, live together for a while, live together for a long time, either as couples or in larger numbers; and the ability to flow easily from one of these states to another as our needs change. Liberation for gay people is defining for ourselves how and with whom we live, instead of measuring our relationship in comparison to straight ones, with straight values. (Wittman 1970)

Queer theory emphasizes difference and the transformative potential of LGBTQ identities as opposed to sameness and assimilation. In "Since When Is Marriage a Path to Liberation?" Paula Ettelbrick's contribution to the 1989 *OUT/LOOK* debate, she offers two major arguments in opposition to same-sex marriage. First, she argues that gaining access to marriage will "force our assimilation into the mainstream, and undermine the goals of gay liberation" (Ettelbrick 1992, 20). Second, she states that prioritizing marriage will foreclose opportunities to validate and fight for alternative intimate and family relationships (Ettelbrick 1992, 20). Ettelbrick's comments draw attention to queerness as a subversive identity capable of challenging dominant narratives and paradigms, and provide a useful lens for evaluating the goals of the liberal marriage equality movement and the reasoning utilized by the Supreme Court in *Obergefell*.

Marriage Equality, Assimilation, and the Consequences for LGBTQ Individuals and Gay Liberation

Queer theory recognizes identity as unstable, fluid, and multifaceted and argues against group-based identity politics as a means of political and legal reform (Butler 1990; Chasin 2000; Duggan 2003). As Ward explains,

The notion that individuals can claim rights based upon self-determined identities is, from this perspective, a distraction from the ways in which identities are given form by the social structures that name and discipline them. Queer theory challenges the notion that identity is the most radical or reliable source of personal or group knowledge and liberations. . . . In this framework, defiant subcultural practices and resistance to various forms of normativity and institutional control become the common ground of queerness, as opposed to a universal collective identity built around same-sex desire. (Ward 2008, 42)

Due to the fact that queer theorists recognize the powerful ways in which institutions both create and constrain identities, they oppose political and legal movements premised on the notion of a shared identity. Accordingly, the suggestion that there is a monolithic gay and lesbian movement leveraging its interests through the courts runs counter to the most basic tenets of queer theory.

Yet, the legalization of marriage equality and the reasoning utilized by a majority of the justices on the U.S. Supreme Court validate the liberal assimilationist strategy over the priorities of radical queer activists, with significant ramifications for the latter. The most immediate consequence of the *Obergefell v. Hodges* decision is that gays and lesbians are now able to enter into legal marriages—pockets of resistance notwithstanding—and receive the benefits and privileges that accrue to married couples and their families. As Stoddard argued in 1989, there is power to be gained from accessing marriage even if it is not an ideal institution (Stoddard 1992, 18–19). Yet, one of the long-term consequences of framing marriage equality as the primary civil rights goal of the LGBTQ community is ignoring and subverting differences within the community in favor of presenting a monolithic gay identity.

The liberal movement's decision to make marriage a civil rights issue presumes and conveys the impression that gays and lesbians are a cohesive group challenging the discrimination that they experience on the basis of their shared identity whereas the reality is that there is no single gay or lesbian identity, and bisexuals and transgender individuals are excluded from this "gay" identity. Queer theory argues that ignoring the racial, ethnic, gender, and class differences within the LGBTQ community enables the development of a gay rights movement that inevitably leaves many within the community "unfree and unequal" (Chasin 2000, 19). As Butler explains, identity politics is by its nature premised on a paradoxical foundation that "presumes, fixes, and constrains the very 'subjects' that it hopes to represent and liberate" (Butler 1990, 148). The successful push for marriage equality by liberal activists is not only premised on an idealized "set of ready-made subjects," but effectively validates these identities and interests moving forward (Butler 1990, 149), and the Supreme Court's decision in *Obergefell* confirmed queer theorists' concerns about the liberal movement's decision to advance a uniform "gay" identity. Justice Kennedy's opinion for the majority explicitly incorporates many of the assimilationist arguments proffered by liberal proponents of marriage equality, and speaks of gays and lesbians as a monolithic group with shared goals.

Yet, the myth of a "gay" movement singularly focused on marriage equality not only obfuscates diversity within the movement but also omits that the benefits of marriage are limited to those who are able to or want to get married. Access to marriage presupposes that one is out and identifies as gay or lesbian in private and public. Yet, as Stein (2013) argues, there are obstacles to individuals identifying themselves as gay and lesbian that are connected to race, class, and cultural considerations that can place the benefits of marriage out of reach for certain individuals (58). In addition, the legalization of same-sex marriage potentially further marginalizes those who do not subscribe to a fixed gender identity. While individuals may now marry the person of their choosing regardless of his or her gender, as currently constructed, marriage lends itself to fixed gender identities and poses challenges for those who have fluid identities.

Marriage equality's promotion of homonormativity and the gender binary enables the assimilation of some members of the LGBTQ community at the expense of others, and those who are unable to or choose not to marry may find that their relationships are considered "less than" legally sanctioned marriages post-*Obergefell* (Warner 1999, 108). For example, those who are unable to enter into marriages will continue to be denied its material benefits and along with those who reject marriage may find that they are further marginalized in society for their failure to conform to homonormative ideals, whereas those individuals within the LGBTQ community who are able to or want to assimilate will receive the explicit benefits that accrue to the institution of marriage as well as the implicit approval and perks that flow to those in the mainstream.

This result logically follows from the liberal focus on gaining access to existing entities such as marriage as opposed to challenging dominant norms and institutions. The majority opinion in *Obergefell* accepts the homonormative ideal and subsequently validates the importance of two-person marriages and nuclear families in society and seems to foreclose opportunities to disrupt or displace the institution. Lisa Duggan calls this development the new homonormativity: "[I]t is a politics that does not contest dominant heteronormative assumptions and institutions, but upholds and sustains them, while promising the possibility of a demobilized gay constituency and a privatized, depoliticized gay culture anchored in domesticity and consumption" (Duggan 2003, 50). Duggan (2003) criticizes national gay civil rights groups and their neoliberal sexual politics for introducing the new homonormativity. The marriage equality movement's successful use of legal arguments predicated on homonormative identity and values makes it more difficult for radicals to challenge sex and gender binaries and make the case for the fluidity of identities and orientations. Rather than fighting for access to heteronormative and sexist institutions, queer theorists argue that the LGBTQ activists should seek to promote "gender trouble" by challenging the "regulatory fictions" of the sex and gender binaries and the accompanying privileging of masculinity and heterosexist stereotypes (Butler 1990, 33).

As an alternative to emphasizing uniformity, many queer theorists favor a queer intersectional framework that acknowledges and privileges difference. As Ward explains it, "'queer intersectionality' is an approach that strives for racial, gender, socioeconomic, and sexual diversity, but also resists the institutional forces that seek to contain and normalize differences, or reduce them to their use value" (Ward 2008, 19). This approach provides opportunities to recognize and validate the diversity of experiences, identities, and perspectives within the LGBTQ movement and to challenge the prevailing homonormative and heteronormative narratives. For queer activists, this pluralist approach is preferable to liberal activists' push for assimilation (Chasin 2000; Polikoff 2008; Ward 2008).

Pluralism and the recognition of difference draw attention to the individual and institutional animus and bigotry that many members of the LGBTQ community experience on a daily basis. In contrast, the liberal movement's strategic calculation comes with real costs because the emphasis on assimilation that is a key facet of the marriage equality litigation strategy is unlikely to gain LGBTQ individuals equal access to a wide array of opportunities and institutions. As Duggan explains, the new homonormativity emphasizes equality, but the term has been narrowed to include access to a few conservative institutions such as marriage, rather than adopting a fuller equal rights agenda (Duggan 2003, 65). As a result, successful assimilation "has only taken place among a segment of the lesbian and gay population, creating a politics that reinforces white, male, gender-conforming middle-class standards of sexuality—in other words, those best positioned to take advantage of the privileges of normalization and assimilation" (Bernstein and Taylor 2013, 16).

The emphasis on marriage equality has monopolized resources and energy at the expense of other issues that are equally if not more important to the LGBTQ community, such as workplace discrimination, systemic racism, violence and abuse, criminalization of transgender identity, and socioeconomic considerations such as poverty (Stewart-Winter 2015). For example, discrimination on the basis of sexual orientation and gender identity is not prohibited by the 1964 Civil Rights Act, and many states do not include sexual orientation and gender identity in their civil rights guarantees. Gaining prohibitions on discrimination on the basis of sexual orientation and gender identity via civil rights legislation is essential in order to reach much of the systemic discrimination that affects members of the LGBTQ community, and may have a more immediate effect on eliminating the day-to-day discrimination experienced by LGBTQ individuals.

As acknowledged by queer activists, one of the limitations of a rights-oriented movement is that legal victories do not undermine homophobia (Vaid 1995, 179). As Vaid explains, "[I]t is clear that gay mainstreaming will remain partial and provisional until the underlying religious, moral and cultural prejudices that stigmatize gay men, lesbians, and bisexuals are transformed. Our movement must strive beyond personal gain to an institutional transformation, beyond mainstreaming ourselves into the center to transforming the mainstream" (Vaid 1995, 180). Thus, while the push for marriage equality was a success and fulfills the personal needs of many within the movement, assimilationist strategies predicated on gaining access to heteronormative institutions such as the recognition of a legal right to marry do not address or eradicate the systemic and intersectional discrimination and homo- and transphobia that many LGBTQ individuals confront on a daily basis.

Furthermore, while liberal activists defended their push for marriage equality as an essential first step in the battle for equal rights for gays and lesbians (Stoddard 1992, 16–18), the Supreme Court's majority opinion in *Obergefell* may be of limited utility moving forward. Initially, one of the perks of pushing for marriage equality and assimilation into the institution of marriage is that it successfully introduced equal protection claims based on discrimination on the basis of sexual orientation into the courts. As Stein explains, in states such as California, Connecticut, and Iowa, the courts held that sexual orientation is entitled to heightened scrutiny in the context of marriage litigation, and this means that future equal protection claims implicating other issues will be bound by these precedents in these states (Stein 2009, 580). In contrast, the majority opinion in *Obergefell* is based on the Due Process Clause and eschews a traditional equal protection analysis.

The Court's failure to engage in an equal protection analysis and utilize standards of scrutiny distinguishes this case from civil rights litigation in the areas of race and sex.[1] Given that the majority opinion in *Obergefell* did not identify sexual orientation as a suspect or quasi-suspect classification or enunciate a standard of review for evaluating alleged equal protection violations, lower courts did not gain precedential guidance for cases involving state-sponsored or -sanctioned discrimination against LGBTQ individuals. This is significant because future allegations of discrimination on the basis of sexual orientation that reach the courts are likely to be based on equal rights claims and not implicate "fundamental" rights and liberties derived from the Due Process Clause. In this way, the absence of a clear and binding equal protection precedent will limit the utility of the *Obergefell* case in future equal protection litigation alleging discrimination on the basis of sexual orientation in the federal courts.

Obergefell, Privileging Marriage, and Future Opportunities for Radical Institutional Change

In the *Obergefell* decision, Justice Kennedy's discussion of the primary role that the institution of marriage plays in contemporary American society confirms its ongoing dominance as an organizing and privileging mechanism in ways that run directly counter to the goals of queer activists. Specifically, the majority opinion validated that "the Nation's traditions make clear that marriage is a keystone of our social order" (*Obergefell v. Hodges*, Slip opinion, 16). Consistent with the liberal assimilationist argument, the Court concluded that

> [t]he States have contributed to the fundamental character of marriage by placing that institution at the center of so many facets of the legal and social order. There is no difference between same- and opposite-sex couples with respect to this principle. Yet by virtue of their exclusion from the institution, same-sex couples are denied the constellation of benefits that the States have linked to marriage. This harm results in more than just material burdens. Same-sex couples are consigned to an instability many opposite-sex couples would find intolerable in their own lives. As the State itself makes marriage all the more precious by the significance it attaches to it, exclusion from that status has the effect of teaching that gays and lesbians are unequal in important respects. It demeans gays and lesbians for the State to lock them out of a central institution of the Nation's society. Same-sex couples, too, may aspire to the transcendent purposes of marriage and seek fulfillment in its highest meaning. (*Obergefell v. Hodges*, Slip opinion, 17)

Clearly, the liberal arguments that same-sex relationships are analogous to opposite-sex relationships and that lesbian and gay individuals deserve the same opportunities as heterosexuals to participate in the institution of marriage proved persuasive for five of the nine justices.

In contrast, queer activists would have advanced an alternative pluralist paradigm that seeks to disrupt and transform traditional stereotypes and institutions. Notably, queer opponents of marriage equality reject efforts to assimilate members of the LGBTQ community into a heteronormative institution. Queer theory draws on feminist critiques of marriage as a patriarchal and sexist institution to inform its own criticism of the institution (Ettelbrick 1992; Polikoff 1993, 2008). For example, self-identified radical lesbian feminist Nancy Polikoff explains, "I believe that the desire to marry in the lesbian and gay community is an attempt to mimic the worst of mainstream society, an effort to fit into an inherently problematic institution that betrays the promise of both lesbian and gay liberation and radical feminism" (Polikoff 1993, 1536). In particular, Polikoff takes issue with the fact that the pro-marriage camp within the lesbian and gay community seeks admission to the institution of marriage as it now stands and does not propose to radically restructure or challenge it (Polikoff 1993, 1541). For radical or queer activists, the decision to mobilize extensive resources to lobby and litigate for access to an inherently conservative and patriarchal institution and its accompanying oppressive sex and gender roles was an ill-advised decision that robs the LGBTQ movement of its radical transformative potential, and privileges those in legally sanctioned monogamous relationships and their families over alternative and less traditional arrangements (Polikoff 2008; Warner 1999, 82, 109).

The *Obergefell v. Hodges* decision validates marriage as a desirable, and perhaps even an ideal, institution and privileges marriage as the mechanism for conferring not only legal but also social and cultural recognition on unions between two people. The Court's holding effectively codifies marriage as the primary tool for legitimating relationships and promotes homonormativity by privileging marriage over other intimate arrangements. At numerous points throughout the majority opinion, Justice Kennedy specifies that the marital union consists of two people—"the right to marry is fundamental because it supports a two-person union unlike any other in its importance to the committed individuals" (*Obergefell v. Hodges,* Slip opinion, 13), and "in forming a marital union, two people become something greater than they once were" (*Obergefell v. Hodges,* Slip opinion, 28)—a specificity that may be interpreted as an attempt to foreclose future litigation challenging state prohibitions on polygamy or arguments in favor of bestowing legal recognition on polyamorous relationships.

This precedent poses a challenge to the radical goal of validating alternative relationships. At a minimum, privileging monogamous relationships over open or polyamorous relationships inhibits sexual liberation and stigmatizes those members of the LGBTQ community who deviate from heteronormative sexual behaviors. As Bernstein and Burke explain,

> Heterosexuality is privileged as the benchmark by which to judge all other forms of sexuality. In this sense, the issue is not simply straight/gay, but also normal/deviant and insider/outsider. Framing the issue in this manner, queer theorists point out that winning the right to marry might improve the lot of same-sex couples who wish to enter into such unions, but overall it will simply redraw the line between normal and deviant a little further in one direction. In other words, simply by demanding this right, same-sex marriage proponents contribute to the normalizing discourse on sexuality. While they struggle to place themselves within the normal insider category, they further reify both the dichotomies and others' positions within them. (Bernstein and Burke 2013, 320–21)

This "normalizing discourse on sexuality" favors certain relationships and sexual behaviors over others, including favoring the "Good Gay" over the "Bad Queer": "the kind who has sex, who talks about it, and who builds with other queers a way of life that ordinary folks do not understand or control" (Warner 1999, 114). As a lesbian and gay politics, homonormativity promotes monogamy and domesticity (Ward 2008, 60)—thereby challenging open sexual cultures (Warner 1999, 113)—and honors the nuclear family. Thus, the push for marriage equality is likely to reify sex and gender binaries and may introduce heterosexist roles and stereotypes into same-sex relationships.

Furthermore, the Court's ruling in *Obergefell* suggests that one of the primary reasons for entering into a marriage is to start a family and thereby privileges reproduction and childrearing over alternative lifestyles. Consistent with the goals of liberal activists, the justices discussed marriage equality as an important tool for strengthening the legal case for same-sex couples' parental rights. A desire to see that children will have a legal attachment to both of their parents clearly informed the majority opinion. Kennedy stated that "[t]he marriage laws at issue here thus harm and humiliate the children of same-sex couples," and he identified the need to protect children of gay and lesbian parents from "the stigma of knowing their families are somehow lesser" as one of the four primary reasons for doing away with prohibitions on same-sex marriage (*Obergefell v. Hodges,* Slip opinion, 15).

The majority's discussion of marriage's role in legitimating families, however, may further the marginalization of alternative organizational structures and conceptions of family (Polikoff 2008). In particular, Justice Kennedy's statement that "[m]arriage also affords the permanency and stability important to children's *best* interests" (emphasis added) sends a clear signal that children are best served by being raised in homes with married parents (*Obergefell v. Hodges,* Slip opinion, 15). He proceeds to state that absent this holding, children "suffer the significant material costs of being raised by unmarried parents, relegated through no fault of their own to a more difficult and uncertain family life" (*Obergefell v. Hodges,* Slip opinion, 15).

Consistent with the fears of radical and queer theorists, this privileging of families with two married parents over other familial organizations and relationships as well as nonnuclear family arrangements may have ramifications for certain communities, including but not limited to poor and working-class communities, where alternative family arrangements are prevalent. There are racial and socioeconomic implications to this, as demonstrated by the way poor single mothers or unmarried couples of color are vilified in the media and society. This social ostracization may extend to gays and lesbians who do not conform to social norms and expectations about marriage and family, including single and/ or unmarried parents. In this way, the *Obergefell* decision may exacerbate inequities within the LGBTQ community and further ostracize or marginalize those individuals (both gay and heterosexual) who do not want to or are unable to enter into traditional nuclear family arrangements.

Finally, the majority opinion in *Obergefell* validated the liberal argument that marriage conveys material and substantive benefits and that the most efficient way for gays and lesbians to gain access to these benefits is via legal marriages (Stoddard 1992, 14–16). In his opinion for the Court, Justice Kennedy states that just as a couple vows to support each other, so does society pledge to support the couple, offering symbolic recognition and material benefits to protect and nourish the union. Indeed, while the States are in general free to vary the benefits they confer on all married couples, they have throughout our history made marriage the basis for an expanding list of governmental rights, benefits and responsibilities. (*Obergefell v. Hodges,* Slip opinion, 17)

He then enumerates these material and substantive benefits at length, and sanctions governments' practice of using marriage as the mechanism for conveying and distributing benefits (*Obergefell v. Hodges,* Slip opinion, 17).

As a result, gays and lesbians who are content with the status quo in their relationships may be pressured to enter into marriages in order to access their partners' benefits. The legalization of same-sex marriage may lead employers and government organizations to mandate that one be legally married in order to qualify for a significant other's benefits. As a result, some couples may be pressured to get married in order to gain economic and health benefits that they previously were able to access under domestic partnership laws (Stein 2009, 587). This type of development runs directly counter to the goals of queer activists who argue in favor of disconnecting benefits from marriage.

With respect to the material benefits that accrue to married couples, queer theorists argue that the goal should be to challenge a system that assigns these benefits to individuals on the basis of narrow and exclusionary definitions of marriage and family. Queer theorists propose working to decouple benefits from these restrictive typologies with a goal of moving beyond a right to marry in favor of systemic change that provides all individuals with access to benefits (Chasin 2000, xvii; Polikoff 1993, 1549). Polikoff explains that as long as special rights accrue to married couples (be they heterosexual or gay and lesbian), all nonmarried couples, regardless of sexual orientation, and nontraditional family units will continue to be denied just treatment (Polikoff 2008, 84). Thus, real change and social justice are furthered not via marriage equality but by changing laws and policies to honor and extend benefits to the full array of families (Polikoff 2008).

Furthermore, while the argument that marriage will enable gays and lesbians to access their spouses' material benefits may be compelling, being able to access these benefits first requires one to have them—health insurance via an employer, an estate to leave to someone else—which is not the case for many individuals (Stein 2013, 56). As a result, this priority reflects the privileged socioeconomic interests of a certain facet of the LGBTQ community. While the Supreme Court's decision legally opens marriage to some gays and lesbians, it also confirms the institution's ongoing role in legitimating those relationships that are deemed to have value and in distributing legal, material, and social benefits.

Conclusion

The Supreme Court's decision in *Obergefell v. Hodges* is the culmination of a lengthy legal and political debate surrounding the right of same-sex couples to enter into legally recognized marriages. While many within the LGBTQ community signficiantly disagree about the wisdom of allocating extensive resources to gaining access to a traditional heteronormative institution, the liberal victory for marriage equality is a milestone for gay civil rights. At the same time, however, the battle for marriage equality was litigated on the basis of assimilationist arguments—gays and lesbians are just like heterosexuals and want access to the same intimate and family associations—and the Court affirmed this approach in its holding: "It would misunderstand these men and women [gays and lesbians] to say they disrespect the idea of marriage. Their plea is that they do respect it, respect it so deeply that they seek to find its fulfillment for themselves. Their hope is not to be condemned to live in loneliness, excluded from one of civilization's oldest institutions" (*Obergefell v. Hodges,* Slip opinion, 28). This reasoning endorses and promotes a homonormative ideal that may be detrimental to those who do not wish to or cannot live within its boundaries. In particular, it is imperative to recognize that certain individuals within the LGBTQ community will be better situated to capitalize on this new right than others and that race, class, and gender-identity privileges are implicated in one's ability and decision to enter into marriage. Those individuals who are unable or unwilling to enter into marriage may find that they are marginalized by government and society for failing to comply with homonormative assimilationist values and that they will continue to be deprived of its benefits.

It remains to be seen whether or not those committed to marriage equality will continue to fight for LGBTQ rights and interests in other areas. As soon as the *Obergefell* decision was announced by the U.S. Supreme Court, liberal leaders of the marriage equality movement such as Evan Wolfson, founder and president of Freedom to Marry, took the opportunity to enunciate next steps for LGBTQ civil rights. In an op-ed piece published in the *New York Times* the day after *Obergefell* was decided, Wolfson stated that the victory for marriage equality "is something to celebrate. And now we must get back to work. Securing protections from discrimination for gay, lesbian, bisexual and transgender Americans needs to be our priority" (Wolfson 2015). This public statement that there is still work to be done is noteworthy, but even more important than words will be the actions of the major leaders and donors within the marriage equality movement. If these individuals identify marriage equality as the pinnacle of the gay civil rights movement and exit the political arena or choose to shift their time and attention to different causes, this will create a resource vacuum that will have significant ramifications for the movement and undermine or slow the push to challenge both private and state discrimination against LGBTQ individuals as well as attempts to address the systemic poverty and violence experienced by many in the community.

Obergefell v. Hodges cannot be the pinnacle legal and political achievement of the gay rights movement. The fight for equality and social justice continues in other areas, including discrimination on the basis of gender identity and expression, workplace discrimination, systemic poverty, intersectional oppression, violence against members of the LGBTQ community, and ongoing homo- and transphobia. While it is clear that the radical LGBTQ vision and its potential to obliterate governing norms, expectations, and institutions are challenged by the increasing mainstreaming of portions of the LGBTQ community, the costs associated with privileging marriage and homonormativity will be felt by those least willing or able to assimilate, and it is queer activists who are uniquely situated to draw attention to the social justice issues and intersectional discrimination experienced by a large portion of the LGBTQ community, including transgender individuals and LGBTQ people of color. Queer theory is able to address intersectional oppression as well as discrimination on the basis of gender identity, and the queer pluralist paradigm is likely to be particularly useful, if not essential, for informing rhetorical, political, and legal strategies in the battle for transgender rights. Thus, while the liberal assimilationist approach may have prevailed in the push for marriage equality, with significant costs for the queer agenda and those members of the LGBTQ community who do not comply with homonormative values and ideals, queer theory is poised to make important contributions in the ongoing battles for LGBTQ rights and remains relevant as a mechanism for drawing attention to and fighting for diverse interests and individuals within the LGBTQ community.

NOTE

1 The majority opinion does, however, reference the "immutable nature" of gays' and lesbians' sexual orientation (*Obergefell v. Hodges,* Slip opinion, 4), an acknowledgement that may prove to be significant in equal protection jurisprudence moving forward.

REFERENCES

Cases Cited
Baehr v. Lewin, 74 Haw. 645, 852 P.2d 44 (1993)
Baker v. Nelson, 409 U.S. 810 (1972)
Baker v. Nelson 291 Minn. 310, 191 N.W.2d 185 (1971)
Baker v. Vermont, 744 A.2d 864 (Vt. 1999)
Bowers v. Hardwick, 478 U.S. 186 (1986)
DeBoer v. Snyder, 973 F. Supp. 2d 757 (E.D. Mich. 2014)
Lawrence and Garner v. Texas, 539 U.S. 558 (2003)
Loving v. Virginia, 388 U.S. 1 (1967)
Obergefell v. Hodges, 576 U.S. ___ (2015)
Turner v. Safley, 482 U.S. 78 (1987)
United States v. Windsor, 570 U. S. ___ (2013)
Zablocki v. Redhail, 434 U.S. 374 (1978)

Other Sources

Allen, Samantha. 2015. "LGBT Leaders: Gay Marriage Is Not Enough." *Daily Beast*, June 26. www.thedailybeast.com.

Bernstein, Mary, and Mary C. Burke. 2013. "Normalization, Queer Discourse, and the Marriage-Equality Movement in Vermont." In *The Marrying Kind? Debating Same-Sex Marriage within the Lesbian and Gay Movement*, Mary Bernstein and Verta Taylor (eds.), 319–43. Minneapolis: University of Minnesota Press.

Bernstein, Mary, and Verta Taylor. 2013. "Introduction: Marital Discord; Understanding the Contested Place of Marriage in the Lesbian and Gay Movement." In *The Marrying Kind? Debating Same-Sex Marriage within the Lesbian and Gay Movement*, Mary Bernstein and Verta Taylor (eds.), 1–36. Minneapolis: University of Minnesota Press.

Butler, Judith. 1990. *Gender Trouble: Feminism and the Subversion of Identity*. New York: Routledge.

Cain, Patricia. 2000. *Rainbow Rights: The Role of Lawyers and Courts in the Lesbian and Gay Civil Rights Movement*. Boulder, CO: Westview.

Chasin, Alexandra. 2000. *Selling Out: The Gay and Lesbian Movement Goes to Market*. New York: St. Martin's.

Duggan, Lisa. 2003. *The Twilight of Equality? Neoliberalism, Cultural Politics, and the Attack on Democracy*. Boston: Beacon.

Ettelbrick, Paula L. 1992. "Since When Is Marriage a Path to Liberation?" In *Lesbian and Gay Marriage*, Suzanne Sherman (ed.), 20–26. Philadelphia: Temple University Press.

Family Equality Council, Colage, and Kinsey Morrison. 2014. "Amicus Curiae Brief in Support of Petitioners, Addressing the Merits and Supporting Reversal." Submitted in *Obergefell v. Hodges*.

Freedom to Marry. 2015. "Amicus Curiae Brief in Support of Petitioners." Submitted in *DeBoer v. Snyder* .

Gerhardstein, Alphonse A., et al. 2014. "Joint Petition for a Writ of Certiorari." Submitted to U.S. Supreme Court in *Obergefell v. Hodges*.

Green, Adam Isaiah. 2013. "Debating Same-Sex Marriage: Lesbian and Gay Spouses Speak to the Literature." In *The Marrying Kind? Debating Same-Sex Marriage within the Lesbian and Gay Movement*, Mary Bernstein and Verta Taylor (eds.), 375–405. Minneapolis: University of Minnesota Press.

Polikoff, Nancy D. 1993. "We Will Get What We Ask For: Why Legalizing Gay and Lesbian Marriage Will Not 'Dismantle the Legal Structure of Gender in Every Marriage.'" *Virginia Law Review* 79, no. 7: 1535–50.

Polikoff, Nancy. 2008. *Beyond (Straight and Gay) Marriage: Valuing All Families under the Law*. Boston: Beacon.

Stein, Arlene. 2013. "What's the Matter with Newark? Race, Class, Marriage Politics, and the Limits of Queer Liberalism." In *The Marrying Kind? Debating Same-Sex Marriage within the Lesbian and Gay Movement*, Mary Bernstein and Verta Taylor (eds.), 39–65. Minneapolis: University of Minnesota Press.

Stein, Edward. 2009. "Marriage or Liberation? Reflections on Two Strategies in the Struggle for Lesbian and Gay Rights and Relationship Recognition." *Rutgers Law Review* 61, no. 3: 567–93.

Stewart-Winter, Timothy. 2015. "The Price of Gay Marriage." *New York Times*, June 26. www.nytimes.com.

Stoddard, Thomas B. 1992. "Why Gay People Should Seek the Right to Marry." In *Lesbian and Gay Marriage*, Suzanne Sherman (ed.), 13–19. Philadelphia: Temple University Press.

Vaid, Urvashi. 1995. *Virtual Equality: The Mainstreaming of Gay and Lesbian Liberation.* New York: Anchor Books.

Ward, Jane. 2008. *Respectably Queer: Diversity Culture in LGBT Activist Organizations.* Nashville, TN: Vanderbilt University Press.

Warner, Michael. 1999. *The Trouble with Normal: Sex, Politics, and the Ethics of Queer Life.* New York: Free Press.

Wittman, Carl. 1970. *The Gay Manifesto,* library.gayhomeland.org.

Wolfson, Evan. 2001. "All Together Now: A Blueprint for the Movement." *Advocate,* Sept. www.freedomtomarry.org.

Wolfson, Evan. 2015. "Gay Rights: What Comes Next." *New York Times,* June 27: A21.

20

The State of Marriage?

How Sociolegal Context Affects Why Same-Sex Couples Marry

ELLEN ANN ANDERSEN

On the morning of June 26, 2015, the Supreme Court ruled that same-sex couples have a fundamental right to marry under the Constitution (*Obergefell v. Hodges* 2015).[1] Within a few hours of the decision, same-sex couples began applying for marriage licenses in those states whose discriminatory marriage laws had just been invalidated. Social and traditional media were filled with images of same-sex weddings.

These images hearken back to an unusual and prominent feature of the marriage equality movement: wedding waves. In many instances in the years preceding *Obergefell*, same-sex couples came together en masse to wed. The most prominent examples occurred in 2004. For four weeks in San Francisco and six in Multnomah County (Portland), Oregon, local officials issued gender-neutral marriage licenses, notwithstanding state laws limiting marriage to different-sex couples. The response was extraordinary. Throngs of same-sex couples queued up for marriage licenses. By the time courts in each state shut down the process, 4,037 couples in San Francisco and 3,022 couples in Portland had seized the opportunity to marry.

Similar wedding waves have occurred in other locations, most commonly in the aftermath of a lower court decision striking down a state's ban on same-sex marriage. For instance, in the sixteen days between December 20, 2013 (when a federal district court struck down Utah's ban on same-sex marriage) and January 6, 2014 (when the Supreme Court stayed the lower court decision), 1,362 same-sex couples applied for marriage licenses in Utah. Over 800 same-sex couples in Indiana took advantage of a similar three-day window of opportunity to marry in 2014, while over 200 couples married in Michigan in the twenty-four hours when licenses were available to them.

These weddings are remarkable in several respects. First, in all instances the opportunity to wed legally came as a surprise. Not only did the opportunity to marry appear suddenly; it threatened to disappear at any moment. Couples who made the decision to wed did so not knowing whether or not officials would still be issuing marriage licenses by the time they had made it downtown to fill out the paperwork.

To add further to the unusual nature of these weddings, they all occurred under a haze of legal uncertainty. The most legally problematic weddings occurred in San Francisco and Portland when local officials chose to disregard state laws restricting marriage to different-sex couples, stepping far outside the limits of their legal authority. And indeed, courts subsequently invalidated the marriage licenses issued by both jurisdictions. Weddings occurring after court rulings were on firmer legal ground. But these decisions remained subject to appeal. Until the litigation ended, same-sex couples could not be sure that their marriages would be deemed valid.

What is it about the chance to marry officially that repeatedly sparked hundreds and sometimes thousands of same-sex couples to drop everything and to descend in waves on city halls? To wait for hours, days, and even weeks for the chance to apply for a marriage license? To wed knowing that there was a real chance that their licenses would subsequently be invalidated? And did the reasons couples participated in a marriage wave vary according to the specific sociolegal contexts of the weddings? That is, did the same-sex couples marrying in Portland in 2004 do so for the same reasons as the couples marrying in Utah in 2013? Or did variations in the political, legal, and/or cultural contexts of the weddings shape motivations to marry?

Existing scholarship provides some purchase on the first set of questions. A handful of studies of wedding waves reveals that participating couples had multiple, often overlapping motivations to marry (see Kimport 2013; Richman 2013; Taylor, Kimport, Van Dyke, and Andersen 2009). They married to strengthen their relationship and to follow the putatively "natural" course of relationships. They married in order to access the rights and benefits that accompany marriage. They married as a way of making a political statement on behalf of LGBT rights or declaring their equal rights as citizens. And they married as a means of establishing their relationships as real and valuable to others.[2]

Unfortunately, almost all empirical studies of motivations to marry are centered on couples in a single location at a single point in time. That makes them incapable of exploring how, or whether, variations in the sociolegal contexts of the wedding waves systemically shape why couples decide to wed. Yet scholarship on mobilization to collective action makes clear that individual decisions to participate are mediated by contextual factors. We know, for example, that people are generally more willing to engage in low-risk than high-risk forms of activism (McAdam 1986). People are more likely to participate when they have personal ties to movement activists or are integrated into particular social and voluntary networks (Diani and McAdam 2003; Kitts 1999; Snow, Zurcher, and Ekland-Olson 1980).

It thus seems likely that individual decisions to participate in a wedding wave were also mediated by contextual factors, including the sociolegal contexts of the weddings themselves. Weddings, of course, are not usually treated as a form of collective action (cf. Taylor, Kimport, Van Dyke, and Andersen 2009). However, the wedding waves were no ordinary weddings; they were intentional and public bids by individuals working in concert to attain a common goal: entry into a profoundly significant legal and cultural rite from which same-sex couples have historically been excluded (van Zyl 2011, 339). As such, they are appropriately classified as political acts.

The sociolegal contexts of the wedding waves varied in three important ways. First: their legal certainty. As noted above, the San Francisco and Portland waves were the most legally problematic, while weddings occurring after court rulings were on firmer legal ground. Couples marrying under conditions of greater legal uncertainty might well be thinking less about the interpersonal meaning of marriage and more about its public dimension, both in terms of seeking recognition and in terms of making a political claim. They might likewise be less focused on marrying in order to obtain legal benefits and protections than their counterparts marrying in more legally definitive circumstances.

Second: the ability of same-sex couples to protect their relationships from external forces. Couples who married in the 2004 San Francisco wedding wave, for example, already had many tools with which to protect their relationships. California permitted same-sex couples to enter into domestic partnerships, which incorporated many of the state-level rights and protections of marriage. Oregon, in contrast, provided no mechanism for same-sex couples to legally link their lives together in the absence of marriage. The legal benefits and protections provided by marriage thus probably loomed larger in the minds of participants in the 2004 Portland wedding wave than in the minds of their San Francisco counterparts.

Third: prevailing beliefs about the relationship between marriage and homosexuality. Couples who married in the 2004 wedding waves were truly breaking new ground. San Francisco and Portland were the first localities in the nation to embrace marriage equality, however temporarily. By the time couples in the Utah, Indiana, and Michigan wedding waves began marrying nearly a decade later, marriage equality was no longer a fringe notion. Over a dozen states permitted same-sex couples to marry. The U.S. Supreme Court had ruled in *United States v. Windsor* (2013) that the federal government was required to recognize validly performed same-sex marriages. Public opinion surveys showed that support for marriage equality had surpassed opposition.

This evolution of sociolegal understandings about the relationship between homosexuality and marriage might well impact same-sex couples' reasons for marrying. As same-sex marriage became more normalized, couples' reasons for marrying may have become more "normalized" as well. That is, their reasons for marrying might more closely mirror the reasons different-sex couples marry. Ironically enough, given the outsized interest in why same-sex couples choose to marry, we know relatively little about why different-sex couples choose to marry. The literature that exists, however, shows no indication that different-sex couples view marriage as a political act (see Kefalas, Furstenberg, Carr, and Napolitano 2011; Smock, Manning, and Porter 2005; Willoughby and Hall 2015).

In the following pages, I draw on mail surveys of participants in three wedding waves as well as a comparison survey of same-sex couples who married in Massachusetts to examine the effects of shifting sociolegal contexts on reasons for marrying. My interest here is in distinguishing among the participants themselves rather than distinguishing between participants and nonparticipants. I show that the specific sociolegal contexts of the wedding waves played a powerful external role in shaping motivations to marry.

The Studies

The data for this study come from four previous studies: three studies of participants in wedding waves (the 2004 San Francisco and Portland waves and the 2013–14 Utah wave) and a comparison study of LGBT people who married in Massachusetts between 2004 and 2007. The vast majority of couples who married in all four locations were residents of the state in which the weddings occurred.

Massachusetts was chosen as a comparison sample because the same-sex weddings there came closest to a "regular" wedding experience in terms of its legal certainty. Couples knew in advance when they would be permitted to marry and, although the weddings were subjects of fraught political contestation both in Massachusetts and across the nation, they also knew that their ability to marry was in no immediate danger of disappearing. The Massachusetts Supreme Judicial Court had ruled that the state's constitution required marriage equality and the only mechanism for reversing the court's decision was a constitutional amendment, which could not make it to the ballot prior to 2006. Any future amendment would probably not affect existing marriages and—even if it did—the amendment under consideration would permit same-sex couples to enter into civil unions, which would provide all the state-level rights and responsibilities of marriage. The political environment around same-sex weddings in Massachusetts was volatile, but the legal environment was stable, at least in the short term.

One thousand couples were randomly selected from San Francisco and Portland, 2,000 couples from Massachusetts, and 587 couples from Utah. (Although the samples were drawn at the couple level, the unit of analysis for each study was the individual.) The San Francisco and Portland couples were surveyed in the fall of 2006, the Massachusetts couples in the fall of 2007, and the Utah couples in the spring of 2015. The first three groups were mailed packets with two questionnaires in them and were given the option of responding via mail or online. The Utah couples were mailed letters containing login information for a web survey hosted by Qualtrics. All respondents were urged to participate in the survey even if their spouse chose not to do so.

At least one questionnaire was returned from 39 percent of the *individuals* from the Portland sample, representing 53 percent of the *households*. Thirty-one percent of the individuals sampled in San Francisco responded, representing 37 percent of the households. The Utah sample had a 32 percent individual response rate and a 41 percent household response rate. Twenty-nine percent of the individuals sampled in Massachusetts returned surveys; the household response rate is not known.[3] Comparison with demographic data collected by San Francisco, Multnomah County, and Massachusetts indicates that all three samples came close to representing the populations from which they were drawn.[4] There is no similar data for the population in Utah.

All surveys asked about the respondents' demographic attributes, political attitudes, and social-movement involvement. They also asked respondents to describe various aspects of their spousal relationships, including how long they had been together prior to marrying, whether they had children, and whether they had ever experienced problems as a result of their lack of legal ties to one another.

All surveys also contained an open-ended question asking respondents to describe their motivations to wed. The San Francisco and Portland questionnaires asked the respondents why they and their spouses had "decide[d] to apply for a [marriage] license." The Massachusetts and Utah questionnaires asked why respondents and their spouses had "decided to marry." The wording difference may have colored the nature of the responses, an issue I discuss further below.

Responses to the San Francisco and Portland questionnaires were analyzed at the same time using thematic analysis, which allows the respondents' own voices to guide the development of themes and categories rather than forcing them to fit their responses into an a priori schema (Boyatzis 1998). Themes and subthemes were identified until saturation was reached and no new themes emerged. Two coders independently analyzed each response. The coding themes developed from those questionnaires were subsequently applied to the Massachusetts and Utah data. Coders were instructed to mark any themes that fell outside the initial coding schema. Two coders independently analyzed each response; no new themes emerged.

Motivations to Marry

No matter where they married, respondents' reasons for doing so fell into four broad categories that mirror the findings of earlier studies. Table 20.1 presents the aggregated responses. The percentages in each category do not sum to one hundred because respondents often indicated that they had multiple motivations to marry. For example, one Massachusetts man said he and his spouse decided to marry for "[l]egal recognition of our relationship. Equality, love, commitment and all that jazz." Motivations to marry are distinguishable analytically, but often woven deeply together in practice.

TABLE 20.1. Percentage of Respondents Articulating
Specific Motivations to Marry

Motivations to marry	% Expressing
Culture of Love	39
Dignity	30
Contestation	47
Legal Protection	41
Other personal	8
"Because we can"	4
N	2576

Culture of Love

Just under 40 percent of the respondents said that they married for reasons that
fall within what Ann Swidler (2013, 5) calls the "culture of love." They married to
express their love for their spouse and to deepen or reaffirm their commitment.
They married because they saw marriage as the "natural progression of our relationship" or the "logical" next step. They married to fill expected cultural roles.
As one man said, he married "[b]ecause my parents have been married for 51
years, my dad's parents have been married 73 years and are both still alive, and
my mom's parents were married for 40 years." Couples married to fill a deep-
seated yearning; the phrase "we've always wanted to marry" was common.

It may seem surprising that six in ten respondents did *not* report marrying
for love. However, a large number of responses *presupposed* the existence of love
and commitment. For instance, one woman said she and her spouse decided to
wed "for the validation associated with the marriage certificate. Our love and
commitment to one another remains unchanged."

Because marrying for love falls far outside our common understandings of
political activism, love-based reasons for marrying are a challenge to the argument that the wedding waves constituted a form of political activism. It is important to note, then, that while around 40 percent of the respondents included love
as a reason to marry, only around 10 percent said love was the *only* reason they
married.

Dignity

Thirty percent of the respondents married as a bid for recognition and inclusion within the dominant society. That is, they were driven by their desire for
dignity. They wanted their relationships to be seen by others as real and valuable, where "others" included their extended families, their communities, and

their government. "Marriage is society's stamp of approval," said one woman. Another woman said she married because she "wanted to feel a part of mainstream America."

Many parents specifically discussed the importance of legitimation to their children. For example, a woman in Oregon said she and her wife married because "our daughter needed to see her family as legitimate." Likewise, a Massachusetts woman said she married because "[i]t was particularly important that our then 4 year old be able to view our relationship as 'on par' to those of our friends."

Contestation

Close to half the respondents couched their motivations to marry in the language of contestation, solidarity, and identity. Many said they married to send messages about equal rights and the value of same-sex relationships. "We did it as a political statement that LGBT people deserve full equality—marriage should be seen as a human right not a heterosexual privilege," one person declared. For many respondents, marrying was a way to deploy their identities publicly and strategically to fight for marriage equality. Many spoke of the power of numbers and their desire to "take a stand." Said one woman who married in Portland, "I felt that if they were issuing licenses, we should have as many people as possible join the effort—demonstrate how many of us do want equal rights, how many of us are out there." Still others drew on oppositional language. As one man put it, he married as an "act of defiance against the social norms in Utah." Many respondents were also aware of the historic nature of their weddings and eager to be part of that history. As one person who married in Portland said, "We wanted to participate in the biggest civil rights issue in our lives."

Legal Protection and Benefits

Just over 40 percent of the respondents said they married to protect their family from disruption and/or to benefit from the web of rights and obligations surrounding marriage. They wed at least in part, they said, to gain access to "rights," "benefits," and "legal protections."

These benefits and protections can be broken down into two main categories: economic and familial. Within the category of economic motivations, there were two main drivers. The first was access to health insurance. One man who married, for instance, did so in the hope that his "partner would be able to get health benefits through my employer." The second driver was the desire to facilitate property transfer and inheritance at the end of life. We "wanted to ensure that what we built together would (without question) belong to the other in the event of a tragedy," one woman wrote.

In terms of familial protections, respondents spoke passionately about desiring to protect the integrity of their spousal relationship against interfering others. Concerns about hospital visitation, medical decision making, and end-of-life care abounded. "I was going into the hospital for surgery and wanted [my wife] to be able to make decisions on my behalf and, if something went wrong, to benefit from my survivor's benefits," one woman explained.

Individuals who had children (or were planning to have children) described their desire to protect their children, and particularly their desire to protect the integrity of the parent-child relationship. A Massachusetts woman explained, "I was pregnant at the time and we wanted to protect our daughter by making sure both of us were linked as her parents, especially because of the religious beliefs held by my father and brothers."

Other Personal Reasons

Eight percent of the respondents indicated that they married for personal reasons that did not fall neatly within the "culture of love" category. One man who married in Portland, for example, explained his motivations this way: "Honestly . . . our best friends were also applying and we went along for the ride. Also, my mother was visiting and she really urged us to go make history." Several respondents said they married "on a whim" or because "it sounded like fun" or because "it seemed like the right thing to do."

"Because We Can"

Four percent of respondents indicated that they married because it was possible to do so without elaborating further. Since phrases like "because we can" are ambiguous in meaning—they might refer to personal or political motivations—simple statements of ability to marry were coded as a separate category.

Location and Motivations to Marry

Figure 20.1 breaks down the respondents' motivations to marry by wedding location. As it shows, the percentage of respondents articulating particular rationales for marrying shifted dramatically across locale, most strikingly so with respect to legal protections. While nearly three-quarters of the participants in the Utah wedding wave indicated that they married at least in part to access the legal rights and benefits that come with the institution, less than a third of the participants in the Portland wedding wave said they married for such pragmatic reasons, and only about a sixth of the San Francisco cohort did. A similar pattern appears when examining love as a motivation to marry, although the divergences are somewhat smaller. Utahans were the most likely to say they married for love

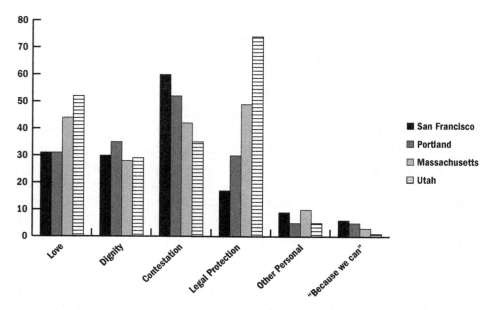

Figure 20.1. Percentage of Respondents in Four Locations Articulating Specific Motivations to Marry

(52 percent), while the San Francisco and Portland cohorts (31 percent) were the least likely to say so.

Results are flipped when the role of contestation is examined. While participants in the San Francisco wedding wave were the *least* likely to say they married for love or legal benefits, they were the *most* likely to say that they married as a form of political contestation. Sixty percent of the San Francisco cohort described their weddings as political actions, while 35 percent of the Utah respondents did. The motivations of the Massachusetts and Portland respondents fell in between, with the latter more likely than the former to describe their motivations to marry in political terms. The only motivation to marry that showed little variation across location was dignity. In every location, roughly 30 percent of the respondents said they married as a bid for recognition and inclusion.

What accounts for the differences in motivations to marry among the wedding waves? Why were the motives of participants in the Utah wedding wave so different from those of their San Francisco and Portland counterparts? While I argue that these differences are largely a product of variations in the sociolegal context of the weddings, one alternative explanation is that the underlying populations of the wedding waves differed and that these differences influenced why people chose to marry. In the following pages I employ multivariate analysis to show that location is the single most important predictor of motivations to marry, even when all other likely explanations are taken into account.

Accounting for Motivations to Marry

Motivations to marry will never be reducible to a set of underlying variables. My aim here is simply to show that location plays an important role in predicting motivations to marry, even when relevant controls are included. In the following analyses, I treat each of the main motivations to marry as separate dependent variables. Because the dependent variables are dichotomous, I use binomial logistic regression.

To account for the effect of location, I include dummy variables for the participants in the San Francisco, Portland, and Utah wedding waves. People who married in Massachusetts serve as the comparison group because the same-sex weddings there came closest to approximating what we might consider a "regular" wedding experience rather than a wedding wave.

I also include an array of variables to control for other factors that arguably influenced the respondents' reasons for marrying, including their age, gender, parenthood status, religiosity, the length of their relationship, and whether or not they had ever experienced a problem because of a lack of legal ties to their partner.[5]

Because of the inherently political nature of the weddings under study, I include two variables designed to capture the respondents' political commitments. Political beliefs were gauged via the standard seven-point liberal-conservative scale. Under the theory that more liberal respondents might be more inclined to see their weddings as a form of political activism, I created a dummy variable called "liberal identity" that represents the 74 percent of respondents identifying themselves as liberal or extremely liberal. Likewise, under the theory that respondents immersed more fully in activist networks might be more likely to see their weddings as a form of political activism, I created a scaled variable called political activism that tracks involvement in eight different causes: AIDS, civil rights, women's rights, the pro-choice movement, the environment, health care, peace, and education.

Findings and Discussion

Table 20.2 shows that the specific location of the wedding was both the strongest and the most consistent influence on the likelihood that a respondent would articulate a particular motivation to marry, even when controls were included. This means that the wide variation in motivations to marry across wedding waves cannot be attributed to differences in the underlying participants. The only reasonable explanation is that the specific political, legal, and/or cultural contexts of the weddings exerted an independent effect on the respondents' motivations for marrying. I break the findings down by marriage wave in the following pages. For ease of interpretation, I convert log odds to odds in my discussion.

TABLE 20.2. Factors Affecting Reasons to Marry, by Particular Motivation
Binomial Logistic Regression with Standard Errors in Parentheses

	Love	Recognition	Politics	Rights
Location of Wedding				
San Francisco (0–1)	−.47 (.12)***	−.10 (.13)	.62 (.12)***	−1.52 (.14)***
Portland (0–1)	−.58 (.12)***	.24 (.12)*	.36 (.11)***	−.84 (.12)***
Utah (0–1)	.37 (.14)**	.03 (.15)	−.23 (.14)	1.15 (.16)***
Control Variables				
years as couple				
0–5 (0–1)	.56 (.12)***	.10 (.13)	−.27 (.12)*	−.28 (.13)*
11–16 (0–1)	−.24 (.13)	.17 (.14)	.05 (.13)	.18 (.14)
17+ (0–1)	−.51 (.14)***	.20 (.15)	.12 (.14)	.17 (.15)
had legal problems (0–1)	−.12 (.09)	.18 (.10)	−.19 (.09)*	.42 (.10)***
parenthood (1 = parent)	−.03 (.10)	−.05 (.10)	−.03 (.09)	.25 (.10)*
age (20–86)	.003 (.005)	−.006 (.006)	−.005 (.005)	−.007 (.006)
highly religious (0–1)	.02 (.12)	.09 (.12)	−.26 (.11)*	.06 (.12)
gender (1 = male)	.01 (.09)	−.09 (.10)	.13 (.09)	.06 (.10)
political activism (0–8)	−.01 (.02)	.04 (.02)*	.08 (.02)***	−.02 (.02)
liberal identity (0–1)	.03 (.10)	.08 (.10)	.30 (.10)**	.02 (.11)
Intercept	−.27 (.27)	−.99 (.28)***	−.41 (.26)	−.06 (.28)
−2 log likelihood	2803.049	2678.255	2921.432	2606.222

Notes: N=2195. *p ≤.05, **p ≤.01, ***p ≤.001.

The San Francisco Wedding Wave

The participants in the San Francisco wedding wave were the least likely to say that the legal aspects of marriage motivated them to wed—80 percent less likely than those who married in Massachusetts. This makes sense. The participants in the San Francisco wedding wave had less practical incentive to wed than any of the other three sample populations. Over three-quarters of the respondents who married in San Francisco were already registered as domestic partners in California. As domestic partners, they already received many of the state-level rights and benefits of marriage. Marriage thus offered relatively little in the way of new legal protections.

While the San Francisco respondents were the least likely to say that they married for practical reasons, they were the most likely to say they married to make a political statement—85 percent more likely than the comparison group of Bay Staters who married. This too makes sense. The San Francisco weddings marked the first time in the United States that a county had enthusiastically instituted a regime of marriage equality, a move then mayor Gavin Newsom made for expressly political reasons. He was quite vocal that his decision to open marriage to same-sex couples was a repudiation of President George W. Bush's 2004 State of the Union address, an address in which the president had staunchly articulated his support for "traditional" marriage and had inveighed against the Massachusetts Supreme Judicial Court's recent decision requiring marriage equality. Much of the frenzied media coverage emphasized the political nature of Newsom's decision. It is reasonable to infer that the hyperpoliticized atmosphere of the San Francisco weddings led to a corresponding emphasis on political reasons to marry.

Less obvious is why participants in the San Francisco wedding wave were more than 35 percent less likely than those who married in Massachusetts to describe their motivations in love-based terms. With due recognition that many people's reasons for marrying presupposed the existence of an enduring love-based bond, the San Francisco respondents were significantly less likely to say that they married for love. The unprecedented nature of the 2004 San Francisco weddings and the chance to participate in the marriage equality movement in a real and meaningful way may simply have overwhelmed other motivations to marry. Alternately, the finding might be an artifact of changes in the questionnaire wording across the four studies. The San Francisco and Portland samples were asked why they decided to apply for marriage licenses. The Utah and Massachusetts samples were asked why they decided to marry. The "decision to marry" wording might have primed respondents to draw on the language of love and commitment to describe their reasons to marry.

The Portland Wedding Wave

The participants in the Portland wedding wave resembled their San Francisco counterparts in many ways. Both groups were significantly more likely than the Massachusetts and Utah samples to say they married for politics and significantly less likely to say they married for legal and love-based reasons. However, Oregonians were about 20 percent more likely to say they married for rights and benefits than Californians and about 40 percent less likely to say they married for politics. Differences in the sociolegal contexts of the two wedding waves help explain these findings.

The Portland weddings were akin to the San Francisco ones in important respects. Portland opened marriage to same-sex couples shortly after San Francisco did, also for expressly political reasons. As with San Francisco, throngs descended on City Hall to stand in lengthy lines in order to obtain marriage licenses of questionable legality. But there were also two key differences in the contexts of the weddings. First, unlike California, Oregon provided no mechanism for same-sex couples to legally link their lives together in the absence of marriage. The Portland weddings offered same-sex couples their first chance— even if a tenuous one—to protect their relationships against external forces. As one Oregonian phrased it, she and her partner married "[i]n the hope that some-day we and our children would be entitled to the benefits available to married couples and their families."

Second, the Portland wedding wave garnered far less media attention than did the San Francisco one. While the San Francisco weddings splashed across the front pages of newspapers across the nation, the Portland weddings received fairly perfunctory coverage. To the extent that the atmosphere of the Portland weddings was thus somewhat less politicized than that of the San Francisco ones, it seems reasonable that participants in the Portland wedding wave might be somewhat less inclined than their San Francisco counterparts to view their wed-dings as political actions.

Participants in the Portland wedding wave differed from all other respondents in one respect: they were about 25 percent more likely than any other group to say that they married to gain recognition and validation of their relationships. I have no ready explanation for this phenomenon.

The Utah Wedding Wave

Participants in the Utah wedding wave were strikingly different from partici-pants in the San Francisco and Portland waves, and somewhat different from LGBT people who married in Massachusetts. They were the most likely to say they married for love or legal reasons and the least likely to say they married for political reasons. To get a sense of the magnitude of the divergence between Utahans and all other participants, I re-ran the regressions displayed in table 20.2 twice, using first San Francisco then Portland as the control variable for location. Table 20.3 is excerpted from those analyses: it shows the odds of a participant in the Utah weddings expressing a particular motivation to marry relative to indi-viduals who married in each of the other three locations, with all other factors held constant.

As table 20.3 shows, Utahans and Bay Staters were just as likely to say they married for political reasons. Utahans, however, were 45 percent less likely than

TABLE 20.3. Odds of Participants in the Utah Wedding Wave Expressing a Particular Motivation to Marry Relative to Odds of LGBT People Marrying in Massachusetts, Portland, and San Francisco Expressing the Same Motivation

Results from Binomial Logistic Regression

	Love	Recognition	Politics	Protection
Massachusetts	1.45**	n.s.	n.s.	3.17***
Portland	2.60***	n.s.	.55***	7.37***
San Francisco	2.32***	n.s.	.43***	14.55***

Notes: N=2195. *p≤.05, **p≤.01, ***p≤.001.

Oregonians and 57 percent less likely than Californians to wed as an expression of politics. Conversely, they were about one and a half times (145 percent) more likely than Bay Staters to say they married for love and well over twice as likely as Oregonians and Californians to do so. But the starkest difference comes in the context of legal rights. Participants in the Utah wedding wave were more than *three* times as likely as those who married in Massachusetts to say they married to secure legal rights. They were over *seven* times as likely as the Portland respondents to say so. And they were more than *fourteen* times as likely to say so as the San Francisco respondents. What accounts for this dramatic differential?

The legal context of the Utah wedding wave assuredly played a significant role. The legal consequences of marrying were greater for Utahans than for any of the other respondents, for two reasons. First, the Utah wedding wave was the only one to take place after the 2013 U.S. Supreme Court decision *United States v. Windsor. Windsor* required the federal government to recognize marriages between same-sex couples, which meant that same-sex couples who married in Utah could expect a significantly expanded set of legal consequences, including the ability to file federal taxes jointly, transfer property between spouses tax free (at the federal level), collect spousal Social Security benefits, and sponsor spouses for immigration.

That alone might spark an increased interest in the legal aspects of marriage. But same-sex couples living in Utah also faced an especially onerous legal regime. Like Oregon, Utah provided no mechanism for same-sex couples to legally link their lives together in the absence of marriage. But unlike Oregon (or California or Massachusetts), Utah law forbade unmarried couples from adopting children. As a result, the *only* way for both same-sex parents to be recognized as parents to their children was to marry or to temporarily relocate to another state and complete the adoption process during that relocation. Same-sex couples in Utah, then, had an impetus to marry that none of the other couples did. Many respondents indicated that they were marrying either because they were planning to have children or because they were seeking to protect the children they already had. The unique legal disadvantage faced by same-sex couples with children was highlighted by one pair of Utah respondents who explained that they had actually ended their romantic relationship prior to marrying. They had wed solely so that the nonbiological mother could legally adopt her own child. Once the adoption was finalized, the women planned to divorce.

Participants in the Utah wedding wave also had more assurance of the legality of their marriage licenses than did the participants in the San Francisco and Portland wedding waves. The Utah weddings occurred under the auspices of a judicial ruling rather than the rogue decision of a county government. Moreover, by the time the Utah weddings occurred, marriage equality was the law in seventeen states and the federal government recognized the validity of same-sex marriages even in some instances when state governments did not. Given the expanded legal consequences of marrying, the particularly poor ability of same-sex couples to protect their families in the absence of marriage, and some level of assurance that the licenses issued in the wedding wave would be treated as legally valid, Utahans' disproportionate emphasis on the web of rights and responsibilities attending legal marriage becomes clearer.

That couples marrying in Utah and Massachusetts were less likely to see their weddings as political actions than the West Coast couples likewise makes some sense. The West Coast wedding waves were both sparked by political decisions of uncertain legality and took place before any state in the nation formally recognized the right of same-sex couples to marry. It is easy to see why many participants in those waves construed their actions within the framework of what Felstiner, Able, and Sarat (1980) term "naming, blaming, and claiming." They were, in fact, standing up en masse to claim a new legal right and doing so in an unprecedented fashion.

If anything, we might have expected Utahans to be less likely than Bay Staters to cite political reasons for marrying. After all, the Massachusetts weddings were themselves unprecedented and occurred in the midst of a political frenzy. By the time the Utah couples married, marriage equality was becoming mainstream in much of the nation. Utah, however, was the first "red" state forced to marry same-sex couples. Many respondents alluded to the distinctively conservative cast of the state and their surprise that marriage equality had arrived. As one person said, "Having lived in Utah as a gay male all of my life, I never thought something this amazingly progressive would ever happen." For such respondents, getting married had a distinctly political cast. One woman said she married partly as a "vindication against the conservative majority; because I thought it would never happen in Utah!" Others spoke of their desire to be part of the movement for marriage equality in Utah, to participate in what one woman called "the historic Utah battle."

We turn finally to the issue of love. Why were respondents from the Utah wedding wave more likely to say they married for love than the other three sets of respondents? Changes in question wording might explain why the West Coast respondents were less likely than Utahans to invoke love, but cannot explain why Utahans were 45 percent more likely than people in Massachusetts to talk about love. I outline two hypotheses here. Exploring them more fully goes beyond the limits of my data. One possibility is that shifts in the way marriage-rights organizations framed the importance of marriage equality may have affected how the respondents thought of their own actions. Through 2008, marriage equality advocates tended to emphasize the legal harms suffered by same-sex couples denied access to marriage (Tadlock, Gordon, and Popp 2007). After the 2008 failure of the "No on 8" campaign, which sought to convince Californians not to amend their constitution to limit marriage to different-sex couples, several organizations began to rethink their approach. Freedom to Marry heavily increased its emphasis on the importance of love, regularly employing two phrases: "love is love" and "all love is equal." The Human Rights Campaign and GLAAD likewise developed campaigns emphasizing the importance of love, family, and children to same-sex couples. It is possible that participants in the Utah wedding wave were exposed to and influenced by this love-based framing (but cf. Harrison and Michelson 2015).

An alternative possibility is that something about the culture of Utah may have primed same-sex couples to view their participation in the wedding wave through the lens of love and commitment. Some respondents indicated that their motives to marry were influenced by the dominant Mormon culture in Utah. As one man said, "We both come from Mormon backgrounds so we're both programmed with strong desires to get married." Although three-quarters of the Utah respondents indicated that they did not currently practice a religion, more than half were raised in the Mormon faith. Immersion in the Mormon culture, or any culture with a heavy emphasis on marriage and family, may make people more likely to think of marriage in terms of expected cultural norms and values.

Conclusion

Wedding waves are an iconic symbol of the marriage equality movement in the United States. Here they serve as a useful venue for exploring how motivations to marry are systematically shaped by external factors. Previous studies have shown that same-sex couples articulate four conceptually distinct motivations to marry, a finding this study confirms. Same-sex couples wed as a way to express their love and commitment. They wed in order to access the myriad of rights and benefits that accompany marriage. They wed to make a political statement on behalf of LGBT rights or to declare their equality as citizens. And they wed as a way of establishing the legitimacy of their relationships. These motivations are not mutually exclusive; indeed, same-sex couples commonly articulate multiple motivations for marrying.

For all their emphasis on exploring why same-sex couples desire to marry, scholars have rarely explored the underlying factors that *shape* those reasons (cf. Richman 2013). This study fills that gap. Most broadly, it reveals that motivations for participating in a wedding wave were shaped by a variety of factors. Some of these factors were individualistic or interpersonal. Couples in relationships of five years or fewer, for example, were more likely to say that they married for love and less likely to say that they married as an expression of politics or to secure legal protections. Individuals deeply immersed in activist networks were more likely to say that they married for political reasons. But the strongest and most consistent mediator of motivations to marry was the specific location of the wedding wave.

These locations, I have argued, serve as a proxy for the particular sociolegal contexts in which the wedding waves occurred. The ability of couples to protect themselves from external forces in the absence of marriage, for example, varied widely among the four groups studied. This disparity in turn appears to have played a major role in shaping their motivations to marry. Couples marrying in San Francisco, a location already offering significant legal protections to same-sex couples, were the least likely of all four groups to point to pragmatic legal concerns as a reason to wed. In contrast, couples marrying in Utah, the location with the most onerous legal regime, were the most likely of all groups to emphasis legal rights and benefits as a motivation to marry. As a gauge of the importance of legal regimes, Utah respondents were *fourteen* times as likely as their San Francisco counterparts to say they married for pragmatic purposes.

This finding drives home the legal importance of marriage. For all that we speak of marriage in the language of love, romance, and commitment, it is also a legal contract creating a web of rights and obligations. George Chauncey (2005, 71) has aptly described it as "the nexus for the allocation of a host of public and private benefits" in the United States. Those who are excluded from this nexus pay a heavy toll, in terms of both the practical difficulties they face protecting their relationships from external disruption and the omnipresent fear that their relationships might be disrupted. This is a weight that the Supreme Court's ruling in *Obergefell* has largely lifted from the shoulders of same-sex couples, but it should not be treated as a historical relic. Parallels can certainly be drawn to the experiences of other legally marginalized groups, perhaps most notably families in which one or more members are legally undocumented.

The findings from this study also speak to the ways differences in the sociolegal contexts of the wedding waves shaped the participants' views of their involvement as *political* acts. Given the nature of the wedding waves, participation in them qualifies as a political act whether or not the participants consciously perceived their actions thusly. But participants in some wedding waves were far more likely to see their actions as having an expressly political meaning. It is important to note that this finding cannot be attributed simply to the passage of time. When other relevant factors were accounted for, participants in the Utah wedding wave were just as likely to say they married as a form of contestation as respondents who married in Massachusetts, between seven and nine years earlier. Participants in the San Francisco wedding wave were significantly more likely than their Portland counterparts to say they married for political reasons, even though the weddings took place within several weeks of each other. And both the Portland and the San Francisco respondents were more likely to say they married as a form of political expression than respondents who married in Massachusetts, even though the Bay State weddings began within months of the others.

A likely explanation is that the politicized atmosphere of the weddings primed respondents to think about their actions in particular ways. Each of the wedding waves occurred in a unique set of circumstances. It is beyond the scope of this study to disentangle precisely how those various circumstances primed respondents to conceptualize their participation as a form of contestation. To what extent did media coverage play a role? Did the sense of breaking new ground in the struggle for marriage equality matter? Did it matter that two wedding waves were precipitated by the elected branches of government while one was precipitated by a judicial ruling (as were the Massachusetts weddings)? And did the legal (un)certainty of the weddings influence participants in the wedding waves to conceptualize their actions as a form of protest?

The important point for the purpose at hand is that the value of marrying—as a statement of love or of politics, as a plea for recognition or as a method for protecting family relationships from outside interference—depended in large part on the relationship between individuals and the state. Marriage is a private institution, but it is emphatically a public one as well. It is intimately connected to American conceptions of citizenship, where citizenship encompasses social status as well as legal status and is a precondition for the enjoyment of civil and social rights (Bosniak 2000; Shklar 1998; Smith 1999). Individuals in positions of systemic power often have the privilege of ignoring the "public" aspect of marriage, instead conceptualizing marriage as a "private" relationship and taking the very real legal and political implications of the institution for granted. As individuals are increasingly marginalized, the public aspect of marriage becomes increasingly important.

It is ironic, then, that a persistent criticism of marriage equality was that (presumably unlike different-sex couples) same-sex couples who sought to marry were seeking marriage for ignoble reasons—as an entrée to rights and benefits—rather than as an enduring expression of love and commitment. As the experiences of many of the same-sex couples in this study make clear, they married for "ignoble" reasons precisely in order to protect their enduring and committed relationships.

NOTES

1   The research for this chapter was supported by funding from the Department of Political Science, University of Vermont, and from the Office of Professional Development and the Dean of the School of Liberal Arts at Indiana University–Purdue University, Indianapolis. I extend my thanks to Matthew Beal, Allie van Sickle, and Brock Gibian for their research assistance and to Susan Burgess, Christine Keating, Marla Brettschneider, Lisa Holmes, and Caroline Beer for their incredibly useful feedback.

2   Other studies exploring why same-sex couples desire to marry have reached similar conclusions. See especially Badgett 2010; Clarke, Burgoyne, and Burns 2007; Hull 2006; Schecter, Tracy, Page, and Luong 2008.

3   Sixteen percent of the packets mailed to couples who married in San Francisco were returned with no forwarding address, as were 20 percent of the packets mailed to couples who married in Portland and 10 percent of the letters mailed to couples who married in Utah. Response rates have been adjusted accordingly. The Massachusetts response rate is unadjusted.

4 Both the San Francisco and the Multnomah County samples were more educated than the underlying population. They were also slightly older. In the San Francisco sample, men were overrepresented by seven percentage points.

5 Race, education, and income had no systemic effect on motivations to marry and were excluded from the analysis in the interests of parsimony.

REFERENCES

Badgett, M. V. 2010. *When Gay People Get Married: What Happens When Societies Legalize Same-Sex Marriage*. New York: NYU Press.

Bosniak, Linda. 2000. "Citizenship Denationalized." *Indiana Journal of Global Legal Studies* 7(2): 447–509.

Boyatzis, Richard E. 1998. *Transforming Qualitative Information: Thematic Analysis and Code Development*. Thousand Oaks, CA: Sage.

Chauncey, George. 2005. *Why Marriage? The History Shaping Today's Debate over Gay Equality*. New York: Basic Books.

Clarke, Victoria, Carole Burgoyne, and Maree Burns. 2007. "Romance, Rights, Recognition, Responsibilities, and Radicalism: Same-Sex Couples' Views on Civil Partnership and Marriage." In *Out in Psychology: Lesbian, Gay, Bisexual, Trans, and Queer Perspectives*, ed. Victoria Clarke and Elizabeth Peel, pp. 173–93. Chichester, England: Wiley.

Diani, Mario, and Doug McAdam. 2003. *Social Movements and Networks: Relational Approaches to Collective Action*. Oxford: Oxford University Press.

Felstiner, William L. F., Richard L. Abel, and Austin Sarat. 1980. "The Emergence and Transformation of Disputes: Naming, Blaming, Claiming . . ." *Law and Society Review* 15(3/4): 631–54.

Harrison, Brian F., and Melissa R. Michelson. 2015. "Everybody Wants Somebody to Love." Paper presented at the Annual Meeting of the Western Political Science Association, Las Vegas, NV.

Hull, Kathleen. 2006. *Same-Sex Marriage: The Cultural Politics of Love and Law*. Cambridge: Cambridge University Press.

Kefalas, Maria J., Frank F. Furstenberg, Patrick J. Carr, and Laura Napolitano. 2011. "'Marriage Is More Than Being Together': The Meaning of Marriage for Young Adults." *Journal of Family Issues* 32(7): 845–75.

Kimport Katrina. 2013. *Queering Marriage: Challenging Family Formation in the United States*. New Brunswick, NJ: Rutgers University Press.

Kitts, James A. 1999. "Not in Our Backyard: Solidarity, Social Networks, and the Ecology of Environmental Mobilization." *Sociological Inquiry* 69(4): 551–74.

McAdam, Doug. 1986. "Recruitment to High-Risk Activism: The Case of Freedom Summer." *American Journal of Sociology* 92(1): 64–90.

Obergefell v. Hodges. 2015. 2015 WL 213646 (Supreme Court).

Richman, Kimberly D. 2013. *License to Wed: What Legal Marriage Means to Same-Sex Couples*. New York: NYU Press.

Schecter, Ellen, Allison J. Tracy, Konjit V. Page, and Gloria Luong. 2008. "Shall We Marry? Legal Marriage as a Commitment Event in Same-Sex Relationships." *Journal of Homosexuality* 54(4): 400–422.

Shklar, Judith N. 1998. *American Citizenship: The Quest for Inclusion*. Cambridge, MA: Harvard University Press.

Smith, Rogers M. 1999. *Civic Ideals: Conflicting Visions of Citizenship in U.S. History*. New Haven, CT: Yale University Press.

Smock, Pamela J., Wendy D. Manning, and Meredith Porter. 2005. "'Everything's There Except Money': How Money Shapes Decisions to Marry among Cohabitors." *Journal of Marriage and Family* 67(3): 680–96.

Snow, David A., Louis A. Zurcher Jr., and Sheldon Ekland-Olson. 1980. "Social Networks and Movements: A Microstructural Approach to Differential Recruitment." *American Sociological Review* 45(5): 787–801.

Swidler, Ann. 2013. *Talk of Love: How Culture Matters.* Chicago: University of Chicago Press.

Tadlock, Barry L., C. Ann Gordon, and Elizabeth Popp. 2007. "Framing the Issue of Same-Sex Marriages: Traditional Values vs. Equal Rights." In *The Politics of Same-Sex Marriage.* Ed. Craig A. Rimmerman and Clyde Wilcox, pp. 193–214. Chicago: University of Chicago Press.

Taylor, Verta, Katrina Kimport, Nella Van Dyke, and Ellen Ann Andersen. 2009. "Culture and Mobilization: Tactical Repertoires, Same-Sex Weddings, and the Impact on Gay Activism." *American Sociological Review* 74(6): 865–90.

United States v. Windsor, 133 S.Ct. 2675 (2013).

Van Zyl, M. 2011. "Are Same-Sex Marriages Un-African? Same-Sex Relationships and Belonging in Post-Apartheid South Africa." *Journal of Social Issues* 67(2): 335–57.

Willoughby, Brian J., and Scott S. Hall. 2015. "Enthusiasts, Delayers, and the Ambiguous Middle Marital Paradigms among Emerging Adults." *Emerging Adulthood* 3(2): 123–35.

21

Queer Sensibilities and Other Fagchild Tools

JERRY D. THOMAS

Marriage for queer citizens is a narrative of assimilation to heteronormativity. Courts legitimate marriage as *the* social institution around which society has been and should be organized. Requiring states to recognize same-sex marriages, courts emphasize queer sameness to heterosexuals, the same as queers whose pastiche imitation of heteronormativity, namely, child rearing, emphasizes and replicates fictions of reproductive futurism. This essay criticizes marriage as privileging heteronormativity in citizenship at the expense of queer sensibilities: that is, marriage privileges some future child that does not exist at the expense of citizen queers who are now here.

Alexis de Tocqueville observed in the 1830s that Americans fascinate themselves with equality because the benefits of equality are immediately felt, its evils less so:

> None but attentive and clear-sighted men perceive the perils with which equality threatens us, and they commonly avoid pointing them out. . . . The evils which extreme equality may produce are slowly disclosed; they creep gradually into the social frame; they are seen only at intervals; and at the moment at which they become most violent, habit already causes them to be no longer felt. (2001, 191)

The benefits of marriage equality prevailed in the marriage discourse despite warnings of marriage equality's evils. This essay is an interval that discloses perils of marriage equality, namely that it further privileges heteronormativity at the expense of queer liberty and difference. Tocqueville also notes that equality criticism often comes from those who already have it: "The taste and the idea of freedom only began to exist and to be developed at the time when social conditions were tending to equality, and as a consequence of that very equality" (2001, 192). I acknowledge this continued tendency: however hypocritical it appears to me, I completed this essay when marriage equality had already manifested in the United States and when I, a fagchild with queer sensibilities, had been married for almost ten years. I begin with the courts.

Courts Legitimate Mainstream Sexual Citizenship Norms

The timing of the Supreme Court's gay and lesbian rights decisions supports the legitimater role of the courts. The Court legitimates prevailing sexual norms in step with public opinion rather than shifting sexual norms toward greater inclusivity ahead of polities' majorities. In the main, the Court is not an institution that advances evolving sexual norms; it is not an institution of social change (Rosenberg 2008). Rather, the Court legitimates majoritarian sexual norms. Marriage illustrates.

In 2014, one year after *Windsor* and one year before *Obergefell*, a majority of Americans supported "legal recognition of marriage for gay and lesbian couples" (Flores 2014, 2015). Public opinion had shifted rather quickly in the previous five years, but it had, nonetheless, tilted in favor of support for same-sex marriage. State recognition of marriage also trended toward inclusivity. Just before *Obergefell* in summer 2015, about three-fourths of the states provided same-sex marriages in some form or degree. Notwithstanding a handful of pending legal challenges and rogue disregards for higher court rulings, the shift toward same-sex marriage had already galvanized in the states. This shift occurred quickly. Massachusetts was first in 2003, followed by eleven states and the District of Columbia within the ten years leading up to *Windsor* in 2013. Within two years of *Windsor*, another half of the states included gays and lesbians in marriage. In 2014, the Court denied certiorari petitions from states challenging circuit court decisions requiring states to recognize same-sex marriages, which left lower-court decisions in place. By summer 2015, *Obergefell* ordered the remaining quarter of states to issue marriage licenses to same-sex couples. By the time the Court decided *Obergefell*, the Court's role, intentionally or not, was to legitimate marriage equality, which had already been accepted into the mainstream.

The *Windsor* Court facilitated state trends, but it did not address sex and sexuality. Two sets of strategic behaviors probably led to success in *Windsor*. First, the Court probably granted certiorari based on an "outcome" model rather than a "jurisprudential" one (Perry 1991). Although we do not know who voted for certiorari, the four liberal justices—Ginsburg, Sotomayor, Kagan, and Breyer—were probably confident of a pro-gay outcome since Justice Kennedy was sure to join them. Justice Kennedy authored the Court's two other opinions legitimating gay and lesbian rights, *Romer* and *Lawrence*. Too, given the messy technicalities about standing and murky federalism issues, it is unlikely that the Court granted certiorari to advance jurisprudential issues about either standing or federalism. Cleaner cases could do this work better. It seems likely that justices voted for certiorari because they were concerned about the outcome of same-sex marriage.

The second set of strategies was external to the Court. Strategists structured legal opportunities by choosing plaintiffs and case facts amenable to appealing to senses of fairness, avoiding sexuality altogether (Andersen 2006). *Windsor* was about taxes, older citizens who could not procreate if they wanted to, women, who are perceived as less threatening than men, and lesbians, who are perceived as less threatening than gay men. It was easy for the public to desexualize Edith Windsor because she could easily be seen as resembling a desexualized grandmother. *Windsor* was not about sex and sexuality; it was about money and fairness. It affronts senses of justice not to give an elderly woman a tax break after the death of the person with whom she had a relationship for nearly fifty years. Edith Windsor was a real plaintiff who suffered real harms, but advancing a case about an elderly lesbian challenging tax laws was palatable to mainstream America, whose majority already supported legal recognition of marriage for gay and lesbian couples. Strategically, Windsor's case was a structured legal opportunity.

The Court's legitimater role in marriage is consistent with its role in other sexual policy areas. When the *Lawrence* Court struck down states' sodomy laws in 2003, it did so for about one-fourth of the states. The other three-fourths had already eliminated sodomy laws. Where sodomy laws still existed, states scarcely enforced them because it was impractical and invasive to police intimate and sexual conduct in citizens' private homes. To do so would have violated popular understandings of privacy. When the *Lawrence* Court legitimated private sexual autonomy, it did so with little controversy or fanfare.

The Supreme Court has not been activist in the sense that it does not deviate far from public opinion concerning sexual citizenship. I am careful not to suggest that public opinion dictated the Court's constitutional underpinnings, only that the timing of the Court's decision coincided with shifts in majority opinion. This timing was probably influenced by Justice Ginsburg's noted experiences with the timing of the Court's abortion decisions, which Chief Justice Roberts cited in his *Obergefell* dissent to bolster his argument that the Court should not decide the case, but should leave it to democratic processes in the states. Justice Ginsburg, in the majority, obviously chose not to side-step deciding the issue for fear that states and citizens would view the decisions as illegitimate. I cannot know Justice Ginsburg's motivations beyond the words of the majority opinion she joined, but as the chief justice notes, she is aware of how timing impacts citizens' acceptance of issues. In relation to *Roe v. Wade*, then Judge Ginsburg wrote, "The political process was moving in the early 1970s, not swiftly enough for advocates of quick, complete change, but majoritarian institutions were listening and acting. Heavy-handed judicial intervention was difficult to justify and appears to have provoked, not resolved, conflict" (1985, 385–86). But *Obergefell* was unlike *Roe v. Wade* in one critical regard: when the Court acted, about one-fourth of states *did not* provide some sort of same-sex marriage compared with about one-fourth of states that *did* provide some sort of abortion beyond instances jeopardizing the mother's life. In response to arguments that same-sex marriage foreclosed democratic processes, Justice Kennedy wrote,

> [T]here has been far more deliberation than this argument acknowledges. There have been referenda, legislative debates, and grassroots campaigns, as well as countless studies, papers, books, and other popular and scholarly writings. There

has been extensive litigation in state and federal courts. . . . Judicial opinions addressing the issue have been informed by the contentions of parties and counsel, which, in turn, reflect the more general, societal discussion of same-sex marriage and its meaning that has occurred over the past decades. As more than 100 amici make clear in their filings, many of the central institutions in American life—state and local governments, the military, large and small businesses, labor unions, religious organizations, law enforcement, civic groups, professional organizations, and universities—have devoted substantial attention to the question. (*Obergefell v. Hodges*, slip op. 23)

Obergefell met considerably more controversy than *Lawrence*, but I do not anticipate *Roe*-type backlash because, in the main, same-sex marriage was vetted more fully in political discourses and accepted by a majority of Americans before the Court acted.

The same *Roe* Court could have recognized same-sex marriages in 1972 when two men challenged Minnesota laws denying them the right to marry. Instead, the Court declined even to recognize that the issue of same-sex marriage involved federal constitutional questions, neither questions of liberty nor questions of equality. The Court dismissed the case "for want of a substantial federal question" (*Baker v. Nelson* 1972). Only three years after Stonewall, public support for same-sex marriage would have been as negligible as the Court suggested. Not until the tide of public support for same-sex marriage tipped 50 percent did the Court grant certiorari for same-sex marriage controversies. In sum, the Court has not been progressive, countermajoritarian, activist, or otherwise at the leading edge of social change for sexual citizenship.

To say that the Court is not an institution for social change is not to say that the role of the Court is unimportant. Contrarily, a central theme in queer theory is the construction of sexualities, among other things, through language. Those who control the language control the discourse and politics of sexual citizenship. Judges are masters of legal and constitutional language. This, coupled with their legitimation role, gives courts considerable influence over the trajectory of sexual citizenship over short and long terms. Legal and political activists and theorists will frame discourses within and against the language of the courts, just as I do in the next part of this essay when I criticize the marriage discourse through queer theory lenses.

Queer Sensibilities

This essay is about peeling back layers of false consciousness in legal and political discourses of marriage. Many of its themes are not new, but it is as if we have yet to learn what queerist Audre Lorde, a black lesbian, counseled in 1979 during the Second Sex Conference's panel titled "The Personal and the Political," when she criticized white heterosexual conference organizers for excluding women who are different—poor, lesbians, Black, and older: "the master's tools will never dismantle the master's house" (1984, 112).

It is impossible to write a detached, impersonal essay, so writing this has involved peeling back layers of my own false consciousness. Bowie-like, I am learning to "turn and face the strange," even when it means facing the strange inside myself. I find consciousness-raising ultimately liberating, but its processes and tools are sometimes painful. My queer sensibilities are, as Professor Warner notes, born of stigmas connected with "gender, the family, notions of individual freedom, the state, public speech, consumption and desire, nature and culture, maturation, reproductive politics, racial and national fantasy, class identity, truth and trust, censorship, intimate life and social display, terror and violence, health care, and deep cultural norms about the bearing of the body" (1993, xiii). These sensibilities showed me that tenaciously held identities, ones I believed essentialized my being—gender, sexuality, race, and god—were all social constructions I could disrupt, cherish, or reimagine in ways of my own choosing. I have learned to embrace a figural role as radical queerist— disrupter, nihilist, parrhesiaste, bearer of bad news—an unsettling role that defines itself against the normal, a role I prefer not to play but understand is my social responsibility to play because I wish someone had told me forty years ago about the fictions that govern queer lives.

The radical queer defines itself against the normal. Inasmuch as heterosexuality, gender, and marriage are normal, queer stands in opposition to them; but queer does not confine and define itself (if there is "self") as narrowly as opposing gender and heteronormativity. Queer theory's antisocial thesis situates queerism more broadly in opposition to society's arrangements and institutions. Gay and lesbian citizens who want to participate fully in heteronormative social institutions such as marriage may find queer theory's nihilistic tendencies off-putting for a number of reasons, such as when *we* are (1) pragmatists who espouse Sisyphus-like futilities in tearing down hegemonic institutions; (2) complacent-turned-complicit political participants, unwilling to do difficult, painful self-reflective constructionist-deconstructionist work that feminism and queerism require because to turn and face the strange risks losing power; or (3) oblivious citizens, unaware of the extent to which societies—transculturally and across time—are constructed by those who control the language and, hence, the politics of the discourse surrounding humanity, including discourses of irrefutable, unquestionable, and concrete knowledges disguised as science, god, and law. Embracing queerness requires tearing down notions of society and social institutions as well as notions of self and tenaciously held identities.

Even when we stand in full awareness of constructivism, as many in the academy stand, we lack the tools, desire, or courage to be *parrhesiastes* who tell it like it is (Foucault 2011). Instead, we aspire to attain privilege in society and social institutions through liberal democracy's promise of equality, often shortsight-edly, as de Tocqueville observed (2001, 191). For equality, liberal gays and lesbians "choose" to assimilate, never realizing there is not much choice to do otherwise and never questioning whether we should.

There is anger in radical queerism. Anger, not assimilation, started the Stone-wall riots in 1969. Lady Bunny reminds,

> Don't you ever discount the drag queens. I get so tired of these conservative gays always saying, "The leather men and the drag queens: that doesn't represent our community." We started your gay rights! It was not the conservative gays that put on a pink t-shirt or a rainbow flag one day a year and then went back to their closeted office jobs. It was drag queens and the street people that were getting the harassment by the police that said, "Uh-uh, Enough! Here's a brick in your fucking face!" (Greenfield-Sanders 2013, 25:31)

We shun and fear anger because it is often conflated with violence. Violence may have started the modern queer movement, but violence did not end it. Queers suffer from violence, but it is unnecessary to meet violence with more violence in order to claim democratic citizenship. We can disarticulate violence without disempowering anger. Anger, like queerness, cannot be shamed into a closet, compartmentalized and severed from the whole with expectations that it will wither and go away. Queerism does not run from its anger. It uses it.

Larry Kramer reminds us that anger is a creative emotion and that AIDS poli-tics epitomizes the manifestation of queer possibilities. In response to unrespon-sive publics that watched gay men die, Kramer notes, "ACT-UP made itself. We began every meeting by announcing who had died since the last meeting. And boy, if that wasn't enough to keep you going, I don't know what" (Greenfield-Sanders 2013, 26:20). In 1989, AIDS activists protested by using civil disobedi-ence during a service in St. Patrick's Cathedral in New York. They turned toward the congregation and repeatedly yelled, "Stop murdering us! Stop murdering us!" Afterwards, AIDS activists worried that people hated them for interfering with their rights to worship; they were crucified in the media. Kramer embraced fear and anger as politically useful:

> They are afraid of us. This is the best thing we have ever done. We are no longer just limp-wristed fairies. We're guys in jeans, in Levis and boots. We're here, we have voices, and we're gonna fight back. It made us, that action at St. Patrick's. Every treatment for HIV that is out there is out there because of us: not from the govern-ment, not from any politician, not from any drug company. We forced all those things into being by our anger and our fear. And that's what anger can get you. *You do not get more with honey than with vinegar.* Anger is a wonderful emotion, very creative, if you know how to do it. (Greenfield-Sanders 2013, 28:40–29:40)

ACT-UP was instrumental in setting in motion federally funded HIV and AIDS research and support, but it took threatening *children* with AIDS before political and government action would become mainstream. In 1990, Congress passed the Ryan White Comprehensive AIDS Resources Emergency (CARE) Act. Ryan White was expelled from his middle school for having AIDS, which he contracted through a blood transfusion to treat his hemophilia. When AIDS claimed a desexualized child as its face, its emblem, Congress acted decisively: the Senate passed cloture, ending debate, by a vote of 95–3; the bill passed in the House 408–14 (HRSA, USDHHS). Almost no one opposed aid for children.

We lost the impulse of AIDS politics; the punctuated equilibrium of heteronormativity was restored. Political science and public law have not yet taught us much from queerism and AIDS politics, despite urgings and suggestions to the contrary (Sherrill et al. 1992). It is as if queer theory is too radical, too uncertain, and too marginal to be taken seriously. Instead, political science and public law, like mainstream gays and lesbians, reward and perpetuate assimilationism. I suspect we lost the impulse of AIDS politics—a queer politics—when we cast aside the messiness of it all in favor of a tidier homonormative politics that allowed us to feel better about ourselves in society. Professor Duggan describes homonormativity as "a politics that does not contest dominant heteronormative assumptions and institutions, but upholds and sustains them, while promising the possibility of a demobilized gay constituency and a privatized, depoliticized gay culture anchored in domesticity and consumption" (2003, 50).

Homonormativity pushed sexuality further into private spheres—domestic spheres—hoping queer disruption would go away, as if monogamous relationships would be a "responsible disease prevention strategy" (Duggan 2003, 53). Michael O'Rourke, the Irish postman and queerist who has greater freedom outside the academy to be a parrhesiaste, writes that the "big secret" about queer theory is that it doesn't like to talk about sex, that it sanitizes itself from the messy: "Queer theory does not—despite what it tells itself—like the icky, sticky, yucky, viscous, gloopy, gunky, mascara-streaked, wet, bloody, sweaty, pissy, shitty, leaky, seeping, weeping, sploshing, spurting, spashing, milky. It needs to carefully mop up the messy, the dirty, the sexually disgusting. In order to remain squeaky clean it has to cast out that which it deems too perverse" (2014, 5). We lost the impulse of AIDS politics when guilty survivors mopped up the messiness of AIDS and queer sex by castigating and castrating our own queernesses and burying them with AIDS victims. Coerced and shamed, we disembodied the bloody and the shitty and traded them for marriage certificates.

Feminism empowers queerism to reclaim the messy. It is futile and naïve to deny embodiment, mortality, vulnerabilities, and ecological limits. Mainstream societies attempt to reconcile these embodiments and limits in the emblem of the child as the symbol of humanity's future that never comes (Edelman 2004). Hedonic queers refuse to deny themselves possibilities for living simply because society insists that their bodies be used for the production and reproduction of future societies. In this important way, queer politics is abortion politics (Edelman 2004). To suggest that we should live for posterity is to value an existing life less than the fictional life of some future child. Hedonic queerism rejects this system of valuation as a way to reconcile embodiment and its limits. Once queers accept the inevitability of their own deaths, they are liberated to live and die autonomously and need not die in ways prescribed by heteronormativity or feminism. Feminist scholars suggest there ought to be more to a theory of sexual citizenship than "if it feels good, do it" (Eichner 2009, 317), where queer logics are reduced pithily to "fuck[ing] our way to freedom" (Glick 2000, 17). Hedonic queerism insists that doing what feels good *is* sufficient, but having claimed embodiments and death—lessons learned in AIDS politics—hedonic queerism says: not only can we fuck our way to freedom, but we can fuck ourselves to death.

I live in my own dying corpse and choose to make it as pleasurable as possible and dare anyone, including myself—a self-censoring, internalized-homophobic self—to tell me otherwise. I choose not to die exhausted from chasing and rearing children who will die exhausted from chasing and rearing future children that never come. Deconstructing and disrupting the hegemony of "reproductive futurism" (Edelman 2004) is daunting, surely; but it is the dysfunctional fiction of the future child, not queerist disruptions to it, that is like Sisyphus's cyclical, futile damnation. Professor Edelman writes,

> [T]he Child has come to embody for us the telos of the social order and come to be seen as the one for whom that order is held in perpetual trust. . . . In its coercive universalization, however, the image of the Child, not to be confused with the lived experiences of any historical children, serves to regulate political discourse—to prescribe what will count as political discourse—by compelling such discourse to accede in advance to the reality of a collective future whose figurative status we are never permitted to acknowledge or address. . . . [W]e are no more able to conceive of a politics without a fantasy of the future than we are able to conceive of a future without the figure of the Child. (2004, 11)

Reproductive futurism, as Edelman describes, "imposes an ideological limit on political discourse as such, preserving in the process the absolute privilege of heteronormativity by rendering unthinkable, by casting outside the political domain, the possibility of a queer resistance to this organizing principle of communal relations" (Edelman 2004, 2). Reproductive futurism dominates the discourse, resulting in the political Left and Right privileging citizens that *might be* over citizens that *are*.

Gays and lesbians are model citizens: homonormativists whose pastiche performances imitate and replicate heteronormativities, including reproductive futurism. Queers create space in popular culture and society by mimicking heterosexualism, often in parody, which on the surface does not threaten heteronormativity but through slippages reveals instabilities in heteronormativity's underpinnings (Burgess 2006). Humor accommodates visibility. Other imitations, as in visual art, are performed not in parody but with pastiche, an imitation more sincere than parody in that the individual performing the imitation does not seek to unsettle the original; instead, the performance replicates and stabilizes what it imitates, often better than the original. Of parody and pastiche, artist and queer theorist Henry Rogers asks, "[W]hat does happen to the parodic manifestation, the satirical impulse, when the laughter stops? What happens when laughter falls to a titter and eventually to nothing more than a smile, when parody is absorbed by mainstream culture, when embraced as simply another representation in the cultural catalogue of representations: does parody, indeed, slip ever so slightly into pastiche?" (2006, 10–11).

For marriage imitation, parody slipped into pastiche in the moments when gays and lesbians who performed marriage, even before legal recognition came to pass, did so not to disrupt it but to perfect it. This is apparent in parenting. In the moments when gays and lesbians as couples, together and openly, had children, they did so under intense scrutiny of communities and polities, pressured to prove their worth as parents. This psychology motivates minorities to become super-citizens. Marginalized, stigmatized queers function as "minority citizens . . . subjected to intense scrutiny [who] must prove their good citizenship and even their humanity" (Riggle et al. 2005, 222). Proof of good citizenship and humanity occurs externally and internally, especially when gays and lesbians suffering from internalized homophobias want to prove to themselves their own worthiness as humans, citizens, parents, and heteronormativists. This political psychology leads minorities to become super-citizens, replicating majority norms with pastiche.

Judge Richard Posner alludes to gays' and lesbians' pastiche replication of parenting in the Seventh Circuit case striking down same-sex marriage bans in Wisconsin and Indiana: "[I]t will enhance the status of these marriages in the eyes of other Americans, and in the long run it may convert some of the opponents of such marriage by demonstrating that homosexual married couples are in essential respects, notably in the care of their adopted children, like other married couples" (*Baskin v. Bogan* 2014, 658). He reasons that gay couples' intentional decisions to parent operate as a selection bias for good parenting since gay couples may not, unlike heterosexual couples, enter parenting unintentionally through accidental pregnancies. Therefore, it becomes illogical to exclude same-sex couples—model parents—from becoming even better parents by recognizing and stabilizing their marriages. He wrote,

> Indiana's government thinks that straight couples tend to be sexually irresponsible, producing unwanted children by the carload, and so must be pressured (in the

form of governmental encouragement of marriage through a combination of sticks and carrots) to marry, but that gay couples, unable as they are to produce children wanted or unwanted, are model parents—model citizens really—so have no need for marriage. Heterosexuals get drunk and pregnant, producing unwanted children; their reward is to be allowed to marry. Homosexual couples do not produce unwanted children; their reward is to be denied the right to marry. Go figure. (662)

Surely it is illogical, as Judge Posner notes, to exclude gays and lesbians from marriage because of their model parenting skills, but even when gays and lesbians mimic heteronormativity in parenting with pastiche, children dominate the political and legal frames.

The issue from the queer perspective is not whether gays and lesbians are model parents, either because they are intentional in their parenting decisions or because they over-perform under the public's intense scrutiny; the issue is whether gay and lesbian citizens are expected to perform as heteronormativists, toeing the line of reproductive futurism in order to receive sexual citizenship. Judge Posner framed the equality question in ways that never questioned marriage and heterosexuality: "[I]n a same-sex marriage case the issue is not whether heterosexual marriage is a socially beneficial institution but whether the benefits to the state from discriminating against same-sex couples clearly outweigh the harms that this discrimination imposes" (655). Reproductive futurism, then, retains a place of unquestioned privilege, where gays and lesbians replicate it, often better than heterosexuals themselves, for the sake of reproductive futurism itself.

To be clear, marriage proponents indeed argued that marriage is not only about children. States allow citizens to marry even if they are unable to procreate. Justice Scalia provided this legal road map in his *Lawrence* dissent: "[W]hat justification could there possibly be for denying the benefits of marriage to homosexual couples? . . . Surely not the encouragement of procreation, since the sterile and the elderly are allowed to marry" (*Lawrence v. Texas* 2003, 604). On one hand, this argument disrupts marriage as solely a child-rearing institution. On the other, the argument is still framed by children. Citizens who can have children retain the unquestioned right to marry. All others—gay, lesbian, elderly, sterile—are granted this privilege as exceptions to the rule, presumably since they would procreate if they were able.

Homonormativity and pastiche parenting do not dissolve sexual hierarchies. Biological families formed through "natural" heterosexuality are privileged over adoptive families formed through technology or law, where the latter is an imitation of the former (Brettschneider 2011, 24, biological families are cast as prototypical models and adoptive families as mere imitations). While Brettschneider correctly identifies hierarchies in family structures and the need to disrupt and dismantle them, a queerer approach disrupts and unsettles not merely the family structure hierarchy but the family structure itself, irrespective of how the structure came to be. Queer theory unsettles not only sexual identities (gay, lesbian, straight) but also heteronormative familial identities (mother, father, parent, child).

In a deliberate effort to forge a gay mainstream, conservative gays explicitly disavowed radical queerisms that sought to unsettle identity and dismantle marriage. Spawned during the Log Cabin National Leadership Conference in 1999, the Independent Gay Forum, a group of gay writers, academics, attorneys, and activists, posted a list of principles on its website under the banner "Forging a Gay Mainstream." Two key principles stated (1) "We deny 'conservative' claims that gays and lesbians pose any threat to social morality or the political order" and (2) "We equally oppose 'progressive' claims that gays should support radical change or restructuring of society."[1] Unabashedly, conservative gays disarticulated queer values by articulating heterosexual values. The *Obergefell* Court legitimated as much when it stated, "It would misunderstand these men and women to say they disrespect the idea of marriage. Their plea is that they do respect it, respect it so deeply that they seek to find its fulfillment for themselves. Their hope is not to be condemned to live in loneliness, excluded from one of civilization's oldest institutions" (2608). While the Court showed concern that excluding gays from marriage would condemn them to live in loneliness, it reflected no concern for queer lives that marriage condemns and alienates.

Conservative gays were successful at forging a gay mainstream not only in the Supreme Court but in lower federal courts. In *Wolfe v. Walker* (2014), Judge Crabb relied on assimilationist arguments painting gays and lesbians as "virtually normal" and in need of the right to marriage, the "fundamental mark of citizenship" (987), without which they would wither since the ability to union with someone is "intrinsic to the notion of human flourishing" (1005). Suggesting that queers are "virtually normal" and that marriage is intrinsic to human flourishing overvalues heteronormativity and the institutions that prop it, meanwhile stigmatizing queer difference (including heterosexuals who choose not to marry) and suggesting that queers will not flourish. These logics are degrading and false.

The radical queer defines itself against the normal; it reacts to and understands its stigmas in relation to others. But radical queerism is not the only choice, even if it is, pragmatically, a feasible and desirable choice. There exists a purer, peaceful, introspective queer—not the disempowered, internalized-homophobic, assimilated, sexually deviant queer who accepts dominant messages about who ze is or how ze ought to act and not the radical queer who disavows dominant messages and does what ze is told ze cannot do. Both versions construct themselves in dominant frames, the former accepting them and the latter rejecting them. There exists an introspective queer that does not define itself against the normal, who creates new tools and frames of living, free of social fictions. At the conclusion of her essay "Master's Tools," Audre Lorde inspires inward reflection to empower that which makes us different. She writes, "Racism and homophobia are real conditions of all our lives in this place and time. *I urge each one here to reach down into that deep place of knowledge inside herself and touch that terror and loathing of any difference that lives there. See whose face it wears.* Then the personal as the political can begin to illuminate all our choices" (1984, 113, emphasis in original). The introspective queer learns a great deal when it lives in isolation and manifests sexuality with its imagining self. Setting aside for the moment issues of "queer phenomenology"—how we experiences ourselves, alone and with objects and others (Ahmed 2006)—one of the things the queer learns when it cannot use the master's tools—the master's penis, women's holes, men's holes—is that the queer must not always wither and cease to exist. It creates its own tools to embody sexuality, to manifest pleasures and discordances with itself and environments untainted with oughts and holes. We can consider, with seriousness, life separate from other citizens, spaces where we need not concern ourselves with dominance feminism and equality questions hog-tied to gender hierarchies, spaces where we can shrug off relational feminism disguised as hedonic feminism in favor of hedonic queerism because the queer, at first disoriented, *can* orient itself in spaces and environments that have nothing to do with holes. Once the child is violently castrated from its mother, once the queer is violently castrated from society, the inevitability of its death does not depend upon its orientation of separateness. It dies. It dies whether it is with its mother or alone. Unfettered because it neither accepts nor reacts to dominant frames, it constructs its own understandings of self. Embodied and situated spatially, it has power to disorient and alter-orient itself, including introspective orientations, as when it fucks itself. No dominance or inequality exists when the queer fucks itself or does not fuck at all.

That a queer should wield this tool in private is of little concern to sexual citizenship in a post-*Lawrence* society that decriminalizes sexual conduct in private spaces; but, unreactive to dominant frames, it is of little concern where the introspective queer expresses itself at all, public or private. The queer constructs sexual introspective spaces in itself, embodied and disembodied at once. Its queerness is with it in all spaces. Other citizens are free to react and define themselves against the queer, free to engage it in its space or free to alter-orient themselves from it in other public and private spaces. Introspective queerism frees the queer in publics using its own introspection, not reacting to extant public-private distinctions. Consequently, it disrupts hierarchies and binarisms—public-private, dominance-submission, parent-child, wealth-poverty, married-single. Once it has been liberated from its mother—castrated, figural or otherwise, but always forcibly as with severed umbilical cords—it exists in itself, in its own liberty, before it exists with others. The primacy of this liberty is its citizenship. Normal loses meaning where there is only the self, undefined against otherness.

Marriage Equality Was Achieved through Pragmatism

Pragmatism rushes in from political lefts and rights, harmoniously, to defend tenaciously held ideologies and identities rooted in consistencies, continuities, and samenesses—historical and futuristic. Pragmatism secured marriage equality for gays and lesbians because marriage and procreation, as we understand them, transcend political orientations. To be outside of marriage and procreation is unthinkable and blasphemous, so pragmatism counsels queers that it is in our best interests to *resolve* sexual citizenship conflicts by choosing options that improve queer lives when we cannot *dissolve* systems that created the conflicts. Coerced, hedonic queerism capitulates, it appears, to pragmatism in liberal democracies.

Pragmatism helps us solve conflicts and double binds in sexual citizenship in two ways: (1) by *resolving* a particular double bind in a nonideal system by choosing temporary backlash over permanent exclusion or (2) by *dissolving* the system that created the double bind in the first place (Radin 1990, 1702). Liberal queerism aligns with the former, radical queerism with the latter. Radical queerism seeks to dissolve norm-based sexual citizenship systems. Fundamentally, the two are at odds: sexual citizenship is defined as adherence to norms, and queerism is defined as transgressing norms. Dissolving the system of sexual citizenship, which, by definition, excludes queers, may mean dissolving the idea of heteronormativity and, concomitantly, queerism itself, since queer defines itself against the normal. In its nonideal world, the pragmatic queer opts to resolve the conflict rather than dissolve the system that created it. Double binds of queer visibility illustrate pragmatism's resolution logic. Visibility invites harassment. Invisibility invites erasure. The temporary backlash of harassment is preferred over erasure, since the latter is a total exclusion from democratic life. In AIDS politics, the equivalent is "silence equals death." The logics of visibility are rooted in normalization. Once queers are commonly visible, they become more normal. The problem as I see it is that pragmatic queers focus on short-term gains, never realizing that normalization also invites death, as Butler notes: "Normalizing the queer would be, after all, its sad finish" (1994, 21). The problem with pragmatism is a misapplication of pragmatism when queers evaluate conflicts solely on the basis of what is doable without assessing the ideal and the nonideal and without realizing that all outcomes point in the same direction: silence equals death, and normalization equals death. Death now or death later? The answer is not rhetorical, since queers might choose short happy lives over long miserable ones.

Normalization of homosexuality served as the backdrop in the 1980s to two developments that placed marriage on the agenda—the AIDS crisis and the lesbian baby boom (Chauncey 2004). Gay liberation, emphasizing visibility and coming out, led to a normalizing of homosexuality in ways that caused gays to see themselves as equal. This growing sense of equality led gay liberationists to question arbitrary denials of rights. Enter AIDS. The response to the AIDS crisis not only denied gay men a litany of dignities, liberties, and equalities from the complacency-complicity of American society and institutions that turned their backs on the epidemic while gay men faced deaths that many citizens believed they ought to face but also denied dying gay men dignities and equalities in relationships they had with caregivers—partners, lovers, close friends, companions. Landlord-tenant relationships and parent-child relationships trumped queer relationships. Chauncey recounts narratives of queer men moving to big cities and contracting AIDS. On their deathbeds, companions had to interact with family members and parents, many of whom did not even know their sons were queer. Surviving companions were locked out of homes and denied personal possessions they shared with the deceased, and they were denied dignities to participate in healthcare decisions and memorial services, sometimes when they themselves were dying of AIDS and often penniless because they had sold most of their possessions to pay for healthcare services. Relationship recognition would not have solved the AIDS crisis, but it would have assuaged its impact.

Through similar injustices and indignities in the 1980s, lesbians perceived the necessities of marriage. Cultural feminists, most of whom rejected marriage as a patriarchal system, were forced to consider formal relationship recognition when the lesbian baby boom witnessed mothers and children estranged from one another after lesbian relationships dissolved or changed through incapacitations, deaths, or permanent separations (Chauncey 2004). Legal institutions privileged grandparent relationships and birth-mother relationships over second-mother relationships, even when the latter relationship was the strongest and its preservation was in the best interests of the child. Separating lesbians from their children forced cultural feminists to embrace marriage as a way to protect themselves and their families (Chauncey 2004).

Through the lens of pragmatism, both developments—the AIDS crisis and the lesbian baby boom—permanently excluded queers from their intimate relationships and families. The double bind was, on one hand, being damned by embracing and capitulating to the patriarchal, heteronormative institution of marriage and, on the other hand, being damned by estrangements from people they most cherished. The solution was to choose temporary backlashes associated with forcing their way into marriage over permanent exclusions from their loved ones. They combated temporary backlashes with homonormativity, assimilation, and pastiche imitations because marriage, we are told, guards against such estrangements. The *Obergefell* Court: "Marriage responds to the universal fear that a lonely person might call out only to find no one there. It offers the hope of companionship and understanding and assurance that while both still live there will be someone to care for the other" (2600).

Pragmatically, queers had little choice in a nonideal world other than to resolve their double binds by embracing marriage. To embrace pragmatism's other prong—dissolving the privilege of the marriage institution that created the double bind in the first place—would have meant assaulting an entrenched system of heteronormativity and facing real risks of dying alone. It is unsurprising that queers chose heterosexual death over queer death.

American pragmatists forced gays and lesbians to choose marriage equality as if there were no other choice, when, in fact, queer theorists offered a number of alternatives, namely, deconstructing marriage so that property rights, economic benefits, parenting, and other conflations are treated as separate matters of law and policy apart from marriage (Warner 1999). A queerer solution would have been to deprivilege marriage by having the state recognize only civil unions, but it violates American sensibilities of equality to have separate institutions for different groups of citizens (marriage for straights, civil unions for gays) because it relegates one group to second-class status. Even if we know that marriage equality will not in one fell swoop dissolve homophobia any more than integrating schools and integrating marriage dissolved racism, this equality logic assumes incorrectly that if you force people into the same institution, they will learn to view and treat one another the same. In these situations, the disempowered must assimilate to the empowered. The lopsidedness of assimilation constitutes erasure.

Even if we succumb to pragmatism's charms, we ignore pragmatic feminism's advice. Professor Radin, echoing Lorde, counsels, "A group that seeks liberation from a dominating system of thought should be very suspicious of adopting its categories" (1990, 1718). Marriage is heteronormativity's tool; it will not dismantle discrimination in sexual citizenship. Queers, as well as courts, adopted and legitimated a category of the dominant group with virtually no suspicion.

Infanticides: Posterity and the Fagchild

Marriage replicates a fiction. Reproductive futurism immures the legal and political debates, because we cannot imagine a future without children, so it is our greatest political concern, heteronormativity says, to protect children and ensure that our posterity has the same world we have or a better one. Straight white men enshrined future children into the Constitution. The Preamble ordains it to "secure the blessings of liberty to ourselves and our posterity." It is political suicide to question whether posterity ought to continue being the thrust of our constitutional democracy, but we allow posterity to eclipse other values, namely, liberty to ourselves and promotion of the general welfare. We overvalue the future child while Black men and Black women, queer and nonqueer, die of AIDS; while Black queers flee for their lives from Uganda and are dropped off, alone, in icy, snowy-white Wisconsin; while citizens complain about the length of Chicago's pride parade celebrating the Supreme Court's marriage decision, probably not knowing that the parade stopped for fifteen minutes because Black queers staged a die-in about Black lives; while Second Amendment and religious libertarians defend the rights of their child who slaughtered forty-nine queer citizens (mostly Black and Latinx) in an Orlando bar; while people who fuck on Florida's beaches go to jail for lascivious and lewd conduct and are stigmatized as sex criminals and shamed on sex offender registries simply because a handful of adults and a three-year-old child see them having sex, even when no one sees genitalia (no penis, no vagina) much less a vagina engulfing a penis, as if seeing other people having sex or even going through motions associated with missionary-style, man-on-woman sex is the most horrible thing a child can witness, a harm so insufferable and deeply rooted that society proscribes, through law, citizens' abilities to express sexuality in the public sphere simply because curious children ask questions and patriarchs are unwilling or unable to discuss sexualities with children, patriarchs who fetishize the pure, untarnished, innocent, desexualized child—the virgin child they claim for themselves as property to ensure that they, through their seed, live in and govern the future; while mean kids bully the fagchild because their fathers bully, terrorize, beat, and murder mothers, queers, and kids; while we slaughter animals and eat them, pretending humanity is supreme in the world rather than a cancer in it; while we pretend we are not vulnerable, that we will not die, and that, disembodied, we will live forever in a future that never comes. Enough. The hedonic queer minimizes suffering and maximizes happiness for the citizens who are now here—Black, Ugandan, animal, fagchild.

I speak not of harms children actually suffer, but of unquestioned fictitious harms children are alleged to suffer, unrealized hypothetical harms—infanticides—that murder queerism in its infancy. I do not damn the child that exists, but the emblem of the future child—the child that never comes—the fictitious child that curtails liberties of the fagchild that is here. Whom shall we murder: posterity's fagchild or the fagchild now here?

Queer Citizen

The Supreme Court established that marriage is a fundamental right. This ship has sailed no matter how much I stand on the same boat encouraging everyone to abandon it. Queers stand in the precarious position of having to defend themselves and offer an alternative to replace what they criticize, a requirement commonly accepted in Kuhnian paradigm shifts; but this position is also the same position of Black women speaking to white women and women speaking to men as Lorde describes in *Master's Tools*: "Women of today are still being called upon to stretch across the gap of male ignorance and to educate men as to our existence and our needs. This is an old and primary tool of all oppressors to keep the oppressed occupied with the master's concerns" (1984, 113). When the status quo plays its trump card—"If not this, what?" (Edelman 2004, 4)—I enter the sexual citizenship discourse feeling like a one-legged man in an ass-kicking contest.

It is one thing to dismantle a house, to be nihilistic and tear down heteronormativity; it is another to create something to replace it. Edelman is right in that we need not propose that some "good" will be assured by queerism, since nothing we call "good" can ever have any assurances. "The embrace of queer negativity, then, can have no justification if justification requires it to reinforce some positive social value; its value, instead, resides in its challenge to value as defined by the social, and thus in its radical challenge to the very value of the social itself" (2004, 6). The value of queerism is in its disruption, so I give myself permission to deconstruct heteronormativity without constructing something to replace it.

Still, I sense an obligation to offer a way forward, on balance with insecurities I feel in knowing . . . well, *knowing* nothing. I look to queerists for guidance. It is probably correct that we cannot dismantle the master's house using the master's tools, but for most of us there are not many other choices for tools. We must first envision our own tools and then have the means to create them. Queer theory does some of this work when it speculates possibilities, but we need more tools.

Queerist filmmaker John Waters—People's Pervert and Prince of Puke, who vied for the title of Filthiest Person Alive—tells us that disrupting from the inside is a better strategy, even though he disrupted from the outside throughout most of his fifty-year career. He was undeterred by the messiness of embodiment; quintessentially, I cannot un-see Divine in *Pink Flamingos* gagging on fresh dog shit squished between her teeth. But in 2015, Waters claimed in a commencement address at Rhode Island School of Design—a mainstream institution honoring his commitments to queer transgressions—that he did not abandon his queerness; the world around him changed and assimilated to him. Still, he advised graduates to transgress not as he did—from the outside—but from the inside. Maybe Waters, like political liberals, eases tensions in Lorde's sister-outsider paradoxes by normalizing the queer, but this leaves us with fewer and fewer secretive, shadowy, Baltimore kink-sex clubs where queer breeds queer. Waters lost his queer edge. He is still edgier than most people, but unlike *Pink Flamingos* (1972), his later films do not show skanky men flexing open and shut their hairy assholes.

Having earned five degrees, educating (assimilating) myself out of ignorance and poverty, I find Waters's advice to disrupt from the inside appealing. I have tools to create queer space in law and politics, if only tiny cracks where other queers can situate crowbars and pry open whatever they can to make life and death better. As a way forward, I want to identify two cracks in *Obergefell* that create space for queer legal theory. First, the Court focuses on liberty rather than equality: it defined marriage as a fundamental right. This is good because focusing on equality would have forced us to wrestle with defining "classes" of citizens for whom equality is sought, perpetuating "identities" and hegemonic assumptions about (and conflations of) the immutability and constructions of sexualities. In sexual citizenship, where the personal is assuredly the political, it is better to focus on individual liberty that allows queerness to thrive rather than equality that demands assimilation. Second, the *Obergefell* Court underscores the Constitution as a living one, stating, "[C]hanged understandings of marriage are characteristic of a Nation where new dimensions of freedom become apparent to new generations, often through perspectives that begin in pleas or protests and then are considered in the political sphere and the judicial process" (2015, 2596). Living constitutions, not constitutions controlled by dead hands, provide space for queer possibilities and disruptions from the inside, within extant legal frameworks.

There is a difference between queers meaningfully disrupting from the inside and dominant majorities allowing coopted tokens and counterfeiters to squawk. It is hard to distinguish the two when one is always on the inside and loses perspective on what it is that people other than dominant majorities actually want and need. Queerist James Franco is instructive: "To have an inside, there always needs to be an outside. The more elite the inside, the more people are on the outside. Get in there, but don't live in there. Be on both sides" (2013).

Meanwhile, I keep going back to Lorde, despite her dead-hand control, because she tells me to search within my queer self for guidance. The citizen-queer is a tool. Citizen-queers, like Lorde's sister-outsiders, exist paradoxically: citizenship defines itself in norm adherence; queer defines itself in norm transgression. Citizen-queers, at once, disrupt and embrace notions of both queer and citizen. Queer theorists incorrectly conceptualize queers operating in peripheries because queers are in the thick of it, always. Citizenship belongs to the queer if it belongs to anyone. American liberalism, hell bent on equality, extends marriage to queer citizens, even the bruised and beaten fagchild, embittered from being forced into submission and conformity, who rejects marriage's patriarchal and heteronormative machinery. If there is solace in queer liberalism's victory or in queer pragmatism's victory, it is that queers who claim marriage can redefine, ignore, destroy, or reconstruct marriage from the inside for their own purposes using their own fagchild tools.

I dedicate this essay to white, cisgendered Matthew, the fagchild I married in Toronto in 2008, and to our five-year-old, multiracial, fagchild nephew, Stacy, who came to live with us in Wisconsin in 2016.

NOTE

1 A full list of original principles is archived at https://igfculturewatch.com/category/general-information. IGF later modified the second principle to read, "We equally oppose 'progressive' claims that the only authentic LGBT position is to support increasing the scope of government, believing this is often at the expense of individual liberty, civil society and voluntary action" (https://igfculturewatch.com/about/, accessed Jan. 22, 2017). For a fuller discussion of IGF's goals and principles related to assimilation and homonormativity, see Duggan (2003, 47–51).

REFERENCES

Ahmed, Sara. 2006. *Queer Phenomenology*. Durham, NC: Duke University Press.

Andersen, Ellen Ann. 2006. *Out of the Closets and into the Courts: Legal Opportunity Structure and Gay Rights Litigation*. Ann Arbor: University of Michigan Press.

Baker v. Nelson, 409 U.S. 810 (1972).

Baskin v. Bogan, 766 F.3d. 648 (7th Cir. 2014).

Brettschneider, Marla. 2011. "Heterosexual Political Science." *PS: Political Science and Politics* 44(1): 23–26.

Burgess, Susan. 2006. "Queer (Theory) Eye for the Straight (Legal) Guy: *Lawrence v. Texas*' Makeover of *Bowers v. Hardwick*." *Political Research Quarterly* 59(3): 401–14.

Butler, Judith. 1994. "Against Proper Objects." *differences: A Journal of Feminist Cultural Studies* 6(2–3): 1–26.

Chauncey, George. 2004. *Why Marriage?* New York: Basic Books.

Duggan, Lisa. 2003. *The Twilight of Equality?* Boston: Beacon.

Edelman, Lee. 2004. *No Future: Queer Theory and the Death Drive*. Edited by M. A. Barale, J. Goldberg, M. Moon, and E. K. Sedgwick. Durham, NC: Duke University Press.

Eichner, Maxine. 2009. "Feminism, Queer Theory, and Sexual Citizenship." In *Gender Equality: Dimensions of Women's Equal Citizenship*. Edited by L. C. McClain and J. L. Grossman. New York: Cambridge University Press.

Flores, Andrew R. 2014. "National Trends in Public Opinion on LGBT Rights in the United States." Los Angeles: Williams Institute.

Flores, Andrew R. 2015. "Examining Variation in Surveying Attitudes on Same-Sex Marriage." *Public Opinion Quarterly* 79(2): 580–93.

Foucault, Michel. 2011. *The Courage of Truth*. Edited by A. I. Davidson and G. M. Burchell. Basingstoke, England: Palgrave Macmillan.

Franco, James. 2013. *Actors Anonymous*. New York: Houghton Mifflin Harcourt.

Ginsburg, Ruth Bader. 1985. "Some Thoughts on Autonomy and Equality in Relation to *Roe v. Wade*." *North Carolina Law Review* 63 (2).

Glick, Elsa. 2000. "Sex Positive: Feminism, Queer Theory, and the Politics of Transgression." *Feminist Review* 64 (Spring): 19–45.

Greenfield-Sanders, Timothy. 2013. *The Out List*. Documentary. HBO.

Health Resources and Services Administration, U.S. Department of Health and Human Services. 2015. *Ryan White CARE Act: A Legislative History* [cited July 19, 2016].

Lawrence v. Texas, 539 U.S. 558 (2003).

Lorde, Audre. 1984. "The Master's Tools Will Never Dismantle the Master's House." In *Sister Outsider*. New York: Ten Speed Press.

Obergefell v. Hodges, 135 S. Ct. 2584 (2015).

O'Rourke, Michael. 2014. "The Big Secret about Queer Theory . . ." *Inter Alia: A Journal of Queer Studies* 9: 1–14.

Perry, H. W. 1991. *Deciding to Decide: Agenda Setting in the United States Supreme Court*. Cambridge, MA: Harvard University Press.

Radin, Margaret Jane. 1990. "The Pragmatist and the Feminist." *Southern California Law Review* 63 (Sept.): 1699–1726.

Riggle, Ellen D. B., Jerry D. Thomas, and S. Rostosky Sharon. 2005. "The Marriage Debate and Minority Stress." *PS: Political Science and Politics* 38(2): 221–24.

Rogers, Henry, ed. 2006. *Art Becomes You: Parody, Pastiche, and the Politics of Art*. Birmingham, England: Article Press (Birmingham City University).

Rosenberg, Gerald N. 2008. *The Hollow Hope: Can Courts Bring About Social Change?* Chicago: University of Chicago Press.

Sherrill, Kenneth S., Carolyn M. Somerville, and Robert W. Bailey. 1992. "What Political Science Is Missing by Not Studying AIDS." *PS: Political Science and Politics* 25(4): 688–93.

Tocqueville, Alexis de. 2001. *Democracy in America*. Edited by R. D. Heffner. New York: Penguin.

U.S. v. Windsor, 133 S. Ct. 2675 (2013).

Warner, Michael. 1999. *The Trouble with Normal*. New York: Free Press.

Warner, Michael, ed. 1993. *Fear of a Queer Planet*. Minneapolis: University of Minnesota Press.

Wolf v. Walker, 986 F. Supp. 982 (W.D. Wisc. 2014).

22

You Don't Belong Here, Either

Same-Sex Marriage Politics and LGBT/Q Youth Homelessness Activism in Chicago

JASON STODOLKA

"Anthony Kennedy is my Spirit Animal" read an optimistic homemade sign being held above the crowd of hundreds gathered on the steps of the U.S. Supreme Court Building on the morning of Friday, June 26, 2015.[1] It was only 9:45 a.m., but already so many had gathered that one lane of First Street had been closed down to accommodate the crowd, and additional spectators were being asked to gather across the street instead. Those assembled—some activists who had worked for years to gain nationwide legal rights to same-sex marriage, others young staffers at the nearby congressional office buildings—were overwhelmingly made up of people anticipating that Justice Kennedy would again side with Justices Ginsburg, Breyer, Sotomayor, and Kagan to expand access to marriage rights in the case of *Obergefell v. Hodges* (2015). Half an hour later, interns ran from the building carrying summaries of the Court's decision to meet the onlookers and the media, and moments later the crowd erupted in cheers as they learned that the Court had indeed split along the expected lines, with Justice Kennedy authoring the decision that proclaimed that the Constitution grants same-sex couples the right to be married. Gathered members of the Gay Men's Chorus of Washington, DC, initiated the singing of "The Star-Spangled Banner," and the chant "Love Conquers Hate" filled the Capitol area. This final resolution to the legal question of same-sex marriage came just days shy of the forty-sixth anniversary of the Stonewall Riots that would be celebrated that weekend, in cities across the globe, as the beginning point of the gay liberation movement.

That same weekend, though, untold thousands of the most needy within the LGBT/Q community were left to sleep on the streets: LGBT/Q youth experiencing homelessness and other unstable housing situations. Some of them, in addition to having nowhere to call home, were cited or arrested for crimes of survival such as public urination, petty theft as they attempted to secure nourishment, or prostitution as they tried to secure some sort of income. Many of these young people have been forced into this condition and struggle on a daily basis to achieve "legitimate" work and housing. The contrast between the celebration of same-sex marriage that occurred on the steps of the Supreme Court Building and the dark realities faced by youth experiencing homelessness illustrates how the concerns of the LGBT mainstream and its overriding focus on same-sex marriage intersect with a self-styled queer subculture within the LGBT/Q social movement that is critical of this myopic outlook. A number of queer theorists have articulated these critiques and suggest that the movement and its vision of a liberationist politics is indeed damaged by the marriage focus. But how does the intersection of these currents in activism look on the ground? Examining how LGBT/Q youth homelessness activists interact with the marriage machine that dominates mainstream activism can bring these ideas into conversation with each other and contribute to an appreciation of how different factions of a social movement can operate in concert with each other, act in opposition to each other, and learn from one another. Additionally, studying the LGBT/Q social movement using social- scientific methods presents opportunities to bring empirical evidence to bear on the theoretical critiques of the role same-sex marriage has played in the movement's development.

Extant literature on social movements provides a good basis from which to begin a social-scientific analysis of the LGBT/Q movement, but also presents the opportunity to imagine how work in this area can help broaden a more general body of knowledge. A significant portion of the scholarship on social movements focuses on measuring movement effectiveness—assessing the ability of social movement actors and organizations to effectively advocate and pressure government to adopt policy as well as affect outcomes beyond policy (McAdam 1999; Andrews 1997). Several of the findings from this work are applicable to the work of the LGBT/Q social movement, especially in regards to the politics of same-sex-marriage recognition and the activism on behalf of queer youth experiencing homelessness, including establishing "organizational repertoires" (Clemmens 1993); affecting changes in the way government treats members of certain groups of people (whether inclusion in decision-making processes or mere awareness of people's interests) (Piven and Cloward 1977; Pellow and Brulle 2005; Kriesi et al. 1995); influencing how government decisions are made by shaping the levels of expertise required by policymakers (Meyer 2009); affecting how the executive branch and bureaucrats implement policy (Ingram and Ingram 2005); altering the information available to policymakers and bureaucrats (Mettler 2005); sharing frames, organizational coalitions, participants, and leadership with other movements (Meyer and Whittier 1994); and affecting conceptualizations of citizenship and democracy by mobilizing on behalf of securing the rights of citizenship for the disenfranchised (Katzenstein 2005; Reese 2005).

Furthermore, scholarship increasingly takes account of the internal dynamics of movements and movement organizations, including inquiry dealing with the importance of identity and identity processes and how they shape and are shaped by the goals, priorities, strategies, tactics, and rhetoric that movements use in pursuit of social and political change.[2] Identity is something inherent within social movement actors—both individuals and groups (collective identity)—that is exercised in the strategic decision making of movements, and movement participants have a multivalent understanding of identity and can embrace, critique, and move beyond their identity (Melucci 1995; Lichterman 1999). The identity process thus informs choices regarding goals, objectives, and strategies, without necessarily determining them. This suggests that groups and organizations identify objectives and strategies based on what their collective identity processes have suggested as desirable.

In the LGBT/Q social movement, and especially regarding same-sex-marriage activism and those who are critical of it, identity manifests itself as a (sometimes real, sometimes imagined) differentiation between the LGBT and the Queer. Appreciating tangible differences between the politics of those who identify as gay, lesbian, bisexual, or transgender, on the one hand, and those who identify as queer, on the other, has become useful to scholars thinking about the role identity plays in social movements. While most in the American mainstream, and many in the gay mainstream, do not even recognize the differences in identity between these two groups, they are having real and meaningful effects on how the queer/gay movement sees itself. The queer subculture within the gay movement is becoming larger and more vocal and making demands of organizations, goals, and strategies. They are affecting what causes the movement takes on and whom the movement sees as its benefactors (e.g., Lichterman 1999).

As many have noted—from John D'Emilio's (1983) study of early organizations like the Mattachine Society and Daughters of Bilitis in the 1950s and 1960s through works on more recent activism such as those of Gary Mucciaroni (2008) and Amy Stone (2012)—there is a consistent and identifiable theme of an assimilationist faction of LGBT people and a liberationist element in opposition. This consistent tension in the LGBT/Q movement also holds significant explanatory power when considering same-sex marriage activism and the queer critique offered by both academics and activists. Assimilationists have long called for viewing lesbians and gay men as "normal," "respectable" Americans, being hardly distinguishable from any other person. Liberationists, though, have sought social change and a reimagination of the place of sexuality in the American consciousness through unapologetically contentious actions that challenge established norms (e.g., D'Emilio 1983; Stein 2000; Johnson 2004; Boyd 2005; Gallo 2006). Furthermore, a historically based sexual shame (Warner 1999) and the growing strength of neoliberalism (Duggan 2003) have contributed to what Duggan (2003) refers to as homonormativity: "a politics that does not contest dominant heteronormative assumptions and institutions, but upholds and sustains them, while promising the possibility of a demobilized gay constituency and a privatized, depoliticized gay culture anchored in domesticity and consumption" (50). The new world order that is envisioned by this homonormativity is one where those lesbians and gays who are able to do so become a part of the new upper-middle-class elite, while the rest of us misbehaving queers become the permanent underclass. This, she argues, runs directly contrary to the political, social, and cultural consciousness that lesbians and gays have tried to build for generations. The fight for same-sex marriage recognition fits firmly within this homonormative politics by offering same-sex couples the trappings of respectability and promoting normative social, familial, and economic production.

The LGBT/Q political universe that these scholars and many others are addressing is one that is divided. On one side is a clearly dominant, moneyed, mainstream LGBT community. While challenging the concepts of heteronormative sexual behavior, this group does little to question other social forces such as male privilege, white privilege, and the privileged position of the wealthy. The political interests of this LGBT mainstream reflect its acquiescence to these ideas; they are largely the interests of upper-middle-class white men. The other side is a queer population that resists the normalizing effects of gay and lesbian identity. Queer is also a political project that advocates changes in political, social, and cultural institutions and processes that achieve social justice for a population that includes LGBT people but also reaches beyond them to include all other people with nonnormative sexual and gender practices and identities as well as women, the poor, racial and ethnic minorities, the physically and mentally disabled, etc. Queer social identity is a resisting of the identity politics practiced by the LGBT mainstream.

Social scientists who have addressed the assimilationist/liberationist split in LGBT/Q activism (and scholarship) are often less critical of the mainstream, offering a more nuanced explanation. Their more sympathetic approach to analyzing both "sides" of the movement is a product of their empirical study of movement organizations and activism and a deeper appreciation of the structural political realities that shape the goals, priorities, tactics, and rhetoric of LGBT/Q organizations. Social science scholarship suggests that queer people have a multidimensional understanding of their own LGBT/Q identity, that their own understanding and expression of that identity vary according to circumstance, and that movement organizations strategically alter emphasis on commonality and difference—that identity can be "deployed at the collective level as a political strategy" (Lichterman 1999; Bernstein 1997). From this perspective, the different goals, priorities, tactics, and rhetoric embraced by the LGBT mainstream and queer radicals are not predominantly a reflection of different visions of what is ideal and right, but rather are significantly influenced by political considerations of what is deemed possible. Both the critique of same-sex-marriage politics that posits it as heternormative and the social-scientific insistence that tactical political considerations are important to movements manifest themselves in the case of youth homelessness activism.

The issue of LGBT/Q youth homelessness both illustrates the pitfalls identified by theorists and activists who are critical of the same-sex-marriage fight and reveals the need for a more complex understanding of marriage as a component of the larger LGBT/Q social movement. In Chicago, youth homelessness gained widespread attention following the Gay Pride celebrations of 2011, which went sour at the end. The morning of Sunday, June 26, went much as it had in previous years: the Pride Parade marched through Boystown while hundreds of thousands of spectators looked on. Bars filled with revelers and private parties ensued. But when night came, all of the expectations of the party planners, the bar owners, and Chicago's gay and lesbian elite were dealt a major blow. Reality had come to roost in Boystown as people from across the city—LGBT, queer, and straight; black, white, and brown—decided they would stay and party too, and not necessarily in the bars. Many stayed and continued the celebration of sexual liberation and queer community in the streets of Boystown, and as more alcohol was consumed, the festivities became louder and less contained. At some point, a "riot" broke out at the intersection of Clark and Belmont Streets, where, it is rumored, a police officer was injured while attempting to control the crowds. The events of the evening were cast alongside a number of stabbings that occurred in the weeks preceding and following the parade as evidence that violence had reached epidemic proportions in the neighborhood and extreme steps were needed to curb the chaos. The target of these cries, it became rapidly clear, was poor and homeless LGBT/Q young people ("Third Boystown Stabbing" 2011; Terri Lin, personal correspondence, August 7, 2013).

As the events surrounding the Pride Parade in 2011 reveal, same-sex-marriage politics did indeed work against queer social-movement activism and a queer politics that addresses issues such as the needs of LGBT/Q youth experiencing homelessness. They affirm theoretical critiques that have been leveled against the so-called marriage-equality activists—that they are elites who advocated on behalf of their own self-interests, that marriage is a flawed institution and should be ignored, that marriage as a goal favors normativity and eschews the nonnormative spaces that the queer community was founded on. The needs of homeless queer youth were being ignored, to a large extent, and certainly underfunded, while millions of dollars were being devoted to the marriage struggle. Even worse than this, though, the same mainstream forces that kept marriage at the top of the LGBT/Q social movement's political agenda were being hostile toward these same homeless youth they were failing to serve. Mainstream LGBT organizations like the Human Rights Campaign and state-level counterparts (Equality Illinois, locally) had long built their work around the marriage issue, and when youth homelessness has been recognized, it has often been paid only lip service and in only a vague and broad sense. On the ground in the community, business owners and mainstream activists used code words like "riff-raff," "hoodlum," and "thugs" to complain about the youth of color who are poor and experiencing homelessness and how they get in the way of the "larger" goals of the community: proving ourselves "normal" and just like straight people and achieving permission to participate in their greatest rite of passage, marriage. Their normalizing agenda knows no bounds. Youth are policed on the streets, kicked out of the gay community center for even minor rules infractions (where the LGBT mainstream, critiques point out, failed to incorporate open-use youth space or activity space in their plans), and barred from local businesses. The irony is lost on bar owners who are openly hostile toward these young people yet encourage us to boycott the vaguely Russian Stolichnaya vodka because the Russian government is harmful to our community.

Community activists estimated that fifteen thousand Chicago young people experience homelessness every year, and that they are disproportionately LGBT/Q—the Center for American Progress (2010) confirms this with their finding that 20–40 percent of the homeless youth population is LGBT/Q (versus 5–10 percent LGBTQ youth in the general population). Furthermore, among these LGBTQ youth who are experiencing homelessness, a disproportionately large number are also people of color and come from households that have experienced long-term economic problems. With fewer than two hundred shelter beds in the city of Chicago to serve all homeless youth, many of the LGBTQ youth see little hope for a safe place to sleep most nights, much less a broader community discussion of the intersectional needs these LGBT and queer youth are facing and the potential for long-term solutions rather than strictly emergency service provision.

The problem of LGBT/Q youth homelessness is not as simple as many might picture, and the term "homeless" itself is often used as a catch-all to describe people experiencing a variety of unstable housing circumstances. The homeless are those who, indeed, are without a home and are forced to sleep on the streets or take their chances accessing a bed at a (sometimes unsafe and homophobic/transphobic) shelter. There are also, though, the borderline homeless who are relying on the goodwill of friends and acquaintances who allow them to sleep on couches and floors—but these situations are highly unstable, often explicitly temporary, and certainly do very little to address the underlying needs that exist in the lives of these individuals. Then, additionally, there are "street youth" who are often categorized as homeless. These are youth who have secured more stable housing but have often faced other, more extreme forms of homelessness, have relationships with friends who are still experiencing homelessness, and still face the same financial hardships that limit access to food and other goods and services. This variation in the forms homelessness takes contributes to the complexity of solving the problem (perhaps partially explaining why many organizations are hesitant to embrace it) and shapes the activism that develops around the issue. There is no "one-off" solution that will ensure that homelessness is no longer a concern for LGBT/Q youth and their supporters.

Two cases help reveal the shapes activism and the movement seeking to address the problem of homelessness among young LGBT/Q people have taken.

The resistance to the group Take Back Boystown demonstrates the negative forces and hostile discourse that brought increased public attention to the plight of youth experiencing homelessness. The efforts of the Safe and Affirming Space Serving Youth (SASSY) and the volunteers that staff its drop-in program show the work that many activists engage in and the array of potential solutions to the problems faced by these youth. Both contribute to a nuanced understanding of youth homelessness and the ways activists work in, around, through, and against more mainstream LGBT/Q political efforts.

Case 1: Take Back Boystown and Resistance

Following the violent and chaotic events of the early summer months in 2011, the Boystown and city-wide LGBT communities erupted with scapegoating and "solutions." The main target of those seeking a clear and easy solution was neighborhood "outsiders"—often young people and (either explicitly or implicitly) people of color. The LGBT community center and other service-providing entities were targeted for supposedly "attracting" violent people to the Boystown area—often explicitly assuming that the violent outsiders were coming to the neighborhood from the south and west sides of the city (predominantly home to people of color). Many of those leading the overtly racist and classist arguments about violence in the area rallied around the nascent group Take Back Boystown, which championed itself as the sane and rational voice of the people living in the Boystown area.

Though Take Back Boystown never really manifested itself as anything more than a page on Facebook, it was instrumental in its earliest mobilizations of those concerned about violence (particularly those interested in placing the blame solely at the feet of homeless young LGBT/Q people of color) and getting them to attend neighborhood association and community policing meetings (Chicago Alternative Policing Strategy—CAPS, a program of the Chicago Police—was central to this process). The banner of Take Back Boystown, both then and now, is used by supporters and detractors as a blanket term that refers not to an organization as such but to a loosely allied group of people with shared conceptions of the problems facing the Boystown community and the appropriate solutions to those problems. In addition to the Facebook page that operates under the Take Back Boystown name, the blog *Crime in Wrigleyville and Boystown* (2015) similarly cites police crime data as "evidence" that there is a problem with outsiders producing chaos and that it must be addressed with more policing of and wariness toward those who spend time in the neighborhood. These efforts have resulted in increased police presence by the Chicago Police Department as well as increased security both at businesses and in public places (on the street) with privately hired security firms. More important in the story of the lives of young LGBT/Q people, especially those of color, was the coalescence around the idea that they were to blame for what other community members saw as an increase in violence.

The racial animus of these "concerned citizens" is clear. Members of the Take Back Boystown group have been quoted as referring to LGBT/Q youth of color as "mobs" with a "ghetto mentality" who are "all black." Characterizing these youth as individuals devolved to referring to them as "thugs" and "fucking monkeys" (Daniel-McCarter 2012; "Third Boyston Stabbing" 2011). Like-minded citizens have been quoted calling youth "hoodlums" and in comments on some articles they refer to "bad youth" who use the LGBT community center as a "day care center for the abandoned south side youths" ("Residents Question" 2011; "Man Stabbed" 2011). Though most offensive Take Back Boystown posts and comments have been removed by the page's moderator, and the Facebook page seems to be all but defunct today (with the last post occurring in July of 2012), other endeavors like the *Crime in Wrigleyville and Boystown* (2015) blog continue to drive the debate of safety and belonging in Boystown. The racist, ageist, and classist comments from the CAPS meetings, community meetings, and online forums come from the same voices central to making same-sex marriage the dominant issue of the LGBT/Q social movement's agenda. Property owners in the area readily identify themselves as gay, as supporters of gay people, and as supporters of gay marriage before they blame people of color and youth experiencing homelessness. Similarly, the owners of gay bars and other businesses—those hosting "marriage equality" fundraisers—announce themselves at meetings as a sort of "back story" to their assertions that policing and punitive actions for loiterers are necessary. These individuals conceive of an LGBT community that is suffering only because of their nonnormative sexual and gender identities. Daniel-McCarter (2012) makes this connection even more directly: "It is the private and business-generated wealth present in 'Boystown' that, in part, created the political power to pass [Illinois'] civil unions statute as well as the financial support to sustain non-profit organizations providing the services young people need" (6). The moneyed and business elite of the community then turns its back on the very people who need the services these organizations provide and for whose "equal rights" they are supposedly fighting. The antagonism that business, bar, and property owners express toward "loitering" youth can be understood to some extent as self-interest, as these community members seek to protect the investments they have made. But this self-interested protectionism that comes at the cost of oppressing young queer people of color is precisely what critics take issue with—a mainstream LGBT consciousness in which individuals cannot or will not look beyond their own immediate interests to recognize the broader good of all LGBT/Q people.

It is important to note that there is a significant community of progressive LGBT and queer activists who resist the mainstream discourse vilifying LGBT/Q youth experiencing homelessness. Indeed, large and influential organizations with a broad policy agenda, such as the Civil Rights Agenda, have been founded to provide a progressive alternative to large mainstream LGBT political organizations. But it is, nonetheless, moneyed LGBT elites, including many business and property owners, who make up the core of the LGBT mainstream—whether through direct activism or through funding. Through access to policy makers and financial resources, these leaders of the LGBT mainstream shaped the discourse on civil unions and same-sex marriage. They similarly shape the discourse surrounding LGBT youth experiencing homelessness—portraying them as villains rather than community members in need.

Segments of the progressive and radical LGBT/Q activist community in Chicago immediately began to push back against the rhetoric of blaming queer homeless youth of color for the "safety" concerns of Boystown residents. In response to the online attacks made by people associated with Take Back Boystown and those who sympathized with that point of view, many used the same online outlets to address the racist, ageist, and classist assumptions that were coloring much of the blame-ridden discourse, while others penned blog posts and opinion pieces in printed and online news publications. Activists also realized the need to organize a critical mass of those who opposed the racist and classist youth blaming to attend community meetings and physically show that there was a segment of the community who did not agree with that simplistic understanding of the problems at play.

One of those voices was that of Terri Lin, an activist working with youth, who took part in the community meetings addressing the "safety" issues as well as contributed to blogs. Terri is a gender-queer-identified individual[3] in their early thirties and of mixed Asian and white racial background. They cite their move to Chicago in their twenties as the dawning of their LGBT activism; they realized they were a "specific kind of minority" that they had very little knowledge of or connection with (lesbian/gay). Seeing unequal treatment of lesbians and gay men, they felt there was not enough being done to address the inequalities. Terri's activism over the past several years has primarily taken place through early work with the Gay Liberation Network in Chicago and later the Safe and Affirming Space Serving Youth (SASSY—discussed below). Their story of activism mirrors that of many other activists working in the area of youth homelessness; they were initially mobilized into activism through the issue of same-sex marriage and later turned their focus to more "queer" issues (Terri Lin, personal correspondence, August 7, 2013).

Terri identifies classism as the biggest issue facing the LGBT/Q community in Chicago, and sees LGBT/Q youth homelessness as a concrete manifestation of this. "What makes this so sad," they say about the mainstream LGBT movement, "is that they're talking about inclusion but they're blind to their own discrimination." They think that most people in the community realize that there is an issue with poverty and homelessness, but the focus on crime and disorder has a negative impact on the openness and inclusivity of Boystown and the whole LGBT/Q community. "People don't realize how much a part of the problem they are," they say (ibid.).

Terri also realizes, though, that their understanding of issues such as racism, classism, and ageism as they affect poverty and homelessness comes as a product of being engaged with the LGBT/Q community and growing as an activist over the previous five years. Their early activist work was as a member of organizations that focused primarily on the issue of same-sex marriage. They were first mobilized to act by Chicago protests of California's Proposition 8 in 2008. Through the initial protests and demonstrations, they were connected to organizations that were participating in the state and national efforts for same-sex relationship recognition (at the time, civil unions were the primary goal locally). Terri later participated, as a member of these groups, in a sit-in at the Cook County Clerk's Office in Chicago protesting the office's refusal to issue marriage licenses to same-sex couples. It was through this activism that Terri became aware of the extent to which inequalities and oppression permeate even the LGBT/Q social movement (ibid.).

As Terri became more aware of the privilege that dominates the mainstream LGBT movement, they began to focus their energies elsewhere. The violence and uproar surrounding the 2011 Pride Parade brought these issues more into focus and allowed them to look outside of the mainstream as an outlet for activist energies. While the groups they were initially involved with were focusing on "gay rights" and military service, Terri was becoming more and more concerned about the racism and classism that were permeating debates over "safety" in the LGBT/Q community. After trying, but failing, to get their groups to change focus, they left. They were becoming more interested in causes that pursue social justice issues—work that uses an intersectional lens to understand inequality and oppression. Terri became involved in efforts like SASSY and others in the Boystown area that seek inclusion and safety for all people—LGBT/Q, the handicapped, people of all ages and income levels. They say that their involvement with these groups and organizations has been guided by their interests, but that their activism has also shaped their interests and concerns as a queer person (ibid.).

Looking back at their direct activism around same-sex marriage and the critique of the marriage fight that they developed along the way, Terri sees both positive and negative. Marriage should be an issue that organizations reluctantly address. Ideally, LGBT/Q organizations should focus on eliminating the legal institution of marriage and making the benefits of marriage available to everyone. Same-sex marriage, though, will be a step along this path. The LGBT/Q community should not be spending all of its time and resources on fighting the marriage battle, though, since there are many other populations that need more attention. They see same-sex marriage as an issue that has both helped and hindered different aspects of the broader movement. Some organizations benefit from the marriage fight; so much national attention on the issue brings validity to the other issues that they address, and using marriage as its activism centerpiece brings in activists (especially first-time activists) attracted to popular and well-publicized issues. Simultaneously, though, other efforts like SASSY (discussed below) are mostly hindered by the marriage debate. SASSY and other entities such as the Crib and Broadway Youth Center (all of which serve youth experiencing homelessness and street youth) engage with the problem of youth homelessness both by providing direct services to those at risk (shelter and meals as well as social work, education, and job-training services) and by engaging in political dialogues in the community and across the city about the needs of LGBT/Q youth. Goals like inclusivity are overshadowed, though, and their projects have had to compete with marriage for limited resources. Terri foresees direct and immediate benefits with the legalization of same-sex marriage—but this is both a blessing and a curse. Marriage rights extend legal benefits and allow the movement as a whole to focus on other issues, they say, but they also allow those with privilege—who see marriage as a sort of final hurdle to achieving full "equality"—to retreat from the social and political work needed to address the needs of all LGBT/Q people, a sentiment reiterated by movement leaders such as NGLTF's Rae Carey (Terri Lin, personal correspondence, August 20, 2013; Carey 2012).

Vicki Rice is another activist who engaged in the resistance to the scapegoating and racism of individuals and groups like Take Back Boystown. Vicki—a Black lesbian in her early fifties—is a leader in the Black LGBT/Q community and served as the executive director of an LGBTQ community group that focuses its energy on Chicago's South Side. She identifies a number of problems facing LGBT/Q Chicago, including many of those cited as central to the crisis of LGBT/Q youth homelessness: employment discrimination, access to healthcare, jobs, school safety, violence, and housing. Through her work within her own organization and her coalitional work with other groups around Chicago, Vicki seeks to raise awareness of these issues in the Black community as well as address potential solutions with other LGBT/Q groups (Vicki Rice, personal correspondence, August 13, 2013).

Concerning the issues of race, LGBT/Q communities of color, and youth homelessness, Vicki was a member of a community task force of LGBTQ community leaders that came together in response to the violence and subsequent neighborhood outcries surrounding the Pride Parade of 2011. The task force was directed by Vicki's own organization, along with two others that focus primarily on service provision for LGBT/Q youth experiencing homelessness and the Institute for Research on Race and Public Policy at the University of Illinois at Chicago (UIC), and was funded through a grant from the UIC Institute for Policy and Civic Engagement. The project—Engaging Chicago LGBTQ Communities in a Community Discussion about Racism, Public Safety, and the Rights of

Young People—issued a report in the summer of 2012 documenting its findings. Youth engaged by the task force cited a notable change in the once safe and accepting Boystown following the violence of the summer of 2011 and the CAPS meetings that took place as a response. The task force also met with youth workers about policing, surveillance, and institutional violence. The report makes three specific policy recommendations:

1. "That people and institutions interested in, and responsible for, addressing neighborhood violence and youth safety involve youth directly and authentically in the process of devising and implementing solutions."
2. "That the suggestions that youth propose [e.g., free spaces where youth are in charge; free education, literacy, and legal resources; financially accessible youth spaces; housing options; cultural institutions; interactive community activities, etc.] be funded and implemented."
3. "That organizations serving youth in the city of Chicago, especially those serving LGBTQ youth of color, develop an internal assessment and policy regarding policing and surveillance of their facilities . . . based on data and research about the impact and research about the consequences of policing on rates of violence and crime, and the effectiveness of policing for violence prevention." (ibid.; UIC IRRPP 2012)

This report has acted as a rallying cry for those in the community who are concerned with youth homelessness, and individuals and organizations have used it to assess the state of current projects to address these concerns, but the undertaking of specific and discrete new projects that the report emphasizes has been slow in coming. As Vicki notes, it has been hard to build sustained efforts to address these concerns with so many dedicating their efforts and resources to same-sex-marriage advocacy (ibid.).

Vicki's views on same-sex marriage reflect both what the queer critique posits and the points made by other activist leaders about the instrumentality of the issue. She says that marriage is certainly not what the LGBT/Q community needs most right now and that it is the product of aloofness on the part of many leaders who fail to recognize the real needs of many in the community. She also says, though, that the marriage issue became more of a hurdle that must be overcome than completely a source of diversion from more important work. She also makes a unique argument about the utility of the marriage issue in a broader political sense. While marriage indeed does not address the most pressing needs of the LGBT/Q community, "in many ways it's a soft punt," she says. It is an issue that everyone else in society can understand, sending a signal that many LGBT/Q people want to assimilate into mainstream American culture and therefore making America as a whole more accepting of all LGBT/Q people and political issues. Indeed, that is the primary reason Vicki herself was involved in marriage activism: the board of directors for the organization she worked for determined that marriage was a useful political goal. She accepted their directive because she also sees the benefit of her membership feeling included in this moment of the overall LGBT/Q movement, a moment for the Black LGBT/Q community to feel connected and be embraced by the mainstream. "So here we are," she says. A lot of the people she worked with and for did not really care much about the specific demands surrounding marriage, but were engaging in the fight for the potential benefits that might be produced (ibid.).

Case 2: Safe and Affirming Space Serving Youth (SASSY)

While Vicki's views of the potential benefits of the marriage debate for the broader movement address the long-term, big-picture goals of LGBT/Q people, one of the immediate, on-the-ground concerns that is repeatedly cited by those working with homeless and street youth is the use of space in Boystown and the lack of adequate space resources for youth. Boystown is primarily an entertainment district that encompasses for-profit enterprises such as a variety of bars and clubs (well over a dozen), restaurants, boutiques, sex shops, a bathhouse, etc. For a variety of reasons, these spaces are not available for the youth: many are not old enough to enter age-restricted spaces (age eighteen for spaces that contain sexually explicit material and twenty-one for those spaces serving alcohol); profound economic hardship often means these youth are unable to partake in consumer interactions, resulting in their being barred from entry; and stigma attached to both youth and homelessness/economic hardship produces unfriendly and unwelcoming environments. Though Boystown is cited as a space that is safe and welcoming for those who resist the social constructions of gender and sexuality that govern mainstream life, in reality it is only a place for those who fit in a narrow segment of nonconformists and can afford to engage in the commercial enterprises that drive the community.

In 2007, after years of fundraising by community leaders, a 175,000-square-foot community center opened in Boystown. In many ways the new center addressed many of the critiques cited above about a lack of noncommercial space in the community for endeavors that did not involve businesses or a consumer-driven interaction with the neighborhood. But the center is still failing homeless youth. The policing by staff at the community center often mirrors that of police on the streets in its insistence on normative standards of appearance and behavior. Likewise, the facility's operators feel pressure to maintain an attractive space and environment that is welcoming to paying patrons of its space (community members must pay, for example, even to use the open gym space), donors, and patrons of the attached grocery store. There is also little free space available that allows homeless youth to just sit and pass their time or interact with friends—whether they are biding their time between events and programs sponsored by the center (from recreation to therapy to job training) or simply escaping harsh conditions outside, youth "loitering" is only allowed in the main lobby and in a remote hallway, where youth are "reminded" to keep quiet or face expulsion from the facility.

In the summer of 2012, the Northalsted Business Alliance (the group of Boystown business owners) made it even clearer that homeless youth of color were not welcome in the area when they hired a private security team to patrol the streets of Boystown, reflecting the broader animus throughout the neighborhood. After the incidents of the previous summer and complaints by area residents noting "large groups of loitering youth," the business alliance brought in the security team to make the area feel more "safe and welcoming" (GoPride. com 2012). As noted above, these actions reflect economic self-interest, but are nonetheless antagonistic toward members of the community this organization claims to represent. The introduction of the new private security measures in the neighborhood became the catalyst for further debate about whether the business owners and residents were more concerned about the safety and security of patrons and residents or whether the true aim was to police queer behavior. As Terri Lin points out, "people—including poor youth—need space to freely explore their gender and sexuality." If they do not have the resources and options available to do this exploration in private, the public becomes the place where their discoveries must unfold. Some complaints by community members about youth of color who are making a lot of noise in public places—perhaps "voguing" or "reading" each other (improvised practices that come from drag culture, often involving verbose and over-exaggerated speech and physicality)—are being leveraged to deny the gender and sexual fluidity and exploration on which a political LGBT/Q consciousness was founded.

Activists working on the issue of youth homelessness seek to expand the social and cultural places where LGBT/Q youth have the freedom to live the loud and idiosyncratic lives that they find attractive. In doing so, they insist that their work must contain two simultaneous components: the public advocacy that challenges the status quo of community operations that are both underserving and antagonistic toward the at-risk youth and the provision of direct services that address these youths' needs. One institution in the community that plays this role is the Safe and Affirming Space Serving Youth (SASSY). SASSY is a biweekly drop-in program operated out of the basement of a Boystown community church. Activists who volunteer with SASSY cook a meal and facilitate the open-use space for several hours every other Saturday. SASSY also incorporates activities such as board games, video games, a nail salon, creative writing sessions, and a "clothes closet" that offers youth free clothing donated by community members. The youth who utilize the program, however, are not required to engage in any activity and can simply use the space for the meal provided and use the time to sleep in a safe and warm facility.

In the winter of 2012–2013, SASSY went through a reorganization to better allow activists and volunteers to address the needs of the youth who were utilizing their services. Central to this reorganization was a more theory- and research-driven understanding of the work they were doing and better training methods for those who volunteer with the program. All SASSY volunteers must attend a training seminar and at least one "trial" SASSY Saturday before they become volunteers. Other trainings in conflict deescalation and antiviolence are offered as well. Central to these trainings is the idea that homeless youth are constantly policed by systems and institutions and therefore SASSY is a place where there is minimal policing, punitive discipline is not used, and the youth who utilize the program are given a voice in how it is managed. Each SASSY Saturday also comes with a very specific set of roles that each volunteer is expected to perform. While this reimagining necessitated a brief stoppage in the drop-in program (instead, carry-out meals were provided to needy youth), the break allowed organizers to revisit their operating procedures and structure their program in a way that addressed the underlying needs of homeless and street youth while also being guided by best practices that advise against over-policing of youth in crisis.

Sid Gordon was one of the leaders of the reimagined SASSY drop-in program. She is a straight woman in her fifties who moved to the Boystown area and became aware of and involved in LGBT/Q youth outreach being performed by others after meeting some homeless and street youth at a chili cook-off being hosted at the church that operates SASSY. After a year of dedicated activism, she was central to the discussions about changing the way the program operated and took on a leadership role as the program reopened. Sid received a small stipend for her (supposedly part-time) work, but often dedicated full-time hours to the project and sometimes spent evenings on the streets of Boystown interacting with youth and encouraging them to come to a SASSY Saturday. Through this work she has come to see trans* activism as one of the most important issues in which the LGBT/Q social movement must engage. Her own experiences of purposefully avoiding groups of homeless and street youth in the early months of her time as a Boystown resident help her understand the reactionary attitudes of other residents. But she also sees how embracing the humanity of these youth leads to a greater appreciation of the difficulties they encounter and makes her want to help (Sid Gordon, personal correspondence, August 15, 2013).

Concerning the issue of same-sex marriage as a focus of the LGBT/Q social movement, Sid says she has always been pro-marriage but was not an active advocate for marriage laws. She sees marriage as an easy target for activism whereas addressing issues like youth homelessness involves implicating the LGBT/Q community itself in contributing to these embarrassing situations. Nonetheless, she sees the two issues as separate entities that have little bearing on each other—youth have little interest in marriage, it being "the least of their worries"; and in her mind marriage advocacy does not seem to have taken away from the actual work of addressing youths' needs. While she would like to see more people engaged in the projects that directly serve the needs of street youth and those with unstable housing, she sees both this work and marriage activism as part of a larger project that aims at creating a society that is fully accepting of LGBT/Q people (ibid.).

Eli Taylor, another volunteer and leader with SASSY, speaks of an outlook that illustrates a queer ethos of human compassion that informs his volunteerism and activism. Eli is a white gay man in his early forties. Though he does not see himself as an activist, he works with SASSY and a number of other efforts that supply meals and other vital resources to needy youth, elderly individuals, and women and children fleeing situations of domestic violence. Like Sid, Eli was part of the impetus behind the restructuring of SASSY to better align the program's practices with antiviolence and antipolicing social work philosophies. Using tactics and ideas learned from working with anti–domestic violence programs, he has contributed most to the leadership structure that the program now uses and has stepped in as the volunteer coordinator (Eli Taylor, personal correspondence, October 7, 2013).

For Eli, same-sex marriage was the number one issue facing the LGBT/Q community and social movement. It was not that same-sex marriage was the most important goal, though; rather, the issue grew so large that it got in the way of other work that needed the movement's attention. He also sees the effects of the issue in his work with youth: the rhetoric of the Right sends the message to already socially disadvantaged youth that their lives and their love is less legitimate than those of straight people, and this message needs to be defeated. With constant attention to the fact that LGBT/Q people did not have equal access to the institution of marriage, the discourse opposing marriage and same-sex love was "just another hammer making them feel like they're not good enough," he says. While he concedes that the marriage fight has diverted money away from LGBT/Q youth programs and that the picture of marital and family bliss is one that many homeless youth cannot identify with, he still finds the antimarriage vitriol of opponents more damning in the lives of these youth. Likewise, while direct service provision attends to some of the immediate needs these youth are experiencing, the fight for same-sex marriage is also important for sending the social/cultural message that LGBT/Q people are "just as good" as—and valued as much as—straight people. The issue of same-sex marriage, he says, has garnered so much attention—with opponents challenging even the worth of LGBT/Q people as human beings—that the fight for marriage rights and recognition was necessary to combat this message and reaffirm to LGBT/Q youth (especially those who have been kicked out of their family homes) that LGBT/Q lives have value (ibid.).

The complex story of the marriage fight's benefits and hindrances to addressing the needs of LGBT/Q youth experiencing homelessness that Sid and Eli note are again reiterated by another member of the SASSY leadership: Carol Thompson. Carol, the pastor at the church that sponsors and houses SASSY, is not only a leader for the program but also an influential voice in the political advocacy for young queer people in the community. Carol's personal story again reflects the common idea that activism around issues such as youth homelessness is part of a journey and an evolutionary process that involves becoming more aware of the issues that need attending to as one becomes an activist. A large part of her motivation to be involved in activist pursuits is an extension of her faith that enlightens her compassion for serving those in need (Carol Thompson, personal correspondence, August 28, 2013).

Carol is a bisexual white woman in her fifties. She grew up in Michigan, where concepts of faith, compassion, and fairness were central components of the values instilled by her parents. As a college student in the wake of the Watergate scandal, Carol turned toward a career in journalism as a way of addressing corruption and exposing the government officials who were abusing the trust of the people they were serving; she envisioned herself as the next Woodward or Bernstein. Upon completing her degree, though, she was offered a job as the press secretary for a member of the Michigan Senate, and over the following two decades Carol worked in a number of positions in and around Michigan state government: doing public relations work for the governor's welfare-to-work program, serving as the press secretary for the Michigan House of Representatives, working as a communications consultant, and serving as a lobbyist for a group advocating prison reform and alternatives to prison (ibid.).

Another scandal, though, heightened a growing cynicism Carol was feeling toward government—this time, Anita Hill and her charges of sexual harassment against her former boss and then U.S. Supreme Court nominee Clarence Thomas. Carol became increasingly "jaded" and left her career in public service. Turning back to the church and reconnecting with both her faith and the sense of justice she had long been drawn to, she began to explore a career in the ministry, moved to Ohio, got married, had children, and was ordained as a minister. These changes also afforded her the opportunity to explore her passion for social justice by becoming active in groups working to protect reproductive freedom and abortion rights, peace and antiwar causes, as well as fledgling gay pride organizations. Working with these groups also increased Carol's awareness of the complexities and problems caused by the American attachment to consumer products and the subsequent power wielded by corporations and their executives. In 2008, Carol was reassigned to a church in Chicago, and since then her social justice activism has taken root in active support for the Chicago Teachers' Union and their attempts to reform public education in the city, for gun control to address proliferating violence, for progressive immigration reform, and for the LGBT/Q community, especially in the areas that most affect LGBT/Q youth experiencing homelessness (ibid.).

By addressing the immediate needs of youth experiencing homelessness in a service-provision capacity as well as addressing the structural hurdles that affect these young people through political advocacy, Carol says she is able to address what she sees as the main issues facing the LGBT/Q community in Chicago. At the top of this list, for her, is transphobia, followed closely by racism, both of which are instrumental in creating the difficulties faced by the homeless youth that Carol interacts with—a population that is disproportionately youth of color who have been forced out of their homes because of transgender identity or gender-nonconforming behavior. Their bodies are policed because they are seen as threatening when their gender identity does not match people's expectations and because they are not able—because of age and/or cost—to engage in the consumer economy that defines Boystown as a consumer and entertainment district, and their lives are criminalized because they engage in crimes of survival and because there is a lack of uniformity in institutional accounting for gender identity. These legal, political, and social attacks operate alongside the larger problem of racism that surrounds the war on drugs and the prison industrial complex. As further evidence that the policing of young homeless queer people of color is based on race and gender expression, Carol noted that in nearby Wrigleyville similar loitering, petty crimes, and even interpersonal violence is often seen as unproblematic when it occurs in a population that is white and gender conforming (ibid.).

Addressing the needs of young people experiencing homelessness and advocating on their behalf has indeed been hampered by the extensive energy and resources funneled into the same-sex marriage battle, Carol finds. Political advocacy often meets with resistance from those favoring normativity as a way of achieving acceptability in social, political, and legal recognition. Fundraising efforts struggle in an environment where potential donors are instead giving to organizations that favor the marriage work being done by other organizations. Nonetheless, Carol notes some benefits that the marriage struggle has had for LGBT/Q youth. For example, she says that other service providers she coordinates with have noted that suicides decreased when same-sex-marriage advances were made and these marriage victories are noted as particularly meaningful by those who are struggling with gender- and sexual-identity issues (ibid.).

The issue of youth homelessness continues to evolve in Chicago's LGBT/Q community and for social movement activists. During the late-fall and early-winter months of 2013, homeless LGBT/Q youth again became the target of Boystown's residents. This time the Southeast LakeView Neighbors neighborhood association was pressuring their alderman and the city to shut down the Broadway Youth Center that was operating out of facilities belonging to an area church. The residents were asking the city to deny the program's special use permit that would allow them to continue operating out of the church (after they had already lost their previous home in a commercial building) because they said the youth frequenting the center were loud, violent, and using drugs. While the city granted the permit over the pleas of the residents, the incident put service providers, activists, and the youth themselves on alert that the Boystown community is still antagonistic toward those suffering from unstable housing situations (Simonette 2014).

In another effort to address the issue of youth homelessness, during the summer of 2014 Tracy Baim, the editor of the *Windy City Times* (Chicago's leading LGBT/Q weekly newspaper) brought together a number of community leaders and activists to host a summit that focused on LGBT/Q homeless youth. The summit included sessions with youth, community leaders, volunteers, and city and state agencies. At the end of the event, the leadership team issued a report that summarized the event and made policy recommendations about how best to address the needs of LGBT/Q homeless youth in Chicago. These recommendation reiterate much of what activists have been looking for: more resources, a multitude of approaches that give struggling youth options, as well as education, jobs, and legal help. The summit was followed up with a LGBT/Q Youth Job Fair in October of 2014 as well as continuing implementation of some of the "small" asks made by youth participants.

The issue of LGBT youth homelessness is a clear empirical example of the truth at the heart of the queer critique of same-sex marriage. The needs of LGBT/Q youth experiencing homelessness have been ignored by a gay and lesbian mainstream movement that has focused on projects that benefit the privileged while leaving many who face drastic conditions out in the cold—sometimes literally. Even when the issues of race and homelessness present themselves, the mainstream continues to underfund necessary social programs and institutions that can address needs. Instead, the institutions of the LGBT community in Chicago literally shut their doors on these youth and vilify them—both for committing petty crimes of survival and also for merely existing and "being in the way." Activists who engage with the homeless youth experience this on a regular basis and are left frustrated when they see the extensive resources that are devoted to the pet projects of the mainstream LGBT movement's leaders.

Still, though, these activists continue to note the importance of the same-sex marriage fight in the work of the LGBT/Q social movement. Youth homelessness activists see same-sex marriage activism and the public discourse around the issue playing several roles in the work they do. Marriage, they say, became more of an inevitable hurdle to overcome before the community as a whole is able to move on to address more important issues than it was a total diversion from those other areas of need. The marriage issue was the entry point through which some activists were mobilized to participate in more queer/less homonormative issue advocacy, and same-sex-marriage work has contributed to a message of love and acceptance that is important to those working with at-risk youth. By bringing the critiques offered by queer theorists and antimarriage queer activists to bear on the study of LGBT/Q politics, we are able to appreciate the ways the movement engages in the processes that both challenge and reify current structures that produce homelessness as well as build a vision of the future in which the movement pushes both the LGBT/Q community and the state to address these concerns.

Extending these findings beyond the case of the same-sex-marriage saga suggests that appreciating the internal dynamics of the LGBT/Q movement—and social movements more generally—contributes to an understanding of how movements see themselves, operate, and succeed. Movement actors and participants are shaped by the struggles they engage with, including becoming more radical. As these individual participants and the organizations with which they are engaged change their perceptions and outlooks, they in turn shape the issues that the movement as a whole tackles, the tactics used, and the outcomes produced.

NOTES

1 The chapter is a version of the author's larger project entitled "For Better or Worse: Same-Sex Marriage Politics and LGBT/Q Social Movement Activism in Chicago." The entire project is covered by Institutional Review Board protocol number 20121078 at the University of Illinois at Chicago. The names of all subjects and organizations subject to this protocol have been changed to protect the privacy of those individuals and groups in accordance with IRB guidelines.

2 An example of this work relating specifically to the LGBTQ movement is Jane Ward, *Respectably Queer: Diversity Culture in LGBT Organizations* (Nashville, TN: Vanderbilt University Press, 2008).

3 Terri uses fluid gender terms and pronouns. To refer to Terri, I use the plural "they"/"them"/"theirs" throughout for the sake of clarity.

REFERENCES

Andrews, Kenneth T. 1997. "The Impact of Social Movements on the Political Process: The Civil Rights Movement and Black Election Politics in Mississippi." *American Sociological Review* 62: 800–819.

Bernstein, Mary. 1997. "Celebration and Suppression: The Strategic Uses of Identity by the Lesbian and Gay Movement." *American Journal of Sociology* 103: 531–65.

Boyd, Nan Alamilla. 2005. *Wide Open Town: A History of Queer San Francisco to 1965.* Berkeley: University of California Press.

Carey, Rae. 2012. "State of the LGBT Movement." National LGBTQ Taks Force. Accessed August 8, 2013. https://thetaskforceblog.org/2012/01/27/rea-carey-delivers-state-of-the-lgbt-movement- at-creating-change/.

Center for American Progress. 2010. "Gay and Transgender Youth Homelessness by the Numbers," www.americanprogress.org. Accessed January 29, 2014.

Clemmens, Elisabeth S. 1993. "Organizational Repertoires and Institutional Change: Women's Groups and the Transformation of U.S. Politics, 1890–1920." *American Journal of Sociology* 98: 755–98.

Crime in Wrigleyville and Boystown. 2015. Accessed June 30, 2015. www.cwbchicago.com, June 30 (last modified).

Daniel-McCarter, Owen. 2012. "Us vs. Them! Gays and the Criminalization of Queer Youth of Color in Chicago." *Children's Legal Rights Journal* 32: 5–17.

D'Emilio, John. 1983. *Sexual Politics, Sexual Communities: The Making of a Homosexual Minority in the United States, 1940–1970*. Chicago: University of Chicago Press.

Duggan, Lisa. 2003. *The Twilight of Equality? Neoliberalism, Cultural Politics, and the Attack on Democracy*. Boston: Beacon.

Gallo, Marcia. 2006. *Different Daughters: A History of the Daughters of Bilitis and the Rise of the Lesbian Rights Movement*. New York: Carroll and Graf.

Giugni, Marco. 1998. "Was It Worth the Effort? The Outcomes and Consequences of Social Movements." *Annual Review of Sociology* 98: 371–93.

GoPride.com. 2012. "Private Security Partol Hired for Boystown: Enhanced Security Team Creates Safer Environment along North Halsted." ChicagoPride.com, July 24, 2012. Accessed February 18, 2013. chicago.gopride.com.

Ingram, Mrill, and Helen Ingram. 2005. "Creating Credible Edibles: The Alternative Agriculture Movement and Passage of U.S. Federal Organic Standards." In *Routing the Opposition: Social Movements, Public Policy, and Democracy*, ed. David S. Meyer, Valerie Jenness, and Helen Ingram, 121–48. Minneapolis: University of Minnesota Press.

Johnson, David K. 2004. *The Lavender Scare: The Cold War Persecution of Gays and Lesbians in the Federal Government*. Chicago: University of Chicago Press.

Katzenstein, Mary Fainsod. 2005. "Rights without Citizenship: Prison Activism in the US." In *Routing the Opposition: Social Movements, Public Policy, and Democracy*, ed. Valerie Jenness, Helen Ingram, and David Meyer. Minneapolis: University of Minnesota Press.

Kriesi, Hanspeter, Ruud Koopmans, Jan Willem Duyvendale, and Marco G Giugni. 1995. *New Social Movements in Western Europe: A Comparative Analysis*. Minneapolis: University of Minnesota Press.

Lichterman, Paul. 1999. "Talking Identity in the Public Sphere: Broad Visions and Small Spaces in Sexual Identity Politics." *Theory and Society* 28: 101–41.

"Man Stabbed in Lakeview, 1 Suspect Caught by Bar's Security." 2011. *Chicago News Report*, June 18. www.chicagonewsreport.com. Accessed January 29, 2014.

McAdam, Doug. 1999. *Political Process and the Development of Black Insurgency, 1930–1970*, 2nd ed. Chicago: University of Chicago Press.

Mellucci, Alberto. 1995. "The Process of Collective Identity." In *Social Movements and Culture*, ed. Hank Johnston and Bert Klandermans, 41–63. Minneapolis: University of Minnesota Press.

Mettler, Suzanne. 2005. "Policy Feedback Effects for Collective Action: Lessons from Veterans' Programs." In *Routing the Opposition: Social Movements, Public Policy, and Democracy*, ed. David S. Meyer, Valerie Jenness, and Helen Ingram. Minneapolis: University of Minnesota Press.

Meyer, David S. 2009. "How Social Movements Matter." In *The Social Movements Reader: Cases and Concepts*, 2nd ed., ed. Jeff Goodwin and James M. Jasper, 417–22. Malden, MA: Wiley-Blackwell.

Meyer, David S., and Nancy Whittier. 1994. "Social Movement Spillover." *Social Problems* 41: 277–98.

Mucciaroni, Gary. 2008. *Same Sex, Different Politics: Success and Failure in the Struggles over Gay Rights*. Chicago: University of Chicago Press.

Pellow, David Naguib, and Robert J. Brulle. 2005. "Power, Justice, and the Environment: Toward Critical Environmental Justice Studies." In *Power, Justice, and the Environment: A Critical Appraisal of the Environmental Justice Movement*, ed. David Naguib Pellow and Robert J. Brulle, 1–19. Cambridge, MA: MIT Press.

Piven, Frances Fox, and Richard A. Cloward. 1977. *Poor People's Movements: Why They Succeed, How They Fail*. New York City: Pantheon.

"Private Security Patrol Hired for Boystown." 2012. *ChicagoPride.com*, July 24. chicagopride.com. Accessed February 18, 2013.

Reese, Ellen. 2005. "Policy Threats and Social Movement Coalitions: California's Campaign to Restore Legal Immigrants' Rights to Welfare." In *Routing the Opposition: Social Movements, Public Policy, and Democracy*, ed. David S. Meyer, Valerie Jenness, and Helen Ingram, 259–87. Minneapolis: University of Minnesota Press.

"Residents Question Neighborhood Safety after Boystown Stabbing." 2011. *Huffington Post*, June 23. www.huffingtonpost.com. Accessed January 29, 2014.

Simonette, Matt. 2014. "SELVN Won't Back Broadway Youth Center Zoning Appeal." *Windy City Times*, January 14, 2014. http://www.windycitymediagroup.com. Accessed January 16, 2014.

Stein, Marc. 2000. *City of Sisterly and Brotherly Loves: Lesbian and Gay Philadelphia, 1945–1972*. Chicago: University of Chicago Press.

Stone, Amy L. 2012. *Gay Rights at the Ballot Box*. Minneapolis: University of Minnesota Press.

Take Back Boystown. N.d. Accessed October 20, 2014. www.facebook.com/TakeBackBoystown.

"Third Boystown Stabbing in as Many Weeks Caught on Video." 2011. *Huffington Post*, July 5. www.huffingtonpost.com. Accessed January 29, 2014.

University of Illinois at Chicago Institute for Research on Race and Public Policy (UIC IRRPP). 2012. "Final Report for the Project: Engaging Chicago LGBTQ Communities in a Community Discussion about Racism, Public Safety, and the Rights of Young People." July 11. http://irrpp. uic.edu. Accessed August 13, 2013.

Ward, Jane. 2008. *Respectably Queer: Diversity Culture in LGBT Activist Organizations*. Nashville, TN: Vanderbilt University Press.

Warner, Michael. 1999. *The Trouble with Normal: Sex, Politics, and the Ethics of Queer Life*. Cambridge, MA: Harvard University Press.

PART V

LGBTQ Politics in Global Context

CHRISTINE KEATING

The essays in this section focus on LGBTQ politics in a global perspective. The global picture of LGBTQ rights is mixed. According to the International Lesbian and Gay Association, for example, there are seventy-five countries that still criminalize same-sex sexual acts between consenting adults. Although that number is discouraging, ten years ago, in 2006, ninety-two countries criminalized same-sex practices—so the number has been reduced by almost 20 percent in ten years. There is growing support among intergovernmental organizations for LGBTQ rights as well: for example, in the past five years the UN Human Rights Council has passed two resolutions in support of LGBTQ rights, the first brought by South Africa and the second by Chile, Colombia, and Brazil.

Globally, LGBTQ movement work takes many different forms across multiple institutional and cultural contexts. The chapters in this section take up this varied landscape of activism and advocacy. In "Political Science and the Study of LGBT Social Movements in the Global South," Julie Moreau examines research on LGBTQ movements in the Global South and their relationship to the state. Analyzing books and journal articles produced over the past twenty-five years, she delineates five areas of investigation that are most prevalent in political science: democratization, human rights, transnationalization, political homophobia, and homonationalism. In her study, she argues that taken together, this research serves to "elucidate the important ways in which Global Southern LGBT movements differ from their northern counterparts, make space for more theoretical contributions based on Global Southern experience, and decenter Western perspectives on sexuality, the state, and social movements."

In "Homonationalism and the Comparative Politics of LGBTQ Rights," Miriam Smith brings together two perspectives on the study of LGBTQ politics in a global perspective that are rarely in conversation with one another. The first perspective grows out of political science and seeks to understand the "evolution of law and public policy on LGBT rights" in comparative perspective. The second perspective grows out of LGBTQ studies and focuses on homonationalism and pinkwashing, that is, the ways in which contemporary states sometimes use the promotion of LGBTQ rights in order to present an image of the state as progressive or to deflect attention from other rights violations that the state is engaging in. Bringing these two literatures together, Smith suggests "a more complex and nuanced view of state politics on LGBTQ rights and the campaigns for and against them, and their effects in domestic and global politics."

In her chapter "Top Down, Bottom Up, or Meeting in the Middle? The U.S. Government in International LGBTQ Human Rights Advocacy," Cynthia Burack looks at the U.S. government's role in working towards LGBTQ human rights across the globe. Burack notes that although the U.S. government was initially slow to join the struggle for LGBTQ rights (or, as it is more often referred to by the international community, "SOGI" rights, that is, rights of those of diverse sexual orientations and gender identities), under the Obama administration, the U.S. government has become one of the leading players in the SOGI rights field. Burack examines different aspects of the U.S. government's approach, detailing the players, programs, and projects that the government is involved in. Contrary to the notion that the United States is able to set or dominate the political agenda of SOGI rights work, Burack argues that the diversity of LGBTQ rights organizations involved in the work on the transnational, national, and local levels makes "it difficult for any one group or community to impose its goals or preferred social, legal, and political strategies on the others or to set human rights agendas."

Finally, in their chapter "Pink Links: Visualizing the Global LGBTQ Network," Christina Kiel and Megan E. Osterbur use hyperlink data to map LGBTQ transnational advocacy networks on both the regional and the global levels. In doing so, they seek to understand the "central actors within regional networks, and organizations that act as conduits between different regions" and argue that such links have important influences on issue framing, policy setting, and the future of the LGBTQ movement. Kiel and Osterbur's chapter illustrates the ways in which digital technologies enable not only new kinds of activism and connections but also new ways to study them.

23

Political Science and the Study of LGBT Social Movements in the Global South

JULIE MOREAU

Recent events have drawn the world's attention to activism around sexuality and sexual identities in the Global South.[1] In South Africa, Argentina, Uruguay, and Brazil, certain lesbian, gay, bisexual, and transgender (LGBT)[2] movements are meeting with success, ranging from the decriminalization of homosexuality to relationship recognition. Yet, in what appears to be a dual trend, movements in other national contexts, such as Russia, Uganda, and Nigeria, are confronting unresponsive or even hostile political climates, reflected in the passage of legislation that further criminalizes same-sex activity and activism.

In 2002, Stephen Brown lamented that gay and lesbian social movements were "vastly understudied" globally. This can no longer be said to be the case, though the topic of sexuality generally remains peripheral in political science (Wilson and Burgess 2007; Mucciaroni 2011). There is now a sizable and growing literature aimed at understanding these divergent political outcomes in the context of the relationship between LGBT organizations and the state in the Global South. Several edited volumes have been published that serve as excellent resources for political scientists (Adam, Duvendak, and Krouwel 1999; Paternotte, Tremblay, and Johnson 2011; Picq and Theil 2015).

Scholars have approached this issue from many disciplinary orientations, as well as diverse theoretical and methodological commitments. As a result, a clear research agenda for political science has yet to materialize. In this review essay, I examine work over the past twenty-five years to understand the contours of this emerging field of study. I briefly provide an overview of my methods and data—research indexed in Worldwide Political Science Abstracts—to give the reader a comprehensive, if not completely exhaustive, picture of scholarship published in English in mainstream political science journals.

I then move to an analytical review of the literature, sometimes drawing from scholarship outside of political science, to group extant research into five research programs: (1) the importance of democratization as a "political opportunity" for the adoption of sexual-minority rights; (2) the prevalence of human rights frames for movements in the Global South when compared to northern movements, as well as their benefits and limitations; (3) the transnationalization of the LGBT movement; (4) the phenomenon of "political homophobia" across contexts, and the limitations of the term "homophobia" when conceiving of hostility toward sexual minorities; and (5) the applicability of the concept of homonationalism to understanding of formal LGBTQ inclusion.

By identifying these five thematic clusters, I not only suggest some future directions that political scientists may take but also aim to elucidate the important ways in which Global Southern LGBT movements differ from their northern counterparts, make space for more theoretical contributions based on Global Southern experience, and decenter Western perspectives on sexuality, the state, and social movements.

Methods and Scope of the Data

I searched Worldwide Political Science Abstracts for all books, journals, and reviews since January 1, 1990, to capture the contours of political science research on this topic over the last twenty-five years. I did a command line search for gay* OR lesbian* OR homosexual* OR bisexual* OR transgender* OR transsexual* OR LGBT AND "social movement" OR "activism" from January 1, 1990, to December 31, 2015.[3] This search returned 502 results. A search for exclusively peer-reviewed publications (predominantly excluding dissertations) revealed 312 results for the same time period. It is worth noting that only twenty-four of these results were published before 2000, indicating that interest in this topic has increased more than tenfold since that year.

These early pieces reveal many of the themes that persist throughout the dataset, including interests in social movement emergence and success, debates over rights, globalization, and identity politics. With respect to this last issue, "queer" is discussed as an emergent politic in relation to U.S. politics, but by later pieces (2011 onwards) it is a more common theoretical framework. The middle pieces (2000–2010) display a concern with right-wing conservatism and religiosity, particularly in the U.S. context (Saponara 1999; Zirakzadeh 2009), as well as same-sex marriage (A.M. Smith 2001; M. Smith 2005a; Egan and Sherrill 2005). The pieces are majority qualitative, though explicitly political theoretical scholarship is rare. Looking at the dataset as a whole, the focus is on North America and Western Europe, with over 190 of the peer-reviewed pieces dealing specifically with North America, Western Europe, Australia, or New Zealand.

Analytical Review of Major Themes and Avenues of Inquiry

Political Opportunities: Democratization and Some Left Turns

What drives this literature is the desire to understand the conditions under which LGBT movements emerge and are successful. Scholars often employ the idea of a "political opportunity structure" (Tarrow 1994) from social movement studies to understand the influence of the political environments in which activists find themselves. Democratic transitions appear to be particularly important for the institutional and legal opportunities they create, as well as increased opportunities for alliances with leftist political parties.

Examination of political opportunity structure has been very useful in understanding LGBT movements in the Global North (Duyvendak 1995; M. Smith 1998; M. Smith 2005b; M. Smith 2008). One particular political opportunity that scholars of Global Southern countries have addressed is a transition to democracy that reconfigures the institutional space. For example, James N. Green (1994) attributes the emergence of the Brazilian gay movement to the democratic opening ("decompression") that began with elections in 1974. Likewise, Stephen Brown (2002) argues that the repressive dictatorship in Argentina (1976–83) led to a decimation of the movement. The transition to democracy, by contrast, saw a proliferation of LGBT organizations in the 1980s and '90s. The Argentine movement took advantage of the new democratic political landscape, including opportunities to protest and influence politicians, as well as the dominance of human rights discourse and increased access to international support. Sheila Croucher (2002) argues that South Africa's democratic transition provided the political opportunity for a relatively small and weak gay movement to secure exceptional gains, and that this mobilization in turn contributed to the deepening of South African democracy.

Transitions to democracy also introduce political opportunities for activists to work with political parties. While historically gays and lesbians have been excluded from leftist parties because of homophobia and parties' class-based organizing model, there is increasing affinity between lesbians and gays and the New Left (Green and Babb 2002). Barry Adam, Jan Willem Duyvendak, and André Krouwel (1999) conclude from a cross-national analysis that support from left-wing parties is strongly associated with movements achieving their goals. In Latin America, the region-wide "left turn" in elected governments has produced connections between leftist parties and LGBT activists, helping activists to advance their causes through state institutions (Lind and Keating 2013; Encarnación 2011; Schulenberg 2013).

Omar Encarnación (2014) argues that the expansion of gay rights in some parts of the world, and their contraction in others, is a product of democratization. Democratization works in several ways: expanding citizenship to include previously marginalized groups; strengthening civil society and intermovement collaboration (gay and lesbian and human rights movements, for example); increasing the strength and importance of the judiciary, which allows for the enforcement of antidiscrimination law; and, finally, providing a socially tolerant environment. Jason Pierceson, Adriana Piatti-Crocker, and Shawn Schulenberg (2010), in their examination of policy adoption of recognition of same-sex relationships in both North and South America, agree that "the return of elected democracies to Latin

America (particularly since the 1990s) seemed to have provided a more open environment that has helped shape progressive policy and contributed to the emergence of traditionally marginalized gay and lesbian NGOs" (10). However, the authors also note that "the degree of democratic consolidation in Latin America does not seem to play a significant role in whether legislation for same-sex couples will or will not be adopted as demonstrated" (Pierceson, Piatti-Crocker, and Schulenberg 2010, 10). This is evidenced by Ecuador and Costa Rica on the one hand and Cuba on the other—a country where relationship recognition has been comparatively well received (Pierceson, Piatti-Crocker, and Schulenberg 2010). With specific reference to relationship recognition, therefore, democratization alone cannot explain why there is variation on this across the Americas. Thus, while the process of democratization may provide a crucial political opening, more work needs to be done to understand the interplay between democratic deepening and sexuality-based claims and organizing.

Furthermore, the case for nondemocracies may not be entirely bleak, and the relationship between the well-being of LGBT individuals and authoritarianism is certainly not clear-cut. Parthiban Muniandy (2012) examines the relationship between social movements and the state in Malaysia, after a police ban was imposed on an annual LGBT awareness exhibition. Muniandy persuasively argues that the LGBT movement, in traditional Islamic authorities, is not confronting an authoritarian monolith but rather a fragmented power structure. This has produced ongoing struggle over "use of public space and democratisation of Islamic discourses" (Muniandy 2012, 584). Social movements are resisting closures in existing political opportunity structures, and creating and taking advantage of fissures (or fragmentations) where they exist.

In the case of Iran, in 2010, the policy regarding military exceptions for transsexuals was changed such that the exemption was classified as a glandular disorder rather than a mental one. The dominant narrative regarding this policy change was that it only altered the way transsexuals were pathologized, and was the product of government's desire to eliminate homosexuality. Afsaneh Najmabadi (2011) argues that this shift was, rather, the product of adept translobbying that included the establishment of alliances in legal and medical fields. For Najmabadi, "the present legitimated legal subject position of transsexuals" was "made possible through the post-1979 coming together of biomedical and psychosexological discourses with Islamic jurisprudential rulings that together establish the legal legitimation of the transsexual subject on the basis of that same sorting system" (540). This policy change, therefore, is not a state initiative that happened to produce benefits for some transsexuals, but is a product of the ongoing process of state formation generally.

LGBT politics offers additional insight to political democratization. Building on well-established political science literature on institutions and society, and social movement literature on political opportunities, scholarship on LGBT issues in the Global South is exploring the consequences of democratic transitions for LGBT movements. Scholars emphasize the importance of democratization as offering opportunities for social movements to influence institutions. Electoral alliances with the Left are one such opportunity. Given increased acceptance of LGBT issues by conservative parties in Europe (Reynolds 2015), the topic of LGBT activism and right-wing political parties globally merits further inquiry. At the same time, recent scholarship is questioning the facile correlation between increased democratization and improvements in the lives of LGBT people. While democratization may present an opportunity for certain kinds of advances, it does not guarantee them. Nor does it mean LGBT gains can only be made in the context of "Western democracy." More analysis is required to understand this process, and research on LGBT social movements in the Global South is uniquely situated to contribute to scholarship in this area.

Rights and Human Rights

A logical extension of the interest in the relationship between LGBT movements and the state is an interest in rights as they mediate and transform this relationship. Drawing on social movement literature on collective action frames (Snow 2004), scholars are concerned with the manner and extent to which rights-based frameworks provide effective and beneficial frames for movement demands, and also with the political limitations of such frames.

In the Global North, sexuality claims have often been framed as civil rights issues (Mertus 2007; Ho and Rolfe 2011; Encarnación 2014). Claims in the Global South, by contrast, have been framed in terms of human rights and make explicit reference to international conventions (Thoreson 2014b; Kollman and Waites 2009). Transnational LGBT rights "brokers" highlight what they understand to be important differences between civil rights frameworks, based in the U.S. experience, and human rights frameworks. They cite human rights as a more "holistic" approach to social justice than mainstream LGBT organizations in the United States (Thoreson 2014b, 117). Further, the coming together of human-rights and sexuality-based social movements has generated a vast network of "researchers, activists, politicians, cultural producers and law-makers to facilitate and develop responses to dialogic negotiation, interpretation and understanding of human rights and cultural values across diverse national contexts" (Offord 2013, 338). Looking at LGBT activism in the Global South, and the intersection of rights discourses and sexual politics transnationally, is necessary in order to understand how the discourse of "gay rights are human rights" (Gross 2013; Encarnación 2011; Friedman 2012) became possible to articulate.

However, scholars are skeptical about the benefits versus the apparent costs of a normalizing (Western) universalism around issues of both sexuality and governance, and many have questioned their socially transformative potential (Wilson

2009; Seckinelgin 2009). Nicole LaViolette and Sandra Whitworth (1994), writing at a time when the criminalization of homosexuality was the norm, discuss the importance of human rights frameworks for conceptualizing violence against lesbians and gays as human rights abuses. However, in this relatively "early" piece in this twenty-five-year literature review, the authors are already skeptical of the limitations of rights-based claims. They are skeptical that human rights "will address or transform the more pervasive and more fundamental manifestations of heterosexism and homophobia in different national contexts. Likewise, it is unclear whether joining the very western notions that dominate human rights discourses to often equally western notions of 'gay men and lesbians' services a progressive and transformative politics" (564). Also skeptical of the predominance of human rights discourse, Matthew Waites (2009) argues that the emergence of sexual orientation and gender identity into human rights discourse is problematic for the way in which it reifies what Butler has called the "heterosexual matrix." Dominant understandings of sexuality and gender remain untouched, particularly the gender binary and the definition of sexualities in relation to this binary (Waites 2009, 138). Because sexual-human-rights discourses do not disrupt this seemingly "new" matrix, according to Waites, they too must be challenged.

Kelly Kollman and Matthew Waites (2009) articulate the human rights critique clearly, citing the appropriateness of human rights for grasping culturally diverse understandings of concepts such as privacy and the family, and sidestepping actual discussions of sexuality. Further, they question the usefulness of rights frames in contexts where "poor individuals lack the education, language or resources to claim and operationalize them, contributing to feelings of disempowerment unless individuals are assisted in developing a sense of ownership of such rights" (7). They also remain critical of the geopolitical context in which rights are deployed. Not only might adoption of human rights frames privilege Western universalisms; they also highlight how the United States and the United Kingdom have invoked human rights violations against women and sexual minorities in their justifications for foreign intervention in Iraq and Afghanistan.

Scott Long (2009) provides examples of such interventions in his critical assessment of Western lesbian and gay groups' responses to the execution of Makwan Mouloudzadeh in Iran in 2007. Misrecognizing the case as one of "homophobia" against a "gay youth," the coverage of the incident in the international press points towards the limitations of insensitive rights framing and identity-based conceptions of sexuality, as well as grievous misreading of non-Western political contexts.

Others argue that rights claims remove sexuality from LGBT demands (Kollman 2007). Kerman Calvo and Gracia Trujillo (2011) argue that the highly visible, more institutionalized wing of the LGBT movement in Spain tends to couch its claims in "desexualized" terms. These claims leave behind explicitly sexual "themes and references" and merge ideas about "the well-being of sexual communities with broader narratives on human rights, citizenship and even nationhood" (Calvo and Trujillo 2011, 565). While this kind of intramovement normalization has been noted in the Global South (Currier 2010), in the case of Spain the authors argue that activists are missing an opportunity to "engage with a transformative dialogue where social categories, ideas about family relations and love could adjust to grassroots diversity and difference" (Calvo and Trujillo 2011, 565).

Relatedly, scholars are concerned with an exclusive focus on rights, and an excessive faith in legal change (Albarracin 2012). While concern regarding the limitations of rights-based frameworks is certainly warranted, it is also important to look at how they are both utilized and subverted by LGBT activists. Cymene Howe (2013), in her ethnographic account of the *lucha* for sexual rights in Nicaragua, addresses the ubiquity of human rights discourses. While rights discourse is pervasive, activists, she argues, do not unquestioningly adopt these frameworks. Rather, they have "translated aspects of the country's revolutionary ethos into terms commensurate with contemporary sexual rights' politics, often reconfiguring translocal political practices so that they resonate more profoundly with local political histories and priorities" (Howe 2012, 167).

While mainstream political-scientific literature on human rights is vast, recent scholarship on LGBT issues in the Global South questions the persistent presumption of the universality of human rights. Scholars emphasize the benefits and limitations of human rights in the hands of LGBT movements as they craft national and transnational demands. In this light, Kollman and Waites (2009) call for a critical conception of human rights, in which their specific content "remains subject to debate and revision" (7). Another important contribution is understanding activists' framing of sexuality-based demands. Scholars on LGBT movements in the Global South note the prevalence of a human rights frame, rather than a civil rights frame, for sexuality-based claims, and more explicit references to international human rights conventions. At the same time, scholars rigorously critique the universalizing and westernizing tendencies of using this frame.

Transnational Dynamics: Power, Adaptation, and Solidarity

A related topic to the one described above is the issue of the transnational dynamics of LGBT social movements. Joseph Massad (2002) argues persuasively that northern donors and nongovernmental organizations (NGOs) impose a Western model of gay sexuality and activism. However, the power dynamics attached to the global circulation of identities like "lesbian" and "gay" and particular models of activism are far from clear-cut. While identities like "gay" may originate in English-speaking Euro-America, same-sex practices exist everywhere and sexuality-based activism is now almost as ubiquitous (Altman 1996; Adam 2002; Thoreson 2014b). Thus, once these terms and ideas are in circulation, Western influence cannot fully explain how identities and tactics manifest themselves.

Elements of discourse and models of organizing may be imposed by Western/ northern actors at the same time that individuals and organizations in the Global South strategically adopt and revise these models for their own purpose and context. Indeed, it is likely that sexual identities manifest themselves as neither strictly a "neocolonial project that undermines local ways of being sexually different" nor a universal foundation that "empowers sexual dissidents anywhere to realize who they 'truly' are" (McAllister 2013, 88). Scholars are exploring the specificities of north-south power dynamics, while not erasing the potential for "adaptation and hybridity" on the part of LGBT activists in the Global South (Thoreson 2014b, 6), nor assuming that influence is unilateral, always "diffusing" from the North to the South (Chabot and Duyvendak 2002).

Barry Adam (2002) argues that it is "something of a fiction" to reference a singular gay and lesbian movement when organizations and goals differ so greatly (134). Further, Adam emphasizes that LGBT subjectivities do not necessary originate "entirely or even primarily, as cultural exports from North/West to the South/East" (2002, 131). On this point, Sean Chabot and Jan Willem Duyvendak (2002) usefully demonstrate the modernist and imperialist assumption underlying much of the literature on globalization and transnationalism: that developments originate in Europe, the United States, and Western democracies generally. We need better understandings of transnational exchange between social movements that avoid what the authors call "essentialist diffusionism" (700).

Moving towards this better understanding, scholars are seeking to understand how LGBT activists take up transnational norms, trends, and discourses and use them for their own ends. For example, Elisabeth Friedman's (2012) work on the diffusion of norms around same-sex marriage between Spain and Argentina adopts such an approach, emphasizing the "receiving context" of norms, as well as the way local actors adapt and transform diffusion items like same-sex marriage legislation. Similarly to Friedman, Encarnación (2013) attributes Argentina's success in passing LGBT-friendly legislation not only to transnational influence but also to the savvy of the domestic movement.

Relatedly, other scholars focus on the manner in which opportunities for social movements are created at both the domestic and transnational level simultaneously. Rafael De la Dehesa (2007) examines the entrance of lesbian and gay activism into the electoral arena in Mexico and Brazil in 1982. He argues for the existence of "global communities" underneath national and international institutions, one being the LGBT movement. Specifically regarding the electoral field, activist strategies are a product of both domestic factors and engagement in the international arena. Dehesa argues that "national factors also constituted a process of selection at work, determining the relative salience and use of particular transnational practices" (31).

Timothy Hildebrant (2012) looks specifically at how opportunities at the national and international levels influence the work of NGOs. The transnational funding from LGBT movements in the Global North may be facilitating the emergence of a Chinese LGBT movement. This is clear in the appearance of mock weddings and drag shows in the Chinese movement's repertoire of collective action and increased use of information technology. However, while local LGBT organizations are benefiting from northern funding, "[T]hese organizations are highly dependent upon the good will of the [Chinese] state in allowing them to exist in the first place. As a result, activists work to preserve ties with the state even if it is at the expense of those with global civil society or other Chinese activists" (845). The result is a complex political opportunity structure confronting Chinese activists, which militates against solidaristic ties at both the national and the transnational levels.

This brings to the fore the negotiation of the power-laden relations of solidarity, both nationally and transnationally (Churchill 2009). Melinda Negrón-Gonzales (2012) examines alliance building in Turkey between secular and religious human rights organizations. For Negron-Gonzales, this kind of solidarity is vital for the consolidation of Turkish democracy, insofar as these solidaristic relationships can help eliminate prejudice and strengthen norms of tolerance (Negron-Gonzales 2012, 415–16). Jon Binnie and Christian Klesse (2012) note the importance of transnational feminist solidarity building to LGBT activisms in Poland. The authors attribute an increase in LGBT visibility since 2004 to the momentum gathered as part of an intermovement coalition around human rights and citizenship. The authors argue that when LGBTQ public demonstrations were attacked, this produced "a broad solidarity movement involving feminists, left-wing or progressive movements, organizations and parties, Jewish community groups, disabled people, artists, workers and transnational actors" (Binnie and Klesse 2012, 456).

However, Ashley Currier (2014) problematizes solidarity for LGBT organizations in Malawi. In the opposite of the Polish case, alliances with LGBT organizations (often tied to transnational LGBT organizations) often prove too costly for local HIV and feminist movements. These alliances are costly for local organizations because of homophobia and because of a loss of domestic legitimacy for their ties to transnational LGBT organizations. While linkages are potentially useful to LGBT organizations in accessing resources, these relations may foreclose solidarity domestically. Therefore, homophobia can both catalyze solidarity and trigger an evaporation of coalitional potential, depending on the circumstances.

Scholarship on LGBT issues in the Global South draws attention to the transnational aspects of LGBT movements, and is particularly attentive to issues of power and influence between the Global North and South. Ideas, policies, and identities do not simply or passively diffuse, nor, however, is the direction of influence always north to south. There is now not only an extensive literature critical of the Western provenance of the terms "gay," "lesbian," "bisexual" and "transgender," but there are also many studies exploring how sexual subjects, both individual and collective, interact with these identities and exercise agency in the construction of their sexual subjectivities. This occurs through both transnational and local dynamics—including funding relationships and solidaristic relationships between the North and the South.

Homophobia? Homophobias? The Radical Right and the Specter of Countermovements

Scholars are exploring the various ways in which antigay sentiment becomes manifest in politics and under what conditions this sentiment gains traction among elites and the larger society. Further, they are interested in how LGBTI social movements and countermovements react to elite and social homophobia, and the strategies they undertake to deal with it.

The political construction and marginalization of sexual minorities is well documented (Tan and Jin 2007; Wong 2013; Wieringa 2000). In order to conceptualize the purposive deployment of explicitly antigay sentiment by politicians, scholars have coined the term "political homophobia." As a strategy of state and nonstate actors, Meredith Weiss and Michael Bosia (2013) argue, political homophobia is an increasingly modular phenomenon. This strategy manifests as a tool of statecraft in Iran (Korycki and Nasirzadeh 2013), EU skepticism in Poland (O'Dwyer 2013), and a politics of postcolonial identity in Uganda (Kaoma 2013). Scholars have also addressed the intersection of homophobia and postcolonial discourses in other countries; Currier (2012) examines how political homophobia occurs in the Namibian context where LGBT activists are reclaiming the discourse of postcolonial identity taken up by elites' homophobic rhetoric to assert their dissatisfaction with the extent of decolonizaton and democratization in the country.

While Weiss and Bosia argue that political homophobia is widespread, Ryan R. Thoreson (2014a) calls for a situated understanding of incidents of what he prefers to call "anti-queer animus." The concept of antiqueer animus allows him to situate various and diverse instances of violence, mistreatment, or antiqueer legislation in their political-economic contexts rather than under the large umbrella of "homophobia." Thoreson's analysis raises questions regarding the extent to which the term "homophobia" has limits of both theoretical and cultural applicability.

Discussion of homophobia raises the issue of anti-LGBT countermovements. Scholarship on the United States has tended to focus specifically on right-wing conservatism and religiosity (Saponara 1999; Smith 2001; Zirakzadeh 2009), though these concerns also apply to Global Southern movements such as the Catholic Church's resistance to same-sex marriage (Pierceson, Piatti-Crocker, and Schulenberg 2010). In the North American context, Burke and Bernstein (2014) argue that it is not necessarily a mainstream LGBT movement bent on normalization that leads to the marginalization of queer discourses in the media. Looking at the case of same-sex marriage in Vermont, the authors argue that more politically radical "queer" discourses on marriage were coopted by opponents of marriage equality (Burke and Bernstein 2014, 830). Jesse Nancarrow Clarke (2003) argues that lesbian and gay groups at the U.N., in Argentina, and in the Philippines alter their collective identity strategies from essentialist to anti-essentialist depending on the form of opposition they receive from Christian conservative attacks. This draws attention to the issue of identity strategies theorized by Mary Bernstein (1997), as well as the importance of countermovements for understanding the context in which sexual identities acquire meaning and strategic utility.

However, not all countermovements require such maneuvering by activists. Thoreson (2008) explains the exceptional success of the LGB movement in South Africa not only through strategic and stable political alliances with the ruling party but also through the failure of the countermovement to galvanize antigay sentiment. While a countermovement seemed like the "biggest threat" to sexual-minority rights ten years ago, this threat has not materialized, in part because African National Congress (ANC) leadership did not take up the issue (unlike other ruling parties and leaders) and in part because of the countermovement's general lack of political adeptness (Thoreson 2008).

The fourth research program discussed here addresses the political conditions under which homophobia gains traction among political elites and (to a lesser extent) the general population. While the marginalization of sexual minorities may prove politically expedient in many different contexts for many different reasons, what may easily be called "homophobia" (Young-Bruehl 2002) in the north/west context has distinctive contours. The context in which homophobia is deployed, or its level of political expediency for political elites and countermovements, has much to do with what homophobia looks like across cases. Scholars working on social movements in the Global South have developed the idea of "political homophobia" to refer to the strategic deployment of homophobia by elites, and are usefully questioning the appropriateness of the term "homophobia" to capture antiqueer sentiment.

Homonationalisms and Sexual Subjects

Extremely influential in queer, feminist, and critical race theorizing is Jasbir Puar's (2007) idea of "homonationalism," or homonormative nationalism. Puar's thesis is that a collusive relationship exists between homosexuals in the United States (and some parts of Europe) with imperial projects such as the "war on terror" in the post-9/11 moment. A certain "brand" of national homosexual signifies the United States' exceptional modernity and legitimates the extermination of certain raced and sexed subjects ("terrorist-monster-fag") both within U.S. borders and without (Puar and Rai 2002; Puar 2007). National queers who conform to the brand become included, but at the expense of racialized "others" who become excluded from citizenship and nationhood, and even denied access to liberal subjecthood. One important element in Puar's critique is that it demonstrates the racialized respectability politics that accompany bids for inclusion in the nation.

While compelling, homonationalism has yet to be fully explored in political science. This oversight is puzzling because homonationalism as a concept relates closely to political-scientific work grappling with the limits of identity politics and inclusionary strategies (Lehr 1994; Gamson 1995; Bernstein 1997). A WPSA keyword search for "homonationalism" in peer-reviewed publications for the date range returned only ten articles. One example is Saffo Papantonopoulou's (2014) examination of the Brand Israel campaign. Papantonopoulou wonders how trans subjects are/will be positioned vis-à-vis homonationalism. Given the amount of attention paid to cis-gender queer subjects in the literature, Papantonopoulou's attention to transsubjectivity is welcome and overdue, as is the argument that trans subjects not merely be included in other already constructed semantic rubrics.

In terms of subjectivities that fall outside the increasingly taken for granted LGBT categorizations, Aniruddha Dutta (2013) explores how the subject is made legible (or illegible) to the state. This illegibility is often a product of simultaneous classing and racializing of subjects. Activism, funding, and state intervention in India, argues Dutta, "construct and delimit gender/sexual minorities through norms of legible identification, failing which marginalized subjects are exposed to state-sanctioned exploitation, neglect and violence" (2013, 496). Subjects who fall outside the parameters of "MSM" labelings, for example, are seen as less legitimate and therefore less able to access the benefits of citizenship (Dutta 2013, 496).

Similarly, Leticia Sabsay (2012) takes up the question of sexual citizenship and the kinds of subjects it produces who are able to claim sexual rights. Similar to Puar's thesis regarding the United States, Sabsay's argument is that the respectability politics of citizenship is constructed "against a myriad of colonised and orientalised 'others'" (618). Further, Sabsay makes a more general claim about the liberal assumptions that underpin sexual citizenship. Specifically, claims for inclusion in citizenship regulate the forms that subjects can take, inherently limiting the field of possible subjectivities that can emerge.

Scholars have been careful not to import the queer critique directly to other contexts. However, queer concerns draw attention to the benefits accrued to the state through policies for inclusion. For example, Hildebrant (2011) argues that the impetus for same-sex-marriage policy adoption in China is unlikely to come from a grassroots movement, but rather from political elites attempting to improve China's human rights reputation. While this may generate benefits such as improved access to sexual healthcare, it could harm the LGBT movement.

Amy Lind and Christine Keating (2013) explore the dynamics of national inclusion and exclusion and their ambivalent manifestations in Ecuador. The authors usefully theorize a phenomenon of "homoprotectionism" to understand the state's paternal relationship towards LGBT citizens. While political homophobia relies on a logic of "othering" sexual minorities, homoprotectionism allows the state "to secure the allegiance of vulnerable groups by offering protection to these groups from other groups within society" (518). Like political homophobia, however, homoprotectionism "can be used to justify the consolidation, extension and centralization of state authority" (518).

Overall, this scholarship examines the process of making gay, lesbian, bisexual, or transgender subjects, alongside generating questions regarding the mechanisms of inclusion and exclusion in (liberal, democratic, settler colonial) states. What are the limits of democratic inclusion? What new subjectivities are created or marginalized in this process? Homonationalism, a highly influential concept in queer and feminist studies, has not yet made a substantial impact on political-scientific thinking on nationalism and sexuality. Homonationalism highlights the mechanisms by which sexual subjects are constructed in and through a process of racialization and nationalization, and how the inclusion of LGBT subjects into the national imaginary accrues substantial benefits to the state. Political scientists would do well to engage with this literature in order to determine the extent to which these concerns apply only to global or regional hegemons and settler colonial states such as the United States, the United Kingdom, Israel, Australia, and South Africa, or whether we can indeed discuss the modular phenomena of both political homophobia and homonationalism. The obstacle is determining the extent to which homonationalism is intertwined with U.S. sexual exceptionalism, or whether similar dynamics exist elsewhere. In general, political science gains significantly from paying attention to interdisciplinary insights from feminist and queer studies.

Conclusion

While the study of sexuality remains relatively marginal in the discipline of political science, there is a rich and growing literature on the study of LGBT social movements. Consideration of the unique dynamics of Global Southern movements and their transnational dimensions are generating cutting-edge scholarship valuable to the study of politics. Institutional configurations, and the ever-shifting relationships between civil and political society, continue to occupy political scientists. Looking at the political opportunities available to LGBT activists remains a fruitful avenue of inquiry and facilitates cross-country comparison. In many cases, democratization, along with its institutional reconfiguration and new opportunities for elite alliances, has proved very important for LGBT movements. While democratization facilitates certain outcomes, it does not guarantee improvement in the lives of LGBT people. Activists are able to renegotiate sexual politics even in authoritarian regimes. Future research can explore stable democracies in other regions where LGBT movements have not emerged with such fervor, such as Botswana, in order to understand the limitations of this variable.

Another consistent avenue of investigation is the mobilization of human rights frameworks to frame LGBT demands. While useful, human rights discourses have important limits. Activists are often able to manipulate this framing. Similarly, the transnationalization of the LGBT movement has become indisputable. What scholars are exploring today are specific power dynamics of transnationalization, including the actual operation of networks such as funding or solidarity.

Homophobias and countermovements will probably continue to be a vibrant strain of research, given the political salience of sexuality and the dual trends of the extension and retraction of LGBT rights. Here, scholars can continue to unpack the diversity of social meanings behind anti-LGBT sentiment, as well as specify the conditions under which political othering of sexualities becomes salient. They might also investigate the mutual imbrication of elite anti-LGBT sentiment and their broader social manifestations.

What has become clear is also the necessity for an interdisciplinary approach to LGBT movements in the Global South. Political scientists cannot afford to overlook the insights of ethnic studies, legal studies, and feminist, postcolonial, anthropological, and sociological insights when seeking to understand the political import of LGBT movements. Future research on homonationalism could proceed in a similar manner to research on homophobias: Are the dynamics of homonationalism specific to the United States? To settler colonies? Is this process unique to LGBT subjects, or is this part of a more general phenomenon of ambivalent inclusion and exclusion as part and parcel of state building?

More work could be done to unpack the political specificities hiding in the LGBT acronym, on specifically trans, lesbian, and intersex organizations (Thoreson 2013) in Global Southern contexts. Movements may work well in this coalitional form, but sometimes there are important divides. Likewise, as political scientists, we often take the nation-state as the default when constructing cases to analyze and compare. This methodological nationalism, or the unquestioned use of the nation-state as an organizing principle (Wimmer and Schiller 2003; Amina, Faist, Schiller, and Nergiz 2012), underlies many approaches to studying LGBT movements. However, national-level perspectives often overlook very important differences in strategy along subnational geographic, race, and class lines (Smith 2004). By delineating these five areas of research, hopefully this chapter has illuminated more avenues for study—avenues that allow the specificity of Global Southern experience to become the focal point for future theorizing.

NOTES

1 I use the terms "Global North" and "Global South" as political signifiers, rather than strict geographical referents, in order to designate the uneven distribution of economic, social, and political power and privilege (Mohanty 2003; Bulbeck 2007). At points, I also use the term "the West" in the same manner.

2 Following the work of Dipesh Chakrabarty (2000), I use the term "sexual minority" to refer not to numerical advantages or disadvantages in a given population but to historically produced constructions of marginalization that can serve as a basis for the critique of power relations. I use "LGBT" throughout the text to refer to the now widespread moniker given to social movements claiming sexuality- and gender-based rights and identities. I refer to "lesbian and gay" (LG) or "lesbian, gay, and bisexual" (LGB) social movements when the authors surveyed here do. I also use the term "queer" if authors use the term, but also to refer to queer theoretical literature. In contrast to the title of this volume, the "Q" rarely appeared in conjunction with LGBT in the indexed political science scholarship on the LGBT movement in the global South.

3 The search was conducted on July 16, 2016.

REFERENCES

Adam, Barry. 2002. "Theorizing the Globalization of Gay and Lesbian Movements." *Research in Political Sociology* 10: 123–37.

Adam, Barry, Jan Willem Duyvendak, and André Krouwel. 1999. "Gay and Lesbian Movements beyond Borders? National Imprints of a Worldwide Movement." Pp. 344–71 in *Gay and Lesbian Movements beyond Borders? National Imprints of a Worldwide Movement*, edited by B. Adam, J. Duyvendak, and A. Krouwel. Philadelphia: Temple University Press.

Albarracin Caballero, Mauricio. 2012. "Social Movements and the Constitutional Court: Legal Recognition of the Rights of Same-Sex Couples in Colombia." *Sur: International Journal of Human Rights* 8(14): 7–31.

Altman, Denis. 1996. "Rupture or Continuity? The Internationalization of Gay Identities." *Social Text* 48: 77–94.

Amina, Anna, Thomas Faist, Nina Glick Schiller, and Devrimsel D. Nergiz. 2012. "Methodological Predicaments in Cross Border Studies." Pp. 1–19 in *Beyond Methodological Nationalism: Research Methodologies for Cross-Border Studies*, edited by A. Amina, D. Nergiz, T. Faist, and N. Schiller. London: Routledge,

Bacchetta, P. 2001. "Extraordinary Alliances in Crisis Situations: Women against Hindu Nationalism in India." Pp. 220–49 in *Feminism and Antiracism*. New York: NYU Press, 2001.

Bernstein, Mary. 1997. "Celebration and Suppression: The Strategic Uses of Identity by the Lesbian and Gay Movement." *American Journal of Sociology* 103(3): 531–65.

Binnie, J., and C. Klesse. 2012. "Solidarities and Tensions: Feminism and Transnational LGBTQ Politics in Poland." *European Journal of Women's Studies* 19(4): 444–59.

Brown, S. 2002. "'Con Discriminación y Repression No Hay Democracia': The Lesbian and Gay Movement in Argentina." *Latin American Perspectives* 29(2): 119–38.

Bulbeck, Chilla. 2007. "Hailing the 'Authentic Other': Constructing the Third World Woman as Aid Recipient in Donor NGO Agendas." *Advances in Gender Research* 11: 59–73.

Burke, M. C., and M. Bernstein. 2014. "How the Right Usurped the Queer Agenda: Frame Co-Optation in Political Discourse." *Sociological Forum* 29(4): 830–50.

Calvo, K., and G. Trujillo. 2011. "Fighting for Love Rights: Claims and Strategies of the LGBT Movement in Spain." *Sexualities* 14(5): 562–79.

Carroll, W. K., and R. S. Ratner. 2001. "Sustaining Oppositional Cultures in 'Post-Socialist' Times: A Comparative Study of Three Social Movement Organisations." *Sociology* 35(3): 605–29.

Chabot, S., and J. W. Duyvendak. 2002. "Globalization and Transnational Diffusion between Social Movements: Reconceptualizing the Dissemination of the Gandhian Repertoire and the 'Coming Out' Routine." *Theory and Society* 31: 697–740.

Chakrabarty, Dipesh. 2000. *Provincializing Europe: Postcolonial Thought and Historical Difference*. Princeton, NJ: Princeton University Press.

Chan, Phil C. W. 2007. "Same-Sex Marriage/Constitutionalism and Their Centrality to Equality Rights in Hong Kong: A Comparative-Socio-Legal Appraisal." *International Journal of Human Rights* 11(1–2): 33–84.

Churchill, Lindsey. 2009. "Transnational Alliances: Radical U.S. Feminist Solidarity and Contention with Latin America, 1970–1989." *Latin American Perspectives* 36(6): 10–26.

Clarke, Jesse Nancarrow. 2003. "Global Movements, Global Opposition: Sexual Rights Claims and Christian Conservatism." *Canadian Journal of Development Studies/Revue canadienne d'etudes du developpement* 24(3): 347–67.

Croucher, Sheila. 2002. "South Africa's Democratisation and the Politics of Gay Liberation." *Journal of Southern African Studies* 28(2): 315–30.

Currier, Ashley. 2010. "The Strategy of Normalization in the South African LGBT Movement." *Mobilization* 15(1): 45–62.

Currier, Ashley. 2012. "The Aftermath of Decolonization: Gender and Sexual Dissidence in Postindependence Namibia." *Signs* 37(2): 441–67.

Currier, A. 2014. "Arrested Solidarity: Obstacles to Intermovement Support for LGBT Rights in Malawi." *WSQ: Women's Studies Quarterly* 42(3–4): 146–63.

De la Dehesa, Rafael. 2007. "Global Communities and Hybrid Cultures: Early Gay and Lesbian Electoral Activism in Brazil and Mexico." *Latin American Research Review* 42(1): 29–51.

Dutta, A. 2013. "Legible Identities and Legitimate Citizens." *International Feminist Journal of Politics* 15(4): 494–514.

Duyvendak, Jan Willem. 1995. *The Power of Politics: New Social Movements in France.* Boulder, CO: Westview.

Egan, Patrick J, and Kenneth Sherrill. 2005. "Marriage and the Shifting Priorities of a New Generation of Lesbians and Gays." *PS: Political Science and Politics* 38(2): 229–32.

Encarnación, Omar. 2011. "Latin America's Gay Rights Revolution." *Journal of Democracy* 22(2): 104–18.

Encarnación, Omar G. 2013. "International Influence, Domestic Activism, and Gay Rights in Argentina." *Political Science Quarterly* 128(4): 687–716.

Encarnación, Omar. 2014. "Gay Rights: Why Democracy Matters." *Journal of Democracy* 25(3): 90–104.

Floyd, K. 2001. "Closing the (Heterosexual) Frontier: Midnight Cowboy as National Allegory." *Science Sexuality* 65(1): 99–130.

Friedman, E. J. 2012. "Constructing 'the Same Rights with the Same Names': The Impact of Spanish Norm Diffusion on Marriage Equality in Argentina." *Latin American Politics and Society* 54(4): 29–59.

Gamson, J. 1995. "Must Identity Movements Self-Destruct? A Queer Dilemma." *Social Problems* 42(3): 390–407.

Goddard, Keith. 2004. "A Fair Representation: GALZ and the History of the Gay Movement in Zimbabwe." *Journal of Gay & Lesbian Social Services* 16(1): 75–98.

Green, J. N. 1994. "The Emergence of the Brazilian Gay Liberation Movement, 1977–1981." *Latin American Perspectives* 21(1): 38–55.

Green, J. N., and F. E. Babb. 2002. "Introduction." *Latin American Perspectives* 29(2): 3–23.

Gross, Aeyal. 2013. "Post/Colonial Queer Globalisation and International Human Rights: Images of LGBT Rights." *Jindal Global Law Review* 4(2): 98–130.

Haider-Markel, Donald P. 2008. "The Lesbian and Gay Movements: Assimilation or Liberation?" *Political Science Quarterly* 123(4): 698–700.

Hildebrandt, T. 2011. "Same-Sex Marriage in China? The Strategic Promulgation of a Progressive Policy and Its Impact on LGBT Activism." *Review of International Studies* 37(3): 1313–33.

Hildebrandt, T. 2012. "Development and Division: The Effect of Transnational Linkages and Local Politics on LGBT Activism in China." *Journal of Contemporary China* 21(77): 845–62.

Ho, S. Iimay, and Megan E. Rolfe. 2011. "Same-Sex Partner Immigration and the Civil Rights Frame: A Comparative Study of Australia, Israel, and the USA." *International Journal of Comparative Sociology* 52(5): 390–412.

Howe, Cymene. 2013. "Epistemic Engineering and the Lucha for Sexual Rights in Postrevolutionary Nicaragua." *Journal of Latin American and Caribbean Anthropology* 18(2): 165–86.

Kaoma, K. 2013. "The Marriage of Convenience: The US Christian Right, African Christianity, and Postcolonial Politics of Sexual Identity." Pp. 75–102 in *Global Homophobia*, edited by M. Weiss and M. Bosia. Urbana: University of Illinois Press.

Kollman, Kelly. 2007. "Same-Sex Unions: The Globalization of an Idea." *International Studies Quarterly* 51(2): 329–57.

Kollman, Kelly. 2009. "European Institutions, Transnational Networks, and National Same-Sex Unions Policy: When Soft Law Hits Harder." *Contemporary Politics* 15(1): 37–53.

Kollman, Kelly, and Matthew Waites. 2009. "The Global Politics of Lesbian, Gay, Bisexual, and Transgender Human Rights: An Introduction." *Contemporary Politics* 15(1): 1–17.

Korycki, K., and A. Nasirzadeh. 2013. "Homophobia as a Tool of Statecraft: Iran and Its Queers." Pp. 174–95 in *Global Homophobia*, edited by M. Weiss and M. Bosia. Urbana: University of Illinois Press.

LaViolette, N., and S. Whitworth. 1994. "No Safe Haven: Sexuality as a Universal Human Right and Gay and Lesbian Activism in International Politics." *Millennium* 23(3): 563–88.

Lehr, V. 1994. "Queer Politics in the 1990s: Identity and Issues." *New Political Science* 30–31: 1–24.

Lind, A. 1997. "Out of the Closet and into La Calle." *NACLA Report on the Americas* 30(5): 6–9.

Lind, Amy, and Christine Keating. 2013. "Navigating the Left Turn." *The Distance between Death and Marriage: Citizenship, Violence and Same-Sex Marriage in South Africa* 15(4): 515–33.

Long, Scott. 2009. "Unbearable Witness: How Western Activists (Mis)Recognize Sexuality in Iran." *Contemporary Politics* 15(1): 119–36.

Mares, M. 2010. "Violence and Ideology: Right-Wing Extremism in the Czech Republic." *Osteuropa* 60(10): 33–50.

Marsiaj, J. 2006. "Social Movements and Political Parties: Gays, Lesbians, and Travestis and the Struggle for Inclusion in Brazil." *Canadian Journal of Latin American and Caribbean Studies* 31(62): 167–96.

Massad, Joseph. 2002. "Re-orienting Desire: The Gay International and the Arab World." *Public Culture* 14(2): 361–85.

Massoud, M. F. 2003. "The Evolution of Gay Rights in South Africa." *Peace Review* 15(3): 1–9.

McAllister, J. 2013. "Tswanarising Global Gayness: The 'UnAfrican' Argument, Western Gay Media Imagery, Local Responses, and Gay Culture in Botswana." *Culture, Health & Sexuality: An International Journal for Research, Intervention and Care* 15(sup1): 88–101.

Mertus, Julie. 2007. "The Rejection of the Human Rights Framings: The Case of LGBT Advocacy in the US." *Human Rights Quarterly* 29(4): 1036–64.

Modood, Tariq. 2008. "Is Multiculturalism Dead?" *Public Policy Research* 15(2): 84–88.

Mohanty, Chandra Talpade. 2003. *Feminism without Borders: Decolonizing Theory, Practicing Solidarity*. Durham, NC: Duke University Press.

Moreno, A. 2008. "The Politics of Visibility and the GLTTTBI Movement in Argentina." *Feminist Review* 89(1): 138–43.

Mucciaroni, Gary. 2011. "The Study of LGBT Politics and Its Contributions to Political Science." *PS: Political Science & Politics* 44(1): 17–21.

Muniandy, P. 2012. "Malaysia's Coming Out! Critical Cosmopolitans, Religious Politics, and Democracy." *Asian Journal of Social Science* 40(5–6): 582–607.

Najmabadi, A. 2011. "Verdicts of Science, Rulings of Faith: Transgender/Sexuality in Contemporary Iran." *Social Research* 78(2): 533–56.

Nardi, P. 1998. "The Globalization of the Gay and Lesbian Socio-Political Movement: Some Observations about Europe with a Focus on Italy." *Sociological Perspectives* 41(3): 567–86.

Negrón-Gonzales, M. 2012. "Cooperation between Secular and Religious Rights Organizations in Turkey." *Turkish Studies* 13(3): 415–30.

O'Dwyer, C. 2013. "Gay Rights and Political Homophobia in Postcommunist Europe: Is There an EU Effect?" Pp. 103–26 in *Global Homophobia*, edited by M. Weiss and M. Bosia. Urbana: University of Illinois Press.

Offord, B. 2013. "Queer Activist Intersections in Southeast Asia: Human Rights and Cultural Studies." *Asian Studies Review* 37(3): 335–49.

Papantonopoulou, S. 2014. "'Even a Freak like You Would Be Safe in Tel Aviv': Transgender Subjects, Wounded Attachments, and the Zionist Economy of Gratitude." *WSQ: Women's Studies Quarterly* 42(1–2): 278–93.

Paternotte, David, Manon Tremblay, and Carol Johnson. 2011. *The Lesbian and Gay Movement and the State: Comparative Insights into a Transformed Relationship*, edited by M. Tremblay, D. Paternotte, and C. Johnson. Surrey, England: Ashgate.

Picq, Manuela Lavinas, and Markus Thiel. 2015. *Sexualities in World Politics: How LGBTQ Claims Shape International Relations*. London: Routledge.

Pierceson, Jason, Adriana Piatti-Crocker, and Shawn Schulenberg. 2010. "Introduction." Pp. 1–13 in *Same-Sex Marriage in the Americas: Policy Innovation for Same-Sex Relationships*, edited by Jason Pierceson, Adriana Piatti-Crocker, and Shawn Schulenberg. Lanham, MD: Lexington Books.

Puar, Jasbir K. 2007. *Terrorist Assemblages: Homonationalism in Queer Times*. Durham, NC: Duke University Press.

Puar, Jasbir, and Amit S. Rai. 2002. "Monster, Terrorist, Fag: The War on Terrorism and the Production of Docile Patriots." *Social Text* 20(3): 117–48.

Reynolds, Andrew. 2015. "Why Does the Republican Party Still Oppose LGBT Rights?" *Washington Post*, June 18. www.washingtonpost.com.

Ripoll, J. L. 2009. "Love in the Time of Cholera: LGBT Rights in Colombia." *Sur: International Journal on Human Rights* 6(11): 73–89.

Roberts, M. W. 1995. "Emergence of Gay Identity and Gay Social Movements in Developing Countries: The AIDS Crisis as Catalyst." *Alternatives Global, Local, Political* 20(2): 243–64.

Sabsay, Leticia. 2012. "The Emergence of the Other Sexual Citizen: Orientalism and the Modernisation of Sexuality." *Citizenship Studies* 16(5–6): 605–23.

Saponara, L. 1999. "Confronting the Logic of the New Right." *Peace Review* 11(1): 69–75.

Schulenburg, Shawn. 2013. "The Lavender Tide? LGBT Rights and the Latin American Left Today." In *Same-Sex Relationship Recognition in Latin America: Promise and Resistance*, ed. Jason Pierceson, Adriana Piatti-Crocker, and Shawn Schulenberg. Landham, MD: Lexington Books.

Seckinelgin, H. 2009. "Global Activism and Sexualities in the Time of HIV/AIDS." *Contemporary Politics* 15(1): 103–18.

Shepard, B. 2001. "The Queer/Gay Assimilationist Split: The Suits vs the Sluts." *Monthly Review* 53(1): 49–62.

Smith, Anna Marie. 2001. "The Politicization of Marriage in Contemporary American Public Policy: The Defense of Marriage Act and the Personal Responsibility Act." *Citizenship Studies* 5(3): 303–20.

Smith, M. 1998. "Social Movements and Equality Seeking: The Case of Gay Liberation in Canada." *Canadian Journal of Political Science* 31(2): 285–309.

Smith, M. 2004. "Resisting and Reinforcing Neoliberalism: Lesbian and Gay Organising at the Federal and Local Levels in Canada." *Policy & Politics* 33(1): 75–94.

Smith, M. 2005a. *A Civil Society? Collective Actors in Canadian Political Life.* Peterborough, Canada: Broadview Press.

Smith, M. 2005b. "The Politics of Same-Sex Marriage in Canada and the United States." *PS: Political Science & Politics* 38(2): 225–28.

Smith, M. 2008. *Political Institutions and Lesbian and Gay Rights in the United States and Canada.* London: Routledge.

Snow, David A. 2004. "Framing Processes, Ideology, and Discursive Fields." Pp. 380–412 in *The Blackwell Companion to Social Movements*, edited by D. Snow, S. Soule, and H. Kriesi. Malden, MA: Blackwell.

Tan, Kenneth Paul, and Gary Lee Jack Jin. 2007. "Imagining the Gay Community in Singapore." *Critical Asian Studies* 39(2): 179–204.

Tarrow, Sidney. 1994. *Power in Movement: Social Movements, Collective Action, and Politics.* Cambridge: Cambridge University Press.

Thoreson, R. R. 2008. "Somewhere over the Rainbow Nation: Gay, Lesbian, and Bisexual Activism in South Africa." *Journal of Southern African Studies* 34(3): 679–97.

Thoreson, R. R. 2013. "Beyond Equality: The Post-Apartheid Counternarrative of Trans and Intersex Movements in South Africa." *African Affairs* 112(449): 646–65.

Thoreson, R. R. 2014a. *Transnational LGBT Activism.* Minneapolis: University of Minnesota Press.

Thoreson, R. R. 2014b. "Troubling the Waters of a 'Wave of Homophobia': Political Economies of Anti-Queer Animus in Sub-Saharan Africa." *Sexualities* 17(12): 23–42.

Ungar, M. 2001. "Lesbian, Gay, Bisexual, and Transgendered International Alliances: The Perils of Success." Pp. 235–48 in *Forging Radical Alliances across Difference: Coalition Politics for the New Millennium*, edited by Jill M. Bystydzienski and Steven P. Schacht. New York: Oxford University Press.

Waites, Matthew. 2009. "Critique of 'Sexual Orientation' and 'Gender Identity' in Human Rights Discourse: Global Queer Politics beyond the Yogyakarta Principles." *Contemporary Politics* 15(1): 137–56.

Weiss, Meredith L., and Michael J. Bosia. 2013. "Political Homophobia in Comparative Perspective." Pp. 1–29 in *Global Homophobia: States, Movements, and the Politics of Oppression*, edited by M. Weiss and M. Bosia. Urbana: University of Illinois Press.

Wieringa, S. 2000. "Communism and Women's Same-Sex Practices in Post-Suharto Indonesia." *Culture, Health, Sexuality* 2(4): 441–57.

Wilson, A. R. 2009. "The 'Neat Concept' of Sexual Citizenship: A Cautionary Tale for Human Rights Discourse." *Contemporary Politics* 15(1): 73–85.

Wilson, A. R., and S. Burgess. 2007. "Sexuality and the Body Politic: Thoughts on the Construction of an APSA Sexuality & Politics Section." *PS: Political Science and Politics* 40(2): 377–81.

Wilson, Bruce M., Rodriguez Cordero, and Juan Carlos. 2006. "Legal Opportunity Structures and Social Movements: The Effects of Institutional Change on Costa Rican Politics." *Comparative Political Studies* 39(3): 325–51.

Wimmer, Andreas, and Nina Glick Schiller. 2003. "Methodological Nationalism and Beyond: Nation-State Building, Migration, and the Social Sciences." *Global Networks* 2(4): 301–34.

Wong, Wai Ching Angela. 2013. "The Politics of Sexual Morality and Evangelical Activism in Hong Kong." *Inter-Asia Cultural Studies* 14(3): 340–60.

Young-Bruehl, E. 2002. "Homophobias: A Diagnostic and Political Manual." *Constellations* 9(2): 263–73.

Zirakzadeh, Cyrus Ernesto. 2009. "Rise of the Right: Exploring Conservative Movements in the United States." *Social Movement Studies* 8(4): 455–59.

24

Homonationalism and the Comparative Politics of LGBTQ Rights

MIRIAM SMITH

In recent years, there has been a growth of scholarship in political science that seeks to explain the evolution of public policy and law on LGBTQ rights, including same-sex marriage, relationship recognition, sodomy law reform, and protection against discrimination. Scholars in this area have developed a number of theoretical perspectives to explain why some countries and jurisdictions have shifted public policies while others have not (Sommer et al. 2013), why policy change has occurred in some areas of LGBTQ rights and not in others within the same country or jurisdiction (Mucciaroni 2008), and how supranational and international forces have enacted LGBTQ-rights recognition and/or influenced domestic policy changes (Kollman 2009). At the same time, in LGBTQ studies, there has been a substantial debate over homonationalism and pinkwashing, sparked in part by the publication of Jasbir Puar's *Terrorist Assemblages* in 2007. Puar and other scholars have argued that the incorporation of LGBTQ rights into normative citizenship has marginalized others, especially racialized others. Homonationalism, it is argued, is a form of nationalism in which the recognition of LGBTQ rights is used to promote a particular version of the nation at the expense of others, sometimes entailing outright racism toward others, especially Muslim others, while pinkwashing is a deliberate technique to vaunt such rights recognition to defuse criticism of the state's actions in oppressing others. "Homonormativity," a term developed by Lisa Duggan (2002), among other scholars, refers to the normalization of a racialized and classed vision of LGBTQ individuals and couples as assimilated into the mainstream of society.

In this chapter, I bring together these two perspectives on LGBTQ politics, the literature on homonationalism, pinkwashing, and homonormativity, and the literature on the comparative politics of LGBTQ rights. I ask what these literatures, which rarely speak directly, can learn from each other. In conducting this analysis, I first describe how scholars of homonationalism and scholars of the comparative politics of LGBTQ rights ask different questions about contemporary LGBTQ politics and use different research methodologies, based on specific assumptions about the relationship between facts and values. Second, I argue that scholars of the comparative politics of the Global North can and should learn from the homonationalist emphasis on racialization and postcolonialism, and I explore some of the ways in which these perspectives can be incorporated into comparative analysis. Scholars of comparative LGBTQ politics should consider how LGBTQ-rights campaigns may exclude racialized people, may reproduce neocolonial assumptions about "other" cultures, or may be used deliberately as fodder in pinkwashing campaigns. In the concluding section of the chapter, I suggest that analyses of these intersections would offer a more complex and nuanced view of state politics on LGBTQ rights and the campaigns for and against them, and their effects on domestic and global politics.

Part I: Homonationalism and Comparative Politics

Discussions of homonationalism, homonormativity, and pinkwashing and literatures on comparative policy development have different assumptions and goals, stemming in part from their different origins. The comparative political development in the LGBTQ area has its origins in the social sciences, especially in comparative politics and international relations, subfields of political science, as well as in political sociology, especially the study of social movements and legal mobilization. In contrast, Puar's concept of homonationalism and much of the associated discussion of pinkwashing and homonormativity stems from the humanities, specifically from cultural studies. In the following section, I present a brief outline of each approach, focusing on the types of research questions posed by each, the types of research methodology that are employed, and the relationship between normative and empirical claims.

Comparative Politics

The comparative politics of sexuality is an emerging field in political science that has been taken up by scholars of American politics, comparative politics, and international relations, as well as by scholars focusing on other areas, including Europe, Canada, Australia and New Zealand, Latin America, Africa, and Asia (e.g., Tremblay et al. 2011; Diez 2015; Haider-Markel 2010; Mucciaroni 2008; Kollman 2009). Much of this scholarship is based on describing the evolution of LGBTQ organizing and social movements, the evolution of public policy on LGBTQ issues, and legal developments at both the national and supranational levels. While this literature includes a broad range of issues and approaches, it tends to focus on a central concern of comparative politics: how we can explain policy outcomes, including policy outcomes over time in a single country or jurisdiction, cross-national similarities and differences in policy outcomes, and similarities and differences across jurisdictions within a country or supranational organization (e.g., differences across states in the United States or differences across countries of the European Union). Given the intensification of globalization in recent decades, coinciding with the rise of LGBTQ movements, scholars from international relations have also focused on describing the growth of LGBTQ organizations at the international and supranational level as well as on explaining policy outcomes at this level, i.e., the adoption (or not) of LGBTQ rights by international and supranational organizations (e.g., the United Nations, the European Union, the International Labour Organization), or describing and evaluating the impact of international or supranational rights recognition on states (Kollman 2009; Kollman and Waites 2009).

This research focuses on a number of different policy areas, including decriminalization of homosexuality, legal protection from discrimination in areas such as employment and housing, parenting and adoption rights, protection from homophobia and bullying in education, protection against hate crime, same-sex relationship recognition, and same-sex marriage. A number of factors have been found to shape policy outcomes, including political culture, public opinion, the role of religion, the impact of political institutions, the impact of partisanship, and the role of courts, among others. In an early study, Frank and McEneaney (1999, 914) identified key social trends that facilitated state recognition of LGBTQ rights and developed the concept of the cultural opportunity structure as a complement to and addition to the political opportunity structure used in political process theory (on political process theory, see Tarrow 2011). By "cultural opportunity," they referred to the emergence of new actors and new frames for action, including individualization, equality for women, and "dense linkages to world society" (i.e., globalization) that create cultural opportunity for LGBTQ-friendly state policies (Frank and McEneaney 1999, 920). Badgett's important 2004 study of cross-national adoption of same-sex-relationship-recognition laws (including civil union, common law recognition, and marriage) explored a range of variables, some of which had been identified in previous studies of variations in LGBTQ legal recognition across the U.S. states as well as comparative studies of the adoption of LGBTQ-positive laws across Europe. These included the strength of LGBTQ social movements or interest groups, political attitudes, religiosity (often measured by church attendance), a culture of tolerance for minorities, and the extent of direct democracy measures in which opponents could stall LGBTQ recognition at the ballot box, among other variables (Badgett 2004, 96–98; see also Barclay and Fisher 2003; Stone 2012).

Unsurprisingly, political scientists have often focused on political and legal institutions, arguing that particular legal and political institutional structures facilitate legal reform and policy change for LGBTQ rights proponents (for example, Smith 2008). Beyond the impact of formal institutions themselves, others have argued for the impact of activist networks in shaping the diffusion of norms in interaction with domestic factors. For example, in comparing LGBTQ rights across European Union (EU) states, Kelly Kollman (2009) argues for the role of social movement networks in shaping policies, focusing on the emergence of LGBTQ transnational activist networks that pressure national and European elites. However, she also considers domestic factors within states that mediate the impact of these activist networks, especially the role of religion and the extent to which international norms are viewed as legitimate by elites and the public. She also finds that pro-LGBTQ norm diffusion through activism is more effective than court decisions per se in influencing national-level policy (Kollman 2009). Sommer et al. (2013) draw on a much larger sample of countries to bring together institutional factors with a consideration of both the impact of dominant religious groups that may oppose LGBTQ rights (e.g., Catholics) and the impact of globalization, which is generally seen to have spread rights consciousness transnationally. They argue that, with respect to the repeal of sodomy laws, these factors have a greater effect on the political branches that are vulnerable to electoral and public pressure, while courts themselves, especially those operating in common law jurisdictions, have a greater chance of reversing previous precedents and repealing sodomy laws, as occurred in the United States in the *Lawrence v. Texas* case. Therefore, their research demonstrates the integration of factors such as religiosity and globalization with institutional and legal factors.

The impact of public opinion on the evolution of LGBTQ rights has also been an important area of research. In a U.S. cross-state study of public opinion and "gay rights," Lax and Phillips (2009) find that public opinion plays a key role in the responsiveness of states to gay rights issues, although policies still lag behind public opinion in some areas. Haider-Markel and Joslyn (2013) have explored a number of dynamics of opposition to LGBTQ rights, especially the extent to which, unlike other civil rights or public policy issues, LGBTQ supporters and opponents hold different views on the causes of homosexuality (Haider-Markel and Joslyn 2013, 607–8). They point out that partisan elites, social movement organizations, and media organize information about the political world, including the causality of homosexuality. Other scholars have explored the dynamics of political advocacy and opposition over time, focusing on the backlash against the recognition of LGBTQ rights. For example, Fetner (2008) argues that the strength of Christian Right organizations in the United States has paradoxically strengthened LGBTQ NGOs in the United States. Keck's important 2009 study of the backlash to same-sex-marriage decisions evaluates the extent of anti-LGBTQ mobilization in response to the recognition of the right to (same-sex) marriage by courts, considering whether the passage of constitutional bans on same-sex marriage resulted in setbacks for LGBTQ rights. All of these works emphasize the extent of political opposition to the recognition of LGBTQ rights in the United States and form key contributions to understanding the evolution of public policy and legal recognition from the perspective of (non-LGBTQ) opponents of LGBTQ rights.

A few pioneering studies have assessed change across policy areas, most notably across the U.S. states (Mucciaroni 2008; see also Lax and Phillips 2009). These studies aim to explain why legal and political change has come more quickly in some areas than in others. For example, Gary Mucciaroni (2008) aims to explain differences across the U.S. states in six issue areas, including sodomy laws, marriage rights, parenting rights, civil rights (including, for example, employment discrimination), hate crimes, and military service. His explanation for these cross-state differences centers on public opinion and the role of political institutions (Mucciaroni 2008, 8–46). David Rayside (2008) points out that efforts to counter homophobia in schooling have made far greater strides in the United States in comparison to the pace of relationship recognition and parenting rights for same-sex couples. Similarly, in the Canadian case, he points out that the opposite holds true as schooling lags far behind legal recognition of same-sex relationships.

This literature makes particular assumptions about facts and values. Very largely, it is based on positivist assumptions and seeks to explain policy development, not evaluate it. Whether same-sex marriage or LGBTQ-rights recognition is good or bad according to some abstract standard is not the concern of this literature, although much of it is clearly sympathetic to and favorable to the recognition of LGBTQ rights in a context in which opponents are viewed as outsiders who are hostile to the LGBTQ communities. This literature does not consider critiques from the LGBTQ communities; it mainly conceives of opponents as those outside the LGBTQ community, typically the Christian Right or other defenders of traditional family who view LGBTQ rights as a violation of religious values or traditional family mores, rather than as internal critics from within LGBTQ communities. For example, Thomas Keck's analysis of the backlash against same-sex marriage litigation in the United States emphasizes the use of defense-of-marriage statutes or state constitutional amendments in rolling back or forestalling recognition of gay marriage. Such measures were mainly backed by right-wing Republicans, sometimes with moderate Democratic support (Keck 2009).

When normative factors do enter into this literature, they often tend not to be about LGBTQ rights themselves but rather about broader questions of democratic politics. For example, the Sommer et al. (2013, 429) comparative study highlights the normative implications of the study in the conclusion. For these authors, the normative implications concern the appropriate role of courts in democratic political systems or, to put it another way, the evaluation of the legitimacy and efficacy of judicial activism, not the question of whether or not repealing sodomy laws is a good idea. Kollman's work explores how norms of LGBTQ recognition circulate and spread across and among the member states of the EU in transnational and supranational circuits of ideas and norms. In this case, Kollman treats norms as the subject of the research. She wants to know how and why norms spread cross-nationally. She is not herself arguing for or against the norms in question in any explicit way, although, again, we can infer from the tone of the article that Kollman is favorable to LGBTQ-rights inclusion.

Nonetheless, with most of these scholars, there is an underlying assumption that they favor the LGBTQ-rights recognition they are exploring and, specifically, that they favor it against the LGBTQ-rights opponents from outside the community, especially the traditional conservatives and the Christian Right. However, this is usually not explicitly mentioned, and it is not the point of their articles. From their methodological perspective, a scholar who is pro-LGBTQ rights (whether LGBTQ person or ally) would reach the same conclusions about the analysis of norm translation and circulation or the role of religiosity in driving opponents of LGBTQ law reform as would a scholar who is opposed to LGBTQ-rights recognition from the political Right or from a traditional conservative perspective. Causal relationships are tested against empirical evidence, and this knowledge is open to anyone, regardless of his or her stance or positionality.

Puar, Homonationalism, and Pinkwashing

In contrast, Jasbir Puar's work on homonationalism, which has been widely cited and discussed in relation to contemporary LGBTQ-rights movements, argues that liberal inclusion of LGBTQ citizens reinforces heteronormativity, as LGBTQ people and same-sex couples are described in normalized terms as similar to straight people and straight couples and, therefore, deserving of rights. While previous work on nationalism and sexuality had described the ways in which LGBTQ rights fit in with nationalist projects (e.g., Stychin 1998), Puar's concept of homonationalism took this a step further by emphasizing how the national and nationalist inclusion of LGBTQ people and same-sex couples marginalized and demonized others, such as those who did not belong to the nation or those who are "other" to the projects of normative sexuality and liberal inclusion (Puar 2007, 50–51).

Puar is centrally concerned with racialization and Islamophobia. The concept of homonationalism is inspired by theorists such as Foucault and, therefore, it has radically different philosophical and theoretical origins than the comparative politics approach. Homonationalism focuses on the valorization of LGBTQ rights at the expense of racialized others, especially Muslims in the wake of the war on terror. Western nations and especially the United States, which is the main focus of Puar's work, are seen as incorporating LGBTQ or queer subjects into a regime of legal and political recognition while, at the same time, drawing a stark contrast with other nations of the world, especially Muslim nations, in which rights for LGBTQ citizens are not recognized. Therefore, the queer subject is normalized as part of the "tolerant" West that forms part of the narrative justifying the war unleashed in Afghanistan and Iraq following 9/11. As Puar argues, homonationalism is more than just state practices but also encompasses the actions of civil society actors such as LGBTQ NGOs that may participate in the construction of a homonationalist narrative, such as equating support for same-sex marriage or the abolition of "don't ask, don't tell" with American military objectives or positing a normalized gay citizen or same-sex couple in contrast to the lack of rights for queers in Muslim countries, including those with which the United States is at war. In other words, homonationalism is not just an affair of states, according to Puar; it is a set of practices that facilitates the Islamophobia that is characteristic of the post–Cold War and post-9/11 period.

However, homonationalism is more than the cynical embrace of gay rights. Puar's analysis also makes clear that the celebration of gay rights involves the sacrifice of the human rights of others. To cite one of Puar's main examples, the fact that the U.S. Supreme Court struck down state sodomy laws in the 2003 *Lawrence* decision is seen as a celebration of liberal individualism, which contrasts sharply with the surveillance and security state of the post-9/11 period. Indeed, there is a contrast between the actions of the U.S. state in engaging in surveillance, drone attacks, and wars in Afghanistan and Iraq, on the one hand, and the celebration of private sexual behavior in *Lawrence*, on the other. These are linked through the U.S. state's deliberate valorization of the tolerance of Western nations in recognizing women's rights and LGBTQ rights in comparison to Muslim societies (Puar 2007, 114–55).

The term "homonationalism" can also be contrasted with pinkwashing, which Puar sees as deliberate actions by states to deploy "gay rights" to depict themselves as virtuous in contrast to their enemies (Puar 2013). The main contrast between homonationalism and pinkwashing is that pinkwashing is a deliberate action of states, while homonationalism is based on a wider range of actions, including the actions and discourse of nonstate actors. In Puar's view, homonationalism is an analytic category "deployed to understand and historicize how and why a nation's status as 'gay-friendly' has become desirable in the first place. Like modernity, homonationalism can be resisted and re-signified, but not opted out of: we are all conditioned by it and through it" (Puar 2013, 336).

Drawing on Foucault, Puar's analysis of homonationalism might best be thought of as a genealogy of the concept, guiding us to consider such questions as, How did the concept arise? How is it used and for what purposes? How does it become part of the truth regime in a given historical context? These questions underscore the specification of the conditions for truth claims, rather than the pursuit of truth per se, i.e., the genealogical project is interested in the meta or epistemological rules that govern the making of truth claims in a particular context. In contrast, the mainstream comparative politics approach takes a traditional social science approach in which claims are tested against empirical developments using specific indicators. In other words, comparative research takes place within what Foucauldians would see as a particular truth regime, which is not itself identified or problematized. From this perspective, it might appear that Puar's analysis and the comparative politics analysis are incommensurable.

While it is true that a genealogical approach differs markedly from a traditional social science approach, social scientists use concepts such as norms, values, discourse, and ideas to describe and explain the ways in which certain norms and discourse become dominant. Analyses of public policy drawing on a range of approaches, including agenda setting (Kingdon 2010), frame analysis (Hulst and Yanow 2016), interpretivism (Fischer 2003), and historical institutionalism (Béland 2009) broadly defined, have all sought to explain why a particular discourse arose at a certain time and how and why it acquired the influence it did. There are some poststructuralists in policy studies—such as Gottweis (1998) and, to a lesser extent, Vivien Schmidt (2008), an advocate of "discursive institutionalism"—who emphasize that concepts cannot be understood as existing outside of the world of ideas and that, in this sense, ideas and interests cannot be separated (see also Fischer 2003). This would be closer to Puar's analysis. However, tellingly, few poststructuralist or interpretivist scholars in comparative politics or comparative public policy have studied LGBTQ topics. There is a striking lack of interest in sexuality as a topic among scholars in this area, thus heightening the gap between Puar's concept of homonationalism and her approach to studying it, on the one hand, and the comparative literature on LGBTQ movements and shifts in LGBTQ public policy, on the other. Nonetheless, there are potential areas for conversation between proponents of the concept of homonationalism and the mainstream approach, in their attention both to discourse and to the role of normative ideas. In the next sections, I will critically assess each approach from the stance of the other and suggest some specific ways in which each could benefit from considering the perspective of the other.

Part II: Critiques

Critique of Puar

Turning to Puar first, from the perspective of comparative politics, Puar's work does not make reference to one of the major political actors that animates the comparative analysis of LGBTQ-rights policies, namely, the political and Christian Right opponents of such recognition. While Puar draws on critiques and debates from queer theory and from within queer communities, her discussion of what she sees as links between homonormativity and racism fails to consider the domestic, transnational, and global mobilization of heterosexual activism against LGBTQ-rights recognition. It is not clear where or how this opposition might fit into Puar's argument. While there are some Arab states that are linked to this agenda and that have occasionally allied with the Roman Catholic Church and with evangelical Protestant organizations in opposition to the international recognition of LGBTQ rights in instruments such as the UN-organized Yogyakarta Principles, systematic explorations of the sources and spread of anti-LGBTQ political mobilization often emphasize the role of American evangelical Protestants, not the Muslim "other" (Buss and Herman 2003).

Because Puar does not explore the role of these active political opponents from outside the LGBTQ community, she does not racialize them. That is, she does not examine the role of race in anti-LGBTQ-rights movements. On the flip side, as I will discuss further below, because the comparative literature does not directly consider the racialization of LGBTQ rights, it does not explore or describe racialization among non-LGBTQ critics and opponents of LGBTQ rights either. The result is that there have been few discussions of the racialization of non-LGBTQ opponents of LGBTQ-rights inclusion. Yet, we see important forms of racialization among such movements. For example, secular conservatives in North America are articulating claims around defending families and protecting women and children's health, all the while aiming to dismantle women's rights as well as LGBTQ rights. These new forms of contention and opposition to LGBTQ rights are themselves highly racialized, i.e., white dominated, although white leaders in these opposition movements also advance narratives that claim to mobilize traditional religious leaders and "ethnic groups" in support of attacks on women's and LGBTQ rights (Saurette and Gordon 2013). For example, in the United States, Republicans have claimed that Hispanics will support their socially conservative agenda, as some Hispanic immigrants to the United States share socially conservative values, including opposition to LGBTQ rights (Valenzuela 2014). Relationships between and among gender, sexuality, race, religion, and "ethnicity" are complex and highly charged. Puar's idea that LGBTQ rights are used by states and other civil society actors such as NGOs or other social institutions to legitimate themselves or to justify their own actions is certainly one important dynamic, but it is not the only one. LGBTQ-rights *opponents* also deploy race, ethnicity, and religion to further their political ends and, in so doing, present a homogenized view of racial, ethnic, and religious groups, analogous to homonationalism itself.

Moreover, the domestic emphasis of much American scholarship on LGBTQ rights is ironically shared by Puar's own work. Scholars outside the United States have adopted the American concept of homonationalism and then applied it to their own contexts, which are often very different, especially with regard to foreign policy. American global hegemony renders American nationalism quite different from Canadian or Dutch nationalism. While these countries certainly encapsulate forms of homonormativity and homonationalism, the concepts need to be adapted for countries that are differently situated in the global power structure, and scholars seeking to use these concepts elsewhere should adapt them to local circumstances in countries that are not hegemonic global superpowers (e.g., Murray 2014). Homonationalism is a concept that can be used comparatively, but it needs to be deployed in relation to specific empirical studies rather than solely as a blunt device of condemnation.

While Puar emphasizes that she conducted interviews and observed LGBTQ activism and discourse, it is not clear that she followed a specific methodology in doing so, and she does not explore or cite the relevant sociological or political science literature on LGBTQ social movements in the United States. Grassroots activism has played an important role in pushing forward litigation and rights-based political campaigns in the United States on LGBTQ rights. An excellent example of this is provided by the case of same-sex marriage. In the early 1990s, lawyers in the United States gathered to consider a legal strategy for the recognition of same-sex couples and, potentially, same-sex marriage. They decided against the pursuit of such a strategy, given that they thought it likely that any cases brought forward would lose. Despite this "decision," made at the top of the LGBTQ movement, plaintiffs came forward to lodge cases claiming that the recognition of same-sex relationships was constitutionally mandated. The concepts of homonormativity and homonationalism risk ignoring the views and agency of ordinary LGBTQ people who are actually responsible for putting these demands into action "from below." LGBTQ NGOs, lawyers, and other elites may not always be able to control and direct the agenda of the movement in a preferred political direction (Wolfson 2007; Becker 2014). The concepts of homonormativity and homonationalism are surprisingly flat and "top down" and fail to capture the contested and complex processes of LGBTQ rights-claiming, either globally or within specific countries. This can be seen in the end point of the homonationalist and homonormative process in which we are forced to distinguish opponents of LGBTQ rights who are non-LGBTQ (e.g., the Christian Right) from those who are LGBTQ (e.g., critics of the rights agenda from within the LGBTQ communities). Yet surely LGBTQ people, even radical critics of same-sex marriage, would be interested in opposing the homophobia of the Christian Right. This is the question posed in a recent article on pinkwashing in the United Kingdom in which critics of homonormativity in the LGBTQ community in London questioned an antihomophobia campaign that targeted racialized people in the community. Others in the LGBTQ community then critiqued this campaign for failing to emphasize the safety of LGBTQ people in the community during a spate of gay bashings (Zanghellini 2012; for another view, see Douglas et al. 2011). This study empirically examines the different points of view at work and highlights the complexities of internal community debates, rather than creating a homogeneous and unitary concept of homonationalism that is disconnected from specific sites.

Another way to understand the concept of homonationalism is to reinterpret its central question. Instead of viewing homonationalism as a concept that is designed to help us understand LGBTQ politics, we can see it as a concept that is designed to help us understand racism, neocolonialism, and Islamophobia. Puar is interested in how the recognition and valorization of LGBTQ rights (and the human rights template in general) has reinforced or sparked Islamophobia and racism. In other words, she is exploring the effects of LGBTQ rights recognition, rather than its causes. The idea of exploring effects, and in particular the effects of recognition for intersectional or other groups and their impact on racialization, is important. In doing so, however, Puar draws on a selective number of examples of discourse around queer rights, without providing any methodological justification for the choice of sites or cases (Puar 2007, xiv–vi).

In her book and in other subsequent work, Puar juxtaposes the recognition of LGBTQ rights in the United States against other actions of the U.S. state, as if to suggest that they are connected to each other because they happened at the same time. In doing so, Puar suggests that one is the condition of the other, i.e., that the racist actions of the U.S. government, for example, are conditions for the recognition of gay rights. While it is evident that, in some times and places, states such as the United States, Canada, the United Kingdom, and other EU countries have deliberately used gay rights and women's rights to depict Muslims as the enemy, these governments have used a range of justifications for the war on terror, gay rights among them. Most observers of U.S. foreign policy would be surprised to hear that LGBTQ rights played any role in the U.S. war in Afghanistan, let alone that it was a necessary condition for the war. A proper analysis of the relationship between LGBTQ rights and Islamophobia or U.S. foreign policy should examine the entire discourse of Islamophobia and/or foreign policy and then situate that discussion of gay rights/women's rights within the universe of Islamophobia or foreign policy, rather than citing selected incidents or elements of discourse to illustrate the proposed association. Despite some of these criticisms, Puar's questions are of central importance and need to be taken up with urgency in the mainstream literature, as I will argue below.

Critiques of Mainstream Literature

In contrast to Puar's work and to the concept of homonationalism, the literature on the comparative politics of LGBTQ rights is not explicitly interested in racism or Islamophobia and largely fails to undertake intersectional analysis of the evolution of LGBTQ rights. Certainly, the comparative politics literature rarely considers or links domestic political developments, especially within the United States, to global and transnational politics or transnational policy mobility or norm circulation. In contrast, Puar is correct to ask us to think through the relationship between domestic legal developments in the United States (e.g., *Lawrence*) and narratives of U.S. foreign policy. The concept of pinkwashing calls attention to the idea that LGBTQ rights can be used as a political cover for other unpalatable policies, a point that is not considered in comparative LGBTQ analyses, which largely neglect the links among policy areas, especially in foreign policy. In addition to this failure to link domestic and international developments, some of the U.S. literature that has made major contributions to understanding the causality of LGBTQ-rights developments are studies of the United States as a single case or comparisons across the U.S. states that do not consider developments in relation to U.S. foreign policy or in relation to the development of LGBTQ politics beyond borders. The exception here is the literature on the recognition of LGBTQ rights in the EU, which, for understandable reasons, has linked domestic developments to those at the supranational level.

Puar's work draws attention to the effects and impact of LGBTQ rights in contributing to the racialization of the other. While she asserts that such rights are recognized at the expense of the other, she implies that there are causal relationships between the recognition of rights and the other dynamics in which she is interested, such as racism, Islamophobia, and neocolonialism. This is an area to which the comparative LGBTQ research could contribute much more systematically than it has to date. Much of the literature focuses solely on the "why" of LGBTQ policy and not on the impact of LGBTQ policy outcomes on social life, whether that is socioeconomic inequality or racism or colonialism. Yet, there are examples of other scholarship that has empirically studied the effects of rights recognition. Among many examples, Rosenberg's *Hollow Hope* (2008) asked if court decisions such as *Brown v. Board* actually resulted in desegregation. The scholarship on the impact of court decisions is an example of the type of research that would take on Puar's intervention on racism and colonialism and potentially integrate it into comparative scholarship. Moreover, the study of comparative LGBTQ rights could take a much broader look at the impact of rights recognition from an intersectional perspective, including the ways in which LGBTQ recognition by the state shapes the politics of race, nation, and class. In addition, studies of racism, racialization, and intersectionality could integrate LGBTQ perspectives into the study of racism, considering and evaluating Puar's claims about the impact of LGBTQ-rights recognition on racism. This type of empirical exploration would permit a more careful evaluation of Puar's claim that LGBTQ-rights recognition contributes to racialization in the United States and, by extension, elsewhere. The political science approach tends to emphasize recognition by states or in formal law as the end point of the LGBTQ-rights struggle, while Puar is considering a much broader set of relationships that extend globally and that place LGBTQ-rights struggles in relation to other actions of states such as state surveillance and war, which would not normally be framed in terms of LGBTQ rights (with the possible exception of the U.S. military policy of "don't ask, don't tell").

In summary, while the work of homonationalism focuses on values and the normative stances that we should take in relation to various claims about race and nationalism that are made in the name of LGBTQ people, comparative politics scholars do not directly discuss values in most cases. Yet, both types of work actually deal with both facts and values but without making this clear. Homonationalism deals with facts and causality and, in fact, is inundated with causal and descriptive assumptions and assertions, despite Puar's roots in cultural studies and interest in the Foucauldian approach. On the other hand, mainstream social science work largely assumes that the recognition of LGBTQ rights is good, but without saying so. Further, mainstream social science does not ask who benefits from the recognition of LGBTQ rights, while Puar asks this question rather pointedly.

Part III: Directions for Future Research

Despite the differences in normative stance highlighted in the last section, there are ways in which the two literatures can learn from each other and in which we can draw on both literatures to highlight the complexities of contemporary LGBTQ politics. We can recognize that, in some places, LGBTQ movements are still beleaguered by right-wing opponents while at the same time recognizing that normative LGBTQ citizenship may have some or all of the deleterious effects cited by scholars of homonationalism and homonormativity. We can recognize that, in terms of normative debate, LGBTQ-rights recognition can be both good and bad for the same groups of people or that it can be good for some and not so good for others. In relation to political science as a discipline, debates on homonationalism and pinkwashing need to be tempered with consideration of the strength of anti-LGBTQ movements and of the ongoing problems with the acceptance of sexuality studies in mainstream social science, especially in political science (Novkov and Barclay 2010). The question of who benefits and who does not from LGBTQ-rights recognition is complicated, and its complexity is not captured by some of the claims of scholars of homonationalism, who present these claims in relatively stark terms. However, this complexity is also not captured by mainstream analyses that fail to take account of race and colonialism. Margaret Denike's analysis of Puar highlights the complexities of the situation:

> [I]n defence of the discourses of rights that Puar's project puts on the line, one of the few tools that has worked to chip away at the hold of homophobia in the public domain, and to grant access for queers to one normative domestic institution at a time, has been local, national and international human rights claims—the form and logic of which are fundamentally dependent on the very identity categories and grounds that Puar's critique of queer theories of subjectivity aims to trouble. While Puar clearly demonstrates the urgency of critically reflecting on the clearly troubled bio-necro context of our discourses and strategies, and on the human cost of rendering others expendable savages and victims, they remain indispensable in temporal and spatial domains where homonationalism is indeed an illusion. (Denike 2010, 98)

In other words, heterosexism and homophobia are still virulent and, therefore, the project of queer human rights is still needed to challenge anti-LGBTQ discourse and mobilization. However, on the other hand, Puar's analysis calls attention to the extent to which LGBTQ rights claims may come at the cost of others by "rendering others expendable savages and victims" (Denike 2010, 98). At the same time, it is important to make a distinction between the extent to which LGBTQ activists deploy the language of turning others into "savages and victims" and the extent to which others deploy this for their own political ends. We see both in operation; we need to distinguish these dynamics empirically and explore the relationship between them. When political and state elites deploy pinkwashing, how does this influence LGBTQ movements and communities? What is the relationship between top-down, state-driven narratives of homonationalism, on the one hand, and the adoption of homonationalist discourse and action by LGBTQ civil society groups or communities, on the other?

Another important question for future research is the relationship between and among different sectors of the LGBTQ communities where pinkwashing campaigns take place or where pinkwashing or homonationalist discourse and actions are questioned, whether within or without the community. In the example of the British pinkwashing campaign (Zanghellini 2012), the LGBTQ community resisted the critique of pinkwashing and homonationalism in the name of asserting concerns about violence against LGBTQ people in the neighborhood. This is one of the few pieces of research that attempts to document the claims and counterclaims among LGBTQ communities and their neighbors in a specific place over pinkwashing and homonationalist claims and counterclaims. These examples highlight a fact overlooked in some of the mainstream LGBTQ political science literature, namely, that the binary focus on advocates and opponents of LGBTQ rights eclipses discussion of the complexities of LGBTQ communities and, in particular, their relationship to particular places and their situatedness in local urban spaces. Traditionally, this would have been told as the story of LGBTQ rights seeking to secure police protection against gay bashing and perhaps to secure a rainbow community policing presence. However, in this case, this traditional narrative is complicated by debates over the nature of policing gay bashing in a multiracial context in which the struggle against gay bashing and homophobic violence may be tied to racialist political agendas at the local level. Puar's work highlights these complexities and calls attention to them; however, the mainstream approach, with its fine-grained empirical methods, can provide useful methodological tools to explore empirically the dynamics of these campaigns. The problem is that the comparative politics literature has not examined these internal debates, especially around race. However, it would be worthwhile to bring the two approaches together in order to produce such an exploration.

Further, it is still centrally important to ensure that a focus on homonationalism does not obscure the continued political role of homophobia. The recent collection *Global Homophobias* (Weiss and Bosia 2013) takes up this type of work. While recognizing homonormativity and homonationalism, the contributors explicitly consider the phenomenon of political homophobia as a deliberate strategy taken up by states in discourse and policy, one that transcends borders in a "modular" way (Bosia and Weiss 2013). The collection explores this phenomenon, considering the interrelation between movement and countermovement and considering cases in which state homophobia precedes LGBTQ organizing (Weiss 2013). These approaches highlight the idea that LGBTQ-rights developments are not linear, that the state can recognize LGBTQ rights in one area while not recognizing rights in other areas, and that some states, like the United States, have a history of deliberately deploying homophobia as well as deliberately deploying homoprotectionism, i.e., the idea of a national government (e.g., the United States) as a protector of LGBTQ rights (Weiss and Bosia 2013; Keating 2013). The contributions in the *Global Homophobias* volume are sensitive to the complex dynamics surrounding the relationship between LGBTQ rights and the state across space and time.

In sum, there is a disciplinary, theoretical, and empirical gap in LGBTQ studies. On the one hand, we have new concepts that have emerged—pinkwashing and homonationalism—that generate new research questions about LGBTQ politics and, especially, about the links between what used to be called domestic and foreign policy and the role of racial, national, and religious diversities within LGBTQ communities and moments. Yet, by and large, empirical scholars in political science have not taken up these questions. At the same time, we have a growth of LGBTQ empirical scholarship that seeks to establish causal relationships among the forces that have facilitated LGBTQ-rights recognition. However, this literature has more or less treated the LGBTQ communities as homogeneous and has not considered the role of rights recognition within particular states (especially the United States) in relation to global politics or transnational and national dynamics of racialization. As a result, even its most important insights about the dynamics of rights recognition have been largely ignored in the literature on homonationalism.

Another area in which these two literatures might speak to each other is with respect to the way in which they pose normative questions. On the one hand, homonationalism critically evaluates the project of LGBTQ rights and asks who is marginalized by such rights recognition while, on the other hand, the empirical literature is interested in why such recognition occurs. The homonationalism literature suggests that the mainstream literature should move beyond the "why" of rights recognition to the impact of rights recognition, including the impact of rights recognition in global politics and in relation to racialization and neocolonialism. This would also deal with some of the weaknesses of Puar's perspective, the way in which it makes causal assumptions while rejecting the methodological and epistemological approaches that would permit a more robust analysis of the dynamics of these causal relations, an empirical project that might actually strengthen its claims and widen its gaze.

The concepts of homonationalism and pinkwashing can be useful to scholars of LGBTQ rights who are interested in the transnational and global circulation of LGBTQ norms. They draw attention to the idea that states are deploying queer rights for the purpose of distracting from other issues or for the purpose of asserting their moral authority in the international community. The process by which states and other international and transnational actors, including international organizations and NGOs, may draw on LGBTQ rights for the purpose of pinkwashing or in the course of advocacy for rights recognition is an area of empirical study that can be taken on by social scientists. In particular, it would be possible to build more conversations around concepts such as homonationalism, pinkwashing, and homonormativity in a comparative public policy approach grounded in poststructuralist or even discursive approaches to policy. In this, it would be useful to distinguish homonationalism and pinkwashing from the recognition of LGBTQ rights or law reforms that extend particular forms of state sanction to same-sex relationships or protection from discrimination to LGBTQ people. It is an empirical question to evaluate the extent to which or the ways in which the changes in public policy amount to pinkwashing or are part of a homonationalist agenda.

This leads to another important direction for future research, which is already underway in social science, namely, the effects of LGBTQ-rights recognition or the effects of changes in state policy for LGBTQ and other communities. Do homonormative policies disadvantage people of color in the same country or community? What are the economic and social implications of recognizing same-sex marriage for those who are economically and socially marginal within LGBTQ and other communities? How are LGBTQ rights used in the service of foreign policy goals or state-sanctioned racialization projects? In particular, building on past work by socio-legal scholars such as Carl Stychin (1998), public policy scholars could consider the relationship between nationalism, especially nationalist claims made by state elites, and the recognition of LGBTQ rights. In addition, exploring how homonormative narratives of state recognition reinforce nationalism in a particular site is also an important potential trajectory of research. Interview material on American and Canadian same-sex couples in relation to the construction of legality in same-sex relationships often emphasizes the extent to which couples seek marriage or marriage-like relationships in order to be the same as everyone else or to fit in with society (Nicol and Smith 2008, 677). This would seem to emphasize the homonormative dynamic of same-sex marriage. On the other hand, some people of color argue that state regulation of same-sex marriage is analogous to laws that prohibited interracial marriage and note the use of state law that dated back to slavery days to prevent the legal recognition of same-sex marriages (see Nicol and Smith 2008, 676). The role of the social scientist should be to present these diverse views and explore connections between and among diverse LGBTQ political and social actors as well as political and social actors outside the LGBTQ community.

Conclusion

The concepts of homonationalism and pinkwashing have become central to the discussion of queer rights in cultural studies and allied disciplines. At the same time, political scientists have increasingly considered the trajectory of LGBTQ-rights recognition in comparative perspective, attempting to explain why some countries have adopted LGBTQ-rights recognition while others have not. This burgeoning comparative literature could benefit from engagement with Puar's ideas and the debates surrounding them. Such an engagement, especially by scholars based in the United States, would encourage the exploration of the relationship between American hegemony and the increasingly global project of LGBTQ-rights recognition. At the same time, comparative scholars would benefit from considering the links among and between LGBTQ-rights recognition, racism, and national claims. These complexities go far beyond the intersectional approaches that are sometimes cited in the socio-legal literature. Indeed, the idea that recognizing the rights of LGBTQ people as citizens in the United States, the EU, and other Western countries or that recognizing global principles of LGBTQ rights such as those encapsulated in the *Yogyakarta Principles* contributes to racism, right-wing nationalism, heightened surveillance, torture, and technologically based warfare is a contention that should be taken seriously by comparative scholars and explored empirically. Further research using the concepts of pinkwashing and homonationalism, more attention to the impact of LGBTQ-rights recognition and not only its causes, as well as more systematic attention to racism as a factor in rights recognition would contribute to a more complex and nuanced understanding of LGBTQ comparative politics. In this sense, Puar's approach has contributed greatly to the contemporary understanding of queer politics and, potentially, to the comparative politics of LGBTQ rights.

REFERENCES

Badgett, M. V. Lee. 2004. "Variations on an Equitable Theme: Explaining International Same-Sex Partner Recognition Laws." In *Same-Sex Couples, Same-Sex Partnerships, and Homosexual Marriages: A Focus on Cross-National Differentials*, edited by Marie Digoix and Patrick Festy. Paris: Institut national d'études démographiques. Pp. 95–114.

Barclay, Scott, and Shauna Fisher. 2003. "The States and the Differing Impetus for Divergent Paths on Same-Sex Marriage, 1990–2001." *Policy Studies Journal* 31(3): 331–52.

Becker, Jo. 2014. *Forcing the Spring: Inside the Fight for Marriage Equality*. New York: Penguin.

Béland, Daniel. 2009. "Gender, Ideational Analysis, and Social Policy." *Social Politics* 16 (4): 558–81.

Bosia, Michael J., and Meredith L. Weiss. 2013. "Political Homophobia in Comparative Perspective." In *Global Homophobia: States, Movements, and the Politics of Oppression,* edited by Meredith L. Weiss and Michael J. Bosia. Urbana: University of Illinois Press. Pp. 1–29.

Buss, Doris, and Didi Herman. 2003. *Globalizing Family Values: The Christian Right in International Politics*. Minneapolis: University of Minnesota Press.

Denike, Margaret. 2010. "Homonormative Collusions and the Subject of Rights: Reading *Terrorist Assemblages*." *Feminist Legal Studies* 18 (1): 85–100.

Díez, Jordi. 2015. *The Politics of Gay Marriage in Latin America: Argentina, Chile, and Mexico.* New York: Cambridge University Press.

Douglas, Stacy, Suhraiya Jivraj, and Sarah Lamble. 2011. "Liabilities of Queer Anti-Racist Critique." *Feminist Legal Studies* 19 (2): 107–18.

Duggan, Lisa. 2002. "The New Homonormativity: The Sexual Politics of Neoliberalism." In *Materializing Democracy: Toward a Revitalized Cultural Politics*, edited by Russ Castronovo and Dana D. Nelson. Durham, NC: Duke University Press. Pp. 175–94.

Fetner, Tina. 2008. *How the Religious Right Shaped Lesbian and Gay Activism*. Minneapolis: University of Minnesota Press.

Fischer, Frank. 2003. *Reframing Public Policy: Discursive Politics and Deliberative Practices*. New York: Oxford University Press.

Frank, David John, and Elizabeth H. McEneaney. 1999. "The Individualization of Society and the Liberalization of State Policies on Same-Sex Sexual Relations, 1984–1995." *Social Forces* 77 (3): 911–43.

Gottweis, Herbert. 1998. *Governing Molecules: The Discursive Politics of Genetic Engineering in Europe and the United States*. Cambridge, MA: MIT Press.

Haider-Markel, Donald. 2010. *Out and Running: Gay and Lesbian Candidates, Elections, and Policy Representation*. Washington, DC: Georgetown University Press.

Haider-Markel, Donald, and Mark R. Joslyn. 2013. "Politicizing Biology: Social Movements, Parties, and the Case of Homosexuality." *Social Science Journal* 50 (4): 603–15.

Hulst, Merlijn van, and Dvora Yanow. 2016. "From Policy 'Frames' to 'Framing': Theorizing a More Dynamic, Political Approach." *American Review of Public Administration* 46 (1): 92–112.

Keating, Christine. 2013. "Conclusion: On the Interplay of State Homophobia and Homoprotectionism." In *Global Homophobia: States, Movements, and the Politics of Oppression*, edited by Meredith L. Weiss and Michael J. Bosia. Urbana: University of Illinois Press. Ch. 11.

Keck, Thomas M. 2009. "Beyond Backlash: Assessing the Impact of Judicial Decisions on LGBTQ Rights." *Law & Society Review* 43 (1): 151–86.

Kingdon, John W. 2010. *Agendas, Alternatives, and Public Policies, Update Edition, with an Epilogue on Health Care*. 2nd edition. Boston: Pearson.

Klawitter, Marieka, and Brian Hammer. 1999. "Spatial and Temporal Diffusion of Local Antidiscrimination Policies for Sexual Orientation." In *Gays and Lesbians in the Democratic Process*, edited by Ellen D. B. Riggle and Barry L. Tadlock. New York: Columbia University Press.

Kollman, Kelly. 2009. "European Institutions, Transnational Networks, and National Same-Sex Unions Policy: When Soft Law Hits Harder." *Contemporary Politics* 15 (1): 37–53.

Kollman, Kelly, and Matthew Waites. 2009. "The Global Politics of Lesbian, Gay, Bisexual, and Transgender Human Rights: An Introduction." *Contemporary Politics* 15: 1 (March): 1–17.

Lax, Jeffrey R., and Justin H. Phillips. 2009. "Gay Rights in the States: Public Opinion and Policy Responsiveness." *American Political Science Review* 103 (3): 367–86.

Mucciaroni, Gary. 2008. *Same Sex, Different Politics: Success and Failure in the Struggles over Gay Rights*. Chicago: University of Chicago Press.

Murray, David. 2014. "The (Not So) Straight Story: Queering Migration Narratives of Sexual Orientation and Gendered Refugee Claimants." *Sexualities* 17 (4): 451–71

Nicol, Nancy, and Miriam Smith. 2008. "Legal Struggles and Political Resistance: Same-Sex Marriage in Canada and the USA." *Sexualities* 11 (6): 667–87.

Novkov, Julie, and Scott Barclay. 2010. "Lesbians, Gays, Bisexuals, and the Transgendered in Political Science: Report on a Discipline-Wide Survey." *PS: Political Science & Politics* 43 (1): 95–106.

Puar, Jasbir. 2007. *Terrorist Assemblages: Homonationalism in Queer Times*. Durham, NC: Duke University Press.

Puar, Jasbir. 2013. "Rethinking Homonationalism." *International Journal of Middle East Studies* 45 (2): 336–39.

Rayside, David M. 2008. *Queer Inclusions, Continental Divisions: Public Recognition of Sexual Diversity in Canada and the United States*. Toronto: University of Toronto Press.

Rosenberg, Gerald N. 2008. *The Hollow Hope: Can Courts Bring About Social Change?* 2nd edition. Chicago: University of Chicago Press.

Saurette, Paul, and Kelly Gordon. 2013. "Arguing Abortion: The New Anti-Abortion Discourse in Canada." *Canadian Journal of Political Science* 46 (1): 157–85.

Schmidt, Vivien A. 2008. "Discursive Institutionalism: The Explanatory Power of Ideas and Discourse." *Annual Review of Political Science* 11 (1): 303–26.

Smith, Miriam. 2008. *Political Institutions and Lesbian and Gay Rights in the United States and Canada*. New York: Routledge.

Sommer, Udi, Victor Asal, Katie Zuber, and Jonathan Parent. 2013. "Institutional Paths to Policy Change: Judicial versus Nonjudicial Repeal of Sodomy Laws." *Law & Society Review* 47 (2): 409–39.

Stone, Amy L. 2012. *Gay Rights at the Ballot Box*. Minneapolis: University of Minnesota Press.

Stychin, Carl F. 1998. *A Nation by Rights: National Cultures, Sexual Identity Politics, and the Discourse of Rights*. Philadelphia: Temple University Press.

Tarrow, Sidney G. 2011. *Power in Movement: Social Movements and Contentious Politics*. Cambridge: Cambridge University Press.

Tremblay, Manon, David Paternotte, and Carol Johnson. 2011. *The Lesbian and Gay Movement and the State: Comparative Insights into a Transformed Relationship*. Farnham, England: Ashgate.

Valenzuela, Ali Adam. 2014. "Tending the Flock: Latino Religious Commitments and Political Preferences." *Political Research Quarterly* 67 (4): 930–42.

Weiss, Meredith L. 2013. "Prejudice before Pride: Rise of an Anticipatory Countermovement." In *Global Homophobia: States, Movements, and the Politics of Oppression*, edited by Meredith L. Weiss and Michael J. Bosia. Urbana: University of Illinois Press. Pp.149–73.

Weiss, Meredith L., and Michael J. Bosia (eds.). 2013. *Global Homophobia: States, Movements and the Politics of Oppression*. Urbana: University of Illinois Press.

Wintemute, Robert. 2001. "Conclusion." In *Legal Recognition of Same-Sex Partnerships: A Study of National, European, and International Law*, edited by Robert Wintemute and Mads Andenaes. Oxford: Hart. Pp. 759–73.

Wolfson, Evan. 2007. *Why Marriage Matters: America, Equality, and Gay People's Right to Marry*. New York: Simon & Schuster.

United Nations. 2008. *Yogyakarta Principles*. www.yogyakartaprinciples.org (accessed May 6, 2015).

Zanghellini, Aleardo. 2012. "Are Gay Rights Islamophobic? A Critique of Some Uses of the Concept of Homonationalism in Activism and Academia." *Social & Legal Studies* 21 (3): 357–74.

25

Top Down, Bottom Up, or Meeting in the Middle?

The U.S. Government in International LGBTQ Human Rights Advocacy

CYNTHIA BURACK

The U.S. Government and SOGI Human Rights

In recent years, a category has been added to those already familiar to students and advocates of human rights: human rights jeopardy based on sexual orientation and gender identity (or SOGI) (Keating and Burack 2016). Officials and agencies of the U.S. government have responded to the integration of SOGI human rights by engaging in programs and projects designed to support and advocate for human rights for LGBTQ people abroad.[1] These programs and projects are executed in cooperation with local LGBTQ groups and activists, national and transnational LGBTQ rights organizations, and other entities, including faith groups, corporations, mainstream human rights organizations, foreign governments, the United Nations, and other civil society organizations (CSOs). In this arena, different LGBTQ organizations bring different goals, competencies, and constituencies to engagement with the U.S. government on SOGI human rights advocacy. But more importantly, the process of engagement between the U.S. government and these diverse groups and advocacy sectors makes it difficult for any one group or community to impose its goals or preferred social, legal, and political strategies on the others or to set human rights agendas.

The U.S. government was not an early adopter of SOGI human rights. However, under the Obama administration the United States has become arguably the "biggest player" in LGBTQ human rights in the world, and I have heard that phrase or some variation of it used to describe the United States by international human rights professionals.[2] Within the U.S. government, the main agency that has taken up the cause of SOGI human rights and integrated these rights into its mandate is the Department of State. And most U.S. government programming on SOGI/LGBTQ human rights is carried out by the State Department's Bureau of Democracy, Human Rights, and Labor (DRL), which also focuses on improving human rights for other "marginalized/vulnerable populations" or "populations at risk." Among these marginalized populations are groups such as women, youth, asylum seekers, disabled people, racial or ethnic minorities, religious minorities, and indigenous people (U.S. Department of State 2015).[3]

Created specifically to address violations of SOGI human rights abroad, the Global Equality Fund (GEF) was announced in Secretary of State Hillary Clinton's 2011 International Human Rights Day speech in Geneva, Switzerland, and implementation commenced in early 2012. The GEF is an umbrella fund that supports three kinds of assistance programs that perform different functions and, in some cases, serve different populations. These three categories of assistance are emergency support; long-term technical assistance and organizational capacity building; and small grants. The GEF is not the only U.S. government funding source that has been available to groups and individuals involved with SOGI human rights, and it is not the only initiative that currently exists to serve members of the LGBTQ community whose human rights are in jeopardy. However, with its three distinct categories of assistance and many partners and grantees around the world, the GEF is the best known of the SOGI human rights programs and initiatives of the U.S. government. It is also a set of programs with which many LGBTQ activists affiliated with the African LGBT organization I address below are familiar.

With regard to the Global Equality Fund and similar programs situated within the State Department, particular terms denote the relationship of the U.S. government to outside entities. For example, "implementing partners" are grantees who receive U.S. government funding. The difference between implementing partners and other "grantees" is that implementing partners are organizations that receive U.S. government funding and then subcontract services and resources to other grantees. "Partners" are organizations, including other governments, that provide resources to implementing partners and grantees (U.S. Department of State 2015).

The first category of assistance is the emergency support provided by Dignity for All. Dignity is a "rapid response" subprogram of GEF that provides emergency funds, advocacy support, and security assistance to LGBTQI individuals or groups under threat or attack due to their sexual orientation or gender identity (U.S. Department of State n.d.[a]). The State Department's implementing partner for the Dignity grants is a consortium of international organizations led by Freedom House, a U.S.-based nonprofit and "independent watchdog organization dedicated to the expansion of freedom around the world" ("About Us" n.d.). Freedom House and its consortium partners disburse emergency funds directly to LGBTQ organizations, human rights defenders, and vulnerable LGBT people for such forms of emergency assistance as security training, medical or legal assistance, trial monitoring, prison visits, and temporary relocation of threatened activists or organizations.

The second category of assistance in the GEF is for long-term capacity-building and technical-assistance grants that either directly fund programs of local, in-country LGBTQ organizations or fund grants to international groups to work with local organizations. Programs help enhance the capacity of pro-LGBTQ CSOs to support their constituencies through, for example, supporting legal challenges and legal reforms, working to expand allies in civil society, and fostering the ability of CSOs to monitor, document, and respond to human rights violations.

The third category of assistance under the GEF consists of small grants of under twenty-five thousand dollars disbursed to local organizations through U.S. embassies for high-impact programs. "Embassy engagement" has been one prong of official U.S. government support for LGBTQ human rights in recent years, and U.S. embassy officials work with LGBTQ advocates and grassroots organizations to support vulnerable populations. Because working closely with local groups and advocates can enable U.S. embassy personnel to acquire knowledge of the needs of local LGBTQ groups and advocates, the Global Equality Fund confers discretion to disburse small grants to those groups and advocates for purposes such as creating educational curricula and training materials and developing civil society networks. Every U.S. embassy has a Human Rights Officer whose responsibility it is to investigate allegations of human rights violations where they serve, and to represent human rights as they have been defined by the Universal Declaration of Human Rights and other treaties and declarations. At the 2015 conference I discuss below, U.S. State Department officials encouraged the human rights advocates in attendance to contact U.S. Embassy Human Rights Officers for assistance with SOGI human rights violations.

In this chapter, I provide a brief overview of major U.S. government SOGI human rights programs that constitute a global arena for cooperation among the U.S. government, local in-country LGBTQ groups, and other human rights organizations. Examining these programs and actors in a particular context, I argue that it is misleading to conceptualize the terms of these programs as being dictated by funders and imposed upon LGBTQ groups abroad. LGBTQ groups often rely on the resources and advocacy of nonindigenous groups, the U.S. government, other governments, and/or human rights organizations and foundations for their fixed costs, programming and legal defense expenses, and many other costs. Additionally, U.S. government officials and agencies formulate policies and design and execute human rights programs upon which many LGBTQI organizations rely. A feature of U.S. government human rights programming and advocacy is that policy constraints set some boundaries to the agendas that can be advanced by U.S. government programs. However, as I hope to show, even the existence of these funding relations and constraints does not ineluctably set the terms of U.S. government engagement with independent, indigenous LGBT groups in a way that places the United States or its representatives in control of human rights agendas. U.S. government SOGI human rights interventions with organizations in the Global South do raise important questions for theories and practices of democracy. As I suggest below, however, these concerns do not conclusively demonstrate that SOGI human rights interventions on the part of the U.S. government are parlous for democracy.

In this analysis I focus on the relationship between State Department officials in the Bureau of Democracy, Human Rights, and Labor and an African LGBTI human rights organization I will call the African Sexual Orientation and Gender Identity Human Rights Organization, or ASOGIHRO—which conveniently can be pronounced "A SOGI HeRO"—for short. Because some ASOGIHRO subscribers and conferees would be likely to suffer negative consequences if their affiliation or participation became public, ASOGIHRO does not advertise its conference online or publish lists of attendees. For that reason, I have given the organization a pseudonym, and in what follows I don't divulge information that would identify the group or the location of its biennial meeting. I learned about the organization, its work, and its relationship with the U.S. State Department when I met the organization's executive officer in Washington, DC, in 2014. In 2015, I was permitted to register for the conference myself and once there, I attended sessions, collected literature from the wide variety of groups whose members represented their organizations at the meeting, and spoke informally with activists and funders, including responding to inquiries about my research. All other information in this chapter is drawn from my field notes for the 2015 meeting, conference literature (2013 and 2015), a 2014 interview and follow-up questions with DRL's director of global programming, and other sources as indicated. By attending the conference and collecting data about the organization and its partnership with the State Department, I hoped to accomplish two tasks relevant to this chapter. The first task was to gain first-hand knowledge of how the U.S. government engages in SOGI human rights advocacy with indigenous LGBTQ groups. And the second was to use my own observations and information collected from the 2015 meeting to verify information about U.S. government SOGI human rights advocacy provided by a State Department official, government documents, and other sources and, thus, to enhance the reliability of this account.

The 2013 Conference

ASOGIHRO is a pseudonym for an indigenous regional LGBTQ advocacy organization that functions as an umbrella group to support civil society activism on sexuality, sexual health, and SOGI human rights in Africa. Besides a commitment to human rights, the organization's vision encompasses such values as gender equality, human dignity, and social justice. ASOGIHRO does not list on its website names of individuals who are connected with the group, a decision that is probably a response to threats that have confronted LGBTQ activists in some African countries in recent years. As an umbrella organization, ASOGIHRO is a grantor that provides resources to sexual-minority groups; it is also a grantee of the U.S. government, and of other human rights and social-justice CSOs.

In early 2013, the executive officer of ASOGIHRO visited Washington, DC, to meet with U.S. government officials, including Patricia Davis (DRL director of Global Programs) and Jesse Bernstein (then senior program officer and team leader for Marginalized Populations).[4] In addition to conversations regarding the GEF, ASOGIHRO's representatives invited Davis and Bernstein to attend ASOGIHRO's 2013 conference. That meeting brought together activists and members of LGBTQ groups from across Africa and members of the international human rights community, African and non-African. The majority of attendees were citizens of African nations; a smaller number of attendees were academics at African universities or representatives of funding organizations. Davis and Bernstein attended as representatives of the State Department—the first instance of U.S. government participation in the conference—and the two were the only government representatives of a foreign state present.

The conference opened with a preconference for donors from a number of organizations: Dutch and Norwegian CSOs, George Soros's Open Society Foundations, the McArthur Foundation, the American Jewish World Service, the Ford Foundation, and Benetech. Of these, Benetech might be less familiar than many large human rights groups. Benetech is a nonprofit umbrella enterprise that, among other activities, hosts a human rights program, the Human Rights Data Analysis Group, and includes Martus: secure software for creating databases for human rights groups and reports that protects the identity of witnesses to human rights abuses. Benetech analysts have provided data analysis and expert testimony in many cases of human rights violations in Latin America, Asia, Africa, Eastern Europe, and the Middle East for such clients as the UN Office of the High Commissioner for Human Rights (Benetech 2013).

A key goal for the ASOGIHRO preconference was determining which "priority populations" donors would serve among the groups of particular interest to the conference organizers: lesbians, gay men, bisexuals, transgender people, men who have sex with men, refugees, and sex workers. With regard to these groups, U.S. policies prohibit international organizations that receive U.S. funding from using those funds to advocate for sex workers' rights or for decriminalization of sex work, although U.S. agencies can fund programs for sex workers on the basis of issues such as sex trafficking, anti-LGBTQ bias, or health (HIV/AIDS, for example). These policies include the Trafficking Victims Protection Reauthorization Act and the United States Leadership against HIV/AIDS, Tuberculosis, and Malaria Act (known as the Global AIDS Act), both passed into law in 2003. The prohibition on U.S. government funds being applied to sex workers' rights advocacy is unpopular in the human rights community because it is widely understood to burden and complicate transnational responsiveness to sex trafficking and to sexual health threats (Ditmore and Allman 2013).[5]

A significant session at the 2013 ASOGIHRO conference, scheduled for the afternoon of the conference's second day, was "Donor Speed Dating," so denoted in the conference program.[6] Conference organizers placed conferees in about a dozen circles of approximately fifteen participants each so that conferees could talk directly with donors about sources of funds and assistance and how to access them. Donors—representatives of human rights organizations and the U.S. State Department—were timed as they circulated from one group to the next, speaking to each group for seven minutes. The DRL's Davis and Bernstein described to conferees the three ways in which the Bureau of Democracy, Human Rights, and Labor could render financial support for LGBTQ people and groups by way of the GEF and took questions. Many activists followed up with private or small-group meetings with Davis, Bernstein, or both about how to access U.S. assistance.

In describing the conference, Davis reported that many, perhaps most, of the activists in attendance had never met with U.S. government representatives and that these activists responded positively to the message that LGBT Africans and human rights advocates would be eligible to receive U.S. human rights assistance. The human rights activists Davis described as having been "very welcoming" to the U.S. delegation and other funders in 2013 were also welcoming in 2015.

The 2015 Conference

For the 2015 meeting, attendance had increased enough that plenary sessions were held in a large tent rather than an indoor space as they had been in 2013.[7] ASOGIHRO's executive officer, whom I met in Washington, DC, in 2014, invited me to the 2015 meeting; thus, I was able to attend, observe events, and meet some African human rights activists, U.S. government grantees, and U.S. government implementing partners. The U.S. delegation attending the conference expanded between 2013 and 2015 to five members: Bernstein, Davis, and Emily Renard from the State Department and Vy Lam and Todd Larson from the U.S. Agency for International Development (USAID). USAID is the U.S. government agency whose mandate is international economic development, poverty relief, and humanitarian assistance. However, under the Obama administration, the State Department and USAID were engaged in efforts to integrate SOGI human rights into development programs; the LGBT Global Development Partnership, of the Center for Transformational Partnerships of USAID's Global Development Lab, has been one such initiative.

In November 2014, between the two ASOGIHRO meetings, the State Department and USAID hosted a Conference to Advance the Human Rights of and Inclusive Development for LGBTI Persons at the State Department in Washington, DC. The conference brought together U.S. officials, LGBTQI human rights activists from around the world, and representatives of foreign governments and human rights organizations. Among the outcomes of the conference was a "Joint Government and Multilateral Agency Communique" that affirmed general commitments to SOGI human rights as well as specific commitments to integrate SOGI into development assistance and to use diplomacy to advance the human rights of LGBTQ people. At the conference, some plenary sessions were made up of U.S. and other government officials, representatives of human rights CSOs, and international LGBTQ human rights activists. Human rights advocates also met separately from government representatives, and the human rights defenders—the majority of whom were leaders and activists representing local or regional LGBTQ organizations outside the United States—produced a document entitled "Civil Society and Non-State Donor Recommendations." This document outlined priorities for SOGI human rights work and provided a detailed explication of policy recommendations, interorganization coordination protocols, and guidelines for designing, implementing, monitoring, and evaluating human rights efforts in cooperation with local advocates and advocacy organizations ("Civil Society and Non-State Donor Recommendations" 2014).

As in 2013, U.S. officials were the only government officials to attend the 2015 conference, although a representative of a Norwegian CSO that works closely with that state attended on behalf of the Norwegian government. In 2015, the donor preconference attracted representatives from organizations that grant funding for SOGI human rights, including Astraea, the Jewish World Service, Wellspring, and the Open Society Foundations. I did not attend the ASOGIHRO preconference, so my account begins with the conference proper. A plenary session on the first day of the ASOGIHRO meeting was entitled "We Don't Know the Answers (but We Have a Few Explanations)." This donor-led session was proposed by State's Bernstein and Davis and featured Davis and representatives of three CSOs that fund SOGI human rights–related projects and programs: U.S.-based Astraea and the American Jewish World Service, and the Deutsche Gesellschaft für Internationale Zusammenarbeit (German Society for International Cooperation). The idea of the panel was for funders to explain to human rights activists and representatives of LGBTQ organizations what specific conditions apply to funding from their organizations, to respond to questions about funding opportunities and constraints, and to suggest ways in which differently situated groups—such as those whose representatives were in attendance at the conference—could assist local and regional LGBTQ human rights organizations.

In 2015, as in 2013, activists and panelists discussed the specific constraint on U.S. government policies that, according to Davis, was a subject of difficult conversations in 2013: U.S. policies that prevent the funding of sex-worker-rights activism by agencies and officials. Davis explained that the constraint does not bar funding for assistance to sex workers as long as that assistance is not related to sex workers' rights or decriminalization of sex work. Although some activists who attended the session pushed back against the sex-worker-rights/decriminalization constraint, Davis noted that the prohibition affects all U.S. government assistance and requires congressional action to reverse. She also explained that the funds and assistance disbursed by the United States to support LGBT human rights originate either from U.S. tax revenue or from contributions of governments, foundations, or other funders. Whatever the source of these resources, when they are managed and disbursed by a U.S. government agency, they are subject to internal government processes of accountability.

In her remarks, Davis set forth goals for cooperation between the U.S. government and grassroots LGBTQI activists: to listen to activists about their needs and issues; to travel to meet activists in locations around the world; to bring activists to meetings in donor countries; to deploy knowledgeable personnel to work closely with activists to meet their needs; to protect the safety and security of grantees and those who benefit from human rights interventions; and to work with grantee activists and organizations to adequately report what they accomplish with the GEF assistance they receive. Two questions addressed to Davis as the U.S. representative focused on the operational needs of organizations. The first criticized a typical model of assistance as geared to prioritizing—and funding—high-profile deliverables rather than meeting the fixed and ongoing costs of advocacy organizations. Davis responded that State Department human rights programs funded through the GEF can, in fact, be used to pay fixed costs such as rent, personnel, and equipment, so that human rights groups are able to function effectively over time. The second operational question concerned the difficulties activists often have with the reporting and administrative demands of managing grants from international funders. In her response, Davis outlined a practice by which the State Department funds a grant to a larger organization as an implementing partner, and the implementing partner then subgrants to the smaller group and agrees to take on the task of administering the grant. This practice provides a cooperative path to funding small LGBT human rights organizations while shifting administrative tasks to groups with more infrastructure and expertise in grant administration.

A key piece of information about U.S. government resources and assistance dedicated to LGBTQ human rights was revealed in the "We Don't Know the Answers" plenary session: under normal circumstances, implementing partners and grantees who receive congressionally appropriated foreign assistance are required to "mark" or "brand" all products of U.S. government assistance at public meetings, on organizations' websites, and on all other materials that might be produced from that assistance (U.S. Department of State n.d.b). However, DRL has received an exemption to this branding requirement because of the sensitive nature of many of its human rights programs and because association with the United States could place many human rights defenders at risk. This exemption is explained in grant agreements that grantees (and implementing partners) sign when they receive aid. The exemption means that grantees are free to reveal their cooperation with the United States, but they are not required to publicize a grantee-grantor relationship with the U.S. government that may leave them open to charges of colluding either with the United States or in Western cultural imperialism. And many are likely to deny such a relationship if denial is in the interest of an LGBTQ organization or the activists affiliated with it.

LGBTQ organizations do make use of the exemption to the State Department's marking policy. For example, even though ASOGIHRO is both a grantee of and an implementing partner with the U.S. government, no information about its relationship with the United States appears on its website or in other materials. As I have researched U.S. government interventions on behalf of LGBTQ human rights, I have discovered that many such in-country advocacy groups have ties with the U.S. State Department that they do not reveal to the public. For example, at a recent LGBTQ human rights conference in a European city, I met one such DRL GEF grantee who leads a Middle Eastern LGBTQ human rights organization. The activist's organization serves as a network hub for and regional partner with other Middle Eastern LGBTQ organizations and does not advertise its relationship with the U.S. State Department.

The second day of the conference included sessions of "Activist-Donor Speed Dating." The conference program promised activists "open engagement" with funders in the "Speed Dating" sessions and, indeed, the discussion was lively and informative in the sessions I attended. Organized differently than it was in the 2013 program, this version of "speed dating" featured two sets of four concurrent sessions. Each one of the first set of sessions concentrated on a region of Africa: North, South, East, and West. Representatives from the State Department, USAID, and other funding organizations spread out and formed a funder panel for each session. These regional sessions were followed by a brief break, after which a new set of topical sessions convened.

The topical session of "Activist-Donor Speed Dating" I attended focused on Sexual Health, and the U.S. government panelist for that session was the State Department's Jesse Bernstein. Bernstein offered the session attendees a quick yet detailed overview of the three types of assistance that make up the Global Equality Fund and represent opportunities for funding and assistance for LGBTQ human rights advocacy. He gave group members examples from funded projects that would be relevant to sexual health advocacy. One activist in this session asked how difficult or bureaucratic the process of applying for GEF funding is, and Bernstein outlined a revised and streamlined grant process designed to be more proposer friendly than previous processes. In this process advocates respond to a solicitation for proposals for particular programs by submitting a two-page statement of interest (SOI) without a budget. Donor representatives review the SOIs and request full formal proposals from activists or organizations for projects that are deemed competitive. At the formal proposal stage, potential grantees can receive further guidance from State Department personnel to complete the proposal, and DRL sometimes encourages activists from smaller organizations to seek partnership with more experienced LGBTQ organizations such as ASOGIHRO.

SOGI human rights advocates attended the ASOGIHRO 2015 biennial meeting from across the continent of Africa. Although I do not have a comprehensive list of national delegations, I know that activists from the following countries attended: Algeria, Angola, Botswana, Burundi, Cameroon, Democratic Republic of Congo, Egypt, Ethiopia, Ghana, Kenya, Liberia, Mozambique, Nigeria, South Africa, South Sudan, Tanzania, Uganda, Zambia, and Zimbabwe. In this chapter, I focus on the discourse and mechanisms of U.S. government advocacy on behalf of LGBTQ human rights, and on the reception of that advocacy by a subset of LGBTQ human rights activists. However, taken as a whole, the conference incorporated presentations and discussions on a variety of topics germane to the concerns of LGBTQ people in different legal, social, and cultural positions in African nations, including the benefits and limitations of litigation; navigating conflict in and among LGBTQ human rights organizations; the role of young people in the movement; promoting transgender rights and awareness; migration, asylum seeking, and refugees; the role of art in the movement; addressing public health concerns of LGBTQ people (including HIV/AIDS); international advocacy; employment and entrepreneurship for LGBTQ people discriminated against in labor markets; building movement sustainability; and LGBTQ people and religion. Funders also attended these sessions throughout the course of the meeting, no doubt learning more about the pressures, challenges, programs, and successes of the LGBTQ movement on the continent.

SOGI human rights interventions of the U.S. government raise broader questions about the theory and practice of democracy. No doubt there are many such questions and implications, but here I will address three. The first is transparency, an issue that becomes salient when government officials don't disclose detailed, specific information regarding, for example, the recipients of U.S. government human rights assistance. A second question often raised by progressive critics of U.S. government interventions with and on behalf of gender and sexual minorities is that the terms of U.S. government assistance, or merely the inequalities that prevail between the United States and poorer nations, may impose a particular understanding of sexual or gendered identity on recipients of human rights aid (Zeidan 2013). Finally, an issue that is explicitly taken up in this volume is that LGBTQ politics have, over time, become shaped and determined more by "funding power" than by "people power," or that the movement—and its agendas and priorities—are imposed from the top down rather than being developed and effectuated from the bottom up.

SOGI Human Rights Advocacy and Democracy

Democratic theorists generally embrace the proposition that government transparency—sometimes called "publicity"—with regard to official acts and communications is crucial to an informed, deliberative, and participatory citizenry (Gutmann and Thompson 1998). Transparency has been understood as a good in and of itself as well as a necessary, though not a sufficient, condition for holding policymakers and other government officials accountable (Naurin 2007).[8] One U.S. LGBTQ activist who has called for more transparency from the State Department on the operation of the Global Equality Fund is Michael Petrelis, whose questions about U.S. government SOGI human rights advocacy exemplify concerns of many advocates of democratic accountability. Petrelis has used his blog, the Petrelis Files, to acquaint readers with his requests for information and his criticism of the State Department's failure to provide detailed information about the GEF and its grantees. Petrelis offers readers a request for information regarding the GEF that he sent to the State Department:

> I wish to learn about the transparency of the Global Equality Fund and need to know where I can find a list of all donors, amounts contributed, expenses, and grants made to LGBT groups since the fund's inception. Where do I obtain this info on the web?
>
> Looking around the State Department site and various government and independent watchdog sites, has not turned up a financial accounting for the public and taxpayers. As both a global gay advocate and transparency activist, I very much wish to see documentation about the money that has flowed in and out of the fund.

Underlining the inadequacy of the response he received to this request, Petrelis makes a classic case for transparency from public officials who oversee and administer the GEF. He emphasizes that "the question before us is how do we follow the money and learn who verifies that the contributions are reaching their intended beneficiaries." Petrelis shares the frustration of many citizens and activists who have tried unsuccessfully to extract information from their government in order to hold policymakers and other public officials accountable when he writes that "the GEF has to engage in respectful dialogue with transparency advocates and immediately release a financial accounting to the public" (Petrelis 2014).

As the circumstances of the ASOGIHRO conferences suggest, in the arena of human rights, an unresolved conflict can prevail between legitimate demands for transparency and the value of protecting the identities of members of marginalized groups. Even before conferees assembled for the 2015 meeting, we were all reminded of the grave conditions in which many LGBTQ individuals and activists live and work. An ASOGIHRO organizer emailed participants traveling to the conference with instructions not to inform anyone of the existence or purpose of the meeting once we arrived in the host country. Organizers arranged transportation from locations in a nearby city to the undisclosed location where the conference would be held. In situations where lives are endangered, DRL officials sacrifice transparency to shield those whose human rights are imperiled. One way to characterize this peril is to say that in the case of SOGI human rights violations, people face double jeopardy: LGBTQ people and human rights defenders may suffer persecution for *being* LGBTQ or an advocate for LGBTQ people, but they may also suffer suspicion and persecution for cooperating—or being perceived to cooperate—with the U.S. government or Western moral degeneracy.

Second, critics of Western hegemony worry that a Western or U.S. understanding of relatively fixed LGBT identities can—or almost certainly does—produce a normalizing effect on local, non-Western human rights advocates and LGBTQ people that may not be a deliberate goal of those who would design and execute programs. This consequence of the power imbalance between Western/U.S. government officials and local, indigenous human rights advocates seeking resources is likely to be a de facto requirement that foreign citizens who engage in sexual relations or in forms of gender presentation or performance that are culturally nonnormative *identify* as gay, lesbian, bisexual, or transgender in order to gain access to resources or forms of protection that U.S. government agencies or entities offer to those whose human rights may be being violated on the basis of their nonconforming gender or sexuality. This anxiety about the imposition of forms of identity or identification is a subset of larger worries about Western cultural imperialism that are central to many personal worldviews, theoretical systems, and practical political programs. Indeed, anxieties about cultural and political imposition have shaped American and other Western feminist theories and practices, in the academy as well as in political organizations and electoral politics.

For these critics, the ASOGIHRO conferences provide an informative example of the operation of U.S. government outreach to those whose human rights are imperiled on the basis of sexuality or gender identity/expression. The conferences are organized by an African LGBTQ organization on behalf of a consortium of African groups, and the U.S. representatives and other funders who attend are guests of the conference organizers. Thus, donors, including U.S. government officials, are in no position to screen possible recipients for their adherence to particular sexual or gender identifications that fit a model preferred by or familiar to Western or U.S. elites. In addition, ASOGIHRO, and the other groups whose members attended the 2015 conference or provided materials there self-consciously employ identifiers such as LGBT, LGBTI, MSM (men who have sex with men), WSW (women who have sex with women), transgender, transwoman, and transman to identify themselves and the objects of their activism.[9]

The empirical question of whether, or under what conditions, U.S. government acts or actors impose particular conceptions or terms related to gender and sexuality on people around the world can be investigated in part by gathering information about the ways in which State Department SOGI human rights programs are designed and administered. In the case of the GEF, as well as other initiatives that are not related to immigration, U.S. agencies and representatives do not screen individual recipients of U.S. human rights resources and assistance for particular configurations of identity. Rather, organizations—often groups in-country and close to LGBTQ people who are served by initiatives like the GEF—serve imperiled individuals and groups without regard for the nuances of how such individuals (or groups) identify themselves or the language they use to do so.

Clearly, men who have sex with men, women who have sex with women, and people who do not identify as conventionally gendered in their own social or cultural context may name themselves using different terms that may signify different cultural meanings or create different group boundaries (Wilson 2004). These cultural differences are important for outsiders to understand for the sake of cultural competency, as well as for pragmatic purposes related to joint efforts on behalf of human rights. However, I observed nothing at ASOGI-HRO to suggest that LGBTQ activists understood these categories of sexual and gender identity to have been imposed on them by outsiders. To the contrary, activists who spoke publicly in conference sessions documented and repudiated the powerful homophobic attributions aimed at them in their own social contexts while identifying themselves and their activism in the terms familiar from SOGI/LGBTQ activism in the United States (see Bosia and Weiss 2013).

Finally, a concern of proponents of democracy about funding and assistance relationships between the U.S. government and local, in-country LGBTQ organizations is that, as a global hegemon, the United States undermines democracy by using its funding and other forms of leverage to impose its will and interests on communities and to degrade their capacity for grassroots activism and democratic decision making. Here again, the ASOGIHRO, its now long-standing relationship with DRL and implementing partners, and its biennial activist conferences shed valuable light on the processes of negotiation through which LGBTQ activist agendas and programs are developed, funded, and executed. At the ASOGIHRO conferences, as well as similar venues throughout the world, U.S. government officials and grassroots human rights advocates meet or renew their acquaintance, share information about the challenges confronting activists, discuss the exigencies activists bring to the table and how their work fits into existing assistance programs, and communicate additional needs that assistance programs might meet. In the 2015 session, "We Don't Know the Answers," one of two applause lines was Davis's plea to the assembled activists to "help me help you" by working with DRL officials to report not only immediate "outputs" associated with assistance but also longer-term "outcomes" that can justify aid and contribute to internal State Department accountability for continued assistance.

As Paisley Currah has pointed out, skeptics of state action on the queer-theoretical Left often tend to "overemphasize a unity of intention on the part of state actors and to imagine the 'the state' as far more monolithic than it is" (Currah 2013). There are many examples of the significance of this internal multiplicity of "the state," including many accounts of the U.S. government simultaneously pursuing and executing contradictory goals and policies. A benign example of such internal multiplicity and contradictoriness of U.S. government policy can be seen in the differences in the grant-making processes of two agencies, USAID and the State Department. USAID has a complex and directive solicitation process (USAID 2013, 2015). By contrast, in its human rights programs, the State Department sets general priorities to serve multiple populations and to be responsive to a wide variety of needs and situations. So, for example, in July 2015, DRL established two priority themes for the year's funding solicitations. These priorities, "friends and allies" and "protecting and promoting the rights of transgender persons," emerged directly from the report drafted by activists and nonstate donors who attended the November 2014 Conference to Advance the Human Rights of and Inclusive Development for LGBTI Persons.

Conclusion

SOGI human rights interventions involving the U.S. State Department and LGBTQ/human rights organizations abroad are devised and executed neither from the top down nor from the bottom up. Both of these metaphors fail to capture the complexity of the negotiations that produce the human rights agenda and the particular projects to which the funding and assistance of the U.S. government, other governments, and CSOs are applied at a particular moment. Neither do these metaphors adequately account for the ways in which exogenous factors (such as U.S. presidential administrations, foreign policy events, executive branch agency norms and agendas) influence current configurations of policy, programming, networks, and forms of solidarity that, together, make up the complex set of conditions for human rights advocacy. Instead, the landscape of U.S. participation in international LGBTQ human rights programming and advocacy is constructed through ongoing negotiation among groups and among human rights advocates.

Although donors and implementing partners fund recipients and provide a variety of kinds of assistance to grantee individuals and organizations, donors and grantees negotiate programming and projects, including the uses of funds and other terms of assistance. These negotiations do not take place in a single venue or at a single stage in a funding process. Instead, it is common for priorities and requests to originate with activists in a variety of formal and informal venues. And after priorities have been set by funders and proposals have been solicited, activists deliver brief SOIs that outline operational needs or program concepts. As Davis put it in the "We Don't Know the Answers" plenary session, at this stage State Department human rights officials are in effect enjoining LGBTQ activists to "tell us what great ideas you have."

One feature of ongoing human rights work, such as that which prevails in the domain of SOGI human rights, is that relationships form not only among activists but also among human rights advocates and funders. In the close quarters of the 2015 ASOGIHRO conference, it was virtually impossible to avoid overhearing conversations that took place among activists and funders during each day and into each night. Throughout the conference, I saw many reunions between activists, as well as between activists and representatives of funding organizations who have developed relationships over time that are based on human rights advocacy. Such phenomena are not the usual domain of political science. However, a complete account of U.S. government SOGI human rights advocacy should take into account not only the policy mechanisms and political environments for human rights interventions but also the relational dimensions of interventions, policies, and practices.

NOTES

1 Especially in international human rights law, "sexual orientation and gender identity" (abbreviated as SOGI) is a common term. A variation is SOGIE, for "sexual orientation and gender identity or expression," which I encountered for the first time in a presentation at the 2015 ASOGIHRO conference.

2 Sweden is the largest contributor to the Global Equality Fund pioneered and administered by the United States, and as of July 2016, the other partner governments are Chile, Croatia, Denmark, Finland, France, Germany, Iceland, the Netherlands, Norway, and Uruguay.

3 Different State Department programs, and thus documents, employ slightly different lists of these groups that are relevant in particular contexts.

4 Information in this section is drawn from 2013 conference material, including the conference program; an interview with Patricia Davis conducted on April 15, 2014; and other sources as identified.

5 A specific element of these policies for many years was an "antiprostitution pledge" ruled unconstitutional by the Supreme Court in 2013 in *Agency for International Development v. Alliance for Open Society International.*

6 Both the 2013 and the 2015 biennial conferences were held in English, and the 2015 conference featured simultaneous translation for speakers of French, Portuguese, and an indigenous African language. The conference programs for both meetings were in English and French.

7 I was unable to obtain an accurate count of conference registrations, but some attendees estimated attendance at between 200 and 250.

8 The European Union has been a prolific site of scholarship and political debate about barriers to transparency and accountability.

9 Added to "LGBT" to denote intersex identity, "I" was occasionally used at the 2015 ASOGIHRO meeting. However, I didn't hear any discussion at the meeting of human rights struggles specifically related to intersex conditions or identification.

REFERENCES

"About Us." N.d. Freedom House, www.freedomhouse.org (accessed June 27, 2015).

Benetech. 2013. Martus: The Global Social Justice Monitoring System. "Resources: Press Room." www.martus.org (accessed July 20, 2013).

Bosia, Michael J., and Meredith L. Weiss. 2013. "Political Homophobia in Comparative Perspective." In Meredith L. Weiss and Michael J. Bosia, editors, *Global Homophobia*. Urbana: University of Illinois Press.

"Civil Society and Non-State Donor Recommendations from the Conference to Advance the Human Rights of and Promote the Inclusive Development for Lesbian, Gay, Bisexual, Transgender (and Intersex)* Persons." 2014. Council for Global Equality, Nov. www.globalequality.org (accessed May 22, 2015).

Currah, Paisley. 2013. "Homonationalism, State Rationalities, and Sex Contradictions" *Theory and Event* 16 (1) (accessed May 29, 2013).

Ditmore, Melissa Hope, and Dan Allman. 2013. "An Analysis of the Implementation of PEPFAR's Anti-Prostitution Pledge and Its Implications for Successful HIV Prevention among Organizations Working with Sex Workers." *Journal of the International AIDS Society* 16 (1): 1–13.

Gutmann, Amy, and Dennis Thompson. 1998. *Democracy and Disagreement*. Cambridge, MA: Harvard University Press.

Keating, Christine, and Cynthia Burack. 2016. "Sexual Orientation and Gender Identity Human Rights." *Human Rights: Politics and Practice*, 3rd edition. Michael Goodhart, editor. Oxford: Oxford University Press.

Naurin, Daniel. 2007. *Deliberation behind Closed Doors: Transparency and Lobbying in the European Union*. Essex, England: ECPR Press.

Petrelis, Michael. 2014. "State Dept's $7.5M Global Equality Fund—Transparency Now!" mpetrelis.blogspot.com, Feb. 1 (accessed June 30, 2015).

United States Agency for International Development. 2013. "Responding to a Solicitation," www.usaid.gov (accessed June 28, 2015).

United States Agency for International Development. 2015. "Training on How to Work with USAID," June 23, www.usaid.gov (accessed June 27, 2015).

United States Department of State. 2015. "Bureau of Democracy, Human Rights, and Labor Request for Proposals: Programs for Human Rights Documentation," March 4, www.state.gov (accessed June 28, 2015).

United States Department of State. N.d.(a). "About the Fund," www.state.gov (accessed June 28, 2015).

United States Department of State. N.d.(b). "Marking Policy," www.statebuy.state.gov (accessed July 9, 2015).

Wilson, Ara. 2004. *The Intimate Economies of Bangkok: Tomboys, Tycoons, and Avon Ladies in the Global City*. Berkeley: University of California Press.

Zeidan, Sami. 2013. "Navigating International Rights and Local Politics: Sexuality Governance in Postcolonial Settings." In Meredith L. Weiss and Michael J. Bosia, editors, *Global Homophobia*. Urbana: University of Illinois Press.

26

Pink Links

Visualizing the Global LGBTQ Network

CHRISTINA KIEL AND MEGAN E. OSTERBUR

The form of a network can have important implications for issue framing, for the network's ability to generate change in policy and/or society, and for expectations for the future of the movement. This chapter uses hyperlink analysis to visualize transnational LGBTQ networks on both regional and global levels. The methods employed here enable us to identify central actors within regional networks, and organizations that act as conduits among different regions. Examining all of the implications is beyond the scope of the chapter; here we provide an initial foray into the form the network takes and propose potential avenues for future research.

There are a number of studies of specific LGBTQ campaigns, e.g., Kollman (2007) on same-sex partnership recognition, Swiebel (2009) on activism at the United Nations, and Ayoub (2013) on European activism. These studies consider the goals and outcomes of campaigns, but spend little time describing the membership and structure of the larger issue network. Certain arguments relating to campaign success depend on the density and connectedness of a network; thus it is important to fill this lacuna in the literature. Elsewhere we argue that those groups that hold positions of power in a network—as measured by the number of connections or their placement as gatekeepers—will be able to affect how the larger network frames its issues (Kiel and Osterbur 2016). We identify such actors.

Organizations active in LGBTQ advocacy are aware of the need to understand who is part of the larger network. Most limit themselves to listing partner organizations on their website. Some are more analytical. For example, in 2008 the LGBT Movement Advancement Project (MAP) published a report cataloging "Major international advocacy organizations who work to secure the rights and welfare of lesbian, gay, bisexual, and transgender (LGBT) people around the globe" (MAP 2008). This particular mapping exercise includes a small sample of organizations (twenty-five), chosen by experts.

Research on transnational advocacy networks (TANs) points to additional ways of describing and evaluating the structure of advocacy networks. Rogers and Ben-David (2008) describe the networks surrounding the Israeli-Palestinian conflict; Montoya (2008) explores the European network countering violence against women; Carpenter et al. (2014) map the human security issue network. Like these and other authors, we use social network analysis approaches, specifically hyperlink analysis, to visualize the connections between organizations with a common purpose, here LGBTQ advocacy.

Hyperlink analysis shows how groups with an online presence link to each other. It assumes that a connection in cyberspace mimics offline interaction. Thus, by visualizing the hyperlinks, we show which groups in which countries connect to each other, to international organizations, and to groups in other states and regions. We describe the method, as well as its advantages and limitations, in more detail in the next section.

The recent shift of public opinion in the United States towards more acceptance of people identifying as LGBTQ is coupled with increased mainstream reporting of LGBTQ issues, both domestic and international. Further, social media campaigns have sprung up addressing LGBTQ violations near and far (e.g., the Avaaz campaign in May 2015 against the criminalization of gay sex in India). This might lead one to believe that LGBTQ issues are now truly international and that rights violations in one country will evoke a global advocacy response. But few campaigns achieve this high-profile status. Most issue networks, from environmental to LGBTQ and other human rights issues, remain regional. People in the same region often face similar challenges. They share information and resources more easily (e.g., through regional organizations), and they are more capable of mobilizing across immediate borders than across oceans and continents. Therefore, we focus our analysis on the regional networks before we attempt to draw a global map of LGBTQ actors.

Our analysis presents only a snapshot of the global LGBTQ TAN, and is necessarily incomplete. But our findings are important in three ways. First, we visualize the existing ties between organizations advocating for LGBTQ rights. Second, the resulting maps, as well as what is missing from them, contribute to a more systematic agenda for LGBTQ research. Third, our findings add to the assimilation vs. liberation debate in the LGBTQ movement. The prominence of international human rights organizations that are non–LGBTQ specific could have important implications for the direction of the movement.

The chapter is organized as follows: in the next section we describe the method used to generate our maps. Then we describe the hyperlink maps of the regions and the results of the global analysis before discussing the implications for LGBTQ research and movement development.

Hyperlink Analysis: Why and How?

The Internet has become an integral tool for TAN members, connecting nongovernmental organizations (NGOs), individual activists, and governmental actors locally, regionally, and internationally (Bimber and Davis 2003; McNutt 2006). A persistent problem in the literature on advocacy networks is their ill-defined nature. Membership is often informal, temporary, and rarely institutionalized. Therefore, no membership lists exist, precluding a complete understanding of the dimensions of the network.

As the importance of the Internet combines with the desire to understand the nature of advocacy networks, scholars have turned to hyperlink analysis to model networks (e.g., Bennett 2003; Lusher and Ackland 2011; Carpenter and Jose 2012). Hyperlink analysis defines network members as communication partners, whereas "communication" is the presence of shared URLs on webpages, which can be identified using a webcrawler.[1] Webpages constitute nodes while the hyperlinks function as the tie that demonstrates communication or resource flow between actors.

The use of hyperlink analysis is predicated on the assumption that communication ties on the web mimic the social structure offline (Park 2003; Bennett 2003). Rogers (2010) asserts the value of using hyperlink analysis as a proxy, claiming that "one can begin to gain a grasp of the very normal politics of association by showing how sites link to each other, and which links are not reciprocal" (245). Using the women's peace and security TAN, Carpenter and Jose (2012) demonstrate the validity of this assumption via interviews with organization elites whose accounts of the network correspond to the model produced via hyperlink analysis. The linking practices within a TAN are comparable to academic citations as the linking behavior of organizations signals which actors in the network have prestige and influence within the group of actors identified as part of the community of shared information (Bennett and Segerberg 2013; Carpenter and Jose 2012).

Given the importance of web presence for organizations' public outreach and advocacy, a webcrawler provides a tool to define community membership and to visualize the network. Its reliability is buttressed by networks' increasing use of the web for mobilization (Bimber and Davis 2003) at a low participation cost for potential activists (Della Porta and Tarrow 2004). For social scientists, the systematic process of webcrawling is appealing, as the data provided from webpages can be analyzed statistically and incorporated into social network analysis (Marres and Weltevrede 2013).

The use of hyperlink analysis is not without limitations, however. Lusher and Ackland (2011) find that in the asylum seeker advocacy network, the online network was more expansive and individual organizations more popular online than offline. Online networks may appear more dense than offline networks when organizations view hyperlinking as cost free. This cautions against seeing the online network as a true portrait of the offline connections. Furthermore, Bennett and Segerberg (2013) have noted the need for caution when studying organizations with incentives to conceal specific ties. They point out that U.S.

congressional candidates are unlikely to link to their covert advisors or large donors on their webpages, although they are certainly central to the influence network.

To what extent do these concerns apply to the global LGBTQ TAN? When one does not specify parameters of exclusion for corporations/organizations that function as donors, these appear in the network. But this comports with the argument that the "pink dollar" advances LGBTQ organizations via appeals to sponsors. Donors in the LGBTQ context would be part of the TAN and would not be expected to conceal their connections.

More worrisome, for certain issue areas, including LGBTQ rights, online cooperation is not cost free. In conservative societies, much advocacy work is clandestine; transnational connections could open both the international NGO and the local partner to criticism of being imperialists or stooges, respectively. Due to these limitations, the hyperlink network may be interpreted as providing evidence of the structure and scope rather than all the details of network behavior (Lang 2013).

We utilize the International Lesbian, Gay, Bisexual, Trans, and Intersex Association (ILGA) 2012 annual report member listing to procure the starting points (seeds) for the webcrawl, which was conducted using Richard Roger's Issue Crawler.[2] Issue Crawler works by systematically identifying URLs within the HTML of the seed sites provided by researchers to determine which sites (or pages) are linking directly to each other (inter-actor analysis) or are connected through a third site (co-link analysis). The webcrawler includes additional actors in the network if they are linked to our originating websites. ILGA was used to establish our network parameters because it acts as a global umbrella organization for local, national, regional, and international LGBTQ groups. In its role as a world federation, it promotes interagency information sharing and facilitates individuals' connections to organizations that claim expertise in LGBTQ issues. ILGA has more than one thousand member organizations from around the world, making its membership directory a legitimate starting point for our analysis. We begin by mapping regional networks using those ILGA member organizations in the 2012 annual report with active websites and subsequently include the regional seeds in the global crawl. The resultant crawls provide evidence for interaction between organizations that may include information exchange, joint relationships, or shared agendas, though the network map alone cannot specify the nature of the interaction. What can be understood from the network maps is the relative dominance of particular TAN actors as well as the capacity to engage in collaborative advocacy within the network (Lang 2013).

We conduct a co-link analysis, as we are interested in organizations that function as hubs or gatekeepers in the network (Carpenter 2011; Lusher and Ackland 2011). Co-link analysis parallels citation analysis in that ties demonstrate a shared inbound link from a third node (website B links to website A *and* website C links to website A, thus B→C as the tie in the network model) (Bennett and Segerberg 2013; Marres 2012). Co-link is preferable to interactor analysis as it provides a higher threshold for centrality (how important is a node to the entire network): actors who share reciprocal links but fail to share links to a third website are omitted from the network. This can reduce the potential for "false positives" in which actors who should not be considered a part of the network appear due to reciprocal linking (Carpenter and Jose 2012).[3]

Webcrawls conducted via Issue Crawler can be manipulated with regard to the depth of the websites crawled, how many pages into a site are analyzed, and the iterations, that is, how far beyond the original seeds the crawl expands. The constraints put on these parameters may alter the shape of the network in important ways. By using a crawl depth of three and three iterations, we aim to be as inclusive as possible while avoiding peripheral actors or commercial ventures that function merely as sponsors. Lang (2013) asserts that crawl depths above three result in the inclusion of peripheral actors as the expectation for the average consumer of a website to venture past three menus is unlikely and information beyond this depth is considered less central by the organization itself. Similarly, a narrow iteration of one or two limits the resultant network to only those that might be properly understood as a solidarity network, while an iteration of three is likely to capture the links that matter to the mission of the TAN (Bennett and Segerberg 2013).

The maps described in the following sections do not present a complete picture of the LGBTQ TAN. Rather, they should be understood as a sample of transnational activity on LGBTQ issues. There are a number of technical limitations to the webcrawl. First, only the top one hundred distinct sites are included in the co-link analysis. If there are more organizations in the network that receive fewer links than the top one hundred nodes, they will not show up. Second, each iteration of the crawl stops after a maximum of URLs (forty thousand) have been fetched. In large networks, that could leave some areas unexplored. And third, some important organizations may be excluded for a number of reasons: they may not use hyperlinks to connect to other organizations; their website address had recently changed or was under development/out of order; they use social media exclusively to forge their networks (social media websites are excluded from our crawls because only the general facebook.com or twitter.com sites would appear, not individual groups' pages).

Another limitation is temporal: we only provide a snapshot of a particular moment in time. However, repeated crawls show that the networks are quite stable over a number of months. Overall, we are confident that hyperlink analysis is a useful tool for LGBTQ TAN research. As we elaborate in our conclusion, additional methods have to be incorporated to make substantial claims about TAN formation, activity, and success. But our maps based on hyperlinks identify central players and important connections within and across geographical regions.

Descriptions of Regional Networks

As a first step to determine the global LGBTQ network, we generate maps for six subnetworks, by regions distinguished in the ILGA 2012 annual report: Africa, Asia, Aotearoa/New Zealand/Australia/Pacific Islands (ANZAPI), Europe, Latin America/Caribbean, and North America. For each network we examine two measures of centrality: degree centrality and betweenness centrality, reported in a separate table for each region. Degree centrality is the sum of the ties between a node and every other node in the network, which measures access between nodes. A higher average degree centrality indicates that communication may travel more quickly through the network. Degree centrality is a measure of the prestige of a node in the network. Betweenness centrality measures the number of shortest paths (a path connecting two actors going through the fewest number of nodes) that go through a particular node. Betweenness indicates the extent to which a node functions as a broker in the network, providing the quickest or only linkages between other nodes. This broker function affords those organizations with large betweenness measures greater social power in the ability to control the flow of resources, particularly to otherwise isolated nodes.

Africa

In 2012, ILGA had ninety-one African member organizations from twenty-two countries. The representation of the countries varies from one (Botswana, Ghana, Rwanda, and others) to twenty (South Africa) members per country. Three groups registered anonymously, all of them in predominantly Muslim countries. Because many organizations have no web presence, and others use free online platforms like Facebook or Blogspot, the crawl starts with thirty-nine seeds from twelve countries. The hyperlink map for Africa (figure 26.1) depicts the one hundred most-connected nodes. The size of the nodes corresponds to

TABLE 26.1. Actor Ranking Africa

Rank	Organization	Indegree	Degree	Betweenness
1	Human Rights Watch	11	12	93.818
2	United Nations	10	13	322.325
3	Amnesty International	10	13	33.644
4	Africa Commission on Human & Peoples' Rights	10	14	66.955
5	Office of the High Commissioner for Human Rights	10	14	439.511

Notes: Average Degree=3.968; Average Path= 3.564.

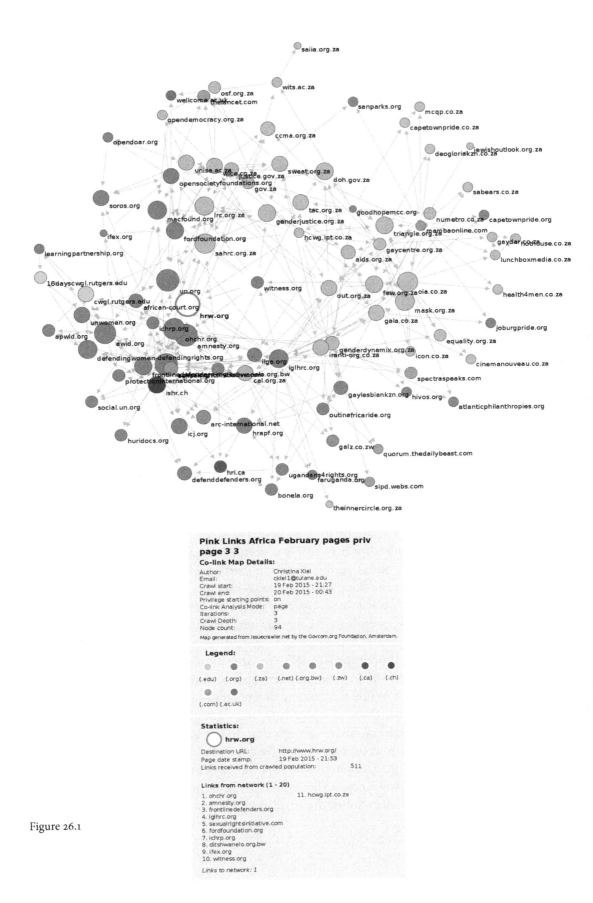

Figure 26.1

inlink count, the number of links received from the crawled population. For example, the circle representing the United Nations website, un.org, is several times larger than the circle for capetownpride.org, indicating that many more organizations linked to un.org than to capetownpride.org (un.org received forty-six links while capetownpride.org received five).

The placement of the node shows its significance relative to other nodes. For example, joburgpride.org is next to capetownpride.org, but removed from un.org, indicating a greater number of webpages linking to both these two local events than to the intergovernmental organization.

Domain names can help identify countries that are represented in the map—to a certain extent. Groups may use a neutral .org extension instead of a national one like .za for South Africa (capetownpride.org is a case in point). What is clear, however, is that South Africa is very strongly represented in this map; twenty-two of the top fifty nodes (as determined by inlink counts) have a South African domain name.

As mentioned above, South Africa is well represented in ILGA, but that cannot be enough to explain its dominance. Of the thirty-nine seeds that start our crawl, only eight have a .za extension. In comparison, four seeds are visibly of Kenyan origin, but none of them receive the necessary two links for inclusion in the co-link map.

In contrast to many other African states, South Africa inscribed strong legislative protections for LGBTQ populations in its 1996 constitution, opening spaces and lessening fear of conservative backlash (Croucher 2002). There are a small number of South African government websites that show up on the map, supporting the view that the government is open for interactions with civil society groups, as they are linking to these points of access.

Kenya is another country that is described as having a relatively strong civil society (Mercer 2002), and it has some participants in the regional network. Uganda, however—which has nine ILGA member organizations, though only one Ugandan organization is depicted on the co-link map—criminalizes homosexuality and suppresses LGBTQ organizations. Similarly, predominantly Muslim countries that are unwelcoming to gay activism are underrepresented in the network. Even though pro-LGBTQ organizations do exist in these societies, we would expect them to operate less openly and connect less frequently on public platforms. While this finding demonstrates that the online network does not always mimic the offline network, we argue that our map still accurately describes the regional TAN—groups that do not use online communication at all will have a harder time connecting offline, too.

While the largest number of nodes originates in South Africa, these are not the most dominant nodes. The largest circles denoting the most central organizations by inlink count of the African LGBTQ network are the website of the

MacArthur Foundation, the African Court on Human and Peoples' Rights, and the African Commission on Human and Peoples' Rights. When nodes are ranked by indegree (counting links from nodes included in the map), the top nodes are Human Rights Watch (eleven), Open Society Foundations (ten),[4] the UN (ten), Amnesty International (AI) (ten), African Commission on Human and Peoples' Rights (ten), and the UN Office of Human Rights (ten) (see table 26.1). Of the top nodes in Africa, only one is regionally based and none are specifically LGBTQ organizations. Human rights organizations whose mission evolves more specifically around LGBTQ rights (International Gay and Lesbian Human Rights Commission with indegree 7; ARC International with 4, and even ILGA with 4) are included in the map, but show lower degree centrality than the more general human rights organizations.

The most prestigious organizations as measured by degree centrality do not have to be the main gatekeepers as measured by betweenness centrality: the betweenness centrality within the African LGBT TAN ranges from 1,648.226 (IGLHR) to zero (Triangle Project). The Ford Foundation is noteworthy as the second-highest-ranking node for betweenness (1,278.156). The high betweenness centrality scores of international organizations and grant-making NGOs in Africa raises questions about how nonregional actors may influence issue framing or campaigns.

The top five nodes represent three of the four main categories of network members: grant-making foundations, international and regional political or judicial institutions, international human rights organizations, and national groups. It makes sense that international actors are prominent in a transnational network. It is therefore not surprising that many websites link to the United Nations and its subsidiaries (i.e., un.org, ohchr.org, unwomen.org). Interestingly, there seems to be a focus on international law as a way to address LGBTQ issues, as both the African Human Rights Court and the International Court of Justice are prominent.

U.S. foundations seem particularly active in the African context. Besides the Open Society (Soros) Foundation, the map includes the MacArthur Foundation, the Ford Foundation, and Atlantic Philanthropies. The map does not show in which countries these grant-giving institutions operate (although the Open Society Foundation has an additional link with a South African local domain extension). But the fact that they are so central in the African regional LGBTQ network is noteworthy.

Another type of organization that is very prominent in the co-link analysis are international nongovernmental human rights organizations, including Human Rights Watch (highest indegree count), Amnesty International, and International Service for Human Rights (indegree 6; betweenness 81.629). We will return to this finding below.

Asia

Fifty of the eighty-seven Asian ILGA members have a web presence and become our seeds for the co-link map (figure 26.2). The resulting network map of Asia (figure 26.2) is a disconnected graph: the displayed nodes form several separate networks. One reason for this is the large number of included countries and the geographical size of this region. For example, one subgraph depicts organizations in Israel that are connected to each other; another includes Japanese groups. A common national domain extension is Singapore, despite this country's small size. Chua's case study of the Singapore gay community explains this finding: Singapore's repressive laws and authoritarian government present a difficult environment for gay activists. After a government crackdown in the late 1990s, groups "suspended physical operations, and coincidently discovered the communications possibilities of the Internet" (Chua 2012, 731). The expectation that the Internet acts as a "shield" leads to proliferation of online activity.

Countries that have a large share of ILGA members, like India and the Philippines, are not represented accordingly, probably in part because of the unreliability of the electric grid affecting webservers (Plumer 2012) that may exclude sites temporarily from a crawl, and possibly also because they do not link as much to other organizations.

The organizations forming the larger network are primarily international nongovernmental organizations (see table 26.2). This means that many of the Asian LGBTQ groups link to NGOs like IGLHCR or Human Rights Watch (indegree 6; betweenness 129.04) and foundations like the Astraea Foundation (indegree 3; betweenness 348.963). The most central node by indegree is IGLHCR.

An interesting cluster includes primarily American organizations that are not known for transnational advocacy: Lambda Legal (indegree 8; betweenness 0.25), PFLAG (indegree 12; betweenness 0) and GLAAD (indegree 6; betweenness 251.254). They connect to the Asian network through international NGOs and through foundations (ARCUS and Astraea). Their betweenness centrality ranges from 0.25 for Lambda Legal to 251.254 for GLAAD. The foundations have

TABLE 26.2. Actor Ranking Asia

Rank	Organization	Indegree	Degree	Betweenness
1	IGLHRC	16	33	2,097.167
2	ILGA	13	13	0
3	PFLAG	12	12	0
4	GLSEN	12	5	154.199
5	National Center for Lesbian Rights	11	16	207.635

Average Degree=4.564; Average Path Length=3.26.

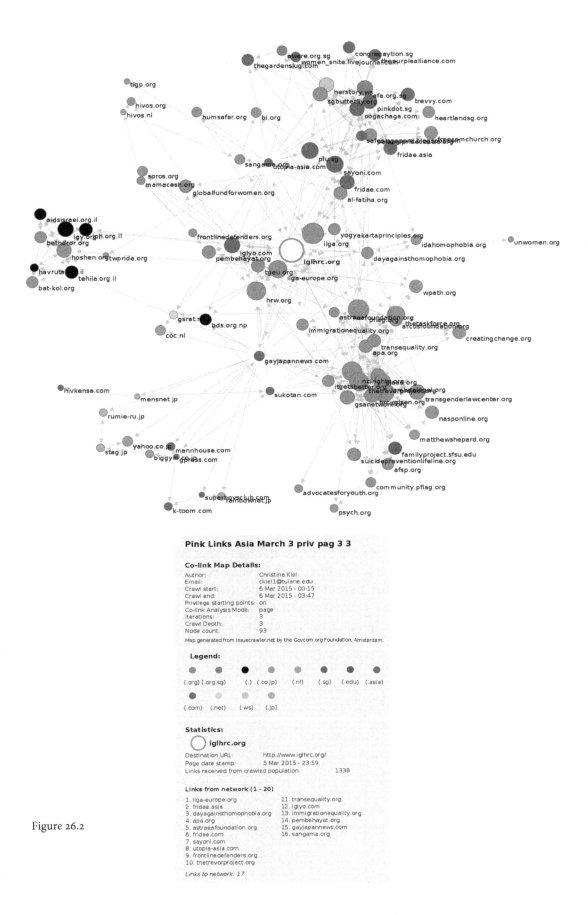

Figure 26.2

betweenness centrality of 101.507 and 348.963, respectively. These foundations support both local (United States) and international social justice programs, which helps explain their bridge-building function.

Of the top five nodes as measured by indegree, three are U.S.-based LGBTQ organizations and the top two are international LGBTQ organizations. The first regional node is Sayoni (8), a queer women's association that is ranked tenth. When turning to betweenness centrality, we find that the gatekeepers in Asia are IGLHRC (2,097.167) followed by Gay Japan News (861.669) and the Trevor Project (812.488). Of these gatekeeper nodes, only one is a regional node, and of the top ten gatekeeper nodes, six are international organizations and one is a U.S.-specific organization (the Trevor Project).

ANZAPI

ILGA combines Australia, New Zealand, and the Pacific region. There are thirty-three member organizations in five countries; twenty-five groups in four countries make the seeds for our crawl. The co-link map (figure 26.3) is exclusively made up of Australian websites. Not only were none of the organizations based in the other countries included in the map; no international NGO, intergovernmental organization, or transnational umbrella group appears. Taking a closer look at the most prominent organizations by indegree (table 26.3), the only LGBTQ organization is ranked third and also engages in general HIV/AIDS outreach (AIDS Council of NSW, indegree 20, betweenness 1,355.608). Two of the five top nodes are government information websites (NSW LawAccess, 20/0, and the Office of the Australian Information Commissioner, 16/177.285). The remaining two top nodes are crisis hotlines (Lifeline, 20/0, and Kids Helpline, 18/261.964). The lack of both ILGA and other transnational nongovernmental organizations in the ANZAPI network coincides with an extremely strong representation of government-hosted websites (twenty of the top fifty nodes have a gov.au extension). Several health-related sites, as well as those addressing human rights, immigration, and legal issues, show up on the map. The dominance of Australian government websites in the hyperlink map could indicate

TABLE 26.3. Actor Ranking ANZAPI

Rank	Organization	Indegree	Degree	Betweenness
1	Lifeline.org.a20u	20	20	0
2	Lawaccess.nsw.gov.au	20	20	0
3	Acon.org.au	20	78	1,355.608
4	Kidshelp.com.au	18	31	261.964
5	Oaic.gov.au	16	26	177.285

Notes: Average Degree=8.848; Average Path Length=2.431

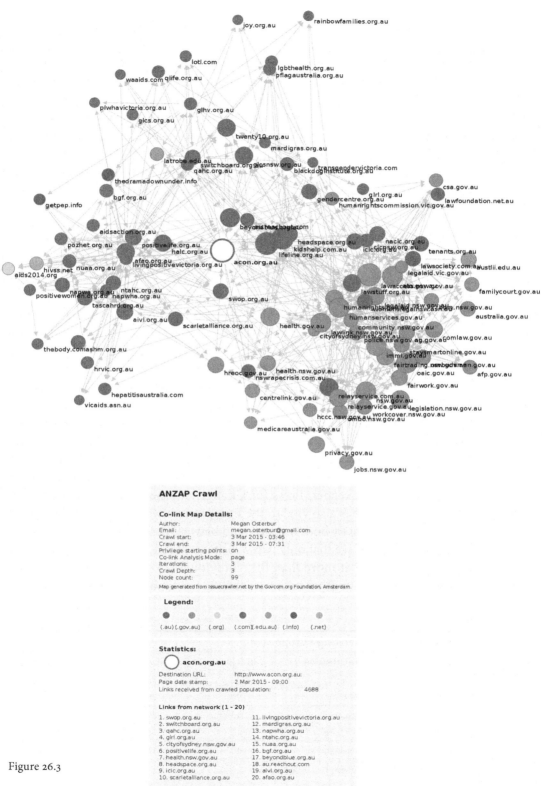

ANZAP Crawl

Co-link Map Details:

Author:	Megan Osterbur
Email:	megan.osterbur@gmail.com
Crawl start:	3 Mar 2015 - 03:46
Crawl end:	3 Mar 2015 - 07:31
Privilege starting points:	on
Co-link Analysis Mode:	page
Iterations:	3
Crawl Depth:	3
Node count:	99

Map generated from Issuecrawler.net by the Govcom.org Foundation, Amsterdam.

Legend:

(.au) (.gov.au)   (.org)   (.com)(.edu.au) (.info)   (.net)

Statistics:

acon.org.au

Destination URL:	http://www.acon.org.au
Page date stamp:	2 Mar 2015 - 09:00
Links received from crawled population:	4688

Links from network (1 - 20)

1. swop.org.au	11. livingpositivevictoria.org.au
2. switchboard.org.au	12. mardigras.org.au
3. qahc.org.au	13. napwha.org.au
4. girl.org.au	14. ntahc.org.au
5. cityofsydney.nsw.gov.au	15. nuaa.org.au
6. positivelife.org.au	16. bgf.org.au
7. health.nsw.gov.au	17. beyondblue.org.au
8. headspace.org.au	18. au.reachout.com
9. iclc.org.au	19. aivl.org.au
10. scarletalliance.org.au	20. afao.org.au

Links to network: 58

Figure 26.3

an openness of the government to LGBTQ issues that makes transnational advocacy connections less urgent. Coupled with Australia's high level of development, which reduces the need for outside funding, and the country's remoteness from other highly developed states interested in networking, the availability of government resources may limit local groups' efforts to connect to international organizations or advocacy campaigns. When we rerun the crawl excluding government websites, the map remains exclusively Australian. We note that the network is less advocacy focused and more concerned with the quality of life of the LGBTQ population, as demonstrated by the dominance of health organizations and helplines noted above.

Europe

ILGA is a Europe-based organization, and its base is on the continent. The umbrella organization had more than four hundred European members from forty-two countries in 2012. The co-link map demonstrates the central place ILGA-EU has in the European LGBTQ network (figure 26.4). It has the most inlinks, has the highest indegree centrality (32), and is centrally located on the map. The central node of ILGA connects to national clusters in the Netherlands, Switzerland, and France. Besides ilga.org and ilga-europe.org, the Dutch COC emerges as a central actor (indegree 10; betweenness 368.961). The European organizations connect to U.S. foundations as well (Open Society, indegree 4; betweenness 13.134), though not as often and as centrally as the African LGBTQ network. By indegree the most prestigious organizations in the network are ILGA-EU, ILGA, Transgender Europe, Ravad, and Inter-LGBT (see table 26.4). ILGA-EU serves as the strongest gatekeeper, based on betweenness, with the second highest gatekeeper, Press for Change, at a betweenness of 1,003.032. Transgender Europe is also vital to the European network as the third-highest-ranking organization by both indegree and betweenness.

It is surprising to see that only two websites with UK extensions are included in the map, given that more than fifty individual UK-based organizations are ILGA members. As in other countries that have a lot of LGBTQ organizations,

TABLE 26.4. Actor Ranking Europe

Rank	Organization	Indegree	Degree	Betweenness
1	ILGA-EU	32	95	4,075.929
2	ILGA	20	20	0
3	Tgeu.org	13	26	405.18
4	Ravad.org	11	26	193.45
5	Inter-lgbt.org	10	16	53.458

Notes: Average Degree=5.122; Average Path Length=2.732.

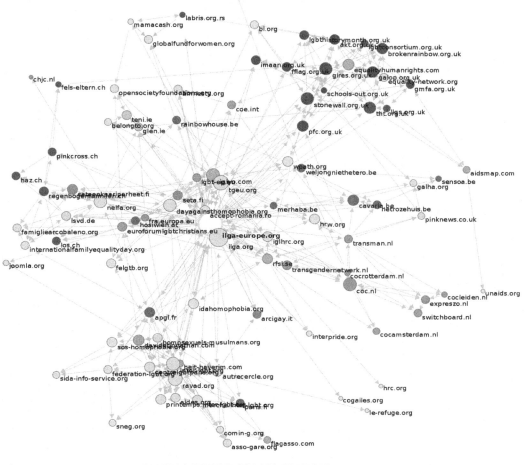

EU-LGBTQ Reader Crawl

Co-link Map Details:

Author: Megan Osterbur
Email: megan.osterbur@gmail.com
Crawl start: 2 Mar 2015 - 19:42
Crawl end: 3 Mar 2015 - 03:46
Privilege starting points: on
Co-link Analysis Mode: page
Iterations: 3
Crawl Depth: 3
Node count: 98

Map generated from Issuecrawler.net by the Govcom.org Foundation, Amsterdam.

Legend:

(.ro)	(.org)	(.com)	(.org.uk)	(.fr)	(.it)	(.be)	(.nl)
(.int)	(.eu)	(.ch)	(.ie)	(.at)	(.org.rs)	(.de)	(.co.uk)
(.se)	(.fi)						

Statistics:

ilga-europe.org

Destination URL: http://www.ilga-europe.org/
Page date stamp: 2 Mar 2015 - 22:53
Links received from crawled population: 3729

Links from network (1 - 20)

1. marche.inter-lgbt.org	11. rfsl.se
2. nelfa.org	12. seta.fi
3. pfc.org.uk	13. lgbt-ep.eu
4. printemps.inter-lgbt.org	14. labris.org.rs
5. ravad.org	15. inter-lgbt.org
6. weljongniethetero.be	16. glen.ie
7. transgendernetwerk.nl	17. davidetjonathan.com
8. tgeu.org	18. federation-lgbt.org
9. teni.ie	19. hosiwien.at
10. sateenkaariperheet.fi	20. homosexuels-musulmans.org

Links to network: 63   < | >

Figure 26.4

this finding underlines that local groups do not always cooperate with each other. Instead, they may work on distinct issues, either localized or thematically. They may also conduct advocacy work abroad. Holzhacker (2012) finds that organizations that achieve their goals domestically branch out and establish transnational coalitions. Lastly, groups with similar missions may see each other as competition for members or funding sources and be reluctant to publicize the other's website.

Latin America and the Caribbean

The Latin America and Caribbean hyperlink crawl starts with a large number of seeds: 250 organizations in 27 countries are ILGA members, yielding 89 seeds. The resulting map (figure 26.5) shows a well-distributed network that clustered less along national lines than in other regions. Here, Argentine, Brazilian, Chilean, and other websites connect to each other. There is no obvious bridge. There are also fewer international LGBTQ NGOs. ILGA and IGLHRC are present, but they are less central than in other regions (indegrees of 3 and 2, respectively). Other major NGOs like AI and HRW and foundations are missing. One possible explanation for this is the dominance of the Catholic Church in the region and its political resistance to the recognition of sexual-orientation- and gender-identity-based organizations in the United Nations Economic and Social Council (ECOSOC) (Swiebel 2009). It may be the case that linking to international organizations makes pursuing policy change domestically more problematic.

Surprisingly, a significant number of organizations in the network are dedicated to an issue unrelated to LGBTQ issues: pro-choice advocacy. Groups from a number of countries (Planned Parenthood and Center for Reproductive Rights in the United States, Aborto Legal in Argentina, and CLADEM in Peru) link to each other, building a network in which women's rights organizations serve as gatekeepers for the LGBTQ TAN (these organizations have high betweenness centrality). Closer investigation shows an overlapping issue network of organizations campaigning for a Convention on Sexual and Reproductive Rights

TABLE 26.5. Actor Ranking Latin America/Caribbean

Rank	Organization	Indegree	Degree	Betweenness
1	UNAIDS	13	20	161.918
2	United Nations	12	10	376.293
3	UNFPA	8	14	160.777
4	Women Using the Law as Tool for Change	7	15	337.871
5	World Bank	7	8	88

Notes: Average Degree 3.385; Average Path 4.672.

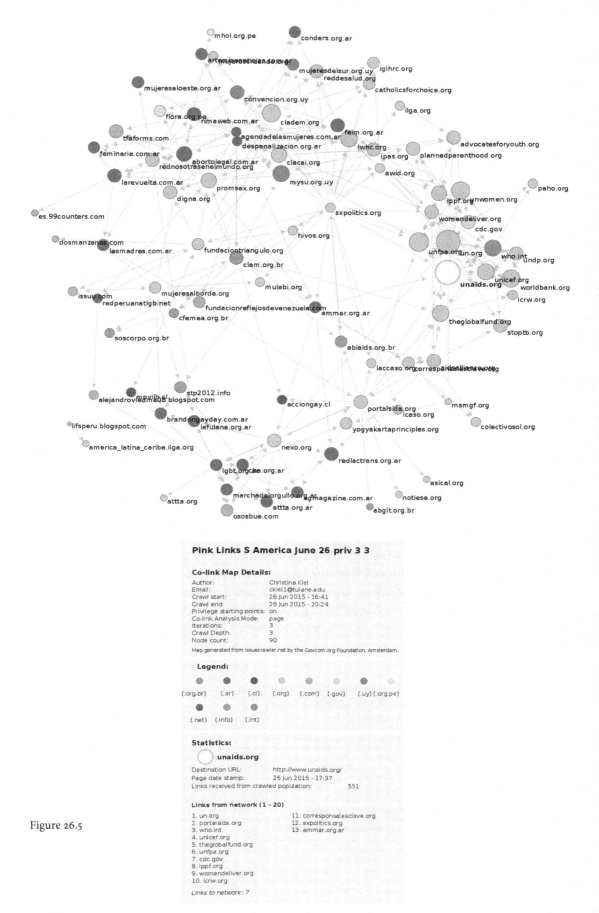

Figure 26.5

(Convencion de los derechos sexuales y los derechos reproductivos, convencion.org.uy). This issue network is also connected to more general women's and health advocacy, including to the dominant cluster (by both degree and betweenness centrality) of intergovernmental organizations—UN, WHO, UN Women, and many more.

The Latin American network's more prestigious nodes by indegree are predominantly international institutions: UNAIDS, UN, UNFPA, and World Bank are all among the top five nodes. The reliance of this network on international institutions and women's rights organizations (the fourth-ranked node is Women Using the Law as a Tool for Change) is noteworthy (see table 26.5). The large betweenness scores indicate that these institutions also serve as important gatekeepers to the network and thus should wield considerable influence.

North America

The North American region consists of only two countries, the United States and Canada.[5] In 2012, ILGA had eighty-six members from this region, sixty-four of which are associated with working hyperlinks.

Not surprisingly given the source for our starting points, ILGA shows up on all maps, with the exception of the ANZAPI region. The organization's bridge-building capacity is most obvious in the North American context. Here two large clusters—one primarily consisting of Canadian nodes and one made up of U.S. organizations—are connected by ILGA and, to a lesser degree, by human rights organizations, e.g., Egale, HRW (figure 26.6). Relatively large nodes, indicating high inlink counts, characterize the Canadian cluster of the network. However, the nodes of U.S. LGBTQ groups have a higher degree of centrality than Canadian nodes, showing more links going towards U.S. organizations, with the top five indegree nodes all from the United States (see table 26.6). The top organizations in terms of betweenness centrality, and thus ability to control information flows, include two Canadian organizations based in Quebec (Fondation Emergence, betweenness 1,130.274, and Arc-en-ciel d'Afrique, betweenness 869.338).

TABLE 26.6. Actor Ranking North America

Rank	Organization	Indegree	Degree	Betweenness
1	National Center for Lesbian Rights	22	29	189.91
2	GLSEN	20	33	236.65
3	Trevor Project	18	28	702.08
4	GSA Network	16	36	499.194
5	Transgender Law Center	16	16	0

Notes: Average Degree=7.16; Average Path Length=3.108.

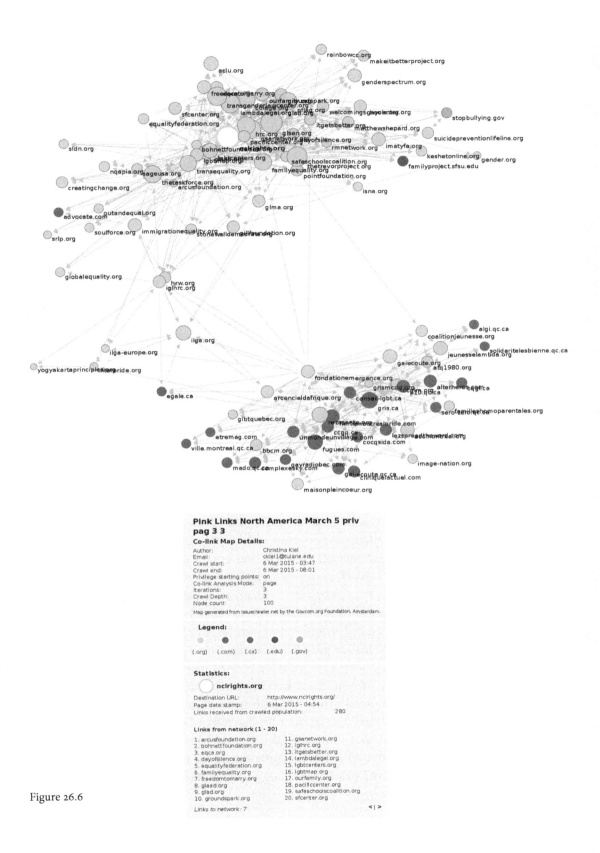

**Pink Links North America March 5 priv
pag 3 3**

Co-link Map Details:

Author: Christina Kiel
Email: ckiel1@tulane.edu
Crawl start: 6 Mar 2015 - 03:47
Crawl end: 6 Mar 2015 - 08:01
Privilege starting points: on
Co-link Analysis Mode: page
Iterations: 3
Crawl Depth: 3
Node count: 100

Map generated from issuecrawler.net by the Govcom.org Foundation, Amsterdam.

Legend:

● ● ● ● ●

(.org) (.com) (.ca) (.edu) (.gov)

Statistics:

◯ **nclrights.org**

Destination URL: http://www.nclrights.org/
Page date stamp: 6 Mar 2015 - 04:54
Links received from crawled population: 280

Links from network (1 - 20)

1. arcusfoundation.org   11. gsanetwork.org
2. bohnettfoundation.org   12. iglhrc.org
3. eqca.org   13. itgetsbetter.org
4. dayofsilence.org   14. lambdalegal.org
5. equalityfederation.org   15. lgbtcenters.org
6. familyequality.org   16. lgbtmap.org
7. freedomtomarry.org   17. ourfamily.org
8. glaad.org   18. pacificcenter.org
9. glad.org   19. safeschoolscoalition.org
10. groundspark.org   20. sfcenter.org

Links to network: 7   < | >

Figure 26.6

This region is a good example of how LGBTQ issue networks remain localized. The interaction rate is higher within countries than across, resulting in denser, though geographically confined, networks. In fact, three out of the five most central nodes are representing organizations based in California (NCLR, the Trevor Project, and the Transgender Law Center).

Comparing Regions

Comparisons of the individual networks lead to some interesting findings:

The average degree varies dramatically. It is much higher for the North American (7.16) and ANZAPI (8.848) regions than for the Latin American (3.385) or African (3.968) regions. This indicates differences in the general level of linking activity among the nodes. The explanation is straightforward: networks that cross fewer international borders are denser as organizations more commonly link to domestic partners. Crawls of regions that encompass many countries more often result in maps that show distinct clusters of groups from the same country (e.g., Europe, Asia). The average path length (how many connections does it take to link two nodes with each other?) is shorter in these denser networks, too. The shortest paths are in the ANZAPI network (2.431), the longest in Africa (3.564) and Latin America (4.672).

Transnational connections are most important for organizations that operate in relative isolation in countries with few national advocacy groups or less activity. The same organizations will have to look outside of their country's borders for financial support. There will be little national government funding for an LGBTQ movement that is fighting for recognition and legitimacy in a hostile or agnostic society (or in economically weak countries). At the same time, groups that have achieved progress on LGBTQ issues in their own country often direct their advocacy across borders. Organizations like COC Nederlands are very active on transnational LGBTQ advocacy (Holzhacker 2012; Kiel and Osterbur 2016).

Additional to LGBTQ-centered transnational organizations, large grant-making institutions have taken up the banner of international LGBTQ rights. Philanthropic organizations from the Open Society Foundations to the Ford Foundation have added grant opportunities for LGBTQ projects, usually through their social justice programs. International grant-making foundations are included in all networks except the ANZAPI map.

The prominence of non-grant-making international NGOs has two explanations. One, large philanthropic organizations based in the United States link to human rights groups like Human Rights Watch and Amnesty International, and vice versa. But more importantly, in countries where LGBTQ organizations operate without a national infrastructure for the movement, connecting to transnational human rights campaigns can provide information, legitimacy, and moral support.

For similar reasons, intergovernmental institutions like the United Nations and the World Health Organization are present in most regional networks. Intergovernmental organizations are great meeting points for TANs, and a number of LGBTQ groups are accredited with the United Nations Economic and Social Council and participate in/observe some UN deliberations. The African TAN in particular includes a number of UN-related nodes (e.g., un.org, unwomen.org, ohchr.org), underlining this network's international outlook.

International Connections

Next we include more than six hundred ILGA members as seeds into the global network crawl. Figure 26.7 shows the network, and the top twenty-five nodes by indegree are listed in table 26.A in the appendix. The resulting map looks substantially different from a combined map of the regional maps. There are a number of explanations for these differences: First, as mentioned above, the crawler stops fetching pages after a certain number of URLs (forty thousand/iteration) have been crawled. A network with so many starting points (six hundred are inadvisable, but possible) could include more hyperlinks that will be left out once the crawl stops.[6] Second, in the global network we exclude pages that have a .gov extension. As demonstrated in the ANZAPI network, governmental actors can be integral to an issue network. They have, however, by definition, a national focus and we want a global map to depict transnational actors. Excluding links with certain extension may cause some co-linking from these nodes to disappear. We also exclude ilga.org to minimize the number of co-linkages that occur only because European organizations are members of both ILGA and ILGA-Europe.

As a consequence, the global map, even more so than the regional ones, has to be understood as a sample of the real-world TAN. We argue, however, that it is representative of the complete hyperlink network, as the most central nodes that occur most frequently will be included.

The map shows a dense center dominated by ILGA-EU. ILGA's European daughter organization has a degree centrality of 66, and a betweenness centrality of 2,709.62, by far the largest in the global network (the next highest degree score is 25; the second highest betweenness score is 896.307). The centrality is to be expected. All our starting seeds have their ILGA membership in common, and most of them will advertise it on their website—and ILGA and ILGA-EU share a database of LGBTQ organizations.

Connected to the central nodes are a number of regional clusters: organizations based in France form one cluster, a few Belgian organizations form another, and British LGBTQ groups form a third. Apart from these regional clusters, the network shows a large number of nodes with .org extensions, many located in the United States. This area of the network map includes non-LGBTQ-specific human rights organizations like HRW, and grant-making foundations.

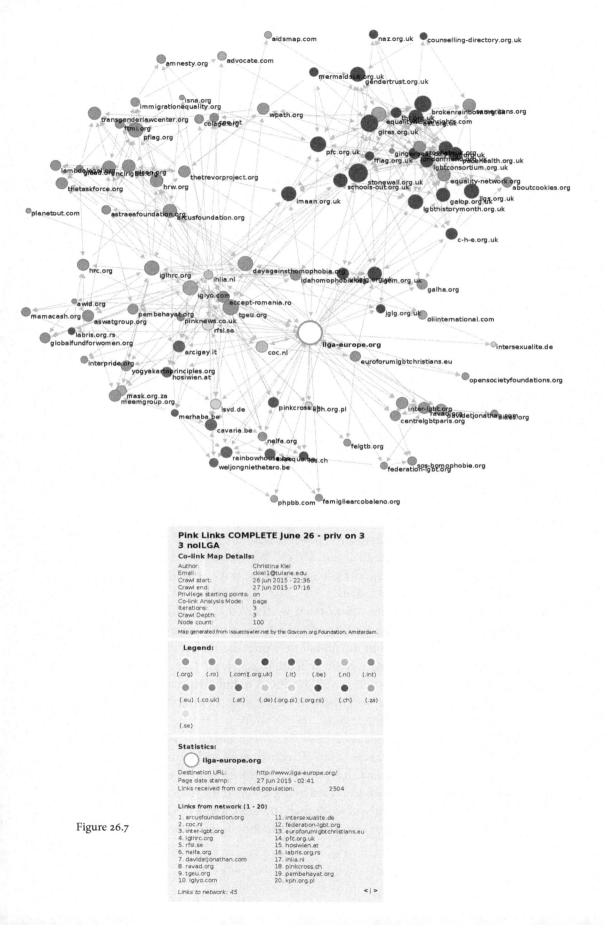

Figure 26.7

The transnational network is dominated by European organizations. In fact, there are no nodes from Asia, the Pacific region, Africa, or Latin America among the top fifty ranked pages (mask.org.za, South Africa, is the first non-Western website with a rank of 75).

What explains this dominance of European organizations? The larger number of starting seeds from Europe is part of the answer. Another explanation is the dominance of European organizations at intergovernmental institutions—most LGBTQ groups that are registered with the United Nations are European, giving them a higher profile and thus higher probability that organizations in another part of the world will link to them.

We further expect the European LGBTQ TAN to follow the prediction that online connections are low cost and therefore plentiful, while in other, less LGBTQ-friendly parts of the world, groups are more cautious about their online presence. And lastly, groups that were successful at home may now focus on international advocacy. For example, the presence of UK-based organizations outside the EU region (e.g., the National Center for Lesbian Rights in Asia and the Wellcome Trust in Africa) can explain the dominance of UK groups in the global map despite their lack of dominance in the EU map. These organizations may be pursuing an international strategy focusing on the Global South.

Actors who drive regional campaigns do not have to participate in global advocacy. And dense networks around health and quality-of-life issues (Australia) do not have international change on their agenda. But the transnational connections visible in figure 26.7 are essential when considering large-scale advocacy efforts, flows of funding for LGBTQ programs, and the ties between some local groups and international human rights organizations.

Non-LGBTQ-Specific Human Rights Organizations in the Network

Highly central nodes in networks may function as policy entrepreneurs, establishing the frames for issues and thus defining problems as well as solutions for the network more broadly. In the global context, the consistent presence of non-LGBTQ-specific human rights organizations and grant-making institutions may have important implications for the LGBTQ movement. Specifically, we would expect that greater dominance by those institutions will move the LGBTQ TAN toward assimilationist politics and a human rights discourse as opposed to a liberationist and sexual-autonomy discourse.

The adoption of the human rights framework has propelled LGBTQ political claims into the mainstream and provided moral leverage for activists and governmental actors alike (Waites 2009; Swiebel 2009; Wilson 2009). Assimilation has been a requisite aspect of this adoption, with established human rights NGOs functioning as gatekeepers who define the parameters of the potential emancipatory project of sexual liberation, usually as a Westernized "gay right"

(Massad 2002; Gross 2013). From the perspective of queer theorists, this form of assimilation serves to reinforce the binaries of gender and hetero/homo and thus limits the scope of the LGBTQ TAN agendas (Moran 2000; Kollman and Waites 2009; Sheill 2009; Waites 2009; Gross 2013).

The above hyperlink analyses of the regional LGBTQ TANs demonstrate the importance of non-LGBTQ organizations to the network in particular through the betweenness centrality of these organizations. As a great number of shortest paths in the network pass through these non-LGBTQ organizations, their ability to facilitate information and resource flows is evident. To the extent that previous scholars point to limitations of the human rights narrative, this has important implications for the future of the movement: assimilation will continue. Future research should continue to examine the network as it evolves, incorporating content analysis and qualitative techniques that consider the framing of goals and strategies of those actors most closely connected to human rights organizations, grant-making institutions, and political institutions relative to those LGBTQ organizations with longer paths.

Non-LGBTQ organizations are less central to the global TAN. The main reason for this is that European organizations are so dominant in this map, and Europe is less connected to general human rights organizations than African and Latin American LGBTQ TANs. This finding poses the question whether assimilation strategies are more common in the Global South, and if so, whether this is the case out of local necessity (to overcome religious and cultural stigma) or due to outside issue framing.

Conclusion

This chapter set out to describe regional LGBTQ TANs, and to give a glimpse of the global connections. Using hyperlink analysis, we visualize major players and note some interesting patterns. The presence of non-LGBTQ organizations—human rights organizations, grant-making institutions, and governmental actors—contributes to our understanding of who is participating in LGBTQ advocacy. The regional maps vary greatly in this regard; for example, non-LGBTQ actors are dominant in Africa, North American organizations that are locally focused are found in the Asia map, and women's human rights organization are prevalent in the Latin America and Caribbean map. It is noteworthy that the global map sees more actors in the top one hundred nodes from regions considered more progressive on LGBTQ rights or with greater web usage in general than actors from other regions.

However, it should be noted that the resulting maps are no more than starting points for substantive analyses of the LGBTQ network. They do not claim to answer questions about TAN activities or successes, strengths, and weaknesses.

Instead, they help us develop a research agenda based on questions that come to mind when looking at the hyperlink maps. For example, the omnipresence of large, established philanthropic foundations poses a number of interesting questions for future research: Can international support make a positive difference in the lives of LGBTQ populations in unfriendly societies? How do power imbalances between small, underfunded local organizations and rich Western groups define their partnership (the Open Society Foundations alone spent $873 million in 2013, $51 million on grants related to international human rights)? Will these donors impact the way LGBTQ issues are framed locally?

Other research questions may grow out of the curious finding that transgender organizations are very central to the European and the global LGBTQ TAN. One might theorize that transgender individuals could feel underrepresented in umbrella LGBTQ organizations, thus increasingly acting though their own groups.

Future research may address these questions via mixed methodology, adding content analysis of the webpages and interviews with organization elites to these network maps (see Carpenter and Jose 2012 for an example of this approach with regard to women's rights). Content analysis in particular may be used to explore the extent to which non-LGBTQ actors in the TANs are advocating an assimilationist human rights frame versus maintaining sexual liberation frames. Interviews with elites in the TANs may provide insight into the funding linkages between organizations.

The maps presented here show that the LGBTQ TAN has some global players, and many regional participants. Activists should keep in mind that networks vary across the globe, and that those groups that are central on the global level may not be the ones generating change locally—and if international organizations dominate campaigns for LGBTQ rights, they may define change as they want to see it, and less as local groups demand.

Beyond the LGBTQ context, advocacy organizations across social movements would benefit from examination of the digital map created by the TAN within which they are working. Such mapping may provide insights into the actors who dominate the online TAN, and in an increasingly digital world, those who dominate cyberspace may also frame the offline debate. As our examination of the LGBTQ TAN maps demonstrates, in some networks key players may be outside of the traditional understanding of movement insiders. TAN research should consider carefully what that means for power relations in networks. At the same time, for advocates within LGBTQ networks, research analyzing the shape of the TAN in digital space can be a useful blueprint for determining where resources may be found and explaining which frames dominate TAN discourse. In these ways, visualizing and measuring the connections across advocacy groups may prove of practical importance for advocacy organization leaders. For scholars

Appendix

TABLE 26.A. Top 25 Nodes from Global Network

	Name of organization	Location	LGBTQ focus	Human rights organization	In-Degree	Degree	Betweenness
1	ILGA-EU	Belgium	X		21	66	2,709.62
2	Stonewall	UK	X		13	24	416.976
3	Gender Identity Research and Education Society	UK	X		11	25	400.365
4	Broken Rainbow	UK	X		10	10	0
5	Press for Change	UK	X		9	17	896.307
6	Transgender Europe	Germany	X		9	16	347.988
7	Equality and Human Rights Commission	UK		X	8	19	237.543
8	Gender Trust	UK	X		8	12	217.319
9	International Gay and Lesbian Human Rights Commission	USA	X	X	8	21	339.34
10	International Gay, Lesbian, Bisexual, Transgender, & Queer Youth Organization	Belgium	X		8	26	527.254
11	Imaan	UK	X		8	8	0
12	Switchboard	UK	X		8	8	0
13	International Day Against Homophobia	USA	X		8	18	412.991
14	LGBT History Month UK	UK	X		8	12	32.641
15	PFLAG	USA	X		8	12	0
16	Albert Kennedy Trust	UK	X		8	19	131.998
17	Arcus Foundation	USA	X	X	7	16	376.578
18	Galop	UK	X		7	16	376.578
19	Lesbian & Gay Christian Movement	UK	X		7	7	0
20	LGBT Foundation	UK	X		7	7	0
21	Pace Health	UK	X		7	15	55.415
22	Schools Out	UK	X		7	21	270.126
23	Equality Network	UK	X		6	9	56.959
24	GLSEN	USA	X		6	12	206.258
25	Human Rights Watch	USA		X	6	6	0

of social movements, the LGBTQ networks mapped here suggest that visualizing the form of the network online may provide insights into the nature of the relationships and power dynamics of other TANs. Our work contributes to the evolving research program on TANs, which is moving beyond case studies of individual organizations or campaigns to include studies of the structure and composition of whole networks.

NOTES

1 Webcrawlers are programs that iteratively and automatically download websites or webpages and extract and collect the URLs on the pages (Thelwall 2001).

2 Issue Crawler is a web-based crawler that has its origins in Netlocator, developed 1999–2000. The full version of Issue Crawler that includes the cluster mapping function we deploy was developed in 2003 (Rogers 2006, 2010).

3 For example, a conservative religious website may link to an LGBT advocacy website with negative content espousing the "dangers of the gay agenda." While the LGBT advocacy website would be considered by TAN activists as part of the network, the religious website would not.

4 Open Society Foundations is not included in the table because its ranking depends on the combined degree count for opensocietyfoundations.org and soros.org.

5 ILGA includes Mexico in the Latin American and Caribbean section.

6 Increasing the ceiling to sixty thousand URLs does not change the network map in any significant way.

REFERENCES

Ayoub, Philip. 2013. "Cooperative Transnationalism in Contemporary Europe: Europeanization and Potential Opportunities for LGBT Mobilization in the European Union." *European Political Science Review* 5, no. 2: 279–310.

Bennett, W. Lance. 2003. "New Media Power: The Internet and Global Activism: Some Strengths and Vulnerabilities of Networked Politics." In *Contesting Media Power*, ed. Nick Couldry and James Curran. Lanham, MD: Rowman & Littlefield. Pp. 17–37.

Bennett, W. Lance, and Alexandra Segerberg. 2013. *The Logic of Connective Action: Digital Media and the Personalization of Contentious Politics*. New York: Cambridge University Press.

Bimber, Bruce, and Richard Davis. 2003 *Campaigning Online: The Internet in U.S. Elections*. New York: Oxford University Press.

Carpenter, Charli. 2011. "Vetting the Advocacy Agenda: Network Centrality and the Paradox of Weapons Norms." *International Organization* 65, no. 1 (2011): 69–102.

Carpenter, Charli, Sirin Duyguly, Alexander Montgomery, and Anna Rapp. 2014. "Explaining the Advocacy Agenda: Insights from the Human Security Network." *International Organization* 68, no. 2: 449–70.

Carpenter, Charli, and Betcy Jose. 2012. "Transnational Issue Networks in Real and Virtual Space: The Case of Women, Peace, and Security." *Global Networks* 12, no. 4: 525–43.

Chua, Lynette. 2012. "Pragmatic Resistance, Law, and Social Movements in Authoritarian States: The Case of Gay Collective Action in Singapore." *Law and Society Review* 46, no. 4: 713–48.

Croucher, Sheila. 2002. "South Africa's Democratisation and the Politics of Gay Liberation." *Journal of Southern African Studies* 28, no. 2: 315–30.

Della Porta, Donatella, and Sidney Tarrow. 2004. *Transnational Protest and Global Activism*. Lanham, MD: Rowman & Littlefield.

Gross, Aeyal. 2013. "Post/Colonial Queer Globalization and International Human Rights: Images of LGBT Rights." *Jindal Global Law Review* 4, no. 2: 98–130.

Holzhacker, Ronald. 2012. "National and Transnational Strategies of LGBT Civil Society Organizations in Different Political Environments: Modes of Interaction in Western and Eastern Europe for Equality." *Comparative European Politics* 10: 23–47.

International Lesbian, Gay, Bisexual, Trans, and Intersex Association (ILGA). 2012. *2012 Annual Report.* Accessed June 15, 2015, www.ilga.org.

Kiel, Christina, and Megan Osterbur. 2016. "A Hegemon Fighting for Equal Rights: The Dominant Role of the COC Nederland in the LGBT Transnational Advocacy Network." *Global Networks.* doi/10.1111/glob.12126/abstract.

Kollman, Kelly. 2007. "Same-Sex Unions: The Globalization of an Idea." *International Studies Quarterly* 51, no. 2: 329–57.

Kollman, Kelly, and Matthew Waites. 2009. "The Global Politics of Lesbian, Gay, Bisexual, and Transgender Human Rights: An Introduction." *Contemporary Politics* 15, no. 1: 1–17.

Lang, Sabine. 2013. *NGOs, Civil Society, and the Public Sphere.* Cambridge: Cambridge University Press.

Lusher, Dean, and Robert Ackland. 2011. "A Relational Hyperlink Analysis of an Online Social Movement." Carnegie Mellon University, accessed November 8, 2014. http://www.cmu.edu.

Marres, Noortje. "The Redistribution of Methods: On Intervention in Digital Social Research, Broadly Conceived." *Sociological Review* 60, no. 1 (2012): 139–65.

Marres, Noortje, and Esther Weltervrede. 2013. "Scraping the Social? Issues in Real-Time Social Research." *Journal of Cultural Economy* 6, no. 3: 313–35.

Massad, Joseph. 2002. "Re-Orienting Desire: The Gay International and the Arab World." *Public Culture* 14, no. 2: 361–85.

McNutt, Kathleen. 2006. "Do Virtual Policy Networks Matter? Tracing Network Structure Online." *Canadian Journal of Political Science* 39, no. 2: 391–405.

Mercer, Claire. 2002. "NGOs, Civil Society, and Democratization: A Critical Review of the Literature." *Progress in Development Studies* 2, no. 1: 5–22.

Montoya, Celeste. 2008. "The European Union, Capacity Building, and Transnational Networks: Combating Violence against Women." *International Organization* 62, no. 2: 359–72.

Moran, Dermot. 2000. *Introduction to Phenomenology* New York: Routledge.

Movement Advancement Project (MAP). 2008. *International LGBT Advocacy Organizations and Programs: An Overview.* Accessed June 15, 2015, www.lgbtmap.org

Park, Han Woo. 2003. "Hyperlink Network Analysis: A New Method for the Study of Social Structure on the Web." *Connections* 25: 49–61.

Plumer, Brad. 2012. "India's Infrastructure Woes, in Two Charts." *Washington Post,* Aug. 6.

Rogers, Richard. 2006. *Mapping Web Space with the Issuecrawler,* available at www.govcom.org.

Rogers, Richard. 2010. "Mapping Public Web Space with the Issuecrawler." In *Digital Cognitive Technologies: Epistemology and the Knowledge Economy,* ed. Bernard Reber and Claire Brossaud. Hoboken, NJ: Wiley.

Rogers, Richard, and Anat Ben-David. 2008. "The Palestinian-Israeli Peace Process and Transnational Issue Networks: The Complicated Place of the Israeli NGO." *New Media & Society* 10, no. 3: 497–528.

Sheill, Kate. 2009. "Losing Out in the Intersections: Lesbians, Human Rights, Law, and Activism." *Contemporary Politics* 15, no. 1: 55–71.

Swiebel, Joke. 2009. "Lesbian, Gay, Bisexual, and Transgender Human Rights: The Search for an International Strategy." *Contemporary Politics* 15, no. 1: 19–35.

Thelwall, Mike. 2001. "A Web Crawler Design for Data Mining." *Journal of Information Science* 27, no. 5: 319–25.

Thelwall, Mike. 2006. "Interpreting Social Science Link Analysis Research: A Theoretical Framework." *Journal of the American Society for Information Science* 57, no. 1: 60–68.

Waites, Matthew. 2009. "Critique of 'Sexual Orientation' and 'Gender Identity' in Human Rights Discourse: Global Queer Politics beyond the Yogyakarta Principles." *Contemporary Politics* 15, no. 1: 137–56.

Wasserman, Stanley, and Katherine Faust. 1994. *Social Network Analysis: Methods and Applications.* Vol. 8. New York: Cambridge University Press.

Wilson, Angela R. 2009. "The 'Neat Concept' of Sexual Citizenship: A Cautionary Tale for Human Rights Discourse." *Contemporary Politics* 15, no 1: 73–85.

PART VI

Queer Futures

CHRISTINE KEATING

During the past twenty years, significant progress around the world has been made towards the goal of ending the persecution of LGBTQ people. Steps that mark this progress include legislation that is geared to protecting LGBTQ people from violence, discrimination, and harassment, as well as measures that work to foster recognition of same-sex relationships and nonnormative gender identities. With these successes—and the challenges that remain—LGBTQ politics is at a critical juncture in terms of next steps. What might the future hold for LGBTQ communities? What could or should be the direction of LGBTQ activism? What are its prospects for success? What challenges does it face? In what ways do our assumptions about politics inform what we think about the future? What would queering our thinking about the future entail?

The essays in this section address these questions in their analyses of alternative futures for LGBTQ politics. In his essay "Whither the LGBTQ Movement in a Post–Civil Rights Era?" Gary Mucciaroni distinguishes between two forms of LGBTQ struggles in the United States: the civil rights struggle and a more inclusive struggle for justice. He argues that the achievement of marriage equality in the United States "marks the beginning of the end of the LGBTQ civil rights struggle" and predicts a future with full legal equality for all LGBTQ Americans (though its achievement will not be effortless or without challenge). Mucciaroni is clear, however, that the achievement of LGBTQ civil rights does not mean that the struggle for LGBTQ justice is over. Instead, he points to an alternative vision for LGBTQ movement, what he calls the "social democratic wish," which links LGTBQ struggles to youth politics, immigration reform, and struggles to end racism, sexism, and classism. In his essay, Mucciaroni analyzes the political feasibility of the social democratic approach to LGBTQ politics.

In her essay "Scouting for Normalcy: Merit Badges, Cookies, and American Futurity," Judy Rohrer analyzes two organizations that are, in her words, "imbued with futurity": the Boy Scouts of America and the Girl Scouts of the U.S.A. Rohrer explores the history of these two organizations themselves, as well as queer engagements with them. Arguing that fun and fantasy are "a critical part of thinking queerly through the politics of futurity," she highlights the importance of irony, camp, and parody as approaches to developing nonnormative strategies and visions for the future.

Although the focus in analyses of LGBTQ politics tends to be on large and relatively powerful organizations such as the Human Rights Campaign Fund, in their essay "Queering the Feminist Dollar: A History and Consideration of the Third Wave Fund as Activist Philanthropy," Melissa Meade and Rye Young explore the relationship among money, politics, and queer activism in the work of the Third Wave Fund, a small, cutting-edge philanthropic organization. In their essay, they consider what it means to invest in feminist and queer futures, arguing that both precarity and resilience mark the organizational underpinnings of innovative work being done that brings together LGBTQ, feminist, antiracist, and anticlassist work. They point to the importance of funding projects that give people the possibility of thinking and practicing potential alternative futures. They call such projects "experiments in queerness" that enable people to do what they call "hypothesis" work in both imagining and trying on new forms of relating and living. In "Single-Sex Colleges and Transgender Discrimination: The Politics of Checking a 'Male' or 'Female' Box to Get into College," Heath Fogg Davis offers historical background to the emergence of women's colleges and the single-sex college-admissions policies that are based on race-sex ideologies. These policies are still in existence today. When assessing the justifications given for maintaining such policies, Fogg Davis argues that while the intersectional feminist goals are legitimate and important, single-sex admissions policies are not necessary for achieving these goals. Instead of single-sex admissions, he argues for school admissions policies that are grounded in the principle of inclusive design. He argues that these policies can serve to minimize the sexist harm that results from sex-classification policies and can help build a queer future in which our "civil right to say who we are in relationship to the social and legal scheme of binary sex" is both recognized and institutionalized.

27

Whither the LGBTQ Movement in a Post–Civil Rights Era?

GARY MUCCIARONI

The adoption of same-sex marriage rights across the United States offers an appropriate occasion to consider the future of the LGBTQ movement. The achievement of marriage equality is not only an important milestone in the history of the movement, but it also heralds the beginning of the end of the LGBTQ civil rights struggle. Full legal equality for all LGBTQ Americans may not be just around the corner, but it is virtually inevitable. Once this equality is accomplished, civil rights must be enforced and vigilantly protected, but the movement's primary preoccupation with civil rights will no longer be justified. Achieving marriage equality has led the movement to have a conversation about the kind of movement it wishes to be in the future, what goals it should seek to pursue, and how it should pursue them. I join this conversation to ask a series of questions: What are the implications of the attainment of marriage equality for the LGBTQ movement? Which issues will take the place of marriage on the LGBTQ agenda? What are the prospects for moving beyond an identity-based, civil rights movement towards one that is more inclusive and geared towards a broader conception of equality and justice? Can aspirations for assimilation and social transformation be accommodated and reconciled?

Two caveats are in order before we begin. First, we should keep in mind that the LGBTQ "movement" in the United States is not a centrally directed or coordinated set of organizations that come to a consensus on goals and strategies and execute a plan. Several movements actually exist, some more reformist and others more radical, some that pursue "insider" and others that pursue "outsider" strategies and tactics (Rimmerman 2008). Even mainstream LGBTQ organizations are diverse and numerous. Second, we should not assume that the LGBTQ movement will be fully in control of its own destiny. The movement is one important actor among several in shaping LGBTQ politics and the movement's success. To paraphrase Karl Marx, social movements make their own histories, but not exactly as they please. The movement's choices and chances for success are contingent on the choices of others and on events that are beyond its control. It is arguable whether, for example, social movement organizations deserve most of the credit for what has been accomplished in terms of LGBTQ freedom and equality up to this point. Largely independently of LGBTQ advocacy organizations, queer individuals took it upon themselves to live openly, and their friends, families, employers, coworkers, and fellow citizens reacted positively in many cases. The media and entertainment industries decided, not just in response to demands from LGBTQ groups, to increase the visibility and variability of portrayals of LGBTQ characters and personalities. Political elites, not simply due to political pressure, made policy decisions at critical moments to push change along. Certainly many different LGBTQ organizations educated the public and policymakers, mobilized supporters, and kept LGBTQ issues on the agenda, but we need to keep their impact in perspective.

I argue, first, that full legal equality for LGBTQ citizens is virtually inevitable, but that accomplishing that goal could take several more years. The structure of the American state, continued resistance from opponents, and the lack of salience of the nondiscrimination issue will frustrate efforts to bring the civil rights era to an end. Next, I consider the political feasibility of a well-known critique and alternative vision of the LGBTQ movement called the "social democratic wish," which calls for going beyond civil rights and identity politics to embrace a broader and more inclusive set of egalitarian and social justice goals. Support for many of these goals has gained traction within the mainstream movement. Yet, efforts to adopt a full-blown social democratic mission would face considerable obstacles, not the least of which are established LGBTQ organizations themselves. A more likely outcome is that the movement will be selective about which goals it will prioritize. I develop a set of criteria for predicting which issues will receive more (and less) attention from the movement in the future. I finish up by discussing the implications of the movement's recent achievements for the perennial debate over "assimilation" versus "liberation."

Moving on from Marriage Does Not Mean Moving on from Civil Rights Quickly

The attainment of marriage equality does not mark the end of the LGBTQ civil rights project, but it heralds the beginning of the end of it. Much of the road toward full legal equality has been traveled. Not only has marriage equality been achieved but also, as of June 2016, Congress has lifted the ban on gays and transgendered individuals serving in the military and passed a federal hate crimes statute; twenty-two states (and hundreds of local jurisdictions) include sexual orientation in their employment nondiscrimination laws (nineteen also include gender identity); only one state (Mississippi) prohibits joint adoptions; and none prohibits second-parent adoption (Human Rights Campaign 2016; Lifelong Adoptions 2016). Furthermore, the question of whether LGBTQ people and their relationships should be accorded equal legal protection has been settled in the court of public opinion. Solid majorities of Americans support laws to protect the rights of LGBTQ citizens in areas like employment and housing (O'Keefe 2013).

Since nondiscrimination in employment, housing, and public accommodations has never been as controversial as gay marriage was, it might be reasonable to assume that the movement would secure civil rights nationwide in relatively short order. Such a scenario is unlikely, however. Completing the civil rights project will not come about anytime soon. As a result, most of the mainstream LGBTQ movement will continue to place it atop its list of priorities (Eckholm 2015). For example, the Equality Federation—a national umbrella organization that is the "strategic partner and movement builder to state-based [LGBT] organizations"—surveyed its members to ask them what goals they considered most important. The results showed that three of their "four top priorities" were civil rights goals: passing "local and/or statewide nondiscrimination legislation," extending nondiscrimination laws "to transgender community," and stopping "anti-LGBT laws/religious liberties legislation" (Equality Federation 2014). For their part, the Human Rights Campaign and Gill Foundation have begun to redirect resources towards those regions of the United States where statewide civil rights laws covering sexual orientation and gender identity do not exist (Wolfman-Arendt 2014).

What will delay completion of the civil rights project? First, despite having lost the war over marriage, LGBTQ opponents, by pursuing "religious freedom" exemptions, persist in efforts to diminish couples' ability to celebrate their unions. Although opposition to same-sex marriage inspired the exemptions, they apply to more than just individuals and businesses that supply wedding-related goods and services. Battles over the exemptions are now part of the broader conflict over how much business owners, landlords, and others should be allowed to discriminate. The reactive posture of the major LGBTQ organizations to the exemptions reflects a long-term pattern of the movement's opponents' helping to shape the movement's agenda (Fetner 2008).[1] As social and religious conservatives (and many Republicans) threaten to undermine the rights that the movement has won, mainstream organizations have responded in a predictably defensive manner. In late 2014, with marriage equality on the horizon, representatives of three foundations that had funded marriage equality campaigns (Overbrook Foundation, Ford Foundation, and Haas Fund) met to discuss what they should do next. According to one report, "[T]he major issue to emerge . . . was the threat of religious exemptions and their power to dilute existing nondiscrimination legislation" (Wolfman-Arent 2014). An examination of the 254 press releases that the Human Rights Campaign (HRC) issued from January through June 2015 reveals, similarly, that religious exemptions were the leading subject of HRC's public communications, with one-quarter of the releases devoted to that topic (see table 27.1).

Second, the fragmentation of the American state will continue to impede the rapid adoption of comprehensive civil rights laws. A growing number of states and localities have protections covering sexual orientation and gender identity,

TABLE 27.1. Press Releases from the Human Rights Campaign, January 1–June 11, 2015 (N=254)

	Percent*	(N)
Religious exemptions to civil rights laws	24%	62
Same-sex marriage	19	49
Civil rights (general)	17	42
Adoption/parenting issues	6	16
International LGBTQ issues	6	16
Transgender issues	6	14
Youth/bullying	4	10
Conversion therapy	4	9
Health and HIV	2	6
Military	1<	2
Other (unrelated to policy issues)	15	39

*Total exceeds 100 percent because some releases included more than one issue. Source: Human Rights Campaign.

but the path to nationwide civil rights protections through the states that do not yet have them will be an arduous process of waging multiple battles on inhospitable terrain. Those states are located in the South and Midwest, where Republicans have consolidated their control since 2010 and religious conservatives remain a potent force. It will almost certainly take the Democratic Party regaining control of both chambers of the U.S. Congress, plus the White House, to assure passage of nationwide, comprehensive, trans-inclusive civil rights protections—the Equality Act (the more comprehensive, trans-inclusive successor to the Employment Non-Discrimination Act, with a more narrow religious exemption). Given the advantages that Republicans have in retaining control over the House of Representatives (through residential patterns and gerrymandering), passage of the Equality Act in the foreseeable future is far from certain. Although the Equal Employment Opportunity Commission, under Title VII of the Civil Rights Act, has inspired an incremental strategy of federal cases to battle employment discrimination (Eckholm 2015), the courts will not be able to play as powerful a role in accomplishing civil rights protections as they did for same-sex marriage.

Third, ironically, the lack of controversy concerning legislation to protect the LGBTQ population from discrimination in employment, housing, and public accommodations makes it difficult to enact such laws wherever Republicans control at least one branch of government. Lack of controversy translates into low issue salience, which permits Republicans and other opponents to vote against LGBTQ nondiscrimination laws with impunity despite the support that their constituents express for them (Lax and Phillips 2009). Fourth, although the public supports giving basic civil rights to the LGBTQ community, most straight Americans do not find the issue as compelling as they did marriage equality. Gould (2009) has shown the importance of emotion in politics. The marriage issue was full of emotion for many LGBTQ people and their loved ones—not just anger at the lack of respect and denial of benefits that LGBTQ couples endured but also feelings of joy, commitment, and love. Discrimination on the job and in the housing market lacks the personal drama and positive vibe of loving couples eager to exchange vows and kisses on the courthouse steps.

Finally, LGBTQ organizations, which have invested heavily in the civil rights project for years, will not reduce their commitment to it and embrace other priorities until it is fully achieved. The continued commitment of mainstream LGBTQ political organizations to civil rights is evident in table 27.1. If we set aside all of the HRC press releases related to the marriage issue, the lion's share of those that remain relate to civil rights (messages concerning the struggle either to enact general civil rights protections or specifically to combat "religious freedom" exemptions).

The movement will continue to need infrastructure to defend against threatened rollbacks on rights after nationwide protections are in place. Civil rights won in one era can be threatened years later, a reality made clear by recent efforts to curtail women's reproductive rights and the voting rights of racial minorities and others. However, how much the right wing will continue to resist LGBTQ rights and how effective they will be is uncertain. In part, again, the calculations of other political actors will be important. The opposition of many large corporations to the religious exemptions arguably has been the most important reason why they have been curtailed, for example. We need to be careful about making predictions based upon the experiences of other movements. Attacks on voting and reproductive rights have made considerably more headway because Republicans see clear partisan advantages in raising barriers for voting groups that support Democrats. The same advantage does not apply to the religious freedom exemptions. Also, abortion rights opponents have gained much more headway than marriage opponents did mainly because public opinion was increasingly behind LGBTQ rights but remains divided over abortion.

As the LGBTQ community gets closer to full legal equality, and as homophobia and heterosexism decline (especially among younger generations), the need for the movement to be as consumed with the attainment of civil rights goals as it was in the past should decline. While the attainment of full legal equality remains in the distance, and even though such battles are never over once and for all, the attainment of full formal legal equality will become a reality. Before that happens, the movement will need to decide in which direction it should head in the post–civil rights era.

What Will a Post–Civil Rights LGBTQ Agenda Look Like?

An alternative vision for the LGBTQ movement, which I label the "social democratic wish," already exists. The social democratic wish is a widely cited critique of the mainstream movement (as it has existed for the past four decades) and an alternative model for reconstituting the movement in a post–civil rights era. It argues that the identity-based, civil rights approaches of the mainstream movement narrow and limit its potential for building a broader, more inclusive political force and pursuing a more ambitious public policy agenda. The identity-based focus isolates the movement, reduces its capacity for building solidarity with other oppressed groups, and truncates its aspirations for social justice. The civil rights approach focuses mainly upon legal equality and is incapable of dealing with forms of inequality rooted in the economy and other institutional structures that are impervious to civil rights remedies (for a discussion of the pros and cons of the civil rights model, see Diller 2000). Mainstream leaders and followers, according to these critics, need to embrace a broader vision by becoming or joining a more inclusive social democratic movement and advocating for a more ambitious set of egalitarian and social justice goals and policies (Vaid 1995; Cohen 1997; Rimmerman 2002).

The struggle for marriage equality has further fueled this critique in recent years, and proponents of the democratic wish have renewed their calls for change in light of the achievement of marriage equality (Vaid 2012; Kunreuther, Masters, and Barsoum 2013). The right to marry disproportionately benefits gay men and lesbians who are white, middle-class, and educated, and who desire to live in conjugal relationships. Individuals in these groups are more likely to marry, and civil marriage, especially in the United States, confers a host of benefits for which unmarried citizens are ineligible. Like their straight counterparts, LGBTQ Americans face the same challenges of living in a society increasingly beset by a lack of opportunity to maintain or reach the middle class. Furthermore, as the critics point out, most Americans, including most LGBTQ individuals, no longer live in nuclear families. Many gays and lesbians either do not wish to marry or they live in communities and family situations where marriage is not a viable option (Beyond Marriage 2006). Even after same-sex couples have been permitted to marry, marriage remains a state-recognized institution for two strangers in a spousal relationship that excludes the other kinds of families and intimate relationships in which two or more individuals care for one another.

Because the campaign for same-sex marriage absorbed a huge proportion of resources and attention, the movement, its allies, the media, and policymakers overlooked or gave short shrift to other worthy, and arguably more pressing, issues. Indeed, when we look back at the period from the mid-1990s to 2015 (and certainly 2003–2015), the dominance of marriage on the LGBTQ agenda is clear. From advocacy to media attention to fundraising, marriage equality eclipsed all other LGBTQ issues. In 2013, when the Supreme Court handed down its land-mark *Windsor* (570 U.S. 2013, 133 S.Ct. 2675) and *Hollingsworth* decisions (570 U.S. 2013, 133 S.Ct. 2652), a check of the Human Rights Campaign blog turned up 385 pages devoted to the marriage issue compared to 31 for "hate crimes" and 81 for "workplace issues." In 2012, 43 percent of the $121.4 million that U.S. foundations contributed to LGBTQ causes went to marriage equality campaigns, which was more than double the amount that went to the next category (health) (Wolfman-Arent 2014). Similarly, the HRC press releases for the first half of 2015 show that the overwhelming focus of the organization's public communications was marriage and the religious freedom exemptions that the adoption of same-sex marriage inspired (see table 27.1).

No issue in the future will so dominate the agenda of the post-marriage LGBTQ movement for such a sustained period as marriage did. As the reality of nationwide marriage equality neared, LGBTQ leaders and followers turned to the question of "what's next?" and came forward with an extensive "still to do" list of issues and goals (see Wolfman-Arendt 2014; Baume 2015; Tillery 2015; Equality Federation 2013). Besides a comprehensive, nationwide nondiscrimina-tion law (inclusive of transgendered and gender-nonconforming individuals), other issues that regularly appear on these lists include

* ending violence and intimidation towards LGBTQ *youth* in schools;
* reforming *immigration* laws so that LGBTQ individuals are not detained or deported to places where they are endangered and to keep families united;
* ensuring that *elderly* LGBTQ individuals can live and be cared for in environments where they are not isolated, disrespected, or harmed;
* meeting the needs of *people of color, the homeless, and the economically disadvantaged*;
* continuing the fight against *HIV/AIDS*;
* fighting against the oppression of *LGBTQ populations living abroad.*

Many LGBTQ activists seem to acknowledge that marriage did not speak to the issues most relevant to many LGBTQ people and have sounded much like the proponents of the democratic wish in their advocacy and plans. A spokesper-son for the Gay and Lesbian Advocates and Defenders (GLAD), which spear-headed much of the drive for same-sex marriage, asserts that "the ultimate prize is not equality, it is justice," and calls for leaving "no one behind, especially the most vulnerable in our community—our youth, our elders, transgender and HIV-positive folks, as well as LGBT people of color, prisoners and immigrants" (Wu 2014). Similarly, a recent report that summarized the views of several dozen "LGBTQ leaders" argued that the movement must shift from a vision that emphasized "equal rights for some to equity and justice for all" (Kunreuther, Masters, and Barsoum 2013, 3). According to the report, "[S]urvey respondents and interviewees described their desire for a vision that embraces a more expansive view of LGBT issues and that strives for inclusion of the full diversity of LGBT people" (4). Similarly, according to the 2013 annual report of the mainstream Equality Federation,

> Marriage equality will not keep LGBT young people in their homes and loved by their families. It will not keep them in school and out of the criminal justice system. It will not ensure transgender people access to accurate identity documents or critical healthcare services. It will not make our streets and our communities safe and free from violence. It will not make our military, our prisons, our immigration system, or our healthcare inclusive and just. It will not erase the vulnerability our community feels as we age in a world without an adequate safety net. Marriage means a lot, but our movement is not finished. It's time for us to go back to the roots of our movement toward our goal of lived equality. Lived equality is about freedom. Freedom from bigotry, freedom to be who we are and live without facing nearly insurmountable obstacles, freedom to love and be loved. This freedom is not only measured in policies and laws; it must also be measured in the lived experience of real people. (Equality Foundation 2013)

The HRC website includes discussions of all of these issues. HRC engages in efforts to educate the public about them and provides LGBTQ constituency groups information about advocacy campaigns that they might join and "self-help" resources to assist them in addressing their personal situations (Human Rights Campaign 2016). It is much more difficult to discern whether HRC is dedicating substantial funds and staff to address the issues. At least rhetorically, many of these organizations understand the partial victory that marriage represents and that marriage does not address the array of injustices that many LGBTQ people continue to experience.

Is the Social Democratic Wish Politically Feasible or Wishful Thinking?

Several features of the present LGBTQ movement suggest that a shift in the direction of social democracy is a plausible alternative. For one, the LGBTQ population is overwhelmingly progressive in its political orientation and thus would be receptive to social democratic appeals. Compared to American voters generally, LGBTQ individuals hold overwhelmingly liberal policy preferences, including issues unrelated to LGBTQ rights (Egan, Edelman, and Sherrill 2008; Egan 2008). They are also among the most consistent supporters of the Democratic Party, which is the closest the United States has to a social democratic party of any political significance at the national level. The left-leaning ideological and partisan unity within the movement helps to counteract the splintering effects of class, race, and gender that make it more difficult to gain consensus on redistributionist goals and policies to benefit marginalized LGBT subgroups. A social democratic approach is well suited to addressing the diverse forms that inequality takes among subgroups of the LGBTQ population.

Leaders of LGBTQ social movement organizations have strong incentives to maintain their relevance and legitimacy. In a post–civil rights era, many organizations will need to remain relevant in order to attract the resources that they will need. Moreover, for a movement based squarely upon the promotion of egalitarian values, equality cannot just mean formal legal equality between the queer community and straight Americans. It demands that the movement is fully inclusive and genuinely concerned with the needs of the entire LGBTQ population, regardless of class, gender, racial, and other differences. LGBTQ leaders, feeling the pressure to maintain their legitimacy, have responded, for example, to complaints from the transgender community about its marginalization in the movement, a marginalization exemplified in the support that mainstream organizations gave to excluding gender identity from a version of the Employment Non-Discrimination Act (ENDA) that passed the House in 2007 (Ochalla 2007). HRC's leader publicly apologized for the organization's treatment of the trans community (see Bernstein 2015, 333).

The movement also has considerable organizational infrastructure at its disposal that it could use to pursue a more social democratic agenda. Political scientists have paid attention to large national political organizations, like HRC, NGLTF, and Lambda Legal (Rimmerman 2002; Anderson 2006), but less to the large number of state and local advocacy groups. They have largely neglected LGBTQ organizations that seek to directly engage and reform civil society institutions in favor of those that work through the state to change public policy. Like other social movements, the LGBTQ movement has recognized that multiple institutions wield power, making it necessary to fight oppression on several fronts (see Armstrong and Bernstein 2008; Gamson 1989). Protest organizations, like ACT-UP, targeted civil society along with the state (Gamson 1989). LGBTQ reformers have targeted schools, corporations, the mass media, the entertainment industry, religious institutions, fraternal organizations, and others in ways that do not involve the police powers of the state. GLAAD, GLSEN, and similar organizations monitor, challenge, and educate major civil society institutions, as have LGBTQ organizations that also engage in litigation, lobbying, and elections. Campaigns for safer schools and better conditions for the elderly, for example, must include a large role for those organizations that monitor civil society institutions and pressure them for change.

Yet, attempts to remake the LGBTQ movement in the image of social democracy would face significant challenges, not the least of which are the mainstream LGBTQ organizations themselves. Long-established organizations generally avoid what they perceive as large-scale changes. Societies and the institutions within them tend to be "path dependent"—preferring to stay on the same trajectory because the costs of getting off one path and onto another outweigh the perceived benefits (Pierson 2000). Getting onto a new path is neither typical nor easy and is usually induced by an exogenous shock. Furthermore, a good deal of research in social psychology suggests that humans are risk averse (they discount the promise of future gains and overestimate the prospects of future losses from change). As a result, organizations often pursue suboptimal goals and strategies rather than embrace the costs and uncertainty of change (Kaheneman and Tversky 1979).

Past success may breed complacency. Those who run the major LGBTQ organizations occupy a comfortable niche in American politics, and their identity-based orientation and civil rights mission have been reasonably successful on their own terms. The movement has provided some common ground for diverse constituencies to rally around a set of goals that, while limited, are far along towards being accomplished. Some of the policies that the LGBTQ movement has pushed have been politically divisive, such as same-sex marriage, but it was able to avoid debates over other measures about which other civil rights movements have found it difficult to form a broad national consensus. Opponents of other identity movements have framed affirmative action and many social welfare programs, for example, as "reverse discrimination" and as efforts to create winners and losers along race and gender lines.

The movement's traditional focus on civil rights had several political advantages. Movement leaders could frame civil rights in ways that resonated with broader social values like individual freedom, equal opportunity, and merit-based treatment of individuals. Civil rights remedies are targeted at individuals who share a set of grievances rooted in their identity and experiences as members of the group. *All* gays, lesbians, bisexuals, and transgendered individuals were subject to discrimination simply because of their sexual orientation or gender identity, regardless of their income, education, race, age, and gender. All were victims of homophobia, heterosexism, traditional gender roles, and fixed notions of gender identity. They joined and supported LGBTQ organizations mostly because they share, to varying degrees, an LGBTQ identity.

Many of the issues included in the social democratic program, by contrast, are not as closely related to LGBTQ identity and cannot be addressed through civil rights remedies easily, or at all in some cases. They are rooted in social conditions that are not primarily related to homophobia and heterosexism. Their impacts vary significantly across LGBTQ subgroups, and many solutions to them will benefit large proportions of the non-LGBTQ population.

LGBTQ movement leaders would probably perceive a full-blown social democratic program as a risky proposition that would depart significantly from the movement's historical focus on civil rights, and more importantly, compromise the identity-based foundation of the movement. The movement consolidated and flourished starting in the 1970s as an identity movement, organizing a diverse array of self-identified LGBTQ individuals for expressive and instrumental purposes, such as gaining recognition and access to material benefits and status (Armstrong 2002). Identity is a powerful tool for social movements, increasing internal solidarity and organizational networks, enabling movements to mobilize those who identify with the group and deploy identity strategically to promote the group's agenda (McGarrey and Jasper 2015; Bernstein 1997).

Proponents of the democratic wish recommend that LGBTQ organizations forge strong alliances with other progressive constituencies, but alliances may be risky. Identity groups face a series of dilemmas when they try to broaden their appeal and join with other groups (Jasper 2006, 2014). Enlarging the group brings more resources and visibility, but it also gets harder to come to agreement and coordinate action; bringing on board powerful groups and individuals has obvious potential benefits, but it also risks giving control over to others who may use the group for their own agenda. Solidarity built upon (LGBTQ) group identity makes it hard to develop solidarity with other groups because most individuals in the non-LGBTQ groups do not share the LGBTQ identity and may demand that LGBTQ groups submerge their interests (although see Bernstein 2002). At the same time, the compromises that may be necessary to partner with non-LGBTQ groups may threaten the internal solidarity of the LGBTQ population.

No doubt, the economic structure and class divisions played a role (often overlooked) in the emergence and development of the LGBTQ movement (D'Emilio 1983; Hetland and Goodwin 2013). But the implications of class and the economy for reconstituting the present-day American movement are mostly negative. Close links between LGBTQ movements and social democracy have emerged mostly in nations, such as those in northern Europe, that have had long histories of strong working-class organizations and relatively weak religious opposition to homosexuality. The backbone of social democracy has been trade unions and social democratic parties. The United States has never had a social democratic party of major significance, trade unions have been under assault and weakened considerably for several decades, and the LGBTQ movement has faced a much more potent religious opposition than in any European nation. A successful protest movement has emerged among fast-food restaurant employees recently, but Republican-controlled state governments have weakened public employee unions and passed right-to-work laws in midwestern industrial states. Without the prospect of forging ties with strong social democratic institutions, it seems unlikely that LGBTQ organizations would prioritize the welfare-state and economic-justice issues that have been at the center of social democracy.

Issue Diversity and Comparative Advantage in the Post–Marriage Equality Era

Short of adopting a comprehensive social democratic program, we might expect the movement to embrace selectively parts of such a program and neglect others. Movement leaders and funders presumably choose issues that they perceive as more central or pressing for the movement and that offer the best chance for being addressed successfully. Which issues are likely to attract greater resources and attention from a post-marriage LGBTQ movement? To provide a plausible answer to this question, we need to develop criteria that LGBTQ organizations might use to decide where to invest resources and then assess each issue to see which ones better meet the criteria. Issues that rank lower on these criteria will have more trouble gaining the visibility and political commitment that will lead to a prominent place on the post-marriage agenda. (N.b.: I do not endorse these as normative criteria that organizations should use, but as predictors of their behavior.)

One criterion would be *universal impact.* The more likely it is that an issue affects all, or a very large proportion of the LGBTQ population, the more likely it is that the movement will adopt the issue as a priority. Universality heightens visibility, interest, and support for addressing an issue because everyone perceives a stake in the outcome.

A second criterion is *middle-class impact.* If an issue directly and significantly affects middle-class and affluent LGBTQ individuals, it is more likely to become a priority. Many leaders of the organizations come from this stratum of society, and middle-class and affluent individuals have higher levels of political efficacy and are able to supply critical resources to LGBTQ organizations, like money and volunteers.

A third criterion is *congruence with LGBTQ identity.* If the problem or grievance arises out of individuals' status as LGBTQ, then leaders and followers have a better appreciation for the problem and can closely identify with the plight of those experiencing it. If the injustice experienced is independent of LGBTQ status and would exist even in its absence, then it is less likely to resonate at an emotional level with those not experiencing it. LGBTQ voters support progressive positions across issues generally, but they will be most moved to engage in actions to address an issue when it taps their own identity.

A fourth criterion is that *society construct the group that experiences the injustice in a positive manner.* Even if organizational leaders and members do not share the negative image of the group, they are less likely to invest their resources if most Americans' affect towards the group is negative or ambivalent.

The final criterion is *the issue's fit with the civil rights model.* The movement will be more likely to adopt the issue as a priority if it can address it using its familiar repertoire of civil rights resources and tools.

These criteria are not exhaustive, and we could think of a lengthier list without much trouble. For example, organizations may prioritize issues that are more amenable to attracting the support of other politically influential groups, or those that are more amenable to developing a consensus on a concrete policy solution.

Which issues perform best on these criteria and stand out as particularly promising ones for the LGBTQ movement to pursue? One is certainly elder care. Virtually all individuals will grow old or look forward to a long life. The problems of old age affect almost everyone, including of course the middle class, and the elderly are a politically active group. Many of those who are not yet old worry about their LGBTQ friends and family members who are elderly. The issue fits well with LGBTQ identity because elderly LGBTQ people are often isolated and discriminated against simply because they do not conform to heteronormative expectations. At the same time, the elderly are a positively constructed group in society, portrayed as people who have spent their lives contributing to society, but who are vulnerable, dependent, and "deserving" of society's help.

Another strong candidate for gaining a prominent place on the LGBTQ agenda is violence, harassment, and isolation experienced by youth in schools and other organizations. All LGBTQ adults were young, and many have young family members, friends, and neighbors who are LGBTQ. All parents of LGBTQ children worry that they may be harmed or feel unwelcome in school. Parents without LGBTQ children may empathize with them. Even queer people who did not experience violence or bullying usually had painful experiences of isolation and rejection, or feared rejection if they "came out." They may have contemplated suicide or dropped out of school. This issue too has a clear connection to LGBTQ identity because the mistreatment arises out of the youth's status as LGBTQ. Society constructs children and minors as dependent and innocent, as society's hope for a better future, and as a group that needs and deserves protection from harm.

The promotion of rights for LGBTQ populations abroad meets several of the criteria as well. Clearly, it fits with LGBTQ identity because the American LGBTQ population can identify (to some degree at least) with the repression that LGBTQ people in other nations experience. Media portrayals of LGBTQ activists abroad are often sympathetic, showing them as innocent victims of state-sponsored or -tolerated violence and discrimination. And the issue fits into the civil rights model because LGBTQ groups abroad seek the same basic human rights that much of the American LGBTQ population enjoys.

Gender equality would be a likely candidate as a focus for the post-marriage LGBTQ movement. Obviously, half of the population is female, including therefore a large segment of the middle class. The women's movement was an important model that the LGBTQ movement followed. Women are generally positively constructed—as our mothers, sisters, daughters, friends, and coworkers. Importantly, gender discrimination is closely entwined with discrimination based upon sexual orientation and gender identity. Discrimination and mistreatment of gays, lesbians, and transgendered individuals are based upon an insistence that everyone must comply with fundamentally sexist and heteronormative traditional gender roles and stereotypes.

Discrimination against transgendered people has reached the agenda recently. Although this was hardly noticed, the military lifted the ban on transgender individuals in the service. More salient has been growing opposition to efforts to allow transgender individuals to use whichever bathrooms they wish rather than the one that corresponds to the gender they were assigned at birth. Voters in Houston overturned such an ordinance and the legislature in North Carolina disallowed the city of Charlotte and other municipalities from adopting them.

The days when the LGBT movement threw the trans community "under the bus" to get a version of ENDA passed should be over, but trans issues related to official documents and healthcare may be more problematic. These issues affect a minority of the LGBTQ population, and middle-class gays, lesbians, and bisexuals probably do not identify as closely with the trans population as with each other. Transgender issues receive more attention, and media portrayals of the trans population are more varied and positive than in the past, but many people remain ignorant of trans issues. Those affected are often ridiculed and pitied, and opponents have sometimes succeeded in stoking fears that their demands to use bathrooms of their choosing will lead to sexual predators having access to women's lavatories.

Other issues, including homelessness, economic inequality, racism, and immigration, will receive less attention from the post-marriage movement. Many LGBTQ Americans today struggle economically and have diminished opportunities for upward mobility, like Americans generally. The discrimination and stigma that LGBTQ people experience increase the chance that some of them will experience homelessness and poverty. LGBTQ individuals who are also members of racial minorities and other historically marginalized groups experience greater discrimination and rejection than if they were white. Nevertheless, homelessness, poverty, racism, and immigrant status are not universally experienced. White, middle-class LGBTQ people do not suffer from these injustices, or they suffer much less. Nor are the poor, the homeless, racial minorities, and immigrants as positively constructed by society as other groups. Thus, many white, middle-class LGBTQ Americans, and their straight allies, will have a harder time relating to the lived experiences of marginalized queer subpopulations and perceiving these injustices as connected to LGBTQ identity. Many will see poverty, homelessness, economic inequality, racism, and immigration as rooted in circumstances that have less to do with sexual orientation and gender identity than with economic and social conditions that go beyond the movement's capabilities and responsibility. Most of these problems are not amenable to civil rights remedies either. For example, racism may be more effectively addressed by reforms that change the cultures of governmental and civil society institutions (such as police forces that engage in racial profiling and the mass media that perpetuates negative images of racial minorities).

What are the implications of this analysis? First, if these predictions prove to be correct, then the gulf between the white, middle-class mainstream of the LGBTQ movement and marginalized LGBTQ groups may widen. Getting the issues that rank lower on these criteria onto the agenda will require, at minimum, much greater efforts at educating mainstream organizations and the public about the injustices that LGBTQ individuals experience. Second, the large number and diversity of the issues on the post-marriage agenda mean that the movement will be more organizationally fragmented and siloed than ever. Third, addressing them will require developing new organizational capacities and shifting resources from one set of approaches and tools to others. The nonmarriage issues are much less amenable to judicial intervention. The courts played a pivotal role in the marriage issue—getting it placed on the agenda at critical junctures, prodding legislatures to remedy marriage inequality, and in many cases nullifying bans on same-sex marriage. None of the issues on the list of priorities of LGBTQ activists in the post-marriage era are as readily remediable through the courts. Although the movement's strengths in political advocacy and legislative lobbying will still be highly relevant, many of the nonmarriage issues will require greater efforts at grassroots mobilization and alliance building than the mainstream movement has heretofore mustered. Also, some issues, including safe schools and elder care, will be less salient than marriage, and thus public support will play a less central role in addressing them.

Implications for the Assimilation versus Transformation Debate

This moment in LGBTQ history is an appropriate time to revisit the decades-old question of whether the movement should try to assimilate into the culture or seek to transform the culture and its institutions. "Assimilationists" largely accept the dominant organization, rules, and norms of society and seek inclusion and full participation in its institutions. "Liberationists" reject those institutions and seek radical change in their structure, rules, and norms, or even their replacement with alternative arrangements. The impact of these alternative visions has varied over time and across organizations and individuals. At particular historical junctures, the movement has sought to change society rather than simply to "fit into" it, such as in the earliest homophile years and the "gay liberation" period of the 1970s. Some organizations, such as Queer Nation, have sought cultural change, while mainstream organizations have sought mainly assimilation. And, of course, in every period some queer people have adhered to one vision while others have embraced the alternative.

Assimilation has been ascendant among most LGBTQ organizations and activists in recent decades, not surprisingly. Seeking radical transformation of the culture runs up against powerful structural obstacles, for example, the "privileged position of business" (Lindblom 1977), the ideological hegemony of capitalism, liberalism, and nationalism, and a fragmented state structure. These forces and ideas have powerful influence even among progressives in American society, who support LGBTQ inclusion and full citizenship. Given these constraints, most political activists in the United States tend toward pragmatism, adopting goals and strategies that they consider practical and politically feasible, opting for reform, compromise, and gradual change. Although many people might entertain radical cultural change if they gave it serious consideration, many LGBTQ people also desire legitimacy in the eyes of society and wish to be able to participate fully as citizens. Like most everyone, LGBTQ people have multiple identities and roles—as workers, family members, members of a neighborhood or local community—and many of them maintain affective ties to members of the non-LGBTQ population. They probably do not see the institutions as intrinsically unjust or that their participation in them perpetuates injustice.

Some critics dismiss civil rights, particularly marriage, as insufficiently relevant to the "lived lives" of many LGBTQ individuals, or as benefiting primarily a narrow subset of white, middle-class couples who will gain from marriage. However, a study that used extensive interview and focus-group data revealed that the mainstream movement's emphasis on marriage and family issues does not make people of color or transgendered individuals feel marginalized within the LGBTQ movement (Hull and Ortyl 2013). Overwhelming numbers of LGBT adults favor allowing same-sex marriage (Pew Research Center 2013). Although Americans are marrying at lower rates today than in the past, most still want to get married (Newport and Wilke 2013), including LGBTQ Americans (60 percent in a recent poll said that they were married or wanted to get married; see Pew Research Center 2013). Younger cohorts have listed marriage as a top priority (Egan and Sherrill 2005). In May 2015, Gallup estimated that about four hundred thousand same-sex marriages existed in the United States, or about 40 percent of all same-sex couples (Gates and Newport 2015). This number is significant and is certain to grow as more couples in more states are now permitted to marry.

Critics correctly point out that marriage contributes to the "normalizing" of LGBTQ individuals and relationships. People will disagree about whether this trend is good or bad for the LGBTQ population. For those who cannot or do not wish to conform, normalizing is irrelevant at best, and at worst will further marginalize them within the movement and society. Proponents of assimilation (many of whom probably feel that they *are* "normal" except for their sexual orientation or gender identity) argue that they deserve the same dignity as everyone else and that a society that is more accepting and inclusive will make life easier and more dignified for married and unmarried openly LGBTQ people alike.

The assimilation-transformation (or liberation) dichotomy is misleading. First, the bare fact of including a historically stigmatized group in an institution transforms it. The mere existence of openly gay, lesbian, bisexual, etc., people in those institutions from which they had been previously excluded transforms the institutions because they are no longer bastions of heterosexual privilege or privilege based upon fixed gender assignment. Mere acceptance and admittance represents significant change. The reason why right-wing opponents of LGBTQ rights fought so hard to exclude queers from the military and marriage is precisely because they used these widely cherished institutions to enforce heteronormativity and stigmatize those who refuse to conform to it.

Second, assimilation holds out the potential for transforming cultural institutions even beyond what mere acceptance and admittance passively accomplish. The presence of openly gay men, lesbians, and trans people in these institutions may transform them over time. Critics of assimilation assume that the relationship between LGBTQ individuals and the institutions in which they seek incorporation is a one-way street in which the institutions influence the LGBTQ community (by normalizing), but not vice versa. Yet, when gays and lesbians insisted upon marriage and adoption rights, they forced a reconsideration of what constitutes a "family," weakened the belief that the functions that families perform are tied to a single type of family structure, and educated the public about who makes for "good" parents. When state-certified gay and lesbian spouses and parents interact with their straight counterparts in everyday life, they broaden the horizons of straight society about different kinds of families and the diminished relevance of traditional family structures and gender roles. According to Bernstein (2015, 329), "To the extent that the lived experiences of same-sex couples challenge hegemonic understandings of gender, sexuality, and family forms and raise children in a more gender-egalitarian manner, same-sex marriage opens the possibility of new types of relationship recognition." Integration in other spheres of life, including the military, may also have a salutary effect, by reducing violence and discrimination based upon homophobia, heterosexism, and traditional gender roles. In short, assimilation and liberation/ transformation are not mutually exclusive goals (Rimmerman 2002). Both can be pursued simultaneously either by different segments of the movement or even by the same organizations and individuals.

Transformation-through-assimilation is by no means a certain route to changing the culture. Assimilation may lead simply to cooptation, conformity, and acceptance of continued injustices as the price for inclusion. A way to avoid this pitfall may be to strengthen and reorient watchdog organizations that have some ability to stand apart from the culture and critique it. For example, a study that examined the press releases of the media watchdog group GLAAD (formerly Gay and Lesbian Alliance Against Defamation) found that the organization put out a mix of messages aimed at the media and other organizations in their portrayal and treatment of the LGBTQ population. Many of the releases simply celebrated or demanded inclusion, fairness, acceptance, equality, understanding, and other assimilationist values, but a fair number were more "disruptive," encouraging LGBTQ individuals, for example, to "be who they are," highlighting the diversity of the LGBTQ population and the visibility of marginalized groups within it, and calling for their "empowerment" (Cabosky 2014, 77–78) .

Organizations that are more separate from the LGBTQ movement and society in general tend to provide more radical alternatives. Instead of trying to bring about change by seeking to influence the state or civil society, "prefigurative" organizations anticipate and create alternative social arrangements by finding spaces that allow participants to live out and realize transformative goals. They "live the revolution" instead of pursuing strategies to influence dominant institutions. These groups embrace nonhierarchical organization, use egalitarian, deliberative, and participatory democratic norms and procedures, and operate by consensus. The heyday for prefigurative organizations was during the days of the New Left in the late 1960s and early 1970s (Breines 1982). Queer versions of prefigurative organizations reject identity politics and socially constructed categories or adopt a fluid and encompassing pan-queer identity. They exist throughout Europe and the United states in the form of "squats," occupations, and festivals (Eleftheriadis 2015).

Conclusion

Predicting a social movement's future is always a hazardous enterprise. It is perhaps easier to make hunches about what will probably *not* happen in the next few decades than to figure out what will happen; but most of us would have placed same-sex marriage in the "not going to happen" column a mere fifteen years ago. Historical logic only becomes clear in hindsight. This is so because, in part, as I have emphasized in this chapter, a social movement's future rides as much on the choices other actors make and on unforeseeable events as they do on the movement's own plans and aspirations. Hopefully the time will come when conditions have changed enough so that LGBTQ people and people everywhere will have less of an urgent need to organize to struggle for equality and justice.

NOTE

1 The movement's opponents are not the only actors in its environment who have forced it into a reactive posture. Major gay rights organizations embraced marriage as a priority only after a handful of same-sex couples and lawyers forced it onto the agenda in Hawaii and Vermont, sparking national media attention and a conservative backlash.

REFERENCES

Anderson, Ellen Ann. 2006. *Out of the Closets and into the Courts: Legal Opportunity Structure and Gay Rights Litigation.* Ann Arbor: University of Michigan Press.

Armstrong, Elizabeth A. 2002. *Forging Gay Identities: Organizing Sexuality in San Francisco, 1950–1994.* Chicago: University of Chicago Press.

Armstrong, Elizabeth A., and Mary Bernstein. 2008. "Culture, Power, and Institutions: A Multi-Institutional Politics Approach to Social Movements." *Sociological Theory* 26 (1): 74–99.

Baume, Matt. 2015. "After Marriage: The Future of the U.S. LGBT Movement." *Unicorn Booty*, April 29, www.unicornbooty.com, retrieved on June 30, 2015.

Bernstein, Mary. 1997. "Celebration and Suppression: The Strategic Uses of Identity by the Lesbian and Gay Movement." *American Journal of Sociology* 103(3): 531–65.

Bernstein, Mary. 2002. "Identities and Politics: Toward a Historical Understanding of the Lesbian and Gay Movement." *Social Science History* 26(3): 531–81.

Bernstein, Mary. 2015. "Same-Sex Marriage and the Future of the LGBT Movement: SWS Presidential Address." *Gender & Society* 29(3): 321–37.

Beyond Marriage. 2006. "Beyond Same-Sex Marriage: A New Strategic Vision for All Our Families and Relationships." July 26, www.beyondmarriage.org.

Breines, Wini. 1982. *The Great Refusal: Community and Organization in the New Left: 1962–1968.* New York: Praeger.

Cabosky, Joseph M. 2014. "Framing an LGBT Organization and a Movement: A Critical Qualitative Analysis of GLAAD's Media Releases." *Public Relations Inquiry* 3(1): 69–89.

Cohen, Cathy J. 1997. "Straight Gay Politics: The Limits of an Ethnic Model of Inclusion." *Nomos* 39: 572–616.

D'Emilio, John. 1983. "Capitalism and Gay Identity." In *Powers of Desire: The Politics of Sexuality,* Ann Snitow, Christine Stansell, and Sharon Thompson, eds. New York: Monthly Review Press.

Diller, Matthew. 2000. "Judicial Backlash, the ADA, and the Civil Rights Model." *Berkeley Journal of Employment and Labor Law* 21(1): 19–52.

Eckholm, Erik. 2015. "Next Fight for Gay Rights: Bias in Jobs and Housing." *New York Times,* June 28, p. 1.

Egan, Patrick J. 2008. "Explaining the Distinctiveness of Lesbians, Gays, and Bisexuals in American Politics." Southern Political Science Association, Midwest Political Science Association, American Political Science Association.

Egan, Patrick J., Murray S. Edelman, and Kenneth Sherrill. 2008. "Findings from the Hunter College Poll of Lesbians, Gays, and Bisexuals: New Discoveries about Identity, Political Attitudes, and Civic Engagement." Hunter College, City University of New York.

Egan, Patrick J., and Kenneth Sherrill. 2005. "Marriage and the Shifting Priorities of a New Generation of Lesbians and Gays." *PS: Political Science & Politics* 38(2): 229–32.

Eleftheriadis, Konstantinos. 2015. "Organizational Practices and Prefigurative Spaces in European Queer Festivals." *Social Movement Studies,* published online April 28. doi: 10.1080/14742837.2015.1029045.

Equality Federation. 2013. *The 2013 Equality Federation Annual Report: Winning at Home.* www.equalityfederation.org, retrieved on June 30, 2015.

Equality Federation. 2014. *State of the States, Part 4: Accomplishing Priorities and the Power of Partnerships,* Dec. 17. www.equalityfederation.org, retrieved on June 30, 2015.

Fetner, Tina. 2008. *How the Religious Right Shaped Lesbian and Gay Activism.* Minneapolis: University of Minnesota Press.

Gamson, Joshua. 1989. "Silence, Death, and the Invisible Enemy: AIDS Activism and Social Movement 'Newness.'" *Social Problems* 36: 351–67.

Gates, Gary J., and Frank Newport. 2015. "An Estimated 780,000 Americans in Same-Sex Marriages." Gallup, www.gallup.com, retrieved on June 30, 2015.

Gould, Deborah. 2009. *Moving Politics: Emotion and ACT-UP's Fight against AIDS.* Chicago: University of Chicago Press.

Hetland, Gabriel, and Jeff Goodwin. 2013. "The Strange Disappearance of Capitalism from Social Movement Studies." In *Marxism and Social Movements,* Colin Barker, et al., eds. Boston: Brill.

Hull, Kathleen E., and Timothy A. Ortyl. 2013. "Same-Sex Marriage and Constituent Perceptions of the LGBT Rights Movement." In *The Marrying Kind?* Marty Bernstein and Verta Taylor, eds. Minneapolis: University of Minnesota Press.

Human Rights Campaign. 2016. www.hrc.org.

Jasper, James. 2006. *Getting Your Way: Strategic Dilemmas in Real Life.* Chicago: University of Chicago Press.

Jasper, James. 2014. *Protest: A Cultural Introduction to Social Movements.* Cambridge: Polity.

Kahneman, Daniel, and Amos Tversky. 1979. "Prospect Theory: An Analysis of Decision under Risk." *Econometrica* 47: 263–91.

Kunreuther, Frances, Barbara Masters, and Gigi Barsoum. 2013. *At the Crossroads: The Future of the LGBT Movement.* Building Movement Project, www.buildingmovement.org.

Lax, Jonathan, and Justin Phillips. 2009. "Gay Rights in the States: Public Opinion and Policy Responsiveness." *American Political Science Review* 103(3): 367–86.

Lifelong Adoptions. 2016. www.lifelongadoptions.com.

Lindblom, Charles E. 1977. *Politics and Markets: The World's Political Economic Systems.* New York: Basic Books.

McGarry, Aiden, and James M. Jasper. 2015. *The Identity Dilemma: Social Movements and Collective Identity.* Philadelphia: Temple University Press.

Newport, Frank, and Joyce Wilke. 2013. "Most in U.S. Want Marriage, but Its Importance Has Dropped." Gallup, www.gallup.com.

Ochalla, Bryan. 2007. "ENDA Vote Postponed over Reaction from Gay Rights Groups," Oct. 3, www.samesexmarriageadvocate.blogspot.com.

O'Keefe, Ed. 2013. "ENDA Explained." *Washington Post,* Nov. 4.

Pew Research Center. 2013. "A Survey of LGBT Americans: Attitudes, Experiences, and Values in Changing Times," www.pewsocialtrends.org, retrieved on June 30, 2015.

Pierson, Paul. 2000. "Increasing Returns, Path Dependency, and the Study of Politics." *American Political Science Review* 94: 251–67.

Rimmerman, Craig A. 2002. *From Identity to Politics: The Lesbian and Gay Movements in the United States.* Philadelphia: Temple University Press, 2002.

Rimmerman, Craig A. 2008. *The Lesbian and Gay Movements: Assimilation or Liberation?* Boulder, CO: Westview.

Tillery, Beverly. 2015. "Planning the Future of the LGBT & HIV Movement," Feb. 3. Lambda Legal, www.lambdalegal.org, retrieved on June 30, 2015.

Vaid, Urvashi. 1995. *Virtual Equality: The Mainstreaming of Gay and Lesbian Liberation.* New York: Anchor Books.

Vaid, Urvashi. 2012. "Still Ain't Satisfied: The Limits of Equality," May, pp. 38–43. www.prospect.org, accessed July 2014.

Wolfman-Arent, Avi. 2014. "Donors to Gay Causes Consider Their Next Steps." Nov. 3. *Chronicle of Philanthropy,* www.philanthropy.com, retrieved on June 30, 2015.

Wu, Janson. 2014. "Equality Is Not the Finish Line," July 29. Gay and Lesbian Advocates and Defenders, www.glad.org.

28

Scouting for Normalcy

Merit Badges, Cookies, and American Futurity

JUDY ROHRER

It is difficult to think of an organization more imbued with American futurity than the Boy Scouts. If "futurity" is the "quality, state, or fact of being future" and "future time," American futurity refers to those U.S. national narratives prescribing a future that compels specific actions by citizens and government in the present. Since the future is often presented as "for the children," the Boy Scouts, as the largest youth organization in the United States, would have had difficulty not being snared by this rhetoric. Their nationalistic, militaristic, heterosexist origins just made this connection that much stronger as they pledged to mold ideal (male) citizens. This contrasts dramatically with the Girl Scouts, who by and large have resisted falling in line as "good" girls/women upholding dominant scripts tying them to normative visions of American futurity.

Given all of this, how do we think about the Boy Scouts of America (BSA) lifting its ban on gay scouts but not gay scout leaders? How do we consider Zach Wahl's leadership of Scouts for Equality and their campaign to get the ban lifted? Wahl, a straight white man and Eagle Scout, was catapulted into the national spotlight with his pro-gay-marriage testimony before the Iowa legislature legitimating his lesbian moms by demonstrating his normalcy. On the other hand, how do we understand the recent protests of the Girl Scouts of the U.S.A. (GSUSA), including cookie boycotts opposing GSUSA's supposed promotion of lesbianism and abortion? And then there is the backlash against a Colorado Girl Scout troop for the admission of a transgender girl. Thinking queerly through recent scouting controversies and how they tie to BSA and GSUSA organizational histories enables us to explore the anxieties and desires that drive approaches to particularized American futurity, and to consider alternatives.

As the controversies demonstrate, there is clearly a critique to be made of homonormativity and homonationalism[1] as they are produced through *boy* scouting as practice, institution, and aspiration. Paralleling the scouting-for-normalcy by gay boy scouting advocates is the policing of normalcy by those outraged that *girl* scouting is not upholding proper girl/womanhood. Both of these initiatives are made in the broader context of U.S. nationalism and reproductive futurity that is particularly pervasive in the BSA. In this chapter I argue that fun and fantasy—especially as practiced via irony, parody, and camp—has been, and can be, a critical part of thinking queerly through the politics of futurity. Since "fun" is highlighted as a key objective of the GSUSA (not so much the BSA), this method seems particularly apt. From queer merit badges to camp parodies to scouting-themed gay male porn to Cub Scout drag kings, I scout (out) alternative strategies and visions for American futurity that push beyond arguments for inclusion of the "good" gay scout/citizen.

In what follows, I explore the histories of the two organizations and how they tie to contemporary firestorms over gender and sexual normativity. Turning to queer culture, which has always been committed to imagining otherwise for survival (including the subsistence that comes through community-based humor), it is not difficult to find examples of queered, camped, parodied scouting. Boy scouting in particular has made itself too easy a target to resist—and the queerest queers rarely resist opportunities for fun. Rather than clamoring toward inclusion via respectability, poking fun at scouting's staunch commitment to normalcy exposes the fear-bound, unimaginative, stagnant quality of dominant notions of American futurity. In response to that exposure, we are encouraged to look elsewhere for possibilities of alternative, dynamic, nonnormative futures. Rather than "no future" for queers (Edelman 2004), this essay argues that the queer rebuke of scouting-for-normalcy indicates that "the future is queerness's domain" (Muñoz 2009).

Boy and Girl Scout His/Herstory

The Boy Scouts began as a way of enforcing imperialism, nationalism, and militarized masculinity and, at the national level, has only deepened those commitments over the past century. The organization was founded in the United States in 1910 but based on an organizational handbook and model developed by Baden Powell, a British imperial military officer who had served in Africa and India. In her comparative study of the BSA and the GSUSA, Barbara Arneil writes, "Like its British counterpart, the BSA was born in a context of general anxiety over 'masculinity' and a particular kind of racialized nation (white, Northern European Protestant) perceived to be at risk from changes in demography and values" (Arneil 2010, 55). Arneil notes that these similarities in perceived context compelled the BSA to adopt the British oath (calling for duty to God, country, law, and helping others), except for one critical departure. Instead of pledging "obedience," the Americans put an emphasis on self-discipline: "[t]o keep myself physically strong, mentally awake and morally straight" (Arneil 2010, 55). The interpretation of the final phrase—being "morally straight"—has been key in the battles over gay scouting.

The BSA has been embroiled in controversy over its exclusionary policies for decades, and it is not just gays who have challenged the organization, but girls and atheists as well. In fact, some in scouting refer to the "three Gs" of their membership policy: "no, girls, godless, or gays" (Ellis 2014, 29). In 1988, after a series of legal challenges, the BSA finally changed its policy to remove gender restrictions on scouting leadership positions, but not on membership (Ellis 2014, 31). While (straight) women can now be scout "masters," the "godless" have not been as lucky. The courts have continually ruled that the Boy Scouts, as a private organization, has a right to limit leadership and membership to those who share its "values" (Ellis 2014, 35). And finally, regarding the third "G," the doggedly defended gay ban looks to be on its last legs, but it took decades of struggle to get to this point.

The ties to a patriotic masculinity and God go beyond exclusionary policies. As Barbara Arneil argues, "At the core of the BSA's identity, and a primary source of its continued defensiveness, was a narrow and unchanging conception of masculinity, Christianity, and patriotism" (Arneil 2010, 59). The BSA has a long history of finding support from the U.S. military in the form of resources, facilities, and transportation. The BSA was chartered by Congress in 1916, and Congress authorized federal agencies to provide it with services and expendable supplies. This has meant that the Department of Defense regularly provides supplies and that there are officials in each branch of the service who carry responsibility for facilitating assistance. For example, local councils frequently use military facilities for BSA activities. And, every U.S. president and commander in chief since William Howard Taft has served as honorary president of the Scouts (Ellis 2014, 69). The strong DOD ties also help explain the current actual president being former defense secretary Robert Gates.

To find God in scouting one needs only to follow the money. Over 70 percent of BSA units are sponsored by religious organizations, and about half of these are Mormon (Ring and Jow 2012). In southern states, these ties are particularly strong with conservative religious denominations, including the Southern Baptists, who have been at the forefront of defending the gay ban. While at times the BSA has had to disassociate itself from religious fanaticism and rabid antigay hate mongering (Ellis 2014), it is historically and financially bound (strongly and without kink) to religious institutions.

The organization has repeatedly gone to court to ensure its power to ban atheists and agnostics, kicking out two Cub Scouts who refused to say the word "God" in the oath and banning another whose father was agnostic (Ellis 2014, 35–37). In fact, so confident was the BSA of the righteousness of this position that in 1993 they tried to get the U.S. Supreme Court to bless the policy, and were sorely disappointed when the Court announced it would not review the case. Comparatively, "at precisely the moment that the Boy Scouts of America were insisting on the exclusion of nonbelievers, the Girl Scouts of America were moving emphatically in the other direction" (Ellis 2014, 37).

As a number of scholars point out, the history of the GSUSA is strikingly different, especially with regard to challenges to normativity. Begun in 1912 and also fashioned on a British model, the Girl Guides, the American version defied the admonitions of the then BSA president and changed its name to the Girl Scouts in 1915. Arneil writes,

> The GSUSA, like its British counterpart, had a contradictory nature. On the one hand, it was a quasi-militaristic organization where values such as loyalty to God and country and traditional gender norms—being supportive, obedient, and "cheerful"—were emphasized. . . . On the other hand, gender roles were challenged and even defied—by insisting on the right to be called "scouts" in the first place and by promoting rugged and traditionally masculine activities. (Arneil 2010, 56)

The early GSUSA did not just defy gender norms but committed itself more broadly to diversity and inclusion. Juliette Gordon Low, the organization's aristocratic founder, was significantly hearing impaired and welcomed girls with disabilities from the start. There is also speculation that the divorced, raucous, and rather butch Gordon Low was a lesbian (Gianoulis 2002–2015). She set the foundation for the organization's multicultural and global perspectives by, among other things, publishing the member handbook in multiple languages. It is also Gordon Low who, from the beginning, required not an oath but a "promise" excluding the BSA language of being "physically strong, mentally awake and morally straight" (Arneil 2010, 56–57). Her legacy lives on and is frequently invoked. For example, Kathy Cloninger, CEO of the GSUSA from 2003 to 2011, stated, "Diversity has been a core value of Girl Scouts since Juliette Gordon Low gathered together the first troop" (Arneil 2010, 56).

While the Promise diverged from the BSA Oath in rejecting the above moralistic and ableist statement, it replicated the language of serving "God and country." However, rather than dig in around these early normative policies as the BSA has done, the GSUSA has been more progressive. For example, as alluded to above, in 1993 the organization voted overwhelmingly to allow members to substitute other words or phrases in the place of "God." Girl Scouts may promise to serve their family, their best friend, Allah, Kali, Beyoncé, Michelle Obama, Olivia Pope . . . It is not then surprising to learn that it is not religious organizations but corporations and foundations that are the primary funders of the GSUSA (including AT&T, Coca-Cola, MetLife, and Rockefeller) (Ring and Jow 2012). With regard to gender, while to my knowledge no boy has sued to gain entry, the girls have also been more open, as discussed in the next section.[2]

The differing orientations of the two organizations are starkly apparent in their mission statements as published on their websites. The BSA states, "The mission of the Boy Scouts of America is to prepare young people to make ethical and moral choices over their lifetimes by instilling in them the values of the Scout Oath and Law." The boys get "ethics," "morals," "values," "Oaths," and "Laws." The GSUSA states, "Girl Scouting builds girls of courage, confidence, and character, who make the world a better place." So, the girls get "courage," "confidence," "character" (one has to admire that alliteration), and "making the world a better place." Which group would you want to join?

The legacy of the GSUSA founder shines through here in the attention to the agency of girls to create positive social change (as opposed to an anxious compulsion to "instill" preset "values"). Gordon Low is said to have had three mantras: (1) don't tell her no; (2) always "take it back to the girls" (i.e., ask them); and (3) make sure it is fun (Girl Scouts of the USA 2010). While "taking it back to the girls" reflects her faith in girls' vision and engagement, "fun" is significant to the argument of this chapter. While it shows up from the establishment of the GSUSA, it is missing in action for the BSA. In notes for one of her speeches, Gordon Low wrote, "When a mother comes to me and asks me, 'Why should my daughter become a Girl Scout?' I just tell her, 'You just ask the girl and she'll tell you. It's because of the fun!'" (Girl Scouts of the USA 2010).

It is significant that this was her primary answer, especially to a parent. There is nothing here about molding ideal future citizens, no compulsion toward nationalist reproductive futurity. Fun is very presentist. It is about now, not later. Gordon Low knew what many queer activists have also known for decades—no one is going to join, and certainly not remain in, your group/organization/movement unless it is fun. Evidence for this on the queer side is on display at any queer action, where the usual self-righteous seriousness of protest politics are often mocked. "We're here, we're queer, we all need a beer." Or, more in the spirit of youth: "If you're queer and you know it, clap your hands—[clap, clap] (repeat)."

Contemporary Firestorms

These his/herstories are played out in contemporary bifurcated controversies involving the two organizations. Generally, the BSA leadership continues to resist change and is under siege by the mainstream Left, while GSUSA leaders tend to embrace change and are under siege by the radical Right. In other words, as Boy Scouts are scouting for normalcy, the Girl Scouts are being policed for challenging normalcy. These politics are most evident in the fight over gay inclusion in boy scouting and right-wing backlashes against feminist and trans-inclusive girl scouting.

The fight for gay scouting has a decades-old history, including a significant milestone in the 2000 Supreme Court case *Boy Scouts of America v. Dale,* which held that the BSA has a constitutional right to exclude gays. The fight has heated up in the last few years and gained attention in a national environment increasingly accepting of gays and lesbians. In 2012 Ryan Anderson of Moraga, California, was denied Eagle Scout status because he was openly gay and therefore in violation of "membership standards." His mother launched a Change.org petition that garnered half a million signatures (Ellis 2014, 251). That same year in Ohio, when den mother Jennifer Tyrell was forced to step down because she is an out lesbian, she also took up the fight. Tyrell has received an outpouring of support from national LGBT organizations, including GLAAD. The BSA defended her dismissal, stating, "Scouting, and the majority of parents it serves, does not believe it is the right forum for children to become aware of the issue of sexual orientation, or engage in discussions about being gay" (James 2012). Notice here the focus on reproductive futurity—purporting to act in the best interests of "the children" by actually "serving" their parents.

The next year, 2013, turned out to be a big one for the BSA. Under the increasing pressure, the organization's national council was slated to take up the issue at its February meeting but opted to delay the vote until May, citing the need for more "deliberation." The Right claimed victory for this delay and it spurred more organizing by both sides. President Obama, several U.S. senators, New York's Mayor Bloomberg, and 1.4 million petition signers weighed in supporting the lifting of the ban. Significantly, given their status as major stakeholders, so did the Mormons. Finally, in May the national council voted by 61 percent to lift the ban on gay members effective January 1, 2014, but to maintain it for adult leaders (Hennessy-Fiske 2013). Despite anxiety about threats of a backlash, not much of one has materialized outside the radical Right. The *Los Angeles Times* reported that less than 2 percent of troops lost their sponsors by December 2013 (Hennessy-Fiske 2013), and the *Washington Post* reported that the impact has been small and mostly felt in southern states (McCartney 2014). Predictably, an antigay spin-off, Trail Life USA, was founded for boys needing safe scouting space free of homos. Still, a mass exodus from the BSA has yet to occur.

In February 2014, Pascal Tessier of Bethesda, Maryland, became the nation's first openly gay Eagle Scout. Tessier came out and joined the fight to change the policy in 2013, putting his candidacy for Eagle Scout at risk but saying it was worth it. When he made Eagle Scout he told the media, "It shows everyone that I'm a capable person—that I'm worth something" (Hennessy-Fiske 2013). When asked about the fact that the ban on gay leaders remains, Tessier remarked, "It's kind of a backhanded acceptance: We accept you for now. It says to you you're a monster of some sort" (Vargas 2014). (Taking up the challenge, the Greater New York Councils of the Boy Scouts announced in April 2015 that it was hiring Tessier to help with, among other things, summer camp.) In his short statements, we see the emphasis on assimilation and respectability ("acceptance," "worthiness," and "capability" all make appearances) that has become central to mainstream LGBT politics.

This assimilationist focus is central to Scouts for Equality, the national organization founded by Zach Wahls after his 2011 testimony before the Iowa House of Representatives catapulted him into the limelight. His statement in support of his lesbian moms and gay marriage relied on his position as a respected young, white, straight man—an Eagle Scout no less—who could "proudly" declare (and reiterated on the jacket cover of his 2012 book, *My Two Moms: Lessons of Love, Strength, and What Makes a Family*), "The sexual orientation of my parents has had zero effect on the content of my character" (Wahls and Littlefield 2012). Speaking of backhanded acceptance . . . Through his organization Wahls has been pivotal in lobbying major corporations to pull their funding of the Scouts, including Lockheed Martin, CAT, UPS, and Intel, and can take partial credit for BSA president Robert Gates's recent indirect statements in support of lifting the ban on gay scoutmasters. Wahls issued an immediate press release announcing his pride in Gates for "charting a course toward full equality" (Wahls 2015). It is illuminating to read Robert Gates's actual remarks, the strongest of which are, "[T]he membership standards cannot be sustained. . . . We must deal with the world as it is, not as we wish it to be" (Crary and Peltz 2015). With friends like this it seems likely that this change will come in the next few years given the pressure (however reluctant), and the clear inconsistency in a policy that says it is okay to be gay until you are eighteen, but not thereafter.

The Girl Scouts, given its history of more flexible and inclusive policies, and a mission supporting the empowerment of girls, has been hit recently with attacks from the Right, rather than the Left. Most notably, two different cookie boycotts were launched: one protesting GSUSA's supposed advocacy of abortion and lesbianism; and the other decrying a Colorado troop's admission of a transgender member. In 2013, conservative pastor and radio host Kevin Swanson announced on air, "I don't want to support lesbianism, I don't want to support Planned Parenthood, and I don't want to support abortion. And if that be the case, I'm not buying Girl Scout cookies." He went on to call the GSUSA a "wicked organization" that does not promote "godly womanhood" and implored his listeners, "Please, I beg of you, do not buy Girl Scout cookies" (Walsh 2013). Not surprisingly, Swanson announced that he expected to see "sodomy merit badges" after the BSA lifted its ban on gay members (Bennett-Smith 2013).

It would be easy to write Swanson off except for the fact that he is not alone. In 2012, Indiana state representative Bob Morris refused to support a resolution commemorating the one-hundred-year anniversary of the Girl Scouts, calling the organization a "tactical arm" of Planned Parenthood (Walsh 2013). (I like the image of Girl Scouts and Brownies in full uniform out in force for clinic defenses.) And a year after Swanson's tirade, we got "CookieCott 2014" with the backing of right-wing heavy hitters such as Concerned Women of America, whose president announced, "[T]he Girl Scouts of America went off track years ago" (Nichols 2014). The "Concerned Women" have been joined in their attack on the GSUSA by Focus on the Family and Family Research Council. The CookieCott alarmism seemed to be tied in part to a tweet from the Girl Scouts about "Incredible Ladies who should be Women of the Year for 2013," which named, among others, Malala Yousafzai, Beyoncé, and pro-choice-filibustering, pink-tennis-shoe-wearing Texas state senator Wendy Davis (Nichols 2014).

In other sectors, news of seven-year-old Bobby Montoya's acceptance (after an initial denial for being transgender) into a Colorado troop in 2011 spurred other calls for cookie boycotts. Websites and Facebook pages titled "Honest Girl Scouts" and "Making Girl Scouts clean again" called for current scouts to go on strike from selling cookies and others to stop buying them until the GSUSA banned transgender members. They fear-mongered via YouTube videos raising the specter of dangerous troop sleepovers with trans scouts who were simply boys pretending to be girls. Three troops across the country in Louisiana decided to disband, so horrified were they by the idea of a trans girl scout (Pasulka 2012). It is important to note that this says much more about the adult troop leaders than the scouts, since the media reported that the scout leaders made the decision—they did not follow Gordon Low's advice to "take it to the girls."

After hearing about the initial denial of Montoya's request to join (including transphobic statements by the troop leader calling Montoya an "it"), the Colorado council reversed the decision, stating, "If a child identifies as a girl and the child's family presents her as a girl, Girl Scouts of Colorado welcomes her as a Girl Scout" and further clarifying that "troops do not require proof of gender" (Murray 2011). And in 2015 the national organization backed up the Colorado decision, stating, "If a girl is recognized by her family, school and community as a girl and lives culturally as a girl, Girl Scouts is an organization that can serve her in a setting that is both emotionally and physically safe." This statement was prefaced with a call back to the organizational foundation set by Juliette Gordon Low (Archibald 2015). Clearly the GSUSA did its homework, referencing current literature on gender identity, which is more than can be said of the BSA's response to advocacy for gay inclusion.

Queering Scouting

Queers have been engaging with scouting in multiple ways for decades. Beyond the fight for inclusion in the BSA, scouting, particularly *boy* scouting, has provided ample material for parody, camp, and fun. For one thing, it is hard to miss the homoerotics of the Boy Scouts. Like sports and the military, the BSA has long provided a safe space for male bonding and homoerotic relations. The vehement protest of gay inclusion and desperate disciplining of boys to be "morally straight" offer clear evidence that the scouting authorities "do protest too much, methinks." Queers have called out that hypocrisy for some time.

In a not-so-surprising twist, a recent biography of Baden Powell, the founder of the Boy Scouts, provides strong evidence that he was a closeted gay man. His strongest emotional bond was to a fellow army officer, he openly admired good-looking, muscular men and boys, attractive women made him extremely nervous, and (wait for it) he often played women's roles in army theatricals (Allen 2012). Out gay men have played upon the homoerotics with camp scouting parodies and, of course, sexual fantasy and porn. For example, after the recent decision accepting gay scouts but not leaders, a porn magazine highlighted a new Men.com "Scout series" with the headline, "Anti-Gay Boy Scouts Get the Gay Porn Parody They Deserve." The magazine declared, "[T]he Boy Scouts still don't accept adult scout leaders who are openly gay, but don't worry, you can watch several adult scouts having a lot of gay sex—openly!" (Zach 2014).

Lesbians have been characteristically less sexual and more serious in their approach to scouting. An important piece of historical scholarship, the 1998 book *On My Honor: Lesbians Reflect on Their Scouting Experience* is a case in point (Manahan 1997). In our defense, we have also had less to parody given the comparative histories of the two organizations. We are, however, not completely humorless, as the Nancy Clue series by Mabel Maney demonstrates. The series is a lesbian spoof of the Nancy Drew and Cherry Ames books. Sherrie Inness points out that the protagonist, Nancy Clue, frequently calls on her Girl Scout training to get her out of a pinch, as in the incident in *The Case of the Not-So-Nice Nurse* when Nancy tied up three villains with a very short rope. She also later survived trapped in a tunnel for three days, noting, "Luckily I had a loaf of bread, chocolate bars, oranges, and some milk in my purse" (Inness 1997, 82). This illustrates the historical tension in girl scouting—being ever prepared, like any experienced butch, but sporting a purse to ensure feminine cover.

While they have not garnered the attention of the queens, drag kings are also masters at parody, sexy reversals, and fun, and scouting has provided them with ample material. The DC Kings of the nation's capital, who claim to be the "longest-running monthly drag king show in the world," include a young new member, Cub Scout, whose performances "always keep you guessing and wanting more" (Kings 2015). Boys R Us, a well-known southwest troupe, notes that their scouting number always drives the crowd wild. They have determined it is something about the Boy Scout uniform and have learned to be particularly cautious with it, lest they get "mauled." In an interview about the show they stated, "We're just having a lot of fun with it right now. I think we went through a period where we got really serious and we discussed some serious issues, and now I think we're more just enjoying ourselves" (D'Andrea 2005).

Susan Sontag, in her early essay on camp, wrote, "[T]he whole point of Camp is to dethrone the serious. Camp is playful, anti-serious. More precisely, Camp involves a new, more complex relation to 'the serious.' One can be serious about the frivolous, frivolous about the serious" (Sontag 1964, 285). Here Sontag is working through her thinking. Dethroning the serious cannot be done through simple reversal; therefore camp is not simply anti-serious, but engages in more complicated dynamics. This describes the drag kings above and the way they always keep us guessing. Are they serious about the potential of being "mauled" by crazed lesbians? Are they frivolous about it? And is the possibility of mauling, both as fantasy and as a reality, serious or frivolous? These queer performers are creating new relationships to the serious and the nonserious, and sometimes this happens by feigning seriousness through their personas. Sontag also writes, "Camp rests on innocence"; it is "naïve" (Sontag 1964, 281). Certainly the persona of Cub Scout is playing on these assumed idyllic characteristics of actual Cub Scouts. He can help me across the street anytime.

Following a recent trend in ironic merit badges spurred by the recent controversies and available for purchase online, gay merit badges are the rage in certain select enclaves. "The Happy Camper" offers a line of gay-themed badges, including Catholic Survivor, Fruit Fly, Drag Queen Diva, Gaydar, BFFS with Ex, Gym Rat, and Bear Pride. Their website states, "Happy Camper badges are equal parts whimsical, serious, self-deprecating, and ridiculous. And, while playfully mocking at times, the badges represent the fact that humor is a great antidote to shame, fear and hate" (Happy Camper 2015). Mary (Mack) Tremonte, self-described printmaker, educator, DJ, and queer scout, has come up with another set of queer scout badges, including Go Gay, Operation Sappho, Holler Back, and Glamarchy (Tremonte 2015). It would take too long to describe the badges, but both sets demonstrate the serious frivolity of camp.

These parodies point to a crucial part of queer politics that has been less visible in the last two decades—the use of humor, fun, parody, and camp. As the mainstream LGBT movement has corralled us into a politics of respectability, politely asking to be allowed to marry,[3] have children, and serve in the military, we have lost the freedom and exhilaration of the outrageous, out-of-control stampede. Stonewall and the Compton Cafeteria rebellions were stampedes of queers (many trans, low-income, and of color) who refused to remain penned up, disrespected, and abused. They were demands for recognition, not inclusion. ACT-UP, Queer Nation, and the Lesbian Avengers, among other groups, built on those rebellions in direct-action politics that claimed space and disrupted (straight) business as usual (rather than entering into it). It is easy to be nostalgic, and this is not meant to be a call back to the radical days of yore. It is meant to open up some space for queers to think about our history, our contemporary politics, and where we think we are going. "Queerness is that thing that lets us feel that this world is not enough, that indeed something is missing" (Muñoz 2009, 1). What possibilities are enabled by queering scouting? How can they help us think differently about queer politics now? How can they help us unsettle normative, exclusionary constructions of American futurity?

The history of boy scouting reveals its foundational and ongoing commitment to the (re)production of "good" masculine citizen-subjects. The desperate attempts to guard against "girls, godless, and gays" reveal the anxiety at the heart of a national identity built on exclusion. That front line has not held: the "three

Gs" are inside, along with many other misfits and oddballs, demanding attention and unsettling who "we" (Americans) think we are and are becoming. The partial lifting of the BSA gay ban is a partial concession to this reality; at the same time it is also the result of liberal assimilationist gay politics and the construction of the "good gay." After all, queer critiques of reproductive futurity have pointed out that the future "for the children" has never included queer, nonwhite, native, noncitizen, or disabled children—in fact, these are exactly the communities who must be excluded, eliminated, or denied to fulfill the teleological narrative of "a better tomorrow" (Berlant 1997; Smith 2010; Kafer 2013; Rodríguez 2014). An LGBT politics of homonormativity and homonationalism has succeeded in sanitizing the most normative among us so that we might experience partial inclusion, as long as we deemphasize our difference, participate in discourses of U.S. exceptionalism, and disassociate from queerer queers.

On the other hand, we have Boy Scout drag kings, gay merit badges, and other forms of parody that successfully emphasize queer exclusion from scouting through exaggerated performative modes of self-styled inclusion. Their goal, as far as I can tell, is not to be included into scouting or dominant American futurity. Cub Scout does not really want to become a scout (and future model citizen) as much as he wants to play with scouting. Further, no one expects the BSA will adopt any of the gay merit badges any time soon, or ever. "Queerness is that thing that lets us feel that this world is not enough" (Muñoz 2009, 1). The Boy Scouts are not enough by a long shot. Rather than trying to become them, these queers help us recognize their inadequacy. They poke fun at the organization's antiquatedness, fear of difference, desire for certitude, compulsion to reproduce the status quo.

The Girl Scouts, being committed to diversity and progressive change, have been more open to admitting that "this world is not enough," and thus more flexible in their programming. This is not to suggest that they are without fault, as the initial denial of Montoya's request for membership demonstrates, but to recognize their foundational difference from the BSA. As the aforementioned *On My Honor* and numerous other sources make clear, the GSUSA has functioned as an important organization in the lives of many lesbian/bi/queer scouts and scout leaders, their participation often simply hidden in plain sight. While my tomboy tendencies led me to a rag-tag 4-H horse club, my mother was a Girl Scout in conservative Prescott, Arizona, in the 1950s. She reflected, "I remember my first leaders were two single women who lived together. Thinking back, I think they might have been lesbians, but no one was concerned in those days. The Protestant church that allowed us to meet in their basement was happy to have women who would volunteer to take on this group of preadolescent girls" (Acevedo 2015). The Girl Scouts still struggle to find adult leaders, and it is worth considering how that is tied to the greater cultural cachet of the BSA and could factor into their inclusivity.

Queer Futurity

The Boy Scouts have always already been gay, even if they adamantly deny it. The Girl Scouts have also always been gay, and have not tried to deny it as much as to point elsewhere. Their organizational histories, recent controversies, and queer satirical responses provide a lens into considering how queer politics might intervene in notions of American futurity. Here I turn to the late José Esteban Muñoz's vision of a queer futurity:

> Queerness is not yet here. Queerness is an ideality. Put another way, we are not yet queer. We may never touch queerness, but we can feel it as the warm illumination of a horizon imbued with potentiality. We have never been queer, yet queerness exists for us as an ideality that can be distilled from the past and used to imagine the future. The future is queerness's domain. (Muñoz 2009, 1)

If "the future is queerness's domain" and if scouting, especially for boys, is all about the construction of a certain normative, prescriptive, reproductive American futurity, then queering scouting offers productive tensions and incommensurabilities through which we can continue to imagine otherwise.

Muñoz's vision of a queer future was in part a response to the antirelationality thesis articulated most pointedly by Lee Edelman in his text *No Future: Queer Theory and the Death Drive.* In his critique of reproductive futurity, Edelman cautions us about the ways investing in dominant notions of a future "for the children" can reproduce injustices in the present. He therefore calls for a radical disassociation with such investments or desires, and also with other people. While Muñoz finds Edelman's book a "brilliant" and "inspiring polemic," he argues against "the seductive sway of the antirelational thesis" as "romances of the negative" (Muñoz 2009, 11). Others have also noted that the subjectless queerness promoted by Edelman reveals his relatively privileged status as a white, able-bodied, middle-class gay man (Smith 2010; Rodríguez 2014). Instead, Muñoz insists "on the essential need for an understanding of queerness as collectivity," writing, "I respond to Edelman's assertion that the future is the province of the child and therefore not for the queers by arguing that queerness is primarily about futurity and hope" (Muñoz 2009, 11).

Not only does he give us permission to desire a future with and for queerness (and he means that in its broadest terms), but Muñoz asserts that queerness is a method that enables our collective desiring and imagining forward. "Queerness is not yet here," but we can feel it as a "warm illumination," a "horizon," an "ideality." In the short chat book/memorial essay *Queer Insists*, Michael O'Rourke shares his own testimonial and those of other leading theorists and activists for whom Muñoz's work has been essential. O'Rourke points out how

Muñoz insisted on queering straight temporalities into "capacious potentiality" (O'Rourke 2014, 43).

Muñoz was famously always late, which was certainly part of his camp academic performance, a refusal of "capitalist time" and its compulsion that we attend to the "late" and the "early." This is what Juana María Rodríguez calls "the performance of Muñozity that erupted whenever José arrived (late of course) . . . a happening that he had helped to create and defile before his entrance" (O'Rourke 2014, 23). Creating and then defiling one's own entrance certainly shows both seriousness and frivolity. Some have said he died too soon, leaving us in 2013 at the age of forty-six. Jack Halberstam disagrees, stating, "[L]like his formulation of queerness as a state of being that is present in its absence, available as a lost past, unreachable as a beckoning future, I would say that Muñoz died as he lived, in a queer time that he may not have chosen but that *insistently* chose him" (O'Rourke 2014, 31). He has not entirely left us as we continue to learn in the afterglow of his luminous spirit.

Muñoz, whose theoretical object of choice was queer of color art and performance, would absolutely appreciate the queer parodies of scouting. I believe he would see in them the possibility of making space for creative reversal, insistent refusal, and movement sideways—"the warm illumination of a horizon imbued with potentiality." He would welcome them as evidence that not all queers are relinquishing the future as the realm for the phantasmic Child (read: homonormative campaigns for marriage, especially those that rely on arguments about what is "good for the children") (Rohrer 2014).

Juana María Rodríguez builds on Muñoz's theorizing and helps in thinking about the tensions among reproductive futurity, assimilationist politics of respectability, and what she terms "queer gestures" toward "alternative sexual cultures, intimacies, logics, and politics" (Rodríguez 2014, 14). Echoing Judith Butler and Jack Halberstam, as well as Muñoz, she writes, "[Q]ueer gestures include the endless sequence of partial moves, interrupted starts, and disheartening breakdowns that occur when we dare to move beyond the possible" (Rodríguez 2014, 8). She weaves queer temporalities with nonlinear movement and failure (or at least the absence of clear success or achievement). Since queer gestures are inherently relational acts, she appreciates Muñoz's insistence on a futurity tied to queer sociality:

> Muñoz connects sociality to futurity, where sociality becomes the means and the condition for the possibility of collective futures. Futurity has never been given to queers of color, children of color, and other marginalized communities that live under the violence of the state and social erasure, a violence whose daily injustices exceed the register of a politics organized solely around sexuality, even as they are enmeshed within a logic of sexuality that is always already racialized through an imagined ideal citizen-subject. (Rodríguez 2014, 11)

The queer gestures Rodríguez wants us to attend to recognize radical queer difference and refuse to relinquish our tomorrows to reproductive futurity, particularly not in a homonormative (white) rainbow wrapper. By asking for inclusion as "good" citizens/spouses/soldiers/parents/scouts, mainstream LGBT politics "sanitize our lives in order to make us palatable as subjects worthy of the rights of citizenship, even as it fails to recognize the multiple vectors of violence and injustice that also constitute our lives as queer subjects" (Rodríguez 2014, 9).

In her refusal of homonormativity, including her attention to the ways it is not even an option for many queers, Rodríguez follows other theorists in bringing sex, desire, and fantasy back in through her attention to "alternative forms of racialized queer female sexuality" (Rodríguez 2014, 14). While campaigns for gay scouting rely on divorcing queerness from a sexuality that is always already read as dangerous (ironic given the recently discovered ongoing and pervasive pedophilia at the hands of straight scoutmasters), as part of a critical queer politics Rodríguez and others embrace sex, sexuality, desire, fantasy, and all of the contradictions that come with that tangled package.

This is incredibly important in a political atmosphere demanding a type of legitimacy and recognizability won through "hypernormative domesticity and proper citizenship." In making her argument Rodríguez writes, "Assimilation into (homo)normative family life means that queerness can no longer be about pleasure, let alone sexual desire. . . . Discourses that define children as the future, as the embodied ideal of youth and national promise, simultaneously produce parents as the opposite: as aging, desexualized caretakers" (Rodríguez 2014, 52). Boy scouting rhetoric provides the master American text for the discourse of "the embodied ideal of youth and national promise."

Zach Wahls mobilized exactly this rhetoric as he skillfully argued for gay marriage by presenting himself as über Scout and ideal future Citizen *in spite of* his lesbian moms. Remember, he stated, and then recently restated, "The sexual orientation of my parents has had zero effect on the content of my character" (Wahls and Littlefield 2012). His moms are not just desexualized; they are eliminated from the equation entirely. That is the case because for many on the Right, as demonstrated earlier, queer sexuality and gender performance are still seen as "wicked" and antithetical to proper citizenship. For these people, queers remain predators who are particularly interested in children. We should never have contact with children as mentors, teachers, coaches, or parents.

For the larger population who consider themselves moderate, sex, sexuality, and gender identity are taboo topics when dealing with children (as if the strategy of not talking about these topics has worked so well). While they may not see queers as predators, because we make these topics visible by representing their nonnormative modalities, we are seen as forcing unwelcomed conversations with, or in relation to, children. Remember the BSA statement regarding Jennifer Tyrell: "Scouting, and the majority of parents it serves, does not believe it is the right forum for children to become aware of the issue of sexual orientation, or engage in discussions about being gay" (James 2012). Hence the hysteria from the Right, and more generalized resistance from moderates, not just to gay Boy Scouts and leaders but also to a trans scout, a feminist role model, a dyke den leader, and so forth.

In spite of "current attempts to assign gay and lesbian families state-recognized respectability," there remain "persistent associations of queerness with perversity and pleasure—in other words, the antithesis of parenting" (Rodríguez 2014, 33). One of the crucial bits lost in these moral panics are the scouts and potential scouts who already fall outside the norm with regard to sexual orientation. With the GSUSA claiming 2.3 million members and the BSA claiming 4.5 million (making it the largest youth-oriented organization in the United States), we can count 680,000 queer or questioning members (assuming the generally agreed on statistic of one in ten). That is a large number of youth who could use support, guidance, and fun, rather than ostracism and exclusion.

The gay male porn and drag king performances that play with scouting themes are exactly the types of queer gestures Rodríguez finds fruitful (pun intended). Rather than beating hasty retreats from queerness, they are successful precisely because they strike at the heart of the matter, mocking and eroticizing the puritanical image of the "good" (gay) scout. They refuse respectability, instead opening up space for possibility through (sexual) relationality. Why is this important? Because, as Judith Butler beautifully articulated, "[F]antasy is what allows us to imagine ourselves and others otherwise; it establishes the possible in excess of the real; it points elsewhere, and when it is embodied, it brings elsewhere home" (Butler 2004, 29).

Just as queerness reminds us that this world is not enough, fantasy "establishes the possible in excess of the real." If some in the BSA are holding tightly to "the real" (as they perceive it), ignoring its rogue excess, it is "possibility," "otherwise," and "elsewhere" that enable others of us to imagine another future. A queer futurity in the style of Muñoz and Rodríguez would include fabulous drag shows at annual BSA jamborees, "Do-si-dos and around she goes" lesbian/bi/trans-friendly Girl Scout cookies, and "Camping It Up" merit badges available to all scouts (boys, girls, and otherwise identified) willing to publicly embrace their fabulous, fun, fantastical selves.

Afterword

Since this chapter was written, a number of things have happened, including the marching of the Girl Scouts in Donald Trump's inaugural parade in spite of sharp criticism by many former scouts and scout parents. This is a good reminder that the GSUSA is far from flawless. The Boy Scouts also announced in January 2017 that they would stop excluding transgender scouts, but their statement was thin and less than welcoming. Additionally, historian Benjamin René Jordan has published a study of manhood and citizenship as constructed via the early period of the BSA that readers may want to explore (Jordan 2016).

NOTES

1 Lisa Duggan coined the term "homonormativity" to name an ideology and practice within the LGBT community that "does not contest dominant heteronormative assumptions and institutions but upholds and sustains them while promising the possibility of a demobilized gay constituency and a privatized, depoliticized gay culture anchored in domesticity and consumption" (Duggan 2003, 50). "Homonationalism" is a more recent term coined by Jaspir Puar describing the symbiotic relationship between the mainstream LGBT movements and nationalism, foreign policy, and, in the United States, narratives of U.S. exceptionalism. "For contemporary forms of U.S. nationalism and patriotism, the production of gay and queer bodies is crucial to the deployment of nationalism, insofar as these perverse bodies reiterate heterosexuality as the norm but also because certain domesticated homosexual bodies provide ammunition to reinforce nationalist projects" (Puar 2007, 39).

2 The progressiveness of the organization has not been without its critics. While I mostly focus on those on the Right, there are others. And some of them bring fun and irony into their critiques. For example, the move to "Digital Cookie" (a Girl Scout cookies app and website) has seen its share of pushback. Comments to an NPR story, "Girl Scouts Bring Cookie Sales On-Line with Sites, App" (Dec. 2, 2014), include the following: "There's a Girl Scout cookie app . . . OK, that's it, I give up, I'm doomed, pass that box of Thin Mints . . . never mind, pass me the whole shipping container" and "'10,000 Girl Scouts freed from cookie factory' . . . lol."

3 While I was in the midst of writing this paper, the U.S. Supreme Court issued its long-anticipated decision on gay marriage. Justice Kennedy's decision certainly reflects the influence of the politics of respectability and assimilation. In it he wrote, "No union is more profound than marriage," and went on to explain that in their appeal to the Court the gay plaintiffs "reveal that they seek not to denigrate marriage but rather to live their lives, or honor their spouses' memory, joined by its bond" (as quoted in Sherman 2015). In other words, queers don't want to challenge marriage or offer alternative forms of kinship but rather to join a historically oppressive institution with a 50 percent failure rate.

REFERENCES

Acevedo, Georgia K. 2015. Personal communication, June 2.

Allen, Brooke. 2012. "Rainbow Merit Badge." *New York Times*, July 19.

Archibald, Andrea Bastiani. 2015. "The Meaning of 'Serving All Girls.'" GSblog, May 14. http://blog.girlscouts.org.

Arneil, Barbara. 2010. "Gender, Diversity, and Organizational Change: The Boy Scouts vs. Girl Scouts of America." *Perspectives on Politics* 8 (1): 53–68.

Bennett-Smith, Meredith. 2013. "Kevin Swanson and Dave Buehner, Christian Radio Hosts, Say 'Sodomy Merit Badge' Next for Boy Scouts." *Huffington Post*, Aug. 20.

Berlant, Lauren Gail. 1997. *The Queen of America Goes to Washington City: Essays on Sex and Citizenship, Series Q*. Durham, NC: Duke University Press.

Butler, Judith. 2004. *Undoing Gender*. New York: Routledge.

Crary, David, and Jennifer Peltz. 2015. "Boy Scouts President Robert Gates Says Ban on Gay Adult Participants 'Cannot Be Sustained.'" *Huffington Post*, May 21.

D'Andrea, Niki. 2005. "The Man Show." *Phoenix New Times*, Aug. 11.

Duggan, Lisa. 2003. *The Twilight of Equality? Neoliberalism, Cultural Politics, and the Attack on Democracy*. Boston: Beacon.

Edelman, Lee. 2004. *No Future: Queer Theory and the Death Drive, Series Q*. Durham, NC: Duke University Press.

Ellis, Richard. 2014. *Judging the Boy Scouts of America: Gay Rights, Freedom of Association, and the Dale Case, Landmark Law Cases, and American Society*. Lawrence: University Press of Kansas.

Gianoulis, Tina. 2002–2015. "Girl Scouts." Last modified June 15, 2015. www.glbtq.com.

Girl Scouts of the USA. 2010. "The Story of Juliette Gordon Low." Last modified May 29, 2015. gsuniversity.girlscouts.org/jglhistory/.

The Happy Camper. 2015. www.happycamperbadges.com.

Hennessy-Fiske, Molly. 2013. "Gay Youths Now 'Safe' in Boy Scouts." *Los Angeles Times*, Dec. 31.

Inness, Sherrie A. 1997. *The Lesbian Menace: Ideology, Identity, and the Representation of Lesbian Life*. Amherst: University of Massachusetts Press.

James, Susan Donaldson. 2012. "Lesbian Cub Leader Fired for Being Gay, Fights Boy Scouts." *ABC News*, April 25.

Jordan, Benjamin René. 2016. *Modern Manhood and the Boy Scouts of America: Citizenship, Race, and the Environment, 1910–1930*. Chapel Hill: University of North Carolina Press.

Kafer, Alison. 2013. *Feminist, Queer, Crip*. Bloomington: Indiana University Press.

Kings, DC. 2015. "Cub Scout." Accessed June 14. dckings.com.

Manahan, Nancy. 1997. *On My Honor: Lesbians Reflect on Their Scouting Experience*. Northboro, MA: Madwoman Press.

McCartney, Robert. 2014. "No, Virginia, Catholic Priest Is in Minority in Region in Breaking with Boy Scouts over Gays." *Washington Post*, Feb. 15.

Muñoz, José Esteban. 2009. *Cruising Utopia: The Then and There of Queer Futurity, Sexual Cultures*. New York: NYU Press.

Murray, Rheana. 2011. "Girl Scouts Troops Disband after Chapter Says It Will Allow Transgendered 7-Year-Old." *New York Daily News*, Dec. 22.

Nichols, John. 2014. "Stand with the Girl Scouts." *Nation*, Feb. 6.

O'Rourke, Michael. 2014. *Queer Insists*. New York: punctum books.

Oxford English Dictionary. 2015. "futurity, n." Accessed June 24. Oxford University Press. www.oed.com.

Pasulka, Nicole. 2012. "The Right-Wing War on a Transgender Girl Scout." *Mother Jones*, Feb. 2.

Puar, Jasbir K. 2007. *Terrorist Assembleges: Homonationalism in Queer Times*. Durham, NC: Duke University Press.

Ring, Trudy, and Lauren Jow. 2012. "3 Big Differences: Boy Scouts versus Girl Scouts." *Advocate*, Dec. 19.

Rodríguez, Juana María. 2014. *Sexual Futures, Queer Gestures, and Other Latina Longings*. New York: NYU Press.

Rohrer, Judy. 2014. *Queering the Biopolitics of Citizenship in the Age of Obama*. New York: Palgrave Pivot.

Sherman, Mark. 2015. "Supreme Court Extends Same-Sex Marriage Nationwide." *Associated Press*, June 26.

Smith, Andrea. 2010. "Queer Theory and Native Studies: The Heteronormativity of Settler Colonialism." *GLQ* 16 (1–2): 41–68.

Sontag, Susan. 1964. "Notes on 'Camp.'" In *Against Interpretation and Other Essays*, edited by Susan Sontag, 275–93. New York: Farrar, Straus & Giroux.

Tremonte, Mary (Mack). 2015. "Queer Scouts." www.mary-tremonte.tumblr.com.

Vargas, Theresa. 2014. "An Openly Gay Eagle Scout Achieves a Milestone in Montgomery County." *Washington Post*, Feb. 10.

Wahls, Zach. 2015. "Boy Scouts President Robert Gates Calls for End to BSA's National Ban on Gay Adults." Scouts for Equality, www.scoutsforequality.org.

Wahls, Zach, and Bruce Littlefield. 2012. *My Two Moms: Lessons of Love, Strength, and What Makes a Family*. New York: Gotham Books.

Walsh, Michael. 2013. "Pastor Blasts 'Wicked' Girl Scouts as Agent of Lesbianism, Abortion." *New York Daily News*, Oct. 23.

Zach. 2014. "Anti-Gay Boy Scouts Get the Gay Porn Parody They Deserve." www.str8upgayporn.com.

29

Queering the Feminist Dollar

A History and Consideration of the Third Wave Fund as
Activist Philanthropy

MELISSA MEADE AND RYE YOUNG

The Third Wave Fund is a self-proclaimed activist philanthropy organization. Based in New York City, it supports youth-led activism for gender justice while challenging orthodoxies of both feminist and LGBTQ philanthropy.[1] When it was created in 1992 as the Third Wave Direct Action Corporation by daughters of second-wave feminism Catherine Gund, Dawn Lundy Martin, Amy Richards, and Rebecca Walker, its initial goal was to harness the burgeoning theories of multicultural and intersectional feminism to inspire young leaders to work together in new justice movements. As it quickly grew into the Third Wave Foundation, its focus became philanthropic, granting and regranting funds to support youth feminism, transform philanthropic institutions, and build philanthropic leaders among women of color and queer, low-income, and transgender activists. After two decades of work in this area, the board voted to close the foundation, citing insurmountable financial challenges. Response to this announcement was swift, however, with founders, early participants, grantees, and other stakeholders assembling to keep Third Wave open. As a stand-alone foundation, it shut its doors, but reopened recently as a smaller fund housed at the Proteus Fund, a clearinghouse for progressive philanthropy.

In this essay we explore the conceptual and political terrain opened up by the closure and reopening of the Third Wave Fund—asking how and when philanthropy is an activist endeavor, as well as how and when feminist and LGBTQ philanthropy work together. The transition from direct-action organization to foundation to activist fund illuminates some critical junctures in the philanthropy for transformative justice. In addition to probing the relationship between philanthropy and social justice, these junctures include recognizing changing power dynamics between grantees and granters and how funding structures can create unintended divisions, hierarchies, priorities, and conceptual constraints. LGBTQ and feminist funding have been artificially separated at times, making it difficult to build effective and strong feminist-queer and queer-feminist initiatives. Third Wave began as an implicitly queer and explicitly feminist organization, and has worked to become explicitly both. In channeling funding to the work of community-based intersectional feminism, Third Wave positions itself as a force for queering feminist philanthropy, and for highlighting the ways in which all philanthropic work concerns gender and sexuality. Gender and sexuality are inextricably linked to our social worlds and material existence, and a queer future of philanthropy is one that pays close attention to how that works.

Our caveat in writing this piece is that both authors are directly involved in the Third Wave organizational structure. Melissa was among the newest members of the board during the time of transition from Foundation to Fund, joining just at the time of its closure. Rye has been with Third Wave since 2008, first as an Abortion Fund intern, then holding several positions before becoming the first executive director of the new Third Wave Fund in January 2014. What follows is a brief history of the organization, followed by a dialogue between the authors about the implications of this history for thinking about queer futures in philanthropy.

Feminist Philanthropic Waves

Although historians of social movements agree that feminist activity has been ongoing in the history of the United States, the metaphor of waves is often conjured to describe particularly salient moments of feminist activism in the United States.[2] The first wave, marked by attention to women's participation in political and public life, culminated with the ratification in 1920 of the Nineteenth Amendment, the amendment granting suffrage for women. Women's activism and philanthropy, however, were generally distinct endeavors. In fact, the law often dictated this separation, interpreting social services as distinct from political work. In the 1897 case of *Garrison v. Little*, the court rejected the legality of a bequeathment left to support women's suffrage, arguing that it was not within the realm of charitable work. The logic of the court was that charitable giving ought not to be in service of advocacy work, that it was for social services, education, and research into social problems. The courts confirmed a split between advocacy and education, between feminism and women's charity.[3]

Women played a large role in charitable giving, however, with the development of more accumulated wealth and attention to social problems. Margaret Olivia Slocum Sage started what is considered to be the first modern foundation in 1907 after the death of her husband, Russell Sage. Sage set up the Russell Sage Foundation to study social problems, and she gave money to education, religion, children's aid, and programs for women's education.[4] She helped professionalize social work, gave generously to both women's and men's colleges, but notably did not give to the suffrage movement.[5] Women's activism in philanthropy was largely directed towards the realms of education, welfare, and healthcare programs, less towards explicitly feminist work.[6]

Feminist activist Matilda Joslyn Gage, who broke from the National Woman Suffrage Association in order to form the more radical Woman's National Liberal Union, connected women's education and political activity and wondered, "Why aren't women of means funding our causes?" She remarked on this false distinction:

> The two great sources of progress are intellect and wealth. Both represent power, and are the elements of success in life. Education frees the mind from the bondage of authority and makes the individual self-asserting. Remunerative industry is the means of securing to its possessor wealth and education, transforming the laborer to the capitalist. Work is itself not power; it is but the means to an end.[7]

Historians, however, have argued that women's volunteerism in the nineteenth and early twentieth centuries helped contribute to the development of feminist consciousness and politics.[8] Indeed, when the second wave of feminism emerged in the 1960s, fueled by advocacy for women's equality in the workplace, the family, the law, and healthcare, activism and philanthropy were more directly connected. It was a resurgence of both a women's movement and women's philanthropy, and often the women's philanthropy was explicitly feminist. The Ms. Foundation for Women, an adjunct of feminist *Ms.* magazine, was founded in 1973 by activists Patricia Carbine, Letty Cottin Pogrebin, Gloria Steinem, and Marlo Thomas. Its intention was to have women lead the movement for equality by funding initiatives for women and girls. In 1977 the Astraea Lesbian Foundation for Justice opened its doors, driving a "philanthropy of inclusion."[9]

LGBTQ and women's funds emerged in the 1980s. Funders for LGBTQ Issues began as a "Working Group on Funding Lesbian and Gay Issues" in 1982 within the National Network of Grantmakers. The working group aimed to both support lesbian and gay organizations and research existing funding structures within LGBTQ communities. The Ms. Foundation awarded it its first grant to do this work, making a clear connection between feminist and LGBTQ grant making.[10] In 1984 the Women's Funding Network was developed at a meeting of the National Black United Fund and the National Committee for Responsive Philanthropy, pulling together more than sixty women's funds across the country.

Marcia Gallo, commenting on histories of lesbian philanthropy in particular, has noted that it is "rooted in a tradition of radical giving." In the mid-twentieth century more explicitly radical community foundations arose (though not necessarily feminist or LGBTQ focused), with a focus on systemic change rather than isolated moments of charity. Gallo argues that these kinds of grassroots funding structures gave rise to LGBTQ philanthropy, and argues for lesbians to "recognize that the intersection between the radical philanthropic movement—which seeks to disrupt the power relations of traditional charitable giving—and the lesbian/gay/bi-sexual/transgender movements—which seek at least to dispel homophobia and at best to disrupt heteronormativity—is where both can become more inclusive, representative, and revolutionary."[11] Too often these funding initiatives have been considered separate, attending to distinct concerns.

The phrase "third wave feminism" appeared in the 1990s. As a body of thought it took as a starting point multiculturalism and postmodernism and what we think of now as intersectionality. In January 1992, Rebecca Walker, daughter of author Alice Walker, in an article in *Ms.* magazine describing a newer generation's interest in feminism and responding directly to Clarence Thomas's appointment to the Supreme Court despite allegations of sexual misconduct, used the term to call women to action: "I write this as a plea to all women. . . . [T]he fight is far from over. Let this dismissal of a woman's experience move you to anger. Turn that outrage into political power. I am not a post-feminist feminist. I am the Third Wave."[12]

Walker continued to build a media presence for this idea of a third-wave feminism, and, along with another recent college graduate, Shannon Liss, organized "Freedom Summer 92." Inspired by the voter registration drives of the early 1960s, this was a twenty-city voter registration campaign targeting young women. The press began to take note of this activity as marking the beginning of a new wave of women's movement and its inchoate organization. For example, the *SF Guardian*, San Francisco's alternative weekly, wrote an article announcing the arrival of Third Wave's Freedom Summer 92 campaign and quoted Walker announcing the Third Wave as "a grassroots resurgence of feminist activism on college campuses that comprises women and men of diverse backgrounds."[13]

From Direct Action to Foundation

In the several years following Walker's declaration of a third wave of U.S. feminism, Walker joined with Amy Richards, Dawn Lundy Martin, and Catherine Gund (née Saalfield, and of the George Gund family of philanthropists) in New York City to form the Third Wave Direct Action Corporation. They worked together to devise activist plans and develop both collective identity and strategy for entering the activist field. The Direct Action Corporation was quickly joined by a Third Wave Fund, housed at the now-defunct Funding Exchange, to raise money for feminist work. In an interview comment reflecting back on that time, Martin suggested, "Most second wave feminist organizations were not friendly places for young eager women to have a say in the movement, so we decided to start our own thing."[14]

The earliest meeting agendas combined professionalized language with open-ended inquiry. Richards brought connections to *Ms.* magazine, where she had worked as an intern, and a burgeoning friendship with Gloria Steinem, who was an early supporter of Third Wave. Agenda items included discussions of "what is 3w really about?" and "who are the other orgs and how do we differ?"[15] They also continued to regularly ask themselves about the state of feminism, what it meant to members, and what Third Wave meant to each other. They agreed that they wanted Third Wave to serve as feminist watchdog, though the focus was still undetermined; initially, the thinking seemed to suggest that the organization would serve as watchdog on politics, but Third Wave would eventually become a feminist watchdog on philanthropy itself. They agreed that a mission of the Third Wave should be to "demystify" feminism for potential activists, and that an organizational strength they had from the outset was their multi-identity lens into feminist activism, or "our multi's," as they called it.[16] The first group of Third Wave members, while sharing common experiences in elite U.S. universities, were a diverse group of women; they were women of color, white women, lesbians, and straight women.

Third Wave had program ideas in 1994 for an underground railroad for abortion services, domestic violence prevention and support, women's literacy development, conferences on the status of women, and consciousness-raising-type discussion groups. In summer 1994 the group published its first newsletter, *3w News*, which included book reviews and information on women's health issues, voter registration drives, and feminist activism more generally.[17] The Third Wave Fund, stemming from the direct-action group, was in nascent form, and in early 1995 the group began consulting with philanthropic experts in a more formal way to learn the logistics of foundation work—how to do budgets, apply for grants, send appeals and letters of inquiry, for example. Richards and the board members saw this move as part of a strategy to become a "communications and networking organization."[18] Above all, they wanted to connect young women in a new third-wave feminism that drew together the multiple and shifting layers of identities informing grassroots politics.

Organizational documents from 1995 reveal a continued search for an identity as an organization, continued interest in expanding and connecting, and an eye towards professional philanthropy. Board members met monthly, served on committees, and volunteered at least five hours each month in the office. They shared feminist reading lists and ideas for growth. They planned for press packets, business cards, and visibility strategies:

> We will concentrate on building a strong membership base. We need to begin to make ourselves more visible. We are building towards being an effective lobbying base on issues concerning young women. We will educate people on issues affecting and concerning young women. We want to build a constituency that will mobilize people around issues that affect young women.[19]

With an explicit interest in becoming a "network organization," Third Wave planned for membership groups in such cities as Boston, Washington, DC, and San Francisco. They had plans for film festivals, feminist parties, an early online presence, and inclusion of high-profile feminists on their advisory board. At the same time as they relied on grassroots participation, they were targeting foundations to raise and distribute money for youth feminist activism.[20] In their third formal board meeting, the board advised each other "to use 'see it, tell it, change it' as our philosophy. We are presently in the 'see it, tell it' phase and are working toward being able to 'change it.'"[21] The founders saw a long-term strategy for the organization that started with communications and moved towards direct action and philanthropy.

The board was reflectively focused on promulgating the idea of a third-wave feminism in the United States and developing a cohesive organizational identity. While a philanthropic ethos was not explicitly articulated in these early documents, there was an implicit philanthropic approach to all of this early organizing. That is, the board was comprised of recently educated women of means beginning to use their resources to acquire capital for a new feminist movement. They occupied a space between movement building and philanthropy. There was always an eye on visibility, not just about funding activist work, but about building coalitions and raising awareness of issues facing young women. Some of the specific issues on their minds included get-out-the-vote campaigns, campus activism, scholarships for women, abortion access, women's healthcare, women's culture and arts (such as the Lilith Fair music festival), advertising for public action campaigns, electoral politics, microloans for women, and legislative policy development.

The Third Wave Foundation

In 1996 the Third Wave Direct Action Corporation moved towards becoming the Third Wave Foundation with the unveiling of the Third Wave Fund. Reminiscent of the first-wave feminists who wondered why women of means were not funding their political and advocacy work, the Third Wave board made sure to highlight that only 6 percent of all philanthropic money was directed toward women and girls, and that the creation of a new feminist community fund "grew out of the need to have young people more involved in the issues that affect them, as well as to create a permanent funding base for young women."[22] The movement Third Wave was building was to redirect philanthropic money to women's needs.

The first grants, administered in 1997 and totaling almost thirteen thousand dollars, largely fit an individual self-empowerment model, with money given to individuals for emergency abortion services, scholarships, and travel to conferences.[23] There were three funding areas identified, with a fourth category designated for projects that would not fit those categories. For the first funding area, Third Wave partnered with the National Network of Abortion Funds to address issues of reproductive rights and abortion access. Thirty-two abortion funds already existed across the country, and Third Wave wanted to contribute to the states that did not yet have a fund set up. Third Wave also wanted to provide funding for emergency abortion services for young women.

The second funding area was a scholarship fund. The third was for small-business and micro-enterprise loans. The goal was "to empower women financially," and the first grant ever received from Third Wave was in this funding area, to members of Eagle Staff for travel to a development conference.[24] The First Nations Development Institute was founded in 1980, and in 1993 its Eagle Staff Fund began its national grant-making program, a Native American–controlled program directed at addressing Native American poverty.[25] The fourth funding area was a general fund. Here Third Wave was interested in responding to growing needs of young feminists, rather than locking itself into categorical funding boxes, "because the issues affecting young women may change from year to year." This category was key in its move from funding individual needs to funding activist groups; this category was also key in considering nimble and responsive ways to conceptualize grant making.

The earliest fundraising strategy outlined three potential sources of resources: individual and corporate donors, Third Wave membership dues, and college students targeted by direct mail campaigns aimed to "increase young women's philanthropic participation."[26] The initial goal was to raise one hundred thousand dollars, which it reached by the end of 1996. For 1997 it increased that goal to five hundred thousand dollars, applying for grants from large foundations and drawing plans to build an endowment with half of all donated money. In its first set of foundation appeals it identified itself as concentrating on regranting to young women, ages fifteen to thirty, nationwide: "The 3W Fund seeks to help young women foster self-confidence and self-sufficiency so they can become the leaders of tomorrow. The TWF will create a permanent funding base for young women."[27] By 1997 Third Wave had twenty-six board members, one part-time staff member, and thirty volunteers. It continued to increase its goals for fundraising and grant making.

In shifting its attention to raising money through large grants, Third Wave moved away from direct-action feminism and into the realm of regranting intermediary philanthropy. The board developed leadership giving goals, though without sustained dedication to this board fundraising development, and focused on grants appeals. The Funding Exchange administered the grants, with Third Wave identifying as the Third Wave Fund, a project "based on the principles of the Third Wave Direct Action Corporation."[28] The direct action newsletter was called *See it? Tell it. Change it!* and the fund newsletter was the *Signal*.

Third Wave worked with other philanthropic organizations to hold convenings that could transform philanthropy itself, and indeed philanthropic activism became a funding area of the organization. In 1998 Third Wave cofounded, with the Tides Foundation and Funding Exchange, "Making Money Make Change," an annual meeting for wealthy young people who want to work in social justice movements.[29] Also in 1998, Third Wave sponsored what was billed as a first annual Young Women's Leadership Forum.[30] By the late 1990s, Third Wave hit its stride, with a functional board of advisors, executive director, and small staff. It had a presence in women's funding circles as well as third-wave feminism nonprofits. Third Wave had small chapters in cities across the United States, and conducted various campaigns such as the "I Spy Sexism" public information campaign, and Reaching Out Across MovementS (ROAMS), a three-year traveling program aiming to connect organizations working for social justice. It was in ROAMS that Third Wave fully expanded its reach into intersectional feminism, connecting activist groups in such arenas as public education, farm labor, lesbian and gay youth organizing, and reproductive rights.

Billed as a series of immersive experiences for youth social justice activists, ROAMS ran from 2000 to 2002, and included road trips through areas in the Southeast, the Pacific Northwest, and the Southwest. On each trip, a dozen or so Third Wave staff members and youth organizers traveled across a region for two to three weeks at a time. They visited community organizations, talked to activists about their work, and compared ideas about organizing feminist politics, making connections, and sharing resources.[31] They were interested in getting the seasoned activists outside of their familiar environments and introducing new activists to a range of organizations. They also aimed to explore connections between rural and urban organizing and investigate particularly underserved geographical areas. And finally, they strove to analyze the ways in which issues of gender and sexuality permeate all community organizing in order to build solid and diverse activist networks.

After these trips, Third Wave sent newsletters and reports back to their community, reporting their findings and building their network. In the 2001 report it was noted, "In keeping with Third Wave's multi-issue approach, we met with organizations working on issues ranging from reproductive rights, day labor organizing, economic justice, sex work advocacy, land rights, race and more."[32] Participants were building an intersectional approach to feminist community work on the ground, strategizing for how to fund the work, and how to build effective coalitions.

Queering Third Wave

Entering the 2000s, Third Wave continued its stride. It was a "by and for" small intermediary foundation, meaning it was run by and for the communities it supported—young women of color, gender-nonconforming youth, and young feminists. Vivien Labaton, the first executive director, left in 2001 after establishing a strong base for the foundation, and several directors and codirectors came through in the following years. While connecting direct-action campaigns with grant making, as an organization Third Wave worked to change philanthropic approaches to thinking about funding activism. Rather than concentrating on recruiting young women into feminism, or funding individual needs of young women, Third Wave had firmly turned to investing in activist nonprofits and movement building. As Third Wave Foundation (rather than Fund) it developed a conceptual framework for bringing women into a third-wave feminist movement while joining the philanthropic community as intermediary fund.

Third Wave widened the scope of its grant-making programs, connecting social justice projects with a feminist lens. That is, while not all the grant recipients were feminist in name, Third Wave highlighted the gender and sexuality issues implicit in their work, adding a feminist dimension with the financial support. Third Wave continued to grant scholarships until 2005, in 2003 adding to the docket a scholarship program for transgender activists in particular. In 2005 the Reproductive Health and Justice Initiative was launched, abetted by the Leila Breitbart Memorial Fund. This new, enlarged focus on justice for reproductive health facilitated connections among the work of the longstanding Emergency Abortion Fund, reproductive health needs for trans and gender-nonconforming youth, lesbians, and young women of color. Through this initiative Third Wave was able to convene meetings of its grantees for peer reflection and growth. In 2006 this group of nonprofits, consisting largely of Third Wave grantees, founded their own coalition network.[33]

Alongside the grant-making programs and convenings, Third Wave embarked on conceptual work at the organizational level to develop a larger frame of gender justice to encompass its broad-sweeping feminist work. In spring 2003 the board and staff began "an organizational discussion on transgender issues and their intersection with third wave feminism," in conjunction with working with grantees working for transgender justice and supporting programs such as an "I Spy Transphobia" public information campaign and trans fem workshops. In October 2005 the board and staff approved a "gender justice plan," which was to include internal trainings, readings, discussion with foundation peers, and plans to produce a comprehensive report documenting the process. The goal of the report would be to share the process and purpose with other foundations.[34] Data were collected and the report was drafted and redrafted, but was never completed or released to the public.

On the heels of Third Wave's work to develop a gender-justice lens for philanthropic work was a keen interest in intersectional feminism across philanthropic circles more generally. Larger organizations looked to Third Wave to release its thoughts on gender justice, and Third Wave participated alongside established foundations and funds to develop the concept of gender justice within funding communities. The National Committee for Responsive Philanthropy issued a report in 2007 advocating for "creating a philanthropic sector that is more responsive to the needs of diverse communities."[35] In 2008 the Catalyst Fund of the Tides Foundation released a resource guide for women of color working in the area of reproductive justice, and the Obama-Biden "Advancing Reproductive Rights and Health in a New Administration" 2008 report adopted social-change-impact language to describe the contemporary climate for this work.[36] Kaiser Family Foundation, Tides Foundation, Ford Foundation, and the Applied Research Center all released reports dealing with intersectional feminism and gender justice in philanthropy between 2009 and 2010.[37]

In 2011, the Third Wave Foundation worked with Real Change Partners LLC to develop a five-year strategic plan. The challenges, values, competencies, strategies, and envisioned future all reflected a professionalized foundation approach to queer feminist philanthropy and to "open[ing] up a space of difference," as J. K. Gibson-Graham has put it when she asked, "What if we were to 'queer' capitalist hegemony and break apart some of its consolidating associations?"[38] Third Wave continued to ask those questions of philanthropy, to try to envision new, queer ways of doing things. Reflecting the fifteen years of grant making, core values were thus articulated:

1. By & For: We believe that lived experience generates wisdom, creativity, and expertise and hold that those most impacted by oppression are best positioned to design and lead solutions to the root causes of social injustice. Third Wave is led by and for the constituencies we serve in strategic partnership with our allies.
2. Justice: We do what we do and how we do it because of a deep belief and commitment to social justice. Our view of justice recognizes that all forms of injustice are inextricably interrelated and create systems of oppression that are felt at the individual, community, and structural levels. With a focus on gender, racial, and economic justice, we work toward personal and structural changes that produce well-being, self-determination, and liberation for all.
3. Transformation: Third Wave embraces and drives transformative change. We ourselves are ever evolving. We build and exert collective power in order to create roadmaps for liberation and transform structural inequalities. Together with our grantee partners, supporters, and allies, we represent the leading edge of national movements for social justice and work to transform policies, systems and practices that impede justice and equity for all.
4. Passion: We believe that by operating with passion for our work, we create a culture of joy, commitment, and accountability that we believe are necessary conditions for fostering growth, leadership, and positive change.[39]

Also articulated were three areas of work for Third Wave. First was strategic grant making, in which Third Wave aimed to work "at the intersections of movements for gender, racial, and economic justice." Second was movement building: "[C]onnecting youth-led organizations from around the country to each other is needed to build a broader, more sustained movement for social justice." And third was philanthropic advocacy. Under this umbrella was the goal to bring attention to underfunded organizations and "help develop progressive and intersectional analyses and funding priorities within social justice philanthropy, ultimately increasing support to youth-led organizations."[40]

At this point less than 7 percent of all philanthropic dollars went to women's and girls' programs, and less than 1 percent were serving transgender youth, so Third Wave's vision was as strong as ever, but its financial situation was not. Losing some key financial grounding led to an unsustainable model of operation, and in early 2013 the board voted to close Third Wave's doors.

On the Future of a Queer Feminist Philanthropy: A Dialogue

In 2014 Third Wave announced Rye Young as it new executive director. After more than a year of intensive strategizing, negotiating, organizing, and thinking, the Third Wave Foundation wound down its operations and the Third Wave Fund emerged. Currently, the Fund no longer has physical space or a large staff, and is hosted by the Proteus Fund, a philanthropic management organization that supports social change in the arenas of human rights, democracy, and peace. The leadership team is new, with new visions of how to organize transformative justice within philanthropy. What follows is a dialogue between Melissa Meade and Rye Young. Melissa is a member of the Legacy Council of the Third Wave Fund, and Rye is currently serving as its executive director. This new iteration of the Third Wave Fund, while building on the history of the Third Wave Foundation, is in its infancy, working on concepts, logistics, and strategies.

MELISSA MEADE: Third Wave struggled for so long with defining and operationalizing the concept of "gender justice" in philanthropy. How is the new iteration of the Third Wave Fund approaching the concept?

RYE YOUNG: Third Wave started as a feminist organization, and Third Wave has always been queer. Even without the language, and even if it wasn't categorized as LGBTQ work, that's what Third Wave has been doing—queering feminism, expanding the scope of feminist work, expanding the notion of LGBTQ, and working at the intersections of where social justice issues are gendered. Here is the way we are thinking about "gender justice," from an excerpt of a forthcoming piece of our website:

Third Wave defines Gender Justice as a movement to end patriarchy, transphobia, and homophobia and to create a world free from misogyny. As gender justice activists, we recognize that gender oppression is tied to classism, racism, ageism, and ableism, so gender justice can only truly be achieved when all forms of oppression cease to exist.

To Third Wave, the Gender Justice movement is (1) multi-issue because no single issue represents all gender oppression and because gender is connected to all aspects of life, (2) community led by those who are directly impacted by oppression, (3) feminist, queer and trans, unapologetically.[41]

MM: In the context of neoliberalism and what's often called the nonprofit industrial complex, I wonder what it means to be an activist fund. In her introduction to the recent *Undoing the Demos: Neoliberalism's Stealth Revolution*, political theorist Wendy Brown begins with a vividly corporeal metaphor for neoliberalism's hold on radical politics: "[M]ore than merely cutting away the flesh of liberal democracy, neoliberalism also cauterizes democracy's more radical expressions."[42] Here the distribution of resources from the private sector suggests not just a tepid politics, but a destructive antipolitics. Can an activist fund intervene, become intravenous even, to further the analogy?

Further, Dylan Rodriguez, in an oft-cited definition, wrote that the nonprofit industrial complex is a "set of symbiotic relationships that link together political and financial technologies of state and owning-class proctorship and surveillance over public political intercourse, including and especially emergent progressive and leftist social movements."[43] And so relationships between funders and grantees become fraught, overprescribed, bureaucratic, and ineffective.

RY: First, we fund activism. The way we choose what to fund—where the money goes—is about being responsive to the needs of activism, and about understanding how movements of activism work. Second, Third Wave is led by activists, in the movements, aware of the legacies of philanthropy and histories of activist movements, and aware of the neoliberal tensions and contradictions inherent in the philanthropic endeavor. Third Wave exists because philanthropy has left gaps in funding, and we see ourselves as contributing to an undoing of this unequal distribution of resources and leadership. We are not working solely within inherited practices and structures; we are attempting to construct new ways of doing philanthropy, ways that are empowering instead of disempowering. We have done away with issue areas, for example, because funding based on issues has often been a way of creating divisions between communities and needs. It artificially separates the ways in which oppression and hierarchies are woven together, so that funders become "feminist," or "queer," or "anti-racist," but not necessarily all together, all at once. Tactics of oppression are always changing and we want to set up our funding structures to be responsive to the changes. We start with communities.

Third, there is an activism in organizing funders to think differently about the ways they approach grantmaking, to think of themselves as being part of social justice movement and not simply donors. Third Wave has always included this part in the work that we do. We ask questions of both grantees and funders—questions about how gender factors into their work, how they think about the ways in which their work has to do with sexuality and gender, alongside labor, race, or literacy. Third Wave has brought together grantees and funders; it's an attempt to collectivize the experience of marginalization. And it's an attempt to re-angle ourselves to listen to what is needed from communities.

As Rickee Mananzala and Dean Spade, in considering tactics of trans resistance, have wisely suggested,

> Trans politics should use a model based on the concept social justice trickles up, not down, prioritizing the needs and concerns of those facing the worst manifestations of gender-based marginalization and exclusion, as well as using a model for social change that centralizes the leadership of trans people of color, trans low-income people, trans immigrants, and others facing intersectional oppression.[44]

MM: And so I want to consider failure. Going through the Third Wave archives I was struck by the precarity of Third Wave's position in the philanthropic world. It has certainly distributed a sizeable amount of grant money, and has had a considerable presence in philanthropic circles dedicated to transformative justice. That said, Third Wave's funding has not always been secure, and its dedication to movement building has never seemed to find solid footing, in terms of philanthropic codification. And, in fact, the board voted to close its doors. After this closure—what we might call failure— however, the new Third Wave Fund has repositioned itself in interesting, vibrant, solid, and ambitious ways.

Jack Halberstam, in the *Queer Art of Failure*, has argued that we ought to name failure "not as the negative space opened up by normalized modes of success but as a habitable space with its own logic, its own practices and the potential for new collectivities." He then goes on to name it as queer, understanding failure as "a practice that builds upon queerness in the sense that queerness is always a failure to conform, to belong, to cohere. Rather than reorienting queerness, we should embrace failure."[45] What do you think of that read of Third Wave?

RY: Third Wave has always existed in a place of precarity and resilience. This is because of its original values—at its starting point valuing multiple perspectives and identities, coinciding issues, complicated and interconnected politics. Third Wave has also valued ongoing reflection and adaptation, a commitment to the margins, to being a fund for the fundless, to being radical in its work. Eighty percent of the organizations we have funded have closed. Is this a systemic failure? Yes, absolutely. Is it a Third Wave failure? I'd argue no. Third Wave has been a project of sending water upstream, finding outcomes in the process, movement building, and communities rather than end results.

Third Wave, the way I see it, will always be susceptible to ups and downs, to the vicissitudes of philanthropy; it will never be too big to fail. At its heart Third Wave is always engaged in hypothesis work, an experiment in normativity and queerness, even as we stand on the ground built by so many other activists. I cannot imagine this project of funding the margins being complete, and if we were to change our values, that would be the ultimate, nonproductive failure.

Epilogue

Third Wave has been a multi-issue feminist organization, and in its history we can clearly see a trajectory of complicating traditionally feminist issues by taking queerness, race, and class as axis points for the conversation and work.

From its start in 1992, Third Wave's goal was to be led by young activists from the communities it supported, and to engage directly in both movement building and grant making. In bringing together feminist and LGBTQ work and articulating an inclusive gender-justice framework for feminist activism and philanthropy, Third Wave can be instructive in thinking about the future of both the feminist and the LGBTQ movements, and the role of radical philanthropy in them. The lived experience of identity does not hinge on gender alone, but is connected explicitly to our multiple and overlapping identities of class location, race, ethnicity, sexual orientation, and more. We must build—and fund—movements that recognize this reality.

NOTES

1 The authors wish to thank Colby-Sawyer College and the Third Wave Fund for supporting this research; the archivists at the Sallie Bingham Center for Women's History and Culture at Duke University's Rubenstein Library; the editors of this important volume; our partners in life and activism; and the Third Wave community of organizers, activists, donors, grant makers, and grant seekers.

2 In 1968 journalist Martha Weinman Lear first used the metaphor (Lear 1968). On organizing U.S. feminism into waves, see, for example, Moynagh and Forestell 2015; Nicholson 1997; Freedman 2003; Siegel 2007; Hewitt 2010; Cobble, Gordon, and Henry 2015.

3 Zunz 2014; Illinois Appellate Court, Smith, and Newell 1898.

4 Crocker 2006; "A Sense of Place" 2010.

5 McCarthy 2007; "A Sense of Place" 2010.

6 Hauser Center n.d.; "A Sense of Place" 2010.

7 Anthony, Stanton, and Gage 1923.

8 See, for example, Freedman 1979; Kerber 1988; Scott 1992.

9 "About Astraea," *Astraea Lesbian Foundation for Justice.* www.astraeafoundation.org.

10 "History," *Funders for LGBTQ Issues.* www.lgbtfunders.org (accessed July 20, 2016).

11 Gallo 2001.

12 Walker 1992.

13 "Third Wave Voter Drive Hits Bay Area," *San Francisco Guardian.* Third Wave Foundation Records, Box 5.

14 "From the Beautiful to the Perverse" 2011.

15 Meeting Agenda, June 7, 1994. Third Wave Foundation Records, Box 5.

16 Ibid.

17 *3w News.* Third Wave Foundation Records, Box 5.

18 Meeting Notes, February 1, 1995. Third Wave Foundation Records, Box 5.

19 Meeting Notes, January 11, 1995. Third Wave Foundation Records, Box 5.

20 Meeting Notes, September 2, 1995. Third Wave Foundation Records, Box 5.

21 Meeting Notes, January 11, 1995. Third Wave Foundation Records. Box 5.

22 Fundraising Documents. Third Wave Foundation Records, Box 5.

23 Ibid.

24 Newsletters. Third Wave Foundation Records, Box 5.

25 First Nations Development Institute. www.firstnations.org.

26 Internal Notes. Third Wave Foundation Records, Box 5.

27 Fundraising letter October 22, 1996. Third Wave Foundation Records, Box 2.

28 Report, August 21, 1997. Third Wave Foundation Records, Box 5.

29 Resource Generation. www.resourcegeneration.org.

30 Report, September 12, 1998. Third Wave Foundation Records, Box 5.

31 For a sense of the breadth in these trips, the following is a partial list of organizations on the Pacific Northwest itineraries: Aradia Women's Health Center, Basic Rights Oregon, Better People, Center for Ethical Leadership, Communities Against Rape and Abuse, Community Coalition for Environmental Justice, Danzine, El Centro de la Raza, Home Alive, Feminist Women's Health Center, Fort Hall Indian Reservation, Idaho Women's Network, Jobs with Justice, Greater Yellowstone Coalition, LELO, Love Makes a Family, Inc., Luz, McKenzie River Gathering Foundation, Montana Community Foundation, Montana Human Rights Network, Northwest Women's Law Center, Northwest Coalition for Human Dignity, Montana People's Action, Peace and Justice Action League, People of Color Against AIDS, Planned Parenthood, Portland Alliance, Pride Montana, Progressive Student Alliance, Rural Organizing Project, SAFES, SAWERA, Seattle Young People's Project, Sisters in Action for Power, South Asian Women's Empowerment, Tribes Project, Resource Alliance, United Vision of Idaho, Washington Alliance for Immigrant and Refugee Justice WEEL (Working for Economic and Employment Liberation), Women of Color Alliance, Workers Organizing Committee, Youth for Justice, Youth for Social and Political Change.

32 "ROAMS 2001 Report." Third Wave Foundation. Third Wave Fund Offices, New York, New York.

33 Reports. Third Wave Foundation Records, Box 5.

34 Internal Documents. Third Wave Foundation Records, Box 5.

35 Cohen 2007.

36 Obama-Biden Transition Project 2008.

37 Kaiser Family Foundation, "Putting Women's Health Disparities on the Map: Examining Racial and Ethnic Disparities at State Level," June 2009. Tides Foundation, "The Opportunity Agenda: Building the National Will to Expand Opportunity in America," 2009. Belden Russonello and Stewart Research and Communications, "Public Opinion Research: How to Discuss Specific Social Justice Issues within a Human Rights Framework," 2009. Applied

Research Center, "Race and Recession: How Inequity Rigged the Economy and How to Change the Rules," 2009. Third Wave Foundation Records Box 5.

38 Graham-Gibson 1999.

39 Third Wave Foundation Strategic Plan, 2012–2016.

40 Ibid.

41 Unpublished Third Wave Fund website. www.thirdwavefund.org.

42 Brown 2015, 9.

43 Rodriguez 2007.

44 Mananzala and Spade 2008, 54.

45 Halberstam 2011.

REFERENCES

Anthony, Susan B., Elizabeth Cady Stanton, and Matilda Joslyn Gage. 1923. "Preceding Causes." *History of Woman Suffrage.* Vol. 1. Kindle edition.

Brown, Wendy. 2015. *Undoing the Demos: Neoliberalism's Stealth Revolution.* Cambridge: MIT Press, Zone Books.

Cobble, Dorothy Sue, Linda Gordon, and Astrid Henry. 2015. *Feminism Unfinished: A Short, Surprising History of American Women's Movements.* New York: Liveright.

Cohen, Rick. 2007. "Strategic Grantmaking: Foundations and the School Privatization Movement." National Committee for Responsive Philanthropy, Nov.

Crocker, Ruth. 2006. *Mrs. Russell Sage: Women's Activism and Philanthropy in Gilded Age and Progressive Era America.* Bloomington: Indiana University Press.

First Nations Development Institute. N.d. www.firstnations.org.

Freedman, Estelle. 1979. "Separatism as Strategy: Female Institution Building and American Feminism, 1870–1930." *Feminist Studies* 5: 512–29.

Freedman, Estelle. 2003. *No Turning Back: The History of Feminism and the Future of Women.* New York: Ballantine Books.

"From the Beautiful to the Perverse: A Talk with Jericho Brown and Dawn Lundy Martin." 2011. *Best American Poetry Blog,* Dec. 16.

Gallo, Marcia M. 2001. "Lesbian Giving—and Getting: Tending Radical Roots in an Era of Venture Philanthropy." *Journal of Lesbian Studies* 5(3): 63–70.

Graham-Gibson, J. K. 1999. "Queer(y)ing Capitalism in and out of the Classroom." *Journal of Geography in Higher Education* 23(1): 80–85.

Halberstam, Judith Jack. 2011. *The Queer Art of Failure.* Durham, NC: Duke University Press.

Hauser Center on Nonprofit Organizations. N.d. *Documentary History of Philanthropy and Volunteerism in the United States, 1600–1900: A Collection of Documents and References.* Cambridge, MA: Harvard University Press.

Hewitt, Nancy A. 2010. *No Permanent Waves: Recasting Histories of U.S. Feminism.* New Brunswick, NJ: Rutgers University Press.

Illinois Appellate Court, Edwin Burritt Smith, Martin L. Newell. 1898. *Reports of Cases Decided in the Appellate Courts of the State of Illinois.* Vol. 75, pp. 402–17. Chicago: Callaghan.

Kerber, Linda. 1988. "Separate Spheres, Female Worlds, Woman's Place: The Rhetoric of Women's History." *Journal of American History* 75: 9–39.

Lear, Martha Weinman. 1968. "The Second Feminist Wave." *New York Times Magazine,* March 10.

Mananzala, Rickke, and Dean Spade. 2008. "The Nonprofit Industrial Complex and Trans Resistance." *Sexuality Research & Social Policy* 5(1): 53–71.

McCarthy, Kathleen D. 2007. "Review of *Mrs. Russell Sage.*" *Enterprise & Society* 8(4): 984–86.

Moynagh, Maureen, and Nancy Forestell, eds. 2015. *Documenting First Wave Feminisms.* Vols. 1 and 2. Toronto: University of Toronto Press.

Nicholson, Linda, ed. 1997. *The Second Wave: A Reader in Feminist Theory.* London: Routledge.

Obama-Biden Transition Project. 2008 "Advancing Reproductive Rights and Health in a New Administration," Nov. Democracy in Action, available at https://www2.gwu.edu.

Resource Generation. N.d. "History." www.resourcegeneration.org.

Rodriguez, Dylan. 2007. "The Political Logic of the Non-Profit Industrial Complex." In *The Revolution Will Not Be Funded: Beyond the Non-Profit Industrial Complex Anthology,* edited by Incite! Boston: South End Press.

Scott, Anne Firor. 1992. *Natural Allies: Women's Associations in American History.* Urbana: University of Illinois Press.

"A Sense of Place: A Short History of Women's Philanthropy in America." 2010. The Women's Philanthropy Institute at the Center on Philanthropy at Indiana University.

Siegel, Deborah. 2007. *Sisterhood, Interrupted: From Radical Women to Girls Gone Wild.* New York: Palgrave Macmillan.

Third Wave Foundation Records, David M. Rubenstein Rare Book & Manuscript Library, Duke University.

Third Wave Foundation Strategic Plan. 2012–2016. Third Wave Foundation Records, David M. Rubenstein Rare Book & Manuscript Library, Duke University.

Walker, Rebecca. 1992. "Becoming the Third Wave." *Ms. Magazine,* Jan./Feb.

Zunz, Olivier. 2014. *Philanthropy in America: A History.* Princeton, NJ: Princeton University Press.

30

Single-Sex Colleges and Transgender Discrimination

The Politics of Checking a "Male" or "Female" Box to Get into College

HEATH FOGG DAVIS

In 2013, Calliope Wong, an Asian American transgender woman, applied for admission to Smith College and was rejected. But unlike the rejection letters received by most applicants to the prestigious women's college, Wong's letter indicated that she was ineligible for admission because she failed to meet the college's definition of being a woman. The letter went on to say that her FAFSA (federal financial aid form) showed her gender as male.[1] In her prior correspondence with Smith, Wong had been informed that she would be eligible for admission as long as her high school records indicated her sex identity as female. Wong complied with this requirement, but she was never informed that a male-marked FAFSA form could also disqualify her from Smith's admission process. The incident brought to public light the fact that many private women's colleges were treating applications from transgender women on an ad hoc basis without any set policies. Smith eventually amended its admissions policy in 2015 to make transgender women eligible for admission, regardless of the sex markers on their personal identity documents. At that point, Wong had already accepted an admissions offer from the University of Connecticut. She declined Smith's retroactive offer of admission. There have been no publicized reports or cases of transgender men seeking admission to the few remaining private men's colleges.

Did Smith do the right thing by stretching its definition of women to include Wong, or should it have abandoned its women-only admissions policy altogether? As Wong's story of rejection became national news, other high-profile women's colleges such as Barnard, Mount Holyoke, and Mills came under similar scrutiny. Lynn Pasquerella, president of Mount Holyoke College, publicly defended Mount Holyoke's exclusion of men on nominal grounds. "At a women's college we have to have some criterion for admission. In addition to academic excellence, it's *being a woman*."[2] Pasquerella meant her statement to be definitive, but instead she ended up raising the very question that resists definition: What does it mean to *be* a woman? One way to answer this question is to say that being a woman means not being a man. But of course that answer begs the question of what it means to be a man. Many people believe that the answers to these questions are so obvious that "it goes without saying."

Transgender experience, however, challenges this assumption. Instead of assimilating and accommodating transgender people into single-sex college admissions, we should use transgender experience, in all of its variation, to fundamentally rethink the relationship between sex classification and the educational missions of single-sex colleges, and indeed, all colleges. At first glance, single-sex college admissions may seem like a narrow issue that affects a small number of people. As of 2016, a mere thirty-nine of the 3,026 four-year U.S. colleges are women-only. And there are just three remaining men-only colleges (Hampden-Sydney, Wabash, and Morehouse). But the definitional question of who qualifies as a woman or a man in a competitive college admissions process is the thin edge of a wedge onto questions that affect *all* prospective college students and their families, as well as those who work in colleges as faculty and staff. Do colleges, both single-sex and co-ed, have a legitimate interest in knowing the sex identity of their applicants? If so, then should this information be required or volunteered by applicants? What definition of sex and/or gender is being invoked when a college prompts a student to check a male or female box? And how should individual colleges use this information? What is the relationship between the gathering of sex-identity information and the legitimate educational goals of particular colleges?

All remaining single-sex colleges should open their admissions processes to everyone. At the same time, women-only colleges should not abandon their important historical and continuing mission of tackling institutional sexism in U.S. higher education. Although women now outnumber men on many college campuses, female students still suffer disadvantageous outcomes in their college experiences, ranging from how often they speak out in classroom discussions to the kinds of praise and criticism they receive in letters of recommendation written by their professors and the professional networks they have access to upon graduation. Remediating these and other forms of institutional sexism in colleges is a legitimate and important educational goal. But the exclusion of all men from admissions is not necessary for—or, in the idiom of antidiscrimination law, "rationally related" to—such goals. Women's colleges should be renamed "historically female colleges," in the same way that we now refer to formerly black colleges and universities as historically black colleges and universities (HBCUs).

Five years before Wong was rejected by Smith on the basis of her inconsistently gender-marked government paperwork, the *New York Times Magazine* ran a story that profiled two white transgender men who had been admitted as women to the women-only colleges of Barnard and Wellesley, respectively, but then changed their sex identities to male after enrollment. The story was featured on the cover of the magazine with the titillating title "When Girls Will Be Boys." The article quoted alumnae who objected to allowing transgender male students to stay enrolled on the grounds that doing so was tantamount to "passively going coed."[3] Seven years later the *New York Times* ran another article on transgender men at women's colleges entitled "When Women Become Men at Wellesley."

The different verb tenses in these two national headlines inadvertently highlight a key issue relevant to college admissions: the timing of a person's sex-identity change or transition. Does being a woman include past experience of *having been* a woman or having been identified by others as female? Drugs that delay the onset of puberty are now available and are being administered to some transgender children to delay the onset of secondary sex characteristics until the young person turns eighteen and can make decisions regarding surgeries and hormone therapy.[4] But a child's access to such medical treatment depends on whether that child has emotionally supportive parents or guardians who can afford such treatment. A five-year-old transgender girl who self-identifies as female and begins taking puberty-blocking hormones may have spent nearly her entire life being and experiencing the world as female by the time she is ready to apply to college. A transgender girl who comes out as transgender during her teenage years may have fewer years being socially recognized as female. But there are other factors to take into account, such as how closely each girl is able to meet hegemonic feminine standards of appearance, comportment, and speech, all of which are shaped by racial expectations. A transgender boy who comes out as transgender at the age of thirteen will have spent his teenage years as male, but he may also have spent a significant period of his childhood as female embodied. Should he be eligible for admission to Smith or Mount Holyoke because he has lived part of his life as a female? Does it make sense to say that a transgender boy who transitions to male at the age of four or five has experienced antifemale sexism—especially given that we acquire much of our gender socialization in early childhood? Is first-hand experience of antifemale sexism the litmus test for qualifying for admission to a women's college? If so, then who decides how much is enough to pass such a test? What about people who self-identify and/or are identified by others as male at the time of their application, but who might transition to female during their time in college? What about people who do not self-identify as male or female, or identify as both—those whom trans legal scholar and activist Dean Spade describes as "administratively impossible"?[5]

What's the Harm?

The way I see it, the harm generated by today's women-only colleges is more about policing the definitional borders of femaleness and maleness than it is about group-based male disadvantage in relationship to female advantage, and vice versa. Women's colleges were founded because men's colleges were unwilling to accept them. The question today is whether women's colleges, and the three remaining men's colleges, should be permitted to continue their tradition of single-sex education in a time when there are a wide variety of colleges to which individual women and men can apply.

Sex-identity discrimination is about gender policing that uses raced notions of hegemonic femininity and masculinity to stipulate who belongs and who does not belong in the binary categories of women and men. On college application forms checked sex- and race-identity boxes are seen and processed by admissions officers. Colleges collect sex- and race-identity information about prospective students via their application forms, and sometimes in-person interviews conducted by alums or school officials. Sex-identity discrimination is pervasive in everyday life, but it becomes especially intense when something socially valuable is at stake such as an elite college education. Hence, it is not surprising that the public interest concerning the challenge posed by transgender experience to single-sex college admissions has focused on a handful of prestigious private women's colleges rather than the majority of private women's colleges and the three remaining private men's colleges, all of which score fairly low on the *U.S. News and World Report* ratings, which is considered the ticker tape of how particular college "brands" are monetized in the U.S. marketplace.

Legal Loopholes

Why in 2016 are some colleges legally permitted to formally exclude prospective students from admission on the basis of sex, while others are not? Why did the negative publicity surrounding Wong's rejection from Smith not put an end to Smith's women-only admissions process? The legal answer lies in a special exemption that was written into Title IX, the federal law that is best known for its impact on collegiate sports but that covers all aspects and levels of federally funded educational programming and includes students, faculty, and staff involved in such programming. Title IX states "that no person in the United States shall, *on the basis of sex* [emphasis added], be excluded from participation in, be denied the benefits of, or be subjected to discrimination under any educational program or activity receiving Federal financial assistance."[6] At the heart of Title IX is a presumptive ban on single-sex educational institutions. This is the case because historically most of these institutions excluded girls and women based on both the false stereotype that they were not as smart as men and the normative stereotype that they should remain in the private sphere of the home. However, the legislation exempts certain kinds of single-sex colleges from this presumptive ban. As Title IX was being debated in Congress in 1972, several elite private women's colleges such as Smith, along with men-only (at the time) colleges such as Harvard and Dartmouth, lobbied for and won a special exemption, which makes it legally possible for private colleges that were founded prior to 1972 and that have "traditionally and continuously" had "a policy of admitting only students of one sex" to maintain their single-sex admissions policies.[7] This exemption only applies to undergraduate college programs, so all graduate educational programs at these institutions must be co-ed. Many private single-sex colleges covered by the exemption voluntarily abandoned their exclusionary admissions policies in the 1960s and 1970s, but forty-three women's colleges and three men's colleges still have sex-based exclusion written into their admissions policies. Religious colleges are exempt from Title IX and may discriminate on the basis of sex.[8]

One could argue that the Title IX exemption should be overturned on the basis that women-only admissions policies disadvantage men, and men-only admissions policies disadvantage women. This would be analogous to cases alleging that the use of race-based affirmative action by colleges disadvantages white and Asian American students.[9] The Supreme Court has ruled that race can be used as one of several factors in college admissions, so long as it is not used as the determining factor in such decision making. The Court has stated that race is a factor in diversity, and that diversity is a legitimate policy goal for colleges to pursue.[10] There have not, however, been any legal challenges to sex-based affirmative action in higher education. Another exemption was written into Title IX that explicitly permits private colleges, even those receiving federal funds, to use gender-based affirmative action in their admissions processes. This exemption has recently come to light as some private colleges have publicly admitted to engaging in affirmative action in favor of men because women now constitute the majority of students on many campuses.

The Supreme Court has ruled on the question of whether a public college's use of a single-sex admission policy violates the Equal Protection Clause of the Fourteenth Amendment. In the 1996 landmark case *United States v. Virginia* the Virginia Military Institute (VMI), founded in 1839, claimed that its men-only admissions policy was necessary because of tradition, and constitutional because it did not disadvantage women in relationship to men. The college argued that its unique "adversative method" of training citizen-soldiers would be compromised by the presence of female students. VMI officials also raised the issue of restrooms and sex-based privacy as reasons for excluding women.[11] In 1995, the military college created the Virginia Women's Institute for Leadership at Mary Baldwin College as an analogous "separate but equal" institution. Justice Ginsburg, writing for the Court, countered that VMI's male-only admissions policy was unconstitutional because it used sex-role stereotypes to place "artificial constraints" on the individual opportunities of women. The statistical stereotype that most women are physically weaker than most men and do not seek out predominantly male, hypermasculine educational settings such as VMI, where they will be physically and psychologically hazed, could not be used to justify the school's male-only admissions policy. Some women do seek out such an experience, and can meet its rigors. But the Court never defined "sex" or "gender." The Court rejected VMI's argument that female cadets could achieve a "separate but equal" military training at Mary Baldwin College.[12]

Is the exclusion of men from women's colleges such as Smith, Mount Holyoke, and Spelman similarly sexist? The defenders of women's colleges make a compelling argument that they are not. The harm done to women by VMI's male-only policy was material: it prevented women from accessing the social, economic, and political capital that has long been available to the men who graduate from patriarchal institutions such as VMI. Indeed, one of the facts that the Court emphasized in *United States v. Virginia* was the high number of VMI alumni that held powerful positions in Virginia's business and political leadership. VMI's goal of producing "citizen-soldiers" was a euphemism for fortifying and replicating male economic and political power within the state. VMI countered this charge by invoking the libertarian claim that women had other comparable options to choose from in Virginia's higher education marketplace. The Court rightly found that argument to be disingenuous. "A purpose genuinely to advance an array of educational options is not served by VMI's historic and constant plan to afford a *unique educational benefit* only to males. However well this plan serves Virginia's sons, it makes no provision whatever for her daughters."[13]

Wong's rejection from Smith raises the question of single-sex admissions in a very different context from that of an all-male military college. It is true that many powerful women have graduated from elite women's colleges, among them Hillary Clinton, Gloria Steinem, and Madeline Albright. Women's college alums make up 20 percent of the women in Congress and 30 percent of *Businessweek*'s list of "rising" women in corporate America, even though only 2 percent of U.S. female college graduates attended women's colleges.[14] These impressive statistics notwithstanding, the idea that men are denied access to social, economic, and political capital in consequence of being shut out of elite women's colleges is a hard sell. Sex-discrimination law protects both women and men from being disadvantaged "because of sex," but the reality is that women, as a group, have suffered disproportionately more than men when it comes to institutional and organizational sexism.

The overwhelming majority of today's single-sex colleges are "women's colleges," meaning that only "women" qualify for consideration in their admissions processes. Some of the oldest and most prestigious women's colleges were the elite "seven sister colleges" of the Northeast, which were chartered in the late nineteenth century before women won the right to vote in 1920. Radcliffe, Vassar, Wellesley, Smith, Mount Holyoke, Barnard, and Bryn Mawr were separate legal entities with their own charters, but each was affiliated with one or more men's Ivy League colleges. Harvard, Yale, Columbia, Brown, Princeton, Dartmouth, Cornell, and the University of Pennsylvania began admitting women in the 1960s and '70s under pressure from the women's liberation movement. Vassar became co-ed in 1969, and is the only seven sister college to have done so. Radcliffe College began offering joint diplomas to female students matriculated at Harvard beginning in 1963, and then executed a "nonmerger merger" with Harvard in 1977. When I graduated from Harvard College in 1993, my diploma listed both Harvard and Radcliffe Colleges. This ended in 1999. Currently, Radcliffe exists as a non-degree-granting institution for advanced women's studies. The five other "seven sister" colleges continue their single-sex admissions policies, and have remained private women's colleges.

How do the remaining single-sex colleges defend their exclusionary admissions policies? The mission statements of most elite single-sex women's colleges draw a causal connection between their women-only institutional identities and their educational values, goals, and benefits. For instance, Mount Holyoke's website declares that it has remained a women-only college "by choice" because "we know that women thrive in an environment where all of the resources are designed for them." To substantiate this claim, the website has a link to social-scientific research showing that female students earning degrees at women's colleges perform better than women graduating from coeducational colleges. They are twice as likely to earn advanced degrees, and are more likely to assume leadership roles, to speak in classroom discussion, and to report greater self-confidence.[15] In the values statement found on its website, Smith states that it "prepares women to fulfill their responsibilities to the local, national, and global communities in which they live." The website includes a host of answers to the question, "Why is Smith a women's college?" For instance, in bold font: "At Smith, women are the focus of *all* the attention and *all* the opportunities"; "At Smith, all of the leaders are women"; "At Smith, the 'old boys network' becomes an ageless women's network."[16] On its website, Barnard describes itself as "[a] liberal arts college in New York City dedicated to the success of women." It notes "the inspiring environment of a women's college," in which students get to "debate ideas with the smartest women you will ever know" in small classes.[17] Here, the link between the sex-identity make-up of the college and success is implied rather than made explicit, as it is on Mount Holyoke's and Smith's websites.

Of the four historically black colleges for women, only Spelman College and Bennett College have remained single-sex.[18] Spelman's mission statement describes the college as "a historically black college and a global leader in the education of women of African descent, [which is] dedicated to academic excellence in the liberal arts and sciences and the intellectual, creative, ethical, and leadership development of its students." It also mentions the strong network that its graduates have access to. In its mission statement, Bennett College describes itself as "a small, private, historically black college for women." It explicitly welcomes "students, staff, and faculty from diverse backgrounds." Prospective students are told that they will leave Bennett with "a greater appreciation of the history and culture of Africa and the African Diaspora, the struggles and accomplishments of women, and a realization of their own ability and the possibilities to help change the world." While both Spelman and Bennett are legally permitted under Title IX's special provision to remain single-sex, neither college is permitted to limit its admission process on the basis of race. Instead, it emphasizes its history as a black college for women, and its present-day specialization in the "history of and culture of Africa and the African Diaspora." Hence, the term "historically black colleges and universities."

The mission statements of the few remaining men's colleges are conspicuously silent on the relevance of a male-only environment to the educational outcomes they market to prospective students and their parents. Wabash College, founded in 1832, only references "men" twice in its three-paragraph mission statement, and it does so only passingly, simply describing the college as "a liberal arts college for men" that offers "qualified young men a superior education, fostering, in particular, independent intellectual inquiry, critical thought, and clear written oral and written expression." The college makes no link between this "superior" education and the absence of young women in its classes or campus life. Hampden-Sydney College, founded in 1732, only references "men" once in its mission statement, statement of purpose, and statement of core values, proclaiming that the college "seeks to form good men and good citizens in an atmosphere of sound learning." In the absence of any sex-based claims, it seems then that the only justification for these colleges to continue their men-only admissions policies is tradition, but it is a quietly stated men-only tradition that avoids the unvarnished sexism and misogyny spewed by VMI and the Citadel officials prior to the court-ordered demise of their male-only admissions policies.

Morehouse College, founded in 1867, differs from Wabash and Hampden-Sydney insofar as it describes itself as "a historically black liberal arts college for men" in its mission statement. Although the overwhelming majority of Morehouse students are African American men, the college, like any school receiving federal funds, cannot deny prospective students from its admissions process on the basis of race. However, as a private college that was founded prior to 1972 and has been continuously single-sex since its founding, Morehouse is legally permitted under Title IX's exemption to bar women from its admissions process. Morehouse can and does market itself as assuming "special responsibility for teaching the history and culture of black people." But it cannot and does not formally market itself as a college "for black men," or a "black male college." Like its historically and still predominantly white counterparts, Wabash and Hampden-Sydney, Morehouse scarcely references sex classification in its mission statement, and draws no causal links between the quality of its education and the absence of female students on campus. In 2010, Morehouse adopted a policy banning its students from wearing women's clothing on campus, but the policy was criticized for being homophobic rather than for being explicitly transphobic.[19]

Assimilation and Accommodation

One approach to solving the discriminatory impact of women-only college admissions on transgender women and men is to preserve the administrative requirement of being a woman and assimilate and/or accommodate transgender and gender-nonconforming prospective students into a more expansive definition of what that means. Mount Holyoke has stretched its definition of "woman" the farthest of all its peer institutions. In 2015 the college amended its sex-based admissions policy to welcome "applications for our undergraduate program from any qualified student who is female or identifies as a woman."[20] On its website, the college lists the sex identities that are included in, and excluded by, its expanded definition of being female or identifying as a woman. The only persons who are ineligible for admission under its new policy are people who were "biologically born male" and self-identify as men at the time of application. Smith and Mills Colleges have stopped short of Mount Holyoke's expansive definition of "woman" but now explicitly include self-defined transgender women as being eligible for admission, regardless of the sex markers that appear on their personal identity documents. Barnard College has changed its admissions policy to include "women who consistently live and identify as women, regardless of the gender assigned them at birth."[21] Bryn Mawr College now considers the eligibility of transgender women on a case-by-case basis based on legal sex documentation.[22] Wellesley College neither explicitly includes nor excludes transgender women in its admissions policies.[23]

Assimilation is arguably also the de facto approach of many nonelite women's colleges that have quietly admitted transgender women and men, and permitted students who transition from female to male after enrollment to graduate on a case-by-case basis without making any formal changes to their admissions policies. Some women's colleges have ducked the issue of publicly stating whether or not they would admit a transgender woman or transgender man by simply stating that their admissions processes are open to "women" and/or "students who identify as female," without disclosing the criteria used for determining who meets these definitions. These policies might be interpreted as being open to transgender women and gender-nonconforming people, as well as transgender men whose personal identity documents have female sex markers. But relying on "legal sex" is problematic because the criteria for changing the sex markers on particular legal identity documents such as birth certificates, driver's licenses, and passports differ so greatly from state to state. And Tennessee legally bans sex-change amendments to birth certificates altogether. And even in cases where all three of these documents bear a female sex marker, there may be other documentation in a person's file that describes that person as male, such as a FAFSA form. This is precisely the problem that befell Calliope Wong when she applied to and was rejected by Smith.

Some women's colleges have focused their attention on making less controversial changes in order to make their campuses more inclusive of matriculated transgender and gender-nonconforming students. For instance, many women's colleges have added the terms "gender identity" and/or "gender expression" to their nondiscrimination and diversity statements.[24] Race and media studies scholar Sara Ahmed points out, however, that too often institutions use diversity statements to proclaim the absence of racism and sexism and other forms of social exclusion in their settings—a move that can effectively foreclose the very work that is needed to combat such exclusion.[25] The provision of services and courses of study that include the term "transgender" might also be construed as signs of a school's acceptance of transgender students. The provision of gender-neutral or "all-gender" restrooms and the adjustment of campus housing policies to accommodate transgender and gender-nonconforming students could also be interpreted as an indication that a college is open to transgender and gender-nonconforming applicants. Other key sex-classification policy nodes within colleges include student housing, name and sex marker changes in bureaucratic record keeping, and the use of gendered pronouns by faculty, staff, and students. Many of these administrative changes are happening at elite liberal arts colleges. One reason for this is probably the presence of strong women's, gender, and sexuality studies academic departments, programs, and student centers. This is especially true at some of the nation's elite women's colleges, where feminist and gender scholars have often served on the committees charged with envisioning and structuring strategic initiatives and institutional change. It matters when students pushing for policy changes have the support of faculty, administrators, and alums. But in the absence of any explicitly affirmative policies, it is difficult to know whether or not that is true. It seems that many women's colleges are delaying for as long as possible taking an official stance on whether and how transgender students fit into their women-only admissions policies. When an institution adopts this kind of stance, it has decided to be reactive instead of taking the opportunity to be innovative and use the challenges posed by transgender identities to reevaluate its use of sex-classification polices across the board.

None of the three private men's colleges have made any adjustments to their admissions policies to explicitly or implicitly assimilate transgender men or women into their institutional core values. This is probably due to the fact that there are so few men's colleges today, and those that remain are not considered as prestigious or elite as the seven sister colleges. It also can be seen as further evidence of the trans-misogyny that Julia Serrano describes as disproportionate fascination with and ridicule of transgender women in the media in comparison to transgender men.[26] Perhaps the prospect of a transgender man attending a men's college does not seem as "titillating" as that of a transgender woman attending a women's college.

Sex and/or Gender

The women's colleges that have been forced or "peer-pressured" to publicly explain their women-only admissions policies express a political definition of "woman" and "female" that focuses on social construction rather than biology. This differs markedly from many of the public arguments in favor of single-sex education at the K-12 level, which are largely based on claims that girls and boys have different learning needs and styles based on biological sex differences. Those arguments often invoke claims that girls and boys have different brains. And when arguments are made about the distraction that the presence of girls poses for boys, there is a thinly veiled presumption that all children are heterosexual. In recent years, that debate has focused specifically on black boys and their putative need to be in all-black male schools with black male teachers to whom they can relate in an environment that is calibrated to their particular learning style. But as education scholar James Earl Davis points out, these kinds of schools do not empower all black boys; in fact, such schools can marginalize and disempower boys whose gender expressions do not conform to hegemonic masculine standards.[27]

There may be some people affiliated with women's colleges who use biological, body-based arguments to defend sex segregation, but the official statements that appear on the websites of prominent women's colleges deliberately avoid essentialist claims that equate female identity and being a woman to physiology and hormones. Mount Holyoke, for instance, acknowledges important changes that have occurred in U.S. feminism:

> Just as early feminists argued that the reduction of women to their biological functions was a foundation for women's oppression, we must acknowledge that gender identity is not reducible to the body. Instead, we must look at identity in terms of the external context in which the individual is situated. It is this positionality that biological women and transwomen share, and it is this positionality that is relevant when women's colleges open their gates for those aspiring to live, learn, and thrive within a community of women.

In focusing on the "external context" of women's "positionality," Mount Holyoke embraces an understanding of sex identity that is reminiscent of the political theorist Iris Marion Young's compelling argument that women are more accurately theorized as a "series" than as an "identity group." Intersecting identities such as race and class mean that there are multiple experiences and self-identities among women. They are not a group, which Young defines as a collection of individuals with common interests and attitudes, in the way that, for example, the National Rifle Association is a group. Instead, she describes women as a series, meaning that they are drawn together by the experience of having to deal with the common political problem of sexism.[28] However, being a woman does not predetermine one's political beliefs about what this sexism entails and how it ought to be addressed.

Mount Holyoke does not explain what it means by "women's positionality." The college asserts a commonality between cisgender and transgender women, but does not explain what exactly these two groups of women have in common. If it is the sort of seriality invoked by Young, does it matter that some transgender women will have been socialized as boys and/or men for certain periods of their lives? Moreover, although transgender men are explicitly mentioned and included in the "frequently asked questions" section of the policy, Mount Holyoke's policy statement makes no mention of them. There seems to be an underlying presumption that transgender men should be included because they have been socialized as girls and/or women, and therefore belong to the series of women. But is socialization the same thing as positionality? As we saw earlier, many variables come into play, such as the age at which the person transitioned from female to male, and whether the person is gender conforming or "gender transforming" in their self-identification and the way they appear to other people in particular contexts.

Ginsburg's conception of "artificial constraint" and statistical sex-role stereotypes can shed light on the ways in which single-sex admissions policies, even those as flexible and expansive as Mount Holyoke's, can and often do produce sex-based disadvantage. The burden should be on the college to prove that the exclusion of biologically born men who identify as men at the time of their application is necessary for the college to carry out its mission of creating an institutional space for its students "to live, learn, and thrive within a community of women." It seems likely that many, and perhaps most, men would not seek the kind of education offered by women's colleges. But some men might seek such an education, and may personally benefit from being in such a learning environment. Women, too, might benefit from being in a female-dominant institution with men. Women's colleges can and should continue to follow their core values and missions. But these legitimate policy goals should be pursued via other means than the continuance of single-sex admissions.

Mount Holyoke went through an important iterative process of explicitly enumerating all the sex-identity groups that may apply for admission. These include "biologically born" females who identify as women, men, or other/they/ze, or do not identify as either women or men; "biologically born" males who identify as female, or other/they/ze when "other/they" means self-identification as a woman; or persons who are "biologically born" with male and female anatomy (intersex) and identify as women. Perhaps the exclusion of "biologically born males" who self-identify as men at the time of their application is needed in order for Mount Holyoke to market itself as a "women's college." But is that really true?

As a practical matter, Mount Holyoke's anti-essentialist definition of what it means to self-identify as female or a woman is undermined by the way it asks prospective students to record their sex identities on its application forms. When an application form prompts a prospective student to check a male or female box, what definition of sex identity is the person being asked to disclose? Is it a first-person self-understanding of maleness or femaleness, or a third-person perception of how others may perceive the person in relation to the social and/or legal scheme of binary sex? What should an applicant do when these two conceptions diverge? What about the person who wants to check both male and female boxes, or neither? On the Common Application, which is used by over six hundred colleges, including Mount Holyoke, a sex-classification question appears on the first screen after the user creates a password for the website. The applicant must select either male or female in order to progress to the rest of the application. To the right of this binary sex question an information icon appears. When the icon is clicked, the following notice appears: "Federal guidelines mandate that we collect data on the *legal sex* of all applicants. Please report the sex currently listed on your *birth certificate*. If you wish to provide more details regarding your gender identity, you are welcome to do so in the additional information section" (emphasis mine). This informational note recognizes that a person's birth-sex designation does not always match that person's sex identity over the course of a lifetime, or more pointedly, at the time of application. When I accessed the Common Application in October 2016, the informational note had been removed. Applicants were now prompted to check a male or female option as their "sex assigned at birth." The next prompt read, "If you would like the opportunity, we invite you to share more about your gender identity below." The invitation to provide further information is a nod to the fact that sex identity can be more complex.

Nevertheless, the mandatory prompt to disclose the sex that appears on our birth certificates is deeply problematic. The sex markers on our birth certificates are based upon a physician's visual inspection of our external genitalia at birth.[29] Also, the requirements for changing birth certificate sex markers vary across states, and can be cumbersome and difficult. In the state of Tennessee such an amendment is legally impossible, so a transgender person born in Tennessee cannot legally align their lived sex identity with their legal sex documentation. Many transgender people have changed some of their identity documents, but not all. Theoretically, an applicant might have a driver's license with a female sex marker and a birth certificate with a male sex marker.

Moreover, sex-classification questions on college application forms presume a fixed and verifiable definition of binary sex identity that fails to take into account transgender and gender- nonconforming experience, which tells us that the sex classification assigned to us at birth is changeable over the course of our lifetimes. The ubiquity of male/female bureaucratic box checking can make this action seem trivial and apolitical. Indeed, most often sex-identity questions appear near the beginning of the bureaucratic form, as if it is a preliminary matter of course, equally as necessary as our name and address. However, the stakes are not trivial. Sex identity is neither straightforward nor easy for everyone faced with college forms, and the consequences of checking a male or female box can mean outright exclusion from a particular educational opportunity. And in other cases, it is unclear how a particular institution or organization will use this information.

A Queer Future: Designing Better Sex-Identity Questions

Transgender and gender-nonconforming experience, in all of its diversity, should prod colleges to critically reflect upon their goals. Women's colleges have a long history of creating higher education environments that are designed to fight institutional sexism. When women were barred from applying to many colleges, this fight meant providing parallel institutions for women. Today, institutional sexism persists, and women's colleges have a vital leadership role to play in paving the way for other colleges to do things differently. But single-sex admissions are not necessary for doing this critical work. The increased visibility of transgender and gender-nonconforming identities is an opportunity for these schools to reflect in a more focused way about the relationship between the collection of sex-identity information and their educational mission. An important place to begin this institutional self-reflection and reform is the sex-classification questions that appear on college application forms.

The idea of "choice architecture" can help administrative policy makers take up this work. In their popular book *Nudge*, legal scholar Cass Sunstein and economist Richard Thaler introduce this term.[30] They argue that we are prompted or nudged to make certain choices on the basis of how those choices are physically presented to us. Consider for example the common practice used in many stores of stocking small sugary snacks at eye level near cash registers. We are visually prompted, but not forced, to purchase these items while we wait in line to pay for things already in our carts or baskets. Sunstein and Thaler recommend rearranging this choice architecture so that we are nudged to make healthier food choices in a supermarket. They base this principle on the political-theory concept of limited paternalism elaborated by the liberal political philosopher John Stuart Mill.[31]

Political theorists Elizabeth Markovits and Susan Bickford apply the idea of choice architecture to feminism. In the supermarket example, the idea was to promote the good of healthier eating. In the context of feminism and the U.S. workplace, Markovits and Bickford propose redesigning the bureaucratic "choice architecture" of human resource paperwork so that individuals are nudged to make choices that promote gender equality. They suggest reconfiguring W-4 forms to give workers the choice of having their paycheck divided between them and a designated partner, or paid fully to them. The important nudge in this example is that the option of splitting the person's salary between the person and his or her spouse or partner is the default option. To have the full payment go to the employee, the employee must actively make a different choice.[32] This reform retains Mill's limited paternalism because it nudges but does not force an individual to make the feminist choice.

What if colleges used the idea of feminist choice architecture to change the way they collect and process sex-identity information from prospective students? The sex-identity questions on college application forms are material artifacts that were conceived, composed, and arranged by people, and thus something that can be rewritten and overwritten by the same people, or their successors. First, colleges should make the sex-identity questions on their application forms voluntary instead of mandatory. This would mean treating sex questions like race questions, which colleges are permitted to ask but cannot require applicants to answer. But application-form designers should not stop there. In asking for information about a candidate's sex and race, colleges should explain what definition of sex identity and racial identity they are invoking. Are they interested in knowing how the candidate self-identifies in relation to these concepts, and/or the person's assessment of their third-person race-sex identification, how others see them? The Common Application provides some direction, but offers no definition of sex beyond the "legal sex" that appears on our birth certificates. This underscores the need for consistent sex-identity public policies in all venues. But in the short term, colleges should further explain why they are asking for applicants' "legal sex" beyond the legalese of "government reporting." A possible legitimate and important reason for a college to ask an applicant to share such information is to achieve and maintain numerical balance between men and women. But colleges should have to articulate this justification so that applicants know why they are being asked.

The sex-identity question(s) on these forms should also explicitly note the temporal nature of such questions. Here is an excellent opportunity for a school to communicate its knowledge that a person's sex classification can change over time. There is also the question of what, if anything, a women's college should do when a matriculated student begins or continues a sex-identity transition after matriculation or graduation. No single-sex college has required a student to leave on these grounds. However, some students who do transition during their college years face difficulties in having their felt sex identities bureaucratically validated. For instance, their diplomas may or may not display their post-transition name. Moreover, some transgender men who do not wish to be out as transgender can face awkward situations when potential employers see a women's college on their transcript or resume.

Women's colleges might consider asking prospective students to reflect upon how their own race-sex identities relate to the college's historical and enduring commitment to fighting institutional sexism. This information could be conveyed in a short essay, and/or in the personal interviews that many elite colleges use in their recruitment processes. And the college could incorporate the analytic framework of intersectionality into its useful description of how feminism has evolved over time. In the revised choice architecture of sex-identity questioning, there should be some discussion about cisgender men. How might the presence of these people help further the college's feminist mission? What are some of the ways in which their presence can threaten and undermine this legitimate and important mission? In the *New York Times* article referenced in the beginning of this chapter, Barnard College president Judith Shapiro "wondered aloud why a transmale or male-identified student 'would want to be in a women's college.'" Shapiro may have been asking that question rhetorically. There seems to be an underlying presumption that the only reason why a man would want to attend a women's college is to invade and dominate. But I believe that there can be other, nonsexist reasons why men would want to be in such an environment. Historically female college should ask male applicants, be they transgender or cisgender, to critically reflect upon and explain how they see themselves contributing to, and benefiting from, being at a feminist college.

In the administrative process of college admissions, race-sex "seeing" is enabled and directed by the seemingly anonymous "choice architecture" of the questions arranged on bureaucratic forms. The boxes that an applicant checks are seen by admissions officers who then have the administrative discretion to use their race-sex perceptions in conjunction with other information to render their admissions decisions. Many elite, highly selective single-sex colleges conduct in-person interviews with prospective students as part of their admissions process. Such interviews give admissions officers a proxy pair of eyes that they can use to visually assess the race-sex identities of particular prospective students. The evaluative judgments about the race-sex perceptions of individual applicants can be negative, positive, or neutral. Judgments will have to be made, so the discretion of admissions officers should be guided by a clear and transparent policy regarding the institutional relevance of prospective students' race-sex identities.

Sex-identity questionnaires envelop many other sex-classification policies. When and how do colleges, both single-sex and co-ed, use sex-marked government identity documents such as driver's licenses, passports, and birth certificates? How does the presence of transgender women and men, and gender-nonconforming students, affect the administration of sex-segregated restrooms on campus, as well as student dormitories and locker rooms for athletics? What are the implications of single-sex colleges for questions about sex-segregated sports? To what extent should sex classification be taken into account when it comes to recruiting, hiring, and promoting faculty and staff at both single-sex and co-ed colleges?

Conclusion

Our race-sex identities are relevant to the diversity goals of colleges, but their institutional relevance must be explained by particular colleges, rather than assumed.

The reason for doing so, to be clear, is not that sex identity is unimportant. On the contrary, it is that our right to say who we are in relationship to the social and legal scheme of binary sex is so important to our self-authority that we should take great care to minimize the institutional opportunities for administrative processes and agents to evaluate this aspect of our lives and possibly overrule our sex-identity self-statements.

The time has come, or is coming, for women's colleges to abandon their single-sex admissions policies, but not their institutional missions to further intersectional feminist values and support female leadership and professional networking. The Title IX exemption should be overturned because it is antithetical to the ethos of Title IX's ban on sex discrimination. Race-sex identity is relevant to these institutional goals, but women-only admissions policies are not the only or best means of achieving them. In the idiom of nondiscrimination law, single-sex admissions policies are not narrowly tailored to meet the legitimate and important institutional policy goals of women's colleges.[33] The institutional self-evaluation that prominent women's colleges have been forced to undertake is something that *all* colleges and universities would benefit from. An important way to implement the results of this institutional self-reflection is to change the way the wording and "choice architecture" of college application forms ask, direct, and nudge prospective students to share information about their sex identities.

NOTES

1 Adalman 2013.
2 Feldman 2014, emphasis mine.
3 Quart 2008.
4 Chen 2015.
5 Spade 2009, 369.
6 "Title IX and Sex Discrimination" 2015.
7 Feldman 2014.
8 Associated Press 2014.
9 Recently, some Asian Americans have argued that they are being discriminated against in the form of admissions quotas limiting their numbers. Sociologists Jennifer Lee and Min Zhou argue that race-based affirmative action is in the best interests of Asian Americans given that they still suffer from institutional racism. Survey data shows that the majority of Asian Americans favor race-based affirmative action. Lee and Zhou 2015.
10 *Regents of the University of California v. Bakke*, 438 U.S. 265 (U.S. Supreme Court 1978).
11 Case 2010, 222.
12 *United States v. Virginia et al.*, 518 U.S. 515 (Supreme Court 1996).
13 Ibid., emphasis mine.
14 Hennessey 2013.
15 Mount Holyoke College n.d.
16 "About Smith" n.d.
17 "Barnard Admissions" n.d.
18 The other two are Barber-Scotia College and Bethune Cookman University.

19 King 2014.

20 Feldman 2014.

21 Harris 2015.

22 Callahan 2014.

23 Padawer 2014.

24 Sara Ahmed cautions that diversity statements can and often do obscure institutional oppression such as racism. Such statements are often used as evidence that an institution does not have the kind of problems that diversity is supposed to solve. Ahmed 2012.

25 Ibid.

26 Serano 2009.

27 Martin and Meyenn 2001.

28 Young 1994.

29 Karkazis 2008.

30 Sunstein and Thaler 2009.

31 Mill 1997.

32 Markovits and Bickford 2014, 92.

33 The Supreme Court articulates its intermediate level of judicial review for sex-classification policies in *Craig v. Boren*, 429 F. Supp 190 (1976).

REFERENCES

"About Smith." N.d. Smith College, www.smith.edu. Accessed December 13, 2015.

Adalman, Lori. 2013. "Prominent Women's Colleges Unwilling to Open Doors to Trans Women." *Feministing*, March 21. www.feministing.com.

Ahmed, Sara. 2012. *On Being Included: Racism and Diversity in Institutional Life*. Durham, NC: Duke University Press.

Associated Press. 2014. "US Women's Colleges Change Admission Policies for Transgender Students." *Guardian*, Sept. 10. www.theguardian.com.

"Barnard Admissions." N.d. Barnard College, www.barnard.edu. Accessed December 13, 2015.

Callahan, Kat. 2014. "Trans Women Offer Women's Colleges a New Way to Support an Old Mission." *ROYGBIV*, Sept. 9. roygbiv.jezebel.com.

Case, Mary Anne. 2010. "Why Not Abolish Laws of Urinary Segregation?" In *Toilet: Public Restrooms and the Politics of Sharing*, edited by Laura Noren Harvey Molotch, 211–25. New York: NYU Press.

Chen, Angus. 2015. "Health Effects of Transitioning in Teen Years Remain Unknown." *NPR*, July 22. www.npr.org. Accessed April 23, 2016.

Craig v. Boren, 429 F. Supp 190 (1976).

Feldman, Kiera. 2014. "Who Are Women's Colleges For?" *New York Times*, May 24. www.nytimes.com.

Harris, Elizabeth A. 2015. "Barnard College, after Much Discussion, Decides to Accept Transgender Women." *New York Times*, June 4. www.nytimes.com.

Hennessey, Rachel. 2013. "What's in a Women's College?" *Forbes*, Feb. 6. Accessed April 20, 2016. www.forbes.com.

Karkazis, Katrina. 2008. *Fixing Sex: Intersex, Medical Authority, and Lived Experience*. Durham, NC: Duke University Press.

King, Aliya S. 2014. "The Mean Girls of Morehouse." *Vibe*, July 5. Accessed December 13, 2015. www.vibe.com.

Lee, Jennifer, and Min Zhou. 2015. *The Asian American Achievement Paradox*. New York: Russell Sage Foundation.

Markovits, Elizabeth K., and Susan Bickford. 2014. "Constructing Freedom: Institutional Pathways to Changing the Gender Division of Labor." *Perspectives on Politics* 12(1): 81–99. doi:10.1017/S1537592713003721.

Martin, Wayne, and Bob Meyenn, eds. 2001. "Transgressing the Masculine: African American Boys and the Failure of Schools." In *What about the Boys? Issues of Masculinity in Schools.* Philadelphia: Open University.

Mill, John Stuart. 1997. "On Liberty." In *Mill: Texts, Commentaries*, edited by Alan Ryan. New York: Norton.

Mount Holyoke College. N.d. "Admission of Transgender Students." Mount Holyoke College, www.mtholyoke.edu.

Padawer, Ruth. 2014. "When Women Become Men at Wellesley." *New York Times*, Oct. 15. www.nytimes.com.

Quart, Alissa. 2008. "When Girls Will Be Boys." *New York Times*, March 16. www.nytimes.com.

Regents of the University of California v. Bakke, 438 U.S. 265 (U.S. Supreme Court 1978).

Serano, Julia. 2009. *Whipping Girl: A Transsexual Woman on Sexism and the Scapegoating of Femininity*. Berkeley, CA: Seal Press.

Spade, Dean. 2009. "Keynote Address: Trans Law and Politics on a Neoliberal Landscape." *Temple Political & Civil Rights Law Review* 18: 353–73.

Sunstein, Cass, and Richard Thaler. 2009. *Nudge: Improving Decisions about Health, Wealth, and Happiness*. New Haven, CT: Yale University Press.

"Title IX and Sex Discrimination." 2015. Policy Guidance, Oct. 15. www2.ed.gov.

United States v. Virginia et al., 518 U.S. 515 (Supreme Court 1996).

Young, Iris. 1994. "Gender as Seriality: Thinking about Women as a Social Collective." *Signs* 19(3): 713–38.

Martha Ackelsberg is William R. Kenan Jr. Professor, emerita, of Government and of the Study of Women and Gender at Smith College. She is the author of *Free Women of Spain: Anarchism and the Struggle for the Emancipation of Women* and the essay collection *Resisting Citizenship: Feminist Essays on Politics, Community, and Democracy*. Within APSA, she has served as program chair and president of the LGBT Caucus and of the Women's Caucus and has been a member of the Committee on the Status of LGBTs in the Profession and chair of the Committee on the Status of Women in the Profession. She also served two terms on APSA Council, and one term as Association Vice-President.

Ellen Ann Andersen is Associate Professor of Political Science and Gender, Sexuality, and Women's Studies at the University of Vermont. Her research has focused primarily on LGBT and HIV/AIDS activism, with a particular focus on the relationship between social movements and the law. She is the author of *Out of the Closets and into the Courts: Legal Opportunity Structure and Gay Rights Litigation* and has published in journals such as the *American Sociological Review*, the *American Journal of Political Science*, *PS*, and *Political Behavior*.

Ben Anderson-Nathe is Associate Professor and Program Director of the Child & Family Studies program in Portland State University's School of Social Work. His scholarship focuses on youth and young adults; critical and qualitative epistemologies; gender and sexuality; and oppression, privilege, and social justice.

B Lee Aultman is a PhD candidate at the Graduate Center, CUNY. Their dissertation, entitled "The Epistemology of Transgender Political Resistance: Embodied Experience and the Practices of Everyday Life," explores how the classificatory schemes of everyday life, including those of political and legal institutions, have distorted the political practices and identities of trans people. Their recent work has appeared in *TSQ: Transgender Studies Quarterly* and *Wagadu: A Journal of Transnational Women's and Gender Studies*.

Mandi Bates Bailey is Associate Professor of Political Science at Valdosta State University in Valdosta, Georgia. Her research has been published in the *American Review of Politics* and the *Social Science Journal*.

Eric A. Baldwin is a PhD student in Political Science and Eugene V. Cota-Robles Doctoral Research Fellow in the Social Sciences at UCLA. His research focuses on the underlying causality of political and collective behavior to understand why and how special interest groups become policy demanders.

Marla Brettschneider is Professor of Political Philosophy joint position in Women's Studies and Political Science at the University of New Hampshire. She is the author of numerous award-winning books and many articles on queer theory and diversity politics such as *The Family Flamboyant: Race Politics, Queer Families, Jewish Lives* and *Jewish Feminism and Intersectionality*.

Cynthia Burack is a political theorist and Professor of Women's, Gender, and Sexuality Studies at Ohio State University. With Jyl J. Josephson, she coedits the Queer Politics and Cultures book series at SUNY Press. Her most recent book is *Tough Love: Sexuality, Compassion, and the Christian Right*, and her current research focuses on U.S. government advocacy for sexual orientation and gender identity (SOGI) human rights abroad.

Susan Burgess is Professor of Political Science at Ohio University. She is the author of *Radical Politics in the United States* (with Kate Leeman); *The New York Times on Gay and Lesbian Issues*; *The Founding Fathers, Pop Culture, and Constitutional Law: Who's Your Daddy?*; and *Contest for Constitutional Authority: The Abortion and War Powers Debates*. Within APSA, she co-organized a new section in Sexuality and Politics in 2007, with Angelia Wilson. She has been a member of the Executive Committee of the Law and Courts section, Coordinator of the Constitutional Law Division, Chair of the LGBT Caucus, as well as a member of the Committee on the Status of Women and the Committee on the Status of LGBTs. As part of the Perestroika movement in political science, her candidacy for a seat on the governing Council triggered an association-wide competitive election, challenging the longstanding system of top-down nominations.

Sean Cahill, PhD, is Director of Health Policy Research at the Fenway Institute. Since 2013, with support from the National Institute of Corrections at the U.S. Department of Justice, and in partnership with colleagues at Brown University's Center for Prisoner Health and Human Rights and at GLAD, Cahill helped develop best practices for managing LGBT and intersex adults in corrections, and LGBTI youth in juvenile justice systems. The analysis here reflects his views and not those of the National Institute of Corrections. He is grateful to Lorie Brisbin, Brad Brockmann, and Vickie Henry for their support in this work.

Paisley Currah teaches political science and women's and gender studies at Brooklyn College and the Graduate Center of the City University of New York. His forthcoming book, *Not the United States of Sex*, explores state policies for sex reclassification, the politics of the transgender-rights movement, and its relation to feminism.

Courtenay W. Daum is Associate Professor in the Political Science Department and Affiliate Faculty with the Center for Women's Studies and Gender Research at Colorado State University. Her recent work has appeared in *New Political Science* and the *Journal of Law, Technology, and Policy*.

Joseph Nicholas DeFilippis is Associate Professor in the Anthropology, Sociology, and Social Work Department at Seattle University. He is founding Executive Director of Queers for Economic Justice, and the former Director of SAGE/ Queens. His work focuses on queer communities, poverty, public policy, social movements, marriage politics, and social justice.

Heath Fogg Davis is Associate Professor of Political Science at Temple University, where he teaches courses on political theory and antidiscrimination law. His book on sex-classification policies is forthcoming in 2017. He also consults with businesses and nonprofit organizations, helping them to develop and implement policies that are transgender inclusive.

Jeremiah J. Garretson is Assistant Professor of Political Science at California State University–East Bay. Winner of the 2009–2011 Best Dissertation Award from the Sexuality and Politics Section of the American Political Science Association, his work has appeared in *Comparative Political Studies*, *Political Research Quarterly*, and the *International Journal of Public Opinion Research*. He is the author of the forthcoming book *Why Tolerance Triumphed: The Origins of Americans' Changing Views on Lesbian and Gay Rights*.

Donald P. Haider-Markel is Professor and Chair of Political Science at the University of Kansas. He is the author or coauthor of many books and articles in a range of issue areas, including civil rights, race and inequality, culture war politics, criminal justice policy, counterterrorism, and environmental policy.

Jyl Josephson is Associate Professor of Political Science and Women's and Gender Studies at Rutgers University-Newark. She is the author of *Rethinking Sexual Citizenship* and is coeditor with Cynthia Burack of the Queer Politics and Cultures series for SUNY Press. Her work has been published in journals such as *Politics and Gender*, *Journal of Poverty*, *New Political Science*, *Perspectives on Politics*, *European Journal of Women's Studies*, and *Trans Studies Quarterly*.

Christine Keating is Associate Professor of Gender, Women's, and Sexuality Studies at the University of Washington. She is the author of *Decolonizing*

Democracy: The Social Contract in Transition in India. Her articles have been published in *Signs, Political Theory, International Journal of Feminist Politics, Hypatia, Women's Studies Quarterly,* and *New Political Science,* as well as in several edited volumes. She is also a codirector of La Escuela Popular Norteña, a popular education collective.

Christina Kiel is Professor of Practice at Tulane University in New Orleans. Her research focus is international conflict studies, mediation, and transnational advocacy movements. Her work has appeared in *Interest Groups and Advocacy* and *Global Networks.*

X. Loudon Manley is a blogger and independent researcher. His research interests include ethnic studies, as well as race and gender politics. He lives in Beverly Hills, California.

Thaís Marques is an MA candidate in Political Science at Rutgers University–Newark. She is a member of the Rutgers University–Newark Chancellor's Commission on Diversity and Transformation and was a founding member of the Newark Students' Union, a student organization dedicated to advocating for quality education in Newark public schools.

Melissa Meade is Associate Professor and Chair of Humanities at Colby-Sawyer College, where she teaches and writes in the areas of media history, law, culture, and feminist media studies. She serves on the Legacy Council of the Third Wave Fund.

Patrick R. Miller is Assistant Professor of Political Science at the University of Kansas. He has been published in numerous peer-reviewed academic journals, and his current research interests focus on political identities, partisanship, political civility, and civic engagement. He earned his PhD at the University of North Carolina at Chapel Hill.

Julie Moreau is a Postdoctoral Research Fellow in the Department of Women's, Gender, and Sexuality Studies at Washington University in St. Louis. Her research interests include transnational queer studies, social movements, and citizenship.

Gary Mucciaroni is Professor of Political Science and Director of the Master of Public Policy Program at Temple University. His publications include *Same Sex, Different Politics: Issues and Institutions in Struggles for Gay and Lesbian Rights.*

Zein Murib is Assistant Professor of Political Science at Fordham University. Murib's work has been published in journals such as *Politics, Groups, and Identities; TSQ: Transgender Studies Quarterly;* and *New Political Science.*

Steven P. Nawara is Assistant Professor of Political Science at Lewis University in Romeoville, Illinois. His work has been published in *Political Behavior, Presidential Studies Quarterly*, and the *Journal of Elections, Public Opinion, and Parties*.

Megan E. Osterbur is Assistant Professor of Political Science at Xavier University of Louisiana. Her research focuses on LGBTQ social movements and public policy relevant to gender and sexuality movements. Her articles have appeared in *Global Networks* and the *International Journal for the Scholarship of Teaching and Learning*.

Ravi K. Perry is Associate Professor of Political Science at Virginia Commonwealth University. His publications include *21st-Century Urban Race Politics: Representing Minorities as Universal Interests, Black Mayors, White Majorities: The Balancing Act of Racial Politics*, and *The Little Rock Crisis: What Desegregation Politics Says about Us*. A member of Kappa Alpha Psi Fraternity, Inc., Perry is President of the National Association for Ethnic Studies and a member of the Executive Council for the Urban Politics Organized Section and the Sexuality and Politics Organized Section of the American Political Science Association. Perry is also a member of the Executive Council with the National Conference of Black Political Scientists. Previously, Perry was a member of the Board of Directors and Affiliate Equity Officer for the ACLU of Mississippi, and was also one of the first openly gay branch presidents of color in the history of the NAACP in Worcester, Massachusetts.

J. Ricky Price is a PhD candidate in Politics at the New School for Social Research in New York City. His work is at the intersection of HIV/AIDS, Political History, Memory Studies, and Science and Technology Studies. He grew up in Wyoming and currently lives in Los Angeles.

Kimala Price is Associate Professor of Women's Studies and Co-director of the Bread and Roses Center for Feminist Research and Activism at San Diego State University.

Judy Rohrer is the Director of the Institute for Citizenship and Social Responsibility and Assistant Professor in Diversity and Community Studies at Western Kentucky University. Her publications include *Haoles in Hawai'i: Race and Ethnicity in Hawai'i*.

Anna Sampaio is Associate Professor in the Department of Ethnic Studies at Santa Clara University. Her publications include *Terrorizing Latina/o Immigrants: Race, Gender, and Immigration Politics in the Age of Security* and, with Carlos Veléz-Ibañez, *Transnational Latino/a Communities: Politics, Processes, and Cultures*.

Shawn Schulenberg is Associate Professor at Marshall University. He was the 2012 Junior Recipient of the Marshall University Distinguished Artists and Scholars Award and currently serves as Director of Sexuality Studies at Marshall University. Schulenberg is the coeditor of *Same-Sex Marriage in the Americas* and *Same-Sex Partnership Recognition in Latin America*, and his work has appeared in the *Journal of Human Rights* and *New Political Science*.

Charles Anthony Smith is Professor of Political Science at the University of California–Irvine. He is the author of *The Rise and Fall of War Crimes Trials: From Charles I to Bush II* and *Gerrymandering in America: The House of Representatives, the Supreme Court, and the Future of Popular Sovereignty*, among other books. He has published articles in the *American Journal of Political Science*, *Political Research Quarterly*, *Law and Society Review*, the *Journal of Human Rights*, *Human Rights Review*, the *International Political Science Review*, *Journal of International Relations and Development*, *Judicature*, and the *Election Law Journal*, among others.

Miriam Smith is Professor in the Department of Social Science at York University. She has published widely on LGBTQ politics in Canada and the United States and is the author of *Political Institutions and Lesbian and Gay Rights in the United States and Canada*.

Paul Snell is a PhD candidate in Political Science at the University of Minnesota.

Jason Stodolka is a PhD Candidate in Political Science, with a concentration in Gender and Women's Studies, at the University of Illinois at Chicago. His research interests focus on intersectional LGBTQ social movement politics and their effect on the policymaking process.

Barry L. Tadlock is Associate Professor of Political Science at Ohio University. He is the coeditor of *Gays and Lesbians in the Political Process: Public Policy, Public Opinion, and Political Representation*, and his work has appeared in *Public Administration Quarterly*, *Legislative Studies Quarterly*, *American Review of Politics*, *Politics and Policy*, *Affilia: Journal of Women and Social Work*, and the *Journal of Children and Poverty*.

Jami K. Taylor is Associate Professor of Political Science and Public Administration at the University of Toledo. With Donald Haider-Markel, she coedited *Transgender Rights and Politics: Groups, Issue Framing, and Policy Adoption*. Her work has also appeared in *Administration & Society*, *State Politics & Policy Quarterly*, *Armed Forces & Society*, and the *American Review of Public Administration*.

Jerry D. Thomas is Assistant Professor of Political Science at University of Wisconsin–Oshkosh, where he specializes in public law and sexual citizenship. His PhD in political science is from the University of Kentucky, and his JD is from Chicago-Kent College of Law. He has received several honors at UWO, including the Willard Smith Distinguished Teaching Award, Outstanding Queer Faculty Award, and the Diversity Leadership Award. He lives in Oshkosh and Chicago.

Angelia R. Wilson is Professor of Politics at the University of Manchester. Previously she served on the APSA Council, the Committee for the Status of LGBTs in the Profession, and the LGBT Caucus. She is currently a member of the Political Studies Association Executive Council. Her most recent publications include *Why Europe Is Lesbian & Gay Friendly (and Why America Never Will Be)* and *Situtating Intersectionality*, as well as numerous academic journal articles. She also is the coeditor of the journal *Politics & Religion*.

Rye Young is Third Wave Fund's Executive Director. He began his career as an abortion fund hotline intern when the organization was known as Third Wave Foundation. Rye served in various program roles at Third Wave, and dedicated himself to developing systems for impact measurement and grant making, while crafting programs that met the needs of Third Wave's grassroots, community-based organizations. Rye serves on the Board of Directors of Funders for LGBTQ Issues and the Groundswell Fund and was a Grace Paley Organizing Fellow with Jews for Racial and Economic Justice. He graduated from Bard College in 2008 with a B.A. in Arabic Language, Culture, and Literature.

INDEX

Abel, Richard L., 388

abortion, 74, 396, 401, 430, 529, 545, 552, 564, 568, 569, 571, 600, 605

Ackelsberg, Martha, 5, 155, 157, 161, 164, 166, 175n5, 177–197, 599

Ackland, Robert, 495, 496

ACT-UP, 60, 65, 178, 249, 256, 258, 263, 399, 400, 533, 554

Adam, Barry, 441

Addelson, Kathryn, 46

adoption rights, 1, 80, 84, 254–256, 266n2, 273, 274, 277–279, 282–287, 335, 387, 460, 526, 528, 541

Affinity Community Services, 13, 111, 115, 123, 125

Affordable Care Act (ACA), 79

Afghanistan, 463

Africa, 459, 480, 481, 485,498, 501, 512, 515, 516, 546, 586, 587; Commission on Human & Peoples' Rights, 498

African Human Rights Court, 501

African National Congress (ANC), 449

African Sexual Orientation and Gender Identity Human Rights Organization (ASOGIHRO), 480

ageism, 423, 573

Ahmed, Sara, 589

AIDS: activism, 1, 63, 65, 68, 155, 178, 179, 188, 213, 259, 383, 599; crisis, 64, 67, 68, 117, 178, 179, 191, 249, 252, 256, 259, 355, 406, 407

Aizura, Aren Z., 37

Alabama, 336

Albright, Madeline, 585

Algeria, 486

Allport, Gordon, 261

American Civil Liberties Union, 34, 150n56, 603

American Foundation for Equal Rights and Freedom to Marry, 284

American Jewish World Service, 481, 483

American Political Science Association (APSA), 1, 177–211; Committee on the Status of Lesbians and Gays (original title), 164, 177–185, 199; Gay and Lesbian Caucus, 159–161, 177–85; New Orleans

siting controversy, 155, 165, 167, 185–187, 196n31, 198–211; Sexuality and Politics section, 177, 236; Task Force on the Status of Gays and Lesbians in the Profession, 179

American Political Science Review, 181

American Psychiatric Association, 31n11, 82

Americans with Disabilities Act, 63

Ames, Cherry, 553

Amnesty International, 498, 501, 512

Andersen, Ellen Ann, 7, 163, 351, 374–393

Anderson-Nathe, Ben, 5, 12, 110–133, 599

Anderson, Ryan, 549

Angola, 486

anti-globalization protests, 4

antihomophobia, 467

anti-LGBT groups and attitudes, 1, 3, 138, 145, 167, 266, 298, 305, 448, 452, 466, 470, 481, 527

Anzaldua, Gloria, 239, 242

Applied Research Center, 111, 572

Arcus Foundation, 81, 502, 518

Arendt, Hannah, 38

Argentine, 441, 508

Arneil, Barbara, 546–548

Asia, 221, 223, 228, 131n9, 459, 481, 498, 502, 504, 512, 515, 516

Asian Communities for Reproductive Justice. *See* Forwardogether

assimilationist strategies, 270

assimilationist values, 272, 370, 539–541

Astraea Lesbian Foundation for Justice, 111, 483, 565

Atlanta, Georgia, 130, 304

Atlantic Philanthropies, 501

attribution theory, 258

Audre Lorde Project (ALP), 13, 111, 114, 117

Aultman, B Lee, 4, 11, 34–52, 599

Australia, 459, 506

Ayoub, Philip, 493

Badgett, M. V. Lee, 391n2, 460

Bailey, Mandi Bates, 7, 12, 334–350, 599

Bailey, Robert (Bob), 159, 162, 178

Baim, Tracy, 432

Baker v. Nelson, 354–356, 371, 397

CPSIA information can be obtained
at www.ICGtesting.com
Printed in the USA
BVOW04s1005261217
503646BV00030B/213/P

9 781479 834099